27th Italian Symposium on Advanced Database Systems (SEBD 2019)

Grosseto, Italy
16-19 June 2019

Editors:

Massimo Mecella
Giuseppe Amato
Claudio Gennaro

ISBN: 978-1-5108-9288-0

Printed from e-media with permission by:

Curran Associates, Inc.
57 Morehouse Lane
Red Hook, NY 12571

Some format issues inherent in the e-media version may also appear in this print version.

Printed by Curran Associates, Inc. (2019)

For permission requests, please contact Italian Symposium on Advanced Database Systems (SEBD 2019) at the address below.

Italian Symposium on Advanced Database Systems (SEBD 2019)

Email: giuseppe.amato@isti.cnr.it

Additional copies of this publication are available from:

Curran Associates, Inc.
57 Morehouse Lane
Red Hook, NY 12571 USA
Phone: 845-758-0400
Fax: 845-758-2633
Email: curran@proceedings.com
Web: www.proceedings.com

SEBD 2019
Italian Symposium on Advanced Database Systems

Proceedings of the 27th Italian Symposium on Advanced Database Systems

Castiglione della Pescaia (Grosseto), Italy, June 16th to 19th, 2019.

Edited by

Massimo Mecella, **Sapienza Università di Roma, Italy**
Giuseppe Amato, **ISTI-CNR, Italy**
Claudio Gennaro, **ISTI-CNR, Italy**

Table of Contents

Session 1: Research Track

Session 2: Ph.D. Session

Preface

The Italian Symposium on Advanced Database Systems (*SEBD – Sistemi Evoluti per Basi di Dati*) is the major annual event of the Italian database research community. The twenty-seventh edition of SEBD was jointly organized by ISTI CNR Pisa, Sapienza Università di Roma, Università della Calabria and ICT-SUD Cosenza, and took place in Castiglione della Pescaia (Grosseto) at Riva del Sole resort from 16th to June 19th 2019.

The symposium program included invited keynote talks by Pavel Zezula (professor at the Masaryk University, Brno, Czech Republic) on similarity management of data, by Divesh Srivastava (head of Database Research at AT&T Labs, USA) on exploring change, and by Carlo Batini (professor at Università di Milano Bicocca) giving a special talk for his retirement. Indeed, SEBD 2019 celebrated the retirements, happened during 2019, of Fausto Rabitti and Carlo Batini, for their great contributions over the years to the Italian database research community. SEBD 2019 also included a doctoral consortium, organized by Fabrizio Falchi, and a tutorial by Andrea Marrella on analysing event data through process mining.

The research track involved presentations of 7 research papers and 39 discussion papers. The latter were short papers mainly devoted to preliminary and ongoing work, system and application descriptions, and new ideas of interest to the SEBD audience. Discussion papers included also extended abstracts of recent publications. The papers covered several research topics, such as searching and retrieval, deep learning and machine learning, ontologies, open data, reasoning techniques, OLAP, visual analytics, stream data management, big data, social media data management, information and data integration, security and blockchain.

We would like to thank the invited keynote speakers and presenter of the tutorial, all authors who submitted papers to the symposium, the members of the program committee, and the additional reviewers for their efforts to produce fair and thorough evaluations of the submitted papers, the general chairs Fausto Rabitti and Sergio Greco, the local organization committee headed by Catherine Bosio and the organizing agency Consulta Umbria, the web and publicity chair Franca Debole, and the publication chair Claudio Gennaro, who helped us in preparing this volume.

Furthermore, we are grateful to the sponsors for their generous support: Centro di Competenza ICT-SUD, ISTI CNR Pisa, Dipartimento di Ingegneria informatica, automatica e gestionale Antonio Ruberti of Sapienza Università di Roma.

Giuseppe Amato and Massimo Mecella
SEBD 2019 Program Chairs

June 2019

Similarity Management of Data
the DISA Experience

Pavel Zezula

FI DISA, Masaryk University, Brno, Czech Republic

Abstract. As the current data is typically weekly structured or unstructured at all, access to objects is only possible through similarity of the object's salient features or properties. Consequently, similarity approach to searching is increasingly playing more and more important role in development of data processing applications. In the last twenty years, the technology has matured and many centralized, distributed, and even peer-to-peer architectures have been proposed. However, the use of similarity searching in numerous potential applications is still a challenge. In the talk, four research directions in developing similarity search applications at Masaryk University DISA laboratory are to be discussed. First, we concentrate on accelerating large-scale face recognition applications and continue with generic image annotation task for retrieval purposes. In the second half, we focus on execution of similarity query streams and finish the talk with an ambition topic of content-based retrieval in human motion-capture data collections. Applications will be illustrated by online prototype implementations.

1 Introduction

In the future, access to digital media stored in memories and circulating among networked computers will have to follow, or at least get much closer in its form, to the behavior of real life evolution and communication between species. There, recognition, learning, and judgment presuppose an ability to categorize stimuli and classify situations by *similarity*, because any event in the history of organism is, in a sense, unique and the specific case of the *exact/partial* match is marginal. As practically any kind of fact can nowadays become a digital part of the networked media – whatever we see, say, measure, observe, test, or otherwise experience, is or at least can be in digital form – computers must provide access to required data through similarity based operations, because it is the similarity that is in the world "revealing".

Similarity in general is determined by *stimuli* materialized as extractions from digital objects in form of *features* (*descriptors*, *properties*, etc.), and the way we grade closeness of objects in user defined *operations* able to satisfy information needs. We can calibrate the stimuli and operations from two different points of view: (1) *effectiveness* concerns the way similarity is defined and the extent to which it reflex the human perception of the relation, and (2) *efficiency* regards the processing speed, costs, or an effort needed to get results independently from scale.

Philosophical and psychological theorizing about similarity has been dominated by the geometric model for much of the twentieth century, see e.g. [22]. Though later criticized by several authors [23,7], it has become important paradigm for developing an *extensible* form of similarity search technology. The central assumption of this type of model is that the similarity can be related by a linear or monotonic decreasing function to inter-point distances in the *metric space* [14], that is, the larger the measure of similarity between two objects, the smaller the distance between the co-responding points in the metric space. Though the origins of the topic in computer science are older, the boom started in the 1990s with the M-tree [4] and resulted in many interesting scientific and technological achievements. The metric space paradigm extends the range of indexable similarity measures but at the same time loses the supportive advantage of coordinate systems to define partitioning of search spaces. The main advantage is that such approach is also able to consider data domains, which are not sortable – typical for a majority of contemporary digital data seen through their content descriptors. Since the similarity is in fact measured as a dissimilarity, specifically a distance, the applied techniques are often designated as *distance searching*.

Several key publications summarize achievements in this area. The first survey [3] includes results till the year 2000. It presents known approaches in original taxonomy with the objective to discover core properties that would allow combination of existing principles to form future better proposals. The second survey [6] divides existing methods for handling similarity search into two classes. The first class directly indexes objects based on distances (distance-based indexing), while the second is based on mapping to a vector space (mapping-based approach). However, the main part of this article is dedicated to a survey of distance-based indexing methods, and the mapping-based methods are only outlined. In 2006, a book named Similarity Search: The Metric Space Approach [24] presented the state-of-the-art in developing index structures and supportive technologies for searching complex data modeled as instances of a metric space. The metric searching problems are also considered in the last edition of the encyclopedic book by Hanan Samet [15] called Foundations of Multidimensional and Metric Data Structures.

2 Similarity Search in Applications

Though a lot of progress has been made [1,12] and several interesting similarity search demonstration prototypes, see Fig. 1 for illustration, are already available, [10,11], the fact still is that the extensibility property – one system used for many applications – of the metric space approach to similarity searching, has not yet been fully exploited [13].

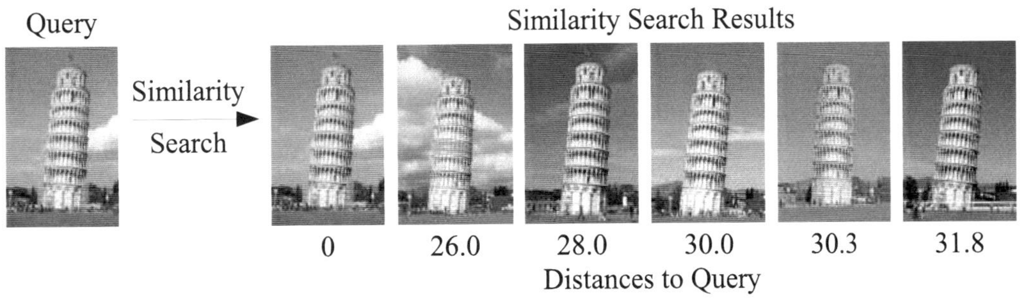

Fig. 1. Image similarity search

An application of similarity searching in several dimensions have been investigated in the Data Intensive Systems and Applications (DISA) Laboratory of Masaryk University, Brno. The first objective is to speedup *face retrieval* in large collections of common photographs. They also develop *image annotation* systems and study mechanisms which should be applied for similarity searching in *data streams*. Finally, they consider a very complex data type, called *motion capture data*, to develop scalable similarity search, filtering and annotation/classification mechanisms. In the following, we shortly outline each of the activities. In the talk, the content-based image similarity search as well as its applications will be demonstrated by on-line demonstrations.

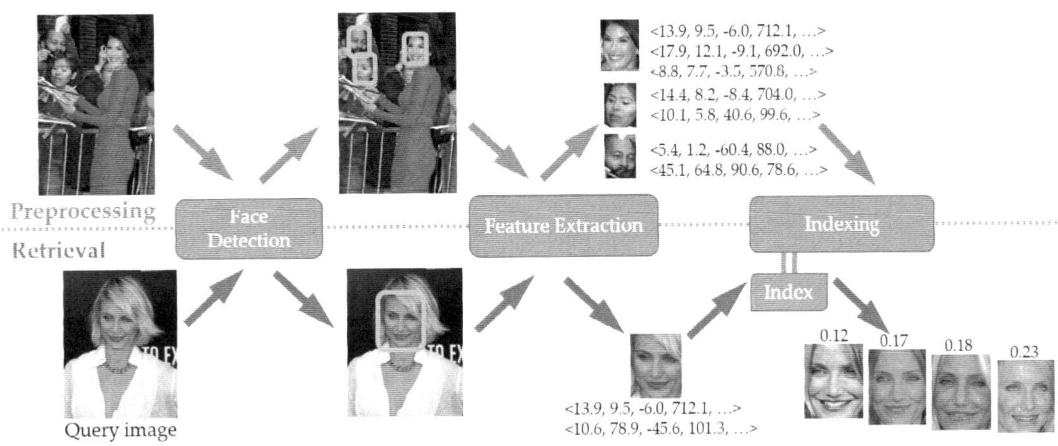

Fig. 2. Face detection and similarity retrieval

2.1 Similarity Searching in Images of Human Faces

Face recognition is a problem of verifying or identifying a face appearing in a given image. In our project, sketched in Fig. 2, we do not develop new face detection or comparison modules but rather demonstrate how a synergic collaboration of existing systems combined with similarity searching can scale into the dimension of large image collections [19]. Specifically, by integrating three OpenCV, NeuroTech and Luxand similarity measures, we achieve high-quality and more stable results, compared to the measures evaluated independently. We also demonstrate, how effectiveness can significantly improve by employing the concept of *multi-face queries* along with optional *relevance feedback*. Finally, a metric indexing structure is applied to achieve scalability of the similarity search.

2.2 Image Annotation

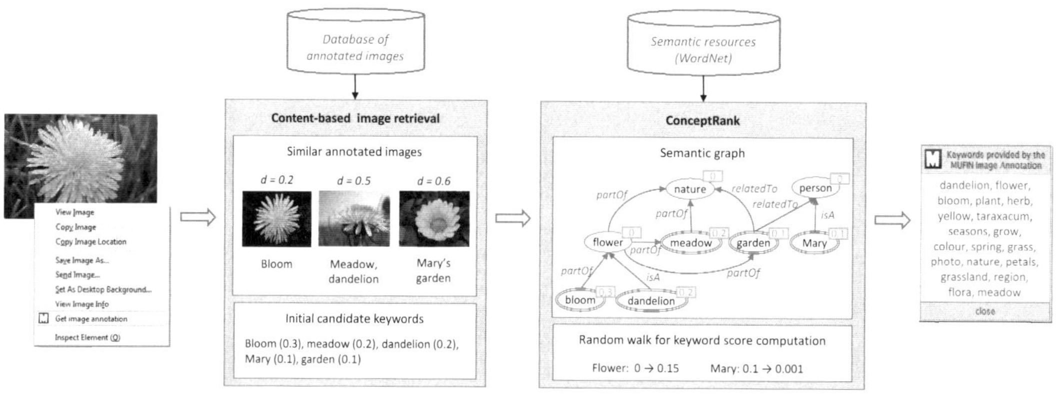

Fig. 3. ConceptRank with search based image annotation

The objective of image annotation is to associate binary images with descriptive metadata that would allow application of text search for content based image retrieval – metadata can also be used for image categorization. Such task has a long tradition in the machine learning field, which approaches the problem by training statistical models for prespecified set of categories. State-of-the-art classification methods of this sort achieve very high accuracy, but their utilization is costly in terms of learning time and requires large amounts of reliably-labeled training data [21]. The proposed strategy, called the *concept-rank* [2], combines information provided by efficient and effective similarity search with semantic information obtained from linguistic resources. Specifically, we first select a set of initial candidate keywords from descriptions of similar already annotated images and give them a probability score proportional to their frequency and the similarity of the respective images to the annotated (query) image. Next, we search for links between these keywords using several semantic relationships defined by the WordNet lexical database, in particular we apply the *hypernymy*, *hyponymy*, *meronymy*, and *holonymy*. We also include new related keywords in consideration for annotation. After the identification of semantic relationships, we run a random-walk-based algorithm over the graph of candidate keywords and their relationships to determine the final probabilities of individual candidates. All the process is illustrated in Fig. 3.

2.3 Stream Processing

The problem of fast executing streams of similarity queries is serious for a large number of applications. For example when annotating large collections of images or when publish-subscribe systems consider incoming documents as queries and test them against user profiles to access the level of agreement between the profile and the processed document (image). The acceleration strategy is based on a pragmatic observation that in large collections the response time to process two random queries is significantly higher that the time needed to process two queries representing similar images [9]. The more similar the queries the shorter the query execution time because a larger portion of the database can be pre-cached from a previous query execution. Then by a clever reordering of queries so that the similarity of two consequent queries is as high as possible, the throughput can significantly be improved. The concept is illustrated in Fig. 4. Further performance improvements can be obtained by a parallel execution for example in cloud computer platforms [8].

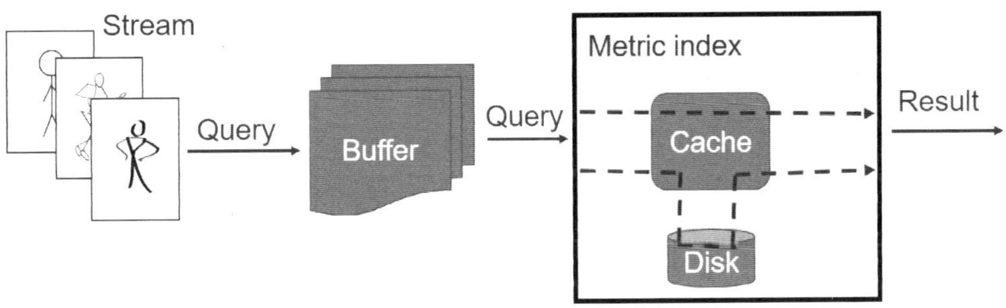

Fig. 4. Similarity query stream processing

2.4 Similarity Searching in Motion Capture Data

Motion capture data is a good example of complex unstructured data. This spatio-temporal data digitally represents human movements in form of 3D trajectories of tracked human body joints. With the recent advances and availability of motion capturing technologies, there is a strong requirement for intelligent management of such data, which has a great potential to be utilized in a number of applications.

To make the content-based management of motion data possible, effective features need to be extracted from 3D skeleton sequences. We propose a 4,096-dimensional vector representation that preserves significant characteristics of original motion sequences [17]. As illustrated in Fig. 5, this representation normalizes and transforms an input sequence into a 2D motion image which is then processed by a convolutional neural network. The last hidden layer of the network is considered as the output feature. The extracted features demonstrate very convenient properties of being (1) of a fixed size, (2) efficiently comparable by the Euclidean distance, and (3) tolerant to a considerable degree of segmentation errors, which is particularly useful for sub-sequence matching.

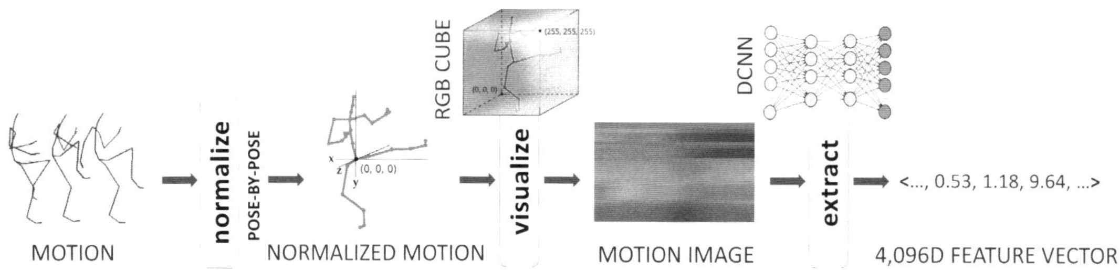

Fig. 5. Feature extraction from 3D human motion sequences.

The extracted features can describe the content of relatively short skeleton sequences taking in order of seconds. This is mainly suitable for recognizing the class of semantic actions using k-nearest neighbor classifiers [20]. In case input sequences are long, the partitioning principle needs to be applied to identify short segments that are better describable by the features. We propose to partition the input sequence into segments of different sizes in a way that an arbitrary sub-sequence overlaps with at least one segment in the majority of frames [16]. This property enables to consider a short query as a single segment and perform efficient sub-sequence searching on a large scale [18]. A similar idea is also used for real-time annotation of pseudo-infinite skeleton sequences [5].

Acknowledgements. This research is supported by the Czech Science Foundation project No. GA19-02033S.

References

1. Batko, M., Novak, D., Falchi, F., Zezula, P.: Scalability comparison of peer-to-peer similarity search structures. Future Generation Comp. Syst. 24(8), 834–848 (2008)
2. Budíková, P., Batko, M., Zezula, P.: Conceptrank for search-based image annotation. Multimedia Tools Appl. 77(7), 8847–8882 (2018), `https://doi.org/10.1007/s11042-017-4777-8`

3. Chávez, E., Navarro, G., Baeza-Yates, R., Marroquín, J.: Searching in metric spaces. ACM Comput. Surv. 33(3), 273–321 (2001)
4. Ciaccia, P., Patella, M., Zezula, P.: M-tree: An efficient access method for similarity search in metric spaces. In: VLDB. pp. 426–435. Morgan Kaufmann (1997)
5. Elias, P., Sedmidubsky, J., Zezula, P.: A real-time annotation of motion data streams. In: 19th International Symposium on Multimedia. pp. 154–161. IEEE Computer Society (2017)
6. Hjaltason, G., Samet, H.: Index-driven similarity search in metric spaces. ACM Trans. Database Syst. 28(4), 517–580 (2003)
7. Krumhansl, C.: Concerning applicability of geometric models to similarity data: The interrelationship between similarity and spatial density. Psychological Review 85 pp. 445–461 (1978)
8. Nalepa, F., Batko, M., Zezula, P.: Model for performance analysis of distributed stream processing applications. In: Database and Expert Systems Applications - 26th International Conference, DEXA 2015, Valencia, Spain, September 1-4, 2015, Proceedings, Part II. pp. 520–533 (2015)
9. Nalepa, F., Batko, M., Zezula, P.: Enhancing similarity search throughput by dynamic query reordering. In: Database and Expert Systems Applications - 27th International Conference, DEXA 2016, Porto, Portugal, September 5 – 8. p. 15 (2016)
10. Novak, D., Batko, M., Zezula, P.: Generic similarity search engine demonstrated by an image retrieval application. In: Proceedings of the 32nd Annual International ACM SIGIR Conference on Research and Development in Information Retrieval, Boston, MA, USA, July 19-23. p. 840 (2009)
11. Novak, D., Batko, M., Zezula, P.: Large-scale image retrieval using neural net descriptors. In: Proceedings of the 38th International ACM SIGIR Conference on Research and Development in Information Retrieval, Santiago, Chile, August 9-13, 2015. pp. 1039–1040 (2015)
12. Novak, D., Batko, M., Zezula, P.: Large-scale similarity data management with distributed metric index. Inf. Process. Manage. 48(5), 855–872 (2012)
13. Novak, D., Kyselak, M., Zezula, P.: On locality-sensitive indexing in generic metric spaces. In: Third International Workshop on Similarity Search and Applications, SISAP 2010, 18-19 September 2010, Istanbul, Turkey. pp. 59–66 (2010)
14. O'Searcoid, M.: Metric Spaces. Springer (2006)
15. Samet, H.: Foundations of Multidimensional And Metric Data Structures. Series in Data Management Systems, Morgan Kaufmann (2006)
16. Sedmidubsky, J., Elias, P., Zezula, P.: Similarity searching in long sequences of motion capture data. In: 9th International Conference on Similarity Search and Applications (SISAP). pp. 271–285. Springer International Publishing, Cham (2016)
17. Sedmidubsky, J., Elias, P., Zezula, P.: Effective and efficient similarity searching in motion capture data. Multimedia Tools and Applications 77(10), 12073–12094 (2018), https://doi.org/10.1007/s11042-017-4859-7
18. Sedmidubsky, J., Elias, P., Zezula, P.: Searching for variable-speed motions in long sequences of motion capture data. Information Systems 80, 148–158 (2019)
19. Sedmidubsky, J., Mic, V., Zezula, P.: 8th International Conference on Similarity Search and Applications (SISAP 2015), chap. Face Image Retrieval Revisited, pp. 204–216. Springer International Publishing (2015), http://dx.doi.org/10.1007/978-3-319-25087-8_19
20. Sedmidubsky, J., Zezula, P.: Probabilistic classification of skeleton sequences. In: 29th International Conference on Database and Expert Systems Applications (DEXA). pp. 50–65. Springer International Publishing, Cham (2018)

21. Szegedy, C., Liu, W., Jia, Y., Sermanet, P., Reed, S.E., Anguelov, D., Erhan, D., Vanhoucke, V., Rabinovich, A.: Going deeper with convolutions. In: IEEE Conference on Computer Vision and Pattern Recognition, CVPR 2015, Boston, MA, USA, June 7-12, 2015. pp. 1–9 (2015)
22. Torgerson, W.S.: Multidimensional scaling of similarity. Psychometrika 30 pp. 379–393 (1965)
23. Tversky, A.: Features of similarity. Psychological Review 84 pp. 327–354 (1977)
24. Zezula, P., Amato, G., Dohnal, V., Batko, M.: Similarity Search: The Metric Space Approach, Advances in Database Systems, vol. 32. Springer (2006)

Analysing Event Data through Process Mining

Andrea Marrella

DIAG, Sapienza University of Rome, Italy
marrella@diag.uniroma1.it

Extended Abstract

Most organizations create business processes, which are sometimes difficult to control and comprehend. Understanding these processes is however an absolute prerequisite prior to taking on any improvement initiative. *Process mining* provides a new perspective that makes easier and faster to get a complete and objective picture of business processes to better control and continuously improve them, by reducing their costs, production time and risks. This is made possible by analysing vast quantities of event data available in today's information systems. Mainly, which activities are performed, when, and by whom.

In that sense, process mining sits between computational intelligence and data mining on the one hand, and business process management on the other hand. The reference framework for process mining focuses on: *(i)* conceptual models describing processes, organizational structures, and the corresponding relevant data; and *(ii)* the real execution of processes, as reflected by the footprint of reality logged and stored by the information systems in use within an enterprise. For process mining to be applicable, such information has to be structured in the form of explicit *event logs*. In fact, all process mining techniques assume that it is possible to record the sequencing of relevant events occurred within an enterprise, such that each event refers to an activity (i.e., a well-defined step in some process) and is related to a particular case

Through process mining, decision makers can discover process models from event logs (*process discovery*), compare expected and actual behaviors (*conformance checking*), and enrich models with key information about their actual execution (*process enhancement*). This, in turn, provides the basis to understand, maintain, and enhance processes based on reality.

In this tutorial, we introduce the process mining framework, the main process mining techniques and tools, and the different phases of event data analysis through process mining, discussing the various ways data and process analysts can make use of the mined models. Finally, we discuss common pitfalls and critical issues, and give suggestions on how to mitigate them.

Writing (and also reading) books reduces (sometimes) the entropy of the universe, but risks to increase (sometimes) the peace of mind in me

Carlo Batini

University of Milano-Bicocca, Italy
batini@disco.unimib.it

Extended Abstract

In the dedication appearing in my book "Information Systems for eGovernment: a Quality of Service Perspective" written with Gianluigi Viscusi and Massimo Mecella, and published by Springer Verlag, I say: To my wife, Barbara, to my brothers Beppe and Mariella, and to all who believe that writing books contributes to reduce the disorder of the universe. During my life I have written (so far) about 35 books (including the three books in preparation), six of them in English. Publishing companies are Springer, Boringhieri, Benjamin and Cummings and subsequently Addison Wesley and Pearson, Editori Riuniti, and others. Six of them are published with Creative Commons licence, so they are accessible and downloadabile by everyone.

In my talk I will make a guided tour on my book production activity, trying to show that my constant not necessarily achieved) goal has been to clarify, to give a structure, to discover and highlight common issues in a topic usually focused on computer science, in the attempt to reduce the disorder and confusion around us in the use of terminologies, concepts and relationships among concepts.

At the same time, writing a book is a time consuming and also complex, strenuous, tirelessly activity; writing books is such as climbing a high, very high mountain, and you have to distribute forces if you want to conquer the summit, sorry, finish the book. Furthermore, when you write the last word of the last chapter, there are at least other two ninety five per cent of effort remaining…….so writing a book is like climbing three mountains, not one. And when I finish the third ninety five per cent of a book, I feel like when I reach the summit of a mountain, my endorfines play a similar role in reaching a state of satisfaction and fullness.

Looking back, I have perceived frequently in book writing what Marcel Proust says in its masterpiece Search for the Lost Time "From a certain age, our memories are so intertwined with each other that the thing we think about, the book we read almost no longer matters. We have put a bit of ourselves everywhere, everything is fruitful, everything is dangerous, and we can make discoveries as important in Pascal's "Thoughts" as in the advertising of a bar of soap."

In a sense, the story of my 35 books, the change in their style, the dedications, can be seen also as a story that tells my life. As to dedications, in books and in student's dissertations, I often say that they are the most important and revealing testimony of the author.

So far, I have always written technical books, namely they address scientific topics. But now, in a time that leads to seniority (let us call the old age with a more polite term..) I'm conceiving books that besides decreasing the disorder of the universe try to decrease the entropy in myself, and try to share with the reader something more than concepts, I mean try to share emotions. This is not easy, since there is a subtle threshold between ostentation and emotional transfert. My plan is to write in the future books that merge my scientific achievements and my emotions and memories.

My life with books retraces from one side the evolution of technologies and from another side my evolution in style. I made a lot of experiences and also experiments. I have written a book using the editor of a mainframe, that had only CAPITAL LETTERS, another recent book is (on purpose) the written transcription of a video course, to achieve the goal of keeping in the text some of the freshness of the oral speech. In the first books I used the typical deductive style, where I first gave definitions and then examples, the last books are instead inductive, first examples and then definitions. I have also tried to introduce some form of interactivity in the last books, posing questions and providing solutions in a different page. As to methodological books, I have written books that have been evaluated as a "big brick", "una mattonata" in roman dialect. I think that is better una mattonata than the jungle. In another book, the only book that I have written alone, "Le basi dell'informatica", I was committed to use only the most frequent five thousand Italian words, so the word "daily" in the first row of the 164 pages has been changed into "every day", you can only imagine the cemetery of corrections in the rest of the 164 pages...

Just to understand my need to write books in all possible variants of settings, I am currently writing three books at the same time, whose titles are

1. Come si progetta un sistema informativo, with title and dedication in italian and text in english.
2. Le basi della scienza dei dati, title and text in Italian, with contributions from Federico Cabitza, Roberto Masiero, Andrea Maurino, Matteo Palmonari, Fabio Stella.
3. Abstractions in models and processes - Conceptual modeling, maps and graphs, with title and text in English, with John Mylopoulos.

Also *reading books* contributes to reduce the entropy of the universe. In an era in which a twitter of Trump reaches in a few seconds millions of followers, the life and survival of books, especially paper books, it's hard. Personally, I reached an equilib-

rium in my library between paper books that take up many centimeters of space and e-books that occupy many orders of magnitude less space. I developed a strategy on the choice of the format, based on what Ella Berthoud e Susan Elderkin say in their book "The Novel Cure: an A to Z of Literary Remedies".
When I ascertain that my paper versions have the size of the characters too small, or else when I think I do not need the paper copy, then I buy subsequently the e-book version, when I want to "see" the book, and want to make a sensorial experience, I buy the paper copy.

I also like to donate books to my friends and colleagues. It is interesting to note that in the past I thought first to the person, and then I chose the book to donate to her/him, now when I read a book or even a review, If I like it then I identify the friend to whom to donate the book.

In Italy, the period of the week in which newspapers publish reviews of books is Saturday (Tuttolibri of La Stampa and Robinson by Repubblica) to Sunday (La Lettura by Corriere della Sera). When I look to the newspaper the first time I come to the conclusion that want to buy all the books reviewed, than the second time only the half of the books. I have decided to apply the policy to wait Sunday evening, so to intercept the natural decay in the attractiveness of books. The experience says that at end I buy on the average two/three books every week.

To conclude, Marguerite Yourcenar says in Memories of Hadrian that (in Italian) "Fondare biblioteche è come costruire ancora granai pubblici, ammassare riserve contro l'inverno dello spirito che da molti indizi, mio malgrado, vedo venire.". "Founding libraries is like building more public granaries, amassing reserves against the winter of the spirit that with a great deal of evidence, in spite of myself, I see coming". She was right.

Fig. 1. My books

References

1. C. Batini - Esercitazioni di programmazione dei calcolatori elettronici - La Goliardica, Roma, 1977.
2. C. Batini - Applicazioni di programmazione in linguaggi assemblativi - La Goliardica, Roma, 1979.
3. C. Batini, F. Ferrara, M. Lenzerini, V. Zecca - Complementi di linguaggi assemblativi - La Goliardica, Roma, 1979.
4. C. Batini, P.Bertolazzi - Introduzione alla struttura degli elaboratori - ESA Editrice, Roma, 1980.
5. C. Batini - Le basi dell' informatica - Editori Riuniti, 1984.
6. C. Batini, S. Breccia, G. Ciccarella, F. Ferrara - Introduzione alle metodologie di programmazione nel linguaggio Fortran - ESA Editrice, Roma 1985.
7. P. Atzeni, C. Batini, V. De Antonellis - La teoria relazionale dei dati - Serie di Informatica, Boringhieri, 1985.
8. C. Batini - Progetto concettuale di basi di dati territoriali: relazione finale - Pubblicazione interna ISTAT, 1985.
9. C. Batini, E. Fortunato - Progetto concettuale di basi di dati territoriali - Pubblicazione ISTAT, 1986.
10. C. Batini, G. De Petra, M. Lenzerini, G. Santucci - La progettazione concettuale dei dati - Franco Angeli Editore, prima edizione 1986.

11. C. Batini, M. Lenzerini, A. Marchetti Spaccamela - Introduzione agli algoritmi e alla programmazione: sei dispense - Corso per il Diploma di Informatica - Consorzio per la Universita' a distanza, 1986.
12. C. Batini, G. Bisogni, P. Gentile Studio Preliminare per la Definizione di uno Schema Generale di Riferimento per lo Sviluppo e la Realizzazione dei Sistemi Informativi nella Pubblica Amministrazione – Istituto Poligrafico e Zecca dello Stato, 1986.
13. S. Ceri, C. Batini, P. Atzeni - Basi di dati - Corso per il Diploma di Informatica - Consorzio per la Università a distanza - 1987.
14. C. Batini – Il Progetto di Sviluppo dei Sistemi Informativi nella Pubblica Amministrazione: la fase di analisi Istituto Poligrafico e Zecca dello Stato, 1987, non disponibile.
15. C. Batini – Struttura e Progetto di un Dizionario Dati Utente per la Banca d'Italia: Relazione finale, Banca d'Italia, 1989.
16. C. Batini – UsER: La Metodologia GESI per il Progetto di Basi di Dati GESI S.r.l., 1989.
17. C. Batini et al. - Quadro metodologico per il progetto di sistemi informativi nella Pubblica Amministrazione - Istituto Poligrafico dello Stato, Ministero del Tesoro, 1990.
18. C. Batini, M.L. Bargellini – Sistemi Informativi per la Diffusione della Informazione: Metodologia di Progettazione – Enea, 1990.
19. C. Batini, L. Carlucci Aiello, M. Lenzerini, A. Marchetti Spaccamela, A. Miola – Fondamenti di Programmazione dei calcolatori elettronici - Franco Angeli Editore, 1990.
20. G. Ausiello, C. Batini, D. Mandrioli, M. Protasi - Modelli e linguaggi dell' informatica - McGrawHill Italia, 1991.
21. C. Batini, S. Ceri, S.B. Navathe - Logical data base design using the Entity Relationship model - Benjamin and Cummings/ Addison Wesley, Palo Alto, California, USA, 1991.
22. P. Ercoli, C.Batini, F. Marozza - L' amministrazione dei sistemi informativi pubblici: Quadro Metodologico di Riferimento - Il Mulino, 1992.
23. P. Ercoli, C. Batini, F. Marozza (a cura di) - Nuove metodologie per i sistemi informativi della Pubblica Amministrazione - Il Mulino, 1993.
24. L. Cabibbo, R. Torlone, C. Batini – Basi di Dati: Progetti ed Esercizi svolti, Pitagora Editrice Bologna, 1995. C. Batini, G. Longobardi, I. Siciliani – Il Repository delle Basi di Dati della Pubblica Amministrazione, Collana Documenti, Autorità per l'Informatica nella Pubblica Amministrazione, 1996.
25. C. Batini, M. Scannapieco, Qualità dei Dati: Concetti, Metodi e Tecniche, Springer Italia, 2008.
26. C. Batini, M. Scannapieco - Data Quality: Concepts, Methodologies, Techniques, Springer Verlag 2006.
27. C. Batini, D. Natale – DG@SOGEI – Metodologia SOGEI sulla Data governance e il Repository degli Schemi Concettuali – Volume I, Sogei, 2007.
28. G. Viscusi, C. Batini, M. Mecella Information Systems for eGovernment: a Quality of Service Perspective – Springer Verlag, August 2010.
29. C. Batini - Course on Database Modeling and Design – Transcriptions of Lessons of the MOOC Course – Creative Commons Licence, 2015.
30. C. Batini, M. Castelli, M. Comerio, M. Cremaschi, L. Iaquinta, A. Torsello, G. Viscusi – The Smart Methodology for the Life Cycle of Services, Creative Commons Licence, 2015.
31. C. Batini, M. Scannapieco - Data and Information Quality: Dimensions, Principles and Techniques, Springer Verlag 2015.

Exploring Change

Tobias Bleifuß[1], Leon Bornemann[1], Theodore Johnson[2], Dmitri V. Kalashnikov[2], Felix Naumann[1], and Divesh Srivastava[2]

[1] Hasso Plattner Institute, University of Potsdam, Germany
{tobias.bleifuss,leon.bornemann,felix.naumann}@hpi.de
[2] AT&T Labs–Research, USA
{johnsont,dvk,divesh}@research.att.com

Abstract. Data and schema in datasets experience many different kinds of change: values are inserted, deleted or updated; rows appear and disappear; columns are added or repurposed, and so on. In such a dynamic situation, users might wonder: How many changes have there been in the recent minutes, days or years? What kind of changes were made at which points of time? How volatile are the values of a specific property or entity? How dirty is the data? The fact that data changed can hint at different hidden processes: a frequently crowd-updated city name may be controversial; a person whose name has been recently changed may be the target of vandalism; and so on. To interactively explore such changes, we present our DBChEx (Database Change Explorer) prototype system [2]. Using two real-world datasets, IMDB and Wikipedia infoboxes, we illustrate how users can gain valuable insights into data generation processes and data or schema evolution over time by a mix of serendipity and guided investigation using DBChEx. Finally, we identify a range of technical challenges that need to be addressed to fully realize our vision of change exploration [1].

References

1. Bleifuß, T., Bornemann, L., Johnson, T., Kalashnikov, D.V., Naumann, F., Srivastava, D.: Exploring change - A new dimension of data analytics. PVLDB **12**(2), 85–98 (2018)
2. Bleifuß, T., Bornemann, L., Kalashnikov, D.V., Naumann, F., Srivastava, D.: DBChEx: Interactive exploration of data and schema change. In: *Proceedings of the Conference on Innovative Data Systems Research* (CIDR) (2019)

Flexible Score Aggregation

(Discussion Paper)

Paolo Ciaccia[1] and Davide Martinenghi[2]

[1]Università di Bologna, Italy, email: `paolo.ciaccia@unibo.it`
[2]Politecnico di Milano, Italy, email: `davide.martinenghi@polimi.it`

Abstract. Ranking objects according to different criteria is a central issue in many data-intensive applications. Yet, no existing solution deals with the case of partially specified score aggregation functions (e.g., a weighted sum with no precisely known weight values).
We address multi-source top-k queries with constraints (rather than precise values) on the weights. Our solution is instance optimal and provides increased flexibility with negligible overhead wrt classical top-k queries.

1 Introduction

Looking for information relevant to decide about the goodness of items of interest (hotels, restaurants, products, services, etc.) has become a common activity, supported by the so-called *multi-source top-k queries* [6]. For instance, the problem of choosing where to eat (possibly with constraints on price, food type, and location) may be addressed by *aggregating* different pieces of information from several sources. It is custom to assume that each such source provides a *ranked list* of results (from best to worst), each coming with a (local) score. Accordingly, objects can be either retrieved sequentially via a *sorted access* or by providing the object's identifier and obtaining the corresponding local score (*random access*). Then, for each object o in the dataset, a *monotone scoring function* f is used to aggregate the local scores yielding the (overall) score $f(o)$.

	a	h	j	d	f	b	e	i	c	g
R_1	9	8	8	7	7	6	6	5	4	4

	i	a	g	j	c	h	f	d	e	b
R_2	10	9	8	8	7	6	5	5	5	4

	c	f	e	i	d	a	b	g	h	j
R_3	9	8	7	7	6	5	5	5	4	3

Fig. 1: A set of ten restaurants ranked by three sources.

Example 1. Consider the scenario depicted in Figure 1, where ten restaurants, a, ..., j, are ordered by $d = 3$ rankings. Assume that the overall score is a weighted sum of the local scores, i.e., $f(o) = \sum_{i=1}^{d} w_i \cdot o[i]$, where $o[i]$ is the score assigned by R_i to object o (e.g., $\mathtt{c}[2] = 7$), and that the $k = 2$ best restaurants are sought. In particular, using the *weight vector* $W_1 = (1/3, 1/3, 1/3)$, the top-2 restaurants are `a` and `i`, with $f(\mathtt{a}) \approx 7.67$ and $f(\mathtt{i}) \approx 7.33$. A different choice of weights, say $W_2 = (0.2, 0.3, 0.5)$, results in `i` and `c` being the top-2 restaurants.

Choosing precise weights in the scoring function is admittedly difficult, and might be the result of learning from users, e.g., via crowdsourcing [4]. A more viable alternative is to specify weights only partially through a set of *constraints*. With reference to Example 1, instead of having fixed weights, it might be interesting to "explore" all the alternatives arising when weights vary around W_2, by, say, ± 0.1. Then, only `a`, `c`, `f`, and `i` can be the possible (top-2) answers.

We study the problem of answering multi-source top-k queries with partially specified weights. This leads to a *family* $\mathcal{F}$ of scoring functions for ranking objects. Existing solutions to the problem with a single scoring function are *Fagin's algorithm* (`FA`) [6] and the *threshold algorithm* (`TA`) [7]. The latter was shown to perform better and to achieve optimal I/O performance. Our proposal, `FSA`, solves the general case and reduces to `TA` for classical top-k queries (i.e, when $\mathcal{F} = \{f\}$) and is *instance optimal for any* $\mathcal{F}$. When no constraints are present, `FSA` behaves like `FA` and returns the so-called k*-skyband* [9], the case $k = 1$ being the *skyline* of the dataset [1].

This paper summarizes the main contributions presented in [3], namely 1) a provably correct and instance optimal algorithm, `FSA`, for answering multi-source top-k queries, 2) several optimization opportunities for improving the execution time of `FSA`, 3) experimental evidence that `FSA` enjoys the flexibility of partially specified weights while incurring little overhead wrt top-k queries.

2 Problem statement

Consider a dataset $\mathcal{D} = \{o_1, \ldots, o_N\}$ where each object $o \in \mathcal{D}$ has $d \geq 2$ *partial scores*, $(o[1], \ldots, o[d])$. For any scoring function f and dataset $\mathcal{D}$, a *top-k* query on $\mathcal{D}$ using f returns a set of k objects with the highest scores according to f (ties arbitrarily broken). Given objects o and o', if $o[i] \geq o'[i]$ holds for all $i = 1, \ldots, d$, at least once strictly, then o *dominates* o', written $o \succ o'$. Notice that $o \succ o'$ implies $f(o) \geq f(o')$ $\forall f \in \mathcal{M}$ ($\mathcal{M}$ being the set of all monotone scoring functions). The *skyline* of $\mathcal{D}$ is the set of undominated objects in $\mathcal{D}$:

$$\textsc{Sky}(\mathcal{D}) = \{o \in \mathcal{D} \mid \nexists o' \in \mathcal{D}.\ o' \succ o\}, \tag{1}$$

but can also be viewed as the set of objects that can be top-1 [8], i.e.:

$$o \in \textsc{Sky}(\mathcal{D}) \iff \exists f \in \mathcal{M}.\ \forall o' \in \mathcal{D}.\ o' \neq o \to f(o) > f(o').$$

The k*-skyband* of $\mathcal{D}$, written $\textsc{Sky}_k(\mathcal{D})$, is the set of all objects in $\mathcal{D}$ that are dominated by less than k objects [9], and thus includes all possible top-k sets.

As a generalization of dominance for a family $\mathcal{F}$ of monotone scoring functions ([2]), we say that object o $\mathcal{F}$*-dominates* object o', $o \neq o'$, denoted by $o \succ_{\mathcal{F}} o'$, iff $\forall f \in \mathcal{F}.\ f(o) \geq f(o')$ and $\exists f \in \mathcal{F}.\ f(o) > f(o')$.

We define the *non-dominated restricted skyband* of $\mathcal{D}$ wrt $\mathcal{F}$, denoted $\textsc{nd}_k(\mathcal{D}; \mathcal{F})$, as the set of objects in $\mathcal{D}$ that are $\mathcal{F}$-dominated by less than k objects:

$$\textsc{nd}_k(\mathcal{D}; \mathcal{F}) = \{o \in \mathcal{D} \mid \nexists o_1, \ldots, o_k \in \mathcal{D}.\quad o_1 \succ_{\mathcal{F}} o \wedge \ldots \wedge o_k \succ_{\mathcal{F}} o\} \tag{2}$$

Clearly, $\textsc{nd}_k(\mathcal{D}; \mathcal{F}) \subseteq \textsc{Sky}_k(\mathcal{D})$. When $\mathcal{F}$ reduces to a single function f, then $\textsc{nd}_k(\mathcal{D}, \{f\})$ includes *all* possible top-k results for f (whereas, in case of ties, top-k queries may nondeterministically discard tuples). From (2) it is evident that if $o \notin \textsc{nd}_k(\mathcal{D}; \mathcal{F})$, then *no scoring function* $f \in \mathcal{F}$ *can make* o *top-k*. We now address the problem of efficiently computing $\textsc{nd}_k(\mathcal{D}; \mathcal{F})$ in a multi-source scenario, for any given dataset $\mathcal{D}$ and set of monotone scoring functions $\mathcal{F}$.

3 Flexible score aggregation with FSA

Fagin's algorithm `FA` was the first to address multi-source top-k queries for arbitrary scoring functions. It consists of three phases: 1) sorted accesses are executed; 2) random accesses are executed on all objects met in phase 1; 3) scores of all fetched objects are computed using a scoring function f and the top-k result determined. The *stopping condition* for phase 1 is to have seen at least k objects on *all* the d rankings. With the scenario depicted in Figure 1, `FA` would stop at *depth* 7 (after 7 sorted accesses per ranking), after seeing `a` and `f` on all rankings. The `FA` algorithm can be adapted to compute $\text{SKY}_k(\mathcal{D})$, since it stops phase 1 independently of f. Therefore, the set S of objects seen when the algorithm stops includes the top-k objects according to *any* possible monotonic scoring function (and, thus, $\text{SKY}_k(\mathcal{D})$, which, in turn, includes $\text{ND}_k(\mathcal{D};\mathcal{F})$).

The `TA` algorithm uses a *threshold value* $f(\tau)$ computed by applying the specific scoring function f to the tuple τ of last scores seen by sorted access on each ranking, which we here call the *threshold point*. A further difference with respect to `FA` is that random accesses are not delayed to a separate phase: after performing d sorted accesses (one per ranking), all the necessary random accesses are executed. The algorithm stops when at least k seen objects have a global score no worse than $f(\tau)$. Thus, for each object o in the result, $f(o) \geq f(\tau)$ holds. In Figure 1, with $k = 2$ and weights $W_2 = (0.2, 0.3, 0.5)$ `TA` would stop at depth 4, where $f(\tau) = 7.3$, since $f(\texttt{i}) = 7.5$ and $f(\texttt{c}) = 7.4$.

Being tailored to a specific f, the stopping criterion of `TA` is (much) more efficient than the one used by `FA`, but now, when `TA` stops, S is only guaranteed to contain the top-k objects according to f, but not necessarily according to other scoring functions.

Let us say that o *weakly $\mathcal{F}$-dominates* o', $o \neq o'$ iff $\forall f \in \mathcal{F}.\ f(o) \geq f(o')$. Then, we can unify `FA` and `TA` according to the following observation.

Observation 1 *`FA` stops executing sorted accesses when k seen objects $o_1, \ldots, o_k$* weakly $\mathcal{M}$-dominate τ. *`TA` stops when k seen objects* weakly $\{f\}$-dominate τ.

Our proposal, `FSA`, applies the notion of $\mathcal{F}$-dominance wrt τ, which includes ($\mathcal{M}$-)dominance and $\{f\}$-dominance as special cases. The extraction performed by `FSA` stops as soon as k objects are seen that $\mathcal{F}$-dominate τ, as all unseen objects are also necessarily $\mathcal{F}$-dominated by these k objects. Notice that `FSA` uses $\mathcal{F}$-dominance rather than weak $\mathcal{F}$-dominance for not discarding ties from $\text{ND}_k(\mathcal{D};\mathcal{F})$. The pseudocode of `FSA` is presented in Figure 1.

Note that the descent performed by `FSA` alternates a single sorted access on the i-th ranking with $d-1$ random accesses on the other rankings. This differs from the strategy adopted by `TA`, which, at each depth, first performs d sorted accesses (one per ranking), thereby retrieving up to d unseen objects, and then completes the scores for these objects with up to $d \cdot (d-1)$ random accesses. However, both algorithms stop at the same depth. Also note that `FA` performs all random accesses at the end; however, such an approach would not be possible for `TA` or `FSA`, since $\{f\}$-dominance and $\mathcal{F}$-dominance generally require knowing all the scores of the objects being compared.

Algorithm 1: FSA algorithmic pattern for computing ND_k.

Input: *Rankings* $R_1, \ldots, R_d$ *for* $\mathcal{D}$*, family of scoring functions* $\mathcal{F}$*, integer* $k > 0$.
Output: $\text{ND}_k(\mathcal{D}; \mathcal{F})$.

let $S := \emptyset$ // *Seen objects*
do
  for i **in** $1 \ldots d$
    let $\langle o, \sigma \rangle :=$ `sortedAccess`(R_i) // *Do a sorted access in each ranking* R_i
    $\tau[i] := \sigma$ // *Update score for threshold* τ
    if $o \notin S$ **then** // *Object* o *is new*
      $o[i] := \sigma$ // *Save score for* o
      for j **in** $1 \ldots d$ // *Extract all other scores for* o *via random access*
        if $j \neq i$ **then** $o[j] :=$ `randomAccess`(R_j, o)
      if $\nexists o_1, \ldots, o_k \in S.\ \ o_1 \succ_{\mathcal{F}} o \wedge \ldots \wedge o_k \succ_{\mathcal{F}} o$ **then** `handle`(o)
while $\nexists o_1, \ldots, o_k \in S.\ \ o_1 \succ_{\mathcal{F}} \tau \wedge \ldots \wedge o_k \succ_{\mathcal{F}} \tau$ // *Stop if* k *objects* $\succ_{\mathcal{F}} \tau$
`clean()` // *Remove from* S *all objects* $\mathcal{F}$*-dominated by* $\geq k$ *others*
return S

Let $I = \langle \mathcal{D}, \mathcal{F}, k \rangle$ indicate an instance of the problem of computing $\text{ND}_k(\mathcal{D}; \mathcal{F})$ wrt a set of monotone scoring functions $\mathcal{F}$ and let $\mathbf{I}$ indicate the class of all such problems. An algorithm A is *correct* (for the computation of ND_k) if, for each instance $I = \langle \mathcal{D}, \mathcal{F}, k \rangle \in \mathbf{I}$, A returns $\text{ND}_k(\mathcal{D}; \mathcal{F})$.

Theorem 1. *FSA is correct for the computation of* ND_k.

Performance in top-k contexts is commonly characterized by the number of objects accessed by sorted access by an algorithm A on an instance I, which we indicate as $\texttt{sumDepths}(A, I)$. Algorithm A is *instance optimal* if there exist constants c_1 and c_2 such that $\texttt{sumDepths}(A, I) \leq c_1 \cdot \texttt{sumDepths}(A', I) + c_2$ for every correct algorithm A' and instance $I \in \mathbf{I}$.

Theorem 2. *FSA is instance optimal.*

4 Algorithmic variants

We now discuss efficient implementations of FSA and focus on the case in which each scoring function is of the form $f(o) = \sum_{i=1}^{d} w_i g_i(o[i])$, where the w_i's are *weights* subject to a set $\mathcal{C}$ of linear constraints and the g_i's are monotone. This form includes, e.g., weighted linear sums and weighted L_p norms. The constraints may be of several kinds (see [5] for an overview), such as

1. *weak rankings*: $w_1 \geq w_2 \geq \ldots \geq w_d$ (relative importance of attributes);
2. *ratio bounds*: $\bar{w}_i(1-\varepsilon) \leq w_i \leq \bar{w}_i(1+\varepsilon)$, $1 \leq i \leq d$ (spread around a weight).

Without loss of generality, we consider the space of normalized weight vectors $\mathcal{W} \subseteq [0,1]^d$, such that, for each $W = (w_1, \ldots, w_d) \in \mathcal{W}$, we have $\sum_{i=1}^{d} w_i = 1$; $\mathcal{W}(\mathcal{C})$ denotes the subset of $\mathcal{W}$ of weight vectors satisfying constraints $\mathcal{C}$.

$\mathcal{F}$-dominance test. There are two main approaches to efficiently check $\mathcal{F}$-dominance [2]. One approach requires solving a linear programming problem encoding the notion of $\mathcal{F}$-dominance. This may be expensive, since every $\mathcal{F}$-dominance test requires solving a different LP problem. A better approach, which we choose for FSA, is based on the $\mathcal{F}$*-dominance region* of an object o, i.e., the set of all points that o $\mathcal{F}$-dominates. Such a region needs to be computed only once for all the tests in which o is the candidate $\mathcal{F}$-dominant object. Testing membership to the $\mathcal{F}$-dominance region is done by *i)* computing the vertices of the convex polytope $\mathcal{W}(\mathcal{C})$, and *ii)* checking the following inequalities:

$$\sum_{i=1}^{d} w_i^{(\ell)} g_i(o[i]) \geq \sum_{i=1}^{d} w_i^{(\ell)} g_i(o'[i]), \quad \ell \in \{1, \ldots, q\}, \tag{3}$$

where each $W^{(\ell)} = (w_1^{(\ell)}, \ldots, w_d^{(\ell)})$, for $1 \leq \ell \leq q$, is a vertex of $\mathcal{W}(\mathcal{C})$, and at least one inequality is strict. Computing vertices may be expensive, but needs to be done only once per dataset.

Memoization of the vertex scores. We call the lhs of (3) the *vertex score* of o for $W^{(\ell)}$, denoted by $v_\ell(o)$ (similarly for o' in the rhs). Each vertex score, once computed, is remembered for subsequent tests (3) involving the same object. We adopt this technique for FSA and call it *memoization.*

Sorting. In FSA, we keep the seen objects topologically sorted wrt the $\mathcal{F}$-dominance relation, so that, in a sequence $o_1, \ldots, o_n$, no object o_i can be $\mathcal{F}$-dominated by an object o_j if $j > i$. We do so by sorting according to weights in the centroid of $\mathcal{W}(\mathcal{C})$. Then, when checking whether an object o should be added to the set S of seen objects (line 10 of Algorithm 1), we only look for k objects $\mathcal{F}$-dominating o among those preceding o in the topological sort.

Pruning. In FSA, object removal can occur within either `handle` or `clean`. With *lazy pruning*, we do not remove objects in `handle` and wait to do it when `clean` is called. With *eager pruning*, when an object o is inserted in S, `handle` also removes all objects in S that are $\mathcal{F}$-dominated by o and were already $\mathcal{F}$-dominated by $k-1$ other objects; `clean` does nothing.

										depth = 3		depth = 4		depth = 5	
ℓ	v_ℓ(a)	v_ℓ(i)	v_ℓ(c)	v_ℓ(h)	v_ℓ(f)	v_ℓ(j)	v_ℓ(g)	v_ℓ(e)	v_ℓ(d)	$v_\ell(\tau_3)$	V_ℓ	$v_\ell(\tau_4)$	V_ℓ	$v_\ell(\tau_5)$	V_ℓ
1	6.6	7.7	7.9	5.0	7.0	5.0	5.8	6.3	5.8	7.4	[f, a]	7.3	[f, a]	6.4	[]
2	7.0	8.0	7.7	5.2	6.7	5.5	6.1	6.1	5.7	7.5	[a, f]	7.4	[a, f]	6.5	[]
3	7.4	7.8	7.2	5.6	6.6	6.0	6.0	6.0	5.8	7.6	[a, c, f]	7.4	[c, f]	6.6	[]
4	7.4	7.3	6.9	5.8	6.8	6.0	5.6	6.1	6.0	7.6	[a, i, c, f]	7.3	[c, f]	6.6	[]
5	6.6	7.2	7.6	5.2	7.2	5.0	5.4	6.4	6.0	7.4	[i, f, a]	7.2	[a]	6.4	[]
6	7.0	7.0	7.1	5.6	7.1	5.5	5.3	6.3	6.1	7.5	[c, f, a, i]	7.2	[c, f, a, i]	6.5	[]

Table 1: Vertex scores for Examples 1 and 2, along with threshold point's vertex scores and vertex lists at depth 3, 4, and 5.

Vertex lists. We observe that τ is $\mathcal{F}$-dominated by an object o iff all vertex scores of o are no less than the corresponding vertex scores of τ, and at least one is greater. We then maintain, for each vertex $W^{(\ell)}$, a list V_ℓ of seen objects whose vertex score is still lower than τ's vertex score $v_\ell(\tau)$. An object o is added to V_ℓ within the call to `handle`(o) and, in V_ℓ, the objects are kept sorted by vertex score. Additionally, for each object o, we maintain a mask of q bits $B_1(o), \ldots, B_q(o)$ such that $B_\ell(o) = 1$ iff $v_\ell(o) \geq v_\ell(\tau)$, plus one extra bit $B_{>}(o)$

that is set to 1 iff at least one inequality holds strictly. Analogously, we also maintain a list $V_>$ of those objects o such that $B_{\not>}(o) = 0$. In this way, when checking which objects $\mathcal{F}$-dominate τ, it suffices to consider, for each $\ell \in \{1, \ldots, q\}$, only the objects in $V_\ell \cup V_>$ and only if $v_\ell(\tau)$ has changed since the last check.

Example 2. Consider again the scenario of Example 1, with $k = 2$ and weight vector $(0.2, 0.3, 0.5) \pm 0.1$ on each weight. The vertices of $\mathcal{W}(\mathcal{C})$ are $W^{(1)} = (0.1, 0.3, 0.6)$, $W^{(2)} = (0.1, 0.4, 0.5)$, $W^{(3)} = (0.2, 0.4, 0.4)$, $W^{(4)} = (0.3, 0.3, 0.4)$, $W^{(5)} = (0.2, 0.2, 0.6)$, $W^{(6)} = (0.3, 0.2, 0.5)$, with centroid $(0.2, 0.3, 0.5)$. At depth 3, the seen objects are a, i, c, f (which will all appear in the result) and h, j, g, e, which are all $\mathcal{F}$-dominated by both i and c and thus not retained. The objects are inserted sortedly in S according to the centroid, with the order: i, c, a, f. Table 1 shows the vertex scores, orderly computed as $\sum_{i=1}^{d} w_i^{(\ell)} o[i]$ (b is not even accessed). To see that, e.g., $\mathtt{i} \succ_{\mathcal{F}} \mathtt{h}$ we observe that $v_\ell(\mathtt{i}) \geq v_\ell(\mathtt{h})$, for $1 \leq \ell \leq q$ (and $v_1(\mathtt{i}) > v_1(\mathtt{h})$). At this point, the seen objects S already coincide with ND_2, but FSA cannot stop yet. The threshold point is $\tau_3 = (8, 8, 7)$; its vertex scores are shown in Table 1, along with the corresponding vertex lists (of objects that still have a vertex score lower than τ_3's). The bit masks $B_{\not>}(o)B_1(o)\ldots B_6(o)$ are computed accordingly; e.g., we have 1110010 for c since c has a worse vertex score than τ_3 on vertices $W^{(3)}$, $W^{(4)}$, and $W^{(6)}$, and thus is present in vertex lists V_3, V_4, and V_6. At depth 4, $\tau_4 = (7, 8, 7)$, but still no object $\mathcal{F}$-dominates it. Finally, at depth 5, $\tau_5 = (7, 7, 6)$, which is now $\mathcal{F}$-dominated by all of i, c, a, f, and then FSA can stop. The subsequent clean procedure does not eliminate anything, since none of the remaining objects is $\mathcal{F}$-dominated by $k = 2$ other objects, thus $\text{ND}_2(\mathcal{D}; \mathcal{F}) = \{\mathtt{i}, \mathtt{c}, \mathtt{a}, \mathtt{f}\}$.

5 Experiments

In this section we evaluate the performance of our implementations of FSA. In particular, we quantify the overhead incurred by the increased flexibility of FSA when compared to the computation of plain k-skybands and top-k queries. For our experiments, we consider three kinds of data distribution (anticorrelated, uniform, and real)[1] and scoring functions taken from weighted L_1 norms with ratio bounds constraints applied on the weights $(1/d(1-\varepsilon) \leq w_i \leq 1/d(1+\varepsilon))$. We report on both effectiveness and efficiency in different scenarios varying by number of rankings d, spread ε, and k, with defaults 4, 20%, and 10, resp.

In order to evaluate the effectiveness of our approach, we compare it to k-skybands, which also retrieve non(-$\mathcal{F}$)-dominated objects but in a way that is agnostic with respect to the set of scoring functions $\mathcal{F}$. The introduction of $\mathcal{F}$ drastically helps to reduce the result set. Figure 2 shows this effect for NBA. In Figure 2a, we vary the spread parameter ε used in ratio bounds constraints and keep default values for all other parameters. As can be seen, the result sets returned by ND_k and SKY_k coincide (985 objects) only when the spread is so high

[1] NBA: 190862 tuples reporting measures of basketball players' performance, available at www.quantifan.com; ANT and UNI have $100K$ tuples.

that each weight can vary in the entire $[0, 1]$ interval ("full"). For all other values of ε, the result set of ND_k is much smaller (from 71 objects when $\varepsilon = 50\%$, to only 12 for $\varepsilon = 1\%$). Note that, when $\varepsilon = 0\%$ ("none"), all weights equal $1/d$ exactly and, thus, there is only one scoring function in $\mathcal{F}$; in that case, the cardinality of the result set is exactly $k = 10$. Figure 2b also reports the cardinality of the result sets, but for different values of k (defaults otherwise). The result set returned by SKY_k is always almost two orders of magnitude larger than that of ND_k, the ratio becoming larger as k increases (from 157/2 when $k = 1$ to 6076/191 when $k = 100$). Finally, Figure 2c shows this when the number of rankings d varies (defaults otherwise). As d increases, the ratio between the cardinalities of the results increases (from 89/15 when $d = 2$ to 27403/63 when $d = 8$). Similar trends can be observed for the UNI and ANT datasets (omitted in the interest of space). Overall, this shows that, thanks to $\mathcal{F}$, ND_k is able to keep the result set within a reasonable cardinality, even for larger or more challenging problem instances, while the cardinality of SKY_k soon diverges.

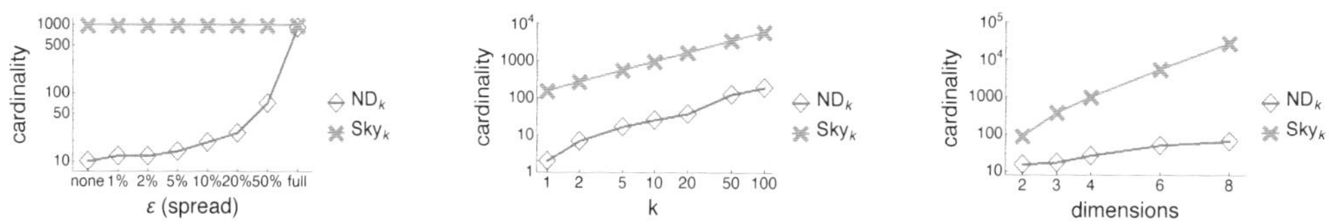

(a) Spread ε varies. (b) k varies. (c) Number of rankings d varies.

Fig. 2: Cardinality of results for the NBA dataset. Varying parameter: ε in (a), k in (b), d in (c).

We consider two variants of the FSA pattern: VEL+ and VEE+, using lazy and, resp., eager pruning, and test them in terms of execution time.

Effect of number of rankings d. Both variants exhibit sub-second execution times in default conditions. The "vertex lists" optimization grants savings of up to one order of magnitude, especially for more complex problem instances. Indeed, for $d > 4$ the number q of vertices increases dramatically, from $q = 6$ with $d = 4$ to $q = 70$ with $d = 8$. Yet, our optimization allows skipping many (already verified) vertex score comparisons between objects and the threshold point, thus leading to a linear behavior as d varies.

Effect of k and spread ε. Figure 3 shows execution times as k and ε vary in all datasets. Clearly, in all scenarios, the problem becomes more challenging as k increases and as ε increases, since, in both cases, more objects need to be extracted and compared. VEL+ and VEE+ show similar performance, with VEE+ slightly prevailing on more challenging instances (e.g., when $k = 100$ or $\varepsilon =$"full"). In such cases, many objects are kept by a lazy strategy and thus the call to the clean procedure weighs more heavily than the eager pruning of objects. In the other cases, the extra cost of pruning objects early is balanced with the reduced cost of calling `clean`. We also observe that, in most scenarios, `VEE+` and `VEL+` incur sub-second execution times, and only exceed $2s$ when $\varepsilon =$"full" (a case in which the result coincides with the k-skyband) in the `ANT` dataset.

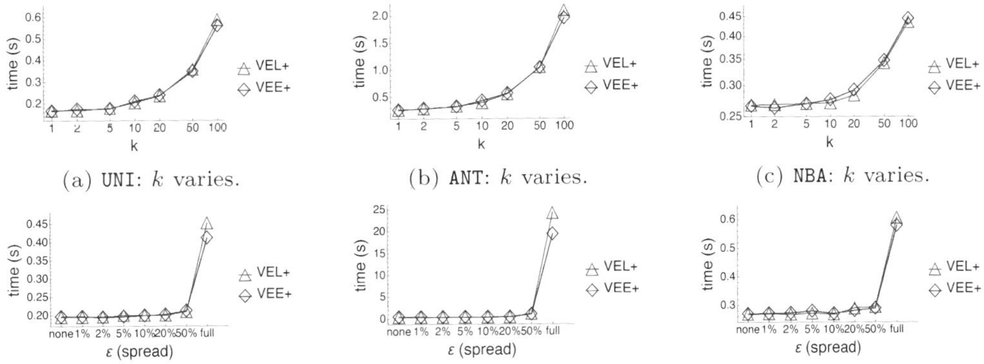

(a) `UNI`: k varies. (b) `ANT`: k varies. (c) `NBA`: k varies.

(d) `UNI`: spread ε varies. (e) `ANT`: spread ε varies. (f) `NBA`: spread ε varies.

Fig. 3: CPU times for computing ND_k. Datasets: `UNI` in (a),(d); `ANT` in (b),(e); `NBA` in (c),(f).

6 Conclusions

We have presented a framework for multi-source top-k queries defined by scoring functions with partially specified weights. This provides the flexibility required in many application scenarios (e.g., online services, crowdsourcing, etc.). Our solution, `FSA`, is a provably instance optimal algorithmic pattern that encompasses both top-k queries (attaining comparable performance) and k-skyband queries.

References

1. S. Börzsönyi, D. Kossmann, and K. Stocker. The skyline operator. In *ICDE*, pages 421–430, 2001.
2. P. Ciaccia and D. Martinenghi. Reconciling skyline and ranking queries. *PVLDB*, 10(11):1454–1465, 2017.
3. P. Ciaccia and D. Martinenghi. FA + TA < FSA: Flexible score aggregation. In *CIKM 2018*, pages 57–66, 2018.
4. E. Ciceri et al. Crowdsourcing for top-k query processing over uncertain data. *TKDE*, 28(1):41–53, 2016.
5. Y. S. Eum et al. Establishing dominance and potential optimality in multi-criteria analysis with imprecise weight and value. *Computers & Op. Res.*, 28:397–409, 2001.
6. R. Fagin. Combining fuzzy information from multiple systems. In *PODS*, pages 216–226, 1996.
7. R. Fagin, A. Lotem, and M. Naor. Optimal aggregation algorithms for middleware. In *PODS*, 2001.
8. N. Meneghetti et al. Output-sensitive evaluation of prioritized skyline queries. In *SIGMOD*, pages 1955–1967, 2015.
9. D. Papadias et al. Progressive skyline computation in database systems. *TODS*, 30(1):41–82, 2005.

Positive Unlabeled Link Prediction via Transfer Learning for Gene Network Reconstruction (Discussion Paper)

Paolo Mignone, Gianvito Pio and Michelangelo Ceci
paolo.mignone@uniba.it, gianvito.pio@uniba.it, michelangelo.ceci@uniba.it

Department of Computer Science - University of Bari Aldo Moro
Via Orabona, 4 - 70125 Bari (Italy)

Abstract. Transfer learning can be employed to leverage knowledge from a source domain in order to better solve tasks in a target domain, where the available data is exiguous. While most of the previous papers work in the supervised setting, we study the more challenging case of positive-unlabeled transfer learning, where few positive labeled instances are available for both the source and the target domains. Specifically, we focus on the link prediction task on network data, where we consider known existing links as positive labeled data and all the possible remaining links as unlabeled data. The transfer learning method described in this paper exploits the unlabeled data and the knowledge of a source network in order to improve the reconstruction of a target network. Experiments, conducted in the biological field, showed the effectiveness of the proposed approach with respect to the considered baselines, when exploiting the *Mus Musculus* gene network (source) to improve the reconstruction of the *Homo Sapiens Sapiens* gene network (target).

1 Introduction

The link prediction task aims at estimating the probability of the existence of an interaction between two entities on the basis of the available set of known interactions, which belong to the same data distribution, the same context and described according to the same features. However, in many real cases, the identical data distribution assumption does not hold, especially if data are organized in heterogeneous information networks [12, 13]. For example, in the study of biological networks, collecting training data is very expensive and it is necessary to build link prediction models on the basis of data regarding different (even if related) contexts. At this regard, *transfer learning* strategies can be adopted to leverage knowledge from a source domain to improve the performance of a task solved on a target domain, for which we have few labeled data (see Figure 1). In the literature, we can find several applications where transfer learning approaches have been proved to be beneficial. For example, in the classification of Web documents, transfer learning approaches can be exploited to classify newly

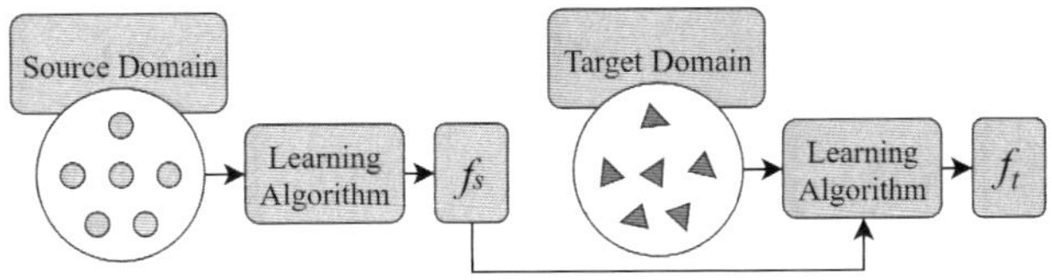

Fig. 1. Knowledge on a source task exploited to solve the target task.

created Web sites which follow a different data distribution [3] (e.g., the content is related to new subtopics). Another example is the work proposed in [9], where the authors exploit transfer learning approaches to adapt a WiFi localization model trained in one time period (source domain) to a new time period (target domain), where the available data possibly follow a different data distribution.

Focusing on the link prediction task, in the literature we can find several works in the biological field, since biological entities and their relationships can be naturally represented as a network. In the specific field of genomics, the working mechanisms of several organisms are usually modeled through gene interaction networks, where nodes represent genes and edges represent regulation activities. Since gene expression data are easy to obtain, several methods have been proposed in the literature that exploit this kind of data [7]. These approaches analyze the expression level of the genes under different conditions. Therefore, most machine learning approaches aiming to solve the link prediction task generally analyze gene expression data, with the final goal of reconstructing the whole network structure (Gene Network Reconstruction - GNR).

While existing methods generally work effectively on sufficiently large training data, a transfer learning approach could favor the GNR of specific organisms which are not well studied, by exploiting the knowledge acquired about different, related organisms. The main contribution of our work [8] is to evaluate the possible benefits that transfer learning techniques can provide to the task of link prediction. In particular, we exploit the available information about a source network for the reconstruction of a target network with poor available data. Moreover, we study the more challenging setting, i.e., the Positive-Unlabeled (PU) setting, where few positive labeled examples are available for both the domains, and no negative example is available [2, 11]. PU learning setting holds in many real contexts (e.g., text categorization, bioinformatics) where it is very expensive or unfeasible to obtain negative examples for the studied concept.

In order to evaluate the performance of the proposed method, we performed experiments in the biological domain. In particular, our experiments focused on the reconstruction of the human (Homo Sapiens Sapiens) gene network guided by the gene network of another, related organism, i.e., the mouse (Mus Musculus).

2 The proposed method

In this section, we describe our transfer learning approach to solve link prediction tasks in network data. Before describing it in details, we introduce some useful notions and formally define the link prediction task for a single domain. Let:

– V be the set of nodes of the network;
– $x = \langle v', v'' \rangle \in (V \times V)$ be a (possible) link between v' and v'', where $v' \neq v''$;
– $e(v) = [e_1(v), e_2(v), \ldots, e_n(v)]$ be the vector of features related to the node v, where $e_i(v) \in \mathbb{R}$, $\forall i \in \{1, 2, \ldots, n\}$;
– $e(x) = [e_1(v'), e_2(v'), \ldots, e_n(v'), e_1(v''), e_2(v''), \ldots, e_n(v'')]$ be the vector of features related to the link $x = \langle v', v'' \rangle$;
– $sim(a, b) \in [0, 1]$ be a similarity function between the vectors a and b;
– $l(x)$ be a function that returns 1 if the link x is a known existing link, and 0 if its existence is unknown;
– $L = \{x \mid x \in (V \times V) \wedge l(x) = 1\}$ be the set of labeled links;
– $U = (V \times V) \setminus L$ be the set of unlabeled links;
– $D = \{\widetilde{X}, P(X)\}$ be the domain described by the feature space $\widetilde{X} = \mathbb{R}^{2n}$, with a specific marginal data distribution $P(X)$, where $X = L \cup U$;
– $w(x)$ $(0 \leq w(x) \leq 1)$ be a computed weight for the link $x \in U$, which estimates the degree of certainty of its existence;
– $f(x)$ be an ideal function which returns 1 if x exists, and 0 otherwise.
The task we intend to solve is then defined as follows:
Given: a set of training examples $\{\langle e(x), w(x) \rangle\}_x$, each of which described by a feature vector and a weight.
Find: a function $f' : \mathbb{R}^{2n} \rightarrow [0, 1]$ which takes as input a vector of features $e(x)$ and returns the probability that x exists. Thus, $f'(e(x)) \approx \mathcal{P}(f(x) = 1)$ or, in other terms, f' approximates the probability distribution over the values of f.

Our method works with two different domains: the source domain $D_s = \{\widetilde{X_s}, P(X_s)\}$, and the target domain $D_t = \{\widetilde{X_t}, P(X_t)\}$, which are described according to the same feature space, i.e., $\widetilde{X_s} = \widetilde{X_t}$, while the marginal data distributions is generally different, i.e., $P(X_s) \neq P(X_t)$.

Given the two sets of labeled examples L_s and L_t, regarding the source and the target domain respectively, the method consists of three stages, that are summarized in Figure 2 and detailed in the following subsections.

Stage I - Clustering. The first stage of our method consists in the identification of a clustering model for the positive examples of each domain (i.e., on L_s and L_t). The application of a clustering method is motivated by the necessity to distinguish among possible multiple viewpoints of the underlying concept of positive interactions. Moreover, a summarization in terms of clusters' centroids becomes useful also from a computational viewpoint, since in the subsequent stages we can compare centroids instead of single instances. We adopt the classical *k-means* algorithm, since it is well established in the literature. However, any other prototype-based clustering algorithm, possibly able to catch specific peculiarities of the data at hand, could be plugged into our method.

Stage II - Instance Weighting. Although an unlabeled link could be either a positive or a negative example, we consider all the unlabeled examples as positive examples and compute a weight representing the degree of certainty in $[0, 1]$ of being a positive example: a value close to 0 (respectively, to 1) means that the

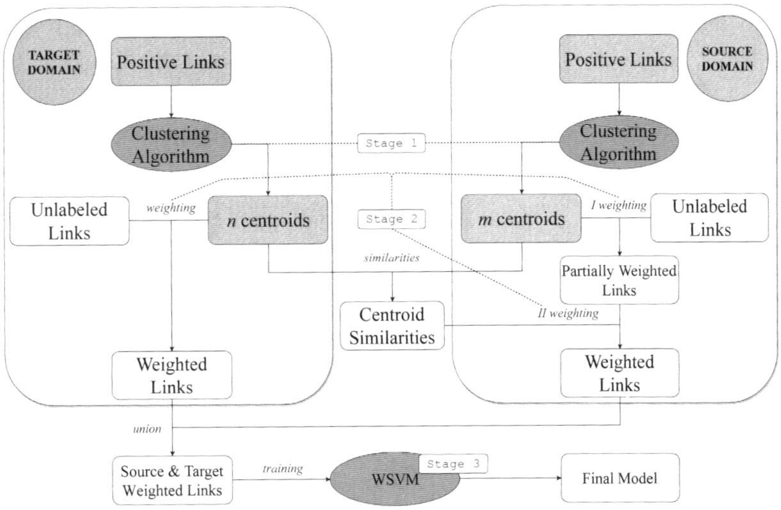

Fig. 2. A graphical overview of the proposed transfer learning approach.

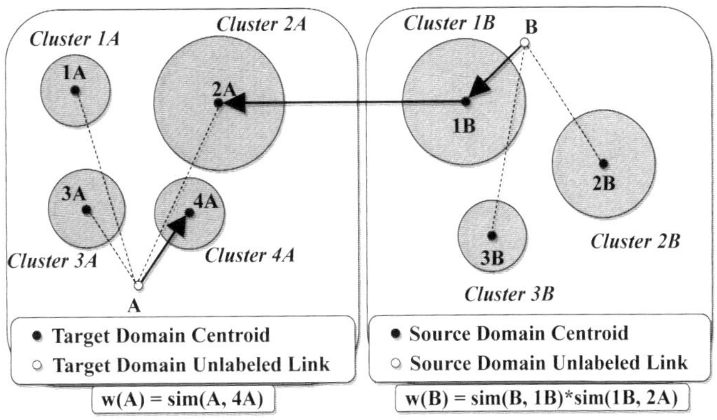

Fig. 3. Weighting process. The instance A is weighted according to the similarity to its most similar centroid (4A), while the instance B is weighted according to the similarity to its most similar centroid (1B), and to the similarity between 1B and 2A.

example is likely to be a negative (respectively, positive) example. The weight associated to the unlabeled instances of both the source and the target domains are computed according to their similarities with respect to the centroids obtained in the first stage. In particular, we identify a different weighting function for the source and target domains, in order to smooth the contribution provided by instances coming from the source domain.

Specifically, an unlabeled link x belonging to the target network (i.e., $x \in V_t \times V_t$) is weighted according to its similarity with respect to the centroid of its closest cluster, among the clusters identified from the target network. Formally:

$$w(x) = max_{c_t \in C_t}(sim(e(x), c_t)), \tag{1}$$

where C_t are the clusters identified from positive examples of the target network.

On the other hand, an unlabeled link x' belonging to the source network (i.e., $x' \in V_s \times V_s$) is weighted by considering two similarity values: *i)* the similarity with respect to the centroid of its closest cluster, computed among the clusters identified from the source network, and *ii)* the similarity between such a centroid and the closest centroid identified on the target network. Formally, let $c' = argmax_{c_s \in C_s}(sim(e(x'), c_s))$ be the closest centroid with respect to x' among the possible centroids C_s identified in the source network. Then:

$$w(x') = sim(e(x'), c') \cdot max_{c'' \in C_t}(sim(c', c'')). \quad (2)$$

As a similarity function, we exploit the Euclidean distance, after applying a min-max normalization (in the range $[0, 1]$) to all the features of the feature vectors. Formally, $sim(e(x'), e(x'')) = 1 - \sqrt{\sum_{k=1}^{n} (e_k(x') - e_k(x''))^2}$.
An overview of the weighting strategy can be graphically observed in Figure 3.

Stage III - Training the classifier. In the third stage, we train a probabilistic classifier, based on linear Weighted Support Vector Machines (WSVM) [14] with Platt scaling [1], from the weighted unlabeled instances coming from both the source and the target networks. We selected an SVM-based classifier mainly because *i)* it has a (relatively) good computational efficiency, especially in the prediction phase, and *ii)* it already proved to be effective (with Platt scaling) in the semi-supervised setting [4]. At the end of the training phase, the WSVM classifier produces a model in the form of an hyperplane function h. Then, by exploiting the Platt scaling, for each unlabeled link x, we compute the probability of being a positive example as $f'(e(x)) = \frac{1}{1+e^{-h(e(x))}}$, where $h(e(x))$ is the score obtained by the learned WSVM. Finally, we rank all the predicted links in descending ordering with respect to the their probability of being positive. A pseudo-code representation of the proposed method is shown in Algorithm 1.

3 Experiments

Our experiments have been performed in the biological field. In particular, the specific task we intend to solve is the reconstruction of the human (*Homo Sapiens Sapiens - HSS*) gene network. As a source task, we will exploit the gene network of another, related organism, i.e., the mouse (*Mus Musculus - MM*).

3.1 Dataset

The considered dataset consists of gene expression data related to 6 organs (lung, liver, skin, brain, bone marrow, heart), obtained by the samples available at Gene Expression Omnibus (GEO), a public functional genomics repository. On overall, 161 and 174 samples were considered for MM and HSS, respectively, involving a total of $45,101$ and $54,675$ genes, respectively, each of which described by 6 features (one for each organ). Accordingly, the interactions among genes were described by 12-dimensional feature vectors, obtained by concatenating the feature vectors associated to the involved genes.

The set of validated gene interactions (verified positive examples) was extracted from the public repository BioGRID (https://thebiogrid.org).

Algorithm 1: PU Link Prediction via Transfer Learning

Data:

$\cdot L_s = \{x_s \mid x_s \in (V_s \times V_s) \wedge l(x_s) = 1\}$: positive links of the source network
$\cdot U_s = (V_s \times V_s) \setminus L_s$: unlabeled links of the source network
$\cdot L_t = \{x_t \mid x_t \in (V_t \times V_t) \wedge l(x_t) = 1\}$: positive links of the target network
$\cdot U_t = (V_t \times V_t) \setminus L_t$: unlabeled links of the target network
$\cdot e(x)$: feature vector of the link x
$\cdot sim(e(x'), e(x'')) = 1 - \sqrt{\sum_{k=1}^{n} (e_k(x') - e_k(x''))^2}$
$\cdot k_1, k_2$: number of positive clusters for the source and the target network, respectively

Result:

$\cdot ranked\_links$: predicted links ordered according to their likelihood

begin
  $C_s \leftarrow kmeans(L_s, k_1)$; $C_t \leftarrow kmeans(L_t, k_2)$;
  $source\_training\_set \leftarrow \emptyset$; $target\_training\_set \leftarrow \emptyset$; $ranked\_links \leftarrow \emptyset$;
  foreach $x_t \in U_t$ **do**
    $w(x_t) \leftarrow max_{(c_t \in C_t)}(sim(e(x_t), c_t))$;
    $target\_training\_set \leftarrow target\_training\_set \cup \{\langle e(x_t), w(x_t)\rangle\}$;
  foreach $x_s \in U_s$ **do**
    $source\_centroid \leftarrow argmax_{(c_s \in C_s)}(sim(e(x_s), c_s))$;
    $partial\_weight \leftarrow sim(e(x_s), source\_centroid)$;
    $centroid\_sim \leftarrow max_{(c_t \in C_t)}(sim(source\_centroid, c_t))$;
    $w(x_s) \leftarrow partial\_weight \cdot centroid\_sim$;
    $source\_training\_set \leftarrow source\_training\_set \cup \{\langle e(x_s), w(x_s)\rangle\}$;
  $training\_set \leftarrow source\_training\_set \cup target\_training\_set$;
  $h(\cdot) \leftarrow WSVM(training\_set)$;
  $f'(\cdot) = \frac{1}{1+e^{-h(\cdot)}}$;
  foreach $x \in U_t$ **do**
    $ranked\_links \leftarrow ranked\_links \cup \{\langle x, f'(e(x))\rangle\}$;
  $ranked\_links \leftarrow sort\_by\_score(ranked\_links)$;
  return $ranked\_links$;

3.2 Experimental Setting

Since our method exploits the k-means clustering algorithm, we performed the experiments with different values for k_1 (i.e., the number of clusters for the MM organism) and k_2 (i.e., the number of clusters for the HSS organism), in order to evaluate the possible effect of such parameters on the results. In particular, we considered the following parameter values: $k_1 \in \{2, 3\}, k_2 \in \{2, 3\}$. We remind that we work in the PU learning setting (i.e., the dataset does not contain any negative example). Therefore, inspired by [10], we evaluated the results in terms of the average recall@k, in a 10 fold CV setting. In particular, in order to quantitatively compare the obtained results, we draw the recall@k curve, by varying the value of k (i.e, the number of top ranked interactions to consider as positive), and compute the area under the curve.

We compared our method, indicated as **transfer**, with two approaches:

- **no_transfer**, which corresponds to the WSVM with Platt scaling learned only from the target network (i.e., from the HSS network). This baseline allows us to evaluate the contribution of the source domain.

- **union**, which is the WSVM with Platt scaling learned from a single dataset consisting of the union of the instances coming from both MM and HSS. This baseline allows us to evaluate the effect of our weighing strategy.

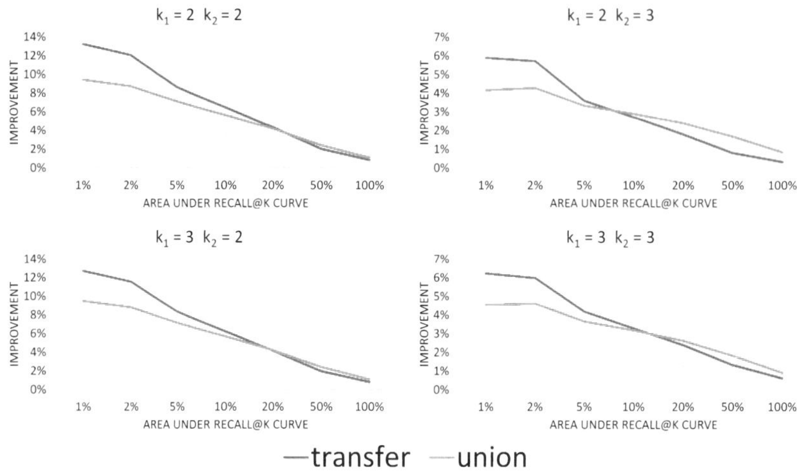

Fig. 4. Improvement over no_transfer, with different values of k_1 and k_2.

Since we are interested in observing the contribution provided by our approach with respect to the non-transfer approach, results will be evaluated in terms of improvement with respect to the **no_transfer** baseline.

3.3 Results

In Figure 4, we show the results obtained with different values of k_1 and k_2. In particular, we considered different percentages of the recall@k curve and measured the area under each sub-curve. This evaluation is motivated by the fact that biologists usually focus their in-lab studies on the analysis of the top-ranked predicted interactions. Therefore, a better result in the first part of the recall@k curve (i.e., at 1%, 2%) appears to be more relevant for the real biological application. The graphs show that both the **union** baseline and the proposed method (**transfer**) are able to obtain a better result with respect to the variant without any transfer of knowledge (**no_transfer**). This confirms that, in this case, the external source of knowledge (the MM gene network) can be exploited to improve the reconstruction of the target network (the HSS gene network).

By comparing the **union** baseline with our method, we can observe that the proposed weighting strategy was effective in assigning the right contribution to each unlabeled instance (coming either from the source or from the target network) in the learning phase. This is even more evident in the first part of the recall@k curve, where our method was able to retrieve about 120 additional true interactions at the top 1% of the ranking with respect to the baseline approaches.

Finally, by analyzing the results with respect to the values of k_1 and k_2, we can conclude that the highest improvement over the baseline approaches has been obtained with $k_1 = 2$ and $k_2 = 2$. This means that clustering can affect the results, and that even higher improvements could be obtained by adopting smarter clustering strategies that can, for example, catch and exploit the distribution, in terms of density, of the examples in the feature space.

4 Conclusion and Future Work

We proposed a transfer learning method to solve the link prediction task in the PU learning setting. By resorting to a clustering-based strategy, our method is able to exploit unlabeled data as well as labeled and unlabeled data of a different, related domain, identifying a different weight for each training instance. Focusing on biological networks, we evaluated the performance of the proposed method in the reconstruction of the Human gene network, supported by the mouse gene network. Results show that our method is able to improve the accuracy of the reconstruction, with respect to baseline approaches. As future work, we plan to implement a distributed version of the proposed method and to adopt some ensemble-based approaches [5, 6] to exploit multiple clusters in the prediction.

Acknowledgments

We would like to acknowledge the European project MAESTRA - Learning from Massive, Incompletely annotated, and Structured Data (ICT-2013-612944).

References

1. J. c. Platt. Probabilistic outputs for support vector machine and comparisons to regularized likelihood methods. In *Advances in large margin classifiers*, 1999.
2. M. Ceci, G. Pio, V. Kuzmanovski, and S. Džeroski. Semi-supervised multi-view learning for gene network reconstruction. *PLOS ONE*, 10(12):1–27, 12 2015.
3. W. Dai, Q. Yang, G. Xue, and Y. Yu. Boosting for transfer learning. In *Proc. of ICML*, pages 193–200, 2007.
4. C. Elkan and K. Noto. Learning classifiers from only positive and unlabeled data. In *Proc. of ACM SIGKDD*, pages 213–220, 2008.
5. J. Levatic, M. Ceci, D. Kocev, and S. Dzeroski. Self-training for multi-target regression with tree ensembles. *Knowl.-Based Syst.*, 123:41–60, 2017.
6. J. Levatic, D. Kocev, M. Ceci, and S. Dzeroski. Semi-supervised trees for multi-target regression. *Inf. Sci.*, 450:109–127, 2018.
7. D. Marbach and J. C. et al. Wisdom of crowds for robust gene network inference. *Nature Methods*, 2016.
8. P. Mignone and G. Pio. Positive unlabeled link prediction via transfer learning for gene network reconstruction. In *ISMIS 2018*, pages 13–23, 2018.
9. S. J. Pan, V. W. Zheng, Q. Yang, and D. H. Hu. Transfer learning for wifi-based indoor localization. *Workshop on Transfer Learning for Complex Task AAAI*, 2008.
10. G. Pio, M. Ceci, D. Malerba, and D. D'Elia. ComiRNet:a web-based system for the analysis of miRNA-gene regulatory networks. *BMC Bioinform*, 16(S-9):S7, 2015.
11. G. Pio, D. Malerba, D. D'Elia, and M. Ceci. Integrating microRNA target predictions for the discovery of gene regulatory networks: a semi-supervised ensemble learning approach. *BMC Bioinform*, 15(S-1):S4, 2014.
12. G. Pio, F. Serafino, D. Malerba, and M. Ceci. Multi-type clustering and classification from heterogeneous networks. *Inf. Sci.*, 425:107–126, 2018.
13. F. Serafino, G. Pio, and M. Ceci. Ensemble learning for multi-type classification in heterogeneous networks. *IEEE Trans. Knowl. Data Eng.*, 30(12):2326–2339, 2018.
14. X. Yang, Q. Song, and Y. Wand. A weighted support vector machine for data classification. In *Int J Pattern Recogn, Vol. 21*, 2007.

Deep Sequential Modeling for Recommendation (DISCUSSION PAPER)

Giuseppe Manco[2], Ettore Ritacco[2], Noveen Sachdeva[1], and Massimo Guarascio[2]

[1] International Institute of Information Technology, Hyderabad, India
noveen.sachdeva@research.iiit.ac.in
[2] ICAR-CNR, Via P. Bucci, 8/9c, Rende, Italy
{name.surname}@icar.cnr.it

Abstract. We propose a model which extends variational autoencoders by exploiting the rich information present in the past preference history. We introduce a recurrent version of the VAE, where instead of passing a subset of the whole history regardless of temporal dependencies, we rather pass the consumption sequence subset through a recurrent neural network. At each time-step of the RNN, the sequence is fed through a series of fully-connected layers, the output of which models the probability distribution of the most likely future preferences. We show that handling temporal information is crucial for improving the accuracy of recommendation.

1 Introduction

Learning of accurate models able to suggest interesting items to the user is an important problem for many scientific and industrial applications. To address this problem,

collaborative filtering approaches to recommendation were extensively investigated by the current literature. Among these, latent variable models [5, 14, 17, 6] gained substantial attention, due to their capabilities in modeling the hidden causal relationships that influence user preferences. Recently, however, new approaches based on neural architectures were proposed, achieving competitive performance with respect to the current state of the art. Also, new paradigms based on the combination of deep learning and latent variable modeling [7, 12] were proven quite successful in domains such as computer vision and speech processing. However, their adoption for modeling user preferences is still unexplored, although recently it is starting to gain attention [9, 8].

The aforementioned approaches rely on the "bag-of-word" assumption: when considering a user and her preferences, the order of such preferences can be neglected and all preferences are exchangeable. This assumption works with general user trends which reflect a long-term behavior. However, it fails to capture the short-term preferences that are specific of several application scenarios, especially in the context of the Web. Sequential data can express causalities and dependencies that require ad-hoc modeling and algorithms. And in fact, efforts to capture this notion of causality have been made, both in the context of latent variable modeling [11, 1, 3] and deep learning [4, 2, 18, 15].

In this paper, we consider the task of sequence recommendation from the perspective of combining deep learning and latent variable modeling. Inspired by the approach in [9], we assume that at a given timestamp the choice of a given item is influenced by a latent factor that models user trends and preferences. However, the latent factor itself can be influenced by user history and modeled to capture both long-term preferences and short-term behavior.

Our contribution can be summarized as follows: (*i*) we extend the framework to the case of sequential recommendation, where user's preferences exhibit temporal dependencies; (*ii*) we evaluate the proposed framework on standard benchmark datasets, by showing that *(a)* approaches not considering temporal dynamics are not totally adequate to model user preferences, and *(b)* the combination of latent variable and temporal dependency modeling produces a substantial gain, even with regard to other approaches that only focus on temporal dependencies through recurrent relationships.

The paper is organized as follows. Sections 2 proposes the modeling of user preferences in a variational setting, by describing how the framework can be adapted to the case of temporally ordered dependencies. The effectiveness of the proposed modeling is illustrated in section 3, and pointers to future developments are discussed in section 4.

2 Variational Autoencoders for User Preferences

The reader is referred to [13] for more details of the approach illustrated here. We shall use the following shared notation: $u \in U = \{1, \ldots, M\}$ indexes a user and $i \in I = \{1, \ldots, N\}$ indexes an item for which the user can express a preference. We model implicit feedback, thus assuming a preference matrix $\boldsymbol{X} \in \{0, 1\}^{N \times M}$, so that $\boldsymbol{x}_u$ represents the (binary) row with all the item preferences for user u. Given $\boldsymbol{x}_u$, we define $I_u = \{i \in I | x_{u,i} = 1\}$ (with $N_u = |I_u|$). Analogously, $U_i = |\{u \in U | x_{u,i} = 1\}|$ and $M_i = |U_i|$.

We also consider a precedence and temporal relationships within $\boldsymbol{X}$. First of all, the preference matrix induces a natural ordering relationship between items: $i \prec_u j$ has the meaning that $x_{u,i} > x_{u,j}$ in the rating matrix. Also, we assume the existence of timing information $\boldsymbol{T} \in \mathbb{R}_+^{M \times N} \cup \{\emptyset\}$, where the term $t_{u,i}$ represents the time when i was chosen by u (with $t_{u,i} = \emptyset$ if $x_{u,i} = 0$). Then, $i <_u j$ denotes that $t_{u,i} < t_{u,j}$, With an abuse of notation, we also introduce a temporal mark in the elements of $\boldsymbol{x}_u$: the term $\boldsymbol{x}_{u(t)}$ (with $1 \leq t \leq N_u$) represents the t-th item in I_u in the sorting induced by $<_u$, whereas $\boldsymbol{x}_{u(1:t)}$ represents the sequence $\boldsymbol{x}_{u(1)}, \ldots, \boldsymbol{x}_{u(t)}$.

The reference model is the Multinomial variational autoencoder (MVAE) proposed in [9]. Within this framework, for a given user u it is possible to devise $\boldsymbol{x}_u$ according to the generative setting:

$$\begin{gathered}\boldsymbol{z}_u \sim \mathcal{N}(\boldsymbol{0}, \boldsymbol{I}_K), \qquad \pi(\boldsymbol{z}_u) \sim \exp\{f_\phi(\boldsymbol{z}_u)\}, \\ \boldsymbol{x}_u \sim \mathit{Multi}\,(N_u, \pi(\boldsymbol{z}_u)). \end{gathered} \tag{2.1}$$

The underlying "decoder" is modeled by $\log P_\phi(\boldsymbol{x}_u|\boldsymbol{z}_u) = \sum_i x_{u,i} \log \pi_i(\boldsymbol{z}_u)$, thus enabling a complete specification of the overall variational framework. Prediction for new items is accomplished by resorting to the learned functions f_ϕ and Q_λ: given a user history $\boldsymbol{x}$, we compute $\boldsymbol{z} = \boldsymbol{\mu}_\lambda(\boldsymbol{x})$ and then devise the probabilities for the whole item set through $\pi(\boldsymbol{z})$. Unseen items can then be ranked according to their associated probabilities.

Ideally, latent variable modeling should be able to express temporal dynamics and hence causalities and dependencies among preferences in a user's history. In the following we elaborate on this intuition. Within a probabilistic framework, we can model temporal dependencies by conditioning each event to the previous events: given a sequence $\boldsymbol{x}_{(1:T)}$, we have

$$P\left(\boldsymbol{x}_{(1:T)}\right) = \prod_{t=0}^{T-1} P\left(\boldsymbol{x}_{(t+1)}|\boldsymbol{x}_{(1:t)}\right).$$

This specification suggests two key aspects:

- There is a recurrent relationship between $\boldsymbol{x}_{(t+1)}$ and $\boldsymbol{x}_{(1:t)}$ devised by $P\left(\boldsymbol{x}_{(t+1)}|\boldsymbol{x}_{(1:t)}\right)$, upon which the modeling can take advantage, and
- each time-step can be handled separately, and in particular it can be modeled through a conditional VAE.

Let us consider the following (simple) generative model

$$\begin{gathered}\boldsymbol{z}_{u(t)} \sim \mathcal{N}\left(\boldsymbol{0}, \boldsymbol{I}_K\right), \qquad \pi\left(\boldsymbol{z}_{u(t)}\right) \sim \exp\left\{f_\phi\left(\boldsymbol{z}_{u(t)}\right)\right\}, \\ \boldsymbol{x}_{u(t)} \sim \mathit{Multi}\left(1, \pi\left(\boldsymbol{z}_{u(t)}\right)\right), \end{gathered} \tag{2.2}$$

which results in the joint likelihood

$$P(\boldsymbol{x}_{u(1:T)}, \boldsymbol{z}_{u(1:T)}) = \prod_t P(\boldsymbol{x}_{u(t)}|\boldsymbol{z}_{u(t)}) P(\boldsymbol{z}_{u(t)}).$$

Here, we can approximate the posterior $P(\boldsymbol{z}_{u(1:T)}|\boldsymbol{x}_{u(1:T)})$ with the factorized proposal distribution

$$Q_\lambda(\boldsymbol{z}_{u(1:T)}|\boldsymbol{x}_{(1:T)}) = \prod_t q_\lambda(\boldsymbol{z}_{u(t)}|\boldsymbol{x}_{(1:t-1)}),$$

where $q_\lambda(\boldsymbol{z}_{u(t)}|\boldsymbol{x}_{(1:t-1)})$ is a gaussian distribution whose parameters $\boldsymbol{\mu}_\lambda(t)$ and $\boldsymbol{\sigma}_\lambda(t)$ depend upon the current history $\boldsymbol{x}_{u(1:t-1)}$, by means of a recurrent layer $\boldsymbol{h}_t$:

$$\begin{aligned}\boldsymbol{\mu}_\lambda(t), \boldsymbol{\sigma}_\lambda(t) &= \varphi_\lambda(\boldsymbol{h}_t) \\ \boldsymbol{h}_t &= \mathit{RNN}_\lambda\left(\boldsymbol{h}_{t-1}, \boldsymbol{x}_{u(t-1)}\right). \end{aligned} \tag{2.3}$$

The resulting loss function can be formalized as follow:

$$\mathcal{L}(\phi, \lambda, \boldsymbol{X}) = \sum_u \sum_{t=1}^{N_u} \left\{ \frac{1}{2} \sum_k \left(\sigma_{\lambda,k}(t) - 1 - \log \sigma_{\lambda,k}(t) + \mu_{\lambda,k}(t)^2 \right) \right.$$
$$\left. - E_{\boldsymbol{\epsilon} \sim \mathcal{N}(\boldsymbol{0}, \boldsymbol{I})} \left[\log P_\phi \left(\boldsymbol{x}_{u(t)} | \boldsymbol{z}_\lambda(\boldsymbol{\epsilon}, t) \right) \right] \right\} .$$

The proposal distribution introduces a dependency of the latent variable from a recurrent layer, which allows to recover the information from the previous history. We call this model SVAE.

Notably, the prediction step can be easily accomplished in a similar way as for MVAE: given a user history $\boldsymbol{x}_{u(1:t-1)}$, we can resort to eq. 2.3 and set $\boldsymbol{z} = \boldsymbol{\mu}_\lambda(t)$, upon which we can devise the probability for the $\boldsymbol{x}_{u(t)}$ by means of $\pi(\boldsymbol{z})$.

The generative model of eq. 2.2 only focuses on the next item in the sequence. The base model however is flexible enough to extend its focus on the next k items, regardless of the time: $\boldsymbol{x}_{u(t:t+k-1)} \sim \mathit{Multi}\left(k, \pi\left(\boldsymbol{z}_{u(t)}\right)\right)$. Again, the resulting joint likelihood can be modeled in different ways. The simplest way consists in considering $\boldsymbol{x}$ as a time-ordered multi-set,

$$P(\boldsymbol{x}_{u(1:T)}, \boldsymbol{z}_{u(1:T)}) = \prod_t P(\boldsymbol{x}_{u(t:t+k-1)} | \boldsymbol{z}_{u(t)}) P(\boldsymbol{z}_{u(t)}) . \quad (2.4)$$

Alternatively, we can consider the probability of an item as a mixture relative to all the time-steps where it is considered:

$$P(\boldsymbol{x}_{u(1:T)}, \boldsymbol{z}_{u(1:T)}) = \prod_t P(\boldsymbol{z}_{u(t)}) \sum_{t-k+1 \leq j \leq t} P(\boldsymbol{x}_{u(t)} | \boldsymbol{z}_{u(j)}), \quad (2.5)$$

where $P(\boldsymbol{x}_{u(t)} | \boldsymbol{z}_{u(j)})$ is the probability of observing $\boldsymbol{x}_{u(t)}$ according to $\pi(\boldsymbol{z}_{u(j)})$. In both cases, the variational approximation is modeled exactly as shown above, and the only difference lies in the second component of the loss function, which has to be adapted according to the above equations.

There is an interesting analogy between eq. 2.5 and the attention mechanism [16]. In fact, it can be noticed in the equation that the prediction of $\boldsymbol{x}_{u(t)}$ depends on the latent status of the k previous steps in the sequence. In practice, this enables to capture short-term dependencies and to encapsulate them in the same probabilistic framework by weighting the likelihood based on $\boldsymbol{z}_{u(t-k+1)}, \ldots, \boldsymbol{z}_{u(t)}$.

3 Evaluation

We evaluate SVAE on some benchmark datasets, by comparing with various baselines and the current state-of-the-art competitors, in order to assess its capabilities in modeling preference data. Additionally, we provide a sensitivity analysis relative to the configurations/contour conditions upon which SVAE is better suited.

We evaluate our model along with the competitors on two popular publicly available datasets, namely *Movielens-1M* and *Netflix*. Movielens-1M is a time series dataset containing user-item ratings pairs along with the corresponding timestamp. Since we work on implicit feedback, we binarize the data, by considering only the user-item pairs where the rating provided by the user was strictly greater than 3 on a range 1:5. Netflix has the same data format as Movielens-1M and the same technique is used to binarize the ratings. We use a subset of the full dataset that matches the user-distribution with the full dataset. The subset is built by stratifying users according to their history length, and then sampling a subset of size inversely proportional to the size of the strata.

Since we are considering implicit preferences, the evaluation is done on top-n recommendation, and it relies on the following metrics.
Normalized Discounted Cumulative Gain. Also abbreviated as *NDCG@n*, the metric gives more weight to the relevance of items on top of the recommender list and is defined as

$$NDCG@n = \frac{DCG@n}{IDCG@n}$$

where $DCG@n = \sum_{i=1}^{n} \frac{r_i}{log_2(i+1)}$ and $IDCG@n = \sum_{i=1}^{|R|} \frac{1}{log_2(i+1)}$. Here, r_i is the relevance (either 1 or 0 within the feedback scenario) of the i-th recommended items in the recommendation list, and R is the set of relevant items.

Precision. By defining $Hits = \sum_i r_i$ as the number of items occurring in the recommendation list that were actually preferred by the user, we have

$$Precision@n = \frac{Hits@n}{n}$$

Recall. defined as the percentage of items actually preferred by the user that were present in the recommendation list:

$$Recall@n = \frac{Hits@n}{|R|}$$

In our experiments, we use the above metrics with two values of n, respectively 10 and 100. The evaluation protocol works as follows. We partition users into training, validation and test set. The model is trained using the full histories of the users in the training set. During evaluation, for each user in the validation/test set we split the **time-sorted** user history into two parts, *fold-in* and *fold-out* splits. The *fold-in* split is used as a basis to learn the necessary representations and provide a recommendation list which is then evaluated with the *fold-out* split of the user history using the metrics defined above. We believe that this strategy is more robust when compared to other methodologies wherein the same user can be in both the training as well as testing sets.

It is worth noticing that Liang et. al [9] follow a similar strategy but they do not consider any sorting for user histories. That is, for the validation/test users, the *fold-in* set doesn't precede the *fold-out* with respect to time.

We compare our model with current state-of-the-art models including recently published neural architectures and we now present a brief summary about our competitors to provide a better understanding of these models.

- **POP** is a simple baseline where the most popular items are recommended.
- **BPR** is a state of the art model based on Matrix Factorization, which ranks items differently for each user [10]. There is a subtle issue concerning BPR: by separating users on training/validation/test as discussed above, the latent representation of users in the validation/test is not meaningful. Then, BPR is only capable of providing meaningful predictions for users that were already exploited in the training phase. To solve this, we extended the training set to include the partial history in *fold-in* for each user in the validation/test. The evaluation takes place on their corresponding *fold-out* sets.
- **FPMC** [11] is a model which clubs both Matrix Factorization and Markov Chains together using personalized transition graphs over underlying Markov chains.
- **CASER** [15] is a convolutional model that uses vertical and horizontal convolutional layers to embed a sequence of recent items thereby learning sequential patterns for next-item recommendation. The authors have shown that this model outperforms other approaches based on recurrent neural network modeling, such as GRU4Rec. We use the implementation provided by the authors and tune the network by keeping the number of horizontal filters to be 16, and vertical filters to be 4.
- **MVAE** from which the SVAE model draws heavily. We use the implementation provided by the authors, with the default hyperparameter settings.

The experiments consider the basic SVAE model and the extensions to the next-k prediction, as discussed in the previous section. The model is trained end-to-end on the full histories of the training users. Model hyperparameters are set using the evaluation metrics obtained on validation users. The SVAE architecture includes an embedding layer of size 256, a recurrent layer realized as a GRU with 200 cells, and two encoding layers (of size 150 and 64) and finally two decoding layers (again, of size 64 and 150). We set the number K of latent factors for the variational autoencoder to be 64. Adam was used to optimize the loss function coupled with a weight decay of 0.01. As for RVAE, the architecture includes user/item embedding layers (of size 128), two encoding layers (size 100 and 64), and a final layer that produces the score $f_\phi(\boldsymbol{z}_{u,i})$. Both SVAE and RVAE were implemented in PyTorch and trained on a single GTX 1080Ti GPU. The source code is available on GitHub.

In a first set of experiments, we compare SVAE with all competitors described above. Table 1 shows the results of the comparison. SVAE outperforms the competitors on both datasets with a significant gain on all the metrics. It is important here to highlight how the temporal *fold-in/fold-out* split is crucial for a fair evaluation of the predictive capabilities: MVAE was evaluated both on temporal and random split, exhibiting totally different performances. Our interpretation is that, with random splits, the prediction for an item is easier if the encoding phase is aware of forthcoming items in the same user history. This severely affects the performance and overrates the predictive capabilities

`https://github.com/noveens/svae_cf`.

of a model: the accuracy of MVAE drops substantially when a temporal split is considered.

By contrast, SVAE is trained to capture the actual temporal dependencies and ultimately results in better predictive accuracy. This is also shown in fig. 1, where we show that SVAE outperforms the competitors irrespective of the size of *fold-in*. The only exception is with very short sequences (less than 10 items), where MVAE gets better results with respect to the sequential models. It is also worth noticing how the performance of both sequential models tend to degrade with increasing sequences, but SVAE maintains its advantage over CASER.

We discussed in the previous section how the basic SVAE framework can be extended to focus on predicting the next k items, rather then just the next item. We analyse this capability in fig. 2, where the accuracy for different values of k is considered according to the modeling in 2.4. On Movielens, the best value is achieved for $k = 4$, and acceptable values range within the interval $1 - 10$.

Model	Movielens						Netflix					
	NDCG		Recall		Precision		NDCG		Recall		Precision	
	@10	@100	@10	@100	@10	@100	@10	@100	@10	@100	@10	@100
POP	4.24	11.30	3.41	22.15	3.98	3.14	3.95	7.61	1.29	12.02	4.26	3.95
BPR*	8.51	16.66	5.20	29.38	7.27	4.51	8.94	12.68	2.63	19.45	8.45	5.89
FPMC	5.65	12.06	3.46	23.10	4.77	3.46	11.01	13.55	3.49	20.82	10.12	6.04
CASER	16.32	27.55	11.35	46.01	13.15	6.45	16.46	19.79	6.33	28.33	14.38	7.54
MVAE	11.69	23.01	9.12	41.43	9.02	5.39	16.15	22.19	7.47	32.72	13.94	8.31
SVAE	**17.81**	**29.93**	**12.48**	**49.09**	**14.40**	**6.93**	**24.64**	**26.77**	**8.93**	**35.58**	**21.93**	**10.55**
MVAE*	27.82	39.79	17.46	59.70	23.01	9.59	35.41	37.70	13.50	47.22	31.39	15.20

Table 1. Results of the evaluation (in percentage). MVAE* considers random splits that disregards the temporal order of user history. BPR* relies on including the *fold-in* subsequences in the training phase.

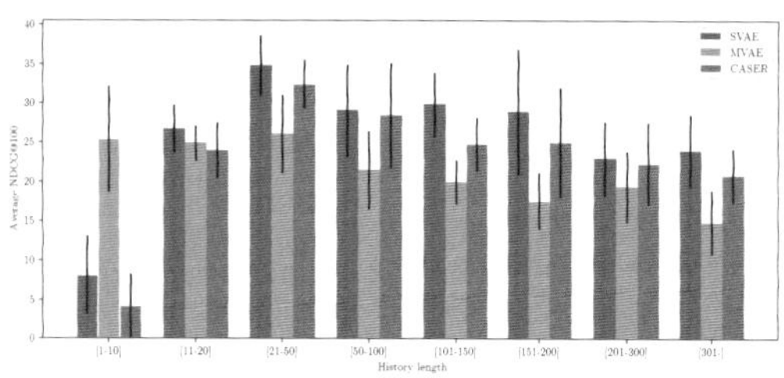

Fig. 1. Average NDCG@100 for MVAE, CASER & SVAE across various history lengths.

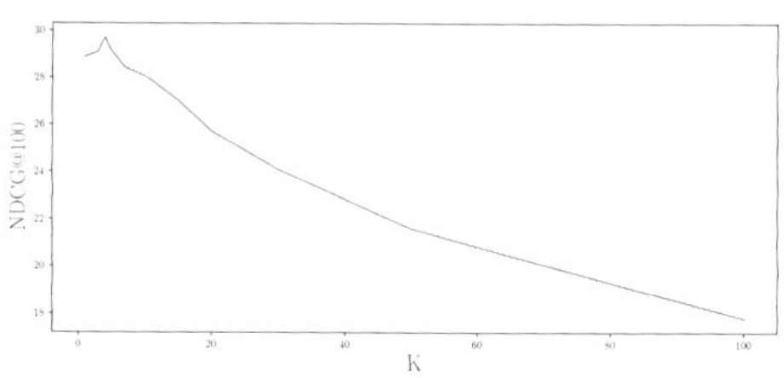

Fig. 2. NDCG@100 values for SVAE on Movielens, across different sizes for the number of items forward in time to predict on.

4 Conclusions and future work

Combining the representation power of latent spaces, provided by variational autoencoders, with the sequence modeling capabilities of recurrent neural networks is an effective strategy to sequence recommendation. To prove this, we devised SVAE, a simple yet robust mathematical framework capable of modeling temporal dynamics upon different perspectives, within the fundamentals of variational autoencoders. The experimental evaluation highlights the capability of SVAE to consistently outperform state-of-the-art models.

The framework proposed here is worth further extensions that we plan to accomplish in a future work. In particular, from an architectural point of view, the attention mechanism, outlined in section 2.5, requires a better understanding and a more detailed analysis of its possible impact in view of the recent developments in the literature.

However, different architectures (e.g. based on convolution or translation invariance are worth being investigated within a probabilistic variational setting.

References

1. Barbieri, N., Manco, G., Ritacco, E., Carnuccio, M., Bevacqua, A.: Probabilistic topic models for sequence data. Machine Learning pp. 1–25 (2013)
2. Devooght, R., Bersini, H.: Long and short-term recommendations with recurrent neural networks. In: UMAP '17. pp. 13–21 (2017)
3. He, R., Kang, W., McAuley, J.: Translation-based recommendation. In: RecSys '17. pp. 161–169 (2017)
4. Hidasi, B., Karatzoglou, A., Baltrunas, L., Tikk, D.: Session-based recommendations with recurrent neural networks. In: ICLR '16 (2016)
5. Hofmann, T.: Latent semantic models for collaborative filtering. ACM Transactions on Information Systems **22**(1), 89–115 (2004)
6. Kabbur, S., Ning, X., Karypis, G.: Fism: Factored item similarity models for top-n recommender systems. In: KDD '13. pp. 659–667 (2013)
7. Kingma, D., Welling, M.: Auto-encoding variational bayes. In: ICLR '14 (2014)
8. Li, X., She, J.: Collaborative variational autoencoder for recommender systems. In: KK '17. pp. 305–314 (2017)
9. Liang, D., Krishnan, R.G., Hoffman, M., Jebara, T.: Variational autoencoders for collaborative filtering. In: WWW '18. pp. 689–698 (2018)
10. Rendle, S., Freudenthaler, C., Gantner, Z., Schmidt-Thieme, L.: Bpr: Bayesian personalized ranking from implicit feedback. In: UAI '09. pp. 452–461 (2009)
11. Rendle, S., Freudenthaler, C., Schmidt-Thieme, L.: Factorizing personalized markov chains for next-basket recommendation. In: WWW '10. pp. 811–820 (2010)
12. Rezende, D.J., Mohamed, S., Wierstra, D.: Stochastic backpropagation and approximate inference in deep generative models. In: ICML '14. pp. 1278–1286 (2014)
13. Sachdeva, N., Manco, G., Ritacco, E., Pudi, V.: Sequential variational autoencoders for collaborative filtering. pp. 600–608. WSDM '19 (2019)
14. Salakhutdinov, R., Mnih, A.: Probabilistic matrix factorization. In: NIPS '08. pp. 1257–1264 (2008)
15. Tang, J., Wang, K.: Personalized top-n sequential recommendation via convolutional sequence embedding. In: WSDM '18. pp. 565–573 (2018)
16. Vaswani, A., Shazeer, N., Parmar, N., Uszkoreit, J., Jones, L., Gomez, A.N., Kaiser, L., Polosukhin, I.: Attention is all you need. In: Advances in Neural Information Processing Systems 30, pp. 5998–6008 (2017)
17. Wang, C., Blei, D.: Collaborative topic modeling for recommending scientific articles. In: KDD '11. pp. 448–456 (2011)
18. Wu, C., Ahmed, A., Beutel, A., Smola, A.and Jing, H.: Recurrent recommender networks. In: WSDM '17. pp. 495–503 (2017)

A Knowledge-Based Platform for the Classification of Accounting Documents*

Alessia Amelio[0000-0002-3568-636X], Alberto Falcone[0000-0002-2660-1432], Angelo Furfaro[0000-0003-2537-8918], Alfredo Garro[0000-0003-0351-0869], Domenico Saccà[0000-0003-3584-5372]

DIMES - University of Calabria
87036 – Rende (CS), Italy
{a.amelio, a.falcone, a.furfaro, a.garro, sacca}@dimes.unical.it

Abstract. Due to the lack of standardization, the task consisting in the classification of invoices' billing entries for accounting purposes has yet not been made fully automatic despite the diffusion of e-invoicing systems. Each accounting firm adopts its own conventions also on the basis of the specific business domain of the invoice owner. Here, we describe a knowledge-based software platform devised to adequately address this issue. The paper focuses on the evaluation of the most appropriate classification algorithms which are suitable to be employed in an adaptive meta-learning approach. The effectiveness of the selected algorithms is experimentally assessed by running them on a real dataset of invoice entries.

Keywords: Automatic Invoice Processing · Meta-Learning · Classification.

1 Introduction

Over the years, business processes and software systems supporting accounting have reached a high level of maturity and, at the same time, have allowed the producers of such systems to achieve an excellent and consolidated level of diffusion in the market. The ever increasing pervasiveness of new ICT technologies, mainly due to the diffusion of mobile devices and "smart" and Internet-enabled objects, has determined, in all application domains, a strong need for innovation for IT products and services, which in turn, has contributed to the increase in competitiveness among companies. Also in the specific domain of systems and

* Supported by project P.O.R. CALABRIA FESR-FSE 2014-2020 - "Smart Electronic Invoices Accounting – SELINA" (CUP J28C1700016006)

services supporting the processing of accounting documents, the demand for innovation has determined the definition of effective strategies to evolve the offer in order to maintain the customer portfolio and potentially increase it.

In this context, one of the aspects most susceptible of innovation is the classification of invoices' billing entries, a process which is not fully automated. One of the main issues is the lack of a standard for the categorization and association of the information related to the invoices entries in the corresponding accounting categories. Often, each accounting firm adopts its own conventions by modifying and adapting them to its client portfolio, to its internal management processes and to other contingent needs.

Most of the scientific works related to the processing of accounting documents has been devoted to the extraction of information from scanned documents, e.g. in [6] a flexible form-reader system has been devised for such purpose. The work described in [4] focuses on the feature extraction process for the supervised classification of scanned invoices obtained from printed documents. An approach based on incremental learning techniques, where some experiments were carried out by applying it to the classification of a small data set of invoices (a learning set of 324 documents, a testing set of 169 documents and 8 classes), has been proposed in [10].

This paper proposes a knowledge-based software platform devised to address the issue of automatic classification of invoices entries which is able to tackle the lack of standardization by allowing the building of specific classification models tailored on the peculiarities/preferences of a given accounting firm. The most appropriate classification algorithms suitable to be employed in such a domain are evaluated and their effectiveness is experimentally assessed by running them on a dataset of 910874 invoice entries. The architecture has been devised to support a meta-learning approach consisting in the integration of more classification algorithms in order to achieve better prediction performances.

The rest of the paper is organized as follows. Section 2 presents the architecture of the proposed classification platform. Section 3 describes the adopted methodology and the dataset used for its validation. Section 4 illustrates the experimental setting whose results are shown in Section 5. Finally, Section 6 draws the conclusions.

2 Platform Architecture

Figure 1 shows the architecture of the proposed platform. It is characterized by a set of modules, each of which is in charge of specific functionalities supporting the classification process of invoices entries.

The *Data Pre-Processing* module aims at performing from the raw input data: (i) cleaning, (ii) numerical feature extraction, and (iii) normalisation. The clean data are used to feed both the *Classification* and *Knowledge update* modules. The first module is composed of a set of classification models, each specifically defined to take into account the details of a given user profile along with related product information (see Section 3) during the classification process (the

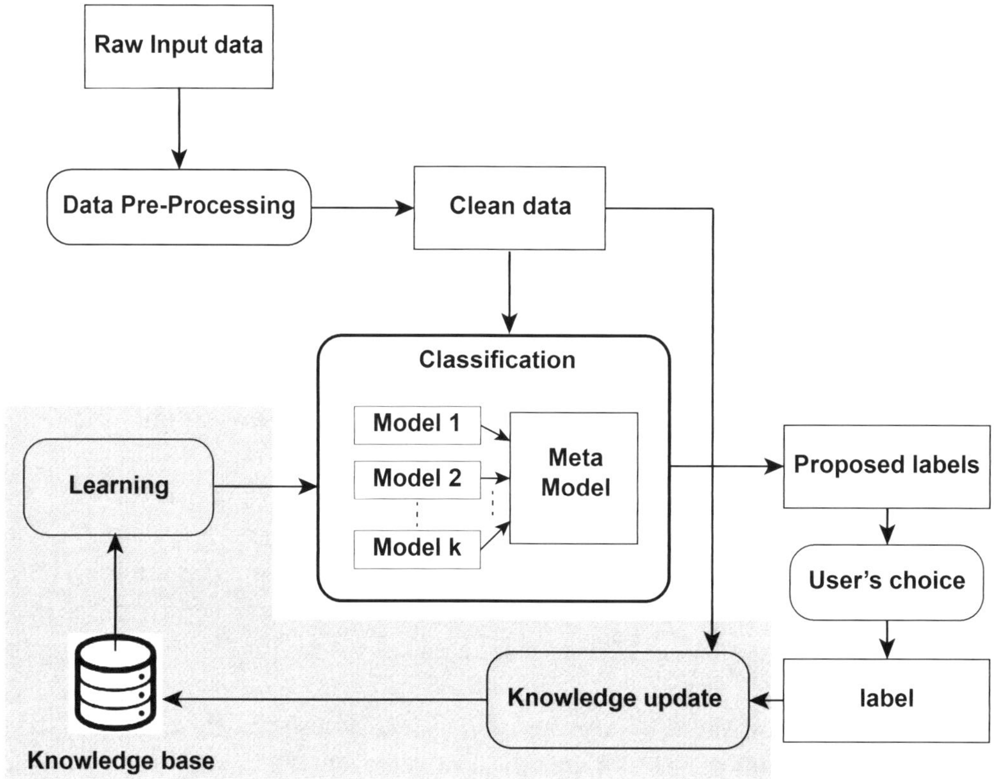

Fig. 1. The architecture of the platform

predicted labels depend on both these information). The second module allows, starting from the *Clean data* and *User's choice*, to update the *Knowledge base* that is exploited by the *Learning* module to re-train the classification models according to the user profiles.

The labels are predicted by the *Classification* module through the *Meta Model* that combines the contributions of each classification model. The *Classification* module produces a ranked list of labels which are fed to the end-user that, in turn, either selects one of them or specifies a new one. In both cases, the resulting labels along with the input data are used by the *Knowledge update* module to update the *Knowledge base*. This feedback allows both to increase the prediction performance of the classification process and to adapt it to *concept drift* issues [15].

3 Data and Methodology

The original dataset consists of a sample of 910874 anonymous invoices' billing entries with 92 numerical and string attributes related to products sold in the period 2016-2018. Specifically, the first 8 are related to the kind of invoice's billing entry along with its occurring date; the following 23 attributes concern the product supplier; the following 2 ones affect the details of the payment;

the next 20 attributes concern the recipient of the goods and related transport details. The latest 39 attributes are related to the product details, i.e. weight, description and the user (invoice owner) information. The group of the invoice entry, which has been defined by the dataset owner, represents the class attribute, for a total of 71 groups.

The dataset keeps information for the following 7 user profiles: (i) *Driver*, (ii) *Change of heading*, (iii) *Direct agent*, (iv) *Fair event*, (v) *Supplier*, (vi) *Internet* and (vii) *Office*.

Starting from the original dataset, the following 2 string attributes have been considered for the analysis: (i) *business activity type* (e.g. "cafe" and "hotel"), and (ii) *description of invoices' billing entry*.

3.1 Preprocessing

The dataset has several missing, invalid and inaccurate values, particularly in correspondence with the product information (e.g. negative weight values, non-homogeneous descriptions and units of measure). To address this issues, it was necessary to perform data cleaning and preparation procedures through the *Data Pre-Processing* module in order to make this data usable for the subsequent classification steps [11].

The data pre-processing task consists of three parts: (i) *data cleaning*, (ii) *feature extraction*, and (iii) *normalization*.

Data Cleaning. The defined *data cleaning* process, which aims to eliminate inaccurate and corrupt data, is composed of three steps which are performed on the 2 selected string attributes:

1. Remove duplicate, redundant and invalid text;
2. Remove useless words and sentences for classification purposes (e.g., "transport cost" or "closed on Tuesday").
3. Identification through regular expressions of invalid text patterns, and further deletion of numbers, symbols, special characters and units of measurement to avoid unexpected behaviours during the classification phases (e.g. overfitting, underfitting).

Feature Extraction. After *data cleaning*, for each entry, a feature vector of 10 numerical values is built from the 2 string attribute values. Specifically, the *business activity type* is characterised by a single word, while the *description of invoices' billing entry* is converted to a sequence of words. All distinct words in the dataset form a vocabulary which associates a unique integer value to each word.

The first element of the feature vector is the integer value in the vocabulary connected with the *business activity type*'s word. The other elements of the feature vector are the integer values in the vocabulary associated with the *description of invoices' billing entry*'s words. Accordingly, the size of the feature vector is equal to 1 plus the size of the longest possible sequence of words composing a *description of invoices' billing entry* in the dataset, which is equal to 9.

Due to the predefined format of the *description of invoices' billing entry* in the dataset, the feature vectors are consistent and comparable. The whole procedure has been performed through the *Tokenizer* utility class provided by the Keras library [12].

Normalisation. In each feature vector, missing numerical values for a given feature are replaced with the mean of the distribution of the remaining ones for that feature. Then, the feature values are bounded to be included in the range $[0, 1]$ using the following *min-max* procedure:

$$\hat{x_i}^j = \frac{x_i{}^j - min_j}{max_j - min_j}, \tag{1}$$

where $x_i{}^j$ is the value of jth feature of feature vector x_i, and min_j and max_j are the minimum and maximum values of jth feature, respectively.

This step is essential for distance-based classifiers to standardize the range of the numerical features so that each feature contributes approximately proportionately to the final distance.

3.2 Classification Models

Although different algorithms have been employed and tested to define the set of classification models composing the *Classification* module, a subset of them were selected which obtained the best performance on the feature vectors related to the different user profiles. Specifically, they are:

- Bayes Net,
- Decision Tree,
- Random Forest,
- K-Nearest Neighbour,
- Deep Neural Network,
- Repeated Incremental Pruning to Produce Error Reduction.

3.3 Bayes Net

A Bayes Net (*BN*) is a probabilistic graphic model that represents a set of stochastic variables with their conditional dependencies through the use of a Direct Acyclic Graph (DAG). In the DAG, each node represents a feature of the dataset, whereas the conditional dependencies among them are represented as edges [14]. The BN model can be used to classify an entry a of the dataset; specifically, a is predicted to belong to the class c whether c maximizes the posterior probability $p(c|a)$.

3.4 Decision Tree

A Decision Tree (*DT*) is a classifier based on a tree structure that is learned from a training dataset. In the tree, leaf nodes represent the class labels, whereas the no-leaf nodes correspond to the feature decision points which spit an entry a of the dataset according to its feature values. After evaluating all the decision points, the entry a is predicted to belong to the class c, which is the leaf node along the path [3].

3.5 Random Forest

A Random Forest (*RF*) generates a set of tree-based classifiers, each of which is built starting from a random subset of the training dataset. A tree-based classifier can be a decision tree as previously described. The classification of an entry a is done by combining the contributions of each tree-based classifier through a majority voting strategy [3].

3.6 K-Nearest Neighbour

A K-Nearest Neighbour (*KNN*) is a classifier that aims at finding the *K-Nearest* entries of the training dataset from a test entry a based on a given distance function. At the end, a is predicted to belong to the class c, which represents the most frequent class in the selected *K-Nearest* entries [2].

3.7 Deep Neural Network

A Deep Neural Network (*DNN*) can be defined as a weighted oriented graph $G =< V, E >$ where nodes represent the artificial neurons $V(G) = \{v_1, v_2, ..., v_n\}$, whereas the weighted edges $E(G) = \{e_1, e_2, ..., e_m\} \subseteq V \times V$ represent the relationships between neurons. A *DNN* is composed of a layer of input neurons, one or more intermediate layers of neurons and a layer of output neurons that provides the classification result. The model learns a non linear-transformation by tuning the layer weights so as to associate the input entry to another space where it becomes linearly separable [2].

3.8 Repeated Incremental Pruning to Produce Error Reduction

Repeated Incremental Pruning to Produce Error Reduction (*RIPPER*) is a rule-based classifier which learns rules by considering all the entries of a given judgment in the training dataset as a class label, and detecting a set of rules that include all the entries belonging to that class. After that, the algorithm continues considering the next class label and does the same steps, iterating until all class labels have been considered [7].

4 Experiments

The classification task consists in predicting the group of invoices' billing entries related to user profiles from the feature vectors in the dataset.

The experiments involving *BN, DT, RF, KNN* and *RIPPER* have been performed in Weka [1], whereas the *DNN* has been implemented in Python through well-known deep learning libraries, i.e. Pandas, Sklearn, Keras with Tensorflows as backend.

For *KNN*, the experimented values for K ranged from 1 to 8. In the end, K was set to 1 since it provided the best results on the given dataset. Concerning the other parameters, they were set to the default Weka values.

The *DNN* has a 1D tensor 10-dimensional input vector (corresponding to the size of the feature vector), an *Embedding* layer that allows to represent words with their meanings, a *Flatten* layer that transforms the output coming from the *Embedding* so as to be exploited by the following *Dense* hidden layer. Also, a *BatchNormalization* layer has been introduced to normalize the activation function of neurons, followed by a *Dropout* layer, which randomly deactivates neurons to prevent overfitting issues [13]. Finally, a *Dense* output layer composed of 71 neurons (corresponding to the number of groups of invoices' billing entries) provides the predicted class. Figure 2 shows the *DNN* architecture.

In order to evaluate the performance of the classifiers, *accuracy*, *error* and *kappa statistics* have been computed from the multiclass confusion matrix. The *accuracy* represents the percentage of correctly classified entries; the *error* quantifies the percentage of incorrectly classified entries; finally, the *kappa statistics* is based on a comparison between the observed and expected accuracy [11].

To make the evaluation independent from the choice of training and test datasets, a k-fold cross validation ($k = 10$) has been used, which is a valuable literature technique to achieve statistically significant results [11].

5 Results

Table 1 reports the classification results obtained by *BN, DT, RF, KNN, RIPPLE* and *DNN* in terms of *accuracy*, *error* and *kappa statistics* for one randomly selected test dataset related to the *Supplier* user profile.

It is worth noting that all the presented classification models obtained an *accuracy* in predicting the group of invoices' entries exceeding 95%. Specifically, *DNN* obtains the best result of 99.20% for *accuracy*, 0.80% for *error* and 0.99 for *kappa statistics*. Hence, it can be definitively adopted as classification model for the *Supplier* user profile. This is followed by *RF*, *KNN*, *DT*, *RIPPLE* and *BN*.

Concerning the best classification method, *DNN*, Figure 3 shows the trend of *accuracy* and *error* over the epochs on training and test datasets.

As depicted in Figure 3, the *error* decreases at each epoch, whereas the *accuracy* increases at each epoch. This is what it is expected using an optimization function based on the descending gradient, which tries to minimize the *error*

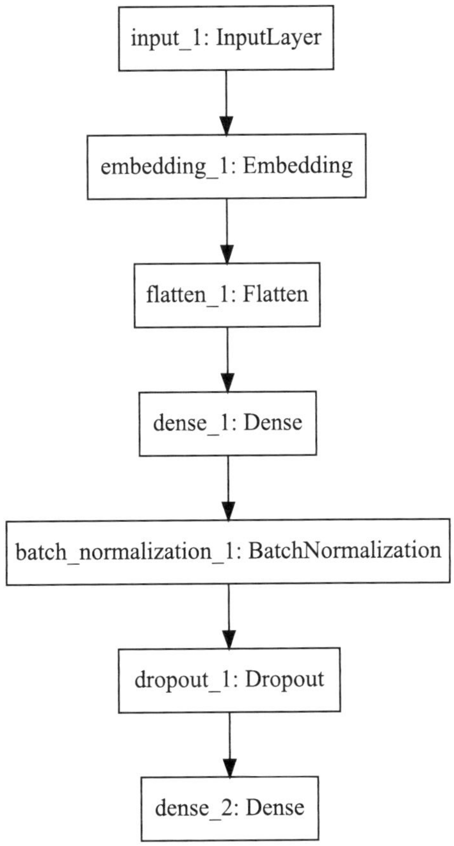

Fig. 2. The architecture of the adopted *DNN*.

Table 1. Classification results for the user profile *Supplier*.

Classification model	Accuracy (%)	Error (%)	Kappa statistics
BN	95.64	4.35	0.95
DT	96.82	3.17	0.96
RF	98.02	1.98	0.98
KNN	97.60	2.40	0.97
RIPPLE	96.58	3.42	0.96
DNN	99.20	0.80	0.99

value at each epoch [13]. An opposite trend can be observed for *accuracy* where its value increases over the epochs. It worth noting that the defined *DNN* is able to learn the key patterns characterizing the dataset already from the first epochs; it is visible from the trend of the *accuracy* and *error* obtained on the dataset which rapidly increases and decreases, respectively, and then does not change significantly over the epochs.

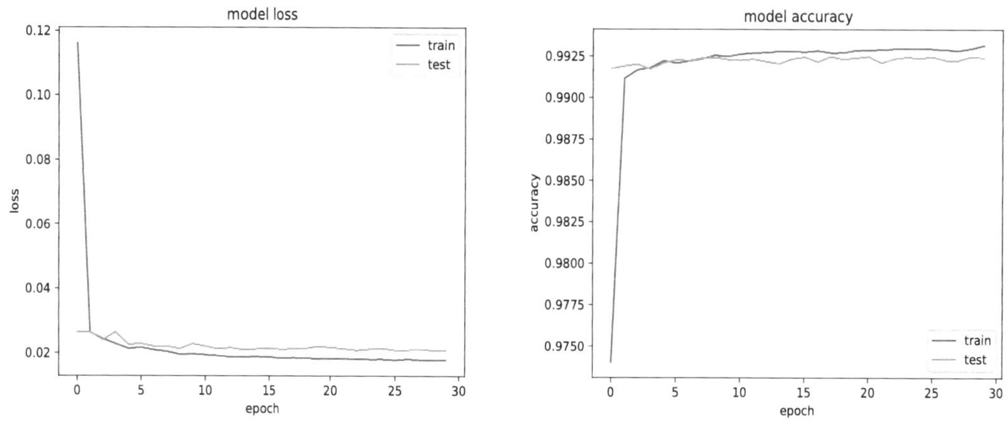

Fig. 3. Accuracy and error obtained by *DNN* on invoices' entries related to the *Supplier* user profile.

6 Conclusions and Future Works

This paper presented the architecture of a platform for the automatic classification of invoice entries for accounting purposes and the evaluation of the performance of the classification algorithms that can be suitably employed in such a domain. The architecture has been designed to enable a meta-learning approach where issues such as adaptation to invoice owner profiles and concept drift can be effectively handled. Toward this goal, the future work will involve the analysis of ensemble learning techniques [15, 16] based on new boosting and bagging strategies to combine the classification results in the *Meta Model*, different feature representations for modelling the invoice entries, and the active learning approach proposed. Another potential future research direction concerns the extension of the architecture in order for it to work in distributed environments e.g. through the use of Model-Driven approaches [5] and its evaluation by means of virtual environments [8, 9].

References

1. Weka 3: Data Mining Software in Java, `https://www.cs.waikato.ac.nz/ml/weka/index.html`
2. Altman, N.S.: An introduction to kernel and nearest-neighbor nonparametric regression. The American Statistician **46**(3), 175–185 (1992)
3. Amelio, L., Amelio, A.: Classification methods in image analysis with a special focus on medical analytics. In: Machine Learning Paradigms, pp. 31–69. Springer (2019)
4. Bartoli, A., Davanzo, G., Medvet, E., Sorio, E.: Improving features extraction for supervised invoice classification. In: Artificial Intelligence and Applications. ACTAPRESS (2010). https://doi.org/10.2316/P.2010.674-040
5. Bocciarelli, P., D'Ambrogio, A., Falcone, A., Garro, A., Giglio, A.: A model-driven approach to enable the distributed simulation of complex systems. In: Complex

Systems Design & Management, Proceedings of the Sixth International Conference on Complex Systems Design & Management, CSD&M 2015, Paris, France, November 23-25, 2015, pp. 171–183. Springer International Publishing (oct 2015). https://doi.org/10.1007/978-3-319-26109-6_13
6. Cesarini, F., Gori, M., Marinai, S., Soda, G.: INFORMys: a flexible invoice-like form-reader system. IEEE Transactions on Pattern Analysis and Machine Intelligence **20**(7), 730–745 (jul 1998). https://doi.org/10.1109/34.689303
7. Cohen, W.W.: Fast effective rule induction. In: Machine Learning Proceedings 1995, pp. 115–123. Elsevier (1995)
8. Furfaro, A., Argento, L., Parise, A., Piccolo, A.: Using virtual environments for the assessment of cybersecurity issues in IoT scenarios. Simulation Modelling Practice and Theory **73**, 43–54 (apr 2017). https://doi.org/10.1016/j.simpat.2016.09.007
9. Furfaro, A., Piccolo, A., Parise, A., Argento, L., Saccà, D.: A cloud-based platform for the emulation of complex cybersecurity scenarios. Future Generation Computer Systems **89**, 791–803 (dec 2018). https://doi.org/10.1016/j.future.2018.07.025
10. Hamza, H., Belaid, Y., Belaid, A., Chaudhuri, B.B.: Incremental classification of invoice documents. In: Proc. of 19th International Conference on Pattern Recognition. IEEE (dec 2008). https://doi.org/10.1109/icpr.2008.4761832
11. Han, J., Pei, J., Kamber, M.: Data mining: concepts and techniques. Elsevier (2011)
12. Ketkar, N., et al.: Deep Learning with Python. Springer (2017)
13. LeCun, Y., Bengio, Y., Hinton, G.: Deep learning. nature **521**(7553), 436 (2015)
14. Solares, C., Sanz, A.M.: Different bayesian network models in the classification of remote sensing images. In: Intelligent Data Engineering and Automated Learning - IDEAL 2007, 8th International Conference, Birmingham, UK, December 16-19, 2007, Proceedings, pp. 10–16. Springer Berlin Heidelberg (2007). https://doi.org/10.1007/978-3-540-77226-2_2
15. Wang, H., Fan, W., Yu, P.S., Han, J.: Mining concept-drifting data streams using ensemble classifiers. In: Proceedings of the ninth ACM SIGKDD international conference on Knowledge discovery and data mining - KDD'03. ACM Press (2003). https://doi.org/10.1145/956750.956778
16. Zhang, C., Ma, Y.: Ensemble machine learning: methods and applications. Springer (2012)

The CRIKE Data-Science Process for Legal Knowledge Extraction
Discussion Paper

Silvana Castano[1], Mattia Falduti[1], Alfio Ferrara[1], and Stefano Montanelli[1]

Università degli Studi di Milano
DI - Via Celoria, 18 - 20135 Milano
{silvana.castano,mattia.falduti,alfio.ferrara,stefano.montanelli}@unimi.it

Abstract. In this paper, we present *CRIKE*, a data-science approach to automatically detect concrete applications of legal abstract terms in case-law decisions. To this purpose, CRIKE relies on the use of the *LATO ontology* where legal abstract terms are properly formalized as concepts and relations among concepts. Using LATO, CRIKE aims at discovering how and where legal abstract terms are applied by judges in their legal argumentation. Moreover, we detect the terminology used in the text of case-law decisions to characterize concrete abstract-term instances.

Keywords: legal ontology, legal-term extraction, case-law analysis

1 Introduction

Law is general and abstract by definition. On the opposite, court case law decisions are specific and concrete, in that they provide a peculiar interpretation of law applied to the considered single cases. Legal interpreters, such as for example judges and lawyers, are daily involved in analysis and evaluation of court case law with the aim to extract/derive possible suggestions for incoming case applications by relying on the experience of past applications that can be considered as a sort of consolidated *legal knowledge*.

According to the Italian law, the legal terminology can be distinguished into three main categories, that are i) *statutory terms*, i.e., terms directly or indirectly defined by law; examples of statutory terms are public officer, illicit drug, and consumer; ii) *descriptive terms*, i.e., terms featuring actions, human activities, and any real-life object; examples of descriptive terms are escape, car, and year; iii) *abstract terms*, i.e., terms featuring something indeterminate that requires a concrete application for being really defined; examples of abstract terms are good faith, long-term cohabitation, and dangerous driving. Consider the abstract schema of a legal action provided in Figure 1. When a new case law is received for

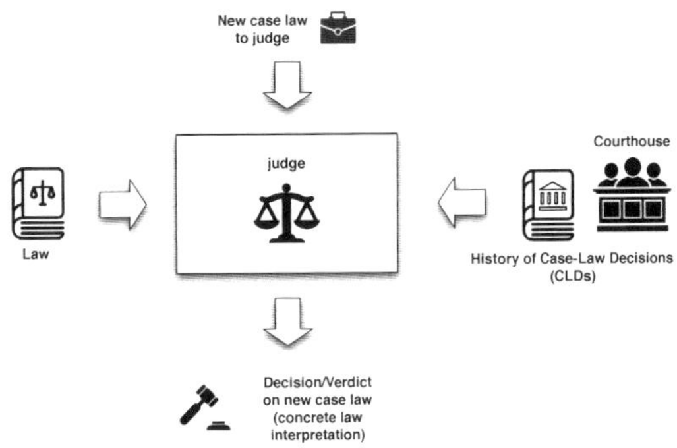

Fig. 1. The abstract schema of a legal action

judgement, the expected evaluation process has to take into account i) the law, for understanding the terms, either statutory, descriptive, or abstract, that can be relevant for the current case, and ii) the history of case-law decisions, for detecting possible relevant interpretations and concrete applications of abstract terms that can be useful to support the decision/verdict to eventually deliver.

In this paper, we present *CRIKE* (CRIme Knowledge Extraction), a data-science approach to detect concrete applications of legal abstract terms in large case-law decisions. To this purpose, CRIKE relies on the use of LATO (Legal Abstract Term Ontology) where legal terms are properly formalized as concepts and relations among concepts. Using LATO, CRIKE aims at discovering how and where legal abstract terms are applied by judges in their legal argumentation.

The paper is organized as follows. In Section 2, the CRIKE approach is introduced. The LATO ontology and the CRIKE techniques for legal knowledge extraction are discussed in Section 3 and 4, respectively. Related work are discussed in Section 5. Concluding remarks are provided in Section 6.

2 The CRIKE approach

The CRIKE approach (see Figure 2) is conceived to support extraction of legal knowledge from a (possibly large) dataset of Case-Law Decisions (CLDs) coming from different, official sources, such as for example First Grade and Court of Appeal judgements. CRIKE embeds the LATO ontology where relevant law concepts of a given domain of interest are properly formalized. To enforce knowledge extraction, CRIKE exploits a given dataset of CLDs in input by adopting a conventional data-science process where each CLD is indexed and stored in a digital format. In particular, the CLDs of our dataset are acquired from the Court and the Court of Appeal of Milan and they are usually provided in image format with highly heterogeneous quality. The indexing and storage activity exploits data cleaning and tokenization techniques to obtain a pure textual version of each CLD as well as a focused set of metadata. By exploiting the indexed CLDs metadata, knowledge extraction is enforced with the aim at classifying a CLD with respect to the LATO ontology knowledge. In particular, extraction

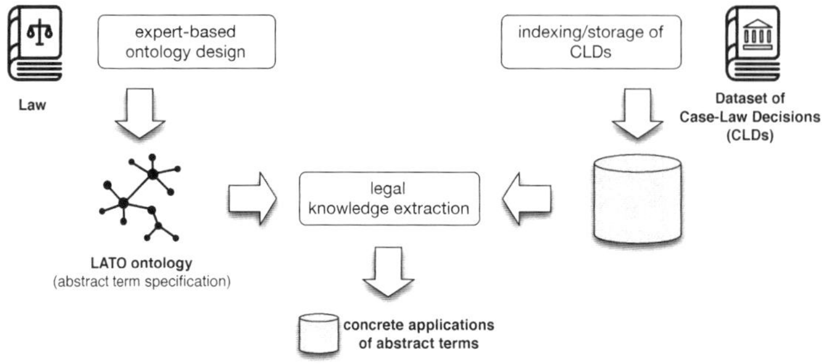

Fig. 2. The CRIKE approach

is focused on detecting the concrete applications of legal abstract terms in the text of the considered CLDs. The crucial idea of CRIKE is that the detection of a given abstract term AT is not only concerned with the recognition of single terms featuring AT, but also with the recognition of terms associated with the ancillary concepts related to AT, that we call *abstract-term context*.

Motivating example. Consider the Italian law about drugs and related drug offenses, as reported in [11]. According to the Italian criminal order, "the Consolidated Law, adopted by Presidential Decree No 309 on 9 October 1990 and subsequently amended, provides the legal framework for trade, treatment and prevention, and prohibition and punishment of illegal activities in the field of drugs and psychoactive substances. Drug use in itself is not mentioned as an offense. [...] The threshold between personal possession and trafficking is determined by the circumstances of the specific case (e.g., the act, possession of tools for packaging, different types of drug possessed, number of doses in excess of average daily use, means of organization). The penalty for supply-related offenses, such as production, sale, transport, distribution or acquisition, depends on the type of drug. However, when the **offenses are considered minor** because of the means, modalities or circumstances, the terms of imprisonment are lower. Evaluating whether or not the offense is minor should take into account a set of "ancillary" elements such as the mode of action, possible criminal motives, quality and quantity of drug possessed, the character of the offender, conduct during or subsequent to the offense, and the family and social conditions of the offender". The notion of **minor offense** is an example of abstract term in the above law quotation. A precise definition of circumstances and related threshold quantities to associate with the notion of minor offense is not available/possible in the (abstract) law. Given a specific criminal charge of drug possession, the final decision/verdict is based on the specific interpretation of the abstract term "minor offense" where the specific circumstances and quantities of the considered case represent a concrete application of the corresponding abstract term.

3 Legal knowledge representation

To formalize the knowledge related to abstract terms and their interpretation, we introduce LATO in CRIKE. LATO is a legal ontology where relevant law terms to exploit knowledge extraction in CLDs are defined; it contains concepts to represent general law terms, either abstract, statutory and descriptive terms.

LATO is manually defined by domain experts and implemented according to the SKOS formalism. In particular, the concept hierarchy is based on a root concept Term with three main subconcepts, namely AbstractTerm, DescriptiveTerm, and StatutoryTerm (see Figure 3(a)). In addition to general law terms, the LATO ontology contains concepts that represent the Italian legislative structure, such as for example the concepts Law, LawArticle, and LawParagraph. Furthermore, the concepts Conviction and Discharge are also specified in LATO to represent the possible Court decisions (i.e., the verdict) of a given case law. In particular, the concept Conviction denotes a verdict in which the Court judges the defendant guilty, while the concept Discharge denotes a verdict in which the facts have a penalty relevance, but no punishment is finally delivered. Finally, the concepts Quantity and UnitOfMeasure are defined in LATO for allowing to represent the quantitative estimation of substances that can appear in legal documents.

AbstractTerm is the core concept of the LATO ontology since it represents the target of the knowledge extraction functionalities of CRIKE. The related construct of SKOS is exploited to enrich the specification of an abstract term AT by formalizing the ontology relationships between AT and the other concepts of the LATO ontology composing its context. In particular, given a considered abstract term AT, related is used to connect AT to ancillary concepts of LATO representing i) an *objective judgment element* OBJ usually expressed through the connection of AT with a descriptive/statutory concept; ii) a *subjective quantitative evaluation* $SUBJ$ usually expressed through a relationship between AT and Quantity/UnitOfMeasure concepts; and iii) a *legislative reference* $LREF$ usually denoted with a connection of AT with a specific law or regulation (i.e., Law, LawArticle, and LawParagraph concepts). According to SKOS, each LATO concept is associated with a *preferred label* (prefLabel) as well as with one or more *alternative labels* (altLabel) and *hidden labels* (hiddenLabel) to enrich the concept definition with a label-set of literal descriptions that is very useful for subsequent knowledge extraction, to capture possible synonyms, acronyms, and abbreviations in the text of CLDs.

Example. An example of SKOS definition for the abstract term $AT =$ MinorOffense is shown in Figure 3(b) according to the Italian drug-trafficking law. MinorOffense is related to the concepts Drug and DrugTraffickingVerb that represent the OBJ relationships since they are subconcepts of StatutoryTerm and DescriptiveTerm, respectively. The relationships with the concepts Quantity and UnitOfMeasure represent the subjective judge evaluations $SUBJ$. The concepts Par5, Art73, and DPR309/1990 are subconcepts of the LawParagraph, LawArticle, and Law, respec-

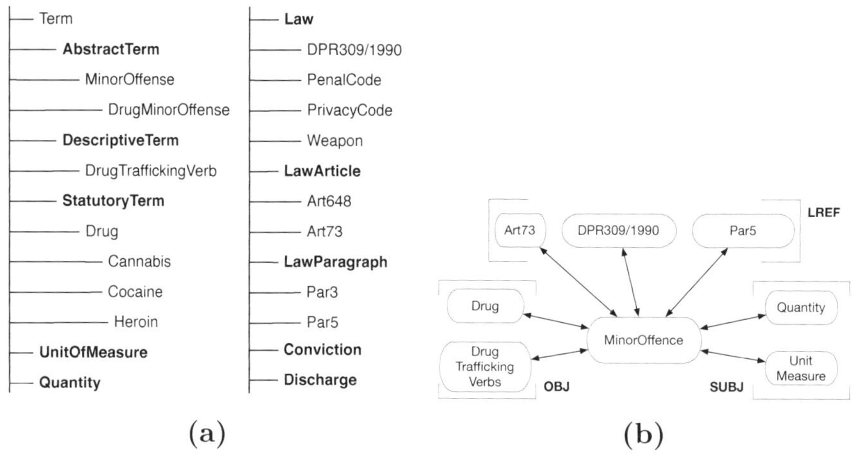

Fig. 3. (a) Excerpt of the LATO concept hierarchy; (b) Example of concept definition for the abstract term MinorOffense

tively, and they express the legal references $LREF$ of MinorOffense in the Italian criminal code where the drug trafficking crime is defined.

4 Knowledge extraction in CRIKE

Knowledge extraction in CRIKE is based on the idea to exploit text analysis techniques for detecting the concrete applications of legal abstract terms belonging to LATO throughout the stored/indexed case-law decisions CLDs. To this end, for a given abstract term AT, we introduce the notion of *abstract-term context* Ctx_{AT} containing, besides the AT term, all the concepts of LATO that are ancillary to AT, namely OBJ, $SUBJ$, or $LREF$ concepts:

$$Ctx_{AT} = \{C_i \mid r(AT, C_i)\}$$

where $r(AT, C_i)$ denotes a SKOS related relationship between the abstract term AT and the concept C_i.

For each concept $C \in Ctx_{AT}$, we define the *concept label set* L_C that contains the whole set of labels, either preferred, alternative, or hidden, associated with C. Furthermore, based on the notion of L_C, we define the *extended label set* $\mathcal{L}_C$ where the concept label set of C is enriched by including the concept label set of the concepts C_j subsumed by C:

$$\mathcal{L}_C = L_C \cup \left\{L_{C_j} \mid C_j \subseteq C\right\}$$

Consider the goal to detect the concrete applications of a certain abstract term AT in a dataset of case-law decisions $CLDs$. CRIKE knowledge extraction is enforced by exploiting the extended label sets $\mathcal{L}_C$ of the concepts in the context Ctx_{AT}. For each document $d \in CLDs$, we define a vector representation $\boldsymbol{d}$ where each element corresponds to a concept in the context Ctx_{AT}. The value $d[i] \in \boldsymbol{d}$ is set to 1 when a *label hit* is detected, meaning that at least one occurrence of a label in $\mathcal{L}_{C_i}$ is found in d for the concept $C_i \in Ctx_{AT}$, and 0 otherwise (i.e., *label miss*). A threshold based mechanism is defined to specify the minimum number of label hits required to consider that a concrete application of the abstract term AT is detected in the document d.

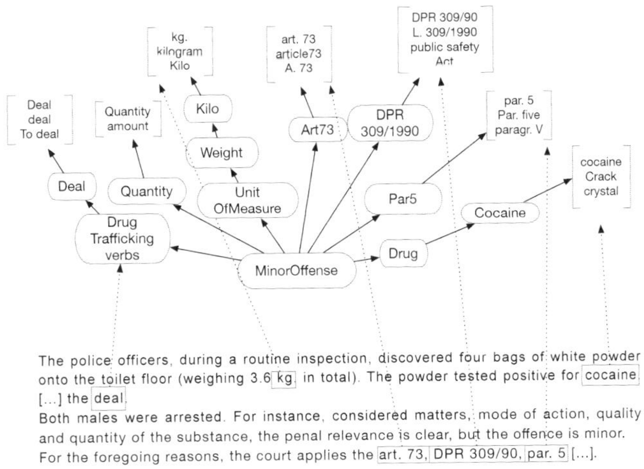

Fig. 4. Example of knowledge extraction for the abstract term MinorOffense

Example. Consider the abstract term AT = MinorOffense and the corresponding context $Ctx_{\mathsf{MinorOffense}} = \{Drug, DrugTraffickingVerb, DPR309/1990, Art73, Par5, Quantity, UnitOfMeasure\}$. Moreover, consider the extended label set $\mathcal{L}_{Drug} = L_{Drug} \cup \{L_{Cocaine}, L_{Heroin}, L_{Cannabis}\}$. In Figure 4, we show an example of knowledge extraction based on the concepts and corresponding extended label sets in the context $Ctx_{\mathsf{MinorOffense}}$. An example of vector-based document representation for the abstract term AT = MinorOffense is shown in Figure 5. If we consider a threshold of 80% of label hits, we have that a concrete

	Drug	DrugTraffickingVerb	DPR309/90	Art73	Par5	Quantity	UnitOfMeasure
d_1	1	0	1	1	1	1	1
d_2	1	1	1	0	0	1	0

Fig. 5. Example of label hits for the abstract term MinorOffense

application of MinorOffense is detected in document d_1 since 6 hits are found over the available 7 concepts in $Ctx_{\mathsf{MinorOffense}}$.

5 Related work

Work related to the issues addressed in CRIKE regards legal argumentation mining and legal ontology design. Legal argumentation mining refers to the capability to automatically detect and classify the role of possible argumentative units within a considered legal case text [1]. In [10], authors propose to mine statutory texts by using natural language processing and supervised machine learning techniques. More recently, the LUIMA approach has been proposed to focus on extraction of evidential reasoning from a court decision dataset [5]. Moreover, a particularly relevant contribution is provided in [9] about extraction of case law sentences for argumentation of statutory terms.

A survey on legal ontology design is presented in [1], where a special focus is given to representation of legal concepts in type systems. In [4], the notion of mutual consensus is introduced to support the specification of concepts and relations about contract formation. An application example based on a corpus of Italian legal texts is presented in [7], where the results of exploiting a learning system are provided. A further specification of a legal ontology using ONTOLINGUA is presented in [13]. Furthermore, in [12], authors present the LOIS project (Lexical Ontologies for Legal Information Sharing), and discuss a methodology for building a multilingual semantic lexicon for law able to be used both as a source of semantic metadata and as an external tool for cross lingual retrieval. On that topic, in [8], a methodology to automatically create an OWL ontology from a set of legal documents is presented. In [3], an automated approach based on statistical analysis is described, for identification of core concepts and relations in a corpus of legal texts. Natural Language Processing (NLP) techniques are proposed in [6], to extract concepts and relations among legal concepts, with the aim to build an ontology for legal information retrieval.

Original contribution of the proposed CRIKE approach is related to the enforcement of a data-science process with the support of an expert-based law ontology to extract knowledge from CLDs. A further peculiar feature of CRIKE is related to the formalization of an abstract term as a legal ontology concept with a corresponding context of related concepts. Ontology concepts with associated contexts are used to drive the identification of concrete applications/interpretations of corresponding abstract terms in the text of CLDs.

6 CRIKE support to practices and concluding remarks

In this paper, we presented the CRIKE approach for legal knowledge extraction. We envisage the following main practices that can be supported by using CRIKE i) **knowledge-assisted verdict writing**, where the concrete terminology extracted for abstract terms can support the judge in the preparation of new case-law decisions; ii) **history-based verdict prediction**, where the knowledge extracted by CRIKE is used to train a machine learning mechanism with the aim to predict the possible decision on a new incoming case-law to judge; and iii) **legal analytics**, where the results of knowledge extraction are exploited to detect possible trends and common abstract-term interpretations.

A preliminary experimentation of CRIKE has been performed based on a dataset provided by the Courthouse of Milan, Italy, whose results are described in [2]. The goal of the experimentation was to analyze the effectiveness of CRIKE in recognizing the concrete applications of the abstract term MinorOffense.

Different research directions are currently being investigated. On the one side, we are working on a bootstrapping approach to enforce enrichment of the LATO ontology, so that the context of abstract terms can be progressively augmented with new relevant terms and literals as long as they are detected in CLDs during extraction. On the other side, machine learning techniques are being developed to enforce a supervised classification of CLDs based on abstract terms, by exploiting a training set of CLDs manually annotated by domain experts.

References

1. Ashley, K.D.: Artificial Intelligence and Legal Analytics: New Tools for Law Practice in the Digital Age. Cambridge University Press (2017)
2. Castano, S., Falduti, M., Ferrara, A., Montanelli, S.: Crime Knowledge Extraction: An Ontology-Driven Approach for Detecting Abstract Terms in Case Law Decisions. In: Proc. of the 17th Int. Conf. on Artificial Intelligence and Law (2019)
3. Francesconi, E., Montemagni, S., Peters, W., Tiscornia, D.: Integrating a BottomUp and TopDown Methodology for Building Semantic Resources for the Multilingual Legal Domain, vol. 6036, pp. 95–121. Springer (2010)
4. Gardner, A.: An Artificial Intelligence Approach to Legal Reasoning. MIT Press, Cambridge, MA, USA (1987)
5. Grabmair, M., Ashley, K.D., Chen, R., Sureshkumar, P., Wang, C., Nyberg, E., Walker, V.R.: Introducing LUIMA: an Experiment in Legal Conceptual Retrieval of Vaccine Injury Decisions Using a UIMA Type System and Tools. In: Proc. of the 15th Int. Conference on Artificial Intelligence and Law. pp. 69–78. ACM (2015)
6. Lame, G.: Using NLP Techniques to Identify Legal Ontology Components: Concepts and Relations, pp. 169–184. Springer Berlin Heidelberg (2005)
7. Lenci, A., Montemagni, S., Pirrelli, V., Venturi, G.: NLP-based Ontology Learning from Legal Texts. A Case Study. In: Proc. of the 2nd Workshop on Legal Ontologies and Artificial Intelligence Techniques. pp. 113–129. Citeseer (2007)
8. Saias, J., Quaresma, P.: A Methodology to Create Legal Ontologies in a Logic Programming Information Retrieval System, pp. 185–200. Springer (2005)
9. Savelka, J., Ashley, K.D.: Extracting Case Law Sentences for Argumentation about the Meaning of Statutory Terms. In: Proc. of the 3rd Int. Workshop on Argument Mining. pp. 50–59 (2016)
10. Savelka, J., Grabmair, M., Ashley, K.D.: Mining Information from Statutory Texts in Multi-Jurisdictional Settings. In: Proc. of the Int. Conference on Legal Knowledge and Information Systems. pp. 133–142. IOS Press (2014)
11. The European Monitoring Centre for Drugs and Drugs Addiction: Italy, Country Drug Report 2018. Tech. rep., The European Monitoring Centre for Drugs and Drugs Addiction (2018)
12. Tiscornia, D.: The LOIS project: Lexical Ontologies for Legal Information Sharing. In: Proc. of the V Legislative XML Workshop. pp. 189–204 (2006)
13. Visser, P., Bench-Capon, T.: The Formal Specification of a Legal Ontology. In: Proc. of the Int. Conference on Legal Knowledge and Information Systems (1996)

GAIA: a Framework for Schema Mapping Reuse (DISCUSSION PAPER)

Paolo Atzeni[1], Luigi Bellomarini[2], Paolo Papotti[3], and Riccardo Torlone[1]

[1] Università Roma Tre, Italy,
[2] Banca d'Italia, Italy,
[3] EURECOM, France

1 Introduction

Schema mappings are widely used as a tool for data exchange and integration. However, although there are systems supporting data architects in the creation of mappings [5], designing them is still a time-consuming task. In this framework, given the overwhelming amount of "enterprise knowledge" stored in traditional data warehouses and in data lakes, reuse is an opportunity of increasing importance [1]. In particular, data transformation scenarios are often defined over schemas that are different in structure but similar in semantics. This is especially true if data sources, which are extremely heterogeneous, have to be mapped to a shared format. It follows that a great opportunity to reduce the effort of transformation design is to *reuse existing schema mappings*. Unfortunately, there is no obvious approach for this problem. Consider the following example.

Example 1. A central bank maintains a register with balance data from all companies in the country (Figure 1). This register has schema **G**, with a relation `Balance` storing, for each company, its gains, zone of operation, and economic sector. External providers send data to the bank in different forms. Provider A adopts a schema $\mathbf{S}_A$, with a relation $\mathtt{R_A}$ for companies (firms), with gains, zone of operation, and economic sector, whose code refers to relation `Activity`. Provider B adopts a schema $\mathbf{S}_B$, with a relation $\mathtt{R_B}$ for companies (enterprises), their gains, sector, capital, and area, whose code refers to relation `Location`. Data is moved from $\mathbf{S}_A$ and $\mathbf{S}_B$ into **G**, by using two schema mappings:

$$\sigma_A\text{: } R_A(f,g,z,s), \text{Activity}(s,d) \rightarrow \text{Balance}(f,g,z,d).$$
$$\sigma_B\text{: } R_B(e,g,s,c,a), \text{Location}(a,n) \rightarrow \text{Balance}(e,g,n,s).$$

The example shows a *data exchange scenario* where the differences in the mappings are due to the structural differences between $\mathbf{S}_A$ and $\mathbf{S}_B$, which are, on the other hand, semantically very similar. Moreover, every new data provider (e.g., $\mathbf{S}_C$ in the figure) would require the manual design of a new, ad-hoc mapping, even if there is a clear analogy with the already defined mappings.

Our goal is to reuse σ_A and σ_B and avoid the definition of a new mapping for $\mathbf{S}_C$. The intuition is to collect all available mappings in a repository; then,

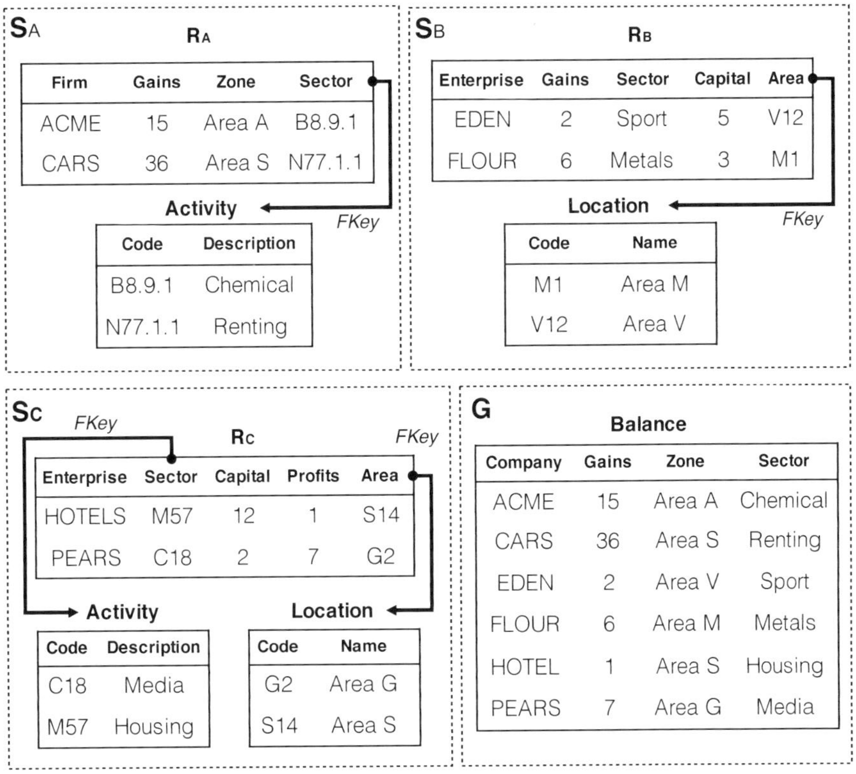

Fig. 1. A data transformation scenario

for any new pair of schemas (e.g., $\mathbf{S}_C$ and $\mathbf{G}$ in the figure), query such repository to retrieve a suitable mapping. Unfortunately, this form of direct reuse is complicated by the nature of schema mappings. A mapping characterizes the constraint between a pair of schemas at a level of detail that enables both logical reasoning and efficient execution. Yet, a simple variation in a schema, such as a different relation or attribute name or a different number of attributes, makes it not applicable. Our experiments show that mappings from a corpus of 1.000 schema mappings can be reused for new, unmapped pairs of schemas only in 20% of cases. To be reusable, a mapping should be described in a way that is independent of its specificities but, at the same time, harnesses the essence of the constraint so as to work for similar schemas.

Example 2. Consider a "generic" mapping Σ_A, obtained from σ_A by replacing names of the relations and attributes with variables. It could be informally described as follows:

Σ_A: *for each* relation r *with* key f and attributes g, a, s
  for each relation r' *with* key s and attribute d
    with a foreign key constraint from s of r to s of r'
  there exists a relation r'' *with* key f and attributes g, a, d.

If instantiated on $\mathbf{S}_A$, the generic mapping Σ_A expresses a mapping to $\mathbf{G}$ that is the same as σ_A. This solution seems a valid compromise between precision, i.e., the ability to express the semantics of the original mapping, and generality, as it can be applicable over different schemas. However, Σ_A falls short of the latter requirement, as it is not applicable on $\mathbf{S}_B$. Indeed, there are no constraints on attribute g and a, and so they could be bound to any of `Gains`, `Sector` and `Capital`, incorrectly trying to map `Capital` into the target.

Example 3. Consider now a more elaborated generic mapping that uses constants to identify attributes:

Σ_B^H: *for each* relation r *with* key e and attributes g, s, c, a
for each relation r' *with* key a and attribute d
with a foreign key constraint from a of r to a of r'
where $g = Gains$, $s \neq Gains$, $s \neq Capital$, $c \neq Gains$, $c \neq Sector$
there exists a relation r'' *with* key e and attributes g, d, s.

This generic mapping is precise enough to correctly describe both σ_A and σ_B and can be re-used with other schemas.

The example shows a combination of attributes, identified by constraints on their names and role, that form a correct and useful generic mapping. Once pinpointed, generic mappings can be stored in a repository, so that it is possible to use them for a new scenario. In our example, given $\mathbf{S}_C$ and $\mathbf{G}$, the generic mapping Σ_B^H can be retrieved from the repository and immediately applied.

There are three main challenges in this approach.

- We need a clear characterization of what it means for a generic mapping to correctly describe and capture the semantics of an original schema mapping.
- As a generic mapping is characterized by a combination of conditions on attribute names and roles, for a given schema mapping there is a combinatorial number of generic mappings. We need a mechanism to generate them.
- For a new scenario (e.g., new schemas), there is an overwhelming number of generic mappings that potentially apply, with different levels of "suitability". We need efficient tools to search through and choose among them.

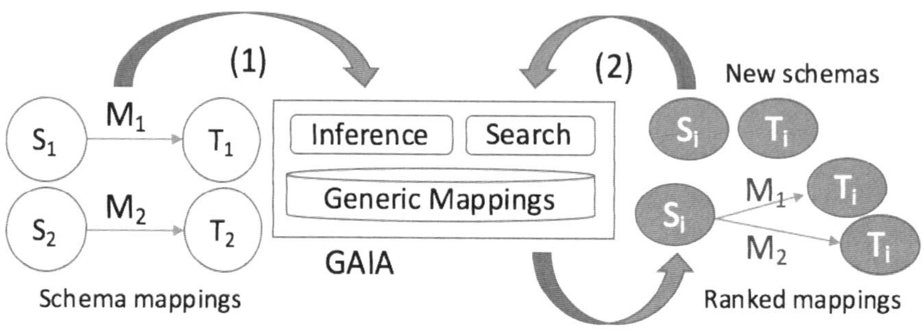

Fig. 2. The architecture of GAIA.

In this work, we address the above challenges with GAIA, a system for mapping reuse. GAIA supports two tasks, as shown in Figure 2: (1) infer generic mappings, called *meta-mappings*, from input schema mappings, and store them in a repository; (2) given a source and a target schema, return a ranked list of meta-mappings from the repository which are used to generate possible mappings between these schemas. GAIA provides the following key contributions:

- The notion of *fitness*: a semantics to precisely characterize and check when a meta-mapping is suitable for a reuse scenario.
- An algorithm to *infer* meta-mappings from schema mappings with an approach that extends previous efforts for the definition of schema mappings by example; this algorithm is used to populate a repository of meta-mappings supporting schema mapping reuse.
- An approach to reuse based on: (i) the search, in the repository of available meta-mappings, for those that *fit* a new pair of source and target schemas and (ii) the construction, from the retrieved meta-mappings, of possible mappings to be proposed to the designer.

Because of space limitation, algorithms and details are in the full version of the paper [2]. In the rest of this paper, we provide examples of meta-mappings (Section 2) and experimental results from an evaluation of our system with more than 20,000 real-world data transformations over 40,000 schemas (Section 3).

2 Mapping and meta-mappings

We recall the notion of schema mapping [6] and introduce that of *meta-mapping*. While the former notion models specific transformations, the latter introduces an abstraction over mappings [7, 8] and models *generic* mappings between schemas. Building on these notions, we illustrate the functionalities of our system.

Schema mappings. Let $\mathbf{S}$ (the source) and $\mathbf{T}$ (the target) be two relational schemas and let $Inst(\mathbf{S})$ and $Inst(\mathbf{T})$ denote the set of all possible instances of $\mathbf{S}$ and $\mathbf{T}$, respectively. A *(schema) mapping* M for $\mathbf{S}$ and $\mathbf{T}$ is a binary relation over their instances, that is, $M \subseteq Inst(\mathbf{S}) \times Inst(\mathbf{T})$ [3].

Without loss of generality, we consider mappings expressed by a single *source-to-target tuple-generating-dependency* (st-tgd) σ: $\forall \mathbf{x}(\phi(\mathbf{x}) \rightarrow \exists \mathbf{y} \psi(\mathbf{x}, \mathbf{y}))$ where $\mathbf{x}$ and $\mathbf{y}$ are two disjoint sets of variables, $\phi(\mathbf{x})$ (the left-hand-side, LHS) is a conjunction of atoms involving relations in $\mathbf{S}$ and $\psi(\mathbf{x}, \mathbf{y})$ (the right-hand-side, RHS) is a conjunction of atoms involving relations in $\mathbf{T}$. The dependency represents a mapping M in the sense that $(I, J) \in M$ if and only if (I, J) satisfies σ. In this case, J is called a *solution* of I under σ. We can compute a suitable J in polynomial time by applying the *chase procedure* to I using σ [6]: the result may have labeled nulls denoting unknown values and is called the *universal* solution, since it has a homomorphism to any possible solution J', that is, a mapping h of the nulls into constants and nulls such that $h(J) \subseteq J'$.

Example 4. Consider the schemas $\mathbf{S}_A$, $\mathbf{S}_B$ and $\mathbf{G}$ of Figure 1, which we recall in Figure 3 with all the formalisms that will be discussed throughout the paper.

A mapping between $\mathbf{S}_A$ and $\mathbf{G}$ is the st-tgd σ_A discussed in the Introduction and reported in Figure 3 (quantifiers are omitted for the sake of readability).

schemas

$\mathbf{S}_A = \{R_A(\underline{Firm}, Gains, Zone, Sector), Activity(\underline{Code}, Description), R_A.Sector \mapsto Activity.Code\}$
$\mathbf{G} = \{Balance(\underline{Company}, Gains, Zone, Sector)\}$
$\mathbf{S}_B = \{R_B(\underline{Enterprise}, Gains, Sector, Capital, Area), Location(\underline{Code}, Name), R_B.Area \mapsto Location.Code\}\}$

mappings

$\sigma_A : R_A(f, g, z, s), Activity(s, d) \rightarrow Balance(f, g, z, d).$
$\sigma_B : R_B(e, g, s, c, a), Location(a, n) \rightarrow Balance(e, g, n, s).$

m-schemas

S_A

Rel

name
R_A
Activity

Key

name	in
Firm	R_A
Code	Activity

Att

name	in
Gains	R_A
Zone	R_A
Description	Activity

FKey

name	in	refer
Sector	R_A	Activity

S_B

Rel

name
R_B
Location

Key

name	in
Enterprise	R_B
Code	Location

Att

name	in
Gains	R_B
Sector	R_B
Capital	R_B
Name	Location

FKey

name	in	refer
Area	R_B	Location

G

Rel

name
Balance

Key

name	in
Company	Balance

Att

name	in
Gains	Balance
Zone	Balance
Sector	Balance

meta-mappings

Σ_A : $\mathsf{Rel}(R)$,$\mathsf{Key}(K_1, R)$,$\mathsf{Att}(A_1, R)$,$\mathsf{Att}(A_2, R)$,$\mathsf{FKey}(F, R, S)$,$\mathsf{Rel}(S)$,$\mathsf{Key}(K_2, S)$,$\mathsf{Att}(A_3, S) \rightarrow$ $\mathsf{Rel}(T)$,$\mathsf{Key}(K_1, T)$,$\mathsf{Att}(A_1, T)$,$\mathsf{Att}(A_2, T)$,$\mathsf{Att}(A_3, T)$
$q_S(\mathbf{x}) = \mathsf{Rel}(R), \mathsf{Key}(K_1, R), \mathsf{Att}(A_1, R), \mathsf{Att}(A_2, R), \mathsf{Att}(A_3, R), \mathsf{FKey}(F, R, S), \mathsf{Rel}(S), \mathsf{Key}(K_2, S), \mathsf{Att}(A_4, S)$
$q_T(\mathbf{x}, \mathbf{y}) = \mathsf{Rel}(T), \mathsf{Key}(K_1, T), \mathsf{Att}(A_1, T), \mathsf{Att}(A_2, T), \mathsf{Att}(A_4, T)$
$\Sigma_B : q_S(\mathbf{x}) \rightarrow q_T(\mathbf{x}, \mathbf{y})$
$\Sigma_B^P : q_S(\mathbf{x}), A_1{=}Gains, A_2{=}Sector, A_3{=}Capital \rightarrow q_T(\mathbf{x}, \mathbf{y})$
$\Sigma_B^N : q_S(\mathbf{x}), A_1{\neq}Sector, A_1{\neq}Capital, A_2{\neq}Gains, A_2{\neq}Capital, A_3{\neq}Gains, A_3{\neq}Sector \rightarrow q_T(\mathbf{x}, \mathbf{y})$
$\Sigma_B^H : q_S(\mathbf{x}), A_1{=}Gains, A_2{\neq}Gains, A_2{\neq}Capital, A_3{\neq}Gains, A_3{\neq}Sector \rightarrow q_T(\mathbf{x}, \mathbf{y})$

Fig. 3. Schemas, m-schemas, mappings, and meta-mappings discussed along the paper.

Intuitively, the application of the chase to the instance of $\mathbf{S}_A$ using σ_A enforces this dependency by generating one tuple in the target for each pair of tuples in the source for which there is a binding to the LHS of the dependency. The result includes the first two tuples in relation `Balance` in Figure 1. Besides, a mapping from $\mathbf{S}_B$ to $\mathbf{G}$ is represented by the s-t tgd σ_B in Figure 3.

Meta-mappings. A *meta-mapping* describes generic mappings between relational schemas and is defined as a mapping over the catalog of a relational database [8]. Specifically, in a relational meta-mapping, source and target are both defined over the following schema, called *(relational) dictionary*: $\mathsf{Rel}(\underline{name})$, $\mathsf{Att}(\underline{name}, in)$, $\mathsf{Key}(\underline{name}, in)$, $\mathsf{FKey}(\underline{name}, in, refer)$ (for the sake of simplicity, we consider here a simplified version of the relational model). An instance S of the dictionary is called *m-schema* and describes relations, attributes and constraints of a (standard) relational schema $\mathbf{S}$. Figure 3 shows the m-schemas of the schemas $\mathbf{S}_A$, $\mathbf{S}_B$, and $\mathbf{G}$ of the running example.

We assume, hereinafter, that, given a schema, its corresponding m-schema is also given, and vice versa. A meta-mapping is expressed by means of an st-tgd over dictionaries that describes how the elements of a source m-schema map to the elements of a target m-schema.

Example 5. Mapping σ_A of Example 4 can be expressed, at the dictionary level, by meta-mapping Σ_A in Figure 3. This st-tgd describes a generic transformation that takes two source relations R and S linked by a foreign key F and generates a target relation T obtained by joining R and S on F that includes: the key K_1 and the attributes A_1 and A_2 from relation R and the attribute A_3 from S.

Given a source m-schema S and a meta-mapping $\mathscr{M}$, a target m-schema T is generated by applying the chase procedure to S using $\mathscr{M}$.

Example 6. The chase of $\mathsf{S_A}$ using Σ_A, both in Figure 3, generates the following target m-schema where $\perp_R$ is a labelled null denoting a relation name.

Rel

name
$\perp_R$

Key

name	in
Firm	$\perp_R$

Att

name	in
Gains	$\perp_R$
Zone	$\perp_R$
Description	$\perp_R$

This m-schema describes the relational schema: $R(\underline{Firm}, Gains, Zone, Description)$

A meta-mapping operates at schema level rather than at data level and thus provides a means for describing generic transformations. Subtleties could arise from the chase procedure in presence of existential quantifications in meta-mappings producing duplications of relations in the result. This is avoided by assuming that, for each existentially quantified variable, there is a target *equality generating dependency* (egd) [6] ensuring that whenever two relations in the target have the same structure, then they coincide.

From meta-mappings to mappings. Given a source schema $\mathbf{S}$ and a meta-mapping Σ, it is possible not only to generate a target schema by using the chase, as shown in Example 6, but also to automatically obtain a schema mapping σ that represents the *specialization* of Σ for $\mathbf{S}$ and $\mathbf{T}$ [8]. The *schema to data exchange transformation* (SD transformation) generates from $\mathbf{S}$ and Σ a complete schema mapping made of $\mathbf{S}$, a target schema $\mathbf{T}$ (obtained by chasing the m-schema of $\mathbf{S}$ with the meta-mapping), and an s-t tgd σ between $\mathbf{S}$ and $\mathbf{T}$. The correspondences between LHS and RHS of σ are derived from the provenance information computed during the chase step, in the same fashion as the provenance computed over the source instance when chasing schema mappings [4].

Example 7. Consider again the scenario in Figure 3. If we apply the SD transformation to the schema $\mathbf{S}_A$ and the meta-mapping Σ_A, we obtain the target m-schema of Example 6 and the following mapping from $\mathbf{S}_A$ to $\perp_R$:

$$\sigma : R_A(f, g, z, s), \text{Activity}(s, d) \rightarrow \perp_R(f, g, z, d).$$

Thus, we get back, up to a renaming of the target relation, the mapping σ_A in Figure 3 from which Σ_A originates.

From mappings to meta-mappings While previous work focused on generating a mapping from a given meta-mapping [8], we tackle the more general problem of *mapping reuse*, which consists of: (i) generating a repository of meta-mappings from a set of user-defined schema mappings, and (ii) given a new pair of source and target schemas, generating a suitable mapping for them from the repository of meta-mappings.

Example 8. For the scenario in Figure 3, our system first generates several fitting meta-mappings from σ_A between $\mathbf{S}_A$ and $\mathbf{G}$. Once $\mathbf{S}_B$ and $\mathbf{G}$ are given as input for a new transformation, the system scans the corpus of existing meta-mappings and identifies Σ_A as a fitting meta-mapping from $\mathbf{S}_B$ to $\mathbf{G}$. This meta-mapping is then instantiated to generate a schema mapping between them, according to the SD transformation above.

3 Experimental evaluation

We implemented GAIA in PL/SQL 11.2 for Oracle 11g. All experiments were conducted on Oracle Linux, with an Intel Core i7@2.60GHz, 16GB RAM.

Datasets and Transformations. We used data transformations that are periodically executed to store data coming from several data sources into the *Central National Balance Sheet* (CNBS) database, an archive of financial information of about 40K enterprises. The schema of CNBS has 5 relations with roughly 800 attributes in total. Source data come from three different providers. The Chamber of Commerce provides data for 20K companies (datasets **Chamber**). While the schemas of these datasets are similar, the differences require one mapping per company between relations of up to 30 attributes with an average of 32 (self) joins in the LHS of the mappings. Data for 20K more companies is collected by a commercial data provider in a single database (**CDP**). This database is different both in structure and attributes names from the schemas in **Chamber** and requires one mapping involving 15 joins in its LHS. Finally, data for further 1,300 companies (**Stock**) is imported from the stock exchange, with each company requiring a mapping with 40 joins on average.

Transformation scenarios. For the inference of the meta-mappings, we consider two configurations: *single*, where a meta-mapping is inferred from one mapping, and *multiple*, where the inference is computed on a group of mappings for companies in the same business sector. We observe that the results stabilize with 10 schema mappings in the group and do not improve significantly with larger numbers, therefore consider 10 mappings for the *multiple* configuration.

Search precision. Let σ be a mapping from a source $\mathbf{S}$ to a target $\mathbf{T}$ and let $\mathcal{Q}$ be the set of meta-mappings inferred from σ. We measure, in terms of *search precision*, the ability of the system to return the meta-mappings in $\mathcal{Q}$ when queried with $\mathbf{S}$ and $\mathbf{T}$, i.e., how well the system retrieves correct cases.

We use a *resubstitution* approach: we populate an initially empty repository by inferring the meta-mappings from a set Θ of mappings. For each schema mapping σ in Θ, we will denote by $\mathcal{Q}_\sigma$ all the meta-mappings inferred from

σ. We then pick a schema mapping σ' from Θ and search the repository by providing as input the source and target schemas of σ'. We then collect the top-10 results according to the coverage and compute the percentage of correctly retrieved meta-mapping, that is, those that belong to $\mathcal{Q}_{\sigma'}$.

We test search precision with a corpus of mappings of increasing size (from 200 to 21,301). In each test, we query the repository of meta-mappings inferred from the given mappings by using 50 different source-target pairs and report their average search precision. The experiment is executed on single and multiple configurations. The largest repository contains about 700K explicit meta-mappings in single configuration and 110K in multiple configuration. In the multiple scenario, the test is considered successful on a mapping σ when the retrieved meta-mapping originates from the group that includes σ. On average, a meta-mapping includes 12 equality and/or inequality constraints.

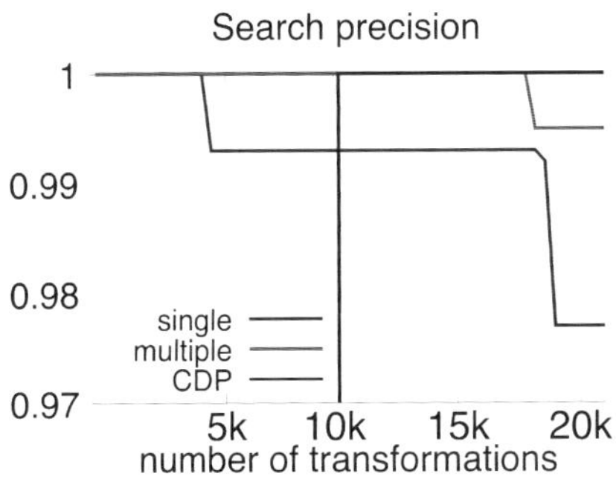

Fig. 4. Search precision.

The plot in Figure 4 shows that search precision decreases with the size of the repository as larger numbers of mappings lead to an increasing number of false positives in the result. We report the search precision for the **CDP** mapping with a separate line. When this mapping is inserted in the repository (after 10K transformations), it is immediately identified with both configurations. This shows that specific structures and constants lead to meta-mappings that are easy to retrieve. Meta-mappings derived from multiple schema mappings improve search precision because are more general than the ones from single mappings, thus reducing the risk of overfitting.

References

1. D. Abadi et al. The Beckman report on database research. *Commun. ACM*, 59(2):92–99, Jan. 2016.
2. P. Atzeni, L. Bellomarini, P. Papotti, and R. Torlone. Meta-mappings for schema mapping reuse. *PVLDB*, 12(5):557–569, 2019.
3. P. A. Bernstein and S. Melnik. Model management 2.0: manipulating richer mappings. In *SIGMOD*, 2007.
4. L. Chiticariu and W. C. Tan. Debugging schema mappings with routes. In *VLDB*, pages 79–90, 2006.
5. R. Fagin, L. M. Haas, M. A. Hernández, R. J. Miller, L. Popa, and Y. Velegrakis. Clio: Schema mapping creation and data exchange. In *Conceptual Modeling*, 2009.
6. R. Fagin, P. Kolaitis, R. Miller, and L. Popa. Data exchange: Semantics and query answering. In *ICDT*, 2003.
7. M. A. Hernández, P. Papotti, and W. C. Tan. Data exchange with data-metadata translations. *PVLDB*, 1(1):260–273, 2008.
8. P. Papotti and R. Torlone. Schema exchange: Generic mappings for transforming data and metadata. *Data Knowl. Eng.*, 68(7):665–682, 2009.

On the Proposal of a Unified Safety Framework for Industry 4.0 Multi-Robot Scenario (DISCUSSION PAPER)

Loris Roveda[1], Blerina Spahiu[2], Walter Terkaj[3]

[1]Istituto Dalle Molle di studi sull'Intelligenza Artificiale (IDSIA), Scuola universitaria professionale della Svizzera italiana (SUPSI), Universit della Svizzera italiana (USI), Via Cantonale 2c - 6928 Manno, Switzerland
loris.roveda@idsia.ch
[2]University of Milano-Bicocca, Viale Sarca, 336 - 20126 Milan, Italy
blerina.spahiu@unimib.it
[3]Institute of Industrial Technologies and Automation (ITIA) of Italian National Research Council (CNR), via Corti, 12 - 20133 Milan, Italy
walter.terkaj@itia.cnr.it

Abstract. Within the context of Industry 4.0, the presence of robotic systems inside the production plant is increasing, thus leading to the need for appropriate safety rules enhancing human-robot interaction. However, without a systematic approach, mapping all the possible scenarios becomes critical. This paper aims at laying the foundations for a unified safety-based semantic approach in cooperative multi-robot industrial environments. The objective of this study is to investigate an approach to organize, store and re-use construction safety knowledge by means of defining a new ontology and the construction of rules for safety application.

1 Introduction

The Industry 4.0 paradigm is driving the innovation of manufacturing and production processes [6] and robotics is a key element enabling such epochal change [11]. The increasing use of robotic systems in industries is enhancing human-robot interaction (*i.e.*, HRI) [13]. Safety is becoming a critical issue since humans and robots interact while sharing working space and tasks. Indeed, standards have already been developed to regulate safety (ISO 20218 [5]). On the basis of such standards, many works investigate the definition of safety algorithms and rules for very specific use-cases, such as for the design of industrial work-cells, physical human-robot interaction for the execution of cooperative applications, etc. However, even if safety rules can be found in the standards, their application is still not straightforward in real industrial environments and no contribution

to a unified safety framework has been proposed to address the complexity of a production plant (*i.e.*, the set of robots, sensors, human workers, tasks, tools and obstacles).
The lack of knowledge related to the tool in use by the robot while cooperating with a human operator may result in unpredictable accidents (*e.g.*, in the case the robot is manipulating a bulky and heavy part with a mechanical gripper while cooperating with a human operator such information is important to define workspace limitations, velocity etc.). Since in common industrial applications such knowledge is not yet available, robots are used under their achievable performance (in order to always ensure safety), resulting in decreasing production capabilities. The combination of the Semantic Web technologies and ontologies (that define concepts of a certain domain and relations between them) can enable such knowledge.

The aim of this paper is to fill this gap and present an initial work toward a unified knowledge framework for the definition of safety rules in production environments by using semantic technologies. Our contributions can be summarized as follows: (i) definition of a framework for the specific case of safety rules; (ii) development of an ontology to describe concepts of the working space; (iii) case study related to a cooperative installation task.
This paper is organized as follows: the application scenarios are introduced in Section 2 while the state-of-the-art is presented in Section 3. The proposed framework is described in Section 4 while conclusions end the paper in Section 5.

2 Application Scenarios

More and more industries are embracing innovation on the process of assembly of their products by means of advanced human-robot collaborative solutions, *i.e.*, i) a Lightweight Mobile Arm (LMA) to perform autonomous transportation of the parts and installation tasks, ii) an empowering robot to perform installation tasks, iii) a sensing solution for cluttered environments to identify human workers inside the working scene.

Considering such multi-robot environment, the definition of a unified safety framework is mandatory. We define three scenarios related to the multi-robot collaborative environment.

Scenario 1 - Exoskeleton Empowering Human Worker: exoskeletons are used to relieve humans from heavy tasks, physically connected to the worker.

Scenario 2 - Empowering Robot for Cooperative Installation Task: the empowering robot is used to install bulky/heavy components (hatracks). Such manipulator, equipped with a force sensor, a mechanical gripper and a vision system (to track humans) is physically interacting with the human operator.

Scenario 3 - LMA for Autonomous Installation Task: the LMA is used to autonomously install medium-size components (e.g., side-wall panels). Such manipulator, equipped with a force sensor, a mechanical gripper and with a vision system (to track humans) should not interact with humans for this task.

3 Related Work

A plethora of EU-funded project have investigated and are currently investigating safety issues at different levels (physical interaction, workspace design, etc.). In the Saphari project[1], collision avoidance and prevention algorithms have been developed to activate collaboration by using human gestures and voice commands [3]. This safety control framework was tested on the lightweight robot LWR-IV, from KUKA [3]. The H2020 COVR project [2] investigates the development of an intuitive toolkit and a range of testing protocols for the validation of safety for cobots.
Standards (e.g. ISO 20218:2011 [5]) have been defined to regulate human-robot collaborative modalities in industrial plants. EU-funded projects[345], together with dedicated research activities [2, 7], have enhanced such developments. Although many works can be found in the state of the art covering safety related topics, only few contributions are devoted to define a unified safety framework [8, 10]. To overcome such limitation in the industrial context, some works are exploiting safety representations applying semantic technologies, *i.e.*, representing safety as an ontology that includes the main concepts of the safety standard and the relationships between the concepts. Applying these concepts, some works have used this representation format in order to exploit semantic technology capabilities for safety assurance and certification. The application of semantic technologies to improve the safety in working environments, *e.g.*, by developing ontologies that represent safety concepts and the relation between them, have been studied in [4]. Specifically for Industry 4.0, the authors in [1] present a method to design new instances of collaborative cells, by taking into account the ISO 15066 and extending the CORA (Core Ontologies for Robotics and Automation) ontology. However, this work is limited to specific cooperative work-cells and it does not take into account the complete and complex production plant environment. The work [12] proposes to integrate task-level planning with semantically represented workplace safety rules, but only a specific application is considered. The authors of [15] address how an Artificial Intelligence technique like Answer Set Programming (ASP) can be applied to support the planning of mobile robot, while explicitly modeling rigid knowledge time-dependent internal knowledge, time-dependent external knowledge, and action knowledge. However, from the analysis of the state-of-the-art, at the best of our knowledge, no contribution has been proposed to define a unified safety framework considering the whole production process involving human-robot cooperation.

---

[1] `http://www.saphari.eu/`
[2] `http://safearoundrobots.com/getcovr`
[3] `http://safearoundrobots.com/getcovr`
[4] `http://www.saphari.eu/`
[5] `http://www.xact-project.eu/`

4 Proposed Approach

The integration of heterogeneous knowledge is required to ensure safety. For instance, the combination of data coming from sensors and from the environment where the robot is operating enables to understand the context where the robot is working, consequently defining appropriate behaviors and safety rules. However, safety depends also on the specific task assigned to the robot and to the tools that the robot is exploiting. This paper proposes a unified robot knowledge approach that considers knowledge coming from sensory data together with context information. Taking inspiration from [8], we introduce an ontology (to conceptualize the environment where the robot is working and formalize the knowledge accessible to the robot in terms of logical rules) with a novel focus on the preservation of safety in the production plant. Robot's knowledge for safety is enhanced by using data coming from sensors with knowledge from reasoning. The framework on top of such approach is shown in Figure 1. Such operation is bidirectional thus enabling to learn from previous situations and taking advantage for further decisions.

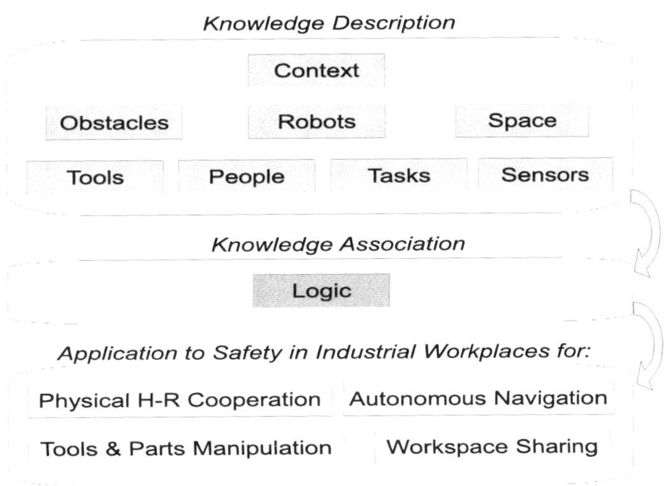

Fig. 1. Unifying framework for safety rules.

4.1 Knowledge Description

A taxonomy provides an ontological structure for human understanding, defining the arrangement of things of interest in a hierarchical structure. Figure 2 shows the taxonomy proposed within a scenario where human and robot should collaborate. This hierarchy takes inspiration from the ifcOWL ontology [9], *i.e.*, the Web Ontology Language (OWL) version of the Industry Foundation Classes (IFC) standard, a widespread open model for the information exchange of Building Information Modeling (BIM) data. Such description allows therefore to define axioms, aiming at identifying the specific cases and the related safety rules for a safe human-robot cooperation inside the production environment. In such taxonomy we unify knowledge from context, obstacles, robots, space, tools, people, sensors and tasks to enhance safety for physical human-robot interaction, workspace sharing, autonomous navigation, tools and parts manipulation. The considered working scenario can be modeled using the following key classes:

- `Object`: a generic tangible (*e.g.*, physical product) or intangible item (*e.g.*, process) that is used to define the global spatial/temporal scenario of the human-robot collaboration (cf. class `IfcObject` in ifcOWL);
- `Person`: defining the human operators that can present in the robot working space (cf. class `IfcActor` in ifcOWL);
- `Task`: defining the actions that the robot/human can perform (*e.g.*, manipulation tasks, assembly tasks, etc.) (cf. class `IfcTask` in ifcOWL);
- `Product`: any object that relates to a geometric or spatial context (cf. class `IfcProduct` in ifcOWL);
- `SpatialElement`: any spatial element that might be used to define a spatial structure or a spatial zones (cf. class `IfcSpatialElement` in ifcOWL);
- `Space`: defining the specific location where the robot is working, *e.g.* assembly lines, storage, corridor, etc. (cf. class `IfcSpace` in ifcOWL);
- `Element`: physically existent object that can be characterized by a placement and 3D representation (cf. class `IfcElement` in ifcOWL).
- `BuildingElement`: any type of static element that may be an obstacle for the robot, *e.g.*, walls, doors, etc. (cf. class `IfcBuildingElement` in ifcOWL);
- `Robot`: defining the robotic systems working inside the production plant, *e.g.* mobile platforms, lightweight manipulators, exoskeletons, etc.;
- `Tool`: defining the specific tool in use to the robot to perform the specific task, *e.g.* mechanical gripper, screwer, etc.;
- `Sensor`: defining different external sensors that the robot can use to perceive the environment, *e.g.* vision systems, force sensors, etc. (cf. class `IfcSensor` in ifcOWL, class `sosa:Sensor` in SSN/SOSA ontology [14]).

The workspace is modeled by tools, the space where they are located and the context where they are used. In fact, a tool can be recognized not only by its characteristics such as shape, size, material, but also by the spatial context where it is located. Moreover, the knowledge of the robots, the sensors, the obstacles and the human operators inside the working scenario and the allocated tasks to the robots are fundamental to model the working scene. Such ontology definition can therefore be applied to the human-robot cooperation in industrial environments, where physical and non-physical cooperation is required.

4.2 Knowledge Association

Knowledge association creates and describes the relationship between ontology classes and properties by means of axioms. Logical inference can be exploited to automatically generate new knowledge starting from generic axioms and specific instances. Such framework enables robot to perceive the environment and the

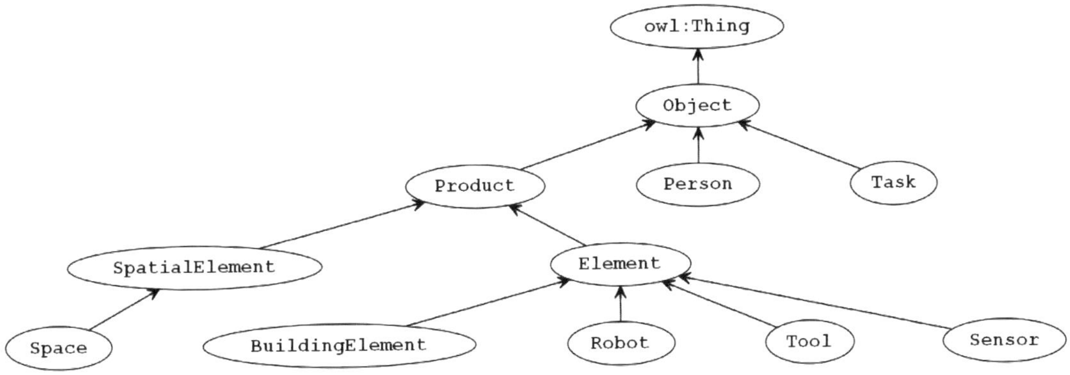

Fig. 2. Taxonomy of the working environment.

context where it is performing in such a way that is easy to avoid obstacles, collisions and to process knowledge coming from other sensors and humans. The axioms are defined using Description Logic (DL) and can be applied also to verify that data are compliant with the ontology schema. Logic representations are defined to identify the specific working scene in which the robot is operating and to consequently define the related safety rules from the standards. Since in the scope of OWL reasoning is monotonic because of the Open World Assumption, the exploitation of other non-monotonic logic languages (*e.g.*, ASP) will be taken in consideration to support the application scenarios.

4.3 Application to Safety

As an example, we describe the three scenarios as in Section 2 and describe the logic representations for defining safety rules for *Scenario 2* in Section 2.

Scenario 1 - Exoskeleton Empowering Human Worker: On the basis of the exoskeleton internal sensors information (*e.g.*, encoders, torque sensors, etc.) it is possible to identify safety-critical situations (such as critical human postures). Moreover, on the basis of the knowledge of the executed task and involved tools, it is possible to on-line check for safety rules to be applied during the task execution.

Scenario 2 - Empowering Robot for Cooperative Installation Task: the complete working scene can be defined having the information related to the tool of the robot, the knowledge about the human operator motion and the safety features implemented by the robot. The related safety rules can be then identified and applied. The examples described by Algorithms 1 and 2 can be exploited, considering the physical HRI installation scenario. Algorithm 1 is considering the use of a safe tool, while Algorithm 2 is considering the use of a non-safe tool. The two proposed scenarios have to apply different safety rules since in the second case the non-safe tool introduces higher safety risks.

Algorithm 1 Scenario 2 - Physical Human-Robot Cooperation with Safe Tool

1: **if** Robot in Installation Area &&
2: Physical Human-Robot Cooperation Task for Installation &&
3: Force Sensor for Human-Robot Cooperation &&
4: Safe Tool &&
5: Human Operator Tracked by Camera Sensor &&
6: Low-Level Safety Emergency Stop **then**
7: Apply Safety Rule for Physical HRI Considering Safe Tool and Low-Level Safe Stop Features

Algorithm 2 Scenario 2 - Physical Human-Robot Cooperation with Safe Tool

1: **if** Robot in Installation Area &&
2: Physical Human-Robot Cooperation Task for Installation &&
3: Force Sensor for Human-Robot Cooperation &&
4: Non-Safe Tool &&
5: Human Operator Tracked by Camera Sensor &&
6: Low-Level Safety Emergency Stop **then**
7: Apply Safety Rule for Physical HRI Considering Non-Safe Tool and Low-Level Safety Stop Features

Scenario 3 - Autonomous Installation Task Performed by Lightweight Manipulator Since the target application is supposed to be autonomous, no physical interaction between the robot and human operators should be established during the task execution. However, the human operator may enter the working area of the manipulator. Therefore, one of the key topic defining the safety rules to be applied in such a case is related to the possibility to track the human motion. The complete working scene can be defined having the information related to the tool in use by the robot, the knowledge about the human operator position and the safety features implemented by the robot. In such a way, the related safety rules can be identified and applied.

5 Conclusions

In this paper a unified safety framework for the Industry 4.0 environment is proposed, including (i) the definition of the framework, (ii) the development of an ontology to describe concepts of the working space, and (iii) the definition of safety rules based on the use cases are proposed. A safety application is detailed to described the adopted approach, for assembly of heavy products in industry. The proposed ontology will be further developed, by integrating existing ontology modules and making extension in the human-robot collaboration context.

Acknowledgments

The work has been partially developed within the H2020 EUROBENCH STEP-bySTEP project.

References

1. D. Antonelli and G. Bruno. Ontology-based framework to design a collaborative human-robotic workcell. In *Working Conference on Virtual Enterprises*, pages 167–174. Springer, 2017.
2. S. Brending, M. Lawo, J. Pannek, T. Sprodowski, P. Zeising, and D. Zimmermann. Certifiable software architecture for human robot collaboration in industrial production environments. *IFAC-PapersOnLine*, 50(1):1983–1990, 2017.
3. A. De Luca and F. Flacco. Integrated control for phri: Collision avoidance, detection, reaction and collaboration. In *Biomedical Robotics and Biomechatronics (BioRob), 2012 4th IEEE RAS & EMBS International Conference on*, pages 288–295. IEEE, 2012.
4. B. Gallina and Z. Szatmári. Ontology-based identification of commonalities and variabilities among safety processes. In *International Conference on Product-Focused Software Process Improvement*, pages 182–189. Springer, 2015.
5. ISO 10218-1:2011: Robots and robotic devices–safety requirements for industrial robots–part 1: Robots. Standard, International Organization for Standardization, Geneva, CH, 2011.
6. H. Lasi, P. Fettke, H.-G. Kemper, T. Feld, and M. Hoffmann. Industry 4.0. *Business & Information Systems Engineering*, 6(4):239–242, 2014.
7. P. A. Lasota, T. Fong, J. A. Shah, et al. A survey of methods for safe human-robot interaction. *Foundations and Trends® in Robotics*, 5(4):261–349, 2017.
8. G. H. Lim, I. H. Suh, and H. Suh. Ontology-based unified robot knowledge for service robots in indoor environments. *IEEE Transactions on Systems, Man, and Cybernetics-Part A: Systems and Humans*, 41(3):492–509, 2011.
9. P. Pauwels, T. Krijnen, W. Terkaj, and J. Beetz. Enhancing the ifcowl ontology with an alternative representation for geometric data. *Automation in Construction*, 80:77 – 94, 2017.
10. S. Ramanathan, A. Kamoun, and C. Chassot. Ontology-based collaborative framework for disaster recovery scenarios. In *Enabling Technologies: Infrastructure for Collaborative Enterprises (WETICE), 2012 IEEE 21st International Workshop on*, pages 104–106. IEEE, 2012.
11. M. Rüßmann, M. Lorenz, P. Gerbert, M. Waldner, J. Justus, P. Engel, and M. Harnisch. Industry 4.0: The future of productivity and growth in manufacturing industries. *Boston Consulting Group*, 9, 2015.
12. A. Shafei, J. Hodges, and S. Mayer. Ensuring workplace safety in goal-based industrial manufacturing systems.
13. P. Tavares, J. A. Silva, P. Costa, G. Veiga, and A. P. Moreira. Flexible work cell simulator using digital twin methodology for highly complex systems in industry 4.0. In *Iberian Robotics conference*, pages 541–552. Springer, 2017.
14. W3C. Semantic Sensor Network Ontology, 2017. Available online: https://www.w3.org/TR/vocab-ssn/ (Last accessed on 10 June 2018).
15. F. Yang, P. Khandelwal, M. Leonetti, and P. Stone. Planning in answer set programming while learning action costs for mobile robots. In *AAAI Spring 2014 Symposium on Knowledge Representation and Reasoning in Robotics (AAAI-SSS)*, March 2014.

Evolution of Financial Time Series Clusters
(Discussion Paper)

Davide Azzalini[1], Fabio Azzalini[1], Mirjana Mazuran[2], and Letizia Tanca[1]

[1] Politecnico di Milano, Italy {name.surname}@polimi.it
[2] Inria, France mirjana.mazuran@inria.fr

Abstract. Nowadays, a huge amount of applications exist that natively adopt a data-streaming model to represent highly dynamic phenomena. A challenging application is constituted by data from the stock market, where the stock prices are naturally modeled as data streams that fluctuate very much and remain meaningful only for short amounts of time. In this paper we present a technique to track *evolving clusters of financial time series*, with the aim of constructing reliable models for this highly dynamic application. In our technique the clustering over a set of time series is iterated over time through sliding windows and, at each iteration, the differences between the current clustering and the previous one are studied to determine those changes that are "significant" with respect to the application. For example, in the financial domain, if a company that has belonged to the same cluster for a certain amount of time moves to another cluster, this may be a signal of a significant change in its economical or financial situation.

1 Introduction

A data stream is an ordered sequence of data elements that are made available over time, and is potentially unlimited. Very interesting data stream applications can be found in finance, where the life of a company evolves with time and, at each time instant, is characterized by different streams of data reporting its stock price, exchange volumes, balance data, and so on. Companies may even appear and disappear from the market, or change their financial behavior.

Several techniques for analyzing streaming data have been studied: many rely on the use of a sliding window, i.e. a model of the data based on a window that moves over time, continuously taking into account the newest data. Also, in the financial context, a variety of clustering methods have been proposed to cluster companies that have the same behavior, w.r.t. prices or other measures.

However, when stock prices are concerned, clusterings done on different windows – even though these might overlap greatly – tend to change a lot, due to the high dynamics of the market and to the scarce permanence of relationships between companies over time. In such a scenario the model tends to fluctuate and remains meaningful only for short amounts of time.

We present PETRA, a *Progressive clustEring TRAcker* where the clustering analysis is iterated over time in order to constantly provide a reliable, stable, up-to-date and consistent model. PETRA also focuses on identifying "significant" changes in the clusterings constructed over time by means of parameters that allow the system to adapt to specific application domains. When applying PETRA to the case of stock prices, we can capture the intrinsic dynamics of the stocks' (and companies') relationships, through the recognition of points in time where their co-movements change, that is, we identify changes in the behavior of a company relatively to the behavior of the other companies of the same cluster. A company changing cluster is a signal to present to investors as well as a building block for more accurate prediction tasks. For example, well-known companies communicate more than small ones, however, small companies are often more interesting for investors since they can bring a higher profit. After clustering we can use the rich information available for the well-known companies in a cluster to obtain some guidelines for the small ones in the same cluster.

PETRA is a part of a broader project: Mercurio [6], whose aim is to support financial investors in their decision process. In particular, PETRA helps investors understand how companies influence each other, for a deeper understanding of the market structure. The system has been designed and optimized for the financial application domain; however, it can be applied to any set of time series with rapidly evolving behaviors, provided that the clustering algorithm, the similarity metrics and some other parameters are appropriately tuned. Figure 1 depicts an example of stock-based companies' clustering.

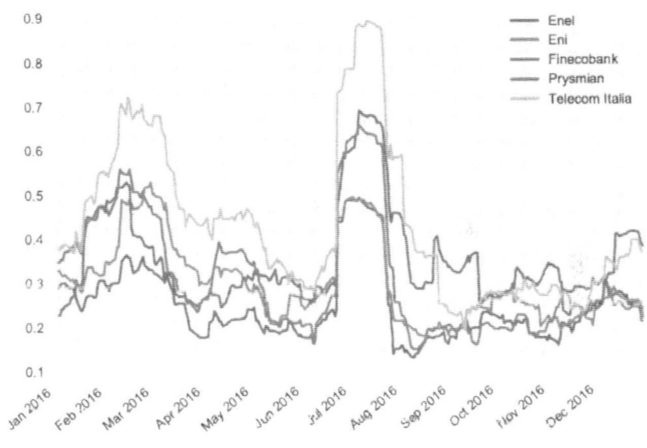

Fig. 1. A cluster of similarly-behaving companies

Most previous works on clustering stock-market firms showed how custom-made clusters outperform traditional industrial grouping criteria [13, 14]. Our work differs from them in that we move from a static to a progressive clustering approach, which allows us to overcome The big problem found when dealing with financial information: stock markets move fast, financial insights expire and get old very quickly. Our progressive clustering provides fresh suggestions daily.

Cluster Tracking in evolving data streams is partially covered by the scientific community. A lot has been done on visually tracking groups of objects [7], e.g., of moving people [8] or facial features [9], and on wireless channel modeling to track multi-path components [10]. Our work is different because we are not interested in tracking the shift in position of a cluster at consecutive time instants; rather, we focus on tracking the membership of each object.

General-purpose techniques [11, 12] exist that face the cluster-tracking problem in terms of outliers, i.e. the clustering is considered valid until the number of outliers crosses a predefined threshold, then re-clustering is needed. In PETRA instead, we re-cluster at each iteration since we are not just interested in having a consistent model but also in detecting as soon as possible the entities that change cluster, and promptly report it.

MONIC [15] also models and monitors cluster transitions. However, PETRA tracks the movements of the companies between clusters in order to generate signals about each company, while MONIC is interested in the transition of the entities between clusters with the scope of drawing conclusion on the lifetime and stability of the clusters. Moreover, MONIC detects the transitions by keeping track of the entity trajectories on spatiotemporal coordinates, while PETRA detects movements by analyzing the contents of the clusters.

Our objective is to dynamically track the evolution of a set of entities $E = (e_1, e_2, ..., e_j, ..., e_N)$ by iteratively clustering their data streams over a sliding window $W_i = [t_{i-w}, t_i]$ of width w. Figure 1 depicts one such cluster and shows how related companies appear inside the cluster. At each time t_i, the sliding window shifts one time-point ahead, and its content is clustered in K clusters $\mathcal{C}^i = (C_1^i, C_2^i, ..., C_K^i)$. Then, $\mathcal{C}^i$ is compared with $\mathcal{C}^{i-1}$ by associating each new cluster with its "previous version". At the end of the procedure PETRA identifies those entities that have made a "persistent" change of cluster[3]. In particular, our method is aimed at clustering time series that: (i) represent entities belonging to the same domain (e.g. stock-market prices of different companies) and are enough to be grouped into clusters; (ii) are sampled at regular intervals, with the same sampling frequency; (iii) contain a number of time points sufficient to allow a sliding window to move along a significant number of positions[4]. Summarizing, our main contributions are: (i) the identification of an approach to generate clusters that are well-balanced w.r.t. the problem under consideration; (ii) the design of a method to trace clusters' behaviors and spot entities' changes of membership; (iii) the definition of a set of rules needed to identify relevant entity switches. Section 2 provides the details about our approach while in Section 3 we show the experimental results.

2 The PETRA Method

We first discuss our design choices and some domain-dependent parameters that need to be set in PETRA, then concentrate on the clustering procedure, and finally show how we track the clusters along time.

Time series clustering algorithms rely on similarity measures for quantifying how homogeneous two observations are. PETRA uses *similarity in time*, which is based on comparing different time series at the same time points, as it is the most suitable one to identify sudden changes in the streams' behaviors.

[3] Note that some changes might be less interesting because being temporary, in the sense that one stream might return to a previous cluster after some time.

[4] Note that the term *significant* is strongly domain-dependent and should be judged by the designer.

```
K ← desired number of clusters;
i ← 0;
repeat
    CORR = computeCorrelationMatrix(W_i)
    D = computeDistanceMatrix(CORR)
    C^i=clusterData(D, K)
    forall change ∈ trackClusters(C^i, C^{i-1}) do
        if change is relevant then
            trigger warning;
        end
    end
    i ← i + 1;
until new data keeps coming;
```

Algorithm 1: The *PETRA* procedure

The similarity measures that can be adopted for clustering time series [1] range from simple ones such as Euclidean distance to more complex ones like Dynamic Time Warping (DTW). DTW is extremely powerful, as it finds a relationship between two time series S_1 and S_2 not only when S_2 is obtained by shifting S_1 in time, but also when S_2 is a contraction or an expansion of S_1; e.g. DTW associates the last week of a company with the last month's behavior of another company. However, this feature is not needed in the financial case, where we need to compare companies on the same time interval and at the same time point, thus, simpler approaches, such as the Euclidean metrics and metrics based on correlation, are sufficiently expressive.

As for the clustering method, PETRA employs hierarchical clustering, since it does not require to set the number of clusters a-priori, and at the same time is well suited for easy visualization. Using the Euclidean distance and hierarchical clustering allows us to use Ward's method for linkage [2], which, as we will see, provides a big advantage in the tracking phase. At each iteration, the Pearson Correlation $corr_{ij}$ [16] between each pair of time series i and j is computed and a global similarity matrix $CORR$ is obtained. Then, to obtain a suitable input for a clustering algorithm, a transformation from correlation coefficients to distances is needed. According to Gower and Legendre[3], if $CORR$ is a positive semidefinite similarity matrix, the dissimilarity matrix D where $d_{ij} = \sqrt{(1 - corr_{ij})}$ is a matrix of euclidean distances. Finally, the width w of the sliding window, and the number of desired clusters K, are left as parameters in PETRA since the best choice strictly depends upon the application goal; in Section 3 we present a possible solution to perform an educated guess; we chose a window of 105 days and a number of clusters equal to 4.

At each new iteration, the distance matrix D is computed for the portions of time series inside the window. Then, the hierarchical clustering using Ward's linkage method is performed, a hierarchy of clusters – represented by means of a dendrogram like in Figure 2 – is obtained, and the dendrogram is cut in order to obtain K clusters. Ward's method promotes the merges of small clusters, which is crucial to the tracking phase since well-balanced clusters are easier to track.

However, depending on the level of the cut, we obtain different numbers of clusters, and a constant-height cut is not suitable in this case: cutting a dendrogram to obtain a fixed number of clusters irrespectively of its general structure is likely to result in highly unstable clusters. Langfelder at al. [4] solved the problem of sub-optimal performances on complicated dendrograms presenting the Dynamic Tree Cut (DTC) algorithm, which provides a dynamic branch-cutting method for detecting clusters in a dendrogram, depending on their shape. Like in the standard dendrogram creation procedure, clusters are merged in a bottom-up fashion, but this merging depends on a set of parametric criteria such as the minimum size of each cluster and the minimum gap between the joining heights. By using DTC we can obtain much more balanced clusters, both in their size and composition, avoiding the downsides of the standard approach and facilitating the tracking phase. Figure 2 shows how, although both cuts identify three clusters, those obtained with the fixed-height cut are highly imbalanced (i.e. there are two clusters of just one element), while DTC cut delivers very balanced clusters.

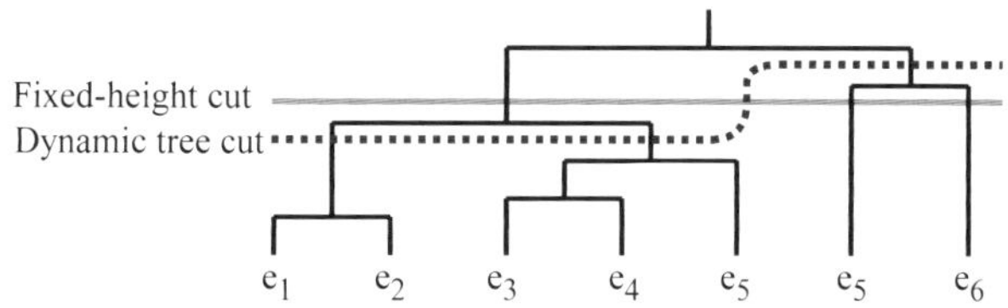

Fig. 2. Fixed-height versus Dynamic Tree Cut

The goal of the tracking phase is to observe how clusters evolve and how the clustered streams change their membership. To track cluster dynamics, we have to recognize the same clusters at different times without relying on any external reference. We address this problem by using the Jaccard similarity index [16] and Linear Programming (LP). Given two clusterings $\mathcal{C}^i$ and $\mathcal{C}^{i-1}$ obtained from the series over two consecutive windows W_i and W_{i-1}, we compute the Jaccard score of each pair of clusters in the two clusterings. The pairs with highest Jaccard score are the most similar clusters, likely representing the same cluster at consecutive time points. Of course, once a cluster is ascribed to one predecessor it cannot be ascribed to any other one: each cluster is linked to one and only one predecessor. This can easily be formalized in LP. Given two clusterings $\mathcal{C}^i = (C_1^i, C_2^i, ..., C_h^i, ..., C_K^i)$ and $\mathcal{C}^{i-1} = (C_1^{i-1}, C_2^{i-1}, ..., C_j^{i-1}, ..., C_K^{i-1})$, we define the square matrix M of dimension K as the matrix of the Jaccard scores of all the possible pairs (C_h^i, C_j^{i-1}) of clusters. Then we define the square matrix X as a decision variable matrix of dimension K, such that x_{hj} is 1 if $Jac(C_h^i, C_j^{i-1})$ in M is chosen by the optimization process, 0 otherwise. The LP model aims to select from M the K values having highest sum, with the strong constraint that each selected value can share neither the row nor the column with the other selected values. This is equivalent to selecting the K cluster pairs with the highest Jaccard scores, without selecting a cluster more than once. The objective function is defined as $maximize\ M \circ X$ (where $\circ$ represents the element-wise matrix product), subject to the constraints: $\sum_j X_{hj} = 1\ \forall h \in [1, K]$, $\sum_h X_{hj} = 1\ \forall j \in [1, K]$, $X_{hj} \in \mathbb{N}\ \forall h, j \in [1, K]$.

At each new iteration PETRA moves its analysis forward of one time point, performs a new clustering and links each new cluster to its "previous version". By doing so, we detect when an entity moves to another cluster. Three types of change are possible:

- *exit*: a company exits the Reference Cluster, moving into a different cluster;
- *re-entry*: an entity re-enters the Reference Cluster;
- *change outside the reference cluster*: an entity moves between two "non-Reference Clusters".

Note that the Reference Clusters strictly depend on the domain under assessment; in our use case the reference clusters turn out to be the industrial sectors. Reference clusters are re-computed every time we move the time window, and are assigned the industrial sector of the majority of the companies inside it. Thus, a cluster that contains mostly banks will be assigned the label "Bank", one that contains mostly automotive companies will be assigned "Automotive", and so on. For example, the industrial sector of Unicredit, a famous Italian bank, is "Bank", thus its reference cluster is the one that contains mostly banks. After an iteration, if most of the companies inside Unicredit's cluster are banks, we say that Unicredit is in its reference cluster, and outside its reference cluster otherwise. This allow us to give more importance to those cluster changes that involve the Reference Cluster.

Note that, when using a sliding window, the change in the new configuration might be caused by the new point added or by the one that has been removed. Our goal is to detect changes that are caused by current events, thus, PETRA triggers warnings only when a change is caused by the new point added. To do so we use the *intersection window* $W_i^{\cap} = [t_{i-w}, t_{i-1}] = W_i \cap W_{i-1}$, and the *union window* $W_i^{\cup} = [t_{i-w-1}, t_i] = W_i \cup W_{i-1}$: by computing the clustering also on the intersection window and comparing it with that of W_i we can say, in case they are different, that the new time point t_i has actually influenced the clustering results. Moreover, by computing the clustering also on $W_i^{\cup}$ and comparing it with that of W_i, if no change has happened, we can also say that the removal of the last point t_{i-w-1} has not contributed to the change, meaning that it is entirely due to the new point added.

3 Experimental Results

To test and validate PETRA in a real application, we perform a market simulation consisting in the purchase and sale of companies' stocks. This is because, since cluster switches are a latent feature, there is no general ground truth to test against and prove their actual relevance directly. However, as far as the financial domain is concerned, we can use the market gain as an indicator for the goodness of the clustering performed by PETRA.

We consider the stock market prices of the 40 most highly capitalized companies in the Italian Stock Exchange [5] between 2008 and 2017. There are 2 values for each trading day: the opening price (*open*) and the closing price (*close*); we cluster based on the *close-open* indicator. Among the 40 companies we randomly select some of them as *leaders*. Leaders are companies whose behaviour we know in advance (i.e. when their price trend changes): for each of them we identify some companies that are "close to the leader" (*friends*) for which we don't know the future behavior. The simulation consists in buying and selling stocks of the friends depending on the behavior of the leaders. If the clustering is correct, the friends' behavior is similar to the leader's one, hence the simulation will buy and sell the stocks at the right time, resulting overall in a profit.

For the validation, since no ground truth for the trend changes of a company's stock price is available, and since the state-of-the-art techniques for segmenting

[5] https://en.wikipedia.org/wiki/FTSE_MIB

time series revealed to be not suitable as they do not lend themselves to a unique parametrization suitable for all the companies, we designed an ad-hoc procedure for identifying the major changes in the price trend of a *leader* a-posteriori. The procedure divides the price timeline of a company into intervals of *up-trend*, *down-trend* and *congestion*[6] according to the position of the company's price w.r.t. three moving averages over the price [6]. For each friend, its closeness to the leader is evaluated using PETRA, thus, we first need to appropriately tune the window length and the number of clusters.

The width of the sliding window is a crucial parameter: a too narrow window would result in an excessive sensitivity providing poor generalization potential, while with a too wide one we risk to miss important events. To identify the best width we analyze each possible width value, that is: (i) for each value n between 2 (the smallest possible window) and 1260 (half of the 2008-2017 period) we divide the companies' time series into segments of width n; (ii) for each n, for each time segment T of length n, and for each pair of companies, we compute the correlation between their segments, and arrange them all into a matrix $A_{T,n}$; (iii) we compute the difference between each correlation matrix and the one at the previous time slot; (iv) we compute their variance and then (v) we average all variances together obtaining a single score for each window width n. We chose the value associated with the smallest score corresponding to 105 days. We estimated the number of clusters through knee/elbow analysis, which suggested an optimal number of 4 clusters. After parameter tuning, the simulation picks 3 leaders and then runs PETRA which, at each iteration, adopts a conservative policy:

- If a leader enters an up-trend phase, pick the 4 closest companies in the same cluster as friends and buy them.
- If a leader enters a down-trend phase, sell all its friends.
- If a friend changes cluster, sell it.

To constitute valuable evidence we run the simulation ten thousand times over different portfolios of leaders and then averaged the profits. Comparing the results to a stock market index is the common practice when it comes to market simulation, thus, we use the FTSE MIB index as a baseline; Figure 3 reports the aggregated results for each year by showing the average profits obtained with PETRA and the FTSE MIB profits for the same year. The profits yielded by our procedure are always positive: even in years like 2008, when the market underwent a severe crisis, our procedure generated profits. Although there are certain years in which FTSE MIB outperforms our approach, our results remains still very comparable, especially when considered on the long term.

The traditional approach [5] to validating Stock Market Clustering is to check if the resulting clusters are consistent w.r.t. the business sectors. Being the industrial sectors static entities, we decided not to use this approach for the validation since the aim of our procedure is to dynamically spot anomalies and changes. Nevertheless our clusters have proved to be consistent also under this point of view. The four clusters identified by our procedure coincide with the sectors: *banking, energy, consumer products* and *industrial products.*

[6] A period in which the price undergoes oscillations without a clear direction.

4 Conclusions and Thanks

We presented a technique to cluster time series where the clustering is iterated over time and, at each iteration, the differences between the current clustering and the previous one are studied to spot significant changes.

We are grateful to U. P. De Vos and to L. Raimondi for taking part in the development of the algorithms and the analysis of the results.

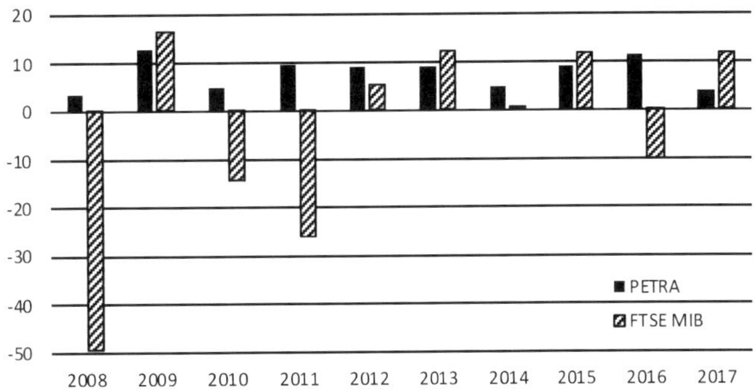

Fig. 3. Average profit (in %) for each year between 2008 and 2017

References

1. S. Aghabozorgi, A. S. Shirkhorshidi, T. Y. Wah: Time-series clustering-A decade review. Information Systems (2015)
2. J. H. Ward Jr.: Hierarchical grouping to optimize an objective function. Journal of the American statistical association (1963)
3. J. C. Gower, P. Legendre: Metric and Euclidean properties of dissimilarity coefficients. Journal of classification (1986)
4. P. Langfelder, B. Zhang, S. Horvath: Defining clusters from a hierarchical cluster tree: the Dynamic Tree Cut package for R. Bioinformatics (2008)
5. M. Gavrilov, D. Anguelov, P. Indyk, R. Motwani: Mining the stock market: Which measure is best?. ACM SIGKDD (2000)
6. D. Azzalini, F. Azzalini, D. Greco, M. Mazuran, L. Tanca: Event Recognition Strategies applied in the Mercurio Project. MIDAS (2017)
7. K. Granstrom, M. Baum, S. Reuter: Extended Object Tracking: Introduction, Overview and Applications. Journal of Advances in Information Fusion (2017)
8. S. J. McKenna, S. Jabri, Z. Duric, A. Rosenfeld, H. Wechsler: Tracking groups of people. Computer vision and image understanding (2000)
9. M. N. Islam, M. Seera, C. K. Loo: A robust incremental clustering-based facial feature tracking. Applied Soft Computing (2017)
10. C. Huang, R. He, Z. Zhong, B. Ai, Z. Zhong: Comparison of Automatic Tracking and Clustering Algorithms for Time-Variant Multipath Components. Globecom Workshops (2017)
11. D. Barbará: Requirements for clustering data streams. ACM SIGKDD Explorations Newsletter (2002)
12. D. Barbará, P. Chen: Tracking Clusters in Evolving Data Sets. FLAIRS Conference (2001)
13. E. J. Edwin, M. J. Gruber: Improved forecasting through the design of homogeneous groups. The Journal of Business (1971)
14. S. Aghabozorgi, T. Y. Wah: Stock market co-movement assessment using a three-phase clustering method. Expert Systems with Applications (2014)
15. M. Spiliopoulou, I. Ntoutsi, Y. Theodoridis, R. Schult: Monic: modeling and monitoring cluster transitions. ACM SIGKDD (2006)
16. J. Han, J. Pei, M. Kamber: Data mining: concepts and techniques (2011)

Information Discovery in Polystores: the Augmented Way (Discussion Paper)

Antonio Maccioni[1] and Riccardo Torlone[2]

[1] Collective[i], New York City, USA
amaccioni@collectivei.com
[2] Roma Tre University, Rome, Italy
riccardo.torlone@uniroma3.it

Abstract. Polystores provide a loosely coupled integration of heterogeneous data sources based on the direct access, with the local language, to each storage engine for exploiting its distinctive features. In this framework, given the absence of a middleware exposing a global schema, it is hard to know if a query to one system can be satisfied by data stored elsewhere in the polystore. We address this problem by illustrating *query augmentation*, a data manipulation operator for polystores based on the automatic enrichment of the answer to a local query with related data in the rest of the polystore. Augmentation can be used to implement *augmented search* and *augmented exploration*: two effective methods for information discovery in polystores that avoid middleware layers, abstract query languages, and shared data models.

1 Introduction

The concept of polyglot persistence, which consists of using different database technologies to handle different data storage needs [9], is spreading within enterprises. Recent research has shown that, on average, each enterprise application relies on at least two or three different types of database engines.

Example 1. Let us consider a company called *Polyphony* selling music online. As shown in Fig. 1, each department uses a storage system that best fits its specific business objectives: (i) the sales department guarantees ACID properties for its transactions database with a relational system, (ii) the warehouse department supports its activities with a document store catalogue, where each item is represented by a JSON document, and (iii) the marketing department uses a graph database of similar-items supporting recommendations. In addition, a key-value store containing discounts on products is shared among the above departments.

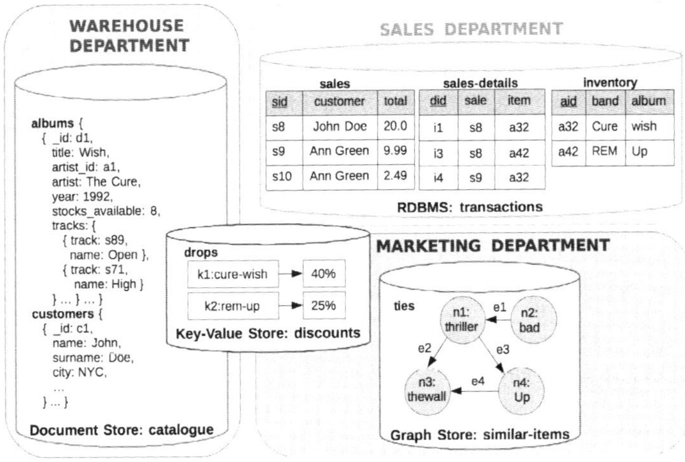

Fig. 1. A polyglot environment.

This approach, however, makes even harder the problem of data integration given the strong heterogeneity of the systems in play [4]. The traditional solution to this issue is based on a middleware layer involving a unified language, a common interface, or a universal data model [10]. However, the addition of this layer to the software stack adds computational overhead at runtime and, more importantly, hides the specificity and functionality for which these systems were adopted. In addition, it is hard to maintain, having an inherent complexity that increases significantly as new database systems take part to the environment.

Polystore systems (or simply, polystores) have been proposed recently as an alternative solution for this approach [12]. The basic idea is to provide a loosely coupled integration of data sources and allow the direct access, with the local language, to each specific storage engine to exploit its distinctive features. This solution meets the requirements of scenarios in which users are often aware of a single (or a few) database only but does not know anything about other databases (neither the content, nor the way to query them and, sometimes, not even their existence). On the other hand, it poses new challenges for accessing and combining all the available data. To recall a discussion about this approach, the issue is that *"if I knew what query to ask, I would ask it, but I don't"* [12].

In this paper, we present (*query*) *augmentation*, a new construct for data manipulation in polystores that, based on a simple notion of probabilistic relationship between objects in different data stores, allows the automatic enrichment of a dataset stored in a local database with data outside the database but available in the polystore. The implementation of this operator does not require the addition of an abstraction layer involving query translation and therefore has a minimal impact on the applications running on top of the data layer. The goal is to provide a soft mechanism for data integration in polystores that complements other approaches, such as those based on cross-db joins [3].

Two effective methods for data access in polystore can be defined with the augmentation construct: *augmented search* and *augmented exploration*.

Augmented search is a form of query relaxation [7] and consists of the automatic expansion of the result of a query over a local database with data that is relevant to the query but is stored elsewhere in the polystore. This is useful in scenarios where information is shared across the organization and the various databases complement or overlap each other. Assume for instance that Lucy, an employee of Polyphony working in the sales department, only knows SQL but needs all the information available on the album "Wish". Then, she just needs to submit, in *augmented* mode, an SQL query over the database transactions in Fig. 1. By exploiting augmentation, the result of the query is the augmented object reported below, revealing details on the product that are not in the database of the sales department, including the fact that it is currently on a 40% discount.

< a32, Cure, Wish > ⇒ (catalogue:{ title: Wish,
⇓ artist_id: a1,
(discounts: 40%) artist: The Cure,
year: 1992,
... })

In an augumented search, each retrieved element e is associated with the probability that e is related to the result of the query. Such probability is derived off-line from integrity constraints and data mining techniques. Colors (as in the example above) and rankings can be used in practice to represent, in a more intuitive way, external data and the degree of relevance.

Augmented exploration makes use of the augmentation operator to provide a more interactive and flexible way to access data, which consists of a guided expansion of the result of a local query. For example, if Lucy submits in *exploratory* mode another SQL query to the database transactions for retrieving all the sales whose total income is greater than 15, she obtains the tuple that follows, in which the links suggest that further information, related to the returned tuple, is available elsewhere and allows her to decide with a click (e.g., on the user name) how to deepen the result. As above, the result is probabilistic.

<s8, John Doe, 20.0 > --on−click--→ ({ _id: c1,
name: John,
surname: Doe,
city: NYC,
... })

This process is iterative and provides a method for database exploration [2], where the user can freely find her way through the polystore, by just clicking on the links as soon as they are made available.

We have implemented our approach in QUEPA[3], a polystore system equipped with the augmentation operator that provides the access methods discussed above and is compatible with most modern database engines. QUEPA operates in a plug-and-play mode and does not affect the access modalities of the various storage systems, thus reducing the need for ad-hoc configurations and for a middleware involving unified query languages or shared data models.

[3] A demo of QUEPA has been shown in [5].

In addition, we have developed an optimization technique that relies on machine learning methods to tune the execution of the augmentation operator.

In the rest of the paper we briefly describe the underlying data model (Section 2), the augmentation mechanism (Section 3), and its implementation (Section 4). Details and experimental results are in the full version of the paper [6].

2 A data model for polystores

In PDM (Polystore Data Model) a polystore $\mathcal{P}$ is made of a set of databases $\mathcal{P} = \{\mathcal{D}_1, \ldots, \mathcal{D}_n\}$ stored in a variety of data management systems $\mathcal{S}_1, \ldots, \mathcal{S}_n$ respectively (relational, key-value, graph, etc.). A database $\mathcal{D} \in \mathcal{P}$ consists of a set of *data collections* each of which is a set of *(data) objects*. An object $o \in C$ is just a key-value pair: $o = \langle k, v \rangle$ where k identifies uniquely o in C and v is an atomic piece of data. A tuple and a JSON document are examples of data objects in a relational database and in a document store of a polystore, respectively.

By definition, given a database $\mathcal{D}$ of a polystore $\mathcal{P}$, a data collection C in $\mathcal{D}$ and a data object $o = \langle k, v \rangle$ in C, we can uniquely identify o in $\mathcal{P}$ by means of k, C and $\mathcal{D}$. We call $\hat{k} = \mathcal{D}.C.k$ the *global-key* of o in $\mathcal{P}$.

Example 2. In the polystore in Figure 1 $\langle \mathsf{d1}, \{\mathsf{\_id} : \mathsf{d1}, \mathsf{title} : \mathsf{Wish}, \ldots\} \rangle$ is an object of the albums collection in the catalogue database whereas $\langle \mathsf{s8}, (\mathsf{s8}, \mathsf{John\ Doe}, 20.0) \rangle$ is an object of the sales collection in the transactions database. The global-key of the latter is transactions.sales.s8.

This model captures polystores involving any database system satisfying the minimum requirement that every stored data object can be identified and accessed by means of a key. Note that the granularity of objects inevitably depends on the designer's choice [1].

The other main ingredient of PDM is the ability to correlate data objects of possibly different databases of the polystore by means of the following basic notion, which we call *p-relation* (for relation in a polystore).

Definition 1 (p-relation). *A p-relation on two objects o_1 and o_2, denoted by $o_1 R_p o_2$, represents the existence of a relation R between o_1 and o_2 with probability p ($0 < p \leq 1$), where R can be one of the following types:*

- *the* identity, *denoted by $\sim$: a reflexive, symmetric and transitive relation (i.e., an equivalence relation), representing the fact that o_1 and o_2 refer to the same real-world entity;*
- *the* matching, *denoted by $\rightleftharpoons$: a reflexive and symmetric relation (not necessarily transitive), representing the fact that o_1 and o_2 share some common information.*

We assume that in a polystore p-relations are "consistent" in the sense that they satisfy the following condition: for each triple of objects o_1, o_2 and o_3 such that $o_1 \rightleftharpoons o_2$ and $o_2 \sim o_3$ it is the case that $o_1 \rightleftharpoons o_3$. While this is a natural condition (two equivalent objects should match the same objects), it guarantees that the augmentation construct behaves consistently with equivalent objects.

Example 3. Consider the polystore in Fig. 1. By denoting the objects with their global keys we have for instance that: catalogue.albums.d1 $\sim_{0.8}$ discount.drop.k1:cure:wish, and transactions.inventory.a32$\rightleftharpoons_1$transactions.sales-details.i4.

Basically, while the identity relation serves to represent multiple occurrences of the same entity in the polystore, the matching relation models general relationships between data different from the identity (e.g., those typically captured by foreign keys in relational databases or by links in graph databases). On the practical side, p-relations are derived from the metadata associated with databases in the polystore (e.g., from integrity constraints) or are discovered using probabilistic mining techniques. For the latter task, we rely on the state-of-the-art techniques for probabilistic record linkage [8], that is, algorithms able to score the likelihood that a pair of objects in different databases match.

3 Augmentation in polystores

The augmentation construct. The basic operator of our approach takes as input an object o of a polystore and returns the augmented set $\alpha^n(o)$, which iteratively returns data objects in the polystore that are related to o with a certain probability. This probability is computed by combining the probabilities of the relationships that connect o with the retrieved objects.

Definition 2. *Let* $\boldsymbol{o}$ *be a set of objects in a polystore* $\mathcal{P}$. *The* augmentation α^n of level $n \geq 0$ *of* $\boldsymbol{o}$ *is a set* $\boldsymbol{o}'$ *of objects* o^p, *where* $o \in \mathcal{P}$ *and* p *is the probability of membership of* o *to* $\boldsymbol{o}'$, *defined as follows* ($m > 0$)*:*

- $\alpha^0(\boldsymbol{o}) = \boldsymbol{o} \cup \{o^p \mid o \sim_p o' \wedge o' \in \boldsymbol{o}\}$
- $\alpha^m(\boldsymbol{o}) = \alpha^{m-1}(\boldsymbol{o}) \cup \{o^{\hat{p}} \mid (o \rightleftharpoons_{p'} o') \wedge (o'^p \in \alpha^{m-1}(\boldsymbol{o})) \wedge (\hat{p} = p \cdot p')\}$

Example 4. Let us consider the polystore in Fig. 2 in which nodes represents objects, ovals represent different databases, solid lines represent identity p-relations, and dashed lines represent matching p-relations. Labels associated with p-relations denote their probability. Then, we have $\alpha^0(\{o_4\}) = \{o_4, o_1^{0.9}\}$, $\alpha^1(\{o_4\}) = \{o_4, o_1^{0.9}, o_7^{0.8}, o_8^{0.7}\}$, and $\alpha^3(\{o_4\}) = \{o_4, o_1^{0.9}, o_7^{0.8}, o_8^{0.7}, o_{10}^{0.7}\}$.

Note that, by construction, for every $k \geq 0$, if $o \in \alpha^k(\mathbf{o})$ then $o' \in \alpha^k(\mathbf{o})$ for each $o' \sim o$. Indeed, if o belongs to $\alpha^k(\mathbf{o})$ because of an object $o'' \in \alpha^{k-1}(\mathbf{o})$ such that $o'' \rightleftharpoons o$, the consistency condition above implies that if $o \sim o'$, we have also that $o'' \rightleftharpoons o'$ and so, by Definition 2, $o' \in \alpha^k(\mathbf{o})$.

The augmented construct can be at the basis of two alternative ways to access a polystore, as described in the following.

Augmented Search. An augmented search consists of the expansion of the result of a query over a local database with data that are relevant to the query but are stored elsewhere in the polystore. Consider again a polystore $\mathcal{P}$ composed of a set of databases stored in different data management systems each equipped with a specific query language. Now, let $Q^{\mathcal{S}}$ denote a query expressed in the query language of the storage system $\mathcal{S}$ and let $Q^{\mathcal{S}}(\mathcal{D})$ be the set of objects in the result of $Q^{\mathcal{S}}$ over a database $\mathcal{D}$ stored in $\mathcal{S}$.

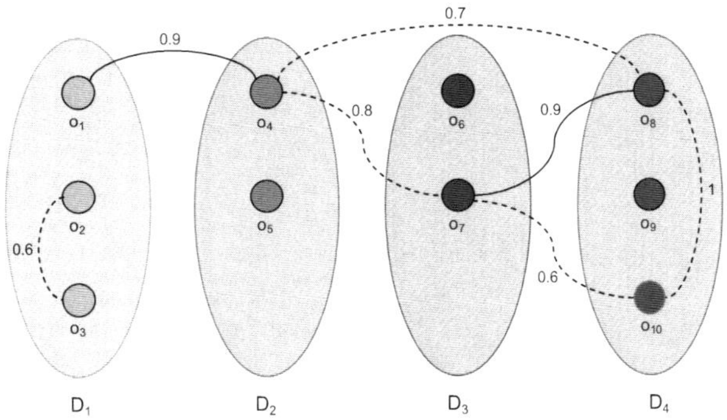

Fig. 2. A set of databases in a polystore

Definition 3. *The* augmentation of level $n \geq 0$ *of a query* $Q^{\mathcal{S}}$ *over a database* $\mathcal{D}$ *stored in* $\mathcal{S}$*, denoted by* $Q^{\mathcal{S}}(n)(\mathcal{D})$*, consists in the augmentation of level* $n \geq 0$ *of the result of* $Q^{\mathcal{S}}$ *over* $\mathcal{D}$ *ordered according to the probability of its elements.*

Example 5. Let Q be a query over the database D_1 in Fig. 2 that returns the objects o_1 and o_2. Then we have $Q(0)(D_1) = \{o_1, o_2, o_4^{0.9}\}$ and $Q(1)(D_1) = (o_1, o_2, o_4^{0.9}, o_7^{0.7}, o_8^{0.6}, o_3^{0.6})$.

Augmented Exploration Exploratory computing is a new trend in big data access that aims at helping users to make sense of very big data sets by means of step-by-step interaction with the system oriented to the progressive refinement of the data retrieval process [2]. The augmentation construct can provide effective support for exploratory computing in a polystore through a process that we call *augmented exploration.* Intuitively, augmented exploration consists of a guided expansion of the result of a query over a local database with related data stored elsewhere in the polystore. It works as follows: we start with a query $Q^{\mathcal{S}}$ expressed in the query language of the storage system $\mathcal{S}$ in the polystore and execute $Q^{\mathcal{S}}$ over a database $\mathcal{D}$ stored in $\mathcal{S}$. We then select, from the answer of the query an object o and apply to o the augmentation construct of level 0 (step 1) and order the result according to the probability of each element. Again, we select, from the result we obtain, an object o_1 and apply to it the augmentation construct of level 1 (step 2) and order the result. We then proceed similarly, by selecting an object o_i from the result of the previous step and apply the augmentation construct of level 1 to o_i, until the user is satisfied with her search. This can be formalized as follows.

Definition 4. *An* augmented exploration *of a polystore* $\mathcal{P}$ *starting from a query* $Q^{\mathcal{S}}$ *over a database* $\mathcal{D}$ *stored in* $\mathcal{S}$ *consists of a sequence of* k *steps:* $[(o_0 \rightarrow \boldsymbol{o}_0); (o_1 \rightarrow \boldsymbol{o}_1); \ldots; (o_k \rightarrow \boldsymbol{o}_k)]$ *where:*

- $o_0 \in Q^{\mathcal{S}}(\mathcal{D})$ *and* $\boldsymbol{o}_0 = \alpha^0(\{o_0\})$,
- $o_i \in \boldsymbol{o}_{i-1}$ *and* $\boldsymbol{o}_i = \alpha^1(\{o_i\})$ $(i > 0)$.

Example 6. Consider the query in Example 5 wich returns the set of objects $\{o_1, o_2\}$. Then, a possible augmented exploration involves the steps:

$$(o_1 \rightarrow \{o_4^{0.9}\}); (o_2 \rightarrow \{o_3^{0.6}\}); (o_4 \rightarrow \{o_7^{0.8}, o_8^{0.7}\})$$

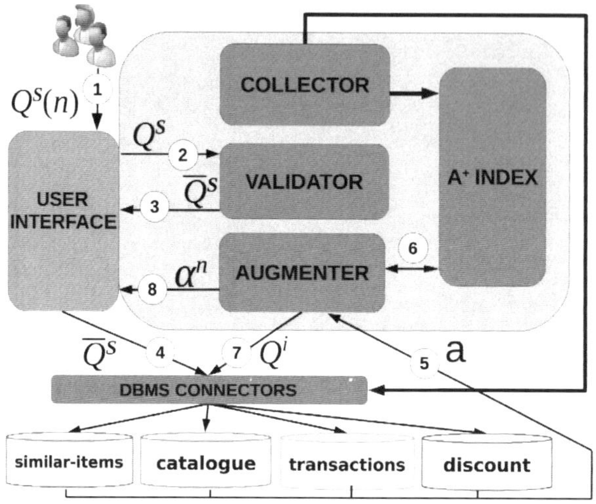

Fig. 3. Architecture of QUEPA.

4 A tool supporting augmentation

We have fully implemented our approach in a system called QUEPA [5]. Its architecture is illustrated in Fig. 3 and includes the main following components:

- *Augmenter:* it implements the augmentation operator and orchestrates augmented query answering. Various smart strategies have been adopted for its optimization aimed at being: (i) network-efficient, by retrieving all the objects from one database with a single query and thus reducing the number of queries to local databases and the communication between them, (ii) CPU-efficient, by assigning independent queries to parallel threads and leveraging the multi-core nature of modern CPU, and (iii) memory-efficient, by suitably caching the last accessed objects and thus reducing the I/O requests. In addition, since traditional cost-based optimizers are difficult to implement in a polystore, given the limited knowledge of each database in play, we have developed an adaptive, rule-based optimizer to dynamically predict the best combination of the above strategies for the the query under consideration.
- A^+ *index:* it is a global, graph-based index in which each global-key is represented in one node and there are two types of edges connecting nodes that represent identity and matching p-relations, respectively.
- *Collector:* it is in charge of discovering, gathering and storing p-relations in the A^+*index*. This is done by collecting fresh metadata, as soon as new datasets are added, and by leveraging existing techniques for record linkage [8]. Specifically, we used BLAST [11] for a non-supervised step of object blocking and DuKe[4] for the following step of pairwise matching. On the basis of the final matching score provided by DuKe, we decide whether a p-relation is an identity or a matching. In addition to the creation of the A^+*index* from scratch, we have developed a simple, yet effective, learning mechanism that

[4] `https://github.com/larsga/Duke`

adds matching p-relations depending on the navigation history of users when they operate in exploratory mode.
- *Connectors:* they are used to interact with the polystore. Each connector is able to communicate with a specific database system by sending queries in the local language and returning the result. Data objects are parsed into an internal representation.
- *Validator:* it is used to pre-evaluate a query and to assess rapidly whether it can be augmented or not.

The *validator* first checks if the query is correct (step ②) and possibly rewrites it (step ③) before its execution over the target database (step ④). The local answer **a** is returned to the *augmenter* which is now ready to compute the augmentation (step ⑤). It gets from the A^+ *index* the global keys of data objects reachable from those in **a** with n applications of the augmentation primitive (step ⑥). These global keys are used to retrieve data objects from the polystore with local queries Q^i (step ⑦). Finally, the augmented answer is returned to the user (step ⑧). The interaction in the augmented exploration is similar but simplified since, at each step, only a single data object is augmented.

A comprehensive campaign of experiments done with QUEPA has shown that our approach is feasible, effective, and, unlike other approaches, scales nicely as the polystore grows in the number of stores and size of databases [6].

References

1. P. Atzeni, F. Bugiotti, L. Cabibbo, and R. Torlone. Data modeling in the NoSQL world. *Computer Standards and Interfaces*, 2016.
2. M. Buoncristiano et al. Database challenges for exploratory computing. *SIGMOD Record*, 44(2):17–22, 2015.
3. J. Duggan et al. The BigDAWG polystore system. *SIGMOD Record*, 44(2):11–16, 2015.
4. L. M. Haas. The power behind the throne: Information integration in the age of data-driven discovery. In *SIGMOD*, page 661, 2015.
5. A. Maccioni, E. Basili, and R. Torlone. QUEPA: QUerying and exploring a polystore by augmentation. In *SIGMOD*, pages 2133–2136, 2016.
6. A. Maccioni and R. Torlone. Augmented access for querying and exploring a polystore. In *ICDE*, pages 77–88, 2018.
7. D. Martinenghi and R. Torlone. Taxonomy-based relaxation of query answering in relational databases. *VLDB J.*, 23(5):747–769, 2014.
8. I. P. Fellegi and A. B. Sunter. A theory for record linkage. *Journal of the American Statistical Association*, 64:1183–1210, 12 1969.
9. P. J. Sadalage and M. Fowler. *NoSQL Distilled: A Brief Guide to the Emerging World of Polyglot Persistence.* Addison-Wesley Professional, 1st edition, 2012.
10. A. P. Sheth and J. A. Larson. Federated database systems for managing distributed, heterogeneous, and autonomous databases. *ACM Computing Surveys*, 22(3):183–236, Sep 1990.
11. G. Simonini, S. Bergamaschi, and H. V. Jagadish. BLAST: a loosely schema-aware meta-blocking approach for entity resolution. *PVLDB*, 9(12):1173–1184, 2016.
12. M. Stonebraker. The case for polystores. ACM SIGMOD Blog. `http://wp.sigmod.org/?p=1629`, July, 2015.

Medical Retrieval using Structured Information Extracted from Knowledge Bases
(Discussion Paper)

Maristella Agosti, Giorgio Maria Di Nunzio, Stefano Marchesin, and Gianmaria Silvello

Department of Information Engineering, University of Padua, Italy
maristella.agosti, giorgiomaria.dinunzio, stefano.marchesin, gianmaria.silvello@unipd.it

Abstract. We investigate how semantic relations between concepts extracted from medical documents, and linked to a reference knowledge base, can be employed to improve the retrieval of medical literature. Semantic relations explicitly represent relatedness between concepts and carry high informative power that can be leveraged to improve the effectiveness of the retrieval. We present preliminary results and show how relations are able to provide a sizable increase of the precision for several topics, albeit having no impact on others. We then discuss some future directions to minimize the impact of negative results while maximizing the impact of good results.

Keywords: Information extraction · Knowledge bases · Medical information retrieval.

1 Motivations

The volume of medical literature published every year keeps growing at a very fast pace. The time required by clinicians to retrieve relevant information from such an amount of literature using standard systems is often prohibitive. Therefore, there has been a strong interest in Clinical Decision Support (CDS) systems [4] designed to produce effective and timely information that can help clinicians in the decision making process for patient care. Within this context, we focus on medical case-based retrieval – i.e., given a medical case of interest, the CDS system should retrieve highly related medical literature from a large collection of medical publications. Due to severe time constraints, clinicians must take fast decisions without having the possibility to thoroughly read the literature; for this reason, medical case-based retrieval favors precision over recall [5].

A key characteristic of the medical literature is the large use of synonyms and context-specific expressions. To address this term heterogeneity, Knowledge Bases (KBs) have often been exploited by Information Retrieval (IR) systems. The current availability of medical KBs offers us the opportunity to develop techniques that better capture the semantics of medical documents, leading to the following research question:

> How can we employ the rich semantic information within medical case reports and related literature to boost retrieval performances and ease the clinical decision process?

Semantic relations are a key aspect within the semantics of a document. They have been mainly used to find relevant concepts to expand a user query, but not as semantic elements to be indexed and retrieved. We hypothesize semantic relations can provide a higher semantic representation of medical cases and literature.

In this work, we present an initial study on the effectiveness of the use of semantic relations for the retrieval of medical literature. We define an approach comprising two methods: a *rule-based* method and a *learning* method. In the rule-based method, we assign a relation to a pair of concepts – contained within the same sentence – when it holds within a reference KB. In the learning method, we train a sentence-level relation extractor that is able to infer relation between a pair of concepts given the sentence context.

We evaluated our approach by using the publicly shared OHSUMED collection [8]. OHSUMED provides rather short queries which represent a hard task for our approach, since limited information – e.g. concepts and relations – can be extracted from them. Testing with OHSUMED allows us to assess the potentials and limitations of the approach. The remainder of the paper is organized as follows: Section 2 presents the background and related work, Section 3 describes the proposed approach, Section 4 presents experiments and results and Section 5 draws some conclusions and outlines future work.

2 Related Work

Concept-based IR aims at making use of external sources (like thesauri and ontologies) to provide additional knowledge and context that may not be explicit in a document collection and users' queries. Concept-based methods can be categorized in two types: (i) methods that use concepts in both indexing and retrieval stages [6], and (ii) methods that apply concept analysis in one specific stage, such as concept-based query expansion [7]. The approach we propose extends the use of concepts to relations and uses them both at the indexing and at the retrieval stages. An approach like the one we adopt is more challenging, but it allows for a finer semantic representation of documents and queries.

In the biomedical domain – where there are authoritative and curated ontologies – concept-based approaches demonstrate consistent improvements over classic keyword-based systems. In [10], 'is-a' relationships between concepts are used to weight documents containing concepts subsumed by the query concepts. [12] proposes a method to represent medical records and queries by focusing only on medical concepts essential for the information need of a medical search task. In [11], queries are expanded by inferring additional conceptual relationships from domain-specific resources as well as by extracting informative concepts from the top-ranked medical records.

The field of Biomedical Information Extraction (BioIE) is highly relevant for CDS. [13] reviews the recent advances in learning-based approaches for BioIE tasks. BioIE tasks comprise entity linking [23], event identification [2] and relation extraction [18, 20]. Being targeted to CDS – i.e. voted to the extraction of key relations that can facilitate clinical decision making – our problem setup is fundamentally different from the conventional biomedical setups. Most of state-of-the-art biomedical relation extraction techniques are developed for specific relations, like protein-protein interactions, gene-disease interactions and so on — which cover only a fraction of the biomedical domain.

Regarding relations in IR, [19] studies the problem of finding human readable descriptions of a given relationship in a knowledge graph. [17] applies supervised relation extraction to documents that are relevant for an information need Q and studies how many of the extracted relations are indeed relevant for Q. [9] explores current state of the art in unsupervised relation extraction (OpenIE) for the task of finding support passages to complement an entity ranking with human-readable explanations of how those retrieved entities are connected to the information need. Conversely, our approach applies supervised relation extraction to extract semantic relations that are used in both the indexing and the retrieval stages. Hence, relations play a pivotal role in the actual retrieval of documents.

3 Methodology

We present a new approach that uses semantic relations for medical case-based retrieval. The methodology is composed of the information extraction step, that is applied both at the indexing and the retrieval stages (Subsection 3.1), and the specific information retrieval stage (Subsection 3.2).

3.1 Information Extraction

The information extraction step is divided into an entity linking component and a relation extraction component.

The entity linking component extracts entity mentions within the text and links them to a reference KB; this reduces the high number of synonyms, abbreviations and context specific expressions that are present in the medical literature. For entity linking we adopt MetaMap,[1] an authoritative tool to detect medical entity mentions in free-text. MetaMap analyses biomedical free-text and identifies concepts belonging to the Unified Medical Language System (UMLS),[2]

[1] https://metamap.nlm.nih.gov/
[2] https://www.nlm.nih.gov/research/umls/

associating each mention with a number of concepts from the UMLS Metathesaurus[3] — which comprises more than 3 million distinct concepts. Within UMLS, a substantial understanding of the medical domain is included, comprising medical concepts, relations, definitions and so on.

The relation extraction component detects semantic relations between pairs of concepts within a sentence. To be consistent with concepts extracted with MetaMap, we consider semantic relations from UMLS Metathesaurus as well. Furthermore, since our task requires a high coverage of the medical domain, considering UMLS Metathesaurus relations – which are coarse-grained relationships that span to a high number of concepts – allows us to increase the recall of extracted relations.

We define two methods for the extraction of relations from documents and queries: a rule-based method and a learning method.

Rule-based: a relation is assigned to a pair of concepts if it relates them within UMLS. We assume that a UMLS relation between two concepts always occurs, even when it is not explicitly mentioned in the sentence containing the two concepts.

Learning: we train a distantly supervised [14] sentence-level Bidirectional Long Short-Term Memory (BiLSTM) neural network to detect if a relation exists between two concepts based on the context of the sentence. The network architecture is composed of an input (word embedding) layer of concatenated word features and positional features. Words are first converted into pre-trained word embeddings trained on 26 million abstracts and citations in PubMed — released by [15]. Then these word features are concatenated with two sets of positional features — to explicitly account for the pairs of words to which we expect to assign relations [21]. We apply a max-pooling layer right after the bidirectional recurrent layer and before the output layer — in order to combine segment-level features that, although not very strong in representing the entire sentence, represent local patterns well [22]. In this way, we try to overcome the tendency of recurrent connections to forget long-term information too quickly, leading the supervision at the end of the sentence to be hardly propagated to early steps in model training (due to gradient vanishing [3]).

3.2 Information Retrieval

Before to be in the condition to retrieve documents, it is necessary to index the documents, so the documents are indexed by considering all terms as in the Bag-of-Words (BoW) representation, but we also extend the BoW representation to both concepts (BoC) and relations (BoR) by considering for the indexing all the extracted concepts and relations respectively. Afterwards the ranking is obtained using Okapi BM25 ranking function [16].

Since relations are extracted at sentence level, we also index passages – i.e. groups of consecutive sentences – by considering all the relations occurring within each group of sentences (passage-level BoR). Relevant passages should contain

[3] https://www.nlm.nih.gov/research/umls/knowledge_sources/metathesaurus/

a higher number of relations related to the information need when compared to non relevant passages — being more similar in their semantic contents to the query. Therefore, documents that contain more relevant passages can be considered more relevant to the query.

We define a weighting scheme such that a document score is computed as the weighted sum of its passages scores, where scores are computed using BM25 as above. The passage-level weighting scheme is as follows:

$$score(q, d) = \sum_{p \in d} \frac{|R_p \cap R_q|}{|R_q|} BM25(p, q) \quad (1)$$

where d is the document, q is the query, p is a passage belonging to document d, R_q is the set of relations extracted from query q and R_p is the set of relations extracted from passage p.

4 Experiments and Results

We employed the OHSUMED test collection which contains 348,566 references from the on-line medical information database MEDLINE,[4] consisting of titles and/or abstracts from 270 medical journals over a five-year period (1987-1991). The available fields are: title, abstract, MeSH[5] indexing terms, author, source, and publication type. There are 106 queries in the collection. Each query is composed of two sentences: title + description. Title is the brief summary of the medical case at hand, description is the information need required to answer a specific question for the case.

Experimental Setup:
We performed two experiments:
i) One using the rule-based method to extract relations out of documents and queries.
ii) The other using the learning method to extract relations out of documents and queries. We compared the results obtained applying BM25 to the three representations (i.e. BoW, BoC and BoR) and we evaluated the results using the nDCG measure.

Results:
i) The rule-based method was able to extract relations from a subset of 44 queries. Therefore, to investigate the effectiveness of relations, we restrict the experiments to this subset only — since the remaining queries lead to no results when considering relations. Of these 44 queries, only 39 have relations matching with some documents. Regarding the relations, we obtained the best results with the passage-level approach. We set the passage length to 2, in order to be compliant with query length. Document score was computed using the formula shown above (1). The nDCG results on these 39 queries are variable – ranging from 0 (18 cases) to 1 (5 cases), as can be seen in Figure 1. Such a variance

[4] https://www.nlm.nih.gov/bsd/medline.html
[5] https://meshb.nlm.nih.gov/search

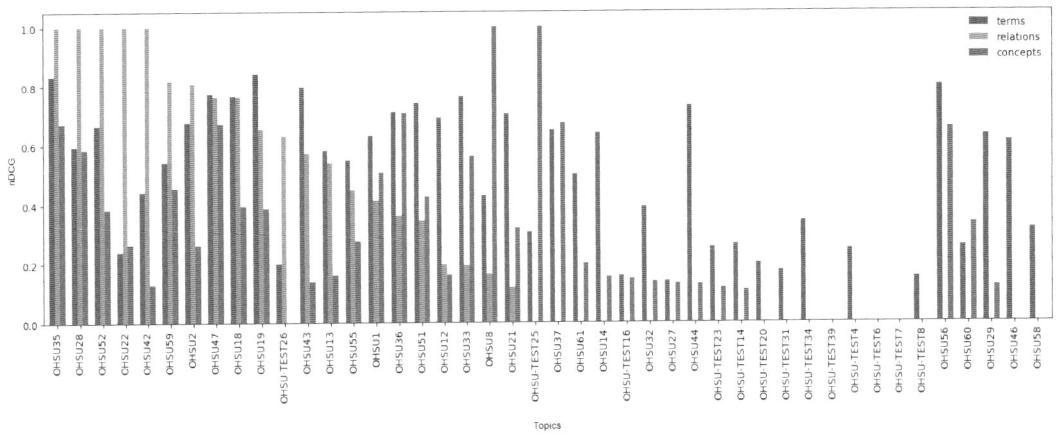

Fig. 1. nDCG values for topics containing relations. OHSU{56,60,29,46,58} returned NA values for the BoR representation. Queries are sorted in descending order first by BoR (relations) nDCG values, then by BoC (concepts) nDCG values.

gives us some hints about the informative power of relations. When properly extracted, relations can be highly effective, indeed; we compared the average nDCG values of concepts and relations on only those topics where relations give a result different than 0 and we found a statistically significant average improvement of 20%. A *t-test* was performed to validate the improvement. Regarding the comparison between relations and terms, the behavior of relations is similar to the one of terms (baseline approach), and there is no statistically significant difference between the two.

ii) The learning method was able to extract relations from a subset of 25 queries. Of these 25 queries, only 12 have relations matching with some documents. The results on these 12 queries are comparable to those presented for the rule-base method, with nDCG values ranging from 0 (in 7 cases) to 1 (in 1 case). The reason for this is two-fold: (a) the shortness of queries that limits the relations that can be extracted; and, (b) the highly different syntactic structure of queries if compared to the sentences within the medical abstracts leading to a mismatch between the query-relations and abstract-relations.

5 Conclusion

In this work, we proposed and evaluated the effectiveness of semantic relations as basic constituents for a CDS system. We defined two methods for extracting relations from queries and documents: a rule-based method and a learning method. We found that relations – when pertinent to the initial information need – are highly valuable, outperforming concepts. The challenge lies in how to limit those cases where relations provide no relevant results for the information need. To this end, considering collections where queries present a long and narrative structure (e.g. TREC CDS tracks[6]) might be a possible direction to balance such issue.

Furthermore, defining more IR-oriented relation extraction approaches that are capable of overcoming the high precision-low recall nature of state-of-the-art methods is a direction that can be investigated.

Finally, we could compare the relation extraction approaches in terms of quality of the results to verify if the extracted relations are semantically correct. This can further clarify whether relations' limited effectiveness in IR tasks lies in current state-of-the-art relation extraction approaches or in the poor representativeness of relations themselves for IR tasks.

An initial version of this paper has been presented at the ACM 12th International Workshop on Data and Text Mining in Biomedical Informatics (DTMBio), held in conjunction with ACM 27th Conference on Information and Knowledge Management (CIKM) [1].

Acknowledgements

The work was partially supported by the CDC-STARS project of the University of Padua, Italy,[7] and by the ExaMode project,[8] as part of the European Union H2020 research and innovation program under grant agreement no. 825292.

References

1. Agosti, M., Di Nunzio, G.M., Marchesin, S., Silvello, G.: A relation extraction approach for clinical decision support. arXiv preprint arXiv:1905.01257 (2019)
2. Ananiadou, S., Pyysalo, S., Tsujii, J., Kell, D.B.: Event extraction for systems biology by text mining the literature. Trends in Biotechnology **28**(7), 381–390 (2010)
3. Bengio, Y., Simard, P., Frasconi, P.: Learning long-term dependencies with gradient descent is difficult. IEEE Transactions on Neural Networks **5**(2), 157–166 (1994)
4. Berner, E.S.: Clinical decision support systems, vol. 233. Springer (2007)
5. Burke, D.T., DeVito, M.C., Schneider, J.C., Julien, S., Judelson, A.L.: Reading habits of physical medicine and rehabilitation resident physicians. American Journal of Physical Medicine & Rehabilitation **83**(7), 551–559 (2004)
6. Egozi, O., Markovitch, S., Gabrilovich, E.: Concept-based information retrieval using explicit semantic analysis. ACM Trans. Inf. Syst. **29**(2), 8:1–8:34 (Apr 2011)
7. Grootjen, F.A., Van Der Weide, T.P.: Conceptual query expansion. Data & Knowledge Engineering **56**(2), 174–193 (2006)
8. Hersh, W., Buckley, C., Leone, T., Hickam, D.: Ohsumed: an interactive retrieval evaluation and new large test collection for research. In: SIGIR'94. pp. 192–201. Springer (1994)

[6] http://www.trec-cds.org/
[7] http://datacitation.dei.unipd.it/
[8] https://www.examode.eu/

9. Kadry, A., Dietz, L.: Open relation extraction for support passage retrieval: Merit and open issues. In: Proceedings of the 40th International ACM SIGIR Conference on Research and Development in Information Retrieval. pp. 1149–1152. ACM (2017)
10. Koopman, B., Zuccon, G., Nguyen, A., Vickers, D., Butt, L., Bruza, P.D.: Exploiting snomed ct concepts and relationships for clinical information retrieval: Australian e-health research centre and queensland university of technology at the trec 2012 medical track. In: The Twenty-First Text REtrieval Conference Proceedings (TREC 2012)[NIST Special Publication: SP 500-298]. pp. 1–8 (2012)
11. Limsopatham, N., Macdonald, C., Ounis, I.: Inferring conceptual relationships to improve medical records search. In: Proceedings of the 10th Conference on Open Research Areas in Information Retrieval. pp. 1–8 (2013)
12. Limsopatham, N., Macdonald, C., Ounis, I.: A task-specific query and document representation for medical records search. In: European Conference on Information Retrieval. pp. 747–751. Springer (2013)
13. Liu, F., Chen, J., Jagannatha, A., Yu, H.: Learning for biomedical information extraction: methodological review of recent advances. arXiv preprint arXiv:1606.07993 (2016)
14. Mintz, M., Bills, S., Snow, R., Jurafsky, D.: Distant supervision for relation extraction without labeled data. In: Proceedings of the Joint Conference of the 47th Annual Meeting of the ACL and the 4th International Joint Conference on Natural Language Processing of the AFNLP: Volume 2-Volume 2. pp. 1003–1011. Association for Computational Linguistics (2009)
15. Pyysalo, S., Ginter, F., Moen, H., Salakoski, T., Ananiadou, S.: Distributional semantics resources for biomedical text processing. In: Proceedings of the 5th International Symposium on Languages in Biology and Medicine, Tokyo, Japan. pp. 39–43 (2013)
16. Robertson, S.E., Walker, S.: Okapi/keenbow at trec-8. In: TREC. vol. 8, pp. 151–162. Citeseer (1999)
17. Schuhmacher, M., Roth, B., Ponzetto, S.P., Dietz, L.: Finding relevant relations in relevant documents. In: European Conference on Information Retrieval. pp. 654–660. Springer (2016)
18. Uzuner, Ö., South, B., Shen, S., DuVall, S.L.: 2010 i2b2/va challenge on concepts, assertions, and relations in clinical text. Journal of the American Medical Informatics Association **18**(5), 552–556 (2011)
19. Voskarides, N., Meij, E., de Rijke, M.: Generating descriptions of entity relationships. In: European Conference on Information Retrieval. pp. 317–330. Springer (2017)
20. Wang, C., Fan, J.: Medical relation extraction with manifold models. In: Proceedings of the 52nd Annual Meeting of the Association for Computational Linguistics (Volume 1: Long Papers). vol. 1, pp. 828–838 (2014)
21. Zeng, D., Liu, K., Lai, S., Zhou, G., Zhao, J.: Relation classification via convolutional deep neural network. In: Proceedings of COLING 2014, the 25th International Conference on Computational Linguistics: Technical Papers. pp. 2335–2344 (2014)
22. Zhang, D., Wang, D.: Relation classification via recurrent neural network. arXiv preprint arXiv:1508.01006 (2015)
23. Zheng, J., Howsmon, D., Zhang, B., Hahn, J., McGuinness, D., Hendler, J., Ji, H.: Entity linking for biomedical literature. BMC Medical Informatics and Decision Making **15**(1), S4 (2015)

Reverse Engineering of Data Services (Extended Abstract)

Gianluca Cima[1], Maurizio Lenzerini[1], Antonella Poggi[1,2]

Sapienza Università di Roma
cima, lenzerini, poggi@diag.uniroma1.it

Abstract. We study the problem of designing reverse engineering techniques for associating semantic descriptions to existing data services. We base our proposal on the Ontology-Based Data Access paradigm, where a domain ontology is used to provide a semantic layer mapped to the data sources of an organization. The basic idea is to perform the reverse engineering of a data service, expressed a query over the data sources, by deriving a query over the ontology that explains the semantics of the data service in terms of the element of the ontology. We illustrate a formal framework for this problem, based on the notion of source-to-ontology rewriting, which comes in three variants, called sound, complete and perfect, respectively. We present a thorough complexity analysis of two computational problems, namely verification (checking whether a query is a source-to-ontology rewriting of a given data service), and computation (computing a source-to-ontology rewriting of a data service).

Introduction

The architecture of many modern Information Systems is based on data services [13], i.e., services deployed on top of data stores, other services, and/or applications to encapsulate a wide range of data-centric operations. In order to realize the promises of data services, in particular to foster their reuse, it is of vital importance to well document and clearly specify their semantics. While most current techniques manually associate APIs (Application Programming Interface) to data services, and describe their intended meaning with ad-hoc methods, often using natural language or complex metadata [5], we propose a new approach, whose goal is to automatically associate formal semantic descriptions to data services. We base our proposal on the *Ontology-Based Data Access* (OBDA) paradigm [11]. An OBDA specification consists of an ontology expressed in Description Logic (DL) [2], the schema of the data sources forming the information system, and a mapping between the source schema and the ontology. The ontology is a formal representation of the underlying domain, and the mapping specifies the relationship between the data at the sources and the concepts in the ontology. With the OBDA specification at hand, we pursue the idea of expressing the semantics of data services using the elements of the domain ontology, which is assumed to be familiar to the consumer of data services.

But how can we automatically produce a semantic characterization of a data service, having an OBDA specification available? The method we propose is to exploit a new reasoning task over the OBDA specification, that works as follows: we express the data service in terms of a query over the sources, and we aim at automatically deriving the query over the ontology that best describes the data service, given the mapping. The following example illustrates this idea.

Example 1. Let $\Sigma = \langle \mathcal{O}, \mathcal{S}, \mathcal{M} \rangle$ be as follows:

- $\mathcal{O} = \{ \text{ErasmusStudent} \sqsubseteq \text{Student}, \text{MathStudent} \sqsubseteq \text{Student} \}$
- $\mathcal{S} = \{ s_1, s_2, s_3, s_4 \}$
- $\mathcal{M} = \begin{array}{l} \{(x) \mid s_1(x)\} \rightarrow \{(x) \mid \text{Student}(x)\} \\ \{(x) \mid s_2(x)\} \rightarrow \{(x) \mid \text{Student}(x)\} \\ \{(x) \mid s_1(x), s_3(x,y)\} \rightarrow \{(x) \mid \text{ErasmusStudent}(x)\} \\ \{(x) \mid s_1(x), s_4(x,y)\} \rightarrow \{(x) \mid \text{MathStudent}(x)\} \end{array}$

and consider the data service expressed as the source query $q_{\mathcal{S}}(x) = \{(x) \mid s_1(x) \vee s_3(x)\}$. It is easy to see that the query that best describes $q_{\mathcal{S}}$ in terms of $\mathcal{O}$ is $q_{\mathcal{O}}(x) = \{(x) \mid \text{Student}(x)\}$.

Note that most of (if not all) the literature about managing data sources through an ontology [9,12] deals with user queries expressed over the ontology, and studies the problem of finding an *ontology-to-source rewriting*, i.e., a query over the source schema that, once executed over the data, provides the answers to the original query. Here, the problem is reversed, because we start with a source query and we aim at deriving a corresponding query over the ontology, called a *source-to-ontology rewriting*. Thus, we deal with a sort of reverse engineering problem, which is novel in the investigation of both OBDA and data integration.

The notions introduced in this paper are relevant in a plethora of scenarios. For the sake of brevity, we mention only two of them. Following the ideas in [6,7], it can be shown that our notions of source-to-ontology rewriting can be used to provide the semantics of open datasets and open APIs published by organizations, which is a crucial aspect for unchaining all the potentials of open data. In [10], the concept of realization of source queries, corresponding to one of the notions studied here, is used for checking whether the mapping provides the right coverage for expressing the relevant data services at the ontology level.

The contributions provided by this paper can be summarized as follows. We propose a formal framework for the problem of semantically characterizing a data service through an ontology (Section 3). We introduce the notions of *perfect*, *sound*, and *complete* source-to-ontology rewritings, and we define two basic reasoning tasks, namely *verification* and *computation*. The former checks whether a given query is a source-to-ontology rewriting of a data service, whereas the latter computes one such rewriting. We show that, although the ideal notion is the one of perfect source-to-ontology rewriting, there are cases where, with the given mapping, no query over the ontology can precisely characterize the data service at hand. Thus, we introduce *maximally sound* and *minimally complete* source-to-ontology rewritings, which intuitively aim at approximating the perfect rewriting of a data service at best, with the goal of either precision (sound rewriting), or recall (complete rewriting).

We study the verification and the computation problem for complete (Section 4) and sound (Section 5) source-to-ontology rewritings in one of the most popular OBDA setting considered in the literature, namely where the ontology language is *DL-Lite*$_{\mathcal{R}}$ [4,3], each mapping assertion maps a conjunctive query (CQ) over the source to a CQ over the ontology, and both the data service and the source-to-ontology rewriting are expressed as unions of CQs. For complete source-to-ontology rewritings we present algorithms for verification and computation, and characterize the complexity of both tasks. For the case of sound rewritings, we do the same for verification, and we precisely determine the cases where a maximally sound rewriting is not guaranteed to exist. For the lack of space, we do not tackle here the case of perfect rewritings, but we point out that results for complete and sound rewritings can be combined to study this case.

To the best of our knowledge, the problem studied in this paper has been (partially) addressed only in [6,10]. The former provides upper bound complexity results for complete rewritings, and the latter focuses on both *DL-Lite*$_{\mathcal{R}}$ and the $\mathcal{EL}$ family of ontology languages, and studies perfect rewritings only, under a slightly different semantics with respect to the one proposed here.

This paper is an extended abstract of [8]. Hence, while we assume basic knowledge about databases [1] and Description Logics (DL) [2], for specific concepts and notations, we refer to the Preliminaries section of [8].

Framework

We implicitly refer to an OBDA specification $\Sigma = \langle \mathcal{O}, \mathcal{S}, \mathcal{M} \rangle$. Intuitively, given a data service expressed as a query $q_\mathcal{S}$ over $\mathcal{S}$, we aim at finding the query over $\mathcal{O}$ that precisely characterizes $q_\mathcal{S}$ w.r.t. Σ. Since the evaluation of queries over $\mathcal{O}$ is based on certain answers, this means that we aim at finding a query over $\mathcal{O}$ whose certain answers w.r.t. Σ and D exactly capture the answers of $q_\mathcal{S}$ w.r.t. D for every $\mathcal{S}$-database D. So, we are naturally led to the notion of perfect source-to-ontology rewriting. In what follows, $q_\mathcal{S}$ refers to a query over $\mathcal{S}$, and $q_\mathcal{O}$ to a query over $\mathcal{O}$ of the same arity.

Definition 1. *$q_\mathcal{O}$ is a* perfect $\mathcal{S}$-to-$\mathcal{O}$ Σ-rewriting *of $q_\mathcal{S}$ if for every $\mathcal{S}$-database D, $Mod_D(\Sigma) \neq \emptyset$ implies $q_\mathcal{S}^D = cert_{q_\mathcal{O},\Sigma}^D$.*

As noted in [6,10] and illustrated in the next example, a perfect source-to-ontology rewriting of $q_\mathcal{S}$ may not exist.

Example 2. Refer to Example 1, and consider the data service exprresed as the source query $q_\mathcal{S}(x) = \{(x) \mid s_1(x)\}$. By inspecting the mappings, one can see that, since the certain answers of Student include the values stored both in s_1 and in s_3, such concept is too general for exactly characterizing $q_\mathcal{S}$. On the other hand, it can also seen that both ErasmusStudent and MathStudent are too specific, and therefore we can conclude that no perfect $\mathcal{S}$-to-$\mathcal{O}$ Σ-rewriting of $q_\mathcal{S}$ exists.

In order to cope with the situations illustrated in the example, we introduce the notions of sound and complete source-to-ontology rewritings, which, intuitively, provide sound and complete approximations of perfect rewritings, respectively.

Definition 2. *$q_{\mathcal{O}}$ is a* sound *(respectively,* complete*) $\mathcal{S}$-to-$\mathcal{O}$ Σ-rewriting of $q_{\mathcal{S}}$ if for every $\mathcal{S}$-database D, $Mod_D(\Sigma) \neq \emptyset$ implies $cert^D_{q_{\mathcal{O}},\Sigma} \subseteq q^D_{\mathcal{S}}$ (resp., $q^D_{\mathcal{S}} \subseteq cert^D_{q_{\mathcal{O}},\Sigma}$).*

Example 3. We refer to Example 2, and observe that $\{(x) \mid \mathsf{ErasmusStudent}(x) \wedge \mathsf{MathStudent}(x)\}$ is a sound $\mathcal{S}$-to-$\mathcal{O}$ Σ-rewriting of $q_{\mathcal{S}}$, whereas $\{(x) \mid \mathsf{Student}(x)\}$ is a complete $\mathcal{S}$-to-$\mathcal{O}$ Σ-rewriting of $q_{\mathcal{S}}$.

Obviously, $q_{\mathcal{O}}$ is a perfect $\mathcal{S}$-to-$\mathcal{O}$ Σ-rewriting of $q_{\mathcal{S}}$ if and only if $q_{\mathcal{O}}$ is both a sound, and a complete $\mathcal{S}$-to-$\mathcal{O}$ Σ-rewriting of $q_{\mathcal{S}}$. There are also interesting relationships between the notions of $\mathcal{S}$-to-$\mathcal{O}$ Σ-rewritings introduced here and the usual notions of rewritings studied in OBDA.

Proposition 1. *$q_{\mathcal{O}}$ is a complete $\mathcal{S}$-to-$\mathcal{O}$ Σ-rewriting of $q_{\mathcal{S}}$ if and only if $q_{\mathcal{S}}$ is an $\mathcal{O}$-to-$\mathcal{S}$ Σ-rewriting of $q_{\mathcal{O}}$. If $q_{\mathcal{S}}$ is a perfect $\mathcal{O}$-to-$\mathcal{S}$ Σ-rewriting of $q_{\mathcal{O}}$, then $q_{\mathcal{O}}$ is a perfect $\mathcal{S}$-to-$\mathcal{O}$ Σ-rewriting of $q_{\mathcal{S}}$.*

It is easy to see that different sound or complete source-to-ontology rewritings of $q_{\mathcal{S}}$ may exist, and therefore it is reasonable to look for the "best" approximations of $q_{\mathcal{S}}$, at least relative to a certain class of queries.

Definition 3. *$q_{\mathcal{O}} \in \mathcal{L}$ is an* $\mathcal{L}$-maximally sound *(respectively,* $\mathcal{L}$-minimally complete*) $\mathcal{S}$-to-$\mathcal{O}$ Σ-rewriting of $q_{\mathcal{S}}$ if $q_{\mathcal{O}}$ is a sound (resp. complete) $\mathcal{S}$-to-$\mathcal{O}$ Σ-rewriting of $q_{\mathcal{S}}$ and no $q' \in \mathcal{L}$ exists such that (i) q' is a sound (resp., complete) $\mathcal{S}$-to-$\mathcal{O}$ Σ-rewriting of $q_{\mathcal{S}}$, (ii) $cert_{q_{\mathcal{O}},\Sigma} \sqsubseteq cert_{q',\Sigma}$ (resp., $cert_{q',\Sigma} \sqsubseteq cert_{q_{\mathcal{O}},\Sigma}$), and (iii) there exists an $\mathcal{S}$-database D s.t. $cert^D_{q_{\mathcal{O}},\Sigma} \subset cert^D_{q',\Sigma}$ (resp., $cert^D_{q',\Sigma} \subset cert^D_{q_{\mathcal{O}},\Sigma}$).*

Example 4. We refer again to Example 2, and observe that while $\{(x) \mid \mathsf{Student}(x)\}$ is the minimally complete $\mathcal{S}$-to-$\mathcal{O}$ Σ-rewriting of $q_{\mathcal{S}}$ in the class of UCQs, both $\{(x) \mid \mathsf{ErasmusStudent}(x)\}$, and $\{(x) \mid \mathsf{MathStudent}(x)\}$ are maximally sound $\mathcal{S}$-to-$\mathcal{O}$ Σ-rewritings of $q_{\mathcal{S}}$ in the class of CQs, while $\{(x) \mid \mathsf{ErasmusStudent}(x) \vee \mathsf{MathStudent}(x)\}$ is so in the class of UCQs.

Given the general framework presented so far, it is natural to consider the following two basic computational problems, for classes $\mathcal{L}_{\mathcal{S}}$ and $\mathcal{L}_{\mathcal{O}}$ of queries:

- *Verification*: given $\Sigma = \langle \mathcal{O}, \mathcal{S}, \mathcal{M} \rangle$, $q_{\mathcal{S}} \in \mathcal{L}_{\mathcal{S}}$ over $\mathcal{S}$ and $q_{\mathcal{O}} \in \mathcal{L}_{\mathcal{O}}$ over $\mathcal{O}$ of the same arity as $q_{\mathcal{S}}$, verify whether $q_{\mathcal{O}}$ is a sound (resp., complete, perfect) $\mathcal{S}$-to-$\mathcal{O}$ Σ-rewritings of $q_{\mathcal{S}}$.
- *Computation*: given $\Sigma = \langle \mathcal{O}, \mathcal{S}, \mathcal{M} \rangle$, and $q_{\mathcal{S}} \in \mathcal{L}_{\mathcal{S}}$ over $\mathcal{S}$ compute any $\mathcal{L}_{\mathcal{O}}$-maximally sound (resp., $\mathcal{L}_{\mathcal{O}}$-minimally complete, perfect) $\mathcal{S}$-to-$\mathcal{O}$ Σ-rewriting of $q_{\mathcal{S}}$, if it exists.

In the rest of this paper, if not otherwise stated, we refer to the most common setting studied in OBDA, i.e., where (i) the ontology is expressed in *DL-Lite*$_{\mathcal{R}}$, (ii) $\mathcal{S}$ is a relational database schema without integrity constraints, and (iii) both $\mathcal{L}_{\mathcal{O}}$ and $\mathcal{L}_{\mathcal{S}}$ denote the class of UCQs. Interestingly, in this case, we have the following.

Proposition 2. *If q_1 and q_2 are two UCQ-minimally complete, or UCQ-maximally sound $\mathcal{S}$-to-$\mathcal{O}$ Σ-rewritings of $q_{\mathcal{S}}$, then they are equivalent w.r.t. Σ.*

Complete source-to-ontology rewritings

In this section, we study both the verification and the computation problem for complete source-to-ontology rewritings.

Verification. Suppose we want to check whether $q_{\mathcal{O}}$ is a complete $\mathcal{S}$-to-$\mathcal{O}$ Σ-rewriting of $q_{\mathcal{S}}$. Obviously, if $q_{\mathcal{S}}$ is contained in $\mathsf{PerfRef}_{q_{\mathcal{O}},\Sigma}$, then for every $\mathcal{S}$-database D consistent with Σ, we have that $q_{\mathcal{S}}^{D} \subseteq cert_{q_{\mathcal{O}},\Sigma}^{D}$ and therefore the answer is positive. However, if $q_{\mathcal{S}}$ is not contained in $\mathsf{PerfRef}_{q_{\mathcal{O}},\Sigma}$, it might be that $q_{\mathcal{O}}$ is still a complete $\mathcal{S}$-to-$\mathcal{O}$ Σ-rewriting of $q_{\mathcal{S}}$, in the case where the non-emptiness of $q_{\mathcal{S}}$ in D reveals the presence of inconsistencies. From this observation, we derive the following characterization.

Proposition 3. *$q_{\mathcal{O}}$ is a complete $\mathcal{S}$-to-$\mathcal{O}$ Σ-rewriting of $q_{\mathcal{S}}(\boldsymbol{t})$ if and only if $q_{\mathcal{S}} \sqsubseteq \mathsf{PerfRef}_{q_{\mathcal{O}},\Sigma} \vee \mathsf{PerfRef}_{\mathcal{V}_{\mathcal{O}}^{\boldsymbol{t}},\Sigma}$.*

The following theorem characterizes the complexity of verification for complete source-to-ontology rewritings.

Theorem 1. *Verification for complete source-to-ontology rewritings is NP-complete.*

Computation. Our algorithm for the computation of minimally complete source-to-ontology rewritings is below.

Algorithm 1
Input: $\Sigma = \langle \mathcal{O}, \mathcal{S}, \mathcal{M} \rangle$, $q_{\mathcal{S}}(\boldsymbol{t}) = q_{\mathcal{S}}^{1}(\boldsymbol{t}) \vee \ldots \vee q_{\mathcal{S}}^{n}(\boldsymbol{t})$ over $\mathcal{S}$
Output: $q_{\mathcal{O}}(\boldsymbol{t})$ over $\mathcal{O}$
begin return $q_{\mathcal{O}} = \{\boldsymbol{t} \mid \mathcal{M}(q_{\mathcal{S}}^{1}) \wedge \top(\boldsymbol{t}) \vee \ldots \vee \mathcal{M}(q_{\mathcal{S}}^{n}) \wedge \top(\boldsymbol{t})\}$ **end**

Intuitively, the algorithm computes the output query as union of CQs obtained by simply applying the mapping $\mathcal{M}$ to each CQ $q_{\mathcal{S}}^{i}$ in $q_{\mathcal{S}}$, using $\top$ to bind the variables that are not involved in the application of $\mathcal{M}$ to $q_{\mathcal{S}}^{i}$.

Theorem 2. *Algorithm 1 computes the UCQ-minimally complete $\mathcal{S}$-to-$\mathcal{O}$ Σ-rewriting of $q_{\mathcal{S}}$.*

The algorithm shows that the UCQ-minimally complete $\mathcal{S}$-to-$\mathcal{O}$ Σ-rewriting of $q_{\mathcal{S}}$ always exists. Moreover, if $q_{\mathcal{S}}$ is a CQ, then it is a CQ. Finally, we observe that the complexity of Algorithm 1 does not depend on $\mathcal{O}$, is in EXPTIME in $\sigma(\mathcal{M})$, and in PTIME in $\sigma(q_{\mathcal{S}})$, where we use $\sigma(x)$ to denotes the size of x. It can be shown that a PTIME algorithm for computing the UCQ-minimally complete source-to-ontology rewriting would imply a PTIME algorithm for CQ containment. So, assuming PTIME $\neq$ NP, computation cannot be solved in PTIME.

Sound source-to-ontology rewritings

We now turn to verification and computation of sound source-to-ontology rewritings.

Verification. Notice that, since for an $\mathcal{S}$-database D consistent with Σ, $\mathsf{PerfRef}_{q_{\mathcal{O}},\Sigma}^{D}$ computes exactly $cert_{q_{\mathcal{O}},\Sigma}^{D}$, checking whether $q_{\mathcal{O}}$ is a sound $\mathcal{S}$-to-$\mathcal{O}$ Σ-rewriting of $q_{\mathcal{S}}$ means checking whether for all $\mathcal{S}$-databases D, either $Mod_{D}(\Sigma) = \emptyset$ or $\mathsf{PerfRef}_{q_{\mathcal{O}},\Sigma}^{D} \subseteq q_{\mathcal{S}}^{D}$. This observation leads to the following characterization.

Proposition 4. *$q_{\mathcal{O}}(\boldsymbol{t})$ is a sound $\mathcal{S}$-to-$\mathcal{O}$ Σ-rewriting of $q_{\mathcal{S}}$ if and only if $\mathit{PerfRef}_{q_{\mathcal{O}},\Sigma} \sqsubseteq q_{\mathcal{S}} \vee \mathit{PerfRef}_{\mathcal{V}^{\boldsymbol{t}}_{\mathcal{O}},\Sigma}$.*

The following theorem characterizes the complexity of the verification problem for sound source-to-ontology rewritings.

Theorem 3. *Verification for sound source-to-ontology rewritings is Π_2^p-complete.*

Computation. We address the problem of computing UCQ-maximally sound source-to-ontology rewritings. Our main result is that there are many cases where a UCQ-maximally sound source-to-ontology rewriting of a query is not guaranteed to exist. To illustrate the result, we introduce a specific setting, that we call *restricted*, obtained from the general one by: (i) limiting the ontology language to *DL-Lite*$_{\mathsf{RDFS}}$, (ii) limiting the mapping to pure GAV, and (iii) limiting $q_{\mathcal{S}}$ to UCQJFEs. The following shows that, surprisingly, as soon as we try to extend such setting, we lose the guarantee of the existence of source-to-ontology rewritings that are maximally sound.

Theorem 4. *UCQ-maximally sound source-to-ontology rewritings of a query $q_{\mathcal{S}}$ may not exist if we extend the restricted setting with each of the following features:* (i) *disjointness axioms in the ontology;* (ii) *inclusion axioms with $\exists R$ as right-hand side in the ontology;* (iii) *LAV mapping assertions, even without joins involving existential variables in the right-hand side;* (iv) *non-pure GAV mapping assertions;* (v) *the fragment of UCQ for $q_{\mathcal{S}}$ beyond UCQJFE.*

Proof sketch. We present the proof for case 5. Consider the OBDA specification $\Sigma = \langle \mathcal{O}, \mathcal{S}, \mathcal{M} \rangle$, where $\mathcal{O}$ has no axiom, and $\mathcal{M}$ is the following pure GAV mapping:

$$\begin{array}{ll} \{(x,y) \mid s_1(y,y) \wedge s_3(x)\} & \rightarrow \{(x,y) \mid R(x,y)\} \\ \{(x,y) \mid s_1(x,y)\} & \rightarrow \{(x,y) \mid R(x,y)\} \end{array}$$

and let $q_{\mathcal{S}}$ be the query $\{() \mid s_1(x,y) \wedge s_1(y,z)\}$. Observe that $q'_{\mathcal{O}} = \{() \mid R(x,y) \wedge R(y,z)\}$ is the complete $\mathcal{S}$-to-$\mathcal{O}$ Σ-rewriting of $q_{\mathcal{S}}$, but is not sound, because the query $q'_s = \{() \mid s_1(x,y) \wedge s_1(z,z) \wedge s_3(y)\}$ is a disjunct of $\mathsf{PerfRef}_{q'_{\mathcal{O}},\Sigma}$ such that $q'_{\mathcal{S}} \not\sqsubseteq q_{\mathcal{S}}$. Conversely, one can verify that each of the following queries is a sound $\mathcal{S}$-to-$\mathcal{O}$ Σ-rewriting of $q_{\mathcal{S}}$:

- $q_0 = \{() \mid R(x,y) \wedge R(y,y)\}$,
- $q_1 = \{() \mid R(x,y) \wedge R(y,z_1) \wedge R(z_1,y)\}$,
- $q_2 = \{() \mid R(x,y) \wedge R(y,z_1) \wedge R(z_1,z_2) \wedge R(z_2,y)\}$,
- $\ldots$

More precisely, if we define q_n to be $\{() \mid R(x,y) \wedge R(y,z_1) \wedge R(z_1,z_2) \wedge \ldots \wedge R(z_{n-1},z_n) \wedge R(z_n,y)\}$, for $n \geq 2$,, then it can be shown that every q_n is a sound $\mathcal{S}$-to-$\mathcal{O}$ Σ-rewriting of $q_{\mathcal{S}}$, and for no pair (i,j), with $i \neq j$, $i,j \geq 0$, $cert_{q_i,\Sigma} \sqsubseteq cert_{q_j,\Sigma}$. It follows that the infinite union q of q_0, q_1, and all q_n's can be shown to be the maximally sound $\mathcal{S}$-to-$\mathcal{O}$ Σ-rewriting of $q_{\mathcal{S}}$ in the class of positive queries. □

We observe that, despite its limitations, the expressive power of the restricted setting is sufficient for several meaningful applications. Indeed, several popular ontologies are expressible in *DL-Lite*$_{\mathsf{RDFS}}$, and the form of pure GAV mapping is exactly the one originally defined in the literature of data integration. Moreover, UCQJFEs capture data services expressible in the famous SPJ (Select, Project, Join) fragment of Relational Algebra, with the only limitation of forbidding projection outside join, which makes them suitable for all tasks related to source profiling. Interestingly, it can be shown that in the restricted setting maximally sound source-to-ontology rewritings always exist.

Conclusion

We have presented a framework for semantically characterizing data services through ontologies, and carried out a comprehensive analysis for the most common OBDA setting. We plan to continue this work along several directions. For example, in the unrestricted setting, we aim at (*i*) studying the problem of checking for the existence of a UCQ-maximally sound source-to-ontology rewriting of a query, and computing it in case it exists, and (*ii*) singling out the minimal class $\mathcal{L}_{\mathcal{O}}$ of queries that guarantees the existence of an $\mathcal{L}_{\mathcal{O}}$-maximally sound source-to-ontology rewritings. Furthermore, we will extend our analysis to OBDA settings based on other DLs as ontology languages.

Acknowlegments. Work supported by MIUR under the SIR project "MODEUS" – grant n. RBSI14TQHQ, and by Sapienza research project "PRE-O-PRE".

References

1. S. Abiteboul, R. Hull, and V. Vianu. *Foundations of Databases*. Addison Wesley Publ. Co., 1995.
2. F. Baader, D. Calvanese, D. McGuinness, D. Nardi, and P. F. Patel-Schneider, editors. *The Description Logic Handbook: Theory, Implementation and Applications*. Cambridge University Press, 2003.
3. D. Calvanese, G. De Giacomo, D. Lembo, M. Lenzerini, and R. Rosati. Tractable reasoning and efficient query answering in description logics: The *DL-Lite* family. *J. of Automated Reasoning*, 39(3):385–429, 2007.
4. D. Calvanese, G. De Giacomo, M. Lenzerini, R. Rosati, and G. Vetere. *DL-Lite*: Practical reasoning for rich DLs. In *Proc. of DL 2004*, volume 104 of *CEUR*, `ceur-ws.org`, 2004.
5. M. J. Carey, N. Onose, and M. Petropoulos. Data services. *Comm. of the ACM*, 55(6):86–97, 2012.
6. G. Cima. Preliminary results on ontology-based open data publishing. In *Proc. of DL 2017*, volume 1879 of *CEUR*, `ceur-ws.org`, 2017.
7. G. Cima, M. Lenzerini, and A. Poggi. Semantic technology for open data publishing. In *Proc. of WIMS 2017*, 2017.
8. G. Cima, M. Lenzerini, and A. Poggi. Semantic characterization of data services through ontologies. In *Proc. of IJCAI 2019*, 2019.
9. M. Lenzerini. Managing data through the lens of an ontology. *AI Magazine*, 39(2):65–74, 2018.
10. C. Lutz, J. Marti, and L. Sabellek. Query expressibility and verification in ontology-based data access. In *Proc. of KR 2018*, pages 389–398, 2018.
11. A. Poggi, D. Lembo, D. Calvanese, G. De Giacomo, M. Lenzerini, and R. Rosati. Linking data to ontologies. *J. on Data Semantics*, X:133–173, 2008.

12. G. Xiao, D. Calvanese, R. Kontchakov, D. Lembo, A. Poggi, R. Rosati, and M. Zakharyaschev. Ontology-based data access: A survey. In *Proceedings of the Twenty-Seventh International Joint Conference on Artificial Intelligence, IJCAI 2018, July 13-19, 2018, Stockholm, Sweden.*, pages 5511–5519, 2018.
13. Z. Zheng, J. Zhu, and M. R. Lyu. Service-generated big data and big data-as-a-service: An overview. In *Proc. of the 2013 IEEE Int. Conf. on Big Data*, pages 403–410, 2013.

An architectural approach for digital factories (Extended abstract)*

Nicola Bicocchi[1], Giacomo Cabri[1], Francesco Leotta[2], Federica Mandreoli[1], Massimo Mecella[2], and Francesco Sapio[2]

[1] Università degli Studi di Modena e Reggio Emilia, Italy
[2] Sapienza Università di Roma, Italy

Abstract. Digital factories comprise a multi-layered integration of various activities along the factories and product life-cycles. A central aspect of a digital factory is that of enabling the product lifecycle stakeholders to collaborate through the use of software solutions. The digital factory expands outside the company boundaries and allows to collaborate on business processes over the whole supply chain. This extended abstract, based on a recently published paper, discusses an interoperability architecture for digital factories. It analyses the key requirements for enabling a scalable factory architecture characterized by access to services, aggregation of data, and orchestration of production processes.

Keywords: digital factories · data sharing and interoperability · service oriented architectures · dynamic supply chains

1 Introduction

Production processes are fragmented across different companies and organised in global multi-tier supply chains. This is the result of the first wave of globalisation, which was partly enabled by the diffusion of Internet-based Information and Communication Technologies (ICTs)in the early 2000s. A recent wave in technology, has led to the fourth industrial revolution - or *Industry 4.0*, whose goal is to increase opportunities for firms, including small and medium enterprises (SMEs) by being able to access global customers. However, this requires the ability to adapt to different requirements and conditions, volatile demand patterns, and fast changing technologies. Therefore, supply chains need to increase their *agility* by adapting to evolving and uncertain business contexts.

---

* This paper is based on Nicola Bicocchi, Giacomo Cabri, Federica Mandreoli, Massimo Mecella (2019): Dynamic digital factories for agile supply chains: An architectural approach. *Journal of Industrial Information Integration*, DOI: https://doi.org/10.1016/j.jii.2019.02.001. The work has been partly supported by the European Commission through the H2020 project FIRST – virtual Factories: Interoperation suppoRting buSiness innovaTion (grant agreement # 734599).

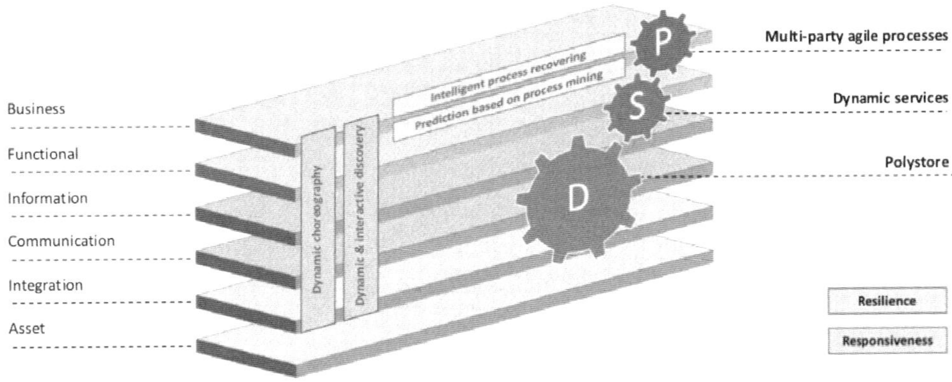

Fig. 1: Our RAMI-based architectural framework

Digital factory is a key paradigm to this end because it uses digital technologies to promote the integration of product design processes, manufacturing processes, and general collaborative business processes across factories and enterprises [2, 6]. An important aspect of this integration is to ensure *interoperability* between machines, products, processes, and services, as well as any descriptions of those. As a result, a digital factory consists of a multi-layered integration of the information related to various activities along the factory and related resources.

The main contribution of this paper is to provide methodological and technological support to agile supply chains in the Industry 4.0 context. It sets forth an architectural framework that the leverages Reference Architectural Model Industrie - RAMI 4.0 [7] and addresses the methodological issue of making RAMI 4.0 capable of enabling agility in supply chains. To address this aim, we propose an architectural framework that enables interoperability via a three-layered architecture where business processes and goal descriptions trigger the discovery of the needed services and data, and their composition in a dynamic, autonomous and adaptive fashion. Lastly, the rest of the paper is organised as follows: Section 2 presents the RAMI 4.0-based architectural framework, and Section 3 concludes the paper and discusses future work.

2 Enabling interoperability

The approach undertaken in this work is based on RAMI 4.0. RAMI is a layered reference architectural framework in the manufacturing industry domain developed in Germany by leveraging EU initiatives and guidelines [3].

RAMI 4.0 consists of six different layers. As shown in Fig. 1, we propose a correspondence between these layers and established technologies, i.e., polystores, dynamic services and multi-party agile processes.

According to RAMI 4.0, data is the bridge towards digitalization and is described in the integration, communication and information layers. In global multi-tier supply chains, data characteristics are: largeness, distribution, and

[3] See `https://ec.europa.eu/futurium/en/system/files/ged/a2-schweichhart-reference_architectural_model_industrie_4.0_rami_4.0.pdf`

heterogeneity. For instance, machines equipped with IoT sensors continuously produce data streams, Online transaction processing - OLTP data are available in DBMSs, Online analytical processing - OLAP data are available in data warehouses, digital manuals are stored in repositories, and so on. To deal with these information, data sources are organised as a dataspace where they can communicate through mappings. The dataspace adhere to the polystore model supporting dynamic configurations (i.e., data sources going in and out the system).

At the functional level, different kinds of services are provided to get information and to perform actions on the manufacturing parts of system (e.g., producing and assembling machines) as well as to enable interoperability with different actors of the supply chain (e.g., order management, warehouse management). Open APIs are exposed by services to control, discover, and compose them in a dynamic way. Rich semantic descriptions of the services should be available to support both the discovery of the services and their execution/invocation. This service layer allows to achieve higher-level goals defined at the business level.

At the business level, business process specifications need to capture not only orchestrated processes but also choreographed processes across different organizations, as a supply chain definition requires. By defining several goals, with different degrees of completeness, the business process model is able to support a resilient and responsive environment, as the involved parties can tune their efforts to reach one of the goals, that is not necessarily the best one. Decisions on the goal to be achieved are driven by the available data [4].

In order to describe our approach we refer to the following scenario.

MyMuffin is a (fictitious) company operating within the EU producing muffins and is expanding its business to allow customers to buy muffins online (in boxes of 4). Clients can customise their muffins by choosing among different combinations of ingredients (e.g., chocolate chips), toppings (icing sugar), and additions to the dough (e.g., honey, yoghurt). The client can also customise the colors of the muffin liners (e.g., pink, yellow) as well as the colors of the box. The muffins are then delivered to a specified location.[4]

The muffin factory collects orders and organises batches of muffin doughs for production. For example, if a client orders 3 boxes of carrot muffins with yoghurt, icing sugar on top, and pink baking paper, whereas another client orders 2 boxes of carrot muffins with yoghurt, nothing on top, and yellow baking paper, the same dough can be used for both orders. Once an order is received, the muffin liners are set-up as in parallel to the dough preparation. In addition, a QR-code is printed on the baking paper to serve as a unique identifier for a specific order. After the dough has been prepared, the muffins are placed in muffin liners and sent to the oven (connected to a QR code reader) for cooking. Muffins are cooked in batches of 1000 muffins. Once the muffins are cooked, toppings are placed, the cart is operated to route the different muffins to the right boxes where they are then ready for delivery. Considering the steps involved here, agility is needed during each stage of process, (e.g., the baking step may overcook some muffins, which therefore are not ready for delivery and should be prepared again).

[4] MyMuffin is a fantasy company, but there are real successful examples of mass customization applied to food likewise Mymuesli, a German company - `https://en.wikipedia.org/wiki/Mymuesli`.

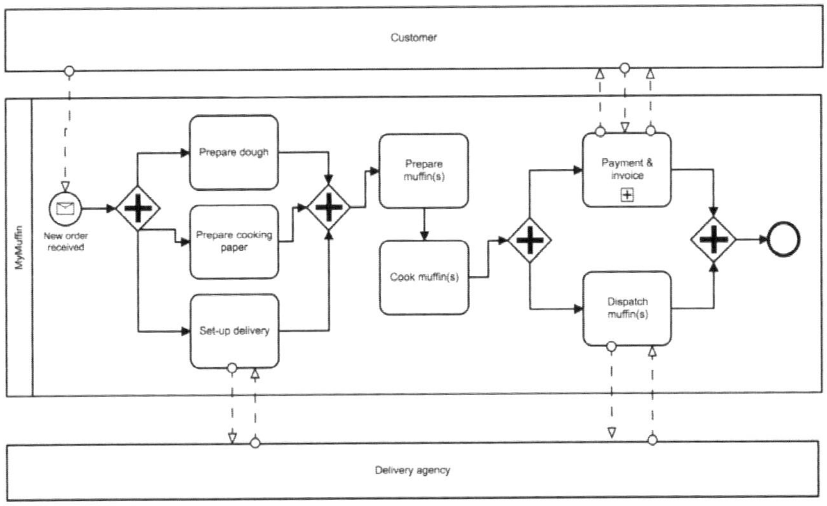

Fig. 2: The BPMN diagram describing the MyMuffin process.

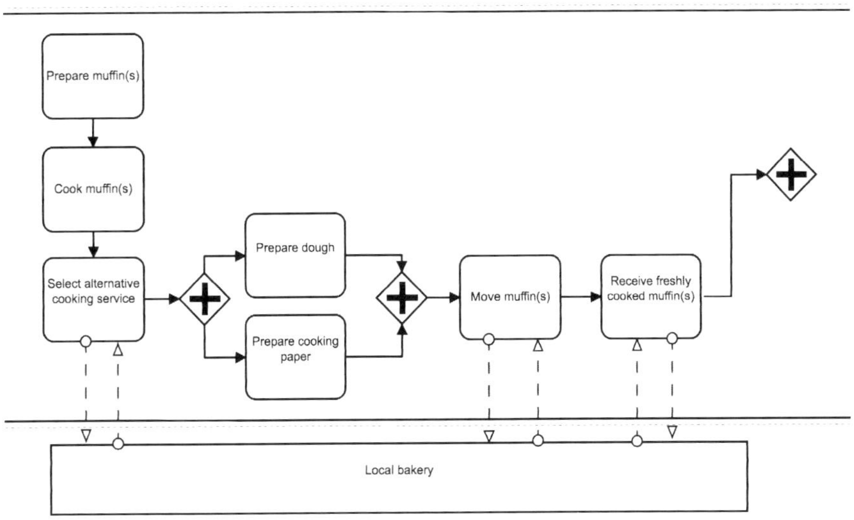

Fig. 3: A fragment of the adapted process.

2.1 Process space layer - goal-oriented process specification

The top layer of the proposed architecture deals with the goals and the processes able to achieve such goals. Figure 2 shows the process behind MyMuffin represented using Business Process Model and Notation (BPMN) [5].

In the MyMuffin example, some goals of the process may be:
[G1] for each order, evade it within 36 hours;
[G2] for each order, the final delivery to the customer should be within 72 hours.

[5] See `http://www.bpmn.org/`

The MyMuffin company adopts a process in which sub-goals might have been defined for specific parts (i.e., goals can in turn be decomposed in sub-goals), e.g., to achieve G1, it should be *[G1.1] muffins should not be overcooked.*

Notably, MyMuffin would like to define, on the basis of such goals, specific KPIs (Key Performance Indicators) that are defined over many aspects (e.g., interactions with external companies being part of the process, maintain a total of less than 24 hours from pick-up to delivery of orders, and to keep a KPI of 95% respected over the week). We can imagine that in a given day, some muffins get overcooked due to an error in the oven. This means that the goal *[G1.1]* is not achieved. Through automated planning techniques, like the one adopted in SmartPM [5], the process can be modified. In particular, as shown in Figure 3, after the original activities *Prepare muffin(s)* and *Cook muffin(s)*, new activities are introduced, to *Select alternative cooking service*, as a local bakery nearby MyMuffin that offers the availability of the oven; then, analogously to the original process, *Prepare dough* and *Prepare cooking paper* are performed, the muffins are moved and finally are received freshly cooked (see *Move muffin(s)* and *Receive freshly cooked muffin(s)* tasks). Finally, the process continues as the original one. Notably, this is only one of the possible adaptations.

2.2 Service space layer - service discovery and composition

Starting from the goals and processes defined in the process layer, services must be dynamically composed to achieve goal(s). In our example, we have different machines that can expose operations such as setting/increasing/decreasing the oven temperature, starting/stopping the dough mixer and providing related data by means of OpenAPIs. Rich semantic descriptions of the services should be available to support both discovery and service execution. The descriptions should include keywords identifying the context of the service (e.g., "food", "cooking"), the equipment (e.g., "oven", "mixer"), the operation (e.g., "turn-on", "speedup"), and the parameters (e.g., "temperature", "speed").

In regards to the discovery phase, semantic descriptions are exploited to search for specific services without knowing their exact names and their syntax a priori. Semantic techniques can be exploited to find synonyms and keywords related to the words searched for in this phase. Searches can be performed either automatically by the process layer or by human operators which may be involved when needed (such as the adaptation techniques realised in the process layer fail, and a human intervention is needed to make the process progress).

Semantic descriptions can be used in the composition phase as well. Being the composition dynamic, the platform must not only find, but also use, the needed service or eventually provide support to human operators. To this purpose, the description of the service parameters is needed to exploit the functionalities of the data layer to adapt the client service invocation to the server syntax. Some proposals and examples of semantic service descriptions are proposed in [1].

As an example, consider a scenario where the oven does not reach the required temperature due to different reasons (e.g., a cold winter day, bad isolation, broken door). The oven service provides the `slowdown():delay` operation, which outputs the delay in percentage (see Fig. 4a); for instance, if the oven was expected to reach the correct temperature in 30 minutes, but it actually needs 45

(a) Adapting to oven performance

(b) Adapting to overcooked muffins

Fig. 4: Service composition.

minutes, a delay of 33% is returned. The operation is then composed with all the services available for reducing the speed of the machines.

As a second example, consider the case where some muffins are overcooked (see Fig. 4b). In this case, the shipping courier must be notified to modify the shipment, and a new set of muffins must be produced starting from the list of ingredients. To this aim, the `overcook():(QRCode,type,num)` overation is available and can be activated either by a monitoring facilities or by human intervention. This operation outputs the type `type` and number `num` of the overcooked muffins and the corresponding order (identified by its `QRCode`), and can be composed with two discovered services: one interacting with the shipping courier (i.e., `shipment(URL)` with the courier service as input) and one activating the dosing machine (i.e., `dosing_machine(setOfIngredients,setOfQuantities)` with ingredients and quantities as input). Essentially, the composition connects the discovered services by making explicit the relationships between the involved service parameters. `?x`, `?y`, `?z`, `?h` are variables and the corresponding values must be discovered in the data space as they represent the input to the two services for shipment and the dosing machine.

2.3 Data space layer - service-oriented mapping discovery

Data are managed and accessed in a data space. The data space must be able to deal with a huge volume of heterogeneous data from autonomous sources and support the different information access needs of the service level. In particular, a large variety of data types should be managed at the data space level. Data can be static such as those available in traditional DBMSs but also highly dynamic like sensor data. Moreover, the data space should accommodate data with different degrees of structure, from tabular to fully textual data. Finally, the data space should cope with the very diversified data access modalities sources offer, from low level streaming access to high level data analytics.

To this extent, the data space is a collection of heterogeneous data sources that can be involved in the processes, both in-factory and out-factory, and that can exchange data through mappings, i.e. declarative specifications describing the relationship between a target data instance and possibly more than one source data instances. Each data source has its data access model that describes the kind of managed data, e.g., streaming data vs. static data, and the supported operators. As an example, Fig. 5a shows a small portion of the MyMuffin data space that can be used in case of overcooking where data are modelled as triples. *Batches* is a data stream that reports the cooking status over time; *Orders* is the

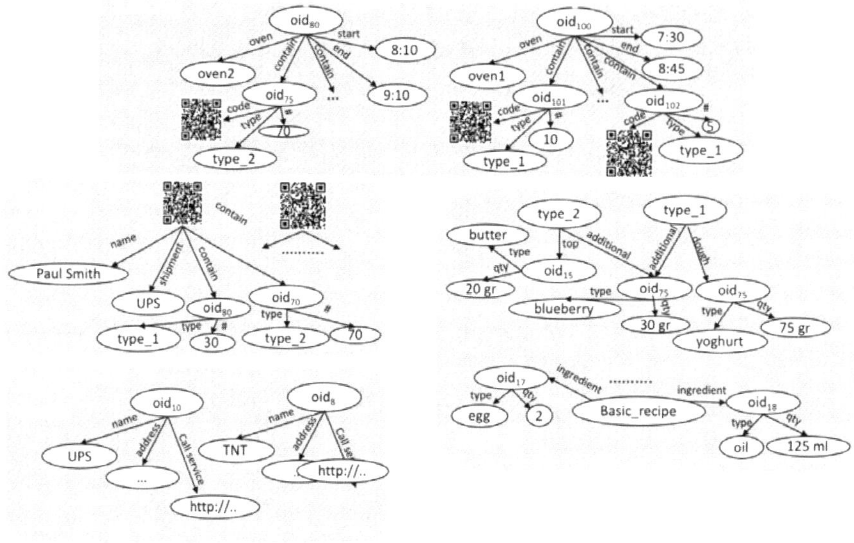

(a) An excerpt of the MyMuffin data space.

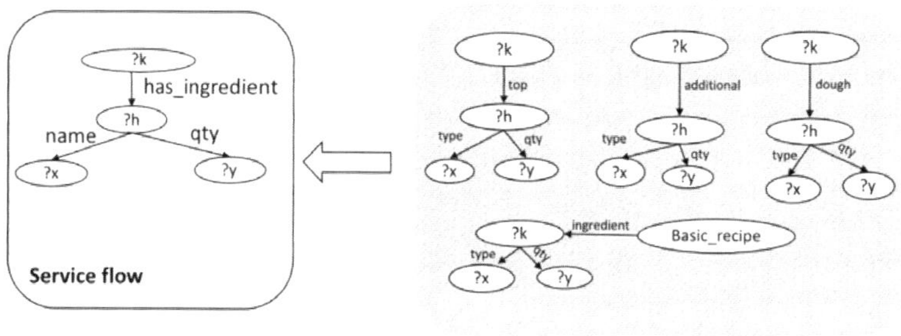

(b) Mapping discovery process

Fig. 5: The data space.

set of records storing the orders made by clients online and the corresponding QR-codes; *Recipes* is a semi-structured data set recording the recipes of the different kinds of muffins; *Yellow pages* is a web-based data source about the couriers and the related Web services.

In this large scale deeply heterogeneous and dynamic integration scenario, unlike traditional approaches, mappings are interactively created and refined according to the needs of service flows and the exclusive role of mappings is to contribute to execute service compositions [3]. Hence, we start from a chain of services with their information needs expressed as inputs and outputs that we attempt to satisfy in the dataspace. For instance the data flow of Fig. 4b indicates that from each `QRCode` returned by the `overcook` service, *(i)* it should be derived the Web service to interact with the delivery agent/courier, whereas *(ii)* from the type of the overcooked muffin it should be derived the list of ingredients together with the required quantities as input to the dosing machine. Therefore, mapping discovery leads to two mappings whose targets are `(QRCode, call, ?z)` and `(type, has_ingredient, ?h)`, `(?h, name, ?x)`, `(?h, qty, num*?y)`. A plausible output to the mapping discovery for the second mapping is shown in

Fig. 5b. This mapping involves the *Recipes* data source, only, and provides all the ingredients of the recipe of the type of the given overcooked muffins. If some muffins of type `type_1` are overcooked then `?k = type_1` and the inputs to the dosing machine will be `(yoghurt,75gr)`, `(blueberry,30gr)`, `(egg,2)`, etc.

3 Conclusion

In this paper, we have outlined an architectural framework for RAMI 4.0-based digital factories. The framework supports agile supply-chains through innovative technological approaches aiming at the dynamic discovery of service and data flows that best fit the requirements expressed in business process specifications and their evolution. The proposed approach relies on a three-level architecture whose aims are to enable the interoperability among the different parts of the real factory and to ease the involvement of humans in the agile management of factory processes. Moreover, the proposed approach leverages the interactions with other actors of the supply chain, making them easier and overcoming the obstacles deriving from the possible different data formats and process management.

Our future work and next steps will mainly consist in the implementation of the proposed architectural framework and proof-of-concept of such an architecture, to be validated in agile supply-chain application scenarios.

Finally, we would like to remark the impact of our research. At the business level, the potential impact of our research can facilitate the information exchange and ability for companies to increase their agility by adapting to changes occurring in the supply chains. As a result, they can offer more customised products and services to the customer. Moreover, agility considers security flaws among the potential risks against which supply chains need to be responsive. Therefore, the adoption of the proposed solution has a fundamental value today as security and privacy of data are one of the most important issues for the public.

References

1. C. Castelli, M. Mamei, A. Rosi, and F. Zambonelli. Engineering pervasive service ecosystems: The sapere approach. *ACM Trans. Auton. Adapt. Syst.*, 10(1).
2. N. Chungoora, R. I. Young, G. Gunendran, C. Palmer, Z. Usman, N. A. Anjum, A.-F. Cutting-Decelle, J. A. Harding, and K. Case. A model-driven ontology approach for manufacturing system interoperability and knowledge sharing. *Computers in Industry*, 64(4):392–401, 2013.
3. F. Mandreoli. A framework for user-driven mapping discovery in rich spaces of heterogeneous data. In *OTM Conf.*, pages 399–417, 2017.
4. A. Marrella, M. Mecella, B. Pernici, and P. Plebani. A design-time data-centric maturity model for assessing resilience in multi-party business processes. *Information Systems*, 2018.
5. A. Marrella, M. Mecella, and S. Sardiña. Supporting adaptiveness of cyber-physical processes through action-based formalisms. *AI Commun.*, 31(1):47–74, 2018.
6. M. P. Papazoglou. Smart connected digital factories - unleashing the power of industry 4.0 and the industrial internet. In *Proc. of CLOSER*, pages 260–271, 2018.
7. F. Zezulka, P. Marcon, I. Vesely, and O. Sajdl. Industry 4.0–an introduction in the phenomenon. *IFAC-PapersOnLine*, 49(25):8–12, 2016.

Entity Resolution and Data Fusion: an integrated approach (DISCUSSION PAPER)

Domenico Beneventano[1], Sonia Bergamaschi[1], Luca Gagliardelli[1], and Giovanni Simonini[2]

[1] University of Modena and Reggio Emilia, Modena, Italy
name.surname@unimore.it
[2] MIT CSAIL, Cambridge, MA, USA
giovanni@csail.mit.edu

Abstract. *Entity Resolution* and *Data Fusion* are fundamental tasks in a Data Integration process. Unfortunately, these tasks cannot be completely addressed by purely automated methods and, then, a "human-in-the-loop" approach, i.e., the interaction with the Integration Designer has to be considered. In fact, the application goal can be relevant to reduce the complexity and the cost of the whole integration process. Moreover, the Entity Resolution and Data Fusion tasks are often considered consecutive and independent of each other: the output of the first step is used as input of the second one.
In this paper, we will show how these tasks have not to be considered independent. In fact, the evaluation of data fusion results is fundamental for the Integration Designer to analyze, and eventually modify, the choices made during the Entity Resolution process. To show this, our highly scalable Entity Resolution tool, `SparkER`, will be extended with post-processing high-quality methods for matching. These methods will be integrated in the MOMIS Data Fusion system, extended as well with metrics for the evaluation of data fusion results.

Keywords: Data Integration · Entity Resolution · Data Fusion

1 Introduction

Data Integration is the problem of combining data residing at different autonomous sources, and providing the user with a unified view of these data. MOMIS (Mediator EnvirOnment for Multiple Information Sources) is an open source Data Integration System [3], characterized by a classical wrapper/mediator architecture, where the local data sources contain the real data, while a Global

Virtual Schema (GVS) provides a reconciled, integrated, and virtual view of the underlying data sources. In particular, MOMIS performs *Data Fusion*, i.e., the process of fusing multiple records representing the same real-world object into a single, consistent, and clean representation; to perform data fusion, several *conflict handling strategies* introduced in [7] are available in the MOMIS system (see section 2.2). As described in several papers MOMIS adopts a semi-automatic approach that retains the "human in the loop" where algorithms and tools are used to assist the Integration Designer performing the Data Fusion task [4, 17].

In the current MOMIS version, the Data Fusion process assumes that *Entity Resolution* (ER) has been already performed and thus a shared object identifier (ID) exists among different sources; in other words, the current version of MOMIS only implements an *exact match*. Multiple records with the same ID are fused by means of the Full Join Merge operator [4].

On 2016, we faced and solved the Entity Resolution problem by developing a set of novel techniques [1, 5, 12, 13, 15, 16]. In particular, we proposed `Blast` [13] (Blocking with Loosely-Aware Schema Techniques), an approach to reduce the ER complexity with indexing techniques aiming to group similar records in blocks and limit the comparison to only those records appearing in the same block. This approach was implemented in `SparkER` [9, 14], a highly scalable Entity Resolution tool designed to be parallelizable on Apache Spark. As highlighted in a very recent demo of `SparkER` [10], the Entity Resolution process can be improved by including the "human-in-the-loop".

On the other hand, the Entity Resolution and Data Fusion steps are often considered consecutive and independent of each other: the output of the first step is used as input of the second one in Data Integration systems. In this paper we will show how these tasks have not to be considered independent. In fact, the evaluation of data fusion results is fundamental for the Integration Designer to analyze, and eventually modify, the choices made during the Entity Resolution process.

In detail, the main contributions of this paper are the following:

- `SparkER` will be extended with post-processing methods to obtain one-to-one matching; such extended `SparkER` will be integrated in the MOMIS framework: the output will be used as input in the MOMIS Data Fusion system;
- `MomisDF`, the module of the MOMIS system which performs Data Fusion, will be extended as well with methods for the evaluation of data fusion results;
- We will show, by an example, how the evaluation of data fusion results can be used by the Integration Designer.

The complete `SparkER-MomisDF` workflow is shown in Figure 1. `SparkER` is composed by two main modules: (i) **blocker**: takes the input records and performs the blocking phase, providing as output the candidate pairs; (ii) **Entity matcher** takes the candidate pairs generated by the blocker and label them as match or no match by comparing pair's similarity with a threshold, so producing a `Match Table` of similar records with their similarity score. The **1-1 Matching** module take as input such `Match Table`, which may contain

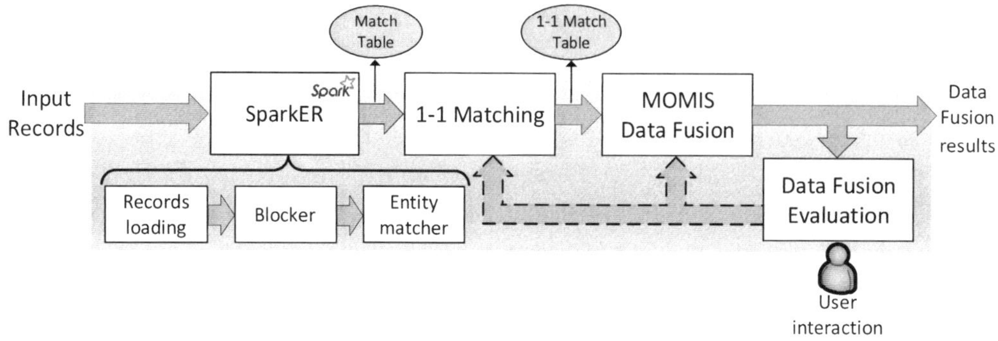

Fig. 1. The `SparkER-MomisDF` workflow

many-to-many matching, and returns a `1-1 Match Table` with only *one-to-one* matching. `MomisDF` performs data fusion of the input records, on the basis of the `1-1 Match Table`.

The structure of the paper is the following. Section 2 contains some preliminaries from literature which we use in our paper. Section 3 shows, by means of an example covering the whole `SparkER-MomisDF` workflow, how the evaluation of fusion results can be useful for the Integration Designer.

2 Preliminaries

This section contains some preliminaries from literature which we use in our paper. Section 2.1 introduces the post-processing methods for one-to-one matching proposed in [8]; section 2.2 introduces the methods for the evaluation of data fusion results proposed in [7].

2.1 Post-processing Methods for one-to-one Matching

As stated in [8] assuming de-duplicated sources, each record can at most match to one record of another source; hence, the matching result should exclusively contain *one-to-one* links as otherwise precision is deteriorated; in other words, in the most common two-source case, it is often desirable for the final matching to be one-to-one [18]. On the other hand, Most ER methods, and in particular, the ones using threshold-based techniques, as `SparkER`, often produce multi-links, i.e., one record is matched to many records of another source. For this reason, the authors of [8] proposed methods that can be executed after any entity resolution process to clean multi-links, i.e., to transform the result such that only *one-to-one* matching occurs in the final result. The following three post-processing strategies are analyzed and implemented in [8]:

- *Symmetric Best Match* (*Max1-both*): the basic idea is that for every record only the best matching record of the other source is accepted.
- *Maximum Weight matching* (MWM): a MWM is a matching that has maximum weight, i.e., that maximizes the sum of the overall similarities between records in the final linkage result.

- *Stable Marriage* (SM): a matching is defined as stable, if there are no two records of the different local classes who both have a higher similarity to each other than to their current matching record.

In [8] a complete evaluation of the different post-processing methods is performed by using both synthetic and real datasets. The linkage quality is assessed by *recall* and *precision*: recall measures the proportion of true-matches that have been correctly classified as matches after the linkage process; precision is defined as the fraction of classified matches that are true-matches. The aim of post-processing is to optimize precision while recall is ideally preserved. The result of the evaluation performed in [8] was that both *Max1-both* and *SM* are able to significantly improve the linkage quality; in general, *Max1-both* can achieve the best linkage quality in terms of precision; for applications favoring recall over precision, a *SM* should be applied.

2.2 Data Fusion Evaluation

To perform data fusion, several *conflict handling strategies* defined in [7] are available in the MOMIS system; in particular, the following strategies:

S1 *Take the information*: prefers values over null values;
S2 *Consider all possibilities*: creates all possible value combinations.

These strategies are implemented as default, i.e., before the intervention of the Designer, that can also apply some *Resolution Strategies* choosing by the *Conflict Resolution Functions* implemented in `MomisDF`, such as, takes an average value and takes the most recent value. The authors of [7] also propose methods for the evaluation of data fusion based on measures of quality of source data, such as *completeness* and *consistency*; for example, the (extensional) completeness is $\mid$ *unique objects in dataset* $\mid / \mid$ *unique objects in universe* $\mid$.
Instead of quality of data sources, we want to evaluate quality of fused data, then we reformulate such measures in terms of the *Global Class* (GC) resulting from the data fusion process (see next section for an example), by considering the following *Data Centric* Evaluation Measures[3]:

- **Density**: measures the fraction of non-NULL values.
  The density of a *Global Attribute* GA in GC is defined as

$$Density_{GA} = \frac{\mid non\text{-}NULL\ values\ in\ GA \mid}{\mid records\ in\ GC \mid}$$

  The density of the whole global class GC is defined as

$$Density_{CG} = \frac{\mid non\text{-}NULL\ values\ in\ GC \mid}{\mid attributes\ in\ GC \mid * \mid records\ in\ GC \mid}$$

[3] Such measures are also introduced in [6]. In our evaluation, the number of objects in the universe is identified with the number of unique entities in the fused data source, and then with the records of the Global Class GC.

– **Consistency**: a data set is consistent if it is free of conflicting information. The consistency of a *Global Attribute* GA in GC is defined as

$$Consistency_{GA} = \frac{|\ non\text{-}conflicting\ values\ in\ GA\ |}{|\ records\ in\ GC\ |}$$

The consistency of the whole global class GC is defined as

$$Consistency_{GC} = \frac{|\ non\text{-}conflicting\ values\ in\ GC\ |}{|\ attributes\ in\ GC\ | * |\ records\ in\ GC\ |}$$

In a similar way, in [11] the concept of *F-quality* is introduced as a measure of quality of fused data rather than source data and two novel algorithms for Linked Data fusion with provenance tracking and quality assessment of fused data are proposed.

Our goal is different, we want to discuss how the evaluation of data fusion results can be used by the Integration Designer to analyze, and eventually modify, the choices made during the Entity Resolution process, to improve the final result. For these reasons, we only consider simple and common conflict handling strategies (i.e. **S1** and **S2**) and the straightforward evaluation defined above.

3 Example and Discussion

This section shows, by means of an example covering the whole SparkER-MOMIS workflow, how the evaluation of fusion results can be useful for the Integration Designer; in particular, this example will show how the evaluation of data fusion results changes by varying the post-processing 1-1 matching method.

We consider two local classes L and R and a global class GC with the same attributes: Surname (S), Name (N), City, Age and Salary (i.e, we assume that the *schema matching* and *global schema generation* phases have already been carried out with the MOMIS framework); moreover L and R have a local ID. An instance of L and R is shown in Figure 2(a).

Let us first consider the simplest case: all the attributes are used to perform Entity Resolution. The ER process performed with `SparkER` (see [10] for a detailed description of the tool) produces the *Match Table* shown in Figure 2(b). Note that the match table provides the pair of local identifiers of each record and their similarity, and that the obtained matching is *many-to-many* (e.g. L1 matches with R1, R2). Now it is possible to apply the three post-processing methods discussed in section 2.1 to obtain a *one-to-one* matching: each of these methods produces a *1-1 Match Table* as shown in Figure 2(b2) (a ✓denotes that the pair is in the *1-1 Match Table*).

Each *1-1 Match Table* is then used to perform Data Fusion; intuitively, two sequential operations are performed:

1. the natural outer join is performed:
   $$Local\ Class\ L ⟗ 1\text{-}1\ Match\ Table ⟕ Local\ Class\ R$$

Local Class L

L_ID	LS	LN	L_CITY	L_AGE	L_SALARY
L1	William	Charlie	NULL	29	NULL
L2	William	Ciarlye	Canton	27	155

Local Class R

R_ID	RS	RN	R_CITY	R_AGE	R_SALARY
R1	Wiliam	Charli	Canyon	28	NULL
R2	Wiliam	Charli	NULL	44	138
R3	Vylian	Carl	Canton	NULL	158

(a) Local Sources

SparkER

Match Table

L_ID	R_ID	sim
L1	R1	0.91
L1	R2	0.86
L2	R1	0.81
L2	R3	0.69

(b1) Match Table

1-1 Match Table

Max1-both	SM	MWM
✓	✓	
		✓
		✓
	✓	

(b2) 1-1 Match Tables

Max1-both

PROV	CITY	AGE	SALARY
L1-R1	Canyon	*{29,28}*	NULL
L2	Canton	27	155
R2	NULL	44	138
R3	Canton	NULL	158

SM

PROV	CITY	AGE	SALARY
L1-R1	Canyon	*{29,28}*	NULL
L2-R3	Canton	27	*{155,158}*
R2	NULL	44	138

MWM

PROV	CITY	AGE	SALARY
L1-R2	NULL	*{29,44}*	138
L2-R1	{Canton, Canyon}	*{27,28}*	155
R3	Canton	NULL	158

(c) Data Fusion result (Global Class Instance)

	Max1-both			SM			MWM		
	CITY	AGE	SALARY	CITY	AGE	SALARY	CITY	AGE	SALARY
Column density	3/4	3/4	3/4	2/3	3/3	2/3	2/3	2/3	3/3
Column consistency	4/4	3/4	4/4	3/3	2/3	2/3	2/3	1/3	3/3
Table density	9/12			7/9			7/9		
Table consistency	11/12			7/9			6/9		

(d) Data Fusion metrics

Fig. 2. The SparkER-MomisDF workflow example

2. the *S1* and *S2* strategies (see Section 2.2) are applied to all the conflicting attributes involved in the Data Fusion process.

For example, the *Max1-Both* Match Table contains only the pair $(L1, R1)$ and only such two local records are fused together so obtaining the first record in the *Max1-Both* Global Class shown in Figure 2(c), where the *PROV* attribute represents the *data provenance* [2], i.e., intuitively, the input local records that contributed to the output global record. Conflicting values obtained by the *S2* strategy are highlighted in yellow. With the other *1-1 Match Tables*, different global class are obtained, as shown in Figure 2(c). Finally, the Integration Designer chooses which attributes to use in the evaluation phase; in our example, suppose they are City, Age and Salary. The Data Fusion evaluation, with the measures density and consistency is shown in Figure 2(d).

In this preliminary work, we have not yet achieved results on significant and real cases. However, some considerations can also be made about the (toy) example. First of all, *Max1-both* achieves the best match quality in terms of column and table consistency. This is consistent with the conclusion reached in [8] that, in general, *Max1-both* can achieve the best linkage quality in terms of precision. On the other hand, it is easy to verify that to increase column and table density, *SM* or *MWM* should be applied, with the obvious consequence that these methods deteriorate column and table consistency. For these reasons, we believe it is important to give the designer the opportunity to analyze and choose the best method. For example, in a context where the Salary attribute has greater importance, the best choice is the *MWM* method that maximizes both density and consistency for such attribute.

In this example we only discussed evaluation of data fusion results to varying of the post-processing 1-1 matching method. On the other hand, it will also be interesting to evaluate the results of the data fusion correspond to the changes in the configurations sparker (and therefore in the different Match Tables produced). In fact, as discussed in [10], the `SparkER` tool can work both in a completely unsupervised mode and in a supervised one. In the first case, the Integration Designer can use a default configuration and perform the process on its data without taking care of the parameters tuning. In the second case, she/he can supervise the entire process, in order to determine which are the best parameters for her/his data, thus producing a custom configuration.

4 Conclusions and future work

We discussed some preliminary ideas about an integrated approach for entity resolution and data fusion. We showed, by an example, how the evaluation of data fusion results can be used by the Integration Designer to analyze, and eventually modify, the choices made during the Entity Resolution process.

As future work, we will perform a complete evaluation of data fusion results with respect to the different post-processing methods, both using real datasets and with other evaluation measures. Another future work is to extend the data fusion evaluation to *Conflict Resolution* Functions, by considering *Ground Truth Based Evaluation* measures, such as the Accuracy, in order to evaluate the fraction of correct values selected by conflict resolution functions chosen by the Integration Designer.

References

1. Benedetti, F., Beneventano, D., Bergamaschi, S., Simonini, G.: Computing inter-document similarity with context semantic analysis. Information Systems **80**, 136–147 (2019). https://doi.org/10.1016/j.is.2018.02.009
2. Beneventano, D., Bergamaschi, S.: Provenance-aware semantic search engines based on data integration systems. Inter. J. of Organizational and Collective Intelligence (IJOCI) **4**(2), 1–30 (Apr 2014). https://doi.org/10.4018/ijoci.2014040101
3. Bergamaschi, S., Beneventano, D., Corni, A., Kazazi, E., Orsini, M., Po, L., Sorrentino, S.: The open source release of the MOMIS data integration system. In: Nineteenth Italian Symposium on Advanced Database Systems (SEBD). pp. 175–186 (2011)
4. Bergamaschi, S., Beneventano, D., Guerra, F., Orsini, M.: Data integration. In: Handbook of Conceptual Modeling - Theory, Practice, and Research Challenges, pp. 441–476. Springer (2011)
5. Bergamaschi, S., Ferrari, D., Guerra, F., Simonini, G., Velegrakis, Y.: Providing insight into data source topics. J. Data Semantics **5**(4), 211–228 (2016). https://doi.org/10.1007/s13740-016-0063-6

6. Bizer, C.: Data quality assessment and data fusion. University Lecture (2018)
7. Bleiholder, J., Naumann, F.: Data fusion. ACM Comput. Surv. **41**(1), 1:1–1:41 (Jan 2009). https://doi.org/10.1145/1456650.1456651
8. Franke, M., Sehili, Z., Gladbach, M., Rahm, E.: Post-processing methods for high quality privacy-preserving record linkage. In: Data Privacy Management, Cryptocurrencies and Blockchain Technology - ESORICS 2018 International Workshops, Barcelona, Spain, September 6-7, 2018, Proceedings. pp. 263–278 (2018)
9. Gagliardelli, L., Zhu, S., Simonini, G., Bergamaschi, S.: Bigdedup: a big data integration toolkit for duplicate detection in industrial scenarios. In: Transdisciplinary Engineering. vol. 7, pp. 1015–1023 (2018)
10. Gagliardelli, L., Simonini, G., Beneventano, D., Bergamaschi, S.: Sparker: Scaling entity resolution in spark. In: Proceedings of the Workshops of the EDBT/ICDT 2019 Joint Conference (EDBT/ICDT), Lisbon, Portugal (2019)
11. Michelfeit, J., Knap, T., Necaský, M.: Linked data integration with conflicts. CoRR **abs/1410.7990** (2014), http://arxiv.org/abs/1410.7990
12. Simonini, G., Bergamaschi, S.: Enhancing entity resolution efficiency with loosely schema-aware techniques. In: 24th Italian Symposium on Advanced Database Systems, SEBD 2016, Ugento, Lecce, Italy, June 19-22, 2016, Ugento, Lecce, Italia, June 19-22, 2016. pp. 270–277 (2016)
13. Simonini, G., Bergamaschi, S., Jagadish, H.V.: BLAST: a loosely schema-aware meta-blocking approach for entity resolution. PVLDB **9**(12), 1173–1184 (2016), http://www.vldb.org/pvldb/vol9/p1173-simonini.pdf
14. Simonini, G., Gagliardelli, L., Bergamaschi, S., Jagadish, H.V.: Scaling entity resolution: A loosely schema-aware approach. Inf. Syst. **83**, 145–165 (2019). https://doi.org/10.1016/j.is.2019.03.006
15. Simonini, G., Papadakis, G., Palpanas, T., Bergamaschi, S.: Schema-agnostic progressive entity resolution. In: 34th IEEE International Conference on Data Engineering, ICDE 2018, Paris, France, April 16-19, 2018. pp. 53–64. IEEE Computer Society (2018). https://doi.org/10.1109/ICDE.2018.00015
16. Simonini, G., Papadakis, G., Palpanas, T., Bergamaschi, S.: Schema-agnostic progressive entity resolution. IEEE Trans. Knowl. Data Eng. **31**(6), 1208–1221 (2019). https://doi.org/10.1109/TKDE.2018.2852763
17. Vincini, M., Beneventano, D., Bergamaschi, S.: Semantic integration of heterogeneous data sources in the MOMIS data transformation system. J. UCS **19**(13), 1986–2012 (2013). https://doi.org/10.3217/jucs-019-13-1986
18. Zhang, D., Rubinstein, B.I.P., Gemmell, J.: Principled graph matching algorithms for integrating multiple data sources. IEEE Trans. on Knowl. and Data Eng. **27**(10), 2784–2796 (Oct 2015). https://doi.org/10.1109/TKDE.2015.2426714

Using a Smart City Ontology to support Personalised Exploration of Urban Data (Discussion Paper)

Devis Bianchini[1], Valeria De Antonellis[1], Massimiliano Garda[1], and Michele Melchiori[1]

University of Brescia, Dept. of Information Engineering
Via Branze 38, 25123 - Brescia (Italy)
devis.bianchini@unibs.it, valeria.deantonellis@unibs.it,
m.garda001@unibs.it, michele.melchiori@unibs.it

Abstract. During the latest years, Smart City projects aimed at driving local governments towards the strong use of technologies to support a higher quality of urban spaces and a better offering of public services. From an information viewpoint, this means enabling different categories of users, including citizens, Public Administration (PA), utility and energy providers, to access the large amounts of data in multiple, heterogeneous Smart City data sources, by adopting new tools and methods to take decisions that might improve city daily life. Aggregation of urban data according to multiple perspectives through the definition of proper indicators enables urban data exploration at different granularity levels for distinct categories of users. Furthermore, Semantic Web technologies may be used to enable interoperability and improve data access. In this paper, we propose a Smart Living Ontology, to provide a semantic-enriched representation of city indicators. On top of the ontology and users' characterisation, a Semantic Layer has been designed to enable personalised access to urban data.

Keywords: urban data exploration, semantic web, smart city ontology

1 Introduction

Smart City projects aim at driving local governments towards the strong use of technologies to support a higher quality of urban spaces and public services [1–3]. From an information viewpoint, different categories of users, including citizens, Public Administration (PA), utility and energy providers, must explore the large amounts of data from multiple, heterogeneous data sources, in order to take decisions that might improve city daily life. In recent research, Semantic Web technologies have been proposed to develop ontology-enabled applications, such as Smart Urban Cockpits and dashboards [8, 10], where proper indicators have been semantically described [6]. Indicators aggregate urban data according to several perspectives and provide a comprehensive view over underlying data without being overwhelmed by the data volume [7].

In this paper, we propose a semantics-enabled framework, which relies on the so-called Smart Living Ontology, to provide a semantic representation of Smart City indicators. The framework also includes the kinds of activities and users' categories for which indicators have been designed to share relevant information. A Semantic Layer, developed on top of the ontology, enables personalised exploration of urban data. The framework has been designed for decision makers, who need to have a view on heterogeneous urban data at different aggregation levels, ranging from energy consumption to garbage collection, pollution levels, citizens' safety. For example, the framework may allow building managers to monitor electrical consumption of administered buildings, by exploiting the indicators hierarchy in the ontology to distinguish electrical consumption according to different perspectives (e.g., consumption in common spaces, consumption of elevators), and to compare average values of consumption with other buildings at district or city level. Furthermore, the framework may enable citizens to make decisions about their activities by observing specific indicators (e.g., to avoid sport activities when pollution levels overtake tolerance thresholds).

This work was performed in the context of the Brescia Smart Living (BSL) Italian project[1], which promotes a holistic view of the city, where different types of data are explored to provide new services to both citizens and PA. The framework has been already presented in [5], where more details about the Smart Living Ontology and the implementation have been described.

This paper is organised as follows: in Section 2 we highlight the cutting-edge features of our approach compared to the literature; in Section 3, motivations are presented; Section 4 presents the Smart Living Ontology; Section 5 describes the Semantic Layer of the framework; in Section 6 we discuss implementation details and preliminary validation; finally, Section 7 closes the paper.

2 Related Work

In literature, the adoption of ontologies in Smart City projects targets *energy management*, where diagnostic models are built to discover energetic losses [11] or to perform optimisation for cost saving [3]; *facility discovery*, to search for city facilities and services [2]; *events monitoring and management* [1]; *Ontology-Based Data Access* (please refer to [12] for a survey and related flagship research projects), to cope with heterogeneous data sources inside the Smart City [4].

With respect to an OBDA perspective, our objective is to focus on data exploration by exploiting a semantic characterisation of Smart City indicators, also considering users' category and activities for which indicators have been

[1] `http://www.bresciasmartliving.eu`

designed. The semantic modelling we pursue also reinforces the characteristics of the BSL project, that if compared to other Smart City projects [1–3] provides a wider spectrum of urban data. Approaches focused on Ontology-Based Data Warehouses (OBDW) store analytical data, indicators, requirements and their semantics [10] or provide a semantic description of metrics used to compute indicators [6], in order to enable meaningful comparison among different aggregated measures. Differently from the aforementioned solutions, our approach is focused on the exploitation of indicators hierarchies and dimensional modelling to guide exploration of aggregated data for multiple categories of users, introducing a semantic relationship between users' profiles and indicators to foster personalised urban data exploration.

3 Motivating scenario

As a motivating example, let's consider John, the manager of several buildings located in different districts of the Smart City. John monitors the electrical consumption of the buildings, in order to implement energy saving policies (e.g., introducing LED lamps in common areas or planning renovation work to increase the energy efficiency class of buildings). Challenging issues are related to the capability of enabling John to fruitfully exploit available information. In this paper, we address such issues as follows.

Semantic specification of city indicators. Indicators are commonly defined to aggregate data according to several dimensions, for different categories of users (e.g., consumption-based indicator of electrical energy use). In our framework, the Smart Living Ontology is defined to provide semantic specification of the indicators, that takes into account indicators scope, in terms of spatial and temporal constraints, their hierarchical organisation and target users.

Personalised data exploration. Given the variety of urban data that can be explored, the selection of proper indicators is personalised taking into account users' profiles, composed of user's category, activities and preferential indicators.

Indicators recommendation to support decision making. Indicators recommendation is provided in order to help users to take decisions in their daily life. For example, John is provided with suggestions about indicators on electrical consumption of the administered buildings. To this aim, indicators scope and hierarchy, as well as filtering based on activities for which the indicators have been designed, are exploited to better focus the exploration.

4 The Smart Living Ontology

Figure 1 reports the main concepts and relationships of the Smart Living Ontology (SLO[2]). In order to face the heterogeneity and complexity of the Smart City

[2] The TBox of the ontology can be found at `https://tinyurl.com/onto-schema` (a free Web Protégé account is required)

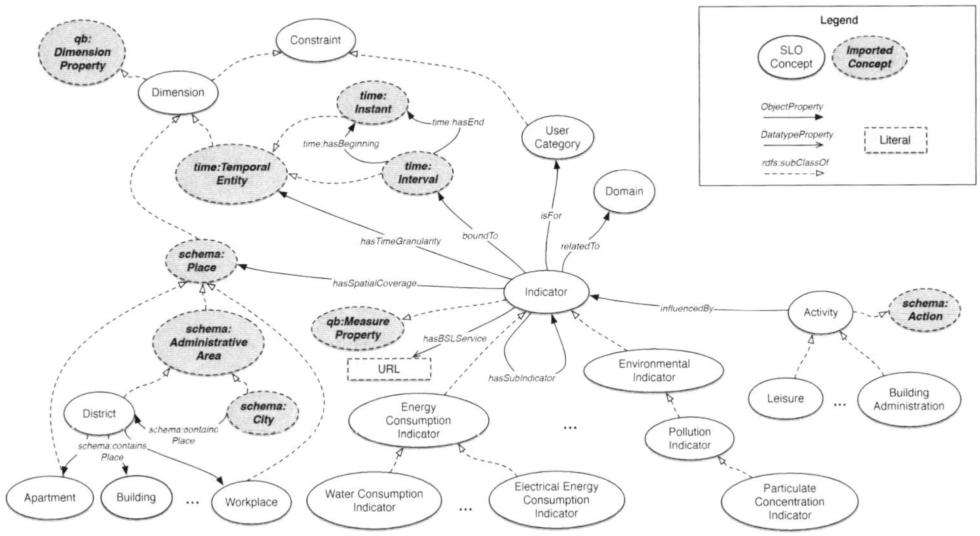

Fig. 1. A portion of the Smart Living Ontology (SLO).

domain, we rely on some foundation ontologies to cover a set of required pivotal concepts: (i) a geospatial mapping of the main structures of the city (e.g., buildings, streets, areas) and their topology; (ii) temporal entities; (iii) other high level concepts, that have been specialised to define the hierarchy of indicators and activities.

Indicators are specified as individuals of the `Indicator` concept or one of its sub-concepts in the indicators hierarchy. An indicator is further `relatedTo` a set of domain individuals (e.g., environment, safety, energy, mobility) to define the indicator scope, and a set of constraints. As shown in Figure 1, in the SLO a constraint can be either a dimension (time and space) or a user's category (e.g., building manager). Specifically, an indicator can be `boundTo` a time interval (e.g., values of electrical consumption available for the year 2017), may have a time granularity (`hasTimeGranularity` relationship), may be defined at city, street, district or more specific levels, such as buildings (`hasSpatialCoverage` relationship). Finally, knowledge about an indicator can be useful to perform specific activities, defined as individuals of the concept `Activity` or its sub-concepts (`influencedBy` property). An indicator is linked to a web-based service of the BSL Platform (`hasBSLService` property) to display the indicator values on the Smart City Dashboard, as explained in Section 6.

BSL users are profiled according to their category, their activities, the types of indicators explored by the user through the interactions with the framework. In the next section we detail how personalised exploration of indicators is performed based on the SLO, with the help of the motivating example.

5 Semantic Layer for Personalised Data Exploration

Personalised data exploration for each user can be achieved by effectively exploiting city indicators, properly selected according to the indicators domains, constraints and profiles of users. Figure 2 reports the steps for semantics-enabled data exploration and the I/O for each step.

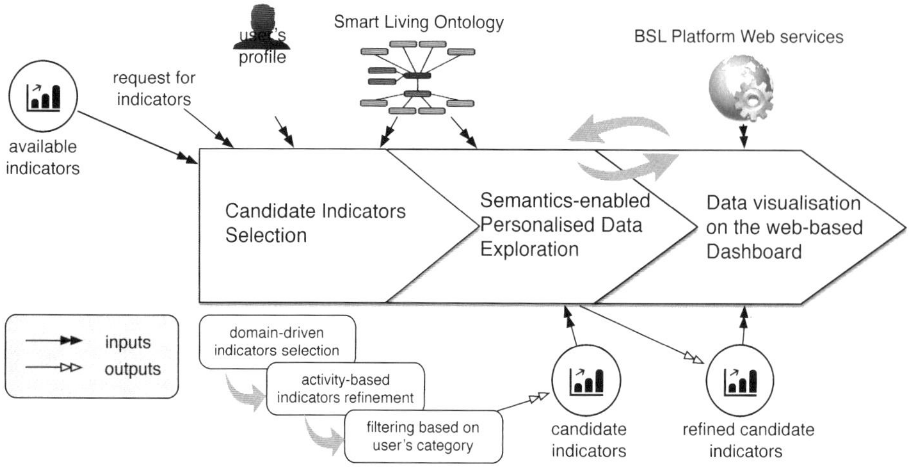

Fig. 2. The steps of semantics-enabled data exploration.

For example, let's consider again the user John in the motivating example, who is the manager of three buildings (namely `Building 1`, `Building 2` and `Building 3`) located in two districts of the city. Since John is usually interested in monitoring buildings, during the registration to the BSL platform, he specifies the activity `Monitoring` in his profile, jointly with his administered buildings, associating them to the districts they are located in.

Candidate indicators selection. In order to have an insight on the status of the buildings, for instance to evaluate whether replacing standard lamps with less energy-demanding LED ones, John issues a request to the framework. To support John in the request formulation, without requiring a detailed knowledge of ontology concepts and individuals, the framework enables him to specify a set of keywords K_r = {`energy`, `consumption`}, processed according to techniques aimed to match the keywords with ontology terms [9] (precisely, individuals of `Domain` and `Indicator` concepts or sub-concepts). The platform processes the request and returns, among the others, the indicator `NormalizedElectrical-EnergyConsumption (NEEC)`, which reports electrical consumption normalised with the number of apartments in the building. The indicator is selected because it is compliant with the keywords given in the request (domain-driven indicators selection), it is associated with the activity `Monitoring` in the ontology (activity-based indicators refinement) and it is compliant with the building manager category (filtering based on user's category). User's exploration history (in terms of formerly inspected indicators) is traced and it is taken into account during indicators suggestion, as it can be exploited to assess the degree of compliance between proposed indicators and user's past exploration preferences. Figure 3 reports the portion of the SLO containing the candidate indicators.

Semantics-enabled personalised data exploration. Starting from `NEEC` indicator (Figure 3), John can further explore other indicators being guided by the semantic relationships in the SLO. Exploration can be performed: (a) over the indicators hierarchy and/or (b) over the indicators dimensions. In the former, John selects the `NEEC` indicator and the framework suggests him more specific indicators (following the `hasSubIndicator` relationship). Exploration over the

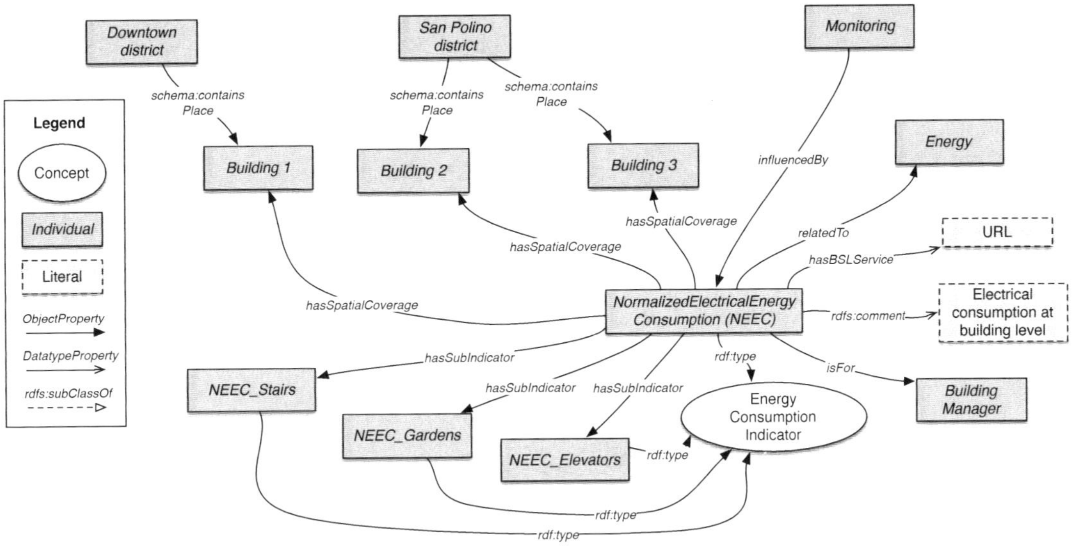

Fig. 3. Example of candidate indicator and related properties.

indicators dimensions exploits both the knowledge on the spatial coverage of indicators and the information stored in the user's profile. Starting from indicators previously selected for the John's building, the containment relationship that relates John's buildings with districts is exploited. Therefore, John could compare his buildings against others having similar characteristics or using different lighting solutions; this may stimulate John to consider the replacement of energy consuming light bulbs with modern LED lamps in shared spaces.

6 Implementation and Preliminary Validation

Figure 4 shows the web-based architecture of the semantics-enabled data exploration framework. The architecture is organised over three layers. Data on field, collected from domain-specific platforms through IoT technologies, as well as data from external sources (e.g., weather and pollution data), are loaded into the BSL platform (*BSL platform Layer*). Data is transferred to the BSL platform using RESTful services, SOAP-based services and MQTT Agents. Data is aggregated into smart city indicators, which are semantically specified in the *Semantic Layer*. The *User Access Layer* includes a web-based Smart City Dashboard to be used by citizens, PA and other users to explore data and take decisions (see [5] for more details). Using the web browser, users can register themselves and update their profile. The framework is implemented in Java and deployed under the Apache TomEE application server. The Smart Living Ontology is deployed in OWL using the Stardog[3] Triplestore. The Stardog module supports domain experts to maintain the ontology (concepts, relations and individuals), interacting with the web-based administration console provided by the module.

Preliminary experiments on the proposed framework, aimed at demonstrating its effectiveness in supporting candidate indicators selection, have been conducted considering a SLO composed of 57 concepts (among them, 30 indicators), 104 individuals, 207 object and datatype properties.

[3] `https://www.stardog.com/`

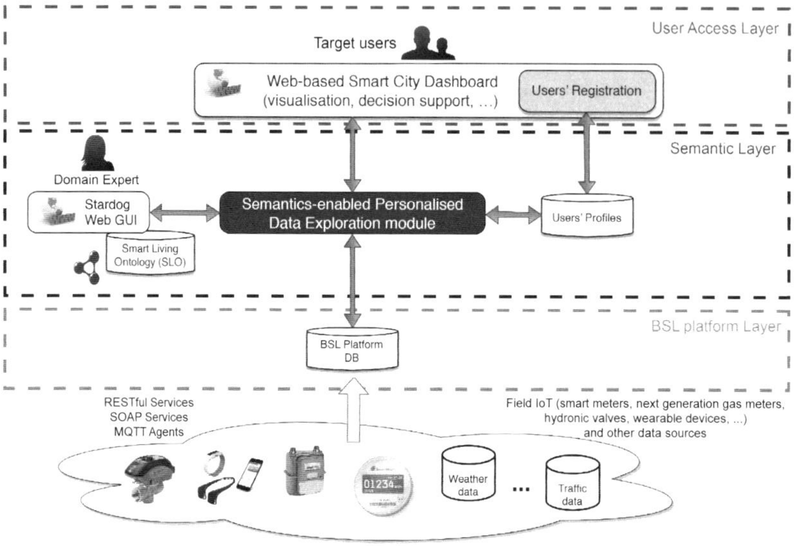

Fig. 4. Web-based architecture of the semantics-enabled data exploration framework.

We considered two kinds of requests: (A) requests where the user specified a set of keywords K_r in order to identify desired domains and indicators, and the user's profile does not contain any activity or preferential indicator; (B) requests where the user presents a richer profile (containing category, activities and preferential indicators), but specifies keywords in K_r, that only correspond to individuals of the `Domain` concept. We compared our ontology-based approach against a keyword-based search, where semantic disambiguation techniques have been applied to K_r [9], but SLO semantic relationships have not been exploited. Average precision and recall values for the keyword-based search are equal to 0.49 and 0.97 for type A (0.33 and 0.27 for type B, resp.), whereas for the ontology-based search they are equal to 0.99 and 0.98 for type A (0.94 and 0.93 for type B, resp.). Candidate indicators selection average execution time for type A is about 2559 ms, whereas for type B is about 1325 ms. Since both the compared approaches use keywords disambiguation techniques and the same keywords have been used during tests, difference in average precision and recall is due to the knowledge structure in the ontology. Usability tests are being performed to check the capability of the framework in facilitating user's access to urban data through the suggestion of candidate indicators. To perform usability tests, we considered metrics such as the number of exploration steps needed to obtain desired data, number of fails, number of successful explorations. Currently, the framework is being tested, with satisfaction, by a sample of users in two districts, a modern one, where new generation smart meters have been installed, and a district in city downtown, more densely populated and presenting older buildings. Usability experiments are being carried on within the Brescia Smart Living project until September 2019.

7 Conclusions

In this paper, we described a semantics-enabled framework composed of: (i) a so-called Smart Living Ontology, apt to provide a flexible representation of Smart City indicators; (ii) a Semantic Layer, to enable personalised exploration of urban data for different categories of users. The framework has been already presented in [5], where more details about the Smart Living Ontology and the implementation have been described. Ontologies represent knowledge structure that can be used to facilitate urban data exploration at different granularity levels and according to different exploration perspectives. Future effort will be devoted to extend the set of semantic relationships in the SLO as follows: (a) further relationships between indicators will be identified (e.g., to assert that two or more environmental indicators must be jointly monitored due to their harmful impact on the ecosystem); (b) strategies to dispense useful recommendations for promoting the users' virtuous behaviours, providing advice for healthy activities that should be practised by users.

References

1. The Res Novae project. `http://resnovae-unical.eu`.
2. The San Francisco Park project. `http://sfpark.org`.
3. The BESOS project. Building Energy decision Support systems fOr Smart cities. `http://besos-project.eu`.
4. Bellini, P., Benigni, M., Billero, R., Nesi, P., Rauch, N.: Km4city ontology building vs data harvesting and cleaning for smart-city services. Journal of Visual Languages & Computing 25(6), 827 – 839 (2014)
5. Bianchini, D., De Antonellis, V., Garda, M., Melchiori, M.: Semantics-enabled personalised urban data exploration. In: Proc. of the 19th International Conference on Web Information Systems Engineering (WISE 2018). pp. 361–376 (2018)
6. Diamantini, C., Potena, D., Storti, E.: Comparison of City Performances Through Statistical Linked Data Exploration. In: Proc. of the 2nd International Conference on ICT Infrastructures and Services for Smart Cities (IISSC 2017). pp. 3–12 (2017)
7. Lanza, J., Sotres, P., Sánchez, L., Galache, J., Santana, J., Gutiérrez, V., Munoz, L.: Managing large amount of data generated by a smart city internet of things deployment. International Journal on Semantic Web and Information Systems 12(4), 22–42 (2016)
8. Psyllidis, A.: Ontology-Based Data Integration from Heterogeneous Urban Systems: A Knowledge Representation Framework for Smart Cities. In: Proc. of the 14th International Conference on Computers in Urban Planning and Urban Management (CUPUM 2014) (2015)
9. Royo, J.A., Mena, E., Bernad, J., Illarramendi, A.: Searching the web: From keywords to semantic queries. In: Third Int. Conf. on Information Technology and Applications (ICITA 2005). pp. 244–249 (2005)
10. Santos, H., Dantas, V., Furtado, V., Pinheiro, P., McGuinness, D.L.: From data to city indicators: A knowledge graph for supporting automatic generation of dashboards. In: Proc. of the 14th European Semantic Web Conference (ESWC 2017). Lecture Notes in Computer Science, vol. 10250, pp. 94–108 (2017)
11. Tomašević, N.M., Batić, M.v., Blanes, L.M., Keane, M.M., Vraneš, S.: Ontology-based facility data model for energy management. Adv. Eng. Inform. 29(4), 971–984 (2015)
12. Xiao, G., Calvanese, D., Kontchakov, R., Lembo, D., Poggi, A., Rosati, R., Zakharyaschev, M.: Ontology-based Data Access: A survey. In: Proc. of the 27th International Joint Conference on Artificial Intelligence (IJCAI 2018). pp. 5511–5519 (2018)

A formal theory to determine scale properties of evaluation measures*

Marco Ferrante[1], Nicola Ferro[2], and Silvia Pontarollo[1]

[1] Department of Mathematics, University of Padua, Italy
{ferrante, spontaro}@math.unipd.it
[2] Department of Information Engineering, University of Padua, Italy
ferro@dei.unipd.it

Abstract. Evaluation measures are the basis for quantifying the performance of information access systems and the way in which their values can be processed to perform statistical analyses depends on the scales on which these measures are defined. For example, mean and variance should be computed only when relying on interval scales.
We define a formal theory of evaluation measures, based on the representational theory of measurement, which allows us to determine whether and when measures are interval scales. We found that common set- based retrieval measures – namely Precision, Recall, and F-measure – always are interval scales in the case of binary relevance while this does not happen in the multi-graded relevance case. In the case of rank-based retrieval measures – namely AP, gRBP, DCG, and ERR – only gRBP is an interval scale when we choose a specific value of the parameter p and define a specific total order among systems while all the other measures are not interval scales.

1 Introduction

Measurement scales play a central role [4,5] since they determine the operations that can be performed with the measured values and, as a consequence, the statistical analyses that can be applied. Stevens [5] identifies four major types of scales with increasing properties: (i) the *nominal scale* consists of discrete unordered values, i.e. categories; (ii) the *ordinal scale* introduces a natural order among the values; (iii) the *interval scale* preserves the equality of intervals or differences; and (iv) the *ratio scale* preserves the equality of ratios.

In experimental evaluation we daily perform operations, such as computing means and variances, which are also the basic "ingredients" of the more sophisticated statistical significance tests we use to compare systems and assess their differences [1]. However, all these operations can be performed only from interval

* Extended abstract of [2]

scales onwards but, due to our limited knowledge of evaluation measures, we do not actually know which scales they rely on.

This paper sets a theory of evaluation measures to formally investigate their properties and to study whether and when they use an interval scale. We frame our work within the *representational theory of measurement* [4], which is the measurement theory adopted in both physical and social sciences. In particular, we develop a fully comprehensive framework, comprising both *set-based* measures – namely Precision, Recall and F-measure – dealing with unordered result lists, and *rank-based* measures – namely, *Average Precision (AP)*, *Discounted Cumulated Gain (DCG)*, *Rank-Biased Precision (RBP)*, and *Expected Reciprocal Rank (ERR)* – dealing with ranked result lists. Moreover, we consider both *binary relevance*, i.e. when documents can be just relevant or not relevant, and *multi-graded relevance* [3], i.e. when documents can have different degrees of relevance, such as not relevant, partially relevant, and highly relevant.

The paper is organized as follows. Section 2 introduces how to determine when a measure is an interval scale, according to the representational theory of measurement; Section 3 introduces our basic formalisms; Sections 4 and 5 discuss set-based and rank-based evaluation measures, respectively; finally, Section 6 wraps up the discussion and outlooks some future work.

2 Representational Theory of Measurement

Given E, a *weakly ordered* empirical structure is a pair $(E, \preceq)$ where, for every $a, b, c \in E$,

- $a \preceq b$ or $b \preceq a$;
- $a \preceq b$ and $b \preceq c \Rightarrow a \preceq c$ (transitivity).

Note that if $a, b \in E$ are such that $a \preceq b$ and $b \preceq a$, then we write $a \sim b$ and we say that a and b are equivalent elements of E for $\preceq$. When the antisymmetric relation holds, that is when $a \preceq b$ and $b \preceq a$ implies that a and b are the same element (namely $a = b$), we talk about a *total order*.

An interval on the empirical structure is an element $(a, b) \in E \times E$ and we introduce a notion of **difference** Δ_{ab} over intervals, to act as a signed distance we exploit to compare intervals. Once we have a notion of difference Δ_{ab}, we can define a weak order $\preceq_d$ between the Δ_{ab} differences and, consequently, among intervals. We can proceed as follows: if two elements $a, b \in E$ are such that $a \sim b$, then the interval $[a, b]$ is null and, consequently, we set $\Delta_{ab} \sim_d \Delta_{ba}$; if $a \prec b$ we agree upon choosing $\Delta_{aa} \prec_d \Delta_{ab}$ which, in turn implies that $\Delta_{aa} \succ_d \Delta_{ba}$, that is there exist a kind of "zero" and the inverse with respect to this "zero".

Definition 1. *Let E be a finite (not empty) set of objects. Let $\preceq_d$ be a binary relation on $E \times E$ that satisfies, for each $a, b, c, d, a', b', c' \in E$, the following axioms:*

i. $\preceq_d$ *is* weak order*;*
ii. if $\Delta_{ab} \preceq_d \Delta_{cd}$*, then* $\Delta_{dc} \preceq_d \Delta_{ba}$*;*

iii. Weak Monotonicity: *if* $\Delta_{ab} \preceq_d \Delta_{a'b'}$ *and* $\Delta_{bc} \preceq_d \Delta_{b'c'}$ *then* $\Delta_{ac} \preceq_d \Delta_{a'c'}$;
iv. Solvability Condition*: if* $\Delta_{aa} \preceq_d \Delta_{cd} \preceq_d \Delta_{ab}$*, then there exists* $d', d'' \in R$ *such that* $\Delta_{ad'} \sim_d \Delta_{cd} \sim_d \Delta_{d''b}$.

Then $(E, \preceq_d)$ *is a* ***difference structure.***

The *representation theorem* for difference structures states:

Theorem 1. *Let* E *be a finite (not empty) set of objects and let* $(E, \preceq_d)$ *be a difference structure. Then, there exist an interval scale measurement* $\mathrm{M} : E \to \mathbb{R}$ *such that for every* $a, b, c, d \in E$

$$\Delta_{ab} \preceq_d \Delta_{cd} \Leftrightarrow \mathrm{M}(b) - \mathrm{M}(a) \leq \mathrm{M}(d) - \mathrm{M}(c) \ .$$

This theorem ensures us that, if there is a difference structure on the empirical set E, then there exists an interval scale M over it.

Therefore, to study whether evaluation measures are interval scales or not, [2] proceeded as follows:

1. Define a total ordering among system runs, which allows us also to introduce the notion of interval among runs;
2. Since this set is graded of a given rank n, there exists a unique rank function ρ which assigns a natural number to each run;
3. Define the length of an interval as the natural distance $\Delta_{ab} := \ell(a, b) := \ell([a, b]) = \rho(b) - \rho(a)$;
4. Check whether the set with the above natural length is a difference structure or not;
5. In this case we have a difference structure and we can define an interval scale M as the rank function ρ itself;
6. We can eventually check whether evaluation measures are a linear positive transformation of this interval scale M and determine whether they are an interval scale.

3 Basic Formalism

Let $(REL, \preceq)$ be a finite and totally ordered set of **relevance degrees**. We set $REL = \{a_0, a_1, \ldots, a_c\}$ with $a_i \prec a_{i+1}$ for all $i \in \{0, \ldots, c-1\}$; REL has a minimum a_0, called the "not relevant" relevance degree. Let us consider a finite set of **documents** D and a set of **topics** T. For each pair $(t, d) \in T \times D$, the **ground-truth** GT is a map which assigns a relevance degree $rel \in REL$ to a document d with respect to a topic t. Let N be a positive natural number called the *length of the run*. We assume that all the runs have same length N, since this is what typically happens in real evaluation settings when you compare systems. We define $D(N)$ as the **set of all the possible** N **retrieved documents**.

A **run** $r : T \to D(N)$ retrieves N documents belonging to $D(N)$ in response to a topic $t \in T$.

Let $R(N)$ be the **set of N judged documents**, that is the set of all the N possible combinations of relevance degrees.

We call **judged run** of length N the function $\hat{r}$ from $T \times D(N)$ into $R(N)$ which assigns a relevance degree to each retrieved document, i.e. a judged run $\hat{r}$ is the application of the ground-truth GT function to each element of the run r.

We define the **gain function** $g : REL \rightarrow \mathbb{R}_+$ as the map that assigns a positive real number to any relevance degree. We set, without loss of generality, $g(a_0) = 0$ and we require g to be strictly increasing.

We define the **indicator function** for the relevance degrees as $\delta_a(a_j) = j \ \forall j \in \{0, \ldots, c\}$. Note that δ_a is a particular gain function.

Given the gain function g, the **recall base** $RB : T \rightarrow \mathbb{R}_+$ is the map defined as $RB(t) = \sum_{j=1}^{|D|} g(GT(t, d_j))$. In the binary relevance case when $c = 1$ and $REL = \{a_0, a_1\}$, the gain function usually is $g(a_1) = \delta_a(a_1) = 1$ and RB counts the total number of relevant documents for a topic.

An **evaluation measure** is a function $\mathrm{M} : R(N) \rightarrow \mathbb{R}_+$ which maps a judged run $\hat{r}$ into a positive real number which quantifies its effectiveness. Note that most of the evaluation measures are normalized and thus the co-domain is the $[0, 1]$ interval.

4 Set-based Measures

Let us start by introducing an order relation $\preceq$ on the set of judged runs. Let $\hat{r}, \hat{s} \in R(N)$ such that $\hat{r} \neq \hat{s}$, and let k be the biggest relevance degree at which the two runs differ for the first time, i.e. $k = \max\{j \leq c : \left|\{i : \hat{r}_i = a_j\}\right| \neq \left|\{i : \hat{s}_i = a_j\}\right|\}$. We strictly order any pair of distinct system runs as follows

$$\hat{r} \prec \hat{s} \Leftrightarrow \left|\{i : \hat{r}_i = a_k\}\right| < \left|\{i : \hat{s}_i = a_k\}\right| . \tag{1}$$

$R(N)$ is a totally ordered set with respect to the ordering $\preceq$ defined by (1). As for any totally order set, $R(N)$ is a poset consisting of only one maximal chain (the whole set); therefore it is *graded of rank* $|R(N)| - 1$, where $\left|R(N)\right| = \binom{N+c}{N}$ since it consists of all the N combinations of $c + 1 = |REL|$ objects with repetition. Since $R(N)$ is graded of rank $|R(N)| - 1$, there exists a unique *rank function* $\rho(\hat{r}) : R(N) \longrightarrow \mathbb{N}$ such that $\rho(\hat{0}) = 0$ and $\rho(\hat{s}) = \rho(\hat{r}) + 1$ if $\hat{s}$ covers $\hat{r}$:

$$\rho(\hat{r}) = \sum_{j=1}^{N} \binom{\delta_a(\hat{r}_j) + N - j}{N - j + 1} , \tag{2}$$

where $\hat{r} = \{\hat{r}_1, \ldots, \hat{r}_N\} \in R(N)$ with $\hat{r}_i \preceq \hat{r}_{i+1}$ for any $i < N$.

The *natural distance* is then given by $\ell(\hat{r}, \hat{s}) = \rho(\hat{s}) - \rho(\hat{r})$, for $\hat{r}, \hat{s} \in R(N)$ such that $\hat{r} \preceq \hat{s}$, and we can define the difference as $\Delta_{\hat{r}\hat{s}} = \ell(\hat{r}, \hat{s})$ if $\hat{r} \preceq \hat{s}$, otherwise $\Delta_{\hat{r}\hat{s}} = -\ell(\hat{s}, \hat{r})$. $(R(N), \preceq_d)$ is a difference structure. Thus the rank function is an interval scale and we are able to define a new measure that follows:

Definition 2. *The Set-Based Total Order (SBTO) measure on* $(R(N), \preceq_d)$ *is:*

$$\mathrm{SBTO}(\hat{r}) = \rho(\hat{r}) = \sum_{j=1}^{N} \binom{\delta_a(\hat{r}_j) + N - j}{N - j + 1} . \tag{3}$$

This measure satisfies the condition imposed by Theorem 1. Thus, SBTO *is an interval scale on* $(R(N), \preceq_d)$.

Let us explore more deeply how the SBTO measure works. The first relevance degree immediately above not relevant, i.e. a_1, always gives a constant contribution, independently from how many a_1 documents are retrieved, since:

$$\binom{\delta_a(a_1) + N - j}{N - j + 1} = \binom{1 + N - j}{N - j + 1} = 1 .$$

However, when we consider higher relevance degrees, i.e. a_k with $k > 1$, the binomial coefficient strictly depends and changes on the basis of how many of them are retrieved. Indeed, $\delta_a(a_k)$ is constant for all the documents with the same relevance degree a_k, but the term $N - j$ decreases as the number of a_k retrieved documents increases due to N being constant and j increasing, i.e. the binomial coefficient is decreasing in the number of a_k retrieved documents. In other terms, each additional a_k retrieved document gives a contribution smaller than the previously retrieved ones by a discount factor j.

4.1 Binary Relevance Case

When $c = 1$, i.e. in the binary relevance case, the ordering (1) just orders judged runs by how many relevant documents they retrieve, i.e. by their total mass of relevance:

$$\hat{r} \preceq \hat{s} \;\Leftrightarrow\; \sum_{i=1}^{N} \delta_a(\hat{r}_i) \leq \sum_{i=1}^{N} \delta_a(\hat{s}_i) ,$$

since there is only one relevant relevance degree a_1.

Therefore the rank function becomes

$$\rho(\hat{r}) = \sum_{i=1}^{N} \delta_a(\hat{r}_i) = \mathrm{M}(\hat{r}) .$$

This follows easily from (3), using the fact that $\delta_a(\hat{r}_i) \in \{0, 1\}$ for any $i \leq N$ when $c = 1$.

Let now g be the gain function, and let us consider *Precision*

$$\mathit{Precision}\ (P)(\hat{r}) = \frac{1}{N} \sum_{i=1}^{N} \frac{g(\hat{r}_i)}{g(a_1)} = \frac{1}{N} \sum_{i=1}^{N} \delta_a(\hat{r}_i) = \frac{\mathrm{M}(\hat{r})}{N} ,$$

since $g(a_0) = 0 = \delta_a(a_0)$ and $c = 1$. Thus Precision is an interval scale, as it is a linear positive transformation of M.

Similarly, *Recall*

$$\textit{Recall (R)}(\hat{r}) = \frac{1}{RB} \sum_{i=1}^{N} \frac{g(\hat{r}_i)}{g(a_1)} = \frac{1}{RB} \sum_{i=1}^{N} \delta_a(\hat{r}_i) = \frac{\mathrm{M}(\hat{r})}{RB}$$

is an interval scale.

The *F-measure*, that is the harmonic mean of Precision and Recall,

$$\mathrm{F}(\hat{r}) = 2\frac{\mathrm{P}(\hat{r}) \cdot \mathrm{R}(\hat{r})}{\mathrm{P}(\hat{r}) + \mathrm{R}(\hat{r})} = \frac{2}{N + RB} \sum_{i=1}^{N} \delta_a(\hat{r}_i) = \frac{2\mathrm{M}(\hat{r})}{N + RB}$$

is an interval scale as well.

4.2 Multi-graded Relevance Case

Neither Generalized Precision nor Generalized Recall are a positive linear transformation of M defined in (3). Indeed, in these measures, the individual contribution of each retrieved document $\hat{r}_j$ is independent from the contribution of any other retrieved document $\hat{r}_k$. However, the previous discussion on the measure defined in (3) pointed out that, for each relevance degree a_k with $k > 1$, the individual contribution of an a_k retrieved document depends on how many a_k retrieved documents there are in the run. Therefore neither gP nor gR are an interval scale, since they cannot be a linear transformation of M.

Moreover they are not even an ordinal scale which, again, implies they cannot be an interval scale too. Indeed, a measure M′ is an ordinal scale on $R(N)$ if, for every $\hat{r}, \hat{s} \in R(N)$, the following statement is true:

$$\hat{r} \preceq \hat{s} \Leftrightarrow \mathrm{M}'(\hat{r}) \leq \mathrm{M}'(\hat{s}) .$$

Let us consider $\hat{r} = \{a_1, \ldots, a_1\}$ and $\hat{s} = \{a_2, a_0, \ldots, a_0\}$, two runs of length N. We have $\hat{r} \prec \hat{s}$. Moreover, since *Generalized Recall (gR)* and *Generalized Precision (gP)* are both proportional to $\mathrm{G}(\hat{v}) := \sum_{i=1}^{N} g(\hat{v}_i)/g(a_c)$, for any $\hat{v} \in R(N)$, we can prove that $\mathrm{G}(\cdot)$ is not on an ordinal scale with respect to the order (1). Since $g(a_0) = 0$, $\mathrm{G}(\hat{r}) = Ng(a_1)/g(a_c)$ while $\mathrm{G}(\hat{s}) = g(a_2)/g(a_c)$. From the fact that the gain function g is a positive strictly increasing function and it is defined independently from the length N of the runs, by choosing a N big enough we can have $\mathrm{G}(\hat{r}) > \mathrm{G}(\hat{s})$.

5 Rank-based Measures

Top-heaviness is a central property in *Information Retrieval (IR)*, stating that the higher a system ranks relevant documents the better it is. If we apply this property at each rank position and we take to extremes the importance of having a relevant document ranked higher, we can define a *strong top-heaviness* property which, in turn, will induce a total ordering among runs.

Let $\hat{r}, \hat{s} \in R(N)$ such that $\hat{r} \neq \hat{s}$, then there exists $k = \min\{j \leq N : \hat{r}[j] \neq \hat{s}[j]\} < \infty$, and we order system runs as follows

$$\hat{r} \prec \hat{s} \Leftrightarrow \hat{r}[k] \prec \hat{s}[k] \; . \tag{4}$$

This order prefers a single relevant document ranked higher to any number of relevant documents, with same relevance degree or higher, ranked just below it

$$(\hat{u}[1], \ldots, \hat{u}[m], a_0, a_c, \ldots, a_c), \prec (\hat{u}[1], \ldots, \hat{u}[m], a_j, a_0, \ldots, a_0) \; ,$$

for any $1 \leq j \leq c$, for any length $N \in \mathbb{N}$ and any $m \in \{0, 1, \ldots, N-1\}$. This is why we call it *strong top-heaviness.*

$R(N)$ is totally ordered with respect to $\preceq$ and is *graded of rank* $(c+1)^N - 1$. Therefore, there is a unique rank function $\rho : R(N) \longrightarrow \{0, 1, \ldots, (c+1)^N - 1\}$ which is given by:

$$\rho(\hat{r}) = \sum_{i=1}^{N} \delta_a(\hat{r}[i])(c+1)^{N-i}, \tag{5}$$

where δ_a is the indicator function.

Let us set $\boldsymbol{\delta_a}(\hat{r}) = (\delta_a(\hat{r}[1]), \ldots, \delta_a(\hat{r}[N]))$. If we look at $\boldsymbol{\delta_a}(\hat{r})$ as a string, the rank function is exactly the conversion in base 10 of the number in base $c+1$ identified by $\boldsymbol{\delta_a}(\hat{r})$ and the ordering among runs $\preceq$ corresponds to the ordering $\leq$ among numbers in base $c+1$.

The *natural distance* is then given by $\ell(\hat{r}, \hat{s}) = \rho(\hat{s}) - \rho(\hat{r})$, for $\hat{r}, \hat{s} \in R(N)$ such that $\hat{r} \preceq \hat{s}$, and we can define the difference as $\Delta_{\hat{r}\hat{s}} = \ell(\hat{r}, \hat{s})$ if $\hat{r} \preceq \hat{s}$, otherwise $\Delta_{\hat{r}\hat{s}} = -\ell(\hat{s}, \hat{r})$. $(R(N), \preceq_d)$ is a difference structure. As done before in the set-based case, an interval scale measure on $(R(N), \preceq_d)$ is given by the rank function itself.

Definition 3. *The Rank-Based Total Order (RBTO) measure on* $(R(N), \preceq_d)$ *is:*

$$\text{RBTO}(\hat{r}) = \rho(\hat{r}) = \sum_{i=1}^{N} \delta_a(\hat{r}[i])(c+1)^{N-i} \tag{6}$$

This measure satisfies the condition imposed by Theorem 1. Thus, RBTO *is an interval scale on* $(R(N), \preceq_d)$.

Let $G = \min_{j \in \{1,\ldots,c\}} (g(a_j) - g(a_{j-1}))/g(a_c) > 0$ be the normalized smallest gap between the gain of two consecutive relevance degrees.

Graded Rank-Biased Precision (gRBP)$_p$ with $p > G/(G+1)$ and other IR measures – namely AP, DCG, and ERR – are not even an ordinal scale on $R(N)$, as the following example shows. Let $\hat{r} = (a_1, a_0, a_2, a_0, a_1)$ and $\hat{s} = (a_1, a_1, a_0, a_0, a_0)$ be two runs on $R(5)$ with $c = 2$ and let us use the indicator function δ as gain function g. We have $\hat{r} \preceq \hat{s}$. Then $\text{DCG}_2(\hat{r}) = 1 + 2/\log_2 3 + 1/\log_2 5 > 1 + 1 = \text{DCG}_2(\hat{s})$; $\text{ERR}(\hat{r}) = 1/4 + 3/16 + 3/320 > 1/4 + 3/32 = \text{ERR}(\hat{s})$; finally, since $g(a_2) = \delta_a(a_2) = 2$, $2\text{gRBP}_p(\hat{r}) = (1-p)(1 + 2p^2 + p^4) > (1-p)(1+p) = 2\text{gRBP}(\hat{s})$ for $p \gtrsim 0.454$, and such an example can be found for any other values of $p > G/(G+1)$, where $G = 1/2$. AP is a binary measure and, just to stay with the same data above, we adopt a lenient mapping of multi-graded to binary relevance degrees setting $g(\mathscr{a}_1) = g(\mathscr{a}_2) = 1$ and thus $RB{\cdot}\mathrm{AP}(\hat{r}) = 1 + 2/3 + 3/5 > 1 + 1 = RB{\cdot}\mathrm{AP}(\hat{s})$, where RB is the recall base.

As a consequence, being not an ordinal scale, gRBP_p with $p > G/(G+1)$, AP, DCG, and ERR cannot be an interval scale too, since an interval scale measure is also an ordinal scale. gRBP_p with $p \leq G/(G+1)$ is interval if and only if $p = G/(1+G) = (c+1)^{-1}$ and the gain function is equal to $g(\mathscr{a}_i) = K\delta_a(\mathscr{a}_i)$, for any $i \in \{0, \ldots, \mathbb{N}\}$ and for any $K > 0$ fixed.

6 Conclusion and Future Works

We developed a theory of evaluation measures to explore whether and when both set-based and rank-based IR measures are interval scales. This is a fundamental question since the validity of the descriptive statistics, such as mean and variance, and the statistical significance tests we daily use to compare IR systems depends on its answer.

We summarize here the main findings of our framework:

- set-based evaluation measures:
  - binary relevance: precision, recall, F-measure are interval scales;
  - multi-graded relevance: gP and gR are neither ordinal nor interval scales;
- rank-based evaluation measures:
  - binary relevance: RBP is an interval scale only for $p = 1/2$ and it is an ordinal scale for $p < 1/2$; RBP for $p > 1/2$ and AP are neither ordinal nor interval scales;
  - multi-graded relevance: gRBP is an interval scale only for $p = G/(G+1)$ and when the gain function is equal to $g(\mathscr{a}_i) = K\delta_a(\mathscr{a}_i)$; gRBP is an ordinal scale when $p < G/(G+1)$; gRBP for $p > G/(G+1)$, DCG, and ERR are neither ordinal nor interval scales.

As future work, we will investigate these new interval scale measures from an experimental point of view, e.g. by performing an analysis of their robustness to pool downsampling or of their discriminative power, as well as the exploration of how they behave in statistical significance testing with respect to the traditional evaluation measures which, instead, violate the interval scale assumption.

References

1. Carterette, B.A.: Multiple Testing in Statistical Analysis of Systems-Based Information Retrieval Experiments. ACM TOIS 30(1), 4:1–4:34 (2012)
2. Ferrante, M., Ferro, N., Pontarollo, S.: A General Theory of IR Evaluation Measures. IEEE TKDE 31(3), 409–422 (March 2019)
3. Kekäläinen, J., Järvelin, K.: Using Graded Relevance Assessments in IR Evaluation. JASIST 53(13), 1120–1129 (November 2002)
4. Krantz, D.H., Luce, R.D., Suppes, P., Tversky, A.: Foundations of Measurement. Additive and Polynomial Representations, vol. 1. Academic Press, USA (1971)
5. Stevens, S.S.: On the Theory of Scales of Measurement. Science, New Series 103(2684), 677–680 (June 1946)

Data fusion with source authority and multiple truth
(Discussion Paper)

Fabio Azzalini, Davide Piantella and Letizia Tanca

Politecnico di Milano, Italy {name.surname}@polimi.it

Abstract. The abundance of data available on the Web makes more and more probable the case of finding that different sources contain (partially or completely) different values for the same item. Data Fusion is the relevant problem of discovering the true values of a data item when two entities representing it have been found and their values are different. Recent studies have shown that when, for finding the true value of an object, we rely only on majority voting, results may be wrong for up to 30% of the data items, since false values are spread very easily because data sources frequently copy from one another. Therefore, the problem must be solved by assessing the quality of the sources and giving more importance to the values coming from trusted sources. State-of-the-art Data Fusion systems define source trustworthiness on the basis of the accuracy of the provided values and on the dependence on other sources. In this paper we propose an improved algorithm for Data Fusion, that extends existing methods based on accuracy and correlation between sources by taking into account also source authority, defined on the basis of the knowledge of which sources copy from which ones. Our method has been designed to work well also in the multi-truth case, that is, when a data item can also have multiple true values. Preliminary experimental results on a multi-truth real-world dataset show that our algorithm outperforms previous state-of-the-art approaches.

1 Introduction

The massive use of user-generated content, the Internet of Things and the tendency to transform every real-world interaction into digital data have lead to the problem of how to make sense of the huge mass of data available nowadays. In this context, not only a source can store a previously unimaginable amount of data, but also the number of sources that can provide information relevant for a query increases dramatically, even in very specific contexts.

With all these conflicting data available on the web, discovering their true values is of primary importance. The solution of this problem is Data Fusion, where the true value of each data item is decided. Redundancy per se is not enough, since it has been shown in [3] that, if we rely only on majority vote, we could get wrong results even in 30% of the times. In order to get more accurate results we propose a Bayesian approach able to evaluate *source quality*.

Data fusion algorithms can be divided into two sub-classes: single-truth and multi-truth, the latter denoting the case when a data item may have multiple true values. Such scenarios are common in everyday life, where many actors can play in a movie or a book can have many authors, like Alice's book "Foundations of Databases"[10] by Serge Abiteboul, Rick Hull and Victor Vianu. We decided to design our model to work also in the multi-truth case.

Currently, many single-truth data fusion algorithms exist in literature, and a few of them exploit Bayesian inference to estimate the veracity of each value and the trustworthiness of sources. TRUTHFINDER [8] applies Bayesian analysis to compute the probability of a value being true, conditioned to the observation of values provided by the sources. ACCU[4] applies a Bayesian iterative approach to compute the veracity of values, assuming uniform distribution of false values for each data item and source independence. These two assumptions have been relaxed by POPACCU[9] and ACCUCOPY[1] respectively.

Less attention has been devoted to studying the problem of multi-truth finding: to our knowledge, only three algorithms try to solve it. MBM[6] approaches multi-truth data fusion with a model that focuses on mappings and relations between sources and sets of provided values, introducing also a copy-detection phase to discover dependencies between sources. DART[5] computes, for each source, a *domain expertise* score relative to the domains of input data. This score is used in a Bayesian inference process to model source trustworthiness and value confidence; sources are assumed to be independent. LTM[7] exploits probabilistic graphical models to find all the true values claimed for each data item.

State of the art systems on Data Fusion define source trustworthiness based on the accuracy of the provided values and on the dependence on other sources. In this paper we propose an improved algorithm for Data Fusion. Our method extends existing methods based on accuracy and correlation between sources taking also into consideration the authority of sources. Authoritative sources are defined as the ones that have been copied by many sources: the key idea is that, when source administrators decide to copy data, they will choose the sources that they perceive as most trustworthy.

To summarize, in this paper we make the following contributions:

- We present a new formula for *domain-aware copy detection* with the goal of determine the probability that source S_i copies, from source S_j, data items belonging to a specific domain. Our copy detection process exploits the *domain expertise* of the sources and can also assign different probabilities to the two directions of copying.
- An urgent need of the truth discovery process is to determine *what sources we can trust*. We present a *fully unsupervised* algorithm that can assign an authority score to each source for each domain. This process is based on the natural habit of choosing, to copy a missing value, the source that provides the correct value with the highest probability - in other words, the most authoritative one.
- We present an improved algorithm for assessing values' veracity in a multi-truth discovery process, exploiting *source authority* in copy detection, positively rewarding sources according to their authority.

In Section 2 we present preliminary information, Section 3 provides the details about our approach and in Section 4 we show the experimental results.

2 Background and Preliminaries

We now present more in details two methods that have been of great importance for our work.

`DART`. This algorithm exploits an iterative domain-aware Bayesian approach to do multi-truth discovery over a dataset composed starting from different sources. Its key intuition is that, in general, a source may have different quality of data for different domains. For each source, they define the *domain expertise score* $e_{d_i}(s)$, measuring the source's experience in a given domain, and assign a confidence $c_s^o(v)$ to each value v provided by a source s, reflecting how much s is convinced that the value v is (part of) the correct value(s) for object o.

The *veracity* $\sigma_o(v)$ of value v for object o is the probability that v is a true value of o, which is better estimated at each iteration of the discovery process. The goal of the `DART` algorithm is to evaluate the probability that a value v is true given the observation of the claimed data $\psi(o)$ (i.e. $P(v|\psi(o))$). Being $P(\psi(o)|v)$ and $P(\psi(o)|\bar{v})$ the probabilities of having the observation $\psi(o)$ when v is true or false respectively, Bayesian inference can be used to express $P(v|\psi(o))$ as shown below:

$$P(v|\psi(o)) = \frac{P(\psi(o)|v)P(v)}{P(\psi(o))} = \frac{P(\psi(o)|v)\ \sigma_o(v)}{P(\psi(o)|v)\ \sigma_o(v)\ +\ P(\psi(o)|\bar{v})(1-\sigma_0(v))} \tag{1}$$

Our main criticism to `DART` is the assumption that sources are independent, which is a clear oversimplification of the real world. We will explain how we have relaxed this assumption in the following section.

`MBM` is a Bayesian algorithm for multi-truth finding that takes into consideration also the problem of source dependence. It computes, for each source and set of values, an *independence score* based on the values provided by all the sources. The *independence score* is then used to discredit, in the voting phase, sources that don't provide their values independently.

Our criticisms to `MBM` are the assumption that there is no mutual copying between sources in the whole dataset and the fact that the algorithm is not able to distinguish the direction of copying. In the following section we will describe how we have relaxed these assumptions.

Table 1 describes the notation that will be used in the following sections.

3 Methodology

We now present `ADAM` (Authority Domain Aware Multi-truth data fusion), a method based on Bayesian inference and source authority that iteratively refines the probability that a provided value for a data item is true.

3.1 Copy detection

Starting from [6], we have devised a *domain-aware* copy detection algorithm to assign different probabilities to the two directions of copy. This model works at *domain granularity*, therefore it can more accurately approximate the real world behaviour of correlated copying [2].

Notation	Description
$O(s)$	Set of all objects provided by source s
$O^d(s)$	Set of objects in domain d provided by source s
$V_s(o)$	Set of all values claimed for object o by source s
$\overline{V_s(o)}$	Set of all values claimed for object o by sources $\neq s$
$S_o^d(v)$	Sources that provide value v for object o in domain d
$S_o^d(\bar{v})$	Sources that don't provide value v for object o in domain d
$e_d(s)$	Expertise of source s in domain d
$\sigma_o(v)$	Veracity of value v for object o
$\tau_d^{rec}(s)$	Recall of source s in domain d
$\tau_d^{sp}(s)$	Specificity of source s in domain d
$c_s^o(v)$	Confidence score of value v of object o related to source s
$s_i \rightarrow s_j$	Source i is copying at object level *from* source j
$s_i \perp s_j$	Sources i and j are independent at object level
$s_i \xrightarrow{d} s_j$	Sources i is copying *from* source j for domain d
Θ_{ij}^d	Set of common objects in domain d between sources i and j
$c_{ij}(o) =: c$	Values provided by both sources i and j for object o
$\psi_{ij}^o =: \psi_c$	Observation of c
$\psi(o)$	Observation of the values provided by object o
$A_d(s)$	Authority of source s in domain d

Table 1. Notation

Scope. Given an object o and two sources s_i and s_j, we denote by ψ_{ij}^o the observation of the common values $c_{ij}(o)$ for a common object $o \in \Theta_{ij}^d$ in domain d provided by two source s_i and s_j.

Assumptions. In our copy detection algorithm we assume that there is no mutual copying *at domain level*, i.e., if source s_1 copies from source s_2 regarding domain $\bar{d}$, then s_2 can copy from s_1 only values for objects in domains $\tilde{d} \neq \bar{d}$; we also assume that two sources can only be either independent or copiers.

Object copying. For each pair of sources i, j, after we have defined the truth probability of the group of values in c as the probability that all the values are correct (Eq. 2), we can compute the likelihood of ψ_c in different cases of source dependence and truthfulness of c. Similarly to [6], we state that if s_i has copied from s_j, or the other way round, then they provide the same common values c, no matter the veracity of c (Eq. 3).

$$\sigma(c) = \prod_{v \in c} \sigma(v) \tag{2}$$

$$\begin{cases} P(\psi_c | s_i \rightarrow s_j,\ c \text{ true}) = P(\psi_c | s_j \rightarrow s_i,\ c \text{ true}) = 1 \\ P(\psi_c | s_i \rightarrow s_j,\ c \text{ false}) = P(\psi_c | s_j \rightarrow s_i,\ c \text{ false}) = 1 \end{cases} \tag{3}$$

Eq.s 4 and 5 define the probabilities that both sources provide the same group of values c independently of each other, in the two cases that c is true and false.

$$P(\psi_c | s_1 \perp s_2,\ c \text{ true}) = \tau^{rec}(s_1)\ \tau^{rec}(s_2)\ [1 - \tau^{sp}(s_1)]\ [1 - \tau^{sp}(s_2)] \tag{4}$$

$$P(\psi_c | s_1 \perp s_2,\ c \text{ false}) = \tau^{sp}(s_1)\ \tau^{sp}(s_2)\ [1 - \tau^{rec}(s_1)]\ [1 - \tau^{rec}(s_2)] \tag{5}$$

Bayesian model. If we apply a Bayesian inference approach we can now compute the probability of two sources being dependent or independent, and in the first case we can also define which of the two is the copier.

With $Y = \{s_i \to s_j;\ s_j \to s_i;\ s_i \perp s_j\}$ we define the three possible outcomes.

$$\begin{aligned} P(y|\psi_c) &= \frac{P(\psi_c|y)\ P(y)}{\sum_{y' \in Y} P(\psi_c|y')\ P(y')} \\ &= \frac{P(y)\left[P(\psi_c|y,\ c\ \text{true})\ \sigma(c) + P(\psi_c|y,\ c\ \text{false})\ (1-\sigma(c))\right]}{\sum_{y' \in Y} P(y')\ \left[P(\psi_c|y',\ c\ \text{true})\ \sigma(c) + P(\psi_c|y',\ c\ \text{false})\ (1-\sigma(c))\right]} \end{aligned} \tag{6}$$

We now have to find a way to estimate the *prior probability* of the Bayesian model: $P(s_i \to s_j)$, $P(s_j \to s_i)$ and $P(s_j \perp s_i)$, that are all the different configurations of *object copying* between sources s_i and s_j. We define this as the probability of the two sources being independent or copiers in the domain of the object we are considering, defined in Eq. 11. For ease of notation we apply the following definition, recalling that d is the same domain of $\Theta_{ij}^d \ni o$ where o is the object of ψ_c that we are analyzing.

$$\begin{cases} P(s_i \to s_j) & =: \rho_{ij}^d \\ P(s_j \to s_i) & =: \rho_{ji}^d \\ P(s_j \perp s_i) & = 1 - \rho_{ij}^d - \rho_{ji}^d \end{cases} \tag{7}$$

and replace Eq.s 7, 2, 3, 4 and 5 into Eq. 6, with the following result:

$$P(s_i \to s_j|\psi_c) = \frac{\rho_{ij}^d}{\rho_{ij}^d + \rho_{ji}^d + \left(1 - \rho_{ij}^d - \rho_{ji}^d\right)\ P_u} \tag{8}$$

where

$$\begin{aligned} P_u \ := \ & \sigma(c)\ \left[\tau^{rec}(s_i) \cdot \tau^{rec}(s_j) \cdot (1 - \tau^{sp}(s_i)) \cdot (1 - \tau^{sp}(s_j))\right] + \\ & + (1 - \sigma(v))\ \left[\tau^{sp}(s_i) \cdot \tau^{sp}(s_j) \cdot (1 - \tau^{rec}(s_i)) \cdot (1 - \tau^{rec}(s_j))\right] \end{aligned} \tag{9}$$

Non-shared values. With Eq. 8 we have expressed the probability that a source s_i has copied from another source s_j their common values c for object o. We now have to take into consideration other possible non-in-common values to opportunely compute the probability that c were really copied. We have chosen to scale the copy probability by the Jaccard similarity of the two sets of values of o claimed by the two sources s_i and s_j, as shown in Eq. 10.

$$J_{ij}(o) = J_{ji}(o) = \frac{\left|V_{s_i}(o) \cap V_{s_j}(o)\right|}{\left|V_{s_i}(o) \cup V_{s_j}(o)\right|} \tag{10}$$

Domain-level copying. We can use the concept of copying an object o to define the act of copying with respect to a domain d as defined in Eq. 11.

$$P\left(s_i \xrightarrow{\text{d}} s_j \middle| \Theta_{ij}^d\right) := \frac{\sum_{o \in \Theta_{ij}^d} P(s_i \to s_j|\psi_c) \cdot J_{ij}(o)}{\left|\Theta_{ij}^d\right|} \tag{11}$$

Initialization. Since in the initialization phase we have no prior knowledge of ρ_{ij}^d, we decided to exploit the fact that sources with high expertise in domain d are less likely to be copiers for domain d and that sources with low expertise in d tend to copy from sources with higher expertise in d. These ideas can be summarized in the initialization expressed in Eq. 12.

$$\rho_{ij}^d = \left[1 - e^d(s_i)\right] e^d(s_j) \cdot \qquad \forall s_i,\ s_j \in \mathcal{S}\ \wedge\ s_i \neq s_j \tag{12}$$

3.2 Source authority

The key idea to define the authority of a source in a specific domain with respect to the outcomes of the copy detection process is that, if many sources copy some values from the same source s_a, it is because s_a is considered authoritative and more trustworthy. For each source $s_j \in \mathcal{S}$, we define $C_d(s_j)$ in Eq. 13 as the set of all the sources that copy *from* source s_j with probability above a given threshold Γ:

$$C_d(s_j) := \left\{ s_i \in \mathcal{S} \middle| \ P(s_i \xrightarrow{\text{d}} s_j | \Theta_{ij}^d) > \Gamma \right\} \quad (13)$$

Qualitatively, the *unadjusted authority score* of source s in domain d is *how much source s is copied in d w.r.t. how much all sources are copied in d* (Eq. 14).

$$a_d(s_j) := \frac{\sum_{s_i \in C_d(s_j)} P(s_i \xrightarrow{\text{d}} s_j | \Theta_{ij}^d)}{\sum_{s_k \in S} \sum_{s_l \in C_d(s_k)} P(s_l \xrightarrow{\text{d}} s_k | \Theta_{kl}^d)} \quad (14)$$

Note that in general the cardinality of $\mathcal{S}$ (i.e. the number of sources) is high and the parameter Γ should not be set too close to 1 to better exploit the variety of outcomes of the copy detection process. This configuration leads to $a_d(s) \ll 1$. We can accordingly apply a linear conversion to $a_d(s)$ in order to map it on the interval $[0; 1]$. We denote this new score as $A_d(s)$ or *authority of source s* in domain d, computed as:

$$A_d(s) := \frac{a_d(s) - a_d^{min}}{a_d^{max} - a_d^{min}} \quad (15)$$

3.3 Veracity

We have extended the DART Bayesian inference model in order to exploit the authority score of each source. Our key idea is to positively reward sources according to their authority, which can be achieved with Eq.s 16 and 17, respectively.

$$P(\psi(o)|v) = \prod_{s \in S_o^d(v)} \tau_d^{rec}(s)^{e_d(s)c_s(v)+A_d(s)} \prod_{s \in S_o^d(\bar{v})} (1 - \tau_d^{sp}(s))^{e_d(s)c_s(v)+A_d(s)} \quad (16)$$

$$P(\psi(o)|\bar{v}) = \prod_{s \in S_o^d(\bar{v})} \tau_d^{sp}(s)^{e_d(s)c_s(v)+A_d(s)} \prod_{s \in S_o^d(v)} (1 - \tau_d^{rec}(s))^{e_d(s)c_s(v)+A_d(s)} \quad (17)$$

In a multi-truth context, *precision* cannot be the only metrics for source trustworthiness [7], but we should use *recall* and *specificity*: *source recall* is the probability that true values are claimed as true (Eq. 18), while *source specificity* is the probability that false values are claimed as false (Eq. 19).

$$\tau_d^{rec}(s) = \frac{\sum_{o \in O^d(s)} \sum_{v \in V_s(o)} \sigma_o(v)}{\sum_{o \in O^d(s)} |V_s(o)|} \quad (18) \qquad \tau_d^{sp}(s) = \frac{\sum_{o \in O^d(s)} \sum_{v' \in \overline{V_s(o)}} (1 - \sigma_o(v'))}{\sum_{o \in O^d(s)} \left|\overline{V_s(o)}\right|} \quad (19)$$

At each iteration of the algorithm veracity scores of values are refined, this leads to a better estimation of copy detection and source authority, that in turn will improve again values' veracity in the next iteration. The algorithm stops iterating when the updates of all veracities are less then a given threshold δ. The output of the algorithm is, for each object o in the dataset, a set of values whose veracities are greater or equal to a given threshold θ.

4 Experimental Results

We now present the result of an experimental comparison between our algorithm, ADAM (Authority Domain Aware Multi-truth data fusion), and the original DART in different configurations of the input data.

4.1 Dataset

We have used as input data a subset of the same *book dataset* that has been used for the evaluation of the DART algorithm, kindly made available by Xueling Lin, one of the authors of [5]. Our goal was to discover the correct values of the multi-truth parameter authors using the category attribute to clusterize books into domains.

For our experiments, we have been able to use a subset of this dataset matching another validated and trustworthy dataset considered as golden truth for the book-authors binding. The dataset used in our experiments is composed by 90,867 tuples from 2,680 sources and 1,958 books, spanning all the 18 domains (i.e. categories of book genres) of the original dataset.

Parameter	Value
α	1.5
Γ	0
δ	0.1
η	0.2
θ	0.5
$\bar{\sigma}$	0.5
$\bar{\tau}^{rec}$	0.8
$\bar{\tau}^{sp}$	0.9

Table 2. Parameters

Our algorithm depends on several parameters; Table 2 reports the value used for each of them. When an indication was present in [5], we used the same provided value to ensure optimal comparability between the two algorithms.

4.2 Results

We have developed in Python 3.7 both an implementation of DART (following as precisely as possible the guidelines expressed in [5]), and our extension ADAM. Even though our interest was in determine the impact of our extensions on DART performances, we have also developed a simple version of MajorityVote as baseline comparison.

ADAM has its F-1 score higher than DART in the 76% of the times. Moreover in our experiments ADAM has required strictly less iterations before convergence in the 65% of the times with respect to DART, in some cases the number of iterations required was less than a half. At first sight this faster convergence might seem to be due only to the increment of $A(s)$ in the exponent in Eq.s 16 and 17 but with a more precise analysis we discover that $A(s) \not\sim 0$ only for a small fraction of the sources, modeling in a correct manner the desired meaning of authority which by definition should be related to only a small subset of objects.

We have run 37 comparison between DART, ADAM and MajorityVote using the same input data for the three algorithms at each run, focusing on both input regarding single and multiple domains. We particularly focus in this section on a subset of 10 runs, reporting in Table 3 the metrics of DART and ADAM of those runs and finally in Table 4 we aggregate the results of all 37 runs reporting the averaged metrics of MajorityVote, DART and ADAM.

Domain	Records	|D|	|O|	|S|	DART			ADAM		
					Prec.	**Rec.**	**F-1**	**Prec.**	**Rec.**	**F-1**
Travels	221	1	44	120	0.9167	1	0.9565	0.9767	0.9545	0.9655
Reference	497	1	19	279	0.6875	0.8148	0.7458	0.84	0.7778	0.8077
History	1639	1	114	565	0.9416	0.8487	0.8927	0.9918	0.8176	0.8963
Arts	1114	1	22	505	0.5161	0.8889	0.6531	0.9545	0.6176	0.75
Random	2764	14	50	615	0.8852	0.9474	0.9153	0.98	0.875	0.9245
Random	2408	13	50	811	0.9016	0.873	0.8871	0.9808	0.85	0.9107
Random	5010	16	100	880	0.8252	0.9147	0.8676	0.9903	0.8361	0.9067
Random	4772	16	100	866	0.837	0.8433	0.8401	0.9706	0.7615	0.8534
Random*	4276	17	100	976	0.5359	0.7366	0.6205	0.9225	0.5265	0.6704
Random	1998	14	50	572	0.9	0.9643	0.931	1	0.9273	0.9623

Table 3. Experimental results (*contains only books with at least 2 authors)

Method	Precision	Recall	F-1
`MajorityVote`	0.9354	0.6958	0.7820
`DART`	0.7953	0.8621	0.8273
`ADAM`	0.9182	0.7727	0.8392

Table 4. Average results of 37 runs

5 Conclusions

We presented `ADAM`, an improved algorithm for multi-truth data fusion. A quicker termination and better results confirm that our idea to reward authoritative sources has led to an increase in the algorithm performance and accuracy.

References

1. Dong, Xin Luna and Berti-Equille, Laure and Srivastava, Divesh: Truth Discovery and Copying Detection in a Dynamic World. VLDB (2009)
2. Blanco, Lorenzo and Crescenzi, Valter and Merialdo, Paolo and Papotti, Paolo: Probabilistic Models to Reconcile Complex Data from Inaccurate Data Sources. Advanced Information Systems Eng (2010)
3. Li, Xian and Dong, Xin Luna and Lyons, Kenneth and Meng, Weiyi and Srivastava, Divesh: Truth Finding on the Deep Web: Is the Problem Solved? CoRR (2015)
4. Dong, Xin Luna and Berti-Equille, Laure and Srivastava, Divesh: Integrating Conflicting Data: The Role of Source Dependence. VLDB (2009)
5. Lin, Xueling and Chen, Lei: Domain-aware Multi-truth Discovery from Conflicting Sources. VLDB (2018)
6. Wang, Xianzhi and Sheng, Quan Z. and Fang, Xiu Susie and Yao, Lina and Xu, Xiaofei and Li, Xue: An Integrated Bayesian Approach for Effective Multi-Truth Discovery. CIKM (2015)
7. Bo, Zhao and Benjamin, Rubinstein and Jim, Gemmell and Jiawei, Han: A Bayesian Approach to Discovering Truth from Conflicting Sources for Data Integration. CoRR (2012)
8. Xiaoxin, Yin and Jiawei, Han and Philip, Yu: Truth Discovery with Multiple Conflicting Information Providers on the Web. TKDE (2007)
9. Dong, Xin Luna and Saha, Barna and Srivastava, Divesh. Less is more: Selecting sources wisely for integration. VLDB (2012)
10. Abiteboul, Serge and Hull, Richard and Vianu, Victor: Foundations of databases: the logical level, Addison-Wesley (1995)

Incremental discovery of functional dependencies with a bit-vector algorithm

Loredana Caruccio, Stefano Cirillo, Vincenzo Deufemia, and Giuseppe Polese

University of Salerno, Department of Computer Science
via Giovanni Paolo II n.132, 84084 Fisciano (SA), Italy
{lcaruccio,scirillo,deufemia,gpolese}@unisa.it

Abstract. Functional dependencies (FDs) were conceived in the early '70s, and were mainly used to verify database design and assess data quality. Nowadays they are automatically discovered from data since they can be exploited for many different purposes, such as query relaxation, data cleansing, and record matching. In the context of big data, the speed at which new data is being created demand for new efficient algorithms for FD discovery. In this paper, we propose an incremental FD discovery approach, which is able to update the set of holding FDs upon insertions of new tuples to the data instance, without having to restart the discovery process from scratch. It exploits a bit-vector representation of FDs, and an upward/downward search strategy aiming to reduce the overall search space. Experimental results show that such algorithm achieves extremely better time performances with respect to the re-execution of the algorithm from scratch.

Keywords: Functional Dependency · Discovery Algorithm · Instance Updating · Incremental Discovery.

1 Introduction

With the advent of Big Data, both industry and research communities have manifested a tremendous interest in technologies capable of extracting information and their correlations among data. One way to represent such relationships is to use functional dependencies (FDs), which represent relationships among database columns that can be used for several advanced database operations, such as query optimisation, data cleansing, and data integration [12].

While FDs were originally specified at database design time, as properties of a schema that should hold on every instance of it, there has been the need to automatically discover them from data for reducing the design effort and for supporting their evolution in the application domains. This is made possible also thanks to the availability of big data collections, and to the contributions of several research areas, such as machine learning and knowledge discovery [9].

The problem of discovering FDs is extremely complex, since the number of holding FDs for a given database instance could be exponential with respect to the number of database columns. In fact, most of the discovery algorithms described in the literature aimed to provide solutions in which the search space complexity is reduced by exploiting the theoretical properties of FDs. However, while the availability of big data collections stimulates the discovery of meaningful FDs from data, the necessity to update them according to the evolution of database instances require that also FDs are updated. In fact, one of the characteristics describing big data is the *velocity*, which includes the fact that data are continuously produced.

In this paper, we propose an incremental discovery approach for FDs, which updates the complete set of holding FDs according to the new added tuples. The approach exploits a bit-vector representation of FDs, and an upward/downward search strategy aiming to prune the search space. Experimental results achieved on twenty-eight datasets show that the proposed approach achieves better time performances with respect to the re-execution of the algorithm from scratch.

The paper is organised as follows. Section 2 reviews the FD discovery algorithms existing in the literature. Section 3 provides some background definitions about FDs and formulates the problem of FD discovery. Section 4 presents the proposed methodology for the incremental discovery of FDs from data, whose evaluation is reported in Section 5. Finally, summary and concluding remarks are included in Section 6.

2 Related Work

The FD discovery problem dates back to the '80s, when the first discovery algorithms were defined [11], and many of the latest proposals are based on theoretical foundations introduced within older solutions [7, 8]. It is a extremely complex problem, since the number of potential FDs can be exponential, and their detection requires analysing a huge number of column combinations [1].

In the literature there are two main categories of methods to automatically discover FDs from data, namely column-based and row-based methods. The former exploit an attribute lattice to generate candidate FDs, which are successively tested to verify their validity. The whole process is made efficient by exploiting valid FDs to prune the search space for new candidates. Examples of top-down approaches include the algorithms TANE [8], FD_Mine [18], and DFD [2]. Row-based methods derive candidate FDs from two attribute subsets, namely *agree-sets* and *difference-sets*, which are built by comparing the values of attributes for all possible combinations of tuples pairs. Examples of bottom-up approaches include the algorithms DepMiner [10], FastFD [17], and FDep [6].

Experimental results show that column-based algorithms usually outperform row-based ones on datasets with many rows and few columns, whereas on datasets with few rows and many columns the row-based algorithms usually perform better [13]. Recently, an hybrid algorithm has been proposed in order to obtain better performance in all cases [14]. It combines row- and column-efficient discovery techniques by managing two separated phases, one in which it calculates FDs on a randomly selected small subset of records (column-efficiency), and the other in which it validates the discovered FDs on the entire dataset.

One of the first theoretical proposal of incremental algorithm for FD discovery has been proposed in 2001 [16]. It exploits the concepts of tuple partitions and monotonicity of FDs to avoid the re-scanning of the database. Another proposal exploits the concept of functional independency in order to maintain the set of FDs updated over time [3]. Finally, in order to discover and maintain functional dependencies in dynamic datasets, the DynFD algorithm has been proposed [15]. It continuously adapts the validation structures of FDs in order to evolve them with batch of inserts, updates, and deletes of data. Some of the methodologies surveyed above (i.e. [16, 3]) are not implemented, whereas others need to store the data structure produced during the discovery process. To this end, the advantage of the proposed methodology is that it relies only on the list of discovered FDs, so it can be applied to any column-based FD discovery algorithm.

3 The Discovery Problem

Before discussing the problem of discovering FDs, let us first recall the definition of the canonical FD. Given a relational database schema $\mathcal{R}$, defined over a set of attributes $attr(\mathcal{R})$, derived as the union of attributes from relation schemas R composing $\mathcal{R}$, assuming w.l.o.g. they all have unique names. For each attribute $A \in attr(R)$, its domain is denoted by $dom(A)$. Moreover, given an instance r of R and a tuple $t \in r$, we use $t[A]$ to denote the projection of t onto A; similarly, for a set X of attributes in $attr(R)$, $t[X]$ denotes the projection of t onto X. An FD over R is a statement $X \rightarrow Y$ (X implies Y) with $X, Y \subseteq attr(R)$, such that, given an instance r over R, $X \rightarrow Y$ is satisfied in r if and only if for every pair of tuples (t_1, t_2) in r, whenever $t_1[X] = t_2[X]$, then $t_1[Y] = t_2[Y]$. X,Y are also named Left-Hand-Side (LHS) and Right-Hand-Side (RHS) of an FD.

The goal of dependency discovery is to find meaningful dependencies holding among columns of a dataset. They represent domain knowledge and can be used to assess database design and data quality [9]. Moreover, discovering dependencies from data permits to capture the evolution of real-world domains.

Discovering FDs over a relation instance r entails finding all the possible column combinations, and for each of them find all the possible partitions forming the LHS and RHS of candidate FDs. Without loss of generality, we can consider only candidates with a single attribute on the RHS. Given this, the FD discovery problem has an extremely large search space. In fact, given a relation r with M attributes and n tuples, we need to consider all the possible combinations of 2 to M attributes, counting each of them as many times as the number of attributes in it, in order to account for the number of different candidates with a single RHS attribute. This complexity is synthesised by the following formula:

$$\sum_{k=2}^{M} \binom{M}{k} k \qquad (1)$$

Since this complexity represents only the number of candidate FDs that could be potentially checked, the discovery algorithms need to tackle several other issues, such as the validation of each candidate whose complexity is linear in the number of tuples.

The general FD discovery problem is described by the following definition.

Definition 1. *Given a relation instance r of a relation R, an* FD *discovery algorithm has to find the minimal cover set of* FDs *holding in r, having the property that tuples equal on the LHS must be equal also on the RHS.*

According to this definition, an FD discovery algorithm has to identify the *minimal cover* of FDs holding on a relation instance r. The minimal cover will contain all valid FDs even if they have low support. Thus, an holding FD does not appear in the minimal cover P only when it can be inferred by other FDs in P. For these reasons, given a set P of all minimal FDs holding on r, and computed at time τ, it is necessary to update P whenever one or more tuples have been added from time τ to time τ', since new tuples can violate one or more FDs of P. Details on how we deal with such a problem are discussed into the next section.

4 Incremental Discovery of Functional Dependencies

This section presents the structure of the proposed incremental approach for FDs discovery by introducing the data representation and the search strategies. Data structures, pruning, and validation processes of FDs will, therefore, be described.

4.1 Incremental Methodology

FD discovery algorithms operating on static datasets require to be re-execute upon the insertion of new tuples. This is a computationally expensive operation, especially for database instances with a large number of rows and columns. The main problem with the database instance evolution is that FDs found at time τ can be invalidated at time τ'. For this reason, it is necessary to implement incremental approaches that reduce the time for searching and validating FDs.

In our study, we propose an incremental discovery approach that takes in input the FDs associated to a relation instance r, represents FDs using bitsets, and performs an upward and downward search strategy. Figure 1 shows the binary representation of an FD with k attributes. In particular, each dependency $X \rightarrow A$ requires two bitsets: the first contains all the LHS attributes, while the second contains the RHS attribute of the FD.

Each location of a bitset B represents an attribute of a relation instance r. In particular, given an FD $X \rightarrow A$ on r, if $B_X[i] = 1$ then the i-th attribute in r belongs to X. The size of each bitset corresponds to the number of attributes of the considered instance r. In this way, it is possible to represent dependencies with hundreds of attributes in a compact and lightweight fashion.

In our methodology, all binary FDs holding on a instance at time τ are stored in a linked ordered hash map. This data structure was used to ensure that information are quickly saved and retrieved. The map uses as key the bit-vector representation of FDs, and as value the next dependency, according to an ordering criteria based on the LHS cardinality. Moreover, two fast arrays link the map in order to reduce the insertion times of the FDs. This data organisation allows to perform a level-wise discovery based on a lattice search strategy. Furthermore, it guarantees an immediate pruning of dependencies that are not minimal.

As said above, inserting new tuples in a relation instance could affect the validity of the FDs. In particular, the main effects that can be produced by new tuples are:

- **Invalidation of functional dependencies**. Let $X \rightarrow A$ be a minimal FD with $X, A \subseteq attr(R)$ at time τ, such that for each pair of tuples (t_1^τ, t_2^τ) belonging to the instance r, whenever $t_1^\tau[X] = t_2^\tau[X]$ then $t_1^\tau[A] = t_2^\tau[A]$. If at time $\tau + 1$ there exist a new tuple $t_3^{\tau+1}$ such that:

$$t_1^\tau[X] = t_3^{\tau+1}[X] \wedge t_1^\tau[A] \neq t_3^{\tau+1}[A]$$

  or two new tuples $t_4^{\tau+1}$, $t_5^{\tau+1}$, which verify the following property:

$$t_4^{\tau+1}[X] = t_5^{\tau+1}[X] \wedge t_4^{\tau+1}[A] \neq t_5^{\tau+1}[A]$$

  then the FD $X \rightarrow A$ is no longer valid.

- **Confirmation of minimality**. If a minimal functional dependency is valid at time τ and has not been invalidated by any tuple at time $\tau + 1$, then this dependency is minimal also at time $\tau + 1$.

Based on these considerations, the methodology considers the first functional dependency extracted at time τ with the smallest LHS cardinality and the attribute partitions of the relation instance. In the pre-processing phase, the FDs holding at time τ are mapped within the linked ordered hash map and the partitions are updated according to the set of new tuples. The use of tuple partitions avoids to access data during the discovery and allows to validate the FDs through the refinement property [8].

Definition 2. ***Refinement.*** *A functional dependency* $X \rightarrow A$ *holds on* r *iff* $|\pi_X| = |\pi_{(X \cup A)}|$, *where* π_X *and* $\pi_{(X \cup A)}$ *are the sets of equivalence classes, i.e., they are the partitions of* r *on* X *and* $X \cup A$.

If a minimal FD $X \rightarrow A$ is invalidated at time $\tau + 1$, then new candidate dependencies need to be analysed. In particular, it is necessary to validate all

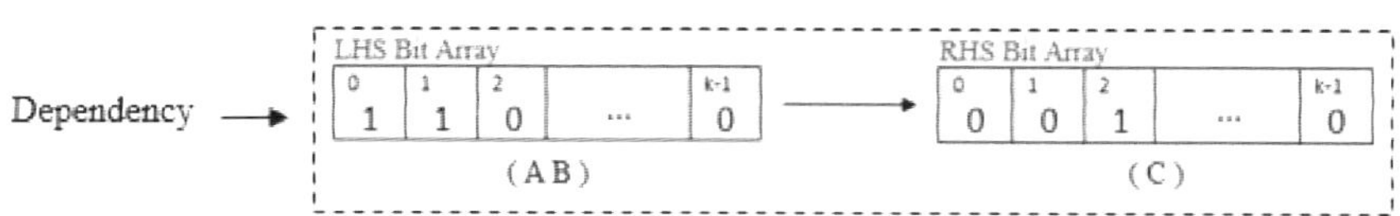

Fig. 1. Bit-vector representation of a functional dependency.

Algorithm 1 Incremental Discovery Algorithm

INPUT: a set Σ_τ of valid and minimal FDs at time τ
OUTPUT: a set $\Sigma_{\tau+1}$ of new valid and minimal FDs at time $\tau + 1$

1: **for all** $X \rightarrow A \in \Sigma_\tau$ **do**
2:     **if** `REFINEMENT`$(X \rightarrow A)$ *is not valid* **then**
3:         $\mathrm{L}_{l+1} \leftarrow$ `NEXTLEVEL`$(X \rightarrow A)$
4:         **for all** $X_{l+1} \in \mathrm{L}_{l+1}$ **do**
5:             **if not** `INFERENCE`$(X_{l+1} \rightarrow A$ **then**$)$
6:                 $\Sigma_\tau \leftarrow \Sigma_\tau \cup \{X_{l+1} \rightarrow A\}$
7:     **else**
8:         $\mathrm{L}_{l-1} \leftarrow$ `PREVLEVEL`$(X \rightarrow A)$
9:         **for all** $X_{l-1} \in \mathrm{L}_{l-1}$ **do**
10:             **if not** `INFERENCE`$(X_{l-1} \rightarrow A)$ **then**
11:                 $\Sigma_\tau \leftarrow \Sigma_\tau \setminus \{X \rightarrow A\}$
12: $\Sigma_{\tau+1} \leftarrow \Sigma_\tau$

non-trivial FDs $XB \rightarrow A$ for each $B \in attr(R)$, with $B \notin X \cup A$. This means that a higher level in the lattice search strategy is considered. In fact, only candidates of higher levels w.r.t. the holding FDs at time τ can hold at time $\tau+1$. Moreover, it is not necessary to verify the dependencies $X \setminus B \rightarrow A$ for each $B \in X$, since such FDs were not valid at time τ, and cannot be valid at time $\tau+1$. However, it is necessary to guarantee the minimality of $XB \rightarrow A$. In fact, such dependency can be considered as minimal at time $\tau + 1$ if and only if it cannot be inferred by other holding FDs at time $\tau + 1$.

Definition 3. ***Inference.*** *A functional dependency $XB \rightarrow A$ is inferred by another dependency $XB \setminus Z \rightarrow A$ with $Z \subseteq XB$ iff $XB \setminus Z \rightarrow A$ holds at time $\tau + 1$, and $Z \neq \emptyset$.*

The inference checking is performed in the proposed search process by exploiting the previously introduced linked ordered hash map. In fact, it is necessary to verify if does not exist an FD, among those already validated at time $\tau + 1$, which is minimal with respect to $XB \rightarrow A$. In particular, in order to speed up the inference checking process, we used a hash map that links the possible FD's RHS with all minimal FDs already validated at time $\tau + 1$. This allows to prune the number of FDs to be checked.

The complete discovery process defined according to the proposed methodology is described by Algorithm 1. In particular, for each FD holding at time τ (line 1), it verifies if $X \rightarrow A$ also holds at time $\tau + 1$ through the `REFINEMENT` function (line 2). Next, if $X \rightarrow A$ is not valid, the algorithm generates new candidate FDs at a higher level, by excluding those that can be inferred (lines 3-6). Instead, if $X \rightarrow A$ is valid, the latter is added to the result set only iff it cannot be inferred by other holding FDs at a lower level (lines 8-11).

In general, the proposed approach can drastically reduce the execution time for two main reasons:

1. the bit-vector representation of FDs permits to quickly process new configurations of FDs by computing the new LHSs in terms of attribute supersets or subsets. In other words, it optimises the downward/upward search strategies;
2. the ordered linked hash map permits to extremely prune the search process, since it guarantees a fast minimality test.

Example 1. Table 1 shows a database instance r in which three new tuples have been added at time $\tau + 1$. Starting from the partitions of the instance r at time τ, that is, $\pi_A = \{[0,1],[3,4],[2]\}$, $\pi_B = \{[3,4],[0],[1,2]\}$, $\pi_C = \{[0,2],[4],[1,3]\}$, $\pi_D = \{[0,3],[4],[2],[1]\}$, the incremental algorithm computes the updated partitions, that is, $\pi'_A = \{[0,1],[3,4,7],[2,5,6]\}$, $\pi'_B = \{[3,4],[0],[6,7],[1,2,\ 5]\}$, $\pi'_C = \{[0,2,5,7],[4],[1,3,6]\}$, $\pi'_D = \{[0,3,5],[7],[4],[2],[6],[1]\}$, and loads the minimal FDs holding at time τ. The latter are represented in terms of bit-vectors and inserted into the ordered linked map.

Figure 2 shows the linked ordered hash map obtained at time $\tau{+}1$ for the new instance of Table 1. It visualises all the considered candidate FDs. In particular, each bit-vector in Figure 2 represents: 1) a minimal FD holding at time $\tau + 1$, 2) a candidate FD that has been invalidated at time $\tau + 1$, or 3) a candidate FD that is not minimal at time $\tau + 1$.

Initially, the dependency with the lowest LHS cardinality is selected by using a fast array to directly link the first dependency with a given LHS cardinality. In Figure 2 this corresponds to $(0110) \rightarrow (0001)$. Using the refinement property, this FD is removed because $|\pi_X| \neq |\pi_{(X \cup A)}|$. Starting from this, the algorithm calculates the next candidates, which consider LHS supersets. For each of them the inference checking is applied, and only those that cannot be inferred are added to the map. Therefore, in the example, the FDs $(1110) \rightarrow (0001)$ and $(0111) \rightarrow (1000)$ are added to the ordered map, also updating the links that preserve the map ordering. The execution proceeds until all FDs are explored. In particular, the FD $(0111) \rightarrow (1000)$ is removed because it is not minimal with respect to $(0101) \rightarrow (1000)$, which has been previously validated. Finally, the algorithm returns the new minimal set of FDs holding on the instance at time $\tau + 1$, so avoiding the re-execution of the discovery algorithm from scratch.

Table 1. An example of a relation instance updated at time $\tau + 1$.

	Row Id	A	B	C	D
	0	Andorra	1	French	French
	1	Andorra	2	English	Russian
	2	San Marino	2	French	Italian
	3	Cipro	4	English	French
	4	Cipro	4	Greek	Spanish
+	5	San Marino	2	French	French
+	6	San Marino	3	English	German
+	7	Cipro	3	French	Arabic

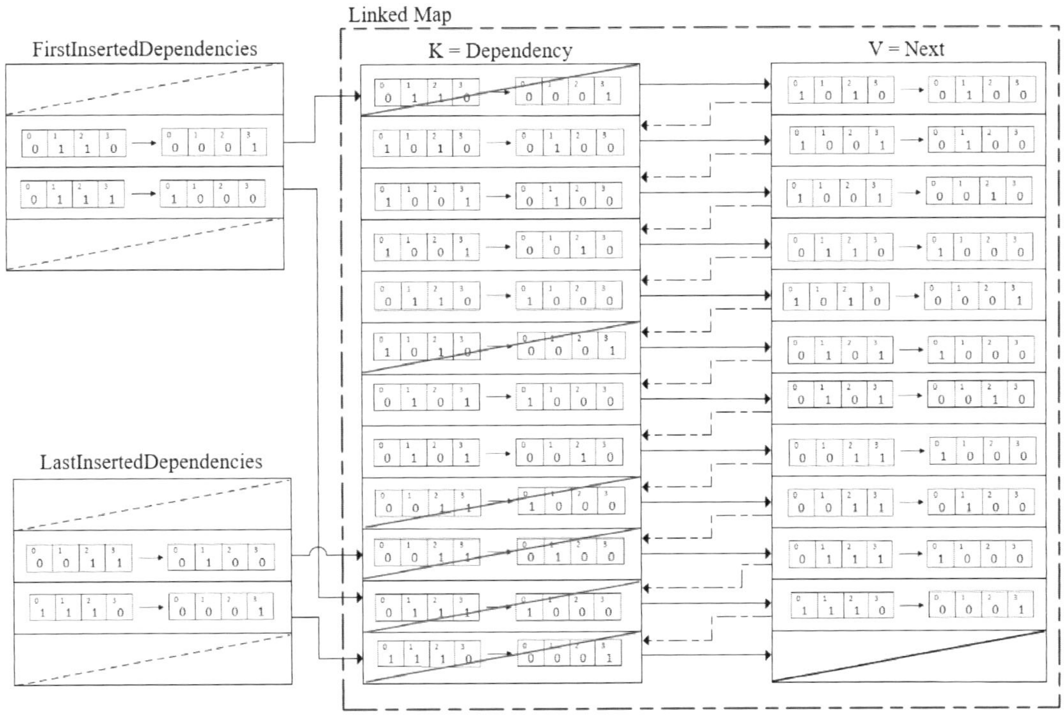

Fig. 2. The Linked Ordered Hash Map related to Example 1.

5 Evaluation

In the following, we present experimental results concerning the performance of the proposed approach in discovering FDs. In particular, the performed tests show how much the new proposed approach can improve time performances with respect to the re-execution of the FD discovery algorithm.

Implementation details. The algorithm has been developed in Java 11.0.2. In particular, in order to improve the performance of the algorithm and avoid the re-calculation of partitions, we also introduced a methodology for caching partitions, since the latter are widely used for the validation of candidate FDs.

Hardware and datasets. The tests has been performed on a Mac with an Intel Xeon processor at 3.20 GHz 8-core and 64GB of RAM. Moreover, to ensure a proper execution on the considered datasets, the Java memory heap size allocation has been set to 40GB to permit a proper execution on datasets with a high number of tuples/attributes.

We evaluated the proposed approach on several real world datasets, previously used for testing FD discovery algorithms [13]. Statistics on the characteristics of the considered datasets are shown in Table 2. Such datasets are composed of one relation, since FD discovery algorithms always consider de-normalised databases.

Table 2. Characteristics of the used datasets and discovery results.

Dataset	Tuples	Attributes	%Inserts	#fds	TANE time(ms)	Incremental time(ms)
Abalone	4176	9	50 %	137	308	**183**
Adult	32561	15	50 %	78	43033	**1085**
Balance-scale	624	5	50 %	1	130	**6**
Breast-cancer-wisc.	699	11	50 %	46	316	**284**
Breast-cancer	285	10	50 %	1	230	**132**
Bridges	108	13	50 %	142	218	**195**
Bupa	344	7	50 %	25	134	**19**
CallIt	10081	3	50 %	1	176	**30**
Cars	407	9	50 %	67	162	**48**
Car_data	1727	7	50 %	1	197	**7**
Chess	1999	7	50 %	6	184	**7**
Citations	1000	9	50 %	76	203	**182**
Citeseer	10K	7	50 %	10	456	**116**
Citeseer	20K	6	50 %	4	721	**816**
Cmc	1472	10	50 %	1	477	**15**
DBLP	20K	8	50 %	28	364	**172**
Echocardiogram	132	13	50 %	538	191	**363**
Ecoli	335	9	50 %	54	139	**24**
Haberman	305	4	50 %	0	110	**1**
Hayes-roth	132	6	50 %	5	119	**2**
Iris	149	5	50 %	4	116	**6**
Letter	20K	17	50 %	61	177087	**6203**
Mammography	960	6	50 %	0	150	**1**
Nursery	12960	9	50 %	1	1065	**45**
Servo	166	5	50 %	1	115	**3**
Tae	150	6	50 %	2	122	**14**
Tax	100K	15	50 %	364	29368	**28598**
Wine	178	14	50 %	1374	209	**131**

Evaluation process. We carried out different tests by using as starting point the minimal FDs extracted through the TANE algorithm [8]. All the tests were performed on datasets split into two parts. The first part represents the relation instance at time τ, and it has been given in input to TANE. The complete dataset represents the relation instance at time $\tau+1$ analysed by the proposed incremental discovery algorithm. Moreover, we re-executed the TANE algorithm on the complete dataset. This allowed us to analyse the resulting FDs, and to compare execution times of our approach w.r.t. a complete re-execution of TANE. Moreover, we executed other two experiments: 1) by varying the number of tuples inserted at time $\tau+1$; 2) by varying the number of rows/columns of the dataset.

Analysis of the results. The first test has been conducted by simulating the insertion of 50% of tuples of the complete dataset. The results are reported in Table 2, where a comparison between the times of TANE and the incremental approach are shown. From the results we can notice that the proposed approach is in general more efficient, despite the variability of the number of rows/columns. This is mainly due to the pruning strategies introduced by the incremental approach. However, there are few cases in which the execution times are equivalent to those of TANE. This happens when there is a huge number of holding FDs at time τ.

The second test aimed to evaluate the relationship between the execution times and the sizes of the datasets. In particular, we selected datasets by varying

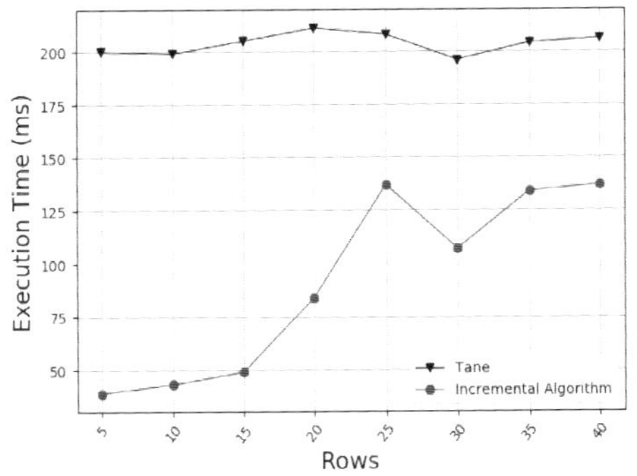

(a) Citations

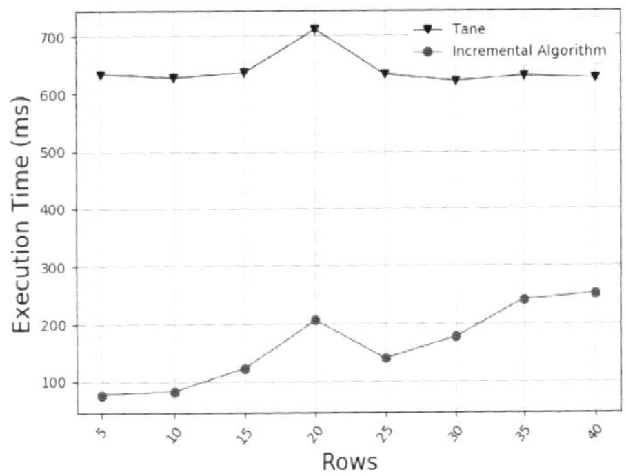

(b) Citeseer

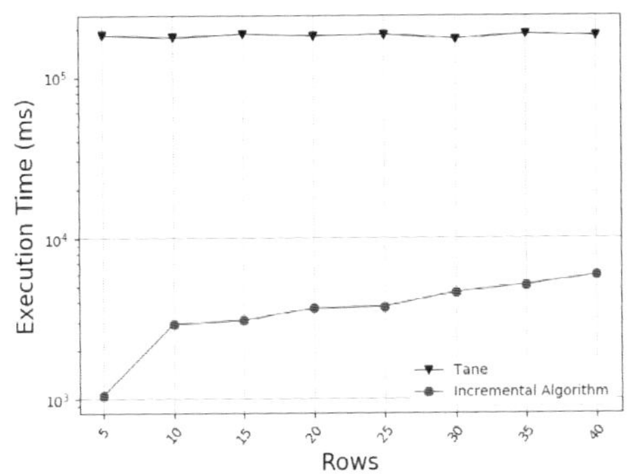

(c) Letter

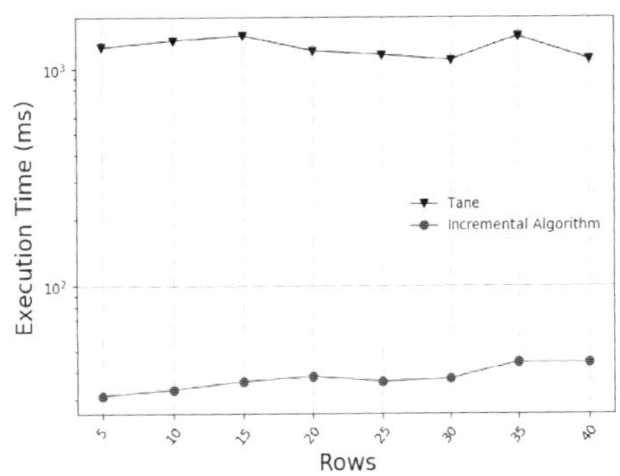

(d) Nursery

Fig. 3. A comparison between execution times of TANE with respect to our proposal by varying the percentage of inserted tuples at time $\tau + 1$.

the number of tuples inserted at time $\tau + 1$ in the range of 5%-40% w.r.t. the complete dataset. Results are shown in Figure 3. In particular, the results for *nursey* (Figure 3(d)) and *citeseer* (Figure 3(b)) show an extremely reduction of the execution times when considering the incremental approach. This is probably due to the fact that the number of minimal FDs at time τ was small. Moreover, although this number is higher for *citations* and *letter*, the time performances of our approach is still lower than the execution of TANE (Figures 3(a) and 3(c)).

The last test allowed us to evaluate the discovery time of the incremental algorithm on datasets with a fixed number of tuples but a variable number of columns (first session), and with a fixed number of attributes but a variable number of tuples within an interval range of $[2000 - 20000]$ tuples with step 2000 (second session). For these experiments *dblp* and *citeseer* datasets have been selected. Table 3 contains the characteristics of the datasets and the results of the experiments with a variable number of attributes. Instead, the results of the second session are shown in the Figure 4. By analysing Table 3, we can notice that the execution times of the proposed approach are always lower than the execution times of TANE. Moreover, we noticed that for our incremental approach the *dblp* dataset is more critical than *citeseer* when the number of attributes increases. Also in this case, this is probably due to the higher number

Table 3. A comparison between execution times of TANE with respect to our proposal by varying the number of attributes.

Dataset	Tuples	Attributes	%Inserts	TANE time(ms)	Incremental time(ms)
DBLP	20K	2	3 %	220	**32**
DBLP	20K	3	3 %	277	**78**
DBLP	20K	4	3 %	293	**126**
DBLP	20K	5	3 %	366	**162**
DBLP	20K	6	3 %	418	**232**
DBLP	20K	7	3 %	490	**245**
Citeseer	20K	2	3 %	175	**2**
Citeseer	20K	3	3 %	203	**2**
Citeseer	20K	4	3 %	360	**3**
Citeseer	20K	5	3 %	376	**45**
Citeseer	20K	6	3 %	435	**73**
Citeseer	20K	7	3 %	456	**89**

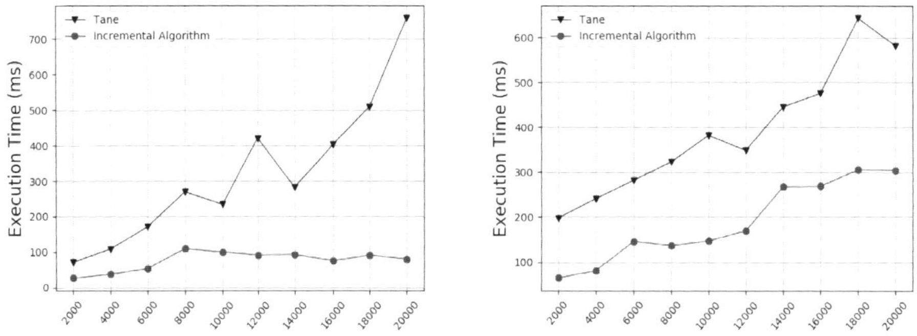

(a) Citeseer (b) DBLP

Fig. 4. A comparison between execution times of TANE with respect to our proposal by varying the number of tuples.

of FDs discovered at time $\tau + 1$. Different results have been obtained when we consider the variation in the number of tuples (Figure 4). In this case, although non monotonic the time trend grows faster for TANE.

6 Final Remarks

In this paper we have proposed an incremental approach for discovering FDs, which permits to update the set of holding FDs without the need of exploring the complete search space. A bit-vector representation of the FDs allowed us to optimise this process. Experimental results show that the proposed approach considerably reduces the execution times with respect to a re-execution from scratch.

In the future, we would like to further improve this approach in order to automatically updates FDs even for other database instance modifications, such as the deletion and the updating of tuples. Another interesting issue concerns the possibility of updating also Relaxed Functional Dependencies (RFDs) [4], for which the discovery process is even more complex [5].

References

1. Abedjan, Z., Golab, L., Naumann, F.: Profiling relational data: a survey. The VLDB Journal **24**(4), 557–581 (2015)
2. Abedjan, Z., Schulze, P., Naumann, F.: DFD: Efficient functional dependency discovery. In: Proceedings of the 23rd ACM International Conference on Information and Knowledge Management. pp. 949–958. CIKM '14 (2014)
3. Bell, S.: Discovery and maintenance of functional dependencies by independencies. In: KDD. pp. 27–32 (1995)
4. Caruccio, L., Deufemia, V., Polese, G.: Relaxed functional dependencies – A survey of approaches. IEEE TKDE **28**(1), 147–165 (2016)
5. Caruccio, L., Deufemia, V., Polese, G.: On the discovery of relaxed functional dependencies. In: Proceedings of 20th International Database Engineering & Applications Symposium. pp. 53–61. IDEAS '16 (2016)
6. Flach, P.A., Savnik, I.: Database dependency discovery: A machine learning approach. AI Commun. **12**(3), 139–160 (1999)
7. Huhtala, Y., Kärkkäinen, J., Porkka, P., Toivonen, H.: Efficient discovery of functional and approximate dependencies using partitions. In: ICDE. pp. 392–401 (1998)
8. Huhtala, Y., Kärkkäinen, J., Porkka, P., Toivonen, H.: TANE: An efficient algorithm for discovering functional and approximate dependencies. The Computer Journal **42**(2), 100–111 (1999)
9. Liu, J., Li, J., Liu, C., Chen, Y.: Discover dependencies from data - A review. IEEE Transactions on Knowledge and Data Engineering **24**(2), 251–264 (2012)
10. Lopes, S., Petit, J.M., Lakhal, L.: Efficient discovery of functional dependencies and armstrong relations. In: Proceedings of the 7th International Conference on Extending Database Technology. pp. 350–364. EDBT '00 (2000)
11. Mannila, H., Räihä, K.J.: Dependency inference. In: Proceedings of the 13th International Conference on Very Large Data Bases. pp. 155–158. VLDB '87 (1987)
12. Naumann, F.: Data profiling revisited. ACM SIGMOD Record **42**(4), 40–49 (2014)
13. Papenbrock, T., Ehrlich, J., Marten, J., Neubert, T., Rudolph, J.P., Schönberg, M., Zwiener, J., Naumann, F.: Functional dependency discovery: An experimental evaluation of seven algorithms. Proceedings of the VLDB Endowment **8**(10), 1082–1093 (2015)
14. Papenbrock, T., Naumann, F.: A hybrid approach to functional dependency discovery. In: Proceedings of the 2016 International Conference on Management of Data. pp. 821–833. ACM (2016)
15. Schirmer, P., Papenbrock, T., Kruse, S., Hempfing, D., Meyer, T., Neuschäfer-Rube, D., Naumann, F.: DynFD: Functional dependency discovery in dynamic datasets. In: To appear in EDBT (2019)
16. Wang, S.L., Shen, J.W., Hong, T.P.: Incremental discovery of functional dependencies using partitions. In: Proceedings Joint 9th IFSA World Congress and 20th NAFIPS International Conference (Cat. No. 01TH8569). vol. 3, pp. 1322–1326. IEEE (2001)
17. Wyss, C., Giannella, C., Robertson, E.: FastFDs: A heuristic-driven, depth-first algorithm for mining functional dependencies from relation instances. In: Procs of Intl Conf. on Data Warehousing and Knowl. Disc. pp. 101–110. DaWaK '01 (2001)
18. Yao, H., Hamilton, H.J., Butz, C.J.: FD_Mine: Discovering functional dependencies in a database using equivalences. In: Proceedings of IEEE International Conference on Data Mining. pp. 729–732. ICDM '02 (2002)

Machine Learning of SPARQL Templates for Question Answering over LinkedSpending *(Discussion Paper)*

Roberto Cocco[1], Maurizio Atzori[1], and Carlo Zaniolo[2]

[1] Department of Math/CS (DMI), University of Cagliari (Italy)
robertococco@outlook.com atzori@unica.it
https://dmi.unica.it/atzori
[2] CS Department, University of California, Los Angeles (USA)
zaniolo@cs.ucla.edu
http://web.cs.ucla.edu/~zaniolo/

Abstract. We present a Question Answering system aimed to answer natural language questions over open RDF spending data provided by LinkedSpeding. We propose an original machine-learning approach to learn generalized SPARQL templates from an existing training set of *(NL question, SPARQL query)* pairs. In our approach the generalized SPARQL templates are fed to an instance-based classifier that associates a given user-provided question to an existing pair, that is used to answer the user question. We employ an external tagger, delegating the Named-Entity Recognition (NER) task to a service developed for the domain we want to question. The problem is particularly challenging due to the small training set size available, counting only 100 questions/SPARQL queries.
We illustrate the results of our new approach using data provided by the Question Answering over Linked Data challenge (QALD-6) task 3, showing that it can provide a correct answer to 14 of the 50 questions of the test set. These results are then compared to existing systems, including QA^3, our previous work where templates were provided by an expert instead of being generated automatically from a training set.

Keywords: Question Answering · SPARQL · Semantic Web · Machine Learning

1 Introduction

The recent years saw a steady growth of structured data made available to the public, with governments giving their contribution by publishing information about public expenses. At the same pace the need grows to make this data available to non-technical users. In this paper, we propose a tool capable of answering a question posed in natural language by a user with no experience of RDF datasets and SPARQL queries. This is a follow-up to our previous template-based question-answering system called QA^3 [1], with the main difference being the way templates are obtained. In fact, while QA^3 requires the templates to be generated by an experienced user, in this paper we present a system that is able to learn new templates from datasets fed to an intelligent template generator. Our system works by processing a dataset containing *(question, SPARQL query)* pairs in input. Specific references contained in each question and its associated SPARQL query are automatically linked by our system, and treated as "variables" that may vary in different user questions. In other words, both questions and SPARQL queries are generalized into templates that can be filled in with different values w.r.t. the instances available in the dataset.

At answering time, the user question is subject to a similar generalization process, whereby it is matched to a list of generalized templates containing the same tags and ordered by the Jaccard Index (also known as *intersection over union*).

The best matching templates, and their associated queries, are then filled in with the data so obtained by tagging the user question. Due to the kind of approach used, in some cases more than a query per template is reconstructed, so we show the user the template question filled in with the highest Jaccard Index and ask the user if this has the same meaning as the original one. This allows our system to exploit user's feedback to further refine the initial training set. Furthermore, the system keeps presenting the user with questions until he/she returns a positive response or no more questions are left to show. This results in a very flexible system, requiring the user to input only non-technical data as long as an initial small training set of question/answer pairs.

RDF. The Resource Description Framework[3] is a set of specifications used to represent graph data. It provides us with a general method to decompose knowledge into triples, composed of a *subject*, a *predicate* and an *object*.

Linked Spending. With more and more governments providing spending data to the public, Linked Spending[4] took on the task of making open spending data available via RDF datacubes, a W3C standard [2]. It now provides more than 2 million planned or carried out financial transactions.

Question answering and QALD. Question answering systems focus on correctly answering questions posed in natural language, instead of retrieving information on the basis of user-generated keywords as traditional search engines do [4] or SQL-like query languages like SPARQL. This problem can be approached in many different ways, but the main challenges can be considered: *(i)* Extracting the relevant information from the questions and mapping it to the datacube, *(ii)* Dealing with terms ambiguity, *(iii)* Working with more than one dataset, *(iv)* Data quality and heterogeneity. In this paper, we leverage

[3] `https://www.xml.com/pub/a/2001/01/24/rdf.html`

[4] `http://linkedspending.aksw.org/`

the award-winning results of QA^3, and focus on automating (through machine learning) the process of generating templates, which previously required a try-and-error approach by a human expert.

Question Answering over Linked Data[5] (QALD) is a series of evaluation campaigns that provides an up-to-date benchmark for assessing and comparing question answering systems that query RDF-based Linked Data. Over the years, QALD has generated a series of training/test sets. The relevant one for this work is Task 3 of QALD6, containing a training set of 100 instances of *(question, SPARQL query)* pairs for LinkedSpending, and another 50 pairs as test set.

Template-based approaches. Template-based approaches to question answering work by constructing templates (or pseudo queries) from a linguistic analysis of the input questions [4]. These templates are neutral, as they contain no reference to the dataset, and they stand in the middle between the natural language question and a query. Since these templates often reflect the linguistic structure of the questions, structural variations must be included, exponentially increasing the number of possible queries to build.

For an extensive review of existing work, please refer to [1].

2 Our Approach

The main three components that compose this template-based approach are the following:

- a *tagger*, that handles the Named-Entity Recognition task, and is provided by QA^3 [1];
- a *template generator*, that handles the induction of templates of both questions and SPARQL queries by processing a given training set of pairs;
- a *template matcher*, that first performs the ranking of templates for the question posed by the user, and then fills-in the best-matching template.

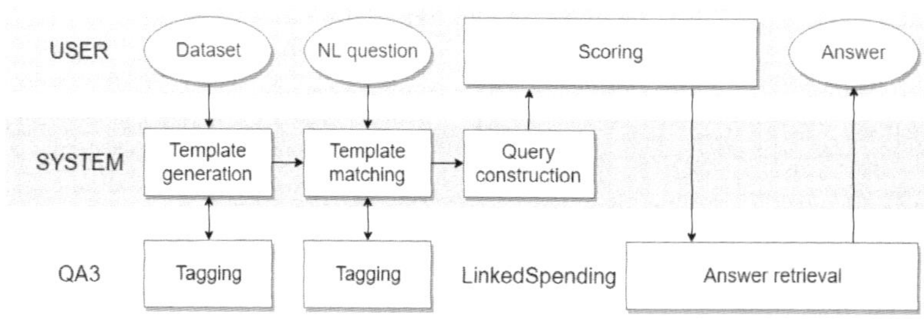

Fig. 1. Our System flow, including tools provided by QA^3 (lower layer) and inputs by the user (upper layer)

[5] `http://qald.aksw.org/`

As shown in Figure 1, a dataset of *(NL question, SPARQL query)* pairs is fed to the *generator*, which, through the *tagger*, outputs a new dataset composed of a list of query templates paired with their respective questions' template. When asked a NL question, the system tags it while the *matcher* extracts similar templates from the templates dataset. From these templates, initial queries and questions can be reconstructed if needed. The scoring of templates w.r.t. a given question is done by the system using semantic similarity, and the system presents the user with successive reconstructed questions until it receives a positive answer, or the list of questions is exhausted. Finally the query, paired with the question chosen by the user, is used to retrieve the answer from the LinkedSpending endpoint[6]. In the following we provide some additional information on each module of the system.

Tagger. The tagger gets the response from a NER service and makes it usable by the system. It sends the end-user question to a service specific for the domain that is being questioned by the user. The service's response usually contains a reference to a datacube, the list of entities found on said datacube, along with the chunk from the question that matched the entity and, optionally, the entity's type.

Generator. The generator creates a template by processing a NL question, a SPARQL query, or both, and removing all the references to the input datacube. It initially gets the list of entities found on the input datacube and the datacube found by the *tagger*. If found in the query, the datacube reference is replaced with the tag (placeholder) <DATASET>. The prefixes are replaced by their expanded form, and aliases and the from clause are removed. Next, the expressions and the supported types (numbers, years) found both on the question and the query are replaced with tags depending on the type of data they represent (e.g. <PROP> for properties, <VALUE> for values, <YEAR> for years, <NUM> for numbers ecc). Finally, the variables get streamlined to a simple naming convention (`varA`, `varB`, ...), and predicates with no matching found in the datacube are replaced by blank nodes. During the filling of a template, the process is basically inverted. The generator still gets from the *tagger* a list of expressions, which in this case were derived from the English question asked by the end-user. Then the template's tags are replaced by the obtained results, based on their types.

Matcher. The matcher, given a question template, returns a list of compatible query templates. This is done by querying a dataset processed by the generator for the tags in the question template. This list, ordered by the Jaccard Index (calculated between the question template, and the question templates associated to the queries in the dataset), will only contain query templates with an equal or lesser number of tags.

[6] `http://linkedspending.aksw.org/sparql`

3 Running Example

In this section, we detail the various steps performed by our prototype and how they work, using a running example associated with the following natural language question: *What was the total Wandsworth spending in 2013 from the housing department?*.

3.1 Data Preprocessing

Data preprocessing is done by feeding a dataset containing *(NL question, SPARQL query)* pairs to the *generator*. The result is a dataset containing a list of query templates associated with a list of question templates and a list of tags. Take a look at Table 1 for an example of such a pair. Pairs that produce the same query template will be joined into an individual entity that references both question templates.

Table 1. An Example of question/SPARQL pair

Question	**SPARQL query**
"What was the total Wandsworth spending in 2013 from the housing department?"	select sum(xsd:decimal(?amount)) { ?obs qb:dataSet ls:wwspending_2013. ?obs lso:wwspending_2013-Department "housing". ?obs lso:wwspending_2013-amount ?amount. }
Question Template	**SPARQL query Template**
"What was the <AGGRA> <DATASET> from the <VALUE1> department?"	select <AGGRA>(xsd:decimal(?varA)) { ?obs qb:dataSet <DATASET> . ?obs [] <VALUE1> . ?obs <MEASURE> ?varA . }

3.2 Question analysis & data matching

These tasks are done by the system's tagger with the aid of a domain-specific NER service, in our case the one provided by the QA^3 tagger. The tagger has the following two goals: (i) finding the correct dataset and (ii) matching question terms with the dataset terminology (NER). Missing the correct dataset or failing to find the correct terms will lead to an incorrect answer, so the NER service's accuracy needs to be very high for our system to work properly.

QA^3 proposed an approach based on choosing "the dataset that better *covers* the question, that is, the one that minimizes the portion of the question not referring to elements in the dataset" [1]. The question-to-dataset terms matching is done by first creating an in-memory index of all literals (labels, comments, and values) for each dataset, and normalizing the textual elements that are keys in the indexes and the questions by removing the stop words.
The response from the NER service usually consists of a dataset and a list of entities, as seen in Figure 2.
We then feed the question and the entities found by the tagger to the *generator* to obtain a template (e.g. *"What was the <AGGRA> <DATASET> from the <VALUE1> department?"*).

```
Dataset: wandsworthspending_2013

Chunk:  What was the total
Chunk:  Wandsworth spending in 2013
        S:  ls:/instance/wandsworthspending_2013
        P:  <http://www.w3.org/2000/01/rdf-schema#label>
        O:  "Wandsworth spending (2013)"
Chunk:  from the
Chunk:  housing
        S:  ls:/instance/observation-wandsworthspending_2013-...
        P:  lso:wandsworthspending_2013-Department
        O: "housing"
Chunk:  department
        S:  lso:wandsworthspending_2013-Department
        P:  <http://purl.org/dc/terms/identifier>
        O:  "Department"
```

Fig. 2. Response's structure

3.3 Query Construction

Inverting the data preprocessing process, the query construction takes a template as input, and returns a query. In this process, the templates are filled-in with the data obtained by the tagger from the NL question. In those cases where the same type of tag appears more than once, or we're working with a template with less tags than the NL question, the system creates a query for every combination, in order to cover different structural variation (e.g., the question *"Which class achieved the highest revenue for the Town of Cary, North Carolina?"* processed as *"Which <PROP0> achieved the <AGGRa> revenue for the <VALUE1>, <VALUE2>?"*, will result in the queries shown in Table 2). This outputs a total of $n!$ queries, where n is the number of times the tag appears in the template, unless templates have fewer tags than the NL question. In this second situation, $n!/m$ templates are returned with m denoting the difference between the number of NL question's tags and the number of template's tags.

Table 2. Example of a query's variations

Query template	select <AGGRa> (?varA) {?obs	<SUB1>	?varA }
Variation A	select max (?varA) {?obs	lso:town_of_cary	?varA }
Variation B	select max (?varA) {?obs	lso:north_carolina	?varA }

3.4 Scoring

The scoring process takes place in two different steps. In the *matcher*, we order the list by the Jaccard Index, for which we can also specify a threshold value. If none of the questions in the list has a value over the threshold, the system widens the search to include templates with fewer tags than the ones on the question. This is done in order to avoid matching unrelated templates, a situation that could occur when more entities are tagged than those that are actually needed. After the query construction, since both the *matcher* and the *generator* can return more than a query, our system ranks them by the Jaccard Index (higher scores first) and presents them one-by-one to the user, until the system gets a positive feedback (Figure 3), in which case the system will proceed to the next step. Otherwise it will terminate refusing to provide an answer.

```
Ask a question:
> Which class achieved the highest revenue for the Town of Cary?

Did you meant "Which class earned the most for the Town of
Cary?" [y, N]
> y

Answer: ['https://openspending.org/town_of_cary_revenues/Class/1']
```

Fig. 3. User feedback exploitation (self-learning)

3.5 Answer retrieval & presentation

The reconstructed query associated to the question picked by the user is executed over the LinkedSpending datacube [3]. The answer obtained by running the SPARQL query computed from the SPARQL query template is run against the LinkedSpending endpoint. Unless the answer is empty, the results are shown to the user as the final answer to the processed question, as in Figure 3.

4 Experiments

We used a simple command line interface, i.e. the one shown in Figure 3, where the user poses a question to the system and is then presented with the questions found in the scoring process. The system executes the query associated with the question chosen by the user. We assume that on the scoring step the user always picks the correct question from the proposed ones if available, or a wrong one in case no correct questions are shown. We think this is the expected scenario whenever the user is practically using the prototype, that is, not in an adversarial worst-case setting. If each proposed question is associated with a query that returns an empty answer, we count the user question as not processed.

QALD-6 Dataset. We tested our system with the datasets of the QALD-6 challenge for statistical question answering over RDF datacubes. It consists in a training dataset of 100 questions, and a test dataset of 50. For each question, both datasets contain the correct answer and other metadata.

Results. The results are obtained by feeding the training dataset to the system generator, and then asking the questions from the training and test datasets respectively. The system scored a total of 14 answers on the test dataset, processing 30 out of 50 questions (precision 47% over processed questions). On the training dataset, it managed to process 59 out of 100 questions, and correctly answered to 41 (69% over processed questions). These results are reported in Table 3. Although precision and recall are lower than our award-winning QA^3 system, we believe these are great results considering that no human expert contributed to this result. In fact, measures are reasonable when compared against existing approaches despite our approach being completely automatic. That is, the system will support new queries as long as at least one example is provided in the training set or the user provide a positive feedback. We believe this represents a significant improvement of the state-of-the-art in unsupervised QA on knowledge bases.

Table 3. Results on training and test datasets, obtained by feeding the training dataset to the system

Dataset	N	Processed	Correctly answered
Training	100	59	41
Test	50	30	14

Table 4. Comparison against other QA systems, as reported by the QALD-6 independent competition

System	Processed	Recall	Precision	F-1
This approach	**30**	**0.41**	**0.47**	**0.44**
QA^3	44	0.62	0.59	0.60
CubeQA	49	0.41	0.49	0.45
SPARKLIS (expert user)	50	0.94	0.96	0.95
SPARKLIS (beginner user)	50	0.76	0.88	0.82

References

1. Atzori, M., Mazzeo, G.M., Zaniolo, C.: QA^3: a Natural Language Approach to Question Answering over RDF Data Cubes. Semantic Web **10**(3), 587–604 (2019). https://doi.org/10.3233/SW-180328, `https://doi.org/10.3233/SW-180328`
2. Cyganiak, R., Reynolds, D.: The RDF Data Cube Vocabulary (W3C Recommendation). `https://www.w3.org/TR/vocab-data-cube/` (Jan 2014)
3. Höffner, K., Martin, M., Lehmann, J.: Linkedspending: Openspending becomes linked open data. Semantic Web **7**(1), 95–104 (2016). https://doi.org/10.3233/SW-150172, `http://dx.doi.org/10.3233/SW-150172`
4. Unger, C., Freitas, A., Cimiano, P.: An introduction to question answering over linked data. In: Reasoning Web. Reasoning on the Web in the Big Data Era - 10th International Summer School 2014, Athens, Greece, September 8-13, 2014. Proceedings. pp. 100–140 (2014)

Mining Microscopic and Macroscopic Changes in Network Data Streams (Discussion Paper)

Corrado Loglisci, Angelo Impedovo, Michelangelo Ceci, Donato Malerba

Dept. of Computer Science, University of Bari "Aldo Moro", Bari, Italy
{corrado.loglisci, angelo.impedovo, michelangelo.ceci, donato.malerba}@uniba.it

Abstract. Network data streams offer an abstraction of complex systems from the real-world, which can be seen as producers of unbounded sequences of complex data generated at high speed. Many complex systems evolve according to stochastic processes which remain unknown to the interested users. As a consequence, changes happen in an unpredictable manner and may involve various portions of the observed complex systems. In this scenario, an interesting problem concerns the identification and characterization of the changes that may concern both the whole structure of a complex system and small parts of it. We conjecture that the former can be explained by the latter and conversely, the latter can trigger the former. This type of problem requires a quite holistic strategy that traditional approaches often do not carry out because they focus on either the whole network or on some portions only. In this discussion paper, we describe a descriptive data mining approach based on frequent pattern discovery that we designed for recent research work. It combines frequent pattern with automatic time-window setting, in order to identify and characterize *macroscopic changes* and *microscopic changes* as changes that have an impact on a substantial part of the network or on specific portions, respectively. We provide arguments of the viability to real-world applications through two case studies, more precisely, telecommunication networks and geo-sensor networks.

Keywords: Change Mining, Network Streams, Frequent Subnetworks

1 Introduction

The dissemination of technologies able to unceasingly record information from real-world applications has lead to the development of systems based on data stream models. Often such systems work in highly dynamic and complex domains where data are naturally interconnected. This is the case of social networks and telecommunication infrastructures. Analyzing data continuously generated in these fields requires data stream mining algorithms that operate on network data. In this scenario, a natural and interesting problem is that of analyzing data streams in order to identify the changes in the network interactions over time. However, in the domains in which human supervision or reference knowledge are not promptly available we cannot learn models able to recognize changing behaviors, and therefore the supervised approaches give way to those unsupervised. The descriptive data mining techniques and, in particular, the pattern-based approaches are gaining great attention thanks to their peculiarities to provide arguments to the change-related discoveries through statistical evidence. In [1], the discovery of *graph evolution rules* starting from sequence of graph snapshots from an evolving graph has been proposed. The rules are graphs in which nodes denote entities while edges are labeled with the time-stamp. However, this approach is only able to represent insertions and not deletions of nodes/edges. In [6], we studied how characterizing the evolution of specific portions of the whole network by introducing the notion of evolution chains. In [9], the authors track changes in the trend of statistical parameters of frequent patterns in social networks. The patterns are mined from descriptive properties of the nodes of the networks and therefore do not provide information on the structural changes.

We addressed the critical points of the aforementioned works through a method, described in detail in [5], which contributes to the problem of change mining in three different perspectives, that is, the task studied, methodological approach and algorithmic solution. As for the task, we argue that changes concerning the global properties of a network can be ascribed to a combination of local variations. Changes of single portions (microscopic changes) can trigger changes in the global properties of the network (macroscopic). More specifically, microscopic changes are associated with subnetworks whose properties change over time, whereas macroscopic changes are associated with composite aggregations of microscopic changes.

As for the methodological approach, we resort to the frequent pattern mining framework to generate a summarizing form of the network data on which identifying evolutions. Therefore, frequent subnetworks are not the primary objective of the paper, but the means to capture two kinds of changes. By using pattern-subnetworks, we can search for changes in an abstract description of the network [4], while alleviating the computational cost that the analysis of raw data would require. So, single frequent subnetworks synthesize specific portions, while sets of frequent subnetworks synthesize larger portions of the network. This methodological decision is motivated by the fact that frequent subnetworks provide arguments for the robustness of our method. Indeed, frequency denotes statistical evidence, therefore, frequently occurring changes turn out to be more interesting than episodic ones, because they are replicated and, probably, well-established over time.

As for the algorithmic solution, the hypothesis on the absence of labeling of the changes suggest us to monitor data streams and decide when new data snapshots exhibit a change, that is, when the network differs from the past. To this end, we use two time-windows, one to collect data snapshots of the "recent past" and the other to collect new data snapshots. This way, we capture the status of the network in two distinct time-windows, keep patterns and their statistical properties updated, and adapt the search strategy to the variations of the underlying data distribution. The combined use of time-windows and frequent subnetworks suggests us to search for *i)* macroscopic changes as variations between sets of frequent subnetworks discovered on two time-windows, and *ii)* microscopic changes as punctual variations of frequent subnetworks occurring at the level of data snapshots. The use of two windows ("recent past" and "new snaphosts") has been studied also for predictive tasks [8].

2 Basics and Problem Statement

In the following, we provide some basic concepts as well as the notions of change of interest for this work. A network data stream is the time-ordered sequence $D = \langle G_1, G_2, \ldots \rangle$ of network snapshots G_i observed at time-point t_i. Each snapshot G_i is labeled graph with labeled edges $G_i \subseteq N \times N \times L$, where N is the set of nodes and L is set of edge labels. In particular a *landmark window* $W = [t_i, t_j]$ of width $|W| = j - i + 1$ is the sequence of consecutive snapshots $\{G_i, \ldots, G_j\}$. Following [3], a (landmark) window W' is successive to another (landmark) window W when they share some initial time-points, that is, $W = [t_i, t_n]$ and $W' = [t_i, t_m]$, with $t_i < t_n < t_m$.

The proposed approach relies on the *frequent pattern mining* framework. In particular, we i) restrict the pattern language to *subnetworks* in which there exists a path between any two nodes, and ii) mine *frequent subnetworks* from snapshots of a window W. The *support* of a subnetwork S in W is defined as $sup(S, W) = \frac{|\{G_i \in W | S \subseteq G_i\}|}{|W|}$. A subnetwork S is *frequent* in W if $sup(P, W) \geq minSUP$, where $minSUP \in [0, 1]$. Then, F_W denotes the set of all the frequent subnetworks discovered from the window W. We consider two types of changes:

Definition 1 (Macroscopic change). *Given* $minMC \in [0, 1]$, *a macroscopic change is found if* $MC(W, W') = \frac{|F_{W'} - F_W| + |F_W - F_{W'}|}{|F_W| + |F_{W'} - F_W|} > minMC$.

Definition 2 (Microscopic change). *Given* $minGR \in [1, +\infty)$, *a subnetwork* S *denotes a microscopic change when i)* $\frac{sup(S,W)}{sup(S,W')} \geq minGR$ *if* $S \in (F_W - F_{W'})$, *or ii)* $\frac{sup(S,W')}{sup(S,W)} \geq minGR$ *if* $S \in (F_{W'} - F_W)$.

where, $W = [t_i, t_n]$ and $W' = [t_i, t_m]$ are two successive windows, F_W and $F_{W'}$ are the sets of frequent subnetworks mined on W and W', respectively.

In these terms, the problem of identifying and characterizing macroscopic and microscopic changes in a network data stream $D = \langle G_1, G_2, \ldots \rangle$ can be interpreted as the search for pairs of successive windows (W, W'), in which the *i)* quantification of the variations between F_W and $F_{W'}$ exceeds the threshold $minMC$ and *ii)* quantification of the variations the support of S (either $S \in (F_W - F_{W'})$ or $S \in (F_W - F_{W'})$) exceeds the threshold $minGR$.

3 The proposed mining approach

In this discussion paper, we discuss the KARMA algorithm proposed in [5], which delivers a computational solution to discover the changes before formulated. The algorithm (Figure 1) iteratively consumes blocks Π of network snapshots coming from the stream D (Step 2) by using two successive landmark windows W and W' (Step 3). This way, it mines frequent subnetworks, F_W and $F_{W'}$, necessary to the identification of both macroscopic and microscopic changes (Steps 4-5). The window grows ($W = W'$, Step 8) with new network snapshots, and the associated set of frequent subnetworks is kept updated until $MC(W, W') > minMC$ and a macroscopic change is found. In that case, the algorithm mines the microscopic changes (Step 6) and drops the content of the window by retaining only the last block of transactions ($W = \Pi$, Step 7). Then, the analysis restarts.

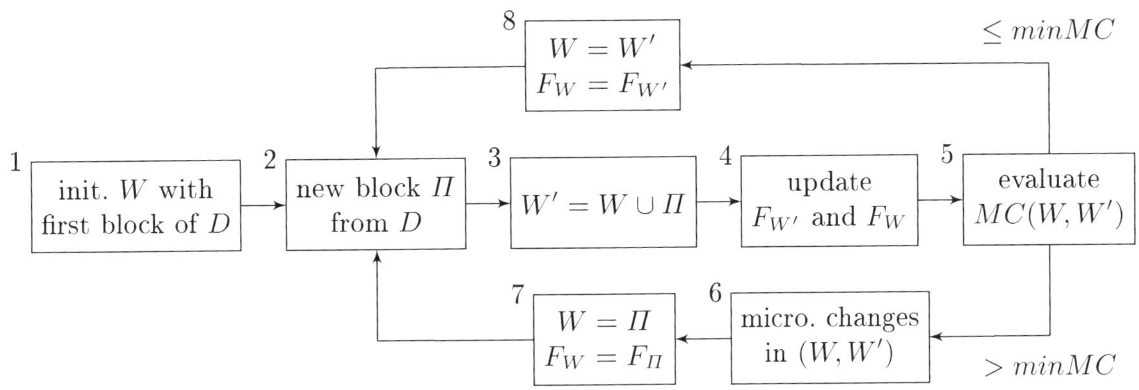

Fig. 1. The KARMA algorithm flowchart

The algorithm relies on the frequent subgraph mining framework, which is intractable for massive datasets due to the combinatorial explosion of the frequent subgraphs. For this reason, the sets F_W and $F_{W'}$ are kept updated and not recomputed from scratch upon the arrival of new transactions. Algorithmically, this is done by means of incremental solutions of frequent pattern mining.

3.1 Macroscopic change mining

When a new block of network snapshots Π is acquired, KARMA builds the window W' ($W' = W \cup \Pi$) and checks if there is a *macroscopic change* by matching W' against W. To do that, KARMA offers two peculiarities: i) identification of relevant changes on a summary of the data (the set of frequent subnetworks) rather than on the raw data, and ii) quantification of the changes in terms of the differences between the set F_W of frequent subnetworks discovered on W and the set $F_{W'}$ of frequent subnetworks discovered on W'. It is desirable to seek for changes on data by looking at frequent subnetworks in order to avoid false alarms, thus achieving higher robustness to noisy data. In this scenario, a single noisy network snapshot (e.g. a noisy outlier) would not affect the set of frequent subnetworks, depending on the minimum support $minSUP$. In fact, the main assumption behind the *macroscopic change* is that the whole network does not exhibit a change between W and W' if the frequent subnetworks, F_W and $F_{W'}$, do not significantly change. To measure the amount of change, KARMA computes the macroscopic change (MC) as $MC(W, W') = \frac{|F_{W'} - F_W| + |F_W - F_{W'}|}{|F_W| + |F_{W'} - F_W|}$. Where W and W' are two successive landmark windows, $|F_W - F_{W'}|$ denotes the number of subnetworks which are frequent in W and infrequent in W', and $|F_{W'} - F_W|$ is the number of subnetworks which are frequent in W' and infrequent in W. The formula quantifies the fraction of subnetworks which have crossed the minimum support threshold $minSUP$, that is, those which were frequent (infrequent) in W and become infrequent (frequent) in W', and which therefore indicate a relevant change in the underlying network data distribution.

3.2 Microscopic change mining

In KARMA, the discovery of *microscopic changes* is performed only when a *macroscopic change* is spotted. Indeed, a microscopic change accounts for the contribution that each subnetwork, which crosses the minimum support threshold $minSUP$, gives to the macroscopic change. To do that, we resort the notion of *emerging pattern* [2], which have been proven useful in the classification setting when mining discriminative patterns between two classes. In KARMA, we mine *emerging subnetworks* whose support significantly spreads between W and W'. This is done by quantifying the *growth-rate* of the subnetwork S, $\frac{sup(S,W)}{sup(S,W')} \geq minGR \quad if \quad S \in (F_W - F_{W'})$ (or alternatively, $\frac{sup(S,W')}{sup(S,W)} \geq minGR \quad if \quad S \in (F_{W'} - F_W)$). Every emerging subnetwork S satisfying the growth-rate inequality denotes a single *microscopic change*. The $minGR$ threshold is a tradeoff between the completeness and the simplicity of the descriptive model. Low values of minGR lead to expressive models, while high values lead to synthetic models about the change.

3.3 KARMA at work

We show the applicability of KARMA for the analysis of a real-world network by discussing some discoveries and commenting on their actionability with respect to facts and events occurred in the domain. In the following, we discuss two case studies: the first39 in the domain of telecommunication networks (NODOBO dataset), and the second in the domain of geo-sensor networks (NOAA dataset).

The *NODOBO*[1] dataset concerns a communication network and contains telecommunication transactions gathered during a study of the mobile phone usage of 27 students of a Scottish state high-school, from September 2010 to February 2011. The students communicate by phone calls, text messages (SMS) and Bluetooth connectivity. When building the network, the nodes represent the students, while the edges represent the different modalities of communication.

[1] http://nodobo.com/release.html

The dataset $NOAA$[2] was developed in the context of the Reanalysis project by the National Center for Environmental Prediction and the National Center for Atmospheric Research. The project aimed at providing new atmospheric analysis by gathering daily measurements of various meteorological quantities (e.g. relative humidity and air temperature) by means of geo-localized sensors equally distributed over space. In this work, we built the network with the measurements of relative humidity of the time-interval January, 1st 1990 - December, 31st 2010, recorded daily on an area that roughly covers North-Central America. The nodes of the network represent the sensors, while the edges are nominal values denoting the relative humidity values measured on the two linked sensors.

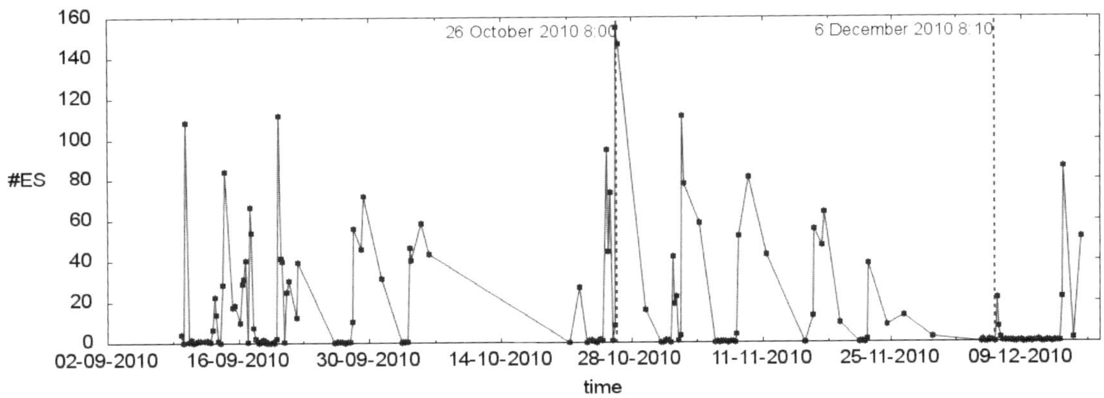

Fig. 2. Number of microscopic changes ($\#ES$) discovered from the NODOBO dataset as a function of time. The values of the $\#ES$ have been multiplied by 10^{-3}.

As for the analysis of NODOBO, in Figure 2, we see a succession of points with a decreasing trend, which has the peak on October 26th, 2010 and the lowest number of microscopic changes on December 6th, 2010. To give a practical interpretation to this behavior, it is useful to say that in Scottish state high-schools there is a holiday period which covers the second and third week of October, thereafter the school activities continue. So, the projection of Figure 2 reveals that, when the school activities resume, there is high variability (many microscopic changes) in the modalities of communication, which, as time goes by, tends to decrease. This may provide indications on the use of mobile phone of the students, which can be exploited, for instance, to plan the school policies and to improve the mobile network services in the area.

Among the microscopic changes associated to the peak, we find the pattern P={(*student_14, student_0, bluetooth*), (*student_18, student_0, bluetooth*), (*student_2, student_0, high_length*)}. It is involved in the strongest macroscopic change (quantified as 0.94), which starts on October 26th 2010 at 3:00 (the time-point after the window [2010 Oct 25-22:00, 2010 Oct 26-2:55]) and terminates on October 26th 2010 at 7:55. Specifically, P denotes the doubling

[2] https://coastwatch.pfeg.noaa.gov/erddap/griddap/esrlNcepRe.html

(growth-rate equals to 2.0) of the occurrences of the associated subnetwork from the window [2010 Oct 25-22:00, 2010 Oct 26-2:55] to the window [2010 Oct 25-22:00, 2010 Oct 26-7:55]. On the contrary, (we verified) P does not appear in the set of microscopic changes corresponding to the successive macroscopic change detected between the landmark windows [2010 Dec 05-22:10, 2010 Dec 06-3:05] and [2010 Dec 05-22:10, 2010 Dec 06-8:05], which may indicate that the modalities of interaction among the three students become stable.

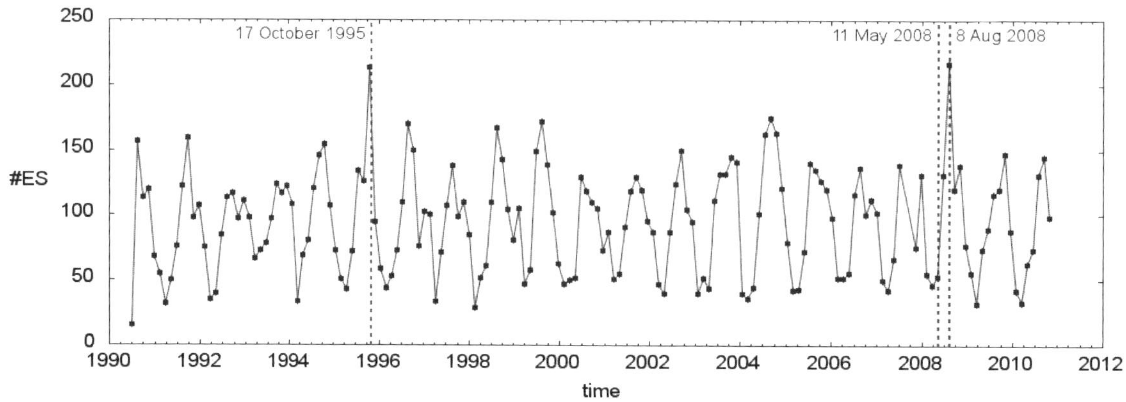

Fig. 3. Number of microscopic changes (*#ES*) discovered from the NOAA dataset as a function of time.

As for the NOAA domain (Figure 3), there are several macroscopic changes, those which have a greater impact on the network are characterized by more than 150 microscopic changes. In particular, there are two macroscopic changes with the highest number, they start on October 17th, 1995 and August 2008, 9th respectively. We deepened the microscopic changes corresponding to the two points and spotted several emerging subnetworks in common, one is $P=\{(<10,300>, <10,305>, \mathit{from\_70\_to\_80}), (<10,300>, <7.5,297.5>, \mathit{from\_80\_to\_90}), (<12.5,297.5>, <7.5,297.5>, \mathit{from\_80\_to\_90})\}$.

By mapping the nodes of P into a geodesic space, we see they identify two regions, both cover approximately the area of the state of Venezuela and part of the Caribbean sea, where there are small differences in terms of relative humidity (the edge labels refer to consecutive ranges). This meteorological scenario becomes less frequent (the growth-rate decreases) over the window [1995 Oct 17, 1995 Nov 30] and [2008 Aug 09, 2008 Sep 22] respectively, which suggests the possibility of different behavior, in the same geographic area, occurred before or after those two macroscopic changes.

4 Conclusions

In this discussion paper, we have investigated the problem of identifying relevant changes in network data streams, where the changes can be distinguished in two categories: macroscopic changes and microscopic changes. The system presented in the paper, called KARMA, is able to simultaneously extract macroscopic changes and microscopic changes by exploiting the fact that they are inevitably related to each other. Two case studies have shown the usefulness and the actionability of the changes in the domain of geo-sensor networks and telecommunication networks. An extensive discussion on the influence of the parameters (minSUP, minMC, minGR) on the results can be found in [5], where a comparative evaluation of the running times is also reported. The interested reader can refer to the journal paper for further details.

For future work, we plan to investigate two main research directions: *i)* use of solutions of big data analytics to detect changes in very large networks, and *ii)* study of the closed patterns [7] to discover non-redundant subnetworks.

References

1. Berlingerio, M., Bonchi, F., Bringmann, B., Gionis, A.: Mining graph evolution rules. In: Proc. of the European Conference on Machine Learning and Knowledge Discovery in Databases: Part I. pp. 115–130. ECML PKDD '09, Springer-Verlag, Berlin, Heidelberg (2009)
2. Dong, G., Li, J.: Efficient mining of emerging patterns: Discovering trends and differences. In: Proceedings of the Fifth ACM SIGKDD International Conference on Knowledge Discovery and Data Mining, San Diego, CA, USA, August 15-18, 1999. pp. 43–52 (1999)
3. Gama, J., Gaber, M.M.: Learning from data streams: processing techniques in sensor networks. Springer (2007)
4. Loglisci, C., Berardi, M.: Segmentation of evolving complex data and generation of models. In: Workshops Proceedings of the 6th IEEE International Conference on Data Mining (ICDM 2006), 18-22 December 2006, Hong Kong, China. pp. 269–273. IEEE Computer Society (2006). https://doi.org/10.1109/ICDMW.2006.144
5. Loglisci, C., Ceci, M., Impedovo, A., Malerba, D.: Mining microscopic and macroscopic changes in network data streams. Knowl.-Based Syst. **161**, 294–312 (2018)
6. Loglisci, C., Ceci, M., Malerba, D.: Relational mining for discovering changes in evolving networks. Neurocomputing **150, Part A**(0), 265 – 288 (2015)
7. Loglisci, C., Malerba, D.: Mining multiple level non-redundant association rules through two-fold pruning of redundancies. In: Perner, P. (ed.) Machine Learning and Data Mining in Pattern Recognition, 6th International Conference, MLDM 2009, Leipzig, Germany, July 23-25, 2009. Proceedings. Lecture Notes in Computer Science, vol. 5632, pp. 251–265. Springer (2009). https://doi.org/10.1007/978-3-642-03070-3_19
8. Loglisci, C., Malerba, D.: Leveraging temporal autocorrelation of historical data for improving accuracy in network regression. Statistical Analysis and Data Mining **10**(1), 40–53 (2017). https://doi.org/10.1002/sam.11336, https://doi.org/10.1002/sam.11336
9. Nohuddin, P.N.E., Coenen, F., Christley, R., Setzkorn, C., Patel, Y., Williams, S.: Finding "interesting" trends in social networks using frequent pattern mining and self organizing maps. Knowl.-Based Syst. **29**, 104–113 (2012)

Data Driven Chatbots: a New Approach to Conversational Applications

Nicoletta Di Blas[1], Luca Lodi[1], Paolo Paolini[1], Barbara Pernici[1], Fabrizio Renzi[2], and Donya Rooein[1]

[1] Politecnico di Milano (DEIB), Milan, Italy
[2] IBM Research, Italy

Abstract. Chatbots and conversational interfaces are becoming ubiquitous and a new HCI paradigm to access applications and information. This paper proposes a novel approach and an innovative technology (iCHAT) for the development of "data-driven chatbots". Key ingredients are "meta-conversation", "conversation tables" (controlling the interface), and a "conversation engine".

Several advantages are envisioned: (i) lower effort for developing new conversational applications; (ii) easiness of maintenance and update, and therefore improved quality; (iii) possibility for content experts of developing conversational applications, without the need of ICT experts. The approach of iCHAT is quite general and it can be applied to all domains. It is being tested by developing a conversational tutor, supporting adaptive learning, for two MOOCs developed at Politecnico di Milano (Italy) in the frame of an EIT program. This paper describes the overall architecture of iCHAT and analyzes its most original aspects: the conversation engine and the conversation tables.

Keywords: Chatbots, Data-driven application development, Educational framework.

1 Introduction and Background

A new paradigm for interfaces is becoming ubiquitous: **conversational interfaces** [1]. Conversations, today, are available via different technologies[1] and different software solutions. Users, especially youngsters, are getting ever more used to conversations as a way to interact with applications. Conversations can be supported by several devices:π computers, phones, home devices (e.g. "Echo"), etc. They can be delivered via text interfaces or audio interfaces (using speech-to-text and/or text-to-speech technologies). The baseline is <the-user-speaks-to-the-chatbot and the chatbot-

[1] See for example www.pega.com/chatbot-revolution

speaks-to-the-user>. Current technologies, such as WATSON by IBM, support quite well the development of specific conversations, by designing a conversation flows.

This paper introduces a new paradigm for designing conversational interfaces, based on two core ideas: A) designing and implementing **chatbots as "data-driven", i.e. controlled via Data Bases and tables**; B) using chatbots as interfaces for **adaptive information intensive applications.** These application allow users to access organized streams of information items.

Conversational interfaces may offer: (i) easiness of use, especially for the younger ones; (ii) lower level of attention required, letting the user focus upon content; (iii) empathic (if not entertaining) interaction, thus improving the user satisfaction; (iv) encouragement to the users to express themselves; (v) possibility to collect "non-functional feedback" (e.g. emotions or feelings) as the interaction process evolves; (vi) possibility to react to unforeseen situations (e.g. to a perceived distress by the learner), etc.

Some important research questions arise: **A) which functionalities** should be supported? **B)** how should the **production process** be organized? **C)** which **technology** should be used to support "A" and "B"?

Question **A** is about **Adaptativity**: what does it mean, from a user point of view, to access adaptively a set of information items? We started investigating Adaptativity in the domain of Education, striving for an adaptive use of material offered by a MOOC. Our approach is exemplified (in the realm of education) by iMOOC, i.e. a methodology for developing and organizing online courses [2]. iMOOC is based upon the assumption that there is a "body of knowledge" represented by a **(large or very large) set of content items**. Items should be properly **tagged and enriched with metadata** (e.g. level of difficulty, time available, type of proffered content, …), in order to make it possible adaptivity. Items are offered to a user arranged into "**learning paths**", i.e. predefined topologies used for traversing the "corpus" of content. Each learning path corresponds to an **"adaptive answer" to a learning need** (according to various criteria, as it will be explained next). Politecnico di Milano has used iMOOC in order to develop two online courses "Recommender Systems Basic" and "Recommender Systems Advanced.", that will be available on Coursera by Summer 2019. They are part of a master of the European Institute of Technology (EIT). The first course consists of 43 items, for a total of 110 minutes of videos; the second course consists 31 items, for a total of 106 minutes of videos.

Question B is about feasibility and sustainability of adaptive conversational applications. The production process must be reasonably efficient, both from an author and a publisher point of view. If the development of a chatbot requires excessive effort by the author, it will not be afforded. We are discussing with major publishers about this issue, but in this paper we only address it indirectly, while describing the technology.

Question C is about technology, but it has a clear impact on "A" (what the chatbot does), and "B" (how the chatbot is designed, implemented and maintained). To address this question, at Politecnico di Milano (in cooperation with IBM Research Italy) we are developing iCHAT [3]. In this paper we are specifically concerned with a portion of the technology: **how to make conversations data-driven**, instead of being explicitly modelled for each application.

In Section 2 we briefly discuss the functionalities of chatbots (for the domain of education) and the overall architecture of iCHAT. In Section 3, we discuss the main theme of this paper: how to use a data-driven approach to design and implement a conversational chatbot. In Section 4 we discuss the state of art. In Section 5 we draw conclusions and sketch future work.

2 iCHAT Architecture for Educational Chatbots

The overall conceptual architecture of iCHAT is shown in Figure 1.

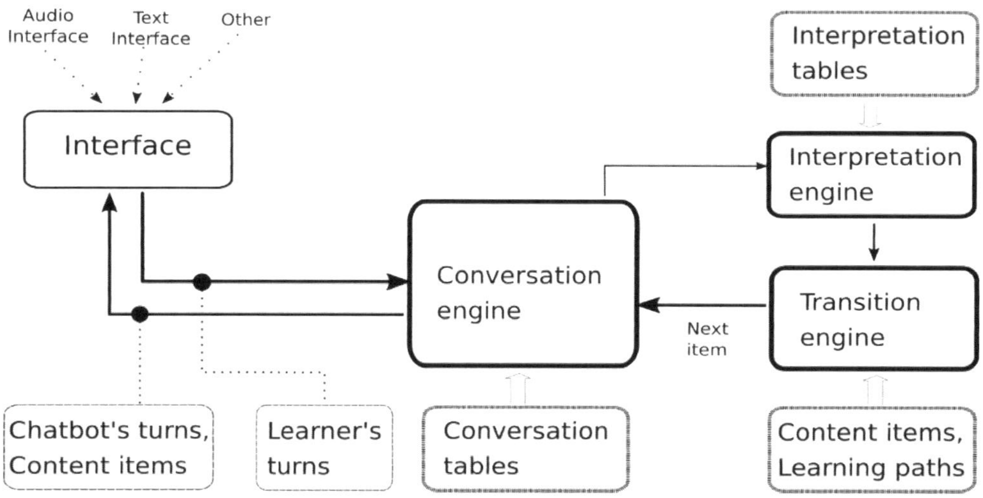

Figure 1: The conceptual architecture of iCHAT

iCHAT entails three main engines: the **conversation engine**, the **interpretation engine**, and the **transition engine**. Since the conversation is the main subject of this paper, for the sake of completeness, we briefly here the other two engines.

The role of the **transition engine** is to control the progress on a learning path (or a pathway of content items in general). When a proper request is received, the transition engine selects the next content item for the user. The transition engine is driven via the "content DB", consisting of the content items (with their tags and metadata) and the pathways (again with their tags and metadata).

The role of the **interpretation engine** is to decide, using the session-variables collected up to a certain moment, how the conversation should move on. A conversation could be "**completed**" (the pathway has been fully covered), "**paused**" (for a later resumption), "**halted**" (with no resumption possible) or "**continued**". In the latter case, a proper request is formulated to the transition engine. The interpretation engine is controlled via a set of rules called "interpretation tables".

The role of the **conversation engine** is to keep effective and efficient the conversation between the user and the chatbot. Users have their turns, and the chatbot has its turns. The most important **turns of the chatbot**, (at least from a learning point of view) are those in which **content items are offered** for "consumption". In our approach, the **chatbot is not an answering machine** but rather a **proactive tutor**. The chatbot has a pathway of content[2] to cover, and a successful conversation is the one leading the user to the completion of the pathway. This is a why the chatbot has to be "empathic" and "persuasive": **the appropriateness of its turns and the quality of the wording are very important**.

The chatbot is **not an expert of a domain**, though it may seem to be to the user. The chatbot, in fact, knows about the content items (title, abstract, metadata, tags, ...), knows about the pathways (content, topology, metadata, ...), knows what the user has done up to a certain point and what still needs to be covered, but it does not actually understand the domain[3]. We can say that the chatbot knows a specific "corpus of content" but not the subject of the course.

Adaptativity of the learning experience comes in tow fashions**. Content Adaptativity**: only suitable content items are offered to the user, and with a suitable organization. This can be very important, for example, for MOOCs [2, 3] or professional training on the job, where there is a large variety of learners, with different learning goals, different backgrounds, different degrees of possible efforts, etc. **Conversation Adaptativity**: the conversation is tuned to the user profile and the specific needs. Different elements can be "adapted": the number of the turns of the chatbot, the subject of those turns, the length of these turns, the wording used by the chatbots, etc. In the next section we focus upon the issue of controlling the Adaptativity of the chatbot.

3 Controlling the conversation of a chatbot: a data-driven approach

In this paper, we mainly examine a **data-driven approach**, in order to control the conversation of a chatbot speaks. Figure 2 shows a sample of a conversation (from the course "Recommender Systems Basic").

Most chatbots, currently, could be considered as "glorified answering machines": the user takes the lead and formulates requests, the chatbot answers in a conversation al fashion (that may take several turns).

For iCHAT, instead, the approach is quite different, since the chatbot is somehow leading the conversation. A conversation goes on as a sequence of "turns" by the chatbot and the user. The turns are not necessarily alternated: the chatbot and the user can take some turns in a sequence[4]. Both for the user and the chatbot there are **solicited turns** (replying to a request) and **unsolicited turns** (autonomous moves). In line 3, for example, the user is replying to a request by the chatbot; in line 7 the user makes an unsolicited comment. In line 10 the chatbot replies to a request by the user [4].

[2] The selection of the proper pathway (among a set of possible pathways on the same content) is not part of the chatbot and it falls outside of the scope of this paper.

[3] And this is different from other approaches aiming at building "smart chatbots".

[4] This creates the problem of avoiding overlapping turns, that we can't discuss here.

1 *Chatbot*: so far you have covered 6 items, for a total of 13 minutes.
2 *Chatbot*: can we move on or do you feel tired?
3 *User*: please, go on
4 *Chatbot*: next item is of **medium** difficulty and it is **recommended** by the teacher. The title is **URM matrix** and it takes **2.5** minutes.
5 *Chatbot*: would you like an abstract of it?
6 *User*: no, move on
... <content consumption of video items>
7 *User*: I found it relatively easy
8 *Chatbot*: so far you are doing well; congratulations....
9 *User:* how much do we have to cover still to complete this learning path?
10 *Chatbot*: there are 9 items, for a total of 17 minutes. 4 items are advanced
....

Figure 2: fragment of a possible conversation for the course "Recommender Systems, Basic"

These are the main elements of our approach

- **The chatbot has an "agenda"** driven by content. In this example, the agenda is a learning path to be covered [3]; in another application (being developed at Politecnico di Milano) [4] the agenda could be a set of activities to be performed by children with special needs.
- The agenda implies that **the chatbot helps the user to go through a set of content items** (arranged in a possibly complex topology). The purpose of the chatbot is therefore to **"persuade"** the user to access (flexibly and adaptively) the maximum number of items (keeping following the indications of the author) and also to **"support"** this consumption of content.
- As a consequence of the above, **the chatbot is quite proactive.** It takes the lead supporting the user in an adaptive course, and also listening to possible specific requests.
- **The user may "interrupt" the chatbot** for different reasons: making comments or expressing feelings (e.g. line 7), requesting additional info (e.g. line 9) or requesting (directly or indirectly) to "suspend" the conversation or to "stop it".
- The fact that the **user can express her feeling** suggests a number of interesting developments: (i) data may suggest another course of action (e.g. accelerating or using a different conversation style); (ii) "non-functional data analytics" (i.e. how the user reacts to interactions with the chatbot) can be harvested and used later to improve content and its organization[5]; (iii) data may suggest ways to improve the conversation styles of the chatbot.

3.1 Chatbots are "data driven"

The most outstanding feature of iCHAT chatbots is the way they are modelled and implemented, justifying the overall label of "data driven".

[5] This would be a sharp improvement over what Learning Management Systems do: they log the actions of the user, but they do not know why the user is performing those actions.

Chatbot technology is currently mainly based upon conversation modelling. Using, for example, WATSON conversation features [5], or a similar platform, the main task is to identify possible inquiries by the user (called "user intents"): they are the possible subjects of the conversation. For each subject, possible continuations of the conversation are identified. The result, overall, is a tree-structure[6] representing the possible evolution of the conversation[7]. It is therefore clear that modelling an application consists into modelling a conversation: data are accessed when needed by the conversation. A negative effect is that for each different problem the conversation must be modeled and implemented: specialists are needed; time is required; costs are high; maintenance is difficult. The goal of iCHAT is to make **chatbot production sustainable**, lowering costs and not requiring extensive intervention by ICT specialists. If a new conversation is needed, the authors or conversation specialists should be able to generate it, without modelling it explicitly, which is a job for ICT specialists. This is the essence, as far as conversation is concerned, of what we call being "**data driven**". The approach of iCHAT is drastically different from the above described conversation modeling.

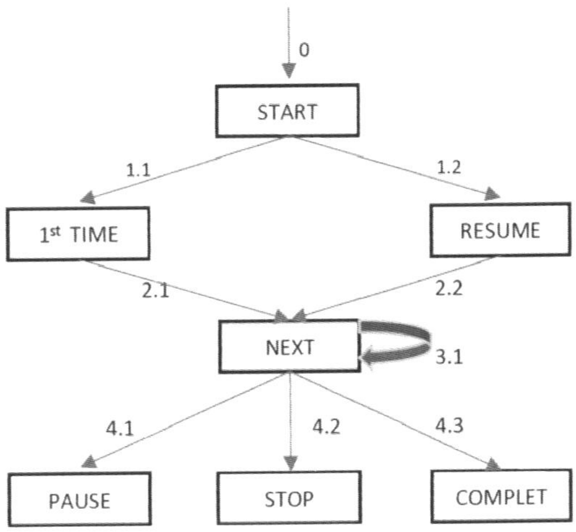

Figure 3 A simplified conceptual representation of the meta-conversation controlling the turns of the chatbot

These are the main features of iCHAT for controlling the chatbot:

a) There is a unique "meta-conversation" model, a simplified version of which is shown in Figure 3. The meta-conversation is content independent and therefore can be used for various applications.

b) Different arcs of the meta conversation corresponds to different states of a "conversation machine". For each "arc" we have defined the possible turns of the chatbot, creating "conversation tables"

[6] Additional mechanism (like "activation rules" or "context variables") allow to deliver conversations that do not appear hierarchical to the user.

[7] More sophisticated, but in essence not dissimilar from hierarchical menu of call-answering software.

c) The turns are purely conversational, and they are totally unrelated to the subject of the conversation. If reference to a specific "corpus of content" is needed[8], this is obtained by using general variables and accessing the content DB.
d) The turns of the chatbot may belong to one out of 11 different categories. Considering the conversation of the example of Figure 2 we use categories like "summary" (line 1), "preview" (lines 4), "proactivity" (lines 2, 5), "reinforcement" (line 8), "forecast" (line 10). For each category we specify: (i) What the chatbot may say (i) The "rule": under which condition it will say it.
e) Users are assigned a "conversational profile". Using a number of variables (as time available, level of background, ...), each user falls into a "stereotype". With stereotype 1, for example, the chatbot keeps the conversation to a minimum (less turns, fewer categories, short formulations). With stereotype 3, the chatbot formulates an extended conversation. Stereotype 2 falls in between.
f) In addition to the "standard" formulation there are alternative formulations for each possible turn, which used to make the chatbot more "human". E.g. line 2 of Figure 2, could be formulated like this: "Now we can move to the next item".
g) Whether a chatbot, in a given situation, will say "x" depends on 3 factors: (i) is "x" appropriate in this situation? (ii) is "x" appropriate for the user profile? (iii) is the current turn "far enough" form the last turn when "x" was uttered? Let us consider, for example. line 8 of Figure 2; it is a reinforcement message, it would sound unnatural (and boring) to repeat it every time that the user gets a content item.
h) In order to make the chatbot "content aware", the turns of the chatbot may embed "templates" and "variables". A turn, for example could be (as in line 4 of Figure 2) "Next item is *<short item description>*". The template "Short item description" is defined in a separate table, as a pattern of words incorporating a number of variable values. Another example is shown at line 10 of Figure 2: the chatbot can speak about what is coming next. Example of variables are: *item_title*, *item_abstract*, *item_length*, etc.
i) Technically speaking, the meta-conversation is content independent, but users may have a different perception. From their point of view, in fact, the chatbot knows the material being covered; (i) the overall organization of the material; (ii) the title and the description of chapters and sections; (iii) the title and the description of each item (including length, level of difficulty, relevance, ...).

Figure 4 shows a simplified sample of "setting" for Arc 3.1, the most important one. (there more than 60 settings for this arc, in reality).

Conversation tables, such as the one shown in Fig. 4, allow relevant results:

- Creating and delivering a chatbot tutor for **a different course**, would require only to create a different content Database.
- Changing the "**wording"** of the various turns, would require only modifying tables like the one shown in Figure 4, without the support of ICT experts.
- Modifying **the turns of the chatbot**, again needs to modify the conversation table, without modelling the conversation again.

---

[8] E.g. the title of an Item or its description.

• Changing **discipline** (e.g. a course in Humanities) would imply also a (possibly minor) revision of the conversation tables, with no need of ICT experts.

CATEGORY ***ASSESSMENT***	*Basic formulation*	*Alternative 1*	*Alternative 2*
Stereotype 1: every M turns	What do you think of this learning session, so far?	How is this learning session going?	What is your opinion on the this learning session?
Stereotype 3: every N turns	*<USER name>*, could you rate the learning session that you have followed so far? What do you think of it?	*<USER name>*, are you happy with what you are learning, so far?	*<USER name>*, I'd like, again, to know your opinion on this learning session. Does it seem useful to you?

Figure 4a A simplified representation of some turns for assessment for ARC3.1

CATEGORY ***PREVIEW***	*Basic formulation*	*Alternative 1*	*Alternative 2*
Before proposing next content-item Stereotype 1: always	Next item is <ITEM title>.	Next item is going to be <ITEM title>	Let's move on to the next item: <ITEM title>.
Before proposing next content-item Stereotype 3: always	Next item is <ITEM description long>.	Next item: <ITEM description long>.	Let's move on to the next item: <ITEM description long>.

Figure 4b A simplified representation of some turns for preview for ARC3.1

CATEGORY REINFORCEMENT	Basic formulation	Alternative 1	Alternative 2
Stereotype 1: never Stereotype 2: every M turns	<USER name>, you are progressing well. Good job!	You are doing great!	It seems that you are doing well, congratulations!
Stereotype 3: every N (turns	<USER id>, you are progressing well. Good job!	You are doing great!	It seems that you are doing well, congratulations!

Figure 4c A simplified representation of some turns for reinforcement for ARC3.1 of Fig. 3

In the next section we briefly analyze the relevant state of art, while in section 5 we sketch the future direction of research.

4 State of the art

Various market technologies are available for the creation of chatbots, almost all sharing a similar approach to the design. Most of the technologies that used in the chatbots are pattern matching techniques and language tricks [6]. IBM Watson Assistants, for example, allows the creation of customized chatbots[9] modeling the conversation as a tree of dialogue nodes, where each node associates a request by the user with a set of replies by the chabot. The use of "context variables" and of "rules" (governing when a reply is appropriate or not) makes the chatbot quite flexible and powerful. Still, two main drawbacks remain.

The first drawback is that chatbots are conceived (and perceived) as "answering machines" [7]. The emphasis is on understanding the user's input, by classifying the user's will in a series of "intents". An intent is defined by several messages' examples. Thus, the most common use cases for this kind of technologies are question/answering and the automation of business tasks. The purpose of the work presented in this paper is instead to build chatbots that can use conversations as a way to support the learning process, as already Carbonell, in 1970 [8], meant to do when he created a Socratic tutor using a semantic network technique. Since the seventies, a number of different efforts have been made in this direction and Pedagogical agents, Educational agents, Learning companions, Virtual Teaching Assistants, Intelligent Tutoring Systems have been designed and deployed. Though not all can be called "chatbots" in strict sense, they all show how the dream of supporting interactive learning has been persistent and resilient [9, 10].

Pedagogical agents (PAs), or Educational Agents, are "lifelike characters in virtual environments that help facilitate learning through social interactions and the virtual real relationships with the learners" [11, 12]. They can be seen as "computer-simulated character, which presents users with human-like characteristics, such as domain competence, emotions, and other personal characteristics" [13]; they can go from making a presentation engaging to interacting on a topic [14]. In contrast to PAs, chatbots provide an interacting interface in a synchronous way with learners to react on individual intents [15]. Learning companions can be seen as "animated digital characters functioning to simulate human-peer-like interaction—might provide an opportunity to simulate such social interaction in computer-based learning" [13, 16]. Virtual Teaching Assistants support teacher in delivering courses (e.g. a programming course: Chou et al [17]). Intelligent Tutoring Systems (ITSs) are "virtual teachers" that can be used for one-to-one tutoring [18-20]. Technology-mediated learning (TML) is an environment to provide learning materials in an interactive way for students [21]. In TML during the learning process students impacted by structural factors such as learning methods [22]. Nowadays chatbots, which are rising a new wave of interest [1, 23-25], are in the same stream.

The second drawback, more relevant for this paper, is that current approaches use conversations explicitly modelled as such; this means that taking up a different application would require to re-do the modeling. Our approach, instead, is totally different: there is a meta-conversation, basically fitting if not all, a quite large number of use

9 https://console.bluemix.net/docs/services/assistant/dialog-overview.html#dialog-overview

cases and each new case requires only to provide a new set of data (mainly a content DB, as described in this paper). The novelty brought about by the iCHAT approach lies mainly in the separation between educational content in strict sense (learning objects, videos, texts…) and conversation: the chatbot engages in a conversation with the user leading it like a teacher would do, allowing the user to express all (and only) the intents ("I'm frustrated, I've understood, this is not clear…") that are relevant for the bot to decide what to show next, following a smart strategy the instructional designer has integrated in the content organization.

5 Conclusions and future work

In this paper we have described a technology for designing and deploying data-driven chatbots. Politecnico di Milano is developing iCHAT, leveraging on WATSON technology, in cooperation with IBM-Research-Italy.

We are striving for a generalized solution, that could be applied for various applications. The current chatbot fully supports two courses (MOOCs) developed by Politecnico di Milano. Learning pathways, currently, are defined taking into account the following criteria: what part of the course needs to be covered; the level of difficulty of the wished items; the relevance of the items (as defined by the teacher). The conversation is profiled according to two criteria: time available and learner's background.

As far as **education** is concerned, these are the most relevant aspects: **conversational interfaces can help into making the learning processes** more effective. Effectiveness should come (i) from **the possibility of better enforcing adaptive learning,** (ii) from the possibility of fostering **longer learning sessions** and also (iii) from the increased "**empathy**" of the interaction, fostering a better mood for the learner. In addition, conversational interaction allows **to collect a number of crucial "non-functional information"** about the learner: how she feels, what she thinks, her cognitive/emotional situation, … This may lead to a very interesting development of **a new generation of learning analytics**, focusing not so much on the "mechanics" of learning (still available, in any case), but rather on the learner reaction to learning.

As for as **technology** is concerned, the most important contribution of iCHAT is the idea that instead of modelling and implementing conversations, chatbots should be **driven by data**. **Conversation tables**, in fact, allow to control the turns of conversation by the chatbot: a) when to speak, when to use a given "category" of what is being said; b) how to use it; c) the specific "message"; d) the specific wording, etc. Conversation tables are used in order to drive a **meta-conversation. Pathways** are another aspect of "data-driven" chatbots: they provide the "agenda" for the conversation.

Another part of the effort, not discussed in this paper, is a set of tables used to understand what the user says ("intents"). In all cases our chatbot does not allow a general conversation; only turns of conversations focused on the learning process (e.g. "I like it", "it was difficult", "I'm tired", …) are recognized. It is clear that only empirical validation with users for an extended period (at least 6 months) will allow to tune the various tables, making the conversations fluid and effective from the user point of view.

Several **technological improvements are planned,** the most important being: (i) improving the ability to understand what the user says; (ii) creation of a friendly authoring environment for conversation tables; (iii) enhancing the transition engine, in order to handle more complex topologies for pathways; (iv) expanding and refining the meta-conversation model, etc.

In terms of applications, IBM and Politecnico are considering to enlarge the scope of iCHAT technology, considering a more general purpose idea: **adaptive streams of information items delivered via adaptive conversational interfaces**. Applications are being investigated for domains like eCulture, eTourism and eFood.

6 References

1. Song, D., E.Y. Oh, and M. Rice. Interacting with a conversational agent system for educational purposes in online courses. in 2017 10th international conference on human system interactions (HSI). 2017. IEEE.
2. Casola, S., et al. Designing and Delivering MOOCs that Fit all Sizes. in Society for Information Technology & Teacher Education International Conference. 2018. Association for the Advancement of Computing in Education (AACE).
3. Akcora, D.E., et al. Conversational support for education. in International Conference on Artificial Intelligence in Education. 2018. Springer.
4. Di Blas, N., Lodi, L., Paolini, P., Pernici, B., Raspa, N., Rooein, D., Renzi, F., Sustainable Chatbots supporting Learning. ED-MEDIA 2019, in World Conference on Educational Multimedia, Hypermedia & Telecommunications,. 2019: Amsterdam.
5. Garzotto, F. and M. Gelsomini, Magic Room: A Smart Space for Children with Neurodevelopmental Disorder. IEEE Pervasive Computing, 2018. 17(1): p. 38-48.
6. Masche, J. and N.-T. Le. A review of technologies for conversational systems. in International Conference on Computer Science, Applied Mathematics and Applications. 2017. Springer.
7. Bollweg, L., et al. When Robots Talk-Improving the Scalability of Practical Assignments in MOOCs Using Chatbots. in EdMedia+ Innovate Learning. 2018. Association for the Advancement of Computing in Education (AACE).
8. Carbonell, J.R., AI in CAI: An artificial-intelligence approach to computer-assisted instruction. IEEE transactions on man-machine systems, 1970. 11(4): p. 190-202.
9. Croxton, R.A., The role of interactivity in student satisfaction and persistence in online learning. Journal of Online Learning and Teaching, 2014. 10(2): p. 314.
10. Person, N.K. and A.C. Graesser, Pedagogical agents and tutors. Encyclopedia of Education, Macmillan, New York, 2006: p. 1169-1172.
11. Davis, R. and P. Antonenko, Effects of pedagogical agent gestures on social acceptance and learning: Virtual real relationships in an elementary foreign language classroom. Journal of Interactive Learning Research, 2017. 28(4): p. 459-480.
12. Page, L.C. and H. Gehlbach, How an artificially intelligent virtual assistant helps students navigate the road to college. AERA Open, 2017. 3(4): p. 2332858417749220.

13. Chou, C.-Y., T.-W. Chan, and C.-J. Lin, Redefining the learning companion: the past, present, and future of educational agents. Computers & Education, 2003. 40(3): p. 255-269.
14. André, E., T. Rist, and J. Müller. WebPersona: a life-like presentation agent for educational applications on the world-wide web. in Proc. of Workshop" Intelligent Educational Systems on the World Wide Web" at AI-ED. 1997.
15. Winkler, R. and M. Söllner, Unleashing the potential of chatbots in education: A state-of-the-art analysis. 2018.
16. Jia, J., CSIEC: A computer assisted English learning chatbot based on textual knowledge and reasoning. Knowledge-Based Systems, 2009. 22(4): p. 249-255.
17. Chou, C.-Y., B.-H. Huang, and C.-J. Lin, Complementary machine intelligence and human intelligence in virtual teaching assistant for tutoring program tracing. Computers & Education, 2011. 57(4): p. 2303-2312.
18. Anderson, J., R. and REISER, B. The LISP tutor: p. 159-175.
19. Economist, T. Mobile services: Bots, the next frontier. 2016, April 8; Available from: Retrieved from www.economist.com/news/business-and-finance/21696477-market-apps-maturing-now-one-text-based-services-or-chatbots-looks-poised
20. Wiley, D., The instructional use of learning objects. Bloomington IN: Agency for Instructional Technology and the Association for Educational Communications and Technology. Online: http://reusability. org/read, 2002.
21. Alavi, M. and D.E. Leidner, Research commentary: Technology-mediated learning—A call for greater depth and breadth of research. Information systems research, 2001. 12(1): p. 1-10.
22. Söllner, M., et al., Process is king: Evaluating the performance of technology-mediated learning in vocational software training. Journal of Information Technology, 2018. 33(3): p. 233-253.
23. High, R., The era of cognitive systems: An inside look at IBM Watson and how it works. IBM Corporation, Redbooks, 2012.
24. Hill, J., W.R. Ford, and I.G. Farreras, Real conversations with artificial intelligence: A comparison between human–human online conversations and human–chatbot conversations. Computers in Human Behavior, 2015. 49: p. 245-250.
25. Kerlyl, A., P. Hall, and S. Bull. Bringing chatbots into education: Towards natural language negotiation of open learner models. in International Conference on Innovative Techniques and Applications of Artificial Intelligence. 2006. Springer.

A System Prototype for Approximate Query Answering over Incomplete Data

(DISCUSSION PAPER)

Nicola Fiorentino, Sergio Greco, Cristian Molinaro, and Irina Trubitsyna

DIMES, University of Calabria
{lastname}@dimes.unical.it

Abstract. Many database applications face the problem of querying incomplete data. In such scenarios, certain answers are a principled semantics of query answering. Unfortunately, the computation of certain query answers is a coNP-hard problem. To make query answering feasible in practice, recent research has focused on developing polynomial time algorithms computing a sound (but possibly incomplete) set of certain answers.

In this paper we present a system prototype implementing a suite of algorithms to compute sound sets of certain answers. The central tools used by our system are conditional tables and the conditional evaluation of relation algebra. Different evaluation strategies can be applied, with more accurate ones having higher complexity, but returning more certain answers, thereby enabling users to choose the technique that best meets their needs in terms of balance between efficiency and quality of the results.

1 Introduction

Incomplete information arises in many database applications, such as ontological reasoning [4, 5], inconsistency management [2, 3, 11, 15], data integration [7, 16], and many others.

A principled semantics of query answering over incomplete databases are *certain answers*, which are query answers that are obtained from all the complete databases represented by an incomplete database [17, 6, 18]. The following example illustrates the notion of a certain answer.

Example 1. Consider the database D consisting of the three unary relations P (Person), S (Student) and E (Employee) reported below, where $\perp$ is a null value.

P
john
mary

E
john
$\perp$

S
mary
bob

Under the missing value interpretation of nulls (i.e., a value for $\perp$ exists but is unknown), D represents all the databases obtained by replacing $\perp$ with an actual value.

A certain answer to a query is a tuple that is an answer to the query for every database represented by D. For instance, consider the query asking for the people who are not employees and students, which can be expressed in relational algebra as $\mathtt{P} - (\mathtt{E} \cap \mathtt{S})$. The certain answers to the query are $\{\langle \mathtt{john} \rangle\}$, because no matter how $\perp$ is replaced, $\langle \mathtt{john} \rangle$ is always a query answer.

For databases containing (labeled) nulls, certain answers to positive queries can be easily computed in polynomial time as follows: first a "standard" evaluation (that is, treating nulls as standard constants) is applied; then tuples with nulls in the result of the first step are discarded and the remaining tuples are the certain answers to the query. However, for more general queries with negation the problem of computing certain answers becomes coNP-hard.

To make query answering feasible in practice, one might resort to SQL's evaluation, but unfortunately, the way SQL behaves in the presence of nulls may result in wrong answers.

Specifically, as evidenced in [18], there are two ways in which certain answers and SQL's evaluation may differ: *(i)* SQL can miss some of the tuples that belong to certain answers, thus producing *false negatives*, or *(ii)* SQL can return some tuples that do not belong to certain answers, that is, *false positives*. While the first case can be seen as an under-approximation of certain answers (a sound but possibly incomplete set of certain answers is returned), the second scenario must be avoided, as the result might contain plain incorrect answers, that is, tuples that are not certain.

The experimental analysis in [13] showed that false positive are a real problem for queries involving negation—they were always present and sometimes they constitute almost 100% of the answers.

Example 2. Consider again the database D of Example 1. There are no certain answers to the query $\mathtt{P} - \mathtt{E}$, as the query answers are the empty set when $\perp$ is replaced with `mary`.

Assuming that `P` and `E`'s attribute is called `name`, the same query can be expressed in SQL as follows:

```
SELECT P.name
FROM P
WHERE NOT EXISTS (
    SELECT *
    FROM E
    WHERE P.name = E.name )
```

The evaluation of the SQL query above returns $\langle \mathtt{mary} \rangle$, which is not a certain answer. The problem with the SQL semantics is that every comparison involving at least one null evaluates to the truth value *unknown*, then 3-valued logic is used to evaluate the classical logical connectives (*AND*, *OR*, *NOT*), and eventually only those tuples whose condition evaluates to *true* are kept.

Going back to the query above, for the first tuple of P, namely john, the nested subquery finds the same tuple in E, and thus john is not returned.

For the second tuple of P, namely mary, the nested subquery gives the empty set and thus ⟨mary⟩ is returned by the overall query. The reason why the nested subquery returns the empty set when mary is considered is that mary is compared with john and the comparison evaluates to *false*, and mary is compared with $\perp$ and the comparison evaluates to *unknown* (because a null is involved). Thus, there is no tuple of E for which the comparison evaluates to *true* and the nested subquery returns the empty set.

Thus, on the one hand, SQL's evaluation is efficient but flawed, on the other hand, certain answers are a principled semantics but with high complexity. To deal with this issue, there has been recent work on evaluation algorithms with *correctness guarantees*, that is, techniques providing a sound but possibly incomplete set of certain answers [13, 17, 18, 12, 8]. The problem of computing sound (but possibly incomplete) sets of *consistent* query answers over inconsistent databases has been addressed in [9], but databases are assumed to be complete, while in this paper we consider incomplete databases with no integrity constraints.

We have developed novel evaluation algorithms with correctness guarantees leveraging conditional tables and the conditional evaluation of relational algebra [12, 8]. In conditional tables each tuple is associated with a condition and the conditional evaluation is a generalization of relational algebra that manipulate conditional tables. Conditions keep track of how tuples are derived and how nulls are used in comparison operators.

The basic idea is illustrated in the following example.

Example 3. Consider again the database and the query of Example 1. The conditional evaluation of the query is carried out by applying the "conditional" counterpart of each relational algebra operator. Rather than returning a set of tuples, the conditional evaluation of a relational algebra operator returns "conditional tuples", that is, pairs of the form $\langle t, \varphi \rangle$, where t is a regular tuple and φ is an expression stating under which conditions t can be derived.

Regarding the query of Example 1, first the conditional evaluation of $\mathtt{E} \cap \mathtt{S}$ is performed, which gives the conditional tuples $\langle \perp, \varphi_1 \rangle$ and $\langle \perp, \varphi_2 \rangle$, where φ_1 is the condition $(\perp = \mathtt{mary})$ and φ_2 is the condition $(\perp = \mathtt{bob})$. This intuitively means that the tuple $\langle \perp \rangle$ is derived when $\perp$ is mary or bob.

Then, the conditional evaluation of the difference operator is carried out, yielding the conditional tuples $\langle \mathtt{john}, \varphi' \rangle$ and $\langle \mathtt{mary}, \varphi'' \rangle$ where φ' and φ'' are the following conditions:

$$\varphi' = \neg((\mathtt{john} = \perp) \wedge (\perp = \mathtt{mary})) \wedge \neg((\mathtt{john} = \perp) \wedge (\perp = \mathtt{bob})),$$
$$\varphi'' = \neg((\mathtt{mary} = \perp) \wedge (\perp = \mathtt{mary})) \wedge \neg((\mathtt{mary} = \perp) \wedge (\perp = \mathtt{bob})).$$

This is the result of the conditional evaluation of the whole query.

Conditions are valuable information that can be exploited to determine which tuples are certain answers. As already mentioned, for a conditional tuple $\langle t, \varphi \rangle$,

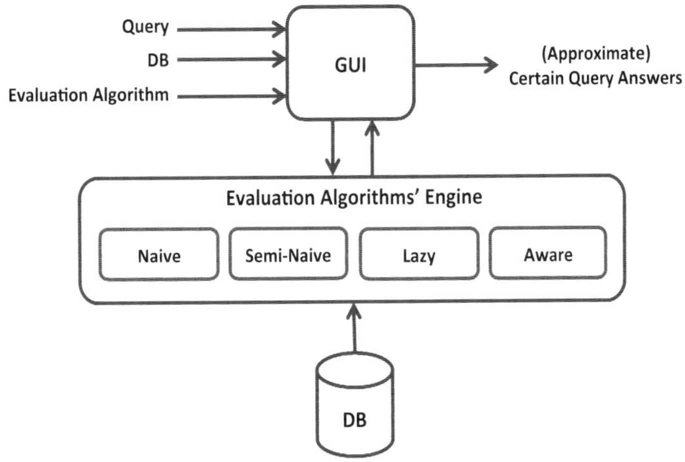

Fig. 1. System Architecture.

the expression φ says under which condition t can be derived. By condition evaluation we mean a way of associating φ with a truth value (*true*, *false*, or *unknown*). The aim is to ensure that if φ evaluates to *true*, then t is a certain answer. For instance, from an analysis of φ' in Example 3 above, one can realize that the condition is always true (i.e., it holds for every possible value $\perp$ stands for), and thus $\langle$`john`$\rangle$ is a certain answer.

Tuples' conditions can be evaluated in different ways: for instance, an eager strategy consists in evaluating conditions right after each relational algebra operator has been evaluated, while an opposite approach consists in evaluating conditions at the very end, that is, after the entire relational algebra query has been evaluated.

We have developed four different strategies leading to different evaluation algorithms, called *naive*, *semi-naive*, *lazy*, and *aware* evaluations. They have been implemented in the ACID system [8], which enables users to query incomplete databases and get under-approximations of the certain answers, choosing the evaluation strategy that is most suitable for the application at hand.

2 System Overview

The ACID system has been implemented in Java. The system architecture is depicted in Figure 1.

There are three main components: a graphical user interface (GUI), the evaluation algorithms' engine, and the database.

The GUI allows user to specify the query to be evaluated, the database, and the type of evaluation to be performed, that is, the approximation algorithm to be applied. The GUI displays the result of evaluating the specified query over the provided database according to the chosen evaluation algorithm. Different filters can be applied to the result (more details are discussed in the next section).

The system's engine supports the four evaluation algorithms mentioned in the previous section, with the naive algorithm being the most efficient but the least accurate one, and the aware algorithm being the most accurate but the least efficient one. The basic ideas of the approximation algorithms are as follows:

- The *naive evaluation* evaluates tuples' conditions right after each relational algebra operator has been applied, using three-valued logic.
- The *semi-naive evaluation* behaves like the naive one, but it better exploits equalities in conditions (by propagating values into tuples and conditions) to provide more accurate results.
- The *lazy evaluation* improves upon the semi-naive one by postponing conditions' evaluation until the set difference operator is encountered in the query.
- The *aware evaluation* provides even more accurate results and behaves as follows: it performs the conditional evaluation of the entire query, then it uses a set of axioms to "simplify" conditions, and eventually it evaluates (simplified) tuples' conditions.

The ACID system manages relational databases possibly containing labeled nulls (in the literature, they have been called *naive tables*, *V-tables*, and *e-tables* [14, 1, 10]). Thus, the same (labeled) null can occur multiple times—e.g., this can be used to express that there are two employees with the *same* unknown salary.

The GUI provides information on the query, the database, and the evaluation strategy to the engine, which computes the approximate certain answers accessing the database. After the evaluation has been carried out, the engine returns the result to the GUI.

The ACID system provides also an API which allow third party applications to interact with the system.

We now go into the details of how to interact with the ACID system (cf. Figure 2).

A typical interaction with the system involves the following steps:

1. The user specifies the input databases. Specifically, for each table in the database, its location in the file system is provided. Tables are supposed to be in csv format.
2. The user specifies the query to be evaluated using standard SQL syntax. Queries can be loaded from and saved to files.
3. The user specifies the evaluation strategy that has to be applied to evaluate the query (indeed, the system supports also the "standard" evaluation mentioned in the introduction and the conditional evaluation of a query).
4. After the evaluation has been launched and has finished, the result and statistics are displayed. Specifically, the result is a set of a tuples, where each tuple is associated with a condition that is either `true` or `unknown`. Tuples associated with `true` are guaranteed to be certain answers to the input query. The result can be filtered with respect to the truth value of the tuples, thus displaying only true or only unknown tuples. The total number of true (resp. unknown) tuples is displayed as well as the execution time. Results can be saved to files.

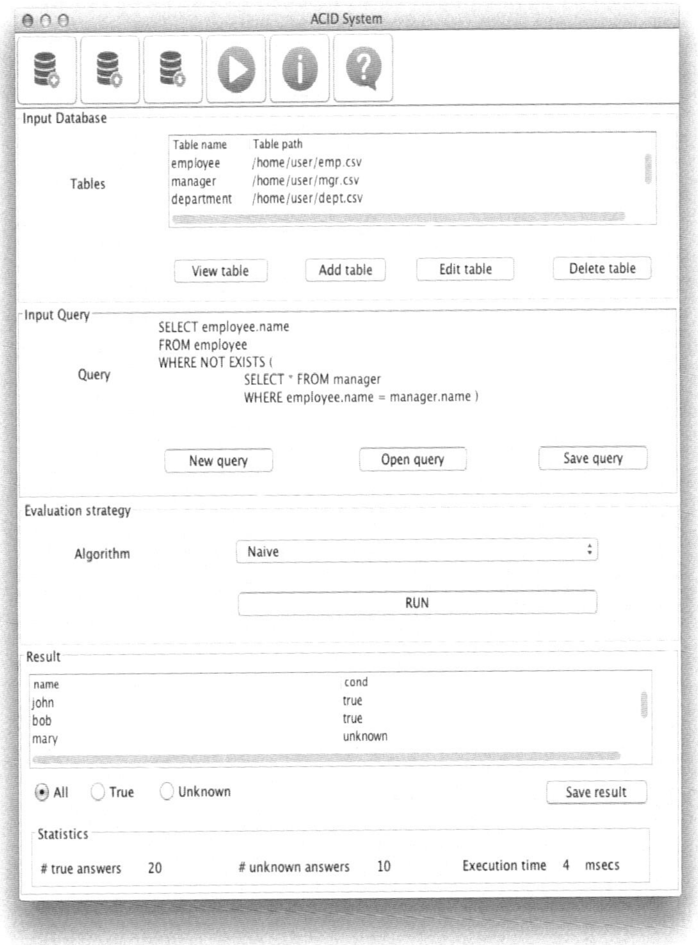

Fig. 2. ACID system's GUI.

3 Trading-off Quality with Runtime

With the same query and database, moving to more accurate strategie, that is, from the naive (resp. semi-naive, lazy) evaluation to the semi-naive (lazy, aware) one, users can see better results, that is, more tuples with condition *true* (i.e., more certain answers), but running times might get higher.

In general, using the system and analyzing the query syntax, users can figure out the strategy that is best suited for their purposes.

As an example, Table 1 reports the execution time, the number of true and unknown answers for three sample queries over a database with the same schema of the one in Example 1, with 1000 tuples per relation and 10% of nulls (randomly generated).

The queries are:

- $Q_{sn} = E - \sigma_{\$1=c}(S)$,
- $Q_{lazy} = P - (E \cap (\sigma_{\$1 \neq c}(S)))$, and

	Q_{sn}			Q_{lazy}			Q_{aware}		
	time	#true	#unk	time	#true	#unk	time	#true	#unk
Naive	518	741	167	788	710	189	2163	100	731
Semi-naive	615	763	145	1090	710	189	2347	100	731
Lazy	661	763	145	1579	737	162	5542	100	731
Aware	3580	763	145	4350	737	162	10376	231	600

Table 1. Runtime (msecs), number of true and unknown answers for three sample queries — 10% of nulls.

- $Q_{aware} = P - (E - S)$,

where c is a value randomly chosen from those in S.

The purpose of the first scenario is to exhibit a query (namely, Q_{sn}) that shows the benefits of going from the naive to the semi-naive evaluation—notice that, in this case, there is no benefit in applying the lazy or aware evaluation, as the structure of the query does not have features that can be exploited by them.

Likewise, the purpose of the second and third scenarios is to show the advantage of using the lazy (resp. aware) evaluation rather than the semi-naive (resp. lazy) one.

4 Conclusion

Certain answers are a principled manner to answer queries on incomplete databases. Since their computation is a coNP-hard problem, recent research has focused on developing polynomial time algorithms providing under-approximations. Leveraging conditional tables, we have developed a suite of novel approximation algorithms.

We have implemented them in the ACID system, which allows users to query incomplete information and get approximate answers with the flexibility of choosing the technique that best meets their needs in terms of balance between efficiency and quality of the result's approximation.

References

1. Abiteboul, S., Grahne, G.: Update semantics for incomplete databases. In: Proc. Very Large Data Bases (VLDB) Conference. pp. 1–12 (1985)
2. Arenas, M., Bertossi, L.E., Chomicki, J.: Consistent query answers in inconsistent databases. In: Proc. Symposium on Principles of Database Systems (PODS). pp. 68–79 (1999)
3. Bertossi, L.E.: Database Repairing and Consistent Query Answering. Synthesis Lectures on Data Management, Morgan & Claypool Publishers (2011)
4. Bienvenu, M., Ortiz, M.: Ontology-mediated query answering with data-tractable description logics. In: Reasoning Web. pp. 218–307 (2015)
5. Calì, A., Gottlob, G., Lukasiewicz, T.: A general datalog-based framework for tractable query answering over ontologies. Journal of Web Semantics **14**, 57–83 (2012)

6. Console, M., Guagliardo, P., Libkin, L.: Approximations and refinements of certain answers via many-valued logics. In: Proc. International Conference on Principles of Knowledge Representation and Reasoning (KR). pp. 349–358 (2016)
7. De Giacomo, G., Lembo, D., Lenzerini, M., Rosati, R.: On reconciling data exchange, data integration, and peer data management. In: Proc. Symposium on Principles of Database Systems (PODS). pp. 133–142 (2007)
8. Fiorentino, N., Greco, S., Molinaro, C., Trubitsyna, I.: ACID: A system for computing approximate certain query answers over incomplete databases. In: Proc. International Conference on Management of Data (SIGMOD). pp. 1685–1688 (2018)
9. Furfaro, F., Greco, S., Molinaro, C.: A three-valued semantics for querying and repairing inconsistent databases. Annals of Mathematics and Artificial Intelligence **51**(2-4), 167–193 (2007)
10. Grahne, G.: The Problem of Incomplete Information in Relational Databases, Lecture Notes in Computer Science, vol. 554. Springer (1991)
11. Greco, S., Molinaro, C., Spezzano, F.: Incomplete Data and Data Dependencies in Relational Databases. Synthesis Lectures on Data Management, Morgan & Claypool Publishers (2012)
12. Greco, S., Molinaro, C., Trubitsyna, I.: Computing approximate certain answers over incomplete databases. In: Proc. Alberto Mendelzon International Workshop on Foundations of Data Management and the Web (AMW) (2017)
13. Guagliardo, P., Libkin, L.: Making SQL queries correct on incomplete databases: A feasibility study. In: Proc. Symposium on Principles of Database Systems (PODS). pp. 211–223 (2016)
14. Imielinski, T., Jr., W.L.: Incomplete information in relational databases. Journal of the ACM **31**(4), 761–791 (1984)
15. Koutris, P., Wijsen, J.: The data complexity of consistent query answering for self-join-free conjunctive queries under primary key constraints. In: Proc. Symposium on Principles of Database Systems (PODS). pp. 17–29 (2015)
16. Lenzerini, M.: Data integration: A theoretical perspective. In: Proc. Symposium on Principles of Database Systems (PODS). pp. 233–246 (2002)
17. Libkin, L.: How to define certain answers. In: Proc. International Joint Conference on Artificial Intelligence (IJCAI). pp. 4282–4288 (2015)
18. Libkin, L.: Certain answers as objects and knowledge. Artificial Intelligence **232**, 1–19 (2016)

Crowdsourced Entity Resolution with Control Queries (Discussion Paper)

Sainyam Galhotra[1], Donatella Firmani[2], Barna Saha[1], and Divesh Srivastava[3]

[1] UMass Amherst {sainyam;barna}@cs.umass.edu
[2] Roma Tre University, donatella.firmani@uniroma3.it
[3] AT&T Labs – Research, divesh@research.att.com

Abstract. Entity resolution (ER) seeks to identify which records in a data set refer to the same real-world entity. Given the diversity of ways in which entities can be represented, ER is known to be a challenging task for automated strategies, but relatively easier for expert humans. Nonetheless, also humans can make mistakes. Our contribution is an error correction toolkit that can be leveraged by a variety of hybrid human-machine ER algorithms, based on a formal way for selecting "control queries" for the human experts. We demonstrate empirically that less recent ER algorithms equipped with our tool can perform even better than most recent ER methods with built-in error correction.

1 Introduction

Entity resolution (ER) is the problem of identifying which records in a data set refer to the same underlying real-world entity [5, 10]. Examples include resolving profiles of people and businesses, or specifications of products and services, from websites and social media. ER can be very intricate, as entities are typically represented in a wide variety of ways that humans can match and distinguish based on domain knowledge, but would be challenging for automated strategies. For these reasons, many frameworks have been developed to leverage humans for performing entity resolution tasks [21, 12], by using, for instance, a crowd-sourcing platform such as Amazon Mechanical Turk. In these frameworks, humans are typically asked questions of the kind "do the record u represent the same entity than the record v?" However, certain record pairs can be challenging to resolve correctly even for humans: take for instance two used iPhones in a retail website, and try to verify whether they are the same model or they have some small differences, for instance in the hardware equipment. Cross-checking human answers can require significant effort, resulting in more money invested in the crowd-sourcing platform or low precision and recall in the computed result.

To this end, we design an error correction toolkit that operates outside the platform, and only requires a small amount of extra questions. Compared to

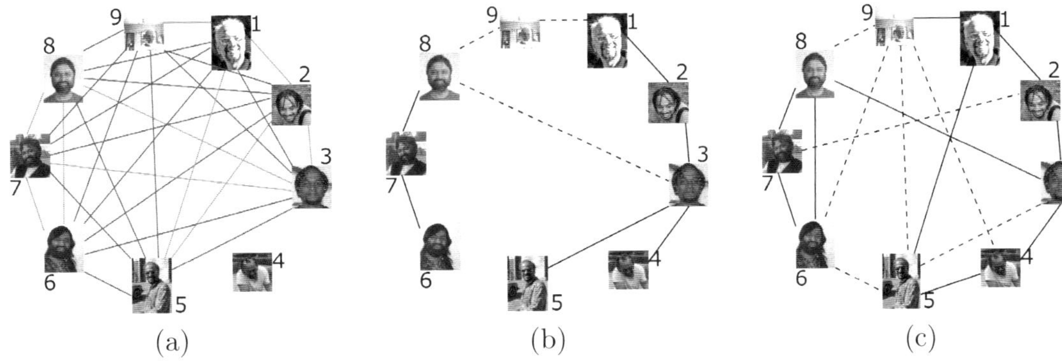

Fig. 1: (a) Example pictures from real web pages. Edges represent matching probabilities (above 0.5 in green). Picture 4 has no face detected. (b-c) Comparison of tree-based (b) with expander-based clusters (c). Positive (negative) answers are represented with solid (dashed) edges, and wrong answers in blue.

other error correction methods, our methodology can be applied to any ER algorithm, boosting its precision and recall and providing formal performance guarantees. In addition, it can be tuned (or even seamlessly turned off) trading off budget for accuracy and adapts to different ER applications.

Main intuition. In literature, there are two main ways to solve ER errors.

- Replicating the same question (i.e. about the same pair) and submitting the replicas to *multiple* humans, until enough evidence is collected for labeling the pair as matching or non-matching (e.g., with voting strategies).
- Using robust clustering techniques for partitioning records into entities, minimizing disagreements between answers (e.g., with correlation clustering).

While recent error-correction works such as [14, 18, 19] provide specific ER algorithms that incorporate both approaches at the same time, we decouple the pair-wise error correction layer from the robust clustering, and focus on which extra-answers would solve disagreements in a principled way, transparently to the underlying ER logic. At the pair level, we can leverage general purpose answer-quality mechanisms already described in the crowd-sourcing literature [2, 23] (that can take advantage of workers meta-data and incentives, to name a few, other than just replicating queries) or use simple majority voting, depending on the application domain. At the cluster level, we proceed as follows.

Expanders. ER strategies based on human experts (e.g., [21, 22, 20, 8]) typically build a *spanning forest* of positive answers for inferring entities via connectivity, based on the assumption that all answers are correct. However, the minimal connectivity of trees yields bad results even in presence of few errors. In a nutshell, we search for queries that can make the connectivity stronger by transforming each tree into an *expander graph*. Graphs with good expansion properties have indeed provably high connectivity and are cheap to build. Intuitively, every edge cut of a graph expander is β times larger than the smallest side of the cut, while every edge of a tree is a cut-edge. This difference is illustrated in Figure 1.

Contributions and outline. We show that the most recent error-correction algorithms can be outperformed by simpler strategies equipped with our expander layer. Section 2 contains an informal overview of our approach. Detailed description of our algorithms and their theoretical basis can be found in [9, 7]. Main experimental results of [9] are reported in Section 3. Finally, Sections 4 and 5 contain related work and our concluding remarks.

2 Overview

We model the pair-wise error correction layer as a black box – that is, a *noisy oracle* – returning already processed pair-wise answers and their corresponding confidence score, possibly labeling some queried pairs incorrectly. We formalize a robust version of the entity resolution problem based on such an oracle and consider *progressive F-measure* [8] as the metric to be maximized in this setting. If one plots a curve of F-measure as a function of the number of oracle queries, progressive F-measure is quantified as the area under this curve.

Problem 1 (Noisy Oracle Strategy) *Given a set of records V, a noisy oracle access to C, and a matching probability function p_m (possibly defined on a subset of $V \times V$), find the strategy that maximizes progressive F-measure.*

Random expansion. Our toolkit guarantees that every cluster – more precisely, the corresponding subgraph induced by positive answers – has good expansion properties. Specifically, every time an ER strategy such as [21, 22, 20, 8] asks a query involving two nodes – say (x, y) – we ask other queries incident to the corresponding clusters c_x and c_y, such as (x_1, y_1) and (x_2, y_2), with $x_1, x_2 \in c_x$ and $y_1, y_2 \in c_y$. Note that extra queries are *not* replicas of (x, y), and they are all distinct. If the answers are positive then the *degree* of nodes within $c_x \cup c_y$ increases, and if the degree gets high enough then we merge c_x and c_y together. We know that random *regular* graphs have good expansion properties [1] in practice, and hence choosing the queries randomly from $c_x \times c_y$ helps us to maintain the required expansion. We refer to our approach as *random expansion.* Technically, we consider *weighted* expanders, where the weight of and edge (x, y) is set to the probability $p_e(x, y)$ that the oracle answer to x, y is erroneous.

Example 1 *In Figure 1 we show the possible result of having an expander ($\beta = 1$) for data in Figure 1a, compared with spanning trees. Both connected components of the left figure (i.e., trees in the spanning forest) and expander graphs of right figure yield the same, correct, clustering $\{1, 2, 3, 4, 5\}, \{6, 7, 8\}, \{9\}$. While connected components only work in absence of errors, expander produces the correct clustering also in presence of plausible human errors such as $(1, 9)$, $(8, 3)$ (false positives) and $(3, 5)$ (false negative). Even though expansion requires more queries than building a spanning forest, it is far from being exhaustive: in the larger cluster out of $\binom{5}{2} = 10$ possible queries, only 5 are asked.*

Algorithm 1 High-level description on `adaptive`(β) pipeline.

1: run *node* ordering equipped with `query_edges`($\beta, \cdot, \cdot$) upon disagreement
2: `boost_fscore`(β)
3: run *edge* ordering equipped with `query_edges`($\beta, \cdot, \cdot$) upon disagreement
4: `boost_fscore`(β)

Expander Toolkit. Our toolkit consists of two methods: `query_edges`() and `boost_fscore`(), as described next. The input includes the parameter β, the matching probability function p_m, and the error probabilities p_e.

- Given a query (u, v) selected by an ER strategy, `query_edges`(β, u, v) provides an intermediate layer between the ER logic and the noisy oracle: instead of asking the selected query (u, v) as the considered strategy would do, `query_edges`(β, u, v) selects a bunch of random queries between the cluster of u and the cluster of v, and returns a YES answer only if the joint error probability of the cut is small.
- The `boost_fscore`(β) method instead provides functionalities for maintaining the expansion properties of subgraphs that were not considered during the execution of the ER process, by either adding new edges to weak cuts or splitting the clusters in expander subgraphs. Running `boost_fscore`(β) at a later phase of the ER process can fix premature decisions.

The parameter β trades off the number of queries for precision: smaller values of β correspond to sparser clusters, and therefore to less queries. $\beta = 0$ is equivalent to using the oracle strategy alone. Greater values of β correspond to denser clusters and to higher precision: we prove that its expected value is $1 - O(1/n^{\beta})$.

Deployment of the toolkit. Consider a *perfect oracle* strategy such as those in [21, 22, 20, 8], assuming all the answers correct and thus asking a spanning forest. As mentioned, `query_edges`() can be used as a substitute of plain connectivity for deciding if two clusters refer to the same entity or not. For instance, in case of *node ordering* based strategies, such as [20], a singleton node is added to a cluster by querying a single edge with it. We can replace that querying step with `query_edges`() which will try to check if the singleton cluster containing the node refers to the same entity as the one it was supposed to be queried with. The *edge ordering* based strategies, such as [22], query the edges in decreasing order of probabilities to decide if the two endpoint clusters ought to be merged or not. Similarly, we can make the same decision by replacing this querying step with `query_edges`() of the two endpoint clusters. We note that the strategy in [8] combines node and edge ordering, and can be modified to apply random expansion similarly. Along with the incorporation of `query_edges`(), any strategy can call `boost_fscore`() towards the end for correcting the errors made in earlier stages. This shows that our toolkit is independent and easy to use.

Adaptive strategy. In the previous paragraph, we have described a simple way to merge the expansion toolkit with a perfect oracle strategies to minimize the effect of error in the noisy setting. One of the main advantages of the above described methods is that they maintain high precision throughout the

dataset	n	k	$\|C_1\|$	ref.	description
`cora`	1.9K	191	236	[16]	Title, author, venue, and date of scientific papers.
`captcha`*	244	69	8	[18]	CAPTCHA images showing four-digit numbers.
`gym`*	94	12	15	[18]	Images of gymnastics athletes in different positions.

Table 1: Datasets used in our experiments. We report the number of records n, number of clusters k (i.e., entities), size of the largest cluster $|C_1|$, and the paper where they appeared first. Datasets with the symbol $\star$ come with a cache of answers from the AMT crowd. `cora` has synthetic noisy oracle answers.

resolution phase. This high precision is achieved at the cost of lower progressive F-score. A close look at the expansion toolkit shows that we can possibly improve this shortcoming as well. To this end, we also provide the `adaptive`() pipeline in Algorithm 1, building on the ideas of the `hybrid`() method in [8]. Let `query_single_edge`(u, v) refer to a pair-wise oracle query of the kind "do the record u represent the same entity than the record v?". The intuition of `adaptive`() is to switch between `query_single_edge`() and `query_edges`() depending on the current answer. Specifically, we call `query_edges`() only if the confidence score returned by the noisy oracle in "disagreement" with the matching probabilities (e.g., a positive answer in case of low matching probability). We make use of `boost_fscore`() between the node and edge ordering phases, for correcting early errors due to the adaptive nature of the strategy. Specifially, `adaptive`() allows temporary non-expander clusters, thus allowing spurious violations of our invariant. However, we observe in practice that such behaviour can provide high gains in progressive F-score without losing on precision.

3 Experiments

We compare our algorithms with the most recent approaches for crowdsourced ER [14, 18, 19]. As a frame of reference, we use the ideal curve with that achieves maximum progressive F-score by progressively growing the true clusters as in [8]. We ran experiments on a machine with two CPU Intel Xeon E5520 units with 16 cores each, running at 2.67GHz, with 32GB RAM. We consider both real and synthetic datasets, as summarized in Table 1. We show performances not only of `adaptive`(), but also of other variants considered in [9], and refer the reader to [9] for a more extensive experimental comparison.

In Figures 2a and 2b, we compare the progressive F-score of our and previous strategies. We set the x axis to the number of *distinct* queries in all the datasets. The plots show that our `adaptive`() pipeline achieves more than 90% F-score with less than 400 queries in case of `gym`. Similarly for `captchas`, the F-score achieved is more than 90% even with the simplest pipeline `lazy`(), which correspond to the ER strategy in [8] equipped with our `boost_fscore`() method at the end. This is due to the zero false positives in the oracle answers for `captchas`. In such scenario, `lazy`() has 100% precision. Benefits of using our expander pipelines become evident with more challenging dataset, such as `gym`.

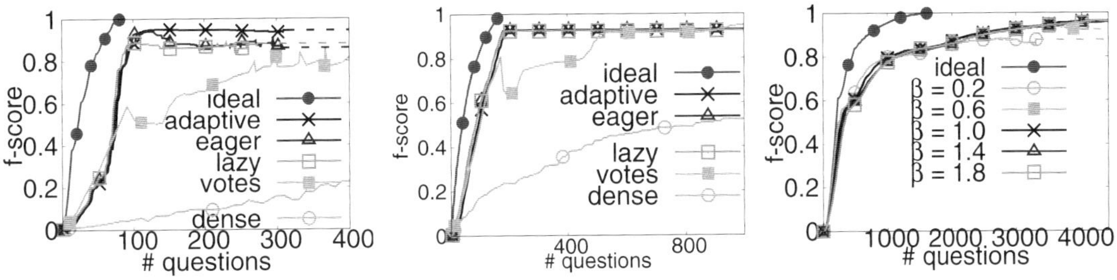

(a) gym (b) captchas (c) cora

Fig. 2: Comparison of the strategies condidered in [9] over datasets of Table 1.

In order to investigate further the effect of oracle answers on gym, we set input probability 1 of a pair (u, v) if and only if (u, v) is matching, and 0 otherwise, and generate synthetic erroneous answers as the error rate for both false positives and negatives varies in the range $[0, 0.3]$. In this setting, we observed that performance of adaptive() is almost ideal up to answer error rate 0.2, which is higher than the error typically observed in real crowd sourcing platforms such as Amazon Mechanical Turk [2]. Figure 2c demonstrates the effect of changing the tuning parameter β on the performance of adaptive() (multiple queries are counted separately). It is evident that the progressive F-score improves as the β value is reduced. The downside of this is that it tries to grow a sparser graph, which has lower precision and the algorithm plateau's out at lower final F-score. On the other hand, higher values of β make the approach conservative to ask more queries and reduces the progressive F-score. The above described behavior is consistent with our theoretical bounds proven in [9].

Alternative forms of expansion. Although random expansion is analytically proven to require less *queries* than deterministic expansion [1], empirically one can make use of alternative forms of expansions for selecting "control queries". The table below compares the number of queries asked by adaptive() on cora with different expansion strategies, dubbed *high*, *low*, and *uncertain*, selecting queries with the closest matching probability to 1, 0, and 0.5 respectively.

F-score	p^+, p^-	random	high p_m	low p_m	uncertain p_m
0.9	0.1	2420	2481	2355	2417
0.85	0.2	3041	4683	4028	3744

Random expansion gets to the same F-score of deterministic alternatives with less or comparable number of queries. We observed similar results for all the considered datasets. Even though cora seems to select *uncertain* as the best deterministic alternative, a deeper look at the experimental data reveals that the 0.5 matching probability bucket is the one containing most edges in cora, and drawing edges from this bucket closely resembles random selection.

4 Related Works

ER has a long history, from the seminal paper by Fellegi and Sunter in 1969 [6], which proposed the use of a learning-based approach, to the recently proposed hybrid human-machine approaches. We focus on the latter line of work, which we refer to *crowdsourced ER*, where we can ask questions to humans about two records representing the same real-world entity.

Perfect oracle strategies. The strategies described in [20, 22, 8] abstract the crowd as a whole by an *oracle*, which can provide a correct YES/NO answer for a given pair of items. This allows for leveraging transitivity: when we know that u matches with v and v matches with w, the matching of u and w is inferred automatically. The strategies focus on different ER logics, which can be formally compared in terms of the number of questions asked for 100% recall [8, 15]. Unfortunately, the strategies do not apply to low quality of answers.

Error-correction methods. In order to deal with erroneous answers by humans, recent approaches typically ask the same query to individual crowd workers, rather than making use of control queries to a crowd abstraction such as the noisy oracle. The strategies in [14] submits the same query to multiple crowd workers, and every answer represents a *vote*. The goal is to achieve a clear majority of YES or NO answers for some pairs (u, v), and use those high confidence pairs for building clusters. The strategies described in [18] assume that every crowd worker has a known *error rate* p^E. In this setting, each YES/NO answer for a given pair of items can be interpreted as a matching probability. Such strategies start from an initial clustering and then refines the solution by asking to the crowd. Finally, the work in [19] uses a combination of k-*node* queries (for instance, with $k = 3$, "are u, v and z the same entity?") and pair-wise queries.

Other Related Works. Wang et al. [21] describe a hybrid human-machine framework CrowdER, that automatically detects pairs that have a high likelihood of matching, which are then verified by humans. Gokhale et al. [12] propose a hybrid approach for the end-to-end workflow, making effective use of active learning via human labeling. In [3] the authors devise a partial ordering based technique to resolve entities, which applies for records of text attributes. Progressive F-score has been discussed in [24, 17, 13]. Finally, estimating or improving crowd accuracy in general, as in [4, 11, 2], is outside the scope of this paper.

5 Conclusions

We address the problem of maximizing progressive F-measure for the crowdsourced ER task. We propose an efficient and cost-effective layer which can be applied on typical ER strategies to make them robust to crowd errors, and present different pipelines that use the expansion toolkit to provide high progressive F-score with provable guarantees. Our experiments over real and synthetic datasets confirm our theory and show the superiority of our pipelines over the techniques proposed in the literature. In our future work, we plan to apply our results to *temporal record linkage*, where error probability is higher as two records are farther in time and very small for nearby records of the same entity.

References

1. N. Alon and J. H. Spencer. *The probabilistic method.* John Wiley & Sons, 2004.
2. J. Bragg and D. S. Weld. Optimal testing for crowd workers. In *AAMAS*, 2016.
3. C. Chai, G. Li, J. Li, D. Deng, and J. Feng. Cost-effective crowdsourced entity resolution: A partial-order approach. In *SIGMOD*, pages 969–984, 2016.
4. N. Dalvi, A. Dasgupta, R. Kumar, and V. Rastogi. Aggregating crowdsourced binary ratings. In *WWW*, pages 285–294, 2013.
5. A. K. Elmagarmid, P. G. Ipeirotis, and V. S. Verykios. Duplicate record detection: A survey. *IEEE Trans. Knowl. Data Eng.*, 19(1):1–16, 2007.
6. I. P. Fellegi and A. B. Sunter. A theory for record linkage. *Journal of the American Statistical Association*, 64(328):1183–1210, 1969.
7. D. Firmani, S. Galhotra, B. Saha, and D. Srivastava. Robust entity resolution using a crowdoracle. *IEEE Data Eng. Bull.*, 41(2):91–103, 2018.
8. D. Firmani, B. Saha, and D. Srivastava. Online entity resolution using an oracle. *PVLDB*, 9(5):384–395, 2016.
9. S. Galhotra, D. Firmani, B. Saha, and D. Srivastava. Robust entity resolution using random graphs. In *SIGMOD*, pages 3–18, 2018.
10. L. Getoor and A. Machanavajjhala. Entity resolution: theory, practice & open challenges. *PVLDB*, 5(12):2018–2019, 2012.
11. A. Ghosh, S. Kale, and P. McAfee. Who moderates the moderators?: crowdsourcing abuse detection in user-generated content. In *EC*, pages 167–176, 2011.
12. C. Gokhale, S. Das, A. Doan, J. F. Naughton, N. Rampalli, J. Shavlik, and X. Zhu. Corleone: Hands-off crowdsourcing for entity matching. In *SIGMOD*, pages 601–612, 2014.
13. A. Gruenheid, X. L. Dong, and D. Srivastava. Incremental record linkage. *PVLDB*, 7(9):697–708, 2014.
14. A. Gruenheid, B. Nushi, T. Kraska, W. Gatterbauer, and D. Kossmann. Fault-tolerant entity resolution with the crowd. *arXiv preprint arXiv:1512.00537*, 2015.
15. A. Mazumdar and B. Saha. A theoretical analysis of first heuristics of crowdsourced entity resolution. *AAAI*, 2017.
16. A. McCallum, 2004. `https://people.cs.umass.edu/~mccallum/data.html`.
17. T. Papenbrock, A. Heise, and F. Naumann. Progressive duplicate detection. *Knowledge and Data Engineering, IEEE Transactions on*, 27(5):1316–1329, 2015.
18. V. Verroios and H. Garcia-Molina. Entity resolution with crowd errors. In *ICDE Conference*, pages 219–230, April 2015.
19. V. Verroios, H. Garcia-Molina, and Y. Papakonstantinou. Waldo: An adaptive human interface for crowd entity resolution. In *SIGMOD Conference*, 2017.
20. N. Vesdapunt, K. Bellare, and N. Dalvi. Crowdsourcing algorithms for entity resolution. *PVLDB*, 7(12):1071–1082, 2014.
21. J. Wang, T. Kraska, M. J. Franklin, and J. Feng. Crowder: Crowdsourcing entity resolution. *PVLDB*, 5(11):1483–1494, 2012.
22. J. Wang, G. Li, T. Kraska, M. J. Franklin, and J. Feng. Leveraging transitive relations for crowdsourced joins. In *SIGMOD Conference*, pages 229–240, 2013.
23. P. Welinder, S. Branson, S. Belongie, and P. Perona. The multidimensional wisdom of crowds. In *NIPS*, pages 2424–2432, USA, 2010. Curran Associates Inc.
24. S. E. Whang, D. Marmaros, and H. Garcia-Molina. Pay-as-you-go entity resolution. *Knowledge and Data Engineering, IEEE Transactions on*, 25(5):1111–1124, 2013.

Greg, ML: Automatic Diagnostic Suggestions
Humanity is Overrated. Or not.

Paola Lapadula [1], Giansalvatore Mecca [1], Donatello Santoro [1], Luisa Solimando [2], and Enzo Veltri [2]

[1] Università della Basilicata – Potenza, Italy
[2] Svelto! Big Data Cleaning and Analytics – Potenza, Italy

(Discussion Paper)

Abstract. Recently machine-learning techniques have been applied in a variety of fields. One of the most promising and challenging is handling medical records. In this paper we present Greg, ML, a machine-learning tool for generating automatic diagnostic suggestions based on patient profiles. At the core of our system there are two machine learning classifiers: a natural-language module that handles reports of instrumental exams, and a profile classifier that outputs diagnostic suggestions to the doctor. After discussing the architecture we present some experimental results based on the working prototype we have developed. Finally, we examine challenges and opportunities related to the use of this kind of tools in medicine, and some important lessons learned developing the tool. In this respect, despite the ironic title of this paper, we underline that Greg should be conceived primarily as a support for expert doctors in their diagnostic decisions, and can hardly replace humans in their judgment.

1 Introduction

The larger availability of digital data related to all sectors of our everyday lives has created opportunities for data-based applications that would not be conceivable a few years ago. One example is medicine: the push for the widespread adoption of electronic medical records [9, 5] and digital medical reports is paving the ground for new applications based on these data.

Greg, ML [8] is one of these applications. It is a machine-learning tool for generating automatic diagnostic suggestions based on patient profiles. In essence, Greg takes as input a digital profile of a patient, and suggests one or more diagnosis that, according to its internal models, fit the profile with a given probability. We assume that a doctor inspects these diagnostic suggestions, and takes informed actions about the patients.

We notice that the idea of using machine learning for the purpose of examining medical data is not new [7, 11, 10]. In fact, several efforts have been taken in this direction [1, 6]. To the best of our knowledge, however, all of the existing tools concentrate on rather specific learning tasks, for example identifying a single pathology – like heart disease [14, 12], or pneumonia [13], or cancer, where results of remarkable quality have been reported [15]. On the contrary, Greg has the distinguishing feature of being a broad-scope diagnostic-suggestion tool. In fact, at the core of the tool stands a generic learning model that allows to suggest large numbers of pathologies, currently several dozens, and in perspective several hundreds.

Greg is a research project developed by Svelto!, a spin-off of the data-management group at University of Basilicata.

The rest of the paper is devoted to introduce Greg, as follows. We discuss the internal architecture of the tool in Section 2. Then, we introduce the methodology and the additional tools in Section 3. We introduce some experimental results based on the current version of the tool in Section 4.

Finally, in Section 5 we conclude by discussing the possible applications we envision for Greg, and discuss a few crucial lessons learned with the tool, which, in turn, have inspired the title of this paper.

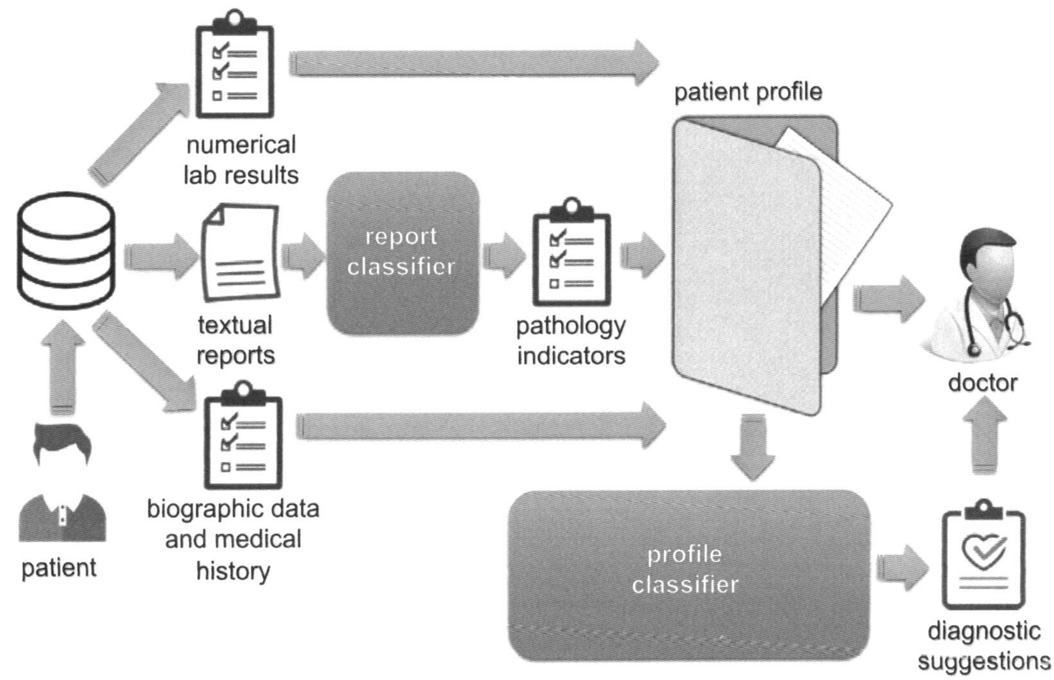

Fig. 1: Architecture of Greg.

2 Architecture of Greg

The architecture and the overall flow of Greg is depicted in Figure 1.

As we have already discussed, at the core of Greg stands a classifier for patient profiles that provides doctors with diagnostic suggestions. Profiles are entirely anonymous, i.e., Greg does not store nor requires any personal data about patients, and are composed of three main blocks:

- anonymous biographical data, mainly age and gender, and medical history of the patient, i.e., past medical events and pathologies, especially the chronic ones;
- result of lab exams, in numerical format;
- textual reports from instrumental exams, like RX, ultrasounds etc.

These items compose the patient profile that is fed to the profile classifier in order to propose diagnostic suggestions to doctors. Notice that, while biographic data, medical history and lab exam results are essentially structured data, and therefore can be easily integrated into the profile, reports of instrumental exams are essentially unstructured. As a consequence, Greg relies on a second learning module to extract what we call *pathology indicators*, i.e., structured labels indicating anomalies in the report that may suggest the presence of a pathology.

The report classifier is essentially a natural-language processing module. It takes the text of the report in natural language and identifies pathology indicators that are then integrated within the patient profile.

The report classifier is, in a way, the crucial module for the construction of the patient profile. In fact, reports of instrumental exams often carry crucial information for the purpose of identifying the correct diagnostic suggestions. At the same time, their treatment is language-dependent, and learning is labor-intensive, since it requires to label large set of reports in order to train the classifier.

Once the profile for a new patient has been built, it is fed to the profile classifier that outputs diagnostic suggestions to the doctor. There are a few important aspects to be noticed here.

- First, Greg is trained to predict only a finite set of diagnoses. This means that it is intended primarily as a tool to gain positive evidence about pathologies that might be present, rather than as a tool to exclude pathologies that are not present. In other terms, the fact that Greg does not suggest a specific diagnosis does not mean that that can be excluded, since it might only be the case that Greg has not be trained for that particular pathology. It can be seen that handling a large number of diagnoses is crucial, in this respect.
- Second, Greg associates a degree of probability with each diagnostic suggestion, i.e., it ranks them with a confidence measure. This is important, since the tool may provide several different suggestions for a given profile, and not all of them are to be considered as equally relevant.

It can be seen how a tool like Greg has an effective as seamless integration with the everyday procedures of a medical institution is. To foster this kind of adoption, Greg can be used as a stand-alone tool, with its own user-interface, but it has been developed primarily as an engine-backed API, that can be easily integrated with any medical information system that is already deployed in medical units and wards. Ideally, with this kind of integration, accessing medical suggestions provided by Greg should cost no more than clicking a button, in addition of the standard procedure for patient-data gathering and medical-record compilation.

3 The Greg Workflow and Ecosystem

As we have discussed in the previous sections, the effectiveness of a system like Greg is strongly related to the number of pathologies which it can provide suggestions for. We therefore put quite a lot of effort in structuring the learning workflow in order to make it lean and easily reproducible. In this section we summarize a few key findings in this respect, that led us to the development of a number of additional tools, which compose the Greg ecosystem.

A first important observation we make is that a system like Greg needs to make reference to a standardized set of diagnosis. As it is common, we rely on the international classification of diseases, *ICD-10 (DRG)* [3]. This, however, poses a challenge when dealing with large and heterogeneous collections of medical records coming from disparate sources, which do not necessarily are associated with a DRG. This poses a standardization problem for diagnosis labels. In fact, standardizing the vocabulary of pathologies and pathology indicators is crucial in the early stages of data preparation. To this end, we leveraged the consolidated suite of data-cleaning tools developed by our research group over the years [2–4].

A second important observation is that we need to handle large and complex amounts of data gathered from medical information systems, including biographical data, admissions and patient medical history, medical records, multiple lab exams, and multiple reports. These data need to be explored, selected and prepared for the purpose of training the learning models. In order to streamline the data-preparation process, we decided to develop a tool to explore the available data. The tool is called Caddy and is essentially a data warehouse build on top of the transactional medical databases. This allowed us to adopt a structured approach to data exploration and data selection, that proved essential in the development of the tool.

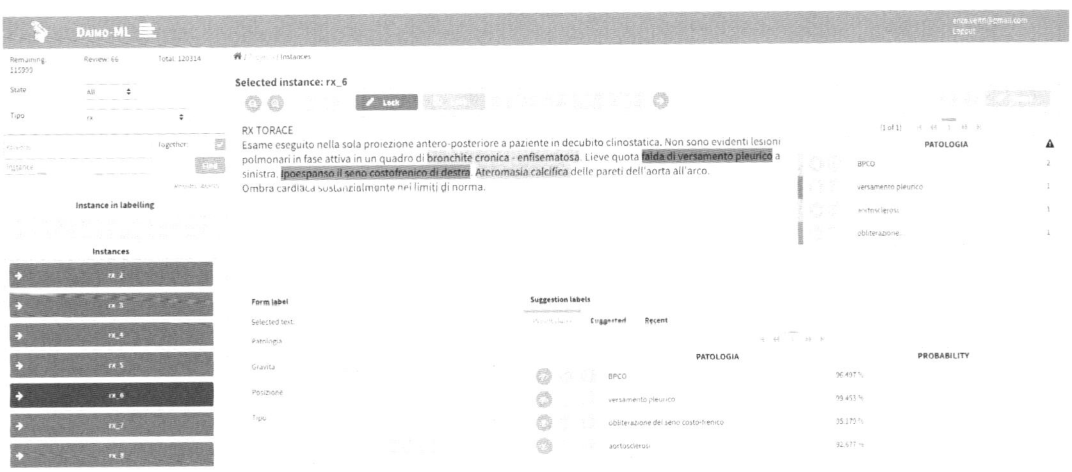

Fig. 2: DAIMO, the ML Labeling Tool.

However, the tool that proved to be the most crucial in the development of Greg is DAIMO, our instance labeler. DAIMO stands for *Digital Annotation of Instances and*

[3] http://www.who.int/classifications/icd/icdonlineversions/en/

Markup of Objects. It is a tool explicitly conceived to support the labeling phase of machine learning projects. A snapshot of the system is shown in Figure 2.

DAIMO is a semi-automated tool for data labeling. It provides a simple and effective interface to explore pre-defined collections of samples to label. Samples may be either textual, or even structured – for example, in tabular format– or even of mixed type. Users that are tasked with labeling can cooperatively explore the samples, pick them, explore existing labels and add more. Figure 2 shows the process of labeling one report. Labels associated with the report are on the right. Each corresponds to a colored portion of the text.

We believe that even only the availability of an intuitive tool to support cooperative labeling-work significantly increases productivity. In addition to this, DAIMO provides additional functionalities that further improve the process.

First, it allows to define *label vocabularies*, in order to standardize the way in which labels are assigned to samples. Users usually search labels within the vocabulary, and add new ones only when the ones they need are not present. When dealing with complex labeling tasks with many different labels, such a systematic approach is crucial in order to get good-quality results.

Second, DAIMO is able to *learn* labeling strategies from examples. After some initial training, it does not only collects new labels from users, but actually suggests them, so that users need only to accept or refuse DAIMO's suggestions. This approach really transforms the labeling process from the inside out, since after a while it is DAIMO, not the user to do most of the work.

In fact, in our experience, working with DAIMO may lower text-labeling times up to one order of magnitude with respect to manual, unassisted labeling.

4 Experimental Results

ID	Diagnosis	GT - D.L.	GT - Doct.
D1	Iron Deficiency	0,18	1,00
D2	Atherosclerosis	0,09	0,98
D3	Cardiomegaly	0,46	0,95
D4	Hepatic Cirrhosis	0,18	0,97
D5	Hypercholesterolemia	0,10	1,00
D6	Prostatic Hyperplasia	0,18	0,97
D7	Hypokalemia	0,10	0,97
D8	Pneumonia	0,63	0,96

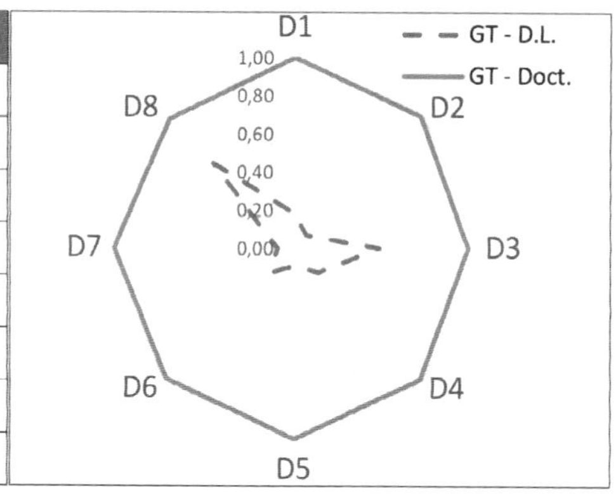

Fig. 3: Experimental Results prior and after Diagnosis Review in terms of F-Measure

We developed an advanced prototype of Greg, used to conduct a number of experiments to assess the feasibility of the overall approach.

We conducted a first preliminary experimental evaluation using 200 medical records over a small set of diagnosis (pneumonia, cirrhosis, anemia, urological infection) [8].

Lately. we used a bigger dataset, containing a total of 22160 medical records and we were able to learn about 50 diagnosis. We used the discharge letters for each medical record as labels. We called this annotated dataset *GT - D.L.* (Ground Truth - Discharge letters). As usually data were split in training, cross-validation and test sets and we measured the F-Measure of Greg predictions. On *GT - D.L.* we obtained poor results, not as good as we would have expected. Some of the results are shown in Figure 3, in terms of F-Measure. Our investigation of the data, however, suggested that in many cases the quality of the results have been underestimated. In essence, in several cases Greg suggested a more thorough set of diagnoses than the one indicated by the doctor in discharge letters. As an example, this happened frequently with patients suffering from anaemia, which is often associated with cirrhosis, even though doctors had not explicitly mentioned that specific diagnosis in the discharge letter.

We therefore conducted a second experiment. We asked our team of doctors to review the set of diagnoses associated with patient profiles used for the test. In essence, our doctors made sure that all relevant diagnoses were appropriately mentioned, including those that the hospital doctors had omitted in the discharge letter. We called this manually annotated dataset *GT - Doct.* (Ground Truth - Doctors). Figure 3 reports Greg's results over this revised dataset. As it can be seen, we obtained an F-Measure for each diagnosis always above the 95%.

To summarize, our preliminary tests show that Greg can effectively achieve high accuracy in its predictions. In addition, it may effectively assist doctors in formulating their diagnoses, by providing systematic suggestions.

5 Conclusions: Opportunities and Lessons Learned

We believe that Greg can be a valid and useful tool to assist doctors in the diagnostic process. Given its ability to learn diagnostic suggestions at scale, we envision several main scenarios of use for the system in a medical facility:

- We believe Greg can be of particular help in ER, during the triage and first diagnostic phase; in particular, based on first evidences about the patient, it may help the ER operator to identify a few pathologies to it is worth exploring, perhaps with the help of specialized colleague.
- Then, we envision interesting opportunities related to the use of Greg in the diagnosis of rare pathologies; these are especially difficult to capture by a learning algorithm, because, by definition, there are only a few training examples to use, and therefore a special treatment is required. Still, we believe that supporting doctors – especially younger ones, that might have less experience in diagnosing these pathologies – in this respect is an important field of application.
- In medical institutions that rely on standardized clinical pathways or *integrated care pathways (ICPs)* – PDTAs in Italy – Greg may be used to quickly suggest which parts of a pathway need to be explored, and which ones can be excluded based on the available evidence.
- Finally, Greg may be used as a second-opinion tool, i.e., after the doctor has formulated her/his diagnosis, for the purpose of double checking that all possibilities have been considered.

While in our opinion all of these represent areas in which Greg can be a valid support tool for the doctor, we would like to put them in context by discussing what we believe to be the most important lessons we have learned so far.

On the one side, the development of Greg has taught us a basic and important lesson: in many cases, probably the majority, the basic workings of the diagnostic process employed by human doctors is indeed reproducible by an automatic algorithm.

In fact, it is well known that doctors tend to follow a decision process that looks for specific indicators within the patient profile – e.g., values of laboratory tests, or specific symptoms – and decides to consider or excludes pathologies based on them. As fuzzy as this process may be, as any other human-thinking process, to our surprise we learned that for a large number of pathologies this process provides a perfect opportunity for the employment of a machine learning algorithm, which, in turn, may achieve very good accuracy in mimicking the human decision process, with the additional advantage of scale – Greg can be trained to learn very high numbers of diagnostic suggestions. In this respect, ironically quoting Gregory House, we might be tempted to state that "Humanity is overrated", indeed.

However, our experiences also led us to find that there are facets of the diagnostic process that are inherently related to intuition, experience, and human factors. These are, by nature, impossible to capture by an automatic algorithm. Therefore, our ultimate conclusion is that humanity is not overrated, and that Greg can indeed provide useful support in the diagnostic process, but it cannot and should not be considered as a replacement of an expert human doctor.

References

1. R. C. Deo. Machine learning in medicine. *Circulation*, 132(20):1920–1930, 2015.
2. F. Geerts, G. Mecca, P. Papotti, and D. Santoro. Mapping and Cleaning. In *Proceedings of the IEEE International Conference on Data Engineering - ICDE*, 2014.
3. F. Geerts, G. Mecca, P. Papotti, and D. Santoro. That's All Folks! LLUNATIC Goes Open Source. In *Proceedings of the International Conference on Very Large Databases - VLDB*, 2014.
4. J. He, E. Veltri, D. Santoro, G. Li, G. Mecca, P. Papotti, and N. Tang. Interactive and deterministic data cleaning. In *Proceedings of the 2016 International Conference on Management of Data, SIGMOD Conference 2016*, pages 893–907, 2016.
5. T. Heinis, A. Ailamaki, et al. Data infrastructure for medical research. *Foundations and Trends in Databases*, 8(3):131–238, 2017.
6. A. Holzinger. Machine learning for health informatics. In *Machine Learning for Health Informatics*, pages 1–24. Springer, 2016.
7. I. Kononenko. Machine learning for medical diagnosis: history, state of the art and perspective. *Artificial Intelligence in medicine*, 23(1):89–109, 2001.
8. P. Lapadula, G. Mecca, D. Santoro, L. Solimando, and E. Veltri. Humanity Is Overrated. or Not. Automatic Diagnostic Suggestions by Greg, ML. In *New Trends in Databases and Information Systems*, pages 305–313. Springer International Publishing, 2018.
9. R. H. Miller and I. Sim. Physicians' use of electronic medical records: barriers and solutions. *Health affairs*, 23(2):116–126, 2004.
10. O. Mohammed and R. Benlamri. Developing a semantic web model for medical differential diagnosis recommendation. *Journal of medical systems*, 38(10):79, 2014.

11. N. Peek, C. Combi, R. Marin, and R. Bellazzi. Thirty years of artificial intelligence in medicine (aime) conferences: A review of research themes. *Artificial intelligence in medicine*, 65(1):61–73, 2015.
12. P. Rajpurkar, A. Y. Hannun, M. Haghpanahi, C. Bourn, and A. Y. Ng. Cardiologist-level arrhythmia detection with convolutional neural networks. *arXiv preprint arXiv:1707.01836*, 2017.
13. P. Rajpurkar, J. Irvin, K. Zhu, B. Yang, H. Mehta, T. Duan, D. Ding, A. Bagul, C. Langlotz, K. Shpanskaya, et al. Chexnet: Radiologist-level pneumonia detection on chest x-rays with deep learning. *arXiv preprint arXiv:1711.05225*, 2017.
14. J. Soni, U. Ansari, D. Sharma, and S. Soni. Predictive data mining for medical diagnosis: An overview of heart disease prediction. *International Journal of Computer Applications*, 17(8):43–48, 2011.
15. I. Steadman. IBM's Watson is better at diagnosing cancer than human doctors. *WIRED*, 2013.

A complex network approach to semantic spaces: How *meaning* organizes itself

Salvatore Citraro[1], Giulio Rossetti[2]

[1] University of Pisa, Italy
salvatorecitraro939@gmail.com
[2] ISTI-CNR, Pisa, Italy
giulio.rossetti@isti.cnr.it

Discussion Paper

Abstract. We propose a complex network approach to the emergence of *word meaning* through the analysis of semantic spaces: NLP techniques able to capture an aspect of meaning based on distributional semantic theories, so that words are linked to each other if they can be substituted in the same linguistic contexts, forming clusters representing semantic fields. This approach can be used to model a mental lexicon of word similarities: a graph $G = (N, L)$ where N are words connected by some type of semantic or associative property L. Networks extracted from a baseline neural language model are analyzed in terms of global properties: they are small world and the probability of degree distribution follows a truncated power law. Moreover, they throw in a strong degree assortativity, a peculiarity that introduces us to the problem of semantic field identification. We support the idea that semantic fields can be identified exploiting the topological information of networks. Several community discovery methods have been tested, identifying from time to time strict semantic fields as crisp communities, linguistic contexts as overlapping communities or meaning conveyed by single words as communities produced starting from a seed-set expansion.

1 Introduction

In this work we assume distributional semantic theories - modeled by semantic spaces[1] - in order to analyze the complex structure of word meaning: words appearing in the same linguistic contexts form clusters representing semantic fields. In semantic spaces words are represented as vectors, whereas similar ones are near in terms of a geometric distance: therefore, it can be possible - through a similarity function - modeling some type of semantic or associative relatedness between words. Moreover, if we represent vectors as nodes, we can connect the

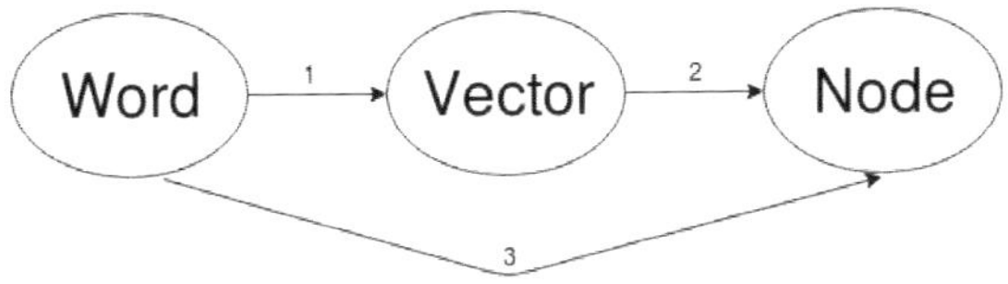

Fig. 1. (1) From texts to semantic spaces (2) From semantic spaces to networks (3) Can a graph have any linguistic reality?

highly similar ones with a link, letting a complex semantic network emerges. The scheme of the approach is summarized in Fig. 1.

The aim of the work is the identification of semantic fields through the exploitable topological information of networks. Treating semantic fields as communities (i.e., set of nodes tightly connected to each other), we want to partition a graph using several community discovery algorithms.

Details about the state-of-art of complex semantic networks will be given in Section 2. Data preparation (i.e., how complex networks have been extracted) will be described in Section 3. Global properties of networks will be analyzed in Section 4 - in terms of degree distribution, small world properties and assortativity. Section 5 will be about the analysis of the different types of semantic fields that we modeled. Section 6 will introduce several futures lines of research.

2 Complex semantic networks and the mental lexicon

The relationship between complex networks and language - in this case, its semantic level - is not trivial. The first metaphors of semantics as network of words refer to the models of semantic memory. Nowadays, they have been using to model a mental lexicon of word similarities, arguing how its structure may result in a complex system[11] as equal to biological, physical, social phenomenons, among others. Network Science offers a paradigm of research capable of determine the complexity of a system. Scale-freeness and small world properties are typical peculiarities of real complex systems: a network is scale-free if its degree distribution follows a power law and it is small world if clustering coefficient is higher and average path length is shorter than those of a random network. Practically, this means that, contrary to a random network, scale-free networks have a few number of highly connected nodes and a long tail of poorly connected ones. Starting from these measures, related works showed how complex semantic networks extracted from lexical databases, thesauri, association norms and treebanks annotated with the role arguments of verbs are scale-free and small world[7][8].

Complex semantic networks are graphs $G = (N, L)$ in which N are words connected by some type of semantic property L. Clarify the type of semantic property helps us to classify complex semantic networks from the aspect of meaning that they are modeling. Practically, in the previous examples nodes are *real words* and semantic properties represent relations like synonymy, hyponymy, hypernymy, free associations or the arguments of verbs, while in network extracted from semantic spaces nodes are vectors connected by an high value of a similarity function. Literature points out how it is hard to verify if networks extracted from semantic spaces are scale-free, although the presence of small world phenomenon: it is argued how degree distributions could follow an exponential distribution[7] as well as a truncated power law[9] or a lognormal one[10] rather than a pure power law. This may be a constraint due to the representational framework necessary for the semantic space construction. However, the literature has concentrated more on global properties than on the meso-scale structure of all this networks, whereas more sensible aspects of word meaning complexity can be captured.

3 Data preparation

Given a training corpus $C = \{w_1, w_2, ..., w_n\}$ as a sequence of tokens and a semantic space as a vector space V in R, the basis of V is the set of the types of the corpus, i.e., the unique occurrence of a token, resulting in a vocabulary $T = \{t_1, t_2, ..., t_n\}$. The dimension of V is $R^{|T|}$, where $|T|$ is the length of vocabulary. Words are first represented as one-hot vectors $v(t_i)$, where 1 is the position of t_i in T. Then, they are embedded in a reduced dense space of dimension R^k, with $k \ll |T|$. Word2vec[12] is a technique to create word embeddings. SkipGram with Negative Sampling is its baseline model, that we used. It predicts a context from a word. Input vectors are one-hot vectors, while output ones are a probability distribution normalized with a softmax function (i.e., a language model). The model creates two types of word embedding from two matrices, W_I of dimension $|T| \cdot k$ and W_0 of dimension $k \cdot |T|$, where each row of W_I defines the embedding of the word t_i, namely h, and each row of W_0 defines the embedding of words when they appear in context with h, namely u. The softmax functions converts u in a probability distribution:

$$y_i = logp(t_{i-2}, t_{i-1}, t_{i+1}, t_{i+2}|t_i) = \frac{exp(u_c)}{\sum_{j \in T} exp(u_j)}$$

where $t_{i-2}, t_{i-1}, t_{i+1}, t_{i+2}$ is the context of a word if the window length was 2, u_c is the probability of the context to maximize and u_j is the rest to minimize. Instead of compute the function on all u_j in the vocabulary, Negative Sampling method does it on a small sample $u_m, m \in E$, where E is sampled using a biased unigram distribution.

Although the complexity of the framework, it can be simply implemented in Python with Gensim[13], a library allowing to tune the value of some hyperparameters like the dimension k of the embedding space (*size*), the length of context (*window*), the number of training words sampled by their frequency in the text (*min_count*) and the dimension of E (*negative*). Corpora used are a light version of *Italian Wikipedia* and *Paisa'*[14], a collection of Italian texts from web, both about 250 million tokens. Lemmas of open class words are used for training (better of lexemes to avoid morphosyntactic relations). Tuned values are $size = 200$, $window = 10$, $negative = 10$ for both corpora, $min\_count = 10$ for *Wikipedia* and $min\_count = 200$ for *Paisa'*. Obtained the word embeddings, the cosine similarity is used to quantify the distance between vectors:

$$sim(\vec{v_1}, \vec{v_2}) = \frac{\vec{v_1} \cdot \vec{v_2}}{\|\vec{v_1}\| \|\vec{v_2}\|}$$

Then, vectors are represented as nodes, with L_{max} as the cosine similarity distribution, namely the number of all distances between all vectors. It is needed a graph in which $L \ll L_{max}$, whereby L must contain strong semantic relations: thus, L is chosen with ϵ-*method*[7], connecting vectors if and only if their cosine similarity exceeds a threshold ϵ. Value of ϵ are 0.5 (only for global network analysis) and 0.65, due to the computational costs of community discovery tasks.

4 Network analysis

Global level is analyzed in terms of degree distribution, small world properties and assortativity by degree. Fig. 2 sums up the analyses on degree distribution and assortativity. As regards first one, it is applied the likelihood-ratio test (LR-test) (also visualized in Table 1) with *powerlaw* library[15]. The LR-test consists of the comparison of the goodness of fit of two models, i.e., how well one of them fits a set of observations: a truncated power law seems to be the better model.

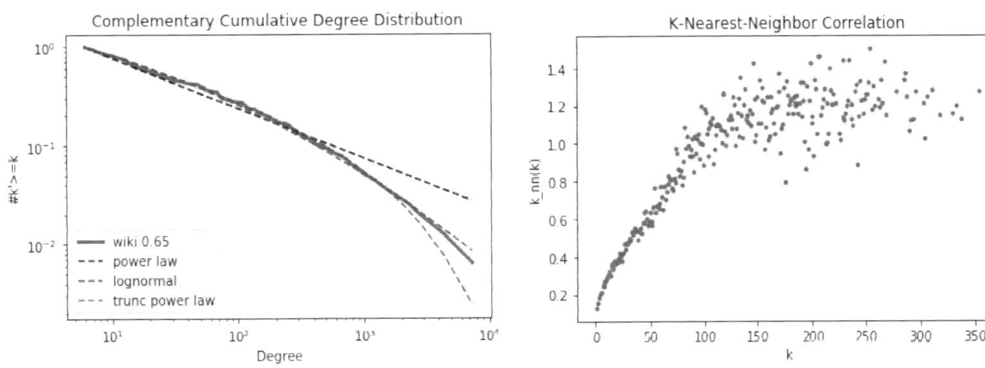

Fig. 2. Complementary cumulative degree distribution and degree assortativity by correlation between k and $k_{nn}(k)$ in *Wikipedia 0.65*

Power law, truncated power law, exponential and lognormal distributions have been compared. Assortativity describes if nodes, on average, connect to nodes with similar degree. Average K-Nearest-Neighbors $k_{nn}(k)$ is used for assortativity, i.e, the average k_{nn} for each node with degree k, where k_{nn} is the average neighbors degree of each node: there is correlation between k and $k_{nn}(k)$, thus networks are assortative. In Table 2 a general description of global network properties shows high global clustering coefficient C and short average path length $\langle d \rangle$, thus networks are small world.

	PL vs. TPL		PL vs. Exp		PL vs. lN		TPL vs. Exp		TPL vs. lN	
Dataset	R	p	R	p	R	p	R	p	R	p
Wikipedia 0.5	-2.54	0.00	4.7	0.00	-1.8	0.00	5.1	0.00	1.09	0.27
Wikipedia 0.65	-1.46	0.04	1.03	0.30	-1.1	0.31	1.95	0.05	1.99	0.04
Paisa' 0.5	-4.96	0.00	8.8	0.00	-3.67	0.00	9.74	0.00	3.0	0.00
Paisa' 0.65	-3.5	0.00	-2.56	0.01	-2.24	0.02	-0.75	0.45	0.07	0.03

Table 1. LR-test (*PL* is for *Power Law*, *TPL* is for *Truncated Power Law*, *Exp* is for *Exponential* and *lN* is for *Lognormal*): if R is positive, the data is more likely in the first distribution; vice versa, if it is negative, and p is the significance value ($p < 0.05$).

Dataset	N	L	$\langle k \rangle$	C	$\langle d \rangle$	d_{max}
Wikipedia 0.5	55244	1702789	61.6	0.39	4.98	13
Wikipedia 0.65	35728	270861	15.1	0.36	7.5	22
Paisa' 0.5	22622	578934	51.5	0.38	4.03	11
Paisa' 0.65	17090	115633	13.5	0.39	6.63	19

Table 2. N is the number of nodes, L is the number of links, $\langle k \rangle$ is the average degree, C is the global clustering coefficient, $\langle d \rangle$ is the average path length, d_{max} is the diameter.

Hubs (i.e, highest degree nodes) suggest that words belong to semantic fields, e.g., in *Wikipedia* networks hubs are words like *iperpiressia, infiammazione, ulcerativo, etc*, while in *Paisa'* ones they are words like *facciata, marmoreo, porticato, etc.* If degrees represent the extent of a semantic field, these words could belong to clusters whose lengths depend on the number of nodes tightly connected to each other:hubs suggest how there might be huge semantic fields lexically richer than others.

Starting from this simple interpretation of degrees, we can think about the lexical richness as a property of semantic fields able to be captured exploiting topological information. Together with other aspects and properties of semantic fields, this will be argument of the next section.

5 Community discovery

Community discovery is the task of the detection of highly connected nodes in complex network structures. In a complex semantic network meso-scale structure is formed by semantic fields.

The idea to represent a semantic fields as a community is so explained: (i) graph clusters are strict semantic fields identified by crisp communities in which a node belongs to one and only one community; (ii) semantic fields are represented by linguistic contexts identified by overlapping communities in which a node belongs to more than one community; (iii) clusters are local semantic fields conveyed by single words, identified by communities produced starting from a seed-set expansion.

Community discovery algorithms produce different types of community on the basis of the specific topological property they choose to detect: e.g., Louvain[2] maximizes a modularity function, Infomap[3] utilizes the map equation framework, Label Propagation[4] uses network structure alone, Demon[5] starts

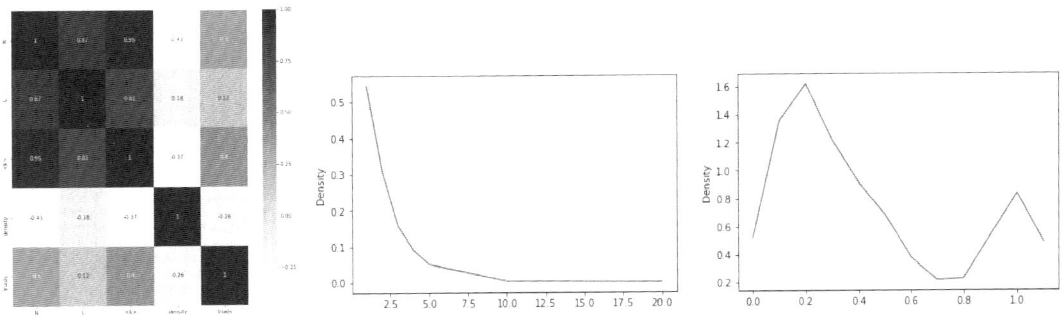

Fig. 3. From left to right (network: *Wikipedia 0.65*), (1) heatmap of correlation of Infomap partition, (2) overlapping distribution of Demon partition, (3) NF1 distribution of comparison between Lemon+Label Propagation and Ground Truth Partition

applying Label Propagation to ego-networks of nodes to merge them in a meso-scale structure, Lemon[6] is based on a seed-set expansion.

As regards crisp communities, Louvain and Infomap got good results. Partitions have been analyzed in terms of dimension N, number of edges L, internal edge density, average degree $\langle k \rangle$ and ratio of triads: Fig. 3, on the left, shows strong correlations between N, L and $\langle k \rangle$, both in Louvain and Infomap partitions. Both algorithms divide the graphs in consistent semantic fields: Louvain captures more general semantic domains while Infomap enhances them with granular partitions, e.g., if the largest community extracted with Louvain from *Wikipedia 0.65* belongs to the field of chemistry, Infomap can break up it in the subdisciplines of chemistry (organic chemistry, biochemistry, pharmacology, etc), consistently with the dataset from which knowledge is extracted. However, limits of crisp partitions are not trivial: the approach is not word-oriented, e.g. *molecola* or *atomo* (in according to graph partitioning, they belong to the chemistry domain) can appear in one and only one community, contrary to their concrete use in more than one domain. We focused on other algorithms capable of produce overlapping communities, in particular Demon. Partitions have been analyzed in terms of overlapping distribution, showed in Fig. 3, in the center. In some cases, the idea of linguistic context as semantic field can be captured. The term *Siria* is one of the nodes with the largest number of communities in a Demon partition with $\tau = 0.5$. A human analysis can easily interprets the communities in which the term is present as two different linguistic context: in the first one its semantics concerns with an *historical geographical entity*, in the second one with a *modern geographical entity*, e.g., a community is composed by terms like *anatolia, babilonese, egitto, eufrate, mesopotamia, persia, sumero*, another one by terms like *arabia, armenia, egitto, iran, iraq, marocco, turchia*. However, even this approach is not totally word-oriented.

In order to focusing on the semantics of single words, communities identified by a seed-set expansion are preferred. The proposed method chains Lemon and Label Propagation algorithms: starting from the seed-centered communities extracted by Lemon for each node, then Label Propagation is applied to break them into smaller and denser word sets. Advantages of this approach focus on the possibility to capture polysemy, i.e., multiple meaning expressed by words. We take account of two terms, *stima* as example of polysemy and *pesca* as example of homonymy. As regards the first term, the partition could be coherent with its polysemic nature, ready to be interpreted both as *the price or value of a possession* (words in communities are *miliardo, dollaro, milione, sterlina, euro*) and as *an approximate measurement* (words in communities are *grossomodo, pressapoco, incirca*), but it is surely mismatched a potential third community composed by words denoting the meaning of *stima* as *an appreciation to others.* As regards the second term, only words related to the sense of the activity of fishing are find, without words related to the sense of the fruit. Then, limits of this approach may be related to the corpora and to the language model themselves, i.e. to the missing textual information and to the bias of word2vec models to create a unique embedding for homonymic words. Moreover, it was performed a Ground Truth Testing to compare and evaluate quality of communities produced in this third approach. Ground Truth Partitions have been extracted from Wikipedia itself, using the disambiguation pages: each hyperlink is a community composed by terms present in the hyperlinked page whose frequency was higher than 1. Filtered networks were compared with NF1 measure, the normalized harmonic mean of Precision and Recall[16], whose distribution is showed in Fig. 3, on the right. As expected, many of communities compared are dissimilar, while in those who get a perfect match the issue concerns the partial terms coverage due to the filtering (i.e., at most six or seven terms compared). Results were interesting but we need deeper quantitative evaluations to test the goodness of partitions: at the state-of-art - this is evident from the approach - there are not valid Ground Truth Partitions for these types of networks.

6 Conclusions

Word meaning has been modeled as a complex system self-organized in semantic fields. The notion of *word meaning* was strictly related to word vectors, i.e., computational representations of meaning. Global properties of networks extracted from word2vec models were consistent with the previous literature.Assortativity might be trace of a context-based representation of word meaning: hubs belongs to few giant semantic fields because they can be substituted in the same wide contexts. A question for future researches could be about interpretations of that: does the assortativity depend on a biased distribution of corpora or on the used language model? Or it reveal real hidden structures of semantic fields in texts? Semantic fields discovery was treated as a task of graph clustering instead of word vectors clustering, namely an alternative approach aiming to model several definitions of semantic field with several community discovery methodologies. We have obtained good results only exploiting the topological information. However, several lines of future research can be followed. Future approach could focus on community discovery methods able to integrate network topology and external information about nodes (e.g., attributes on their frequencies in texts or on the age in which they are learned or on their categories in other levels of language analysis) to better represent a community structure in a complex semantic network.

Acknowledgment

This work is partially supported by the European Community's H2020 Program under the funding scheme "INFRAIA-1-2014-2015: Research Infrastructures" grant agreement 654024, http://www.sobigdata.eu, "SoBigData".

References

1. A. Lenci, *Distributional models of word meaning,* Annual Review of Linguistics, vol. 4, pp. 151171, 2018.
2. V. D. Blondel et al., *Fast unfolding of communities in large networks,* Journal of statistical mechanics: theory and experiment, 2008.
3. M. Rosvall and C. Bergstrom, *Maps of random walks on complex networks reveal community structure,* Proc Natl Acad SciUSA, vol. 105(4), p. 11181123, 2008.
4. U. N. Raghavan, R. Albert and S. Kumara, *Near linear time algorithm to detect community structures in large-scale networks,* Physical review E, vol. 76(3), 2007.
5. M. Coscia, G. Rossetti, F. Giannotti, D. Pedreschi, *Uncovering hierarchical and overlapping communities with a local-first approach,* ACM Transactions on Knowledge Discovery from Data (TKDD), vol. 9(1), 2014
6. Yixuan Li et al. *Uncovering the small community structure in large networks: A local spectral approach,* Proceedings of the 24th international conference on world wide web. International World Wide Web Conferences Steering Committee, 2015.
7. M. Steyvers and J. B. Tenenbaum, *The large-scale structure of semantic networks: Statistical analyses and a model of semantic growth,* Cognitive science, vol. 29, pp. 4178, 2005.
8. H. Liu, *Statistical properties of chinese semantic networks,* Chinese Science Bulletin, vol. 54, pp. 27812785, 2009.
9. A. Utsumi, *A complex network approach to distributional semantic models,* PLoS ONE, vol. 10(8), 2015.
10. I. Kajic and C. Eliasmith, *Evaluating the psychological plausibility of word2vec and glove distributional semantic models,* 2018.
11. S. De Deyne et al., *Large-scale network representations of semantics in the mental lexicon,* in M. N. Jones (Ed.), Frontiers of cognitive psychology. Big data in cognitive science, pp. 174-202, New York, NY, US: Routledge/Taylor & Francis Group, 2017.
12. T. Mikolov et al., *Distributed representations of words and phrases and their compositionality* Proceedings of the 26th International Conference on Neural Information Processing Systems, vol. 2, pp. 31113119, 2013.
13. R. Řehůřek and P. Sojka, *Software Framework for Topic Modelling with Large Corpora,* Proceedings of the LREC 2010 Workshop on New Challenges for NLP Frameworks, 45-50, 2010.
14. V. Lyding et al., *The PAISA' corpus of italian web texts,* Proceedings of the 9th Web as Corpus Workshop (WaC-9), pp. 3643, 2014.
15. J. Alsto, E. Bullmore, and D. Plenz, *powerlaw: A python package for analysis of heavy-tailed distributions,* PLoS ONE, 2014
16. G. Rossetti, L. Pappalardo, S. Rinzivillo, *A novel approach to evaluate algorithms detection internal on ground truth,* Complex Networks VII, 2016

Using CalcuList To MapReduce Json Documents

(DISCUSSION PAPER)

Domenico Saccà and Angelo Furfaro

DIMES Dept, Università della Calabria, 87036 Rende, Italy
sacca@unical.it, a.furfaro@unical.it

Abstract. CalcuList (*Calcu*lator with *List* manipulation), is an educational language for teaching functional programming extended with some imperative and side-effect features, which are enabled under explicit request by the programmer. As the language natively supports json objects, it may be effectively used to implement generic MapReduce, which is a popular model in distributed computing that underpins many NoSQL systems. As a list a jsons can be thought of as a dataset of a document NoSQL datastore, it turns out that CalcuList can be used as a tool for teaching advanced query algorithms for document datastores such as MongoDB and CouchDB.

Keywords: MapReduce, Document Databases, Query Languages, Functional Language, Imperative Features

1 Introduction

Pure functional programming designates a functional programming paradigm that treats all computation as the evaluation of mathematical functions. This paradigm forbids changing-state and mutable data so that functions will only depend on their arguments, regardless of any global or local state (i.e., it has no *side effects*).

An important member of the purely functional languages is Haskell [5, 4], which provides relevant features including polymorphic typing, static type checking, lazy evaluation and higher-order functions. Other functional languages are less pure (*impure*), as they contain imperative features. For instance, most of the languages of the Lisp Family [14] were designed to be multi-paradigm, mainly because the use of side-effects, in some cases, simplifies the developed code or even results in a better computational efficiency.

CalcuList (*Calcu*lator with *List* manipulation) is an *educational* programming language for teaching the functional paradigm, suitably extended with

The full version of this paper is published in [11] and can be downloaded as an open access publication from https://dl.acm.org/citation.cfm?doid=3216122.3216164

some imperative features involving side effects [10]. Thus, CalcuList essentially belongs to the family of "impure" functional languages but it may be use as a *pure* functional language, in that side effects are required to be explicitly enabled.

CalcuList syntax is rather similar to that of Python [13] and natively supports processing of strings, lists and json objects. Json (*JavaScript Object Notation*) [3] is language-independent data interchange format, which has been originally introduced as a subset of the JavaScript scripting language and is now widespread in many applications, e.g. web-services, and support for it has been added to the standard libraries of many programming languages.

The language is strongly typed, but type checking is mainly dynamic as most of the type checking is done at run-time. An interactive computation session with the user is established by means of a REPL (*Read-Evaluate-Print-Loop*) shell. During a session, a user may define a number of global variables and functions and run suitable computations on them as queries, that are computed and displayed on the fly. CalcuList expressions and functions are first compiled and then executed each time a query is issued.

In this paper we shall illustrate powerful features of CalcuList to support *MapReduce*, which is a programming model for processing and generating large data sets, inspired by the functions map and reduce commonly used in functional programming and introduced by Google to support parallel computations on large data sets spread over clusters of computers. Nowadays MapReduce is considered a popular "Data-Oriented" model in distributed computing that processes data simultaneous data sources in two primary steps: *Map* and *Reduce*. The first step maps the input data into intermediate data sets and the second step aggregates the intermediate results in a consolidated result.

MapReduce is mainly used to implement applications for a *document store* (also called document database or document-oriented database), which is a subset of a type of NoSQL database systems that have been released and widely adopted in many domains poorly served by relational databases [7]. A document store is used for storing, retrieving, and managing semi-structured data, mainly organized as jsons. In this paper we show how to use CalcuList to implement MapReduce programs on jsons and we argue that suitable interfaces could make CalcuList a powerful query environment for popular document stores such as CouchDB [12] and MongoDB [1].

The remainder of this paper is organized as follows. Section 2 introduces basic notions about the CalcuList functional core, illustrates higher-order functions and their usage to define MapReduce queries, and describes the imperative aspects of the language and their usage for some situations where they may simplify the definition of MapReduce code or even result in a better computational efficiency. Section 3 focus on the manipulation of json structures in CalcuList and on the usage of higher-order functions to implement MapReduce queries on a document datastore represented bya list of jsons. Finally, Section 4 draws the conclusions and discusses future work.

2 An Overview of CalcuList

The main interface to CalcuList, like other languages (e.g. Python, Scala), is a REPL environment where the user can define functions and issue valid expressions (queries in CalcuList), which in turn are parsed, evaluated and printed before the control is given back to the user.

The basic types for CalcuList are six: (1) *double*, (2) *int* , (3) *char*, (4) *bool* (with values *true* or *false*), (5) *null* (that has a unique value named `null` as well) and (6) *type* (whose values are all the other types: *double*, *int*, etc.).

Three compound types are supported: string, list and json. A string in CalcuList is an immutable sequence (possibly empty) of characters – two strings can be concatenated by the overloaded operator `+` returning a new string and slice operators à la Python are available to extract a substring. Jsons will be described in Section 3. Next we provide some insights on lists.

The *list* is a powerful compound data type used by CalcuList for constructing dynamic data structures and implementing recursive algorithms. A list `L` consists of a number (possibly zero) of comma-separated elements between square brackets. As in Python, the elements can be of any type, including list and json, and heterogeneous. They are numbered with an index starting from zero: the first element (called the *head* of the list) is `L[0]` (also denoted simply by `L[.]`), the second element is `L[1]` and so on.

A list can be extended by adding additional comma-separated elements on top, followed by the append operator (the bar "`|`") - the syntax has been inspired by Prolog [2]. For instance, given a list `L`, `M=[x,y|L]` extends `L` by adding two new elements, `x` and `y`, on top of `L`. Another operator on a list `L` is `L[>]`, which returns the (possibly empty) *tail* of `L`, i.e., the list starting from the element `L[1]`. Slice operators on a list `L` (say with n elements) are deep in the sense that they clone the elements. In particular, `L[:]` clones the whole list `L` whereas `L[i:]`, $\texttt{L}[\texttt{i}_1\texttt{:i}_2]$ and `L[:i]` clone suitable sublists.

The syntax for an expression is like in Java. An expression e is either *simple* or *conditional* with format e_1 `?` e_2 `:` e_3, where e_1 is a logical (i.e., with type *bool*) expression and e_2 and e_3 are expressions (possibly conditional in their turn). The meaning of a conditional expression is: its value is equal to the value of e_2 if e_1 evaluates to *true* or, otherwise, to the value of e_3.

The language allows the user to define global variables. A *global variable* V is defined as "$V = e$", where e is an expression: the type of V is inferred from the type of e and its value is kept until a later re-definition, which may change also the type. A *query* is an expression e prefixed by the `^` symbol and prints the value of the expression at the current state.

A function is defined by giving it a name, followed by: its comma-separated parameter names (included in parentheses), the colon symbol "`:`" and the (typically conditional) expression that computes the value of the function. Parameters as well as the return value of a function are defined without specifying types for them, so that static type checking is performed only for constant operands. A function is compiled while it is defined and, as for Python, the type checking is done at run time, after its call, when all the types become available.

No side effects are allowed in the basic definitions of functions, i.e., functional operations do not modify current global variables and always create new data objects. Differently from Python, global variables are not accessible inside a function so that a possible change of state does not affect the function behavior.

```
>>member(x,L): L !=[] && (x==L[.] || member(x,L[>]));
>>sumL(L) : L==[]? 0: L[.]+sumL(L[>]);
>>range(x1,x2): x1>x2? []: [x1|range(x1+1,x2)];
>>R16= range(1,16); /* global variable */
>>^sumL(R16); /* compute the sum of the elements in R16*/
136
```

Fig. 1. *Functions on Lists*

Figure 1 presents a work session with CalcuList that consists of a number of basic functions for handling lists. The first one is the classical `member` function that checks wether an element belongs to a list. The `sumL` function sums the elements of a list and the `range` function generates the lists of the integers in a given range. Next, a list R16 with elements in the range from 1 to 16 is defined and the query to compute the sum of all such elements is issued.

2.1. Higher-Order Functions and MapReduce Definitions

CalcuList supports higher-order functions since a function parameter can also be a function and a function may return a function. A function parameter `f` is written as `f/`n, where n is the arity of the function `f`. In addition, adding /n after a function head `g(...)` prescribes that the function `g` must return a function with arity n.

Some examples of higher-order functions implementing MapReduce computations are presented in Figure 2. The function `map` receives a list `L` and two functions as parameters, both with arity 1: `f` checks whether an element has a certain property and, in case the test succeeds, `m` maps the element into another value. The function `map` scans all elements of `L`, for each of them it performs the possible mapping and eventually returns the list of the results. The first map query filters all numbers divisible by 2 or by 3 (see function `d2or3`) in the range from 1 to 10 and replaces each of these values with their cube (see the lambda function) – let M denote the result of this query. Note that lambda functions are written in Python like syntax.

The subsequent function `reduce` receives a list `L`, a function parameter `f` (mapping two values into another value) and an initial value that is returned at final stage of the recursion, when `L` reduces to an empty list. Then `reduce` applies `f` to two actual parameters: the list head and the result of `reduce` for the list tail. Therefore, the list is eventually reduced to a single value by recursively applying `f` from right to left. The first reduce query computes the sum of all elements in M (the list returned by `map`), whereas the second one computes the product of the squares (see second lambda function parameter) of all integers in the range from 1 to 10 that are divisible both by 2 and by 3.

```
>>map(L,f/1,m/1) : L==[]?[]: f(L[.])?
   [m(L[.])|map(L[>],f,m)]:  map(L[>],f,m);
>>d2or3(x) : x%2==0 || x%3==0;
>>^map(R16,d2or3,lambda x: x*x*x);
[ 8, 27, 64, 216, 512, 729, 1000, 1728, 2744, 3375, 4096 ]
>>reduce(L,f/2,in): L==[]? in: f(L[.],reduce(L[>],f,in));
>>sum(x,y):x+y;
>>^reduce(map(range(1,10),d2or3, lambda x: x*x*x),sum,0);
14499
>>^reduce(map(range(1,10),lambda x:x%2==0&&x%3==0,
   lambda x:x*x),lambda x,y: x*y,1);
5184
```

Fig. 2. *High-Order Functions and MapReduce Definitions*

2.2. Imperative Features of CalcuList

CalcuList has a *pure* functional programming core but it also allows the programmer to define a function with side effects by adding * next to its name (*star function*). In this way, the usage of global variables inside a function is enabled (provided that they are explicitly listed in its definition body) and they may have assigned new values during the function execution, as in an imperative programming language. Actually also parameter values can be modified during the execution of a star function.

Global variables and parameters can be updated inside a function by means of the so-called *global setting commands* (GSC). A *GSC* is an assignment of an expression value to a labeled global variable or to a function parameter and represents an imperative statement with side effects. GSCs can be inserted both before and after the expression defining the star function. In case of a conditional expression, GSCs may be also inserted before and after each sub-expression. The usage of GSCs has been inspired by the semantic rules of an Attribute Grammar [6].

An example of star function is shown in Figure 3. The function is `reduceCount` that takes a list L of possibly duplicated elements and returns a list LC of pairs $[e, n]$, where e is an element in L and n is the number of occurrences of e in L. The subsequent query returns the list of characters and their numbers of occurrences in the string `"Hello_World"`. Note that `"Hello_World"@list` transforms the string in a list of characters.

3 Definitions of Jsons and Manipulation of Json Lists

CalcuList natively supports json objects (referred to simply as *json*), which are at runtime represented as (possibly empty) sequences of fields separated by comma and enclosed into curly braces. A field is a pair (key, value) separated by a colon: *key* is a string and *value* can be of any type, including json.

```
>>rc1*(_,_) : null;
>>rc2*(L,M,C) : M==[]? rc1(L[>],[[L[.],1]|C]):
  L[.]==M[.][0]?{!M[0][1]+=1!} rc1(L[>],C): rc2(L,M[>],C);
>>rc1*(L,M) : L==[]? M: rc2(L,M,M);
>>reduceCount*(L) : rc1(L,[]);
>>^reduceCount("Hello_World"@list);
[ [ 'H', 1 ], [ 'e', 1 ], [ 'l', 3 ], [ 'o', 2 ],
>>^reduceCount(map(R16,lambda x: true,
  lambda x: x%2==0? "even": "odd"));
[ [ "even", 8 ], [ "odd", 8 ] ]
```

Fig. 3. *Star Functions*

```
>>emps = [ { "name": "e1", "age": 30 },
 {"name":"e2","age":32,"proj":["p1","p2"],"bonus":10},
 {"name":"e3", "age":28, "proj":["p1","p3"] } ];
>>^emps[2]["proj"];
[ "p1", "p3" ]
>>^emps[0]["proj"] %*;
null
```

Fig. 4. *Json Definition and Manipulation in CalcuList*

In Figure 4 we define a variable `emps` as a list of three jsons, each representing an employee. For instance, `emps[1]` is the employee with name `"e2"`, aged 32 and working for the projects `"p1"` and `"p2"`. Given a json J and a key k, $J[k]$ denotes the value of the field of J with key equal to k – if there is no such a field then the value *null* is returned as it happens for `^emps[0]["projects"]` (the string `%*` next to the query is a display option to force the writing of the null value). Given a value v, $J[k] = v$ modifies the value for the field if J includes the key k or otherwise, J is extended with a new field with key k and value v.

Figure 5 presents a high-order function to filter the jsons that satisfy some conditions in one of the fields: `jsFilter`, whose filtering condition parameter is expressed by a function `filterC`, that receives the current json and a field, say with key K and value V, to be used for the evaluation. Next, the figure shows two implementations for `filterC`: (1) `selKV`, which checks whether the json has a field equal to (K, V), and (2) `selKinV`, which checks whether the value V is included in the list of elements that represents the value for the the field K in the json. Two queries on the variable `emps` defined in Figure 4 are issued: the first one filter all employees with age 28 and the second one the employees that work for at least the project `"p1"`.

Figure 5 also presents a classical map function that scans all employees to produce the list of all projects for which they work – note that, by adding the option `[:]` to `E[.]["proj"]`, the project lists are cloned to avoid their

```
>>jsFilter(LJ,filtC/3,K,V):LJ==[]?[]:filtC(LJ[.],K,V)?
    [LJ[.]|jsFilter(LJ[>],filtC,K,V)]:
    jsFilter(LJ[>],filtC,K,V);
>>selVeqK(J,K,V): J[K]!=null && J[K]==V;
>>^jsFilter(emps,selVeqK,"age",28);
[ {"name":"e3",  "age":28, "proj":["p1","p3"] } ]
>>selVinK(J,K,V) : J[K]!=null && member(V,J[K]);
>>^jsFilter(emps,selVinK,"proj","p1") ;
[{"name":"e2","age":32,"proj":["p1","p2"],"bonus":10},
 {"name":"e3","age":28,"proj":["p1","p3"] } ]
>>mapProj(E) : E==[]? []: E[.]["proj"] != null?
    E[.]["proj"][:]+mapProj(E[>]): mapProj(E[>]);
>>^reduceCount(mapProj(emps));
[ [ "p1", 2 ], [ "p2", 1 ], [ "p3", 1 ] ]
```

Fig. 5. *Higher Order Functions on Jsons*

coalescence. The query calling the function `reduceCount`, defined in Figure 3, reduces the list by storing each project once as a pair: project name and number of its occurrences (i.e., the total number of employees working for it).

Figure 6 includes a star function that updates a list of jsons. As a list of jsons can be though of as a collection in a documentary database, star functions have the crucial role of updating the database. As an example we have written the function `giveBonus` that assigns a bonus of a given amount to all employees in a list – the amount is incremented if an employee already has a bonus. Obviously the function has side effects as it updates the elements in the parameter `emps`. We present a query that assigns a bonus of 100 Euro to all employees in the global variable `emps` (defined in Figure 4) who work in project `p1`.

```
>>aBonus*(E,v):E==[]?true:E[.]["bonus"]==null?
    {! E[0]["bonus"]=v !} giveBonus(E[>],v):
    {! E[0]["bonus"]+=v !} giveBonus(E[>],v);
>>^aBonus(jsFilter(emps,selVinK,"proj","p1"),100);
true
>>^emps;
[{"name": "e1", "age": 30},
 {"name":"e2", "age":32, "proj":["p1","p2"], "bonus":110},
 {"name":"e3", "age":28, "proj":["p1","p3"], "bonus":100}
]
```

Fig. 6. *Functions with Side Effects on Jsons*

4 Conclusion

In this paper we have presented a new educational functional programming language extended with imperative programming features: CalcuList, whose imperative features are enabled under explicit request by the programmer. CalcuList expressions and functions are first compiled and then executed each time a query is issued. The CalcuList programming environment has been implemented as a small-sized Java project in Eclipse 4.4.1 with 6 packages and 20 classes all together. The Jar File for using Calculist may be dowloaded from the link in [8]. The size of this file is rather small: 134 kb. The draft of a tutorial on CalcuList may be dowloaded from the link in [9].

References

1. K. Chodorow. *MongoDB: The Definitive Guide.* O'Reilly Media, Inc., 2013.
2. W. F. Clocksin and C. S. Mellish. *Programming in Prolog (2Nd Ed.).* Springer-Verlag New York, Inc., New York, NY, USA, 1984.
3. ECMA Int. The JSON Data Interchange Format. Standard ECMA-404, Ecma International, 2013.
4. P. Hudak, J. Hughes, S. Peyton Jones, and P. Wadler. A History of Haskell: Being Lazy with Class. In *Proceedings of the Third ACM SIGPLAN Conference on History of Programming Languages*, HOPL III, pages 12–1–12–55, New York, NY, USA, 2007. ACM.
5. S. Marlow. Haskell 2010 Language Report.
6. J. Paakki. Attribute Grammar Paradigms – a High-level Methodology in Language Implementation. *ACM Comput. Surv.*, 27(2):196–255, June 1995.
7. V. Reniers, D. Van Landuyt, A. Rafique, and W. Joosen. On the State of NoSQL Benchmarks. In *Proceedings of the 8th ACM/SPEC on International Conference on Performance Engineering Companion*, ICPE '17 Companion, pages 107–112, New York, NY, USA, 2017. ACM.
8. D. Saccà. The CalcuList Environment, Release 4.1.0. https://github.com/saccad/CalcuList/blob/master/CalcuList_R_4_1_0.jar, 2017.
9. D. Saccà. The CalcuList Release 4.1 Tutorial, Version 1. https://github.com/saccad/CalcuList/blob/master/CalcuList_Tutorial_Release_4_v3_5.pdf, 2017.
10. D. Saccà and A. Furfaro. CalcuList: a Functional Language Extended with Imperative Features. *CoRR*, abs/1802.06651, 2018.
11. D. Saccà and A. Furfaro. Using calculist to mapreduce jsons. In B. C. Desai, S. Flesca, E. Zumpano, E. Masciari, and L. Caroprese, editors, *Proceedings of the 22nd International Database Engineering & Applications Symposium, IDEAS 2018, Villa San Giovanni, Italy, June 18-20, 2018*, pages 74–83. ACM, 2018.
12. C. Team. *CouchDB 2.0 Reference Manual.* Samurai Media Limited, United Kingdom, 2015.
13. G. van Rossum and J. Fred L. Drake. *The Python Language Reference Manual (version 3.2).* Network Theory Limited, 2011.
14. P. Winston and B. Horn. *LISP. Second edition.* Addison Wesley Pub.,Reading, MA, Jan 1986.

Anna: a Virtual Assistant to interact with Puglia Digital Library (Discussion Paper)

Vito Walter Anelli[1], Tommaso Di Noia[1], Eugenio Di Sciascio[1], and Azzurra Ragone[2]

[1] Polytechnic University of Bari, Bari, Italy
[2] Independent researcher, Milan, Italy
{name.surname}@poliba.it, azzurraragone@gmail.com

Abstract. In the last years, a huge amount of data has been released by private and public bodies as Linked Open Data. By their inner nature, these data contain rich semantic information that can be automatically processed by software agents and explored by humans via visual tools or structured SPARQL queries. Although they result useful for many tasks, these latter approaches miss the simplicity of the interfaces based on interactions via natural language implemented in modern virtual assistants. In this paper, we present a system able to assist the user in exploring the knowledge exposed by the *Puglia Digital Library* containing information and data associated with digital goods related to the Apulia region in Italy. We show how to interact with the Digital Library by means of a virtual assistant and how, thanks to its publication as Linked Open Data, it is possible to easily integrate it on-the-fly with external knowledge sources such as geographical ones.

Keywords: Linked Open Data, Chatbot, Vocal Assistant, Digital Libraries

1 Introduction

In 2012, Google announced its Knowledge Graph[3] as a new tool to improve the identification and retrieval of entities in return to a search query. Most of the knowledge encoded in Google Knowledge Graph originally came from Freebase which was a crowd-sourced effort to create a base of facts in all possible knowledge domains. Alongside with the development of the above-mentioned initiatives, following the original idea of a Semantic Web [4], new technologies have been developed and released with the aim of embedding structured knowledge with unambiguous semantics into Web pages in order to allow software agents to consume and elaborate information in an automated way. The original idea has been modified over the years thus making possible the creation of a full stack of semantic technologies and, more remarkably, gave birth to the

[3] https://googleblog.blogspot.it/2012/05/introducing-knowledge-graph-things-not.html

Linking Open Data initiative[4] where a community of researchers and practitioners devoted an enormous effort to build publicly available knowledge bases of machine-understandable data. By exploiting Semantic Web technologies, a knowledge base is then represented through a graph (knowledge graph) in which entities are linked to each other by binary relationships. The Linked Data initiative deserves credit for setting best practices[10] for releasing *Open Data* on the Web, and for linking different open, and structured datasets. Linked Data practices are particularly well-suited to associate high quality meta-data to resources. This is a classic issue [17] of Digital Libraries (DLs), which are complex information systems shouldering the preservation of digital documents, intellectual property right management, information filtering, information retrieval, and query answering [8]. Linked Data technologies let DLs realize a fully data-centric, and metadata-based approach in describing their resources [2]. Meta-data and thesauri are already commonly used in DLs' resources descriptions. However, linking these meta-data to Linked Open Data cloud[5] improves reusability and integration of DLs [5]. In this direction some successful examples are the German National Library[6], the British National Library[7], the National Library of Spain[8], the National Library of France[9]. Linked meta-data comes with many benefits [16] as easy cataloging, information discovery, and the possibility to build third-party applications to explore data.

Despite the efforts, technical issues prevent citizens to consume *Open Data*. In most cases *Open Data* are consumed through data-visualization tools, and tables, built upon the released data. The drawback of this approach is that, within a large catalog of items (the default case with DLs), hardly citizens will be able to discover new resources they could be interested in.

In this paper, we report the experience in making accessible the *Puglia Digital Library*[10] (PDL) through **Anna**: a virtual assistant able to explore the knowledge graph behind PDL via natural language-based interactions. In the proposed approach, speech recognition is delegated to Google Assistant, whereas Dialogflow[11] is adopted to manage the interaction with the user.

2 Related work

Chatbots are software agents specifically designed to make the interaction with the user as natural as possible, usually providing a textual and/or vocal interface to gives the user the impression of speaking to a human. This feeling was suggested by [1] who anticipated the key role of chatbots in humanizing machines. A chatbot copes with the natural way of interacting of the user, defining a new category of interfaces, Conversational User Interfaces (CUIs) [13]. The design of a chatbot involves many non-trivial operations that include NLP, pattern

[4] `http://linkeddata.org`
[5] `https://lod-cloud.net/`
[6] `http://www.dnb.de/EN/`
[7] `http://www.bl.uk/bibliograpic/datafree.html/`
[8] `http://datos.bne.es/`
[9] `http://data.bnf.fr`
[10] `http://www.pugliadigitallibrary.it/`
[11] `https://dialogflow.com/`

matching, parsing, artificial intelligence, and ontologies. In [1] a logical scheme is depicted: responder (interface), classifier (transformation), and graphmaster (knowledge extraction). The responder corresponds to the interface that is exposed to the user.

In the last years, DLs gave birth to a flourishing research field, in which a notable number of vocabularies, metadata standards, thesauri, have been designed. The number of collective and small initiatives and DLs [8] that have been put in place make almost impossible to depict the overall field. In 2000s several initiatives were put in place with the aim of managing and organizing DLs, like for instance, a global library cooperative OCLC[12], which has thousands of library members and offers services to support them. On the other side, Europeana[13] [9] is an aggregator of meta-data about more than 58 millions digital resources. Europeana represents all these digital objects through a common format and schema [5], Europeana Data Model[14] (EDM) bases on Semantic Web Languages. The Europeana data model respects these standards and ensures consistency and interoperability even though sometimes the expressiveness of original data is lost [5]. The standardization of meta-data is absolutely not a new topic in Digital Libraries field in which different organization tried to define rigorous cataloguing principles [2] like AACR, MARC[15], ISBD[16] [19], FRBR[17] [20], RDA [6]. The need for DLs to make their content freely accessible, sharable, and re-usable led generally to the adoption of `Linked Open Data`. Pioneers were the Library of the Congress, and Staford University Library, followed by Europeana and British Library [9, ?]. The different DLs take advantage of common `Linked Open Data` vocabularies that fit the need of describing the specific resources they host. In the case of digital resources like images, video, web pages, the most generally adopted vocabulary is definitely Dublin Core Metadata [12] by DCMI which is usually adopted to ensure interoperability between the different metadata vocabularies. Although there is an increasing number of chatbots that retrieve information from relational databases, the usage of *Open Data* as a knowledge source for chatbots, is an almost unexplored research direction. In [14], a question answering system is built using a question generation framework [11]. The knowledge is extracted as plain text from PDF documents using OCR techniques, whereas the matching patterns are defined using Artificial Intelligence Markup Language (AIML). OntBot [18] takes advantage of a mapping between an ontology and the knowledge stored in a relational database. Finally in [15], the authors design a chatbot to query a `Linked Open Data` dataset released by the Italian Ministry of Transport. They took advantage of IBM Bluemix and Watson Conversation to realize their query answering system.

---

[12] `https://www.oclc.org/`

[13] `https://www.europeana.eu/`

[14] `https://pro.europeana.eu/resources/standardization-tools/edm-documentation`

[15] `https://www.loc.gov/standards/marcxml/`

[16] `https://www.ifla.org/files/assets/cataloguing/isbd/isbd-cons_20110321.pdf`

[17] `https://www.ifla.org/files/assets/cataloguing/frbr/frbr_2008.pdf`

3 Puglia Digital Library

Puglia Digital Library is a multimedia archive of books, magazines, newspapers, photographs, sounds, videos. The aim of *Puglia Digital Library* is to preserve and to share the regional digital heritage. *Puglia Digital Library* provides an online platform to store and expose its data. The resources are accessible through a Web Portal that lets the user download the resource, consume it (preserving the integrity of fragile museum resources), and read a description. From 2016 *Puglia Digital Library* became a producer of `Linked Open Data` [7] concerning museum objects, historic, and artistical sites. In order to favor interoperability, *Puglia Digital Library* adopted several sets of meta-data[18] and controlled vocabularies, such as: DCMIType (DCMI Type Vocabulary), PICO (Thesaurus that allow interoperability with Cultura Italia), Vocabularies ICCD (Italian standard for cataloging), AAT (Art & Architecture Thesaurus), TGN (Thesaurus of Geographic Names). The ontology chosen for resources description is CIDOC-CRM[19] (ICOM[20]). However, in order to overcome some representational limitations of the above mentioned ontologies and to enrich the linking with external Linked Data datasets, other ontologies were adopted: Dublin Core[21], DBpedia[22] ,Schema.org[23] , Foaf[24] , SKOS[25], LinkedGeoData[26] and Geonames[27].

4 Anna's Architecture

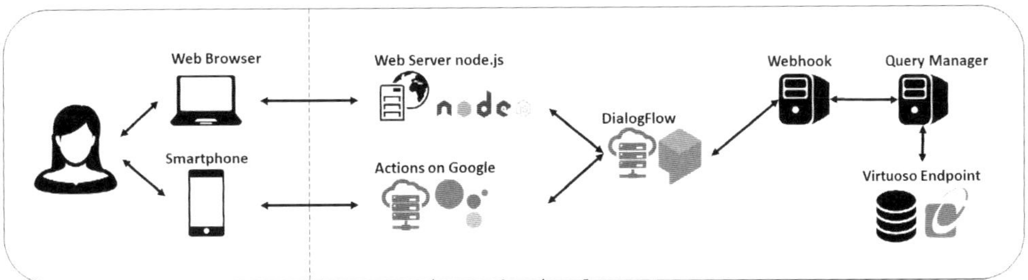

Fig. 1: Anna's Architecture

The software ecosystem behind the chatbot Anna is depicted in Figure 1. The first step to create Anna consisted of creating a SPARQL endpoint to retrieve information from the PDL knowledge base [7] in an effective way. A Virtuoso server instance was created with a SPARQL 1.1 endpoint that allows humans,

[18] DC, DDI, EAC-CPF, EAD, FGDC, ISO 19115 2003, LC-AV, LOM, MARC, MAG, METSRIGHTS, MODS, NISOIMG, PREMIS, TEIHDR, TEXTMD, VRA

[19] `http://www.cidoc-crm.org/`

[20] `http://icom.museum/`

[21] `http://dublincore.org/`

[22] `http://dbpedia.org`

[23] `http://schema.org`

[24] `http://www.foaf-project.org/`

[25] `https://www.w3.org/2004/02/skos/`

[26] `http://linkedgeodata.org/`

[27] `http://www.geonames.org/ontology`

and automated agents to query the underlying Knowledge Graph using SPARQL queries. Differently from SQL queries, SPARQL is based on the idea of graph matching. SPARQL query language lets the user express a graph pattern (in which one or more parts of the triple are substituted by variables), to retrieve the necessary knowledge.

The user can interact with the system using a Web browser or a mobile phone with the Italian Google Assistant. The Web App was implemented in `node.js` and deployed on a specific server. The Google Assistant is an *Actions on Google* project that enables users to interact with *DialogFlow*, converting the speech to text. The Web App copes with the communication protocol adopted by Google Assistant to provide a unified communication protocol. The DialogFlow module handles the conversation itself: each interaction moves the conversation from a state to another, called contexts, in which a specific choice is made by the user (intent). Contexts, and intents are at the core of the interaction mechanism and are depicted in Figure 2. The Webhook keeps the history of the iterative

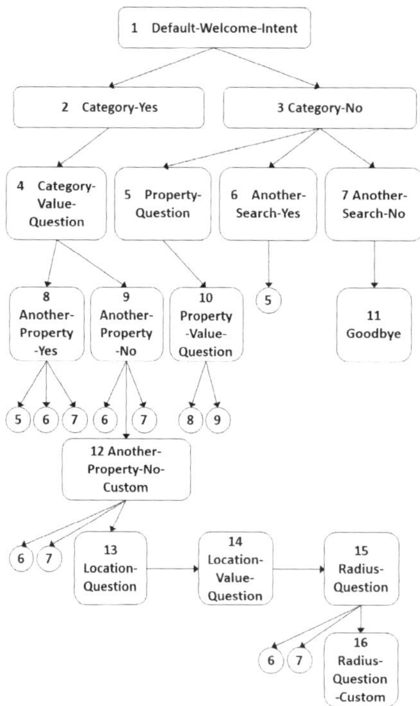

Fig. 2: Intents' Graph

queries of the user, in order to refine the final query. If any further knowledge is required, the Webhook sends a message with the needed information to the Query Manager, which poses the query against the remote SPARQL endpoint. Finally, for the sake of privacy, the Webhook itself does not store any information, and once the session is terminated that specific user history is deleted. In Figure 2 the most important intents are depicted. The directed rows show the outgoing contexts. Whenever the user operates a choice, her input is analyzed and the conversation is moved to a new context. Intents basically defines the usability of the tool, hence the intents'scheme was defined under the instructions of *Puglia Digital Library* users, and managers.

4.1 A typical conversation with Anna

In order to understand the subtle interactions of the Anna ecosystem, a very effective way is to explore a real conversation. The user invokes the chatbot saying "*Talk with Digital Library*". Google Assistant opens a connection with the chatbot which greets to the user and asks if she is interested in a particular topic (Fig. 2 - Intent 1, see also `https://goo.gl/LjFZd2`). Let us suppose she answers *Yes*. This answer is sent from the chatbot to the Webhook, and then to the Query Manager. It sends a query against the Virtuoso Endpoint looking for all the possible topics for the resources stored in the knowledge base. The Query Manager extracts the results from the server's response and the Webhook prepares and sends the results to DialogFlow. At this point, Anna shows a list of available topics (Fig. 2 - Intent 2, see also `https://goo.gl/UoP1US`). User chooses "*History and Traditions*". This information is sent to the Webhook to update the constraint for this search session (Topic:*History and Traditions*). Anna asks if the user wants to choose other properties (Fig. 2 - Intent 4, see also `https://goo.gl/b3eoe9`). User says *Yes*. Anna sends this information to the Webhook, that sends all the session data to the Query Manager. This will compose a query that looks for all the properties that resources (with *"History and Traditions"* as the topic) have. Anna returns a list of options (Fig. 2 - Intent 8, see also `https://goo.gl/gzi513`) composed by "Subject", "Category", "Location". User chooses *"Subject"*. This information is sent to the Query Manager, that will look for all the possible values for the predicate *"Subject"*, considering only those resources that have *"History and Traditions"* as the topic. The results are returned to DialogFlow. Now Anna will show a long list of available topics (Fig. 2 - Intent 5, see also `https://goo.gl/fpMBFK`). User chooses "*Sanctuaries*". This information is sent to the Webhook, which stores a new association, Subject:Sanctuaries. Anna asks the user for more properties (Fig. 2 - Intent 10, see also `https://goo.gl/n1pSc5`). User says *No*. This is the signal the chatbot awaits to prepare the query for the resources. All the available information (*Topic*:*History and Traditions*; *Subject*:*Sanctuaries*) are sent to the Query Manager, which composes the query and sends it against the SPARQL endpoint. The query requires also additional resources' information: label with full name, url address of the resource, url address of the preview image, description of the resource, latitude, and longitude. This information is parsed and stored in a structured form associated to the session by the Webhook. The Webhook also prepares the carousel and sends it back to the user. Now Anna will return the carousel(Fig. 2 - Intent 9, see also `https://goo.gl/Rrjpz1`) containing: *"The Ripalta sanctuary"*, and *"Santissima Maria di Ripalta"*. User selects the first result. The Webhook receives the input of the user and prepares a card about that resource. Anna will return a Card (Fig. 2 - Intent 12, see also `https://goo.gl/vsdC9e`) containing a preview of the digital resource, the name of the selected resource and a complete description. At the end of the card (see `https://goo.gl/rfNB2x`) the user will find a link to the *Puglia Digital Library* corresponding page, with some buttons related to *"Nearest places"*, *"Another search"*, and *"Thank you"*. User selects *"Nearest places"*. Anna sends the request to the Webhook, which extracts and returns the list of considered locations' categories. Anna will return the list (Fig. 2 - Intent 13, see also `https://goo.gl/4jBeuY`): *Hotels*, *Restaurants*, *Cafes*, *Museums*. User is interested in *Restaurants*. In order to prepare a geospatial query Anna asks the user for the distance to be considered (Fig. 2 - Intent 14, see also `https://goo.gl/o4QbCa`). The user answers *"10 km"*, which is sent to the Query Manager to prepare the a special query which is sent against the LOSM [3] endpoint to retrieve this geo-referenced information in real-time. LOSM returns a list of available locations, within the considered radius, together with their coordinates. This information is used to create a new carousel. This carousel, with a list of available places (Fig. 2 - Intent 15, see also `https://goo.gl/rAJ7EV`), is returned to the user. The user chooses the *"Di Muzio"* Restaurant. Once again, the Webhook takes the input sent by the user, extracts the coordinates of the Restaurant, and prepares a card with a valid link to get directions with Google Maps. Thus Anna returns a card (Fig. 2- Intent 16, see also `https://goo.gl/hr6aBg`) with a direct link to navigate towards the Restaurant using Google Maps. At the end of this interaction the user can quit the conversation or begin a new one.

5 Conclusion

In this work, we presented Anna, a vocal assistant built upon the Linked Open Data datasets of *Puglia Digital Library*. The interface was implemented in two different ways: a web application, with a textual interaction, and through Actions on Google, which provides a mixed textual/vocal interaction. The vocal/textual interface is an innovative way of accessing *Open Data* that eases the technological barriers of modern Semantic Web technologies. A common issue for broadcasting these disruptive technologies is the lack of well-established NLP tools for languages different from English. Taking advantage of speech recognition APIs we were able to design the Assistant to be consumed by Italian citizens (the audience of *Puglia Digital Library*) in a natural way. Future work includes the creation of new vocal assistants to provide information for other digital libraries. Moreover, we want to evaluate extensively the usability of the assistant to improve the overall user experience.

Acknowledgments. The authors acknowledge partial support of the following projects: Innonetwork APOLLON, Innonetwork CONTACT, PON FLET 4.0.

References

1. Abdul-Kader, S.A., Woods, J.: Survey on chatbot design techniques in speech conversation systems. International Journal of Advanced Computer Science and Applications **6**(7) (2015).
2. Alemu, G., Stevens, B., Ross, P., Chandler, J.: Linked data for libraries: Benefits of a conceptual shift from library-specific record structures to rdf-based data models. New Library World **113** (01 2012).
3. Anelli, V.W., Calì, A., Di Noia, T., Palmonari, M., Ragone, A.: Exposing open street map in the linked data cloud. In: International Conference on Industrial, Engineering and Other Applications of Applied Intelligent Systems. pp. 344–355. Springer (2016)
4. Berners-Lee, T., Hendler, J., Lassila, O.: The semantic web. Scientific american **284**(5), 34–43 (2001)

5. de Boer, V., Wielemaker, J., van Gent, J., Hildebrand, M., Isaac, A., van Ossenbruggen, J., Schreiber, G.: Supporting linked data production for cultural heritage institutes: The amsterdam museum case study. In: Simperl, E., Cimiano, P., Polleres, A., Corcho, Ó., Presutti, V. (eds.) The Semantic Web: Research and Applications - 9th Extended Semantic Web Conference, ESWC 2012, Heraklion, Crete, Greece, May 27-31, 2012. Proceedings. Lecture Notes in Computer Science, vol. 7295, pp. 733–747. Springer (2012).
6. Coyle, K., Hillmann, D.: Resource description and access (RDA): cataloging rules for the 20th century. D-Lib Magazine **13**(1/2) (2007).
7. Di Noia, T., Ragone, A., Maurino, A., Mongiello, M., Marzocca, M.P., Cultrera, G., Bruno, M.P.: Linking data in digital libraries: the case of puglia digital library. In: Proceedings of the 1st Workshop on Humanities in the Semantic Web co-located with 13th ESWC Conference 2016 (ESWC 2016). pp. 27–38 (2016)
8. Fox, E.A., Marchionini, G.: Toward a worldwide digital library - introduction. Commun. ACM **41**(4), 28–32 (1998).
9. Gradmann, S.: Knowledge = information in context: on the importance of semantic contextualisation in europeana pp. 1–19 (01 2010)
10. Heath, T., Bizer, C.: Linked Data: Evolving the Web into a Global Data Space. Synthesis Lectures on the Semantic Web, Morgan & Claypool Publishers (2011).
11. Heilman, M., Smith, N.A.: Question generation via overgenerating transformations and ranking. Tech. rep., CARNEGIE-MELLON UNIV PITTSBURGH PA LANGUAGE TECHNOLOGIES INST (2009)
12. Initiative, D.C.M., et al.: Dublin core metadata element set, version 1.1 (2012)
13. McTear, M.F.: Spoken dialogue technology - toward the conversational user interface. Springer (2004),
14. Pichponreay, L., Kim, J.H., Choi, C.H., Lee, K.H., Cho, W.S.: Smart answering chatbot based on ocr and overgenerating transformations and ranking. In: Ubiquitous and Future Networks (ICUFN), 2016 Eighth International Conference on. pp. 1002–1005. IEEE (2016)
15. Porreca, S., Leotta, F., Mecella, M., Vassos, S., Catarci, T.: Accessing government open data through chatbots. In: Garrigós, I., Wimmer, M. (eds.) Current Trends in Web Engineering - ICWE 2017 International Workshops, Liquid Multi-Device Software and EnWoT, practi-O-web, NLPIT, SoWeMine, Rome, Italy, June 5-8, 2017, Revised Selected Papers. Lecture Notes in Computer Science, vol. 10544, pp. 156–165. Springer (2017).
16. Southwick, S.B., Lampert, C.K., Southwick, R.: Preparing controlled vocabularies for linked data: Benefits and challenges. Journal of Library Metadata **15**(3-4), 177–190 (2015).
17. Tani, A., Candela, L., Castelli, D.: Dealing with metadata quality: The legacy of digital library efforts. Inf. Process. Manage. **49**(6), 1194–1205 (2013).
18. Vegesna, A., Jain, P., Porwal, D.: Ontology based chatbot (for e-commerce website). International Journal of Computer Applications **179**(14), 51–55 (Jan 2018).
19. Willer, M., Dunsire, G., Bosancic, B.: Isbd and the semantic web. JLIS. It. Rivista italiana di biblioteconomia, archivistica e scienza dell'informazione **1**(2), 213–236 (2010).
20. Žumer, M.: Functional requirements for bibliographic records: Frbr: The end of the road or a new beginning. Bulletin of the American Society for Information Science and Technology.

Querying Large Expressive Horn Ontologies
(discussion paper)

Carlo Allocca[3], Mario Alviano[1], Francesco Calimeri[1,2], Cristina Civili[3], Roberta Costabile[1], Bernardo Cuteri[1], Alessio Fiorentino[1], Davide Fuscà[1], Stefano Germano[2], Giovanni Laboccetta[2], Nicola Leone[1], Marco Manna[1], Simona Perri[1], Kristian Reale[2], Francesco Ricca[1], Pierfrancesco Veltri[2], and Jessica Zangari[1,2]

[1] Department of Mathematics and Computer Science, University of Calabria, Italy
{alviano,calimeri,r.costabile,cuteri,fiorentino,fusca,
leone,manna,perri,ricca,zangari}@mat.unical.it
[2] DLVSystem L.T.D., Polo Tecnologico Unical, Italy
{calimeri,germano,laboccetta,reale,veltri}@dlvsystem.com
[3] Samsung R&D Institute, UK
{c.allocca,c.civili}@samsung.com

Abstract. In the development of the Semantic Web researchers and industry experts agree that scalability can only be obtained by reducing standard reasoning tasks to query evaluation over (deductive) databases. From a theoretical viewpoint much has been done. Conversely, from a practical point of view, only a few reasoning services have been developed, which however typically can only deal with lightweight ontologies. To fill the gap, the paper presents OWL2DLV, a modern Datalog system for evaluating SPARQL queries over very large OWL 2 knowledge bases. OWL2DLV builds on the well-known ASP system DLV by incorporating novel optimizations sensibly reducing memory consumption and a server-like behavior to support multiple-query scenarios. The high potential of OWL2DLV is outlined by the results of an experiment on data-intensive benchmarks, and confirmed by the interest of a major international industrial player, which has stimulated and partially supported the work.

Keywords: Datalog · Ontology-based query answering · DLV

1 Introduction

In large-scale Semantic Web scenarios, it is convenient to reduce standard reasoning tasks to query evaluation over (deductive) databases. From a theoretical viewpoint much has been done: in many ontological settings, the problem of evaluating a conjunctive query (CQ) over a *knowledge base* (KB) consisting of an *extensional dataset* (ABox) paired with an *ontology* (TBox) can be reduced to the evaluation of a Datalog query (i.e., a Datalog program, possibly nonrecursive and including strong constrains, paired with a union of CQs, both constructed only from the original query and the TBox) over the same ABox [14,17,22,29,33]. From a practical viewpoint the situation is not so rosy. Many Datalog reasoners, such as CLINGO [18] and DLV [26], are based on one-shot executions performing heavy operations (e.g., loading and indexing) multiple times and hence are rather unsuited. Also, only a few services with a server-like behavior, such as MASTRO [13], ONTOP [12], and RDFOX [28], have been developed, which however can only deal with lightweight TBoxes. To fill the gap, the paper presents OWL2DLV, a modern Datalog system, based on the aforementioned rewriting approach, for evaluating SPARQL CQs [32] over very large OWL 2 KBs [15].

Reasoning over OWL 2 is generally a very expensive task: fact entailment is already 2NEXPTIME-hard, while decidability of CQ answering is even an open problem. To balance expressiveness and scalability, the W3C identified three tractable profiles —OWL 2 EL, OWL 2 QL, and OWL 2 RL— exhibiting good computational properties: the evaluation of CQs over KBs falling in these fragments is in PTIME in data complexity (query and TBox are considered fixed) and in PSPACE in combined complexity (nothing is fixed) [30]. To deal with a wide variety of ontologies, OWL2DLV implements the Horn-$\mathcal{SHIQ}$ fragment of OWL 2, which enjoys good computational properties: CQs are evaluated in PTIME (resp., EXPTIME) in data (resp., combined) complexity. Moreover, it is also quite expressive: it generalizes both OWL 2 QL and OWL 2 RL, while capturing all OWL 2 EL constructs except role chain [25].

From the technical side, OWL2DLV builds on the well-known ASP system DLV [26], and in particular its most recent incarnation DLV2 [2], by incorporating a server-like modality, which is able to keep the main process alive, receive and process multiple user's requests on demand, and restore its status thanks to an embedded persistency layer. Following the approach proposed by Eiter et al. [17], a Horn-$\mathcal{SHIQ}$ TBox paired with a SPARQL query are rewritten, independently from the ABox, into an equivalent Datalog query.

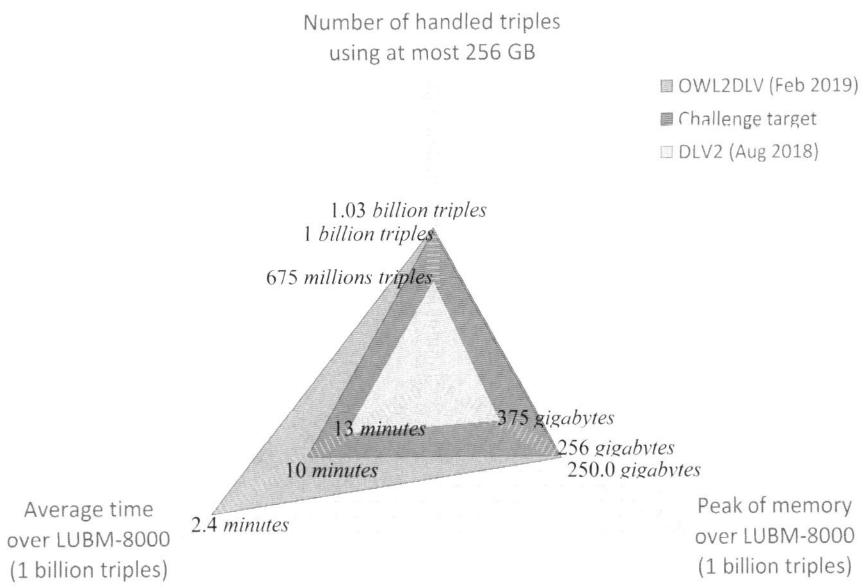

Fig. 1: OWL2DLV – performance and enhancements.

The high potential of OWL2DLV is outlined by the results of an experiment on data-intensive benchmarks, and confirmed by the direct interest of a big international industrial player, which has partially supported this work and also stimulated the evolution of the system with a major *challenge*: "deal with LUBM-8000 —the well-known LUBM [19] standard benchmark for ontological reasoning collecting about 1 billion factual assertions upon 8,000 universities— over machines equipped with 256GB RAM and with an average query evaluation time of at most 10 minutes". Eventually, not only the system was able to widely win the general challenge as reported in Figure 1; but, amazingly, the average time taken by OWL2DLV on the ten (out of fourteen) *bound* queries —i.e., queries containing at least one constant— of LUBM-8000 was eventually less than one second.

2 Background

OWL 2. In Description Logic (DL) terminology, let $\mathsf{N_I}$ (*individuals*), $\mathsf{N_C} \supset \{\top, \bot\}$ (*atomic concepts*) and $\mathsf{N_R}$ (*role names*) be pairwise disjoint discrete sets. A *role* r is either a role name s or its *inverse* s^-. A *concept* is either an atomic concept or of the form $C \sqcap D$, $C \sqcup D$, $\neg C$, $\forall r.C$, $\exists r.C$, $\geqslant nr.C$ or $\leqslant nr.C$, where C and D are concepts, r is a role, and $n \geq 1$. *General concept inclusions* (GCIs), *role inclusions* (RIs), and *transitive axioms* (TAs) are respectively of the form $C_1 \sqsubseteq C_2$, $r_1 \sqsubseteq r_2$, and $Tr(r)$, where: $\sqcup$ is disallowed in C_2, $\geqslant nr$ and $\leqslant nr$ are disallowed in C_1, and they are disallowed also in C_2 in case r is transitive. A Horn-$\mathcal{SHIQ}$ TBox is a finite set of GCIs, RIs and TAs satisfying some non-restrictive global conditions [21,23]. An instance I is a set of assertions of the form $C(a)$ and $r(a,b)$, where $C \in \mathsf{N_C}$, $r \in \mathsf{N_R}$, and $a, b \in \mathsf{N_I}$. An ABox is any finite instance. A KB $\mathcal{K}$ is a pair $(\mathcal{A}, \mathcal{T})$, where $\mathcal{A}$ is an ABox and $\mathcal{T}$ is a TBox.
SPARQL. It is the standard language in the Semantic Web for querying OWL 2 KBs [32]. As in databases, the most important class of SPARQL queries are the *conjunctive* ones, which syntactically are quite similar to SQL queries. More generally, when querying OWL 2 KBs the TBox plays the role of a fist-order theory and it has to be taken into account properly, as described next.
OBQA. By adopting the *unique name assumption*, a *model* of a KB $\mathcal{K} = (\mathcal{A}, \mathcal{T})$ is an instance $I \supseteq \mathcal{A}$ satisfying all the axioms of $\mathcal{T}$, written $I \models \mathcal{T}$ [6]. The set of all models of $\mathcal{K}$ is denoted by $\mathsf{mods}(\mathcal{K})$. To comply with the *open world assumption*, I might contain individuals that do not occur in $\mathcal{K}$. The *answers* to a query $q(\bar{x})$ over an instance I is the set $q(I) = \{\bar{a} \in \mathsf{N_I}^{|\bar{x}|} \mid I \models q(\bar{a})\}$ of $|\bar{x}|$-tuples of individuals obtained by evaluating q over I. Accordingly, the *certain answers* to q is the set $\mathsf{cert}(\mathcal{K}, q) = \bigcap_{I \in \mathsf{mods}(D,\Sigma)} q(I)$. Finally, ontology-based query answering (OBQA) is the problem of computing $\mathsf{cert}(\mathcal{K}, q)$.

3 Query Answering in OWL 2 via Datalog

As said, to perform OBQA, OWL2DLV follows the approach of Eiter et al. [17]. From an OWL 2 Horn-$\mathcal{SHIQ}$ TBox $\mathcal{T}$ and a SPARQL CQ $q(\bar{x})$, OWL2DLV runs Algorithm 1 to build a Datalog program $P_\mathcal{T}$ and a union of CQs $Q_{q,\mathcal{T}}(\bar{x})$ such that, for each ABox $\mathcal{A}$, the evaluation of $Q_{q,\mathcal{T}}(\bar{x})$ over $\mathcal{A} \cup P_\mathcal{T}$ produces the same answers as the evaluation of $q(\bar{x})$ over $\mathcal{A} \cup \mathcal{T}$.

Algorithm 1: TBox and Query Rewriting

Input: An OWL 2 Horn-$\mathcal{SHIQ}$ TBox $\mathcal{T}$ together with a query $q(\bar{x})$
Output: The Datalog program $P_\mathcal{T}$ together with the query $Q_{q,\mathcal{T}}(\bar{x})$
1. $\mathcal{T}' \leftarrow \mathsf{Normalize}(\mathcal{T})$;
2. $\mathcal{T}^* \leftarrow \mathsf{EmbedTransitivity}(\mathcal{T}')$;
3. $\Xi(\mathcal{T}^*) \leftarrow \mathsf{Saturate}(\mathcal{T}^*)$;
4. $P_\mathcal{T} \leftarrow \mathsf{RewriteTBox}(\Xi(\mathcal{T}^*))$;
5. $Q_{q,\mathcal{T}}(\bar{x}) \leftarrow \mathsf{RewriteQuery}(q(\bar{x}), \Xi(\mathcal{T}^*))$;

Consider a TBox $\mathcal{T}$. Step 1 transforms $\mathcal{T}$ into an equivalent TBox $\mathcal{T}'$ containing only "simple" axioms [21]. Step 2 transforms $\mathcal{T}'$ into $\mathcal{T}^*$ by replacing TAs with suitable GCIs including new atomic concepts. Step 3 exhaustively applies inference rules to derive new entailed axioms. The new TBox including this extra axioms is denoted by $\Xi(\mathcal{T}^*)$. Step 4, identifies the DL axioms with no existential restrictions in the right-hand side and transforms them into Datalog rules. Finally, given a CQ $q(\bar{x})$, Step 5 rewrites it into the union of CQ (UCQ) $Q_{q,\mathcal{T}}(\bar{x})$ by incorporating parts of $\Xi(\mathcal{T}^*)$.

The pair $(Q_{q,\mathcal{T}}(\bar{x}), P_\mathcal{T})$ returned by Algorithm 1 is further optimized by a *pruning strategy* followed by the so-called *Magic Sets rewriting* —the latter is already in use in DLV2 but it has been further improved due to the specific nature of $P_\mathcal{T}$. The result of this phase consists of the pair $(\mathsf{opt}(Q_{q,\mathcal{T}}(\bar{x})), \mathsf{opt}(P_\mathcal{T}))$.

Pruning Strategy. Pairs of GCIs of the form $C_1 \sqsubseteq C_2$ and $C_2 \sqsubseteq C_1$ give rise to Datalog queries containing rules with multiple predicates having the same extensions: $C_1(X) :- C_2(X)$ and $C_2(X) :- C_1(X)$. The same happens with RIs. During the evaluation of the query, however, this can be considerably expensive. Hence, we adopt the following pruning strategy. Let $\mathcal{E} = \{E_1, ..., E_k\}$ be a set of equivalent concepts or roles. First, we remove from $P_\mathcal{T}$ all the rules of the form $E_i(X) :- E_j(X)$ with $1 < i \leq k$ and $1 \leq j \leq k$. Second, let $P^1_\mathcal{T}$ be the subset of $P_\mathcal{T}$ containing only rules of the form $E_1(X) :- E_j(X)$ with $2 \leq j \leq k$, for each $i \in \{2, ..., k\}$, we replace each occurrence of E_i by E_1 both in $Q_{q,\mathcal{T}}(\bar{x})$ and in each rule of $P_\mathcal{T}$ that does not belong to $P^1_\mathcal{T}$. An analogous technique is applied over RIs of the form $r \sqsubseteq s^-$ and $s^- \sqsubseteq r$ by taking into account, in this case, that the first argument of r (resp., s) maps the second one of s (resp., r).

Magic Sets Rewriting. To optimize the rewriting, OWL2DLV performs two novel steps: (1) Eliminate rules that have a magic atom with predicate $\mathtt{m\#p\#}\alpha$ if $\alpha \neq \mathtt{f}\cdots\mathtt{f}$ and $\mathtt{m\#p\#f}\cdots\mathtt{f}$ also occurs in the rewritten program; and (2) Remove every rule r_1 whenever it is subsumed by some other rule r_2 ($r_1 \sqsubseteq r_2$), namely there is a variable substitution mapping the head (resp., body) of r_2 to the head (resp., body) of r_1. To avoid the quadratic number of checks, OWL2DLV associates each rule with a suitable hash value of size 64 bits. Then, $r_1 \sqsubseteq r_2$ is checked only if the bit-a-bit equation $hash(r_1)\ \&\ hash(r_2) == hash(r_2)$ is satisfied.

4 System architecture

The OWL2DLV architecture is depicted in Figure 2. The system features four main modules: Loading, Rewriting, Query Answering, and Command Interpreter. Clients

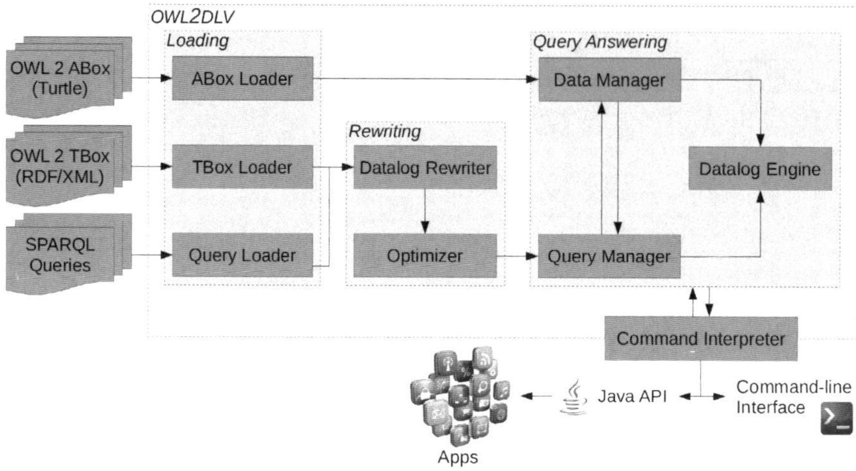

Fig. 2: System Architecture

interact with the system through the latter one. This module allows to "keep alive" the system, and execute multiple commands (e.g., loading, warmup, data updates, and query evaluations) without having to instantiate a new process for each client request. The Loading module processes an OWL 2 ABox encoded in Turtle [8] via the ABox Loader. The result of the parsing phase are Datalog-like facts stored in the OWL2DLV data structures handled by the Data Manager. Concerning the TBox, OWL2DLV supports OWL 2 Horn-$\mathcal{SHIQ}$ ontologies encoded in RDF/XML [15]. The input is parsed by the TBox Loader using the OWL API [20] and loaded in DL-like data structures. The system supports a set of SPARQL CQs via the Query Loader. Then, the Rewriting module implements Algorithm 1 via the Datalog Rewriter submodule and optimize —by applying the *pruning strategy* and the *Magic Sets rewriting*— its output via the Optimizer. The Rewriting module is in charge of evaluating Datalog queries over the parsed ABox, and producing the answers. Finally, the Query Answering module represents an extension of I-DLV [10] (the grounder of DLV2). The overall evaluation procedure is based on a bottom-up process based on a semi-naïve approach [31] empowered with optimizations working in synergy [10,11] and extended via techniques devised to manage efficiently large sizes of data.

5 Experimental Evaluation

We report the results of an experimental evaluation of OWL2DLV over LUBM [19] and DBpedia [5]. Note that, by focusing on the few ready-to-use OWL 2 reasoning services with a server-like behavior, neither MASTRO nor ONTOP nor RDFOX fully support query answering in both domains: all of them do not process some LUBM axioms. Further experiments with computationally intensive benchmarks, such as LUBM$^{\exists}$ [27] and UOBM [24], will be part of an extended version of this paper. Moreover, a comparison against MASTRO, ONTOP and RDFOX on lightweight ontologies as well as a comparison against modern Datalog-based systems like VADALOG [9] and GRAAL [7] for query existential rules [3,4] is also in our agenda.

	LUBM-8000				DBpedia			
	CQ name	*informed*	*responsive*	*dynamic*	CQ name	*informed*	*responsive*	*dynamic*
	q01	0.00	0.00	71.77	**q01**	0.18	0.32	2.51
	q02	194.48	179.65	295.74	**q02**	0.17	0.29	2.15
	q03	0.00	0.00	160.95	**q03**	0.22	0.32	2.29
	q04	0.01	0.01	379.22	**q04**	0.21	0.30	0.33
	q05	0.03	0.03	19.60	**q05**	0.20	0.29	7.52
	q06	844.65	854.35	978.46	**q06**	0.19	0.29	0.38
	q07	0.01	0.01	5.07	**q07**	0.19	0.38	0.79
	q08	0.40	0.32	0.50	**q08**	0.18	0.32	0.31
	q09	972.63	1,008.43	1,053.82				
	q10	0.00	0.01	4.66				
	q11	0.00	0.00	0.00				
	q12	0.03	0.03	0.03				
	q13	6.32	6.69	8.13				
	q14	14.64	14.50	14.12				
Max Memory		250.0	251.0	249.3		63.6	96.4	106.2
Loading		5,226.8	5,196.4	5,186.8		3,845.3	3,719.0	3,811.2
Warmup		4,144.4	3,102.3	1,303.8		226.5	1,136.3	595.5
Query Answering (all)		145.2	147.4	238.9		0.2	0.3	2.0
Query Answering (bound)		0.7	0.7	106.2		0.2	0.3	2.0

Table 1: Experimental evaluation of OWL2DLV in different scenarios. Bound queries are reported in bold. The rows "Query Answering (all)" and "Query Answering (bound)" show, respectively, the average evaluation time computed over all queries and bound queries only. Times are expressed in seconds and memory peaks in GB.

Benchmarks. LUBM is the prime choice of our industrial partner for the challenge. It describes a very-large real-world application domain encoded in OWL 2 Horn-$\mathcal{SHIQ}$ with customizable and repeatable synthetic data. The benchmark incorporates 14 SPARQL queries, 10 of which are *bound* (i.e., containing at least a constant). When rewritten together with the TBox, each LUBM query gives rise to a Datalog query consisting of about 130 rules. Data generation is carried out by the LUBM data generator tool (UBA) whose main parameter is the number of universities to consider: 8,000 in our case, for a total number of about 1 billion triples. This dataset is next referred to as LUBM-8000. Concerning DBpedia, it is a well-known KB created with the aim of sharing on the Web the multilingual knowledge collected by Wikimedia projects in a machine-readable format. For this benchmarks, we inherited a set of queries from an application conceived to query DBpedia in natural language applying the approach [16]. When rewritten together with the TBox, each DBpedia query gives rise to a Datalog query of almost 5400 rules. The latest release of the official DBpedia dataset consists of 13 billion pieces of multilingual information (RDF triples). Here, we focus on the information extracted from the English edition of Wikipedia that is composed by about half a billion triples (https://wiki.dbpedia.org/public-sparql-endpoint).

Results and Discussion. The machine used for testing is a Dell server with an Intel Xeon Gold 6140 CPU composed of 8 physical CPUs clocked at 2.30 GHz, with 297GB of RAM, and running a Linux Operating System. According to the challenge, a memory limit of 256GB has been set during all tests. Table 1 shows the results of our analysis; bound queries are reported in bold. The upper part of the table reports times taken by OWL2DLV to answer queries under the three scenarios: *informed*, *responsive*, *dynamic*; the second part shows extra statistics about peaks of memory, loading and warmup times, and average answering times computed over all queries and over bound queries only. In the *informed* scenario —where we assume that the TBox and the template queries are known in advance— we obtain the best performance. Despite the large ABox sizes, on LUBM almost all bound queries are answered in less than 0.1 seconds leading to an average time of about 0.7 seconds, while on DBpedia the average evaluation time over all queries is about 0.2 seconds. These results show the effectiveness of the Magic Sets technique to dramatically reduce the part of the dataset needed to answer the query, together with all other optimization strategies discussed through the paper. In the *responsive* scenario —where only the TBox is known in advance— the system performance is comparable with the one obtained in the *informed* scenario, although in general the evaluation time is a bit higher. These results confirm that the warmup policy of this setting has a positive impact on the system performance although queries are not known. Finally, in the *dynamic* scenario —where nothing is known— the parsimonious indexing policy is adopted since 256GB are not enough to use the aggressive one. Uniformly, the same policy is also used for DBpedia although not expressly needed. This produces a general gain in the warmup phase later unavoidably paid during the query evaluation due to some missing index that has to be computed on-the-fly. For further details we refer to [1].

Acknowledgments. This work has been partially supported by Samsung under project "Enhancing the DLV system for large-scale ontology reasoning", by MISE under project "S2BDW" (F/050389/01-03/X32) – "Horizon2020" PON I&C2014-20 and by Regione Calabria under project "DLV LargeScale" (CUP J28C17000220006) – POR Calabria 2014-20.

References

1. Allocca, C., Calimeri, F., Civili, C., Costabile, R., Cuteri, B., Fiorentino, A., Fuscà, D., Germano, S., Laboccetta, G., Manna, M., Perri, S., Reale, K., Ricca, F., Veltri, P., Zangari, J.: Large-scale reasoning on expressive horn ontologies. In: Datalog 2.0. CEUR-WS.org (2019)
2. Alviano, M., Calimeri, F., Dodaro, C., Fuscà, D., Leone, N., Perri, S., Ricca, F., Veltri, P., Zangari, J.: The ASP system DLV2. In: LPNMR (2017)
3. Amendola, G., Leone, N., Manna, M.: Finite model reasoning over existential rules. TPLP **17**(5-6), 726–743 (2017)
4. Amendola, G., Leone, N., Manna, M., Veltri, P.: Enhancing existential rules by closed-world variables. In: IJCAI. pp. 1676–1682 (2018)
5. Auer, S., Bizer, C., Kobilarov, G., Lehmann, J., Cyganiak, R., Ives, Z.G.: Dbpedia: A nucleus for a web of open data. In: ISWC. pp. 722–735. LNCS (2007)
6. Baader, F., Calvanese, D., McGuinness, D.L., Nardi, D., Patel-Schneider, P.F. (eds.): The Description Logic Handbook. C.U.P. (2003)
7. Baget, J., Leclère, M., Mugnier, M., Rocher, S., Sipieter, C.: Graal: A toolkit for query answering with existential rules. In: RuleML. pp. 328–344 (2015)
8. Beckett, D., Berners-Lee, T., Prud'hommeaux, E., Carothers, G., Machina, L.: Rdf 1.1 turtle – terse rdf triple language. W3C Recommendation (2014)
9. Bellomarini, L., Sallinger, E., Gottlob, G.: The vadalog system: Datalog-based reasoning for knowledge graphs. PVLDB **11**(9), 975–987 (2018)

10. Calimeri, F., Fuscà, D., Perri, S., Zangari, J.: I-DLV: the new intelligent grounder of DLV. Intelligenza Artificiale **11**(1), 5–20 (2017)
11. Calimeri, F., Perri, S., Zangari, J.: Optimizing answer set computation via heuristic-based decomposition. TPLP p. 126 (2019)
12. Calvanese, D., Cogrel, B., Komla-Ebri, S., Kontchakov, R., Lanti, D., Rezk, M., Rodriguez-Muro, M., Xiao, G.: Ontop: Answering SPARQL queries over relational databases. Semantic Web **8**(3), 471–487 (2017)
13. Calvanese, D., De Giacomo, G., Lembo, D., Lenzerini, M., Poggi, A., Rodriguez-Muro, M., Rosati, R., Ruzzi, M., Savo, D.F.: The MASTRO system for ontology-based data access. Semantic Web **2**(1), 43–53 (2011)
14. Carral, D., Dragoste, I., Krötzsch, M.: The combined approach to query answering in horn-alchoiq. In: KR. pp. 339–348. AAAI Press (2018)
15. Carroll, J., Herman, I., Patel-Schneider, P.F.: Owl 2 web ontology language rdf-based semantics (second edition) (2012)
16. Cuteri, B., Reale, K., Ricca, F.: A logic-based question answering system for cultural heritage. In: JELIA. LNCS, Springer (to appear) (2019)
17. Eiter, T., Ortiz, M., Simkus, M., Tran, T., Xiao, G.: Query rewriting for horn-shiq plus rules. In: AAAI (2012)
18. Gebser, M., Kaminski, R., Kaufmann, B., Ostrowski, M., Schaub, T., Wanko, P.: Theory solving made easy with clingo 5. In: ICLP TCs. pp. 2:1–2:15 (2016)
19. Guo, Y., Pan, Z., Heflin, J.: LUBM: A benchmark for OWL knowledge base systems. J. Web Semant. **3**(2-3), 158–182 (2005)
20. Horridge, M., Bechhofer, S.: The OWL API: A java API for OWL ontologies. Semantic Web **2**(1), 11–21 (2011)
21. Kazakov, Y.: Consequence-driven reasoning for horn SHIQ ontologies. In: IJCAI. pp. 2040–2045 (2009)
22. Kontchakov, R., Lutz, C., Toman, D., Wolter, F., Zakharyaschev, M.: The combined approach to ontology-based data access. In: IJCAI (2011)
23. Krötzsch, M., Rudolph, S., Hitzler, P.: Complexities of horn description logics. ACM Trans. Comput. Log. **14**(1), 2:1–2:36 (2013)
24. Ledvinka, M., Kremen, P.: Object-uobm: An ontological benchmark for object-oriented access. In: KESW. vol. 518, pp. 132–146. Springer (2015)
25. Leone, N.: The AI system DLV: ontologies, reasoning, and more. In: IC3K. pp. 5–16 (2018)
26. Leone, N., Pfeifer, G., Faber, W., Eiter, T., Gottlob, G., Perri, S., Scarcello, F.: The DLV system for knowledge representation and reasoning. TOCL (2006)
27. Lutz, C., Seylan, I., Toman, D., Wolter, F.: The combined approach to OBDA: taming role hierarchies using filters. In: ISWC. pp. 314–330 (2013)
28. Nenov, Y., Piro, R., Motik, B., Horrocks, I., Wu, Z., Banerjee, J.: Rdfox: A highly-scalable RDF store. In: ISWC. vol. 9367, pp. 3–20 (2015)
29. Stefanoni, G., Motik, B., Horrocks, I.: Small datalog query rewritings for EL. In: DL. CEUR Workshop Proceedings, vol. 846 (2012)
30. Stefanoni, G., Motik, B., Krötzsch, M., Rudolph, S.: The complexity of answering conjunctive and navigational queries over OWL 2 EL knowledge bases. J. Artif. Intell. Res. **51**, 645–705 (2014)
31. Ullman, J.D.: Principles of Database and Knowledge-Base Systems, Volume I. Computer Science Press (1988)
32. W3C: SPARQL 1.1 entailment regimes. https://www.w3.org/TR/sparql11-entailment/ (2013)
33. Xiao, G., Calvanese, D., Kontchakov, R., Lembo, D., Poggi, A., Rosati, R., Zakharyaschev, M.: Ontology-based data access: A survey. In: IJCAI (2018)

Investigating the scope of a thing in a multiple Internet of Things scenario

Francesco Cauteruccio[1], Luca Cinelli[1], Giorgio Terracina[1], Domenico Ursino[2], and Luca Virgili[2]

[1] DEMACS, University of Calabria
[2] DII, Polytechnic University of Marche

Abstract. In this paper, we investigate the scope of a thing in a multiple IoT scenario. First we introduce the concept of scope in general, and we illustrate how it has been investigated and applied in social networking. Then, we define the scope of a thing in a Multi-IoT scenario, modeled as an extension of a Social Internetworking System, and we propose a formalization of scope allowing the computation of its values. Finally, we present a possible application of scope and describe some tests that we performed for evaluation purposes.

Keywords: Scope; Social Object; Internet of Things; Multiple IoTs; Trust Degree; Neighborhood of a Thing

1 Introduction

In the Concise Oxford Dictionary [1], *scope* is defined as "*the extent of the area or subject matter that something deals with or to which it is relevant*". Scope has certainly some similitudes with several other concepts investigated in sociology, such as influence, power, centrality, impact, reliability, and so forth. However, it goes beyond each of these terms and, at the same time, summarizes all of them and is influenced by each of them.

In the past, scope has been studied in the context of social networks. For instance, in [12], the authors investigate the scope of users and hashtags in Twitter, whereas in [10, 13–15, 18, 19], the authors propose approaches to computing some aspects of scope (e.g., influence, trust, reliability) for users and/or hashtags. In the meantime, the social network scenario has become increasingly complex and we have passed from social networking to social internetworking [17, 7]. In this last case, several social networks simultaneously coexist and cooperate through specific users, called bridges, who join more social networks.

Parallel to the transition from social networking to social internetworking, in the last few years, we are experiencing the presence of objects that are becoming increasingly smart and social. This phenomenon is revolutionizing the Internet of Things. As a proof of this, more and more authors are starting to study the behavior of things, to talk about their profiles and their social interactions. In fact, different architectures implementing these ideas are frequently proposed in the current literature. Social Internet of Things (hereafter, SIoT [4]), Multiple IoT Environment (hereafter, MIE [5]) and Multiple Internets of Things (hereafter, MIoT [6]) are only three of the latest architectures with these characteristics. In particular, MIoT is the latest of them and, therefore, takes into account the most recent results obtained in the IoT research. A MIoT can be seen as a set of Internets of Things interacting with each other through specific objects, called "cross objects", that belong to more IoTs. The MIoT paradigm represents the extension of the ideas underlying social internetworking to the IoT.

In spite of this enormous interest that increasingly numerous researchers are posing on the IoT, to the best of our knowledge, no analysis about the scope of a thing in a Multi-IoT, or at least in an IoT, scenario has been presented yet. Certainly, several aspects someway related to the scope have been considered in the IoT or, in limited cases, in the SIoT scenario. As an example, in [16], the authors investigate information diffusion in a narrowband IoT with the goal of optimizing information flow at network level. In [3], the authors investigate the adoption of context-aware information diffusion to alert messages in 5G mobile social networks. Context-aware information is collected from different devices deployed in the environment. An interesting approach to content dissemination in the Internet of Vehicles (IoV) is described in [21]. Here, the authors analyze how to combine the information coming from the physical layer with the one regarding the social layer to perform a rapid content dissemination in IoV networks. In [11], the authors present an IoT application in the context of smart cities, a scenario in which an IoT system can reach large scale dimensions. [11] also introduces the concept of IoT hub. This aggregates the information coming from related devices and, therefore, contributes to improve the interoperability between things in a urban-scale IoT system. Furthermore, different approaches on recommender systems and services in IoT have been proposed in the literature; an overview of them is presented in [8]. In particular, in [9], the authors propose a multi-agent recommender system for the IoT aiming at producing a set of significant suggestions for a user with specific characteristics. Here, things are represented through bit vectors, called thing descriptors, managed by cyber-agents. Things can be linked together and, then, can be managed by neighbor cyber-agents. In [20], the authors propose an approach that integrates the concept of social networks of users and Internet of Things. It merges information coming from social networks of users and correlation networks of things by learning shared latent factors. To perform this task, it exploits a technique for probabilistic matrix factorization.

All the approaches mentioned above are extremely interesting; furthermore, several other related approaches proposed in the past to evaluate the relevance or the impact of a node in the Internet of Things could be mentioned. However, none of them has been conceived to operate in a complex scenario consisting of multiple IoTs, which interact with each other through smart and social objects that simultaneously belong to more of them and act as "bridges".

In this paper, we aim at providing a contribution in this setting by proposing an approach to computing the scope of a thing in a MIoT. Specifically, after having provided an overview on the MIoT paradigm (Section 2), we present a definition of scope along with a formalization allowing the computation of the corresponding values (Section 3). Then, we illustrate an application of scope in the context of smart cities, where it can play a key role (Section 4). Thereafter, we present some tests conceived to understand its main features (Section 5). Finally, we draw our conclusions and have a look at some possible future developments of our ideas (Section 6).

2 The MIoT paradigm

In this section, we provide an overview of the MIoT paradigm, described in detail in [6]. A MIoT $\mathcal{M}$ consists of a set of m Internets of Things. Formally speaking:

$$\mathcal{M} = \{\mathcal{I}_1, \mathcal{I}_2, \cdots, \mathcal{I}_m\}$$

where $\mathcal{I}_k$ is an IoT.

Let o_j be an object of $\mathcal{M}$. We assume that, if o_j belongs to $\mathcal{I}_k$, it has an instance ι_{j_k}, representing it in $\mathcal{I}_k$. The instance ι_{j_k} consists of a virtual view (or, better, a virtual agent) representing o_j in $\mathcal{I}_k$. For example, it provides all the other instances of $\mathcal{I}_k$, and the users who interact with this IoT, with all the necessary information about o_j. Information stored in ι_{j_k} is represented according to the format and the conventions adopted in $\mathcal{I}_k$.

A MIoT $\mathcal{M}$ can be also represented by means of a graph-based notation. In particular, a graph $G_k = \langle N_k, A_k \rangle$ can be associated with an IoT $\mathcal{I}_k$ of $\mathcal{M}$. In this case:

- N_k is the set of the nodes of G_k; there is a node n_{j_k} for each instance $\iota_{j_k} \in \mathcal{I}_k$, and vice versa. Since there is a biunivocal correspondence between a node and an instance, in the following we shall use these two terms interchangeably.
- A_k is the set of the arcs of G_k; there is an arc $a_{jq_k} = (n_{j_k}, n_{q_k})$ if there exists a link from n_{j_k} to n_{q_k}. A label can be associated with a_{jq_k}; it stores the set $tranSet_{jq_k}$ of the transactions performed from ι_{j_k} to ι_{q_k} in the past.

Finally:

$$\mathcal{M} = \langle N, A \rangle$$

Here:

- $N = \bigcup_{k=1}^{m} N_k$;
- $A = A_I \cup A_C$, where $A_I = \bigcup_{k=1}^{m} A_k$ and $A_C = \{(n_{j_k}, n_{j_q}) | n_{j_k} \in N_k, n_{j_q} \in N_q, k \neq q\}$.

A_I is the set of the inner arcs (hereafter, *i-arcs*) of $\mathcal{M}$; they link instances (of different objects) belonging to the same IoT. A_C is the set of the cross arcs (hereafter, *c-arcs*) of $\mathcal{M}$; they link instances of the same object belonging to different IoTs. A node connected to at least one c-arc is called *c-node*; otherwise, it is called *i-node*.

In $\mathcal{M}$, an object o_j has associated *a set MD_j of metadata*. Our metadata model refers to the one of the IPSO (Internet Protocol for Smart Objects) Alliance [2]. Specifically MD_j consists of three subsets, namely: *(i)* MD_j^D, i.e., the set of *descriptive metadata*; *(ii)* MD_j^T, i.e., the set of *technical metadata*; *(iii)* MD_j^B, i.e., the set of *behavioral metadata*. All details about these metadata can be found in [6].

Now, we can define the set $tranSet_{j_k}$ of the transactions activated by ι_{j_k} in $\mathcal{I}_k$. Specifically, let $\iota_{1_k}, \iota_{2_k}, \cdots, \iota_{w_k}$ be all the instances belonging to $\mathcal{I}_k$. Then:

$$tranSet_{j_k} = \bigcup_{q=1..w, q\neq j} tranSet_{jq_k}$$

In other words, $tranSet_{j_k}$ is given by the union of the sets of the transactions from ι_{j_k} to all the other instances of $\mathcal{I}_k$.

3 Scope definition

In this section, we present the definition of the scope of an instance ι_{j_k} in an IoT $\mathcal{I}_k$ and of the scope of an object o_j in a MIoT. For this purpose, we must introduce some preliminary concepts.

The first of them is the one of neighborhood of an instance ι_{j_k} in $\mathcal{I}_k$. Specifically, the neighborhood $nbh(\iota_{j_k})$ of ι_{j_k} is defined as:

$$nbh_{j_k} = out\_nbh_{j_k} \cup in\_nbh_{j_k}$$

where:

$$out\_nbh_{j_k} = \{n_{q_k} | (n_{j_k}, n_{q_k}) \in A_I, |tranSet_{jq_k}| > 0\}$$

and

$$in\_nbh_{j_k} = \{n_{q_k} | (n_{q_k}, n_{j_k}) \in A_I, |tranSet_{qj_k}| > 0\}$$

In other words, nbh_{j_k} comprises those instances directly connected to ι_{j_k} through an incoming or an outgoing arc, which shared at least one transaction with ι_{j_k}. In the following of this paper, we are interested only to $out\_nbh_{j_k}$; as a consequence, when we will use the term "neighborhood", we will implicitly mean "out_neighborhood".

Now, we need to introduce *the neighborhood of level t* of an instance ι_{j_k} in its IoT $\mathcal{I}_k$. It is an extension of the concept of $out\_nbh_{j_k}$ and is defined as follows:

$$out\_nbh^t_{j_k} = \begin{cases} out\_nbh_{j_k} & if\, t = 0 \\ \{\iota_{r_k} | \iota_{r_k} \in out\_nbh_{q_k}, \iota_{q_k} \in out\_nbh^{t-1}_{j_k}, \iota_{r_k} \notin out\_nbh^w_{j_k}, 0 \leq w < t\} & if\, t > 0 \end{cases}$$

The concept of $out\_nbh^t_{j_k}$ will be extremely important later. In the meantime, we introduce a new concept, namely the one of minimum path π_{jq_k} from an instance ι_{j_k} to an instance $\iota_{q_k} \in nbh^t_{j_k}$. π_{jq_k} is defined as the succession $\{\iota_{0_k}, \iota_{1_k}, \ldots, \iota_{t_k}\}$ of instances such that $\iota_{0_k} = \iota_{j_k}$, $\iota_{t_k} = \iota_{q_k}$, $\iota_{w_k} \in out\_nbh_{(w-1)_k}$ for $1 \leq w \leq t$.

After this, we must introduce the definition of the Trust Degree TD_{qj_k} of an instance ι_{q_k} in the instance ι_{j_k} in $\mathcal{I}_k$. It can be defined as the fraction of the transactions sent by ι_{j_k} to ι_{q_k} that have been requested by ι_{q_k} or that ι_{q_k} did not request but it has considered so interesting to repost or to elaborate them[3]. In order to formalize TD_{qj_k}, we must introduce:

- the set $reposted_{q_k}$ of the transactions received by ι_{q_k} of $\mathcal{I}_k$ and reposted by it;
- the set $elaborated_{q_k}$ of the transactions received by ι_{q_k} whose contents it elaborated for its purposes;
- the set $requested_{q_k}$ of the transactions explicitly requested by ι_{q_k}.

If ι_{q_k} belongs to $out\_nbh_{j_k}$, TD_{qj_k} can be expressed as:

$$TD_{qj_k} = \frac{|tranSet_{jq_k} \cap (requested_{q_k} \cup reposted_{q_k} \cup elaborated_{q_k})|}{|tranSet_{jq_k}|}$$

Starting from this definition and from the concept of $out\_nbh^t_{j_k}$, we can proceed with the transitive closure of TD_{qj_k} in such a way as to extend it to the case in which ι_{q_k} is indirectly connected to ι_{j_k}. In particular, the general definition of TD_{qj_k} is as follows:

$$TD_{qj_k} = \begin{cases} \frac{|tranSet_{jq_k} \cap (requested_{q_k} \cup reposted_{q_k} \cup elaborated_{q_k})|}{|tranSet_{jq_k}|} & if\, \iota_{q_k} \in out\_nbh_{j_k} \\ \prod_{w=1}^{t} TD_{((w-1)w)_k} & if\, \iota_{q_k} \in out\_nbh^t_{j_k},\ t > 0, \\ & \quad \pi_{jq_k} = \{\iota_{0_k}, \iota_{1_k}, \cdots, \iota_{t_k}\} \end{cases}$$

The next step regards the definition of the concept of Impact Degree ID_{j_k} of an instance ι_{j_k} in $\mathcal{I}_k$. It is defined as the average of the Trust Degrees that all the instances belonging to $out\_nbh_{j_k}$ have in ι_{j_k}. It can be formalized as follows:

$$ID_{j_k} = \frac{\sum_{\iota_{q_k} \in out\_nbh_{j_k}} TD_{qj_k}}{|out\_nbh_{j_k}|}$$

We are now able to define the Scope $Sc^t_{j_k}$ of level t of an instance ι_{j_k} of $\mathcal{I}_k$. Specifically, $Sc^t_{j_k}$ is defined as the weighted sum of the Impact Degrees of the

[3] Clearly, it might happen that an unrequested transaction of $tranSet_{jq_k}$ is not considered interesting by ι_{q_k}. In this case, ι_{q_k} neither posts nor elaborates it.

instances belonging to $out\_nbh^t_{j_k}$, where the weights are the trust values that these instances have in ι_{j_k}. This sum is then averaged by the number of the instances belonging to $nbh^t_{j_k}$. Formally speaking:

$$Sc^t_{j_k} = \frac{\sum_{\iota_{q_k} \in out\_nbh^t_{j_k}} TD_{qj_k} \cdot ID_{q_k}}{|out\_nbh^t_{j_k}|}$$

Now, we can define the Scope Sc^t_j of level t of an object o_j in the MIoT. It is obtained by averaging the Scope of level t of its instances in the corresponding IoTs. Specifically, let $Inst_j = \{\iota_{j_1}, \iota_{j_2}, \cdots, \iota_{j_l}\}$ be the instances of o_j in the IoTs of the MIoT. Then:

$$Sc^t_j = \frac{\sum_{\iota_{j_k} \in Inst_j} Sc^t_{j_k}}{|Inst_j|}$$

From the definitions of TD_{qj_k}, ID_{qj_k}, Sc^t_{jk} and Sc^t_j it emerges that each of these parameters belongs to the real interval $[0, 1]$.

4 Applications

In a scenario characterized by the pervasive diffusion of increasingly intelligent and social objects, our approach can have a large variety of applications. Two very interesting ones regard smart cities and shopping centers. Due to space limitations, we describe in detail only the first one.

Consider some public areas (such as parks, squares, shopping centers, etc.) in a (smart) city, and assume that a set of people actively visits these areas. Each area is equipped with several smart objects for monitoring weather, air quality, traffic conditions, level of noise, etc., along with several actuators, such as smart lamps or information hubs provided as online services. Each person may be provided with several smart devices, such as smartwatches, smartphones, other wearable devices, and so forth. Persons and places can interact with each other through the corresponding smart objects.

Such a scenario can be modeled through a MIoT $\mathcal{M}$ consisting of a set $\{\mathcal{I}_1, \mathcal{I}_2, \cdots, \mathcal{I}_m\}$ of IoTs, each representing a public area. The set of the objects of $\mathcal{M}$ comprises the smart objects installed in the public areas and the set of personal devices of people visiting them. If an object o_j of the MIoT is active in the kth public area, it has an instance ι_{j_k} in the IoT $\mathcal{I}_k$. Clearly, when a person with a smart object o_j moves around different public areas corresponding to different IoTs, o_j will have different instances, one for each IoT.

Each visitor of an area is generally interested to a certain kind of activity; for instance, she could be a fitness runner. The final goal of the MIoT is supporting people to get the best experience from their activities. In this setting, scope can play a role in reaching this objective. In the following, we report some possible usage scenarios.

Assume that a person wants to go out for a run. First, she needs to choose the best area for the run, based on weather conditions, traffic and other parameters that she considers relevant. To carry out her choices, she can check data provided by the sensors of each public area of her interest, the information hubs or other trusted runners. The choice of the data sources to consult is usually related to the corresponding trustworthiness and the easiness of getting desired information from them. These two properties are clearly strictly correlated to the scope of the source; indeed, this scope can be seen as a "summary" of these two parameters and some other related ones, such as accuracy, reputation, impact, etc. Once the person has performed her choice, she can send information to the MIoT in such a way as to serve, in her turn, as information provider for the community.

A similar activity flow may happen in several other circumstances, in which there is a decision to made, e.g., when a user must choose the best shopping center where she can buy a given object, the best cinema where she can see a movie, etc.

In all these cases, data regarding user choices can be coupled with those registered during the activities she performed therein (e.g., data coming from personal smart wears) in such a way as to confirm the correctness of the choice or, on the contrary, to alert the other users of the evaluation errors. For instance, imagine a scenario in which a person verifies that the weather was actually too cold for the clothes she had selected; interestingly, this information could be automatically detected and sent by the sensors in her smart wears. In this case, the scope of the smart wears is useful to understand how extended and how strong is its capability of influencing the decision of the other users. In other words, the scope of an object o_j in this scenario determines how many users are impacted by the data sent by it and how much strong this impact is.

It is worth pointing out the relevance of scope in this context. As a matter of fact, knowing the objects with the highest impact in the MIoT allows the improvement of the efficiency and the effectiveness of the information disseminated through the network. At a higher abstraction level, some smart objects of the MIoT could assume the role of reliable information hubs for the whole MIoT if their scope is particularly strong and large over time.

5 Experiments

In order to perform our experiments, since real MIoTs with the dimension and the variety handled by our model do not exist yet, we constructed a MIoT simulator. This tool starts from real data and returns simulated MIoTs with certain characteristics specified by the user.

The MIoTs created by our simulator follow the paradigm described in Section 2. Our simulator is also provided with a suitable interface allowing a user to "personalize" the MIoT to build by specifying the desired values for several parameters, such as the number of nodes, the maximum number of instances of an object, and so forth.

To make "concrete" and "plausible" the created MIoTs, our simulator leverages a real dataset. It regards the taxi routes in the city of Porto from July 1st 2013 to June 30th 2014. It can be found at the address `http://www.geolink.pt/`

ecmlpkdd2015-challenge/dataset.html. Each route contains several Points of Interests corresponding to the GPS coordinates of the vehicle.

We partitioned the city of Porto in six areas and associated a real IoT with each area. Our simulator associates an object with a given route recorded in the dataset and an object instance with each partition of a route belonging to an area. It creates a MIoT node for each instance and a c-arc for each pair of instances belonging to the same route. Furthermore, it creates an i-arc between two nodes of the same IoT if the length of the time interval between the corresponding routes is less than a certain threshold th_t. The value of th_t can be specified through the constructor interface. Clearly, the higher th_t the more connected the constructed MIoT.

The MIoT for this experiment, which we constructed through our simulator, consisted of 1256 nodes. This number of nodes is much higher than the ones presently characterizing real MIoTs. However, we preferred to construct such a large MIoT because we think that, with the enormous development of the IoT, in the future there could exist MIoTs consisting of thousands of nodes. On the other side, we did not adopt larger MIoTs because they required excessive computation times without providing more knowledge on scope than the one we could have acquired with a MIoT of about 1000 nodes. The six IoTs of the MIoT had 128, 362, 224, 280, 98 and 164 nodes, respectively. The constructed MIoT is returned in a format that can be directly processed by the cypher-shell of Neo4J. The interested reader can find the MIoT adopted in the experiments described here at the address http://daisy.dii.univpm.it/miot/datasets/scope.

We carried out all the tests presented in this section on a server equipped with an Intel I7 Quad Core 7700 HQ processor and 16 GB of RAM with the Ubuntu 16.04 operating system. To implement our approach we adopted:

- Python, as programming language;
- Neo4J (Version 3.4.5), as underlying DBMS.

In these experiments, we aimed at investigating the trend of the scope against the neighborhood level t. In particular, for each instance ι_{j_k} of the MIoT, we computed $Sc^t_{j_k}$ when t increases from 1 to the diameter of $\mathcal{I}_k$. After this, we grouped the instances of our MIoT in several ways (one for each test), based on some specific rationales, and we computed the variation of the average values of the scope for each group.

As a first task of this activity, we computed the variation of the average values of the scope for each IoT of the MIoT. This is equivalent to say that the instances of the MIoT were grouped in the corresponding IoTs (one group for each IoT). The obtained results are reported in Figure 1. From the analysis of this figure, we can observe that, in each IoT, the scope decreases quite quickly. Indeed, it is extremely high when $t = 1$ in all the IoTs. When $t = 2$, the scope is high for the largest IoTs, whereas it has an intermediate value for the other ones. In any case, the scope becomes very low when t is greater than or equal to 4 for small networks and when t is greater than or equal to 5 for the large ones.

As a second task, we computed the variation of the average values of the scope for the whole MIoT. This is equivalent to say that we had a unique group

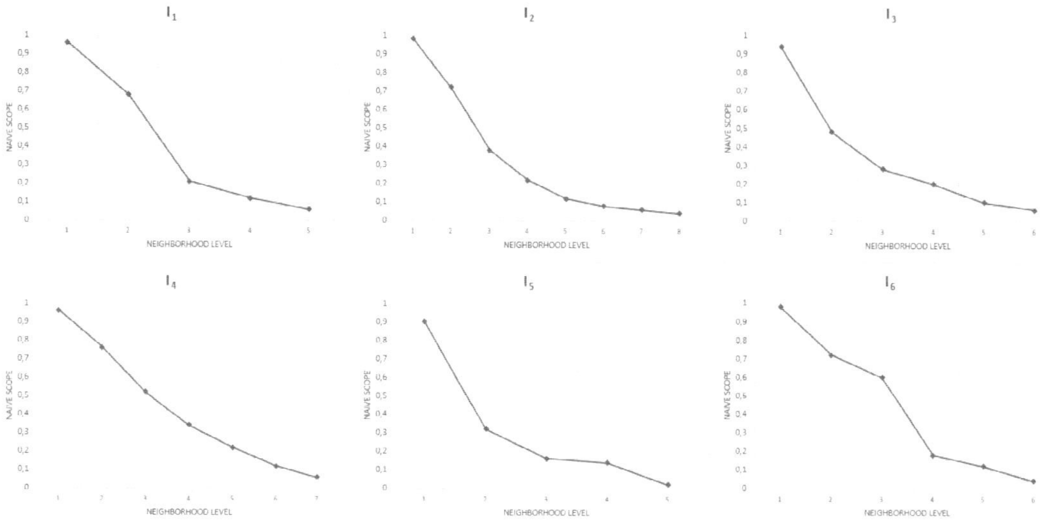

Fig. 1. Variation of the average scope for each IoT of the MIoT against the neighborhood level

comprising all the instances of the MIoT. The obtained results are reported in Figure 2. From the analysis of this figure, we can conclude that the scope presents a trend similar to the one of the largest IoTs of Figure 1. In particular, it is very high for $t = 1$; it is high for $t = 2$; it has an intermediate value for $t = 3$, whereas it is very low for $t > 5$.

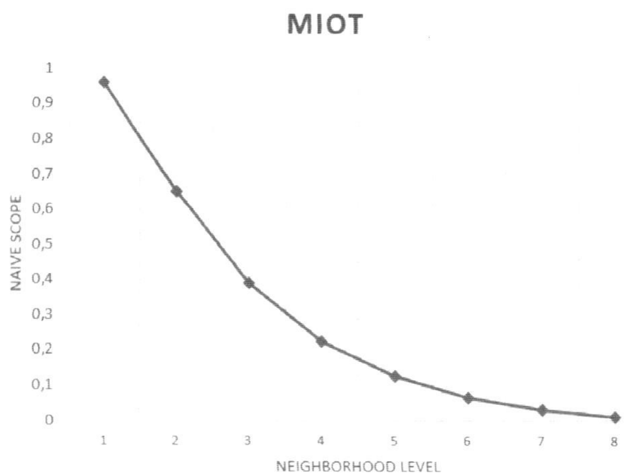

Fig. 2. Variation of the average scope for the whole MIoT against the neighborhood level

As a final task, we subdivided all the instances of the MIoT in two groups containing i-nodes and c-nodes, respectively. Then, we computed the variation of the average values of the scope for the two groups. The final goal of this task was to verify if i-nodes and c-nodes showed different behaviors as far as their scope is concerned. The obtained results are reported in Figure 3. From the analysis of this figure, we can observe that the scope decreases for both i-nodes and c-nodes. However, the trends are different. Indeed, the decrease is much smother for i-nodes than for c-nodes. In particular, for c-nodes, the decrease is very steep because the scope is less than 0.2 already for $t = 3$. This can be explained by considering that, analogously to what was made in all the past approaches, our definition of neighborhood (which plays a key role in our definition of scope) considers as neighbors of a node only other nodes of the same IoT. In other words, it takes only i-arcs into account. Actually, we believe (and the results of Figure 3 represent a confirmation) that it is worthwhile to investigate the role of c-arcs in the computation of the neighborhood of a node and we plan to make this investigation in the future.

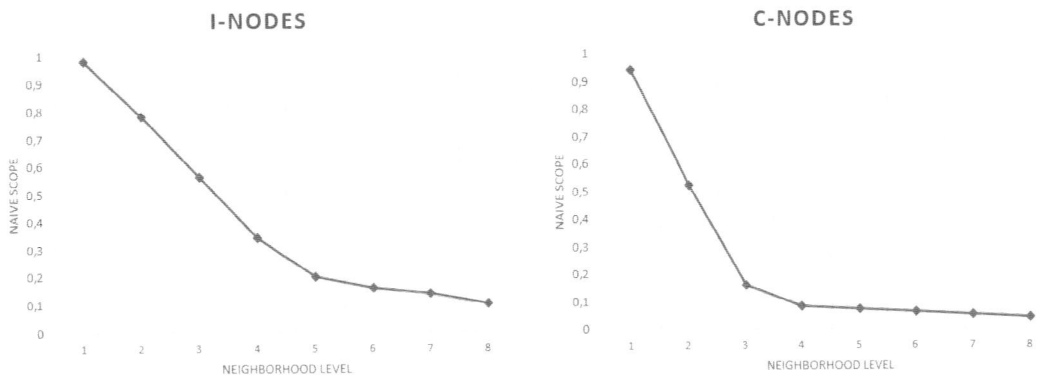

Fig. 3. Variation of the average scope for the i-nodes and the c-nodes of the MIoT against the neighborhood level

As for the investigation of the values of the scope for objects, we observe that they are obtained by averaging the values of the scope of the corresponding instances. As a consequence, it does not make sense to perform the first and the final tasks of the previous activity. The only task that makes sense is the second one; in this case, the variation of the average values of the scope of objects for the whole MIoT is reported in Figure 4. As we could have expected, this trend is very similar (or, better almost identical) to the one of Figure 2.

6 Conclusion

In this paper, we have seen that social internetworking and the Internet of Things are becoming more and more contiguous and are giving rise to several social and/or multiple IoTs paradigms. In this new scenario, we have introduced the concept of scope of a thing in a MIoT, along with a formalization allowing the computation of the corresponding values. Then we have illustrated one possible application along with some experiments aiming at evaluating the variation of scope against the value of the neighborhood level.

Fig. 4. Variation of the average scope for the objects of the MIoT against the neighborhood level

This paper should not be considered as an ending point. Instead, it could be the starting point of many researches in this field. Indeed, there are several future related investigations that could be made in this context. First, we would like to analyze the role of possible constraints on network nodes or arcs in the definition of scope. Then, we plan to study the role of scope in the detection of anomalies and, even more, for understanding the extension and the importance of the damage caused by them. Finally, we would like to analyze the exploitation of scope in predictive maintenance, that is currently one of the most important research issues in the manufacturing industry.

References

1. Concise Oxford Dictionary. `https://en.oxforddictionaries.com/`, 2019.
2. IPSO Alliance. `https://www.ipso-alliance.org/`, 2019.
3. G. Araniti, A. Orsino, L. Militano, L. Wang, and A. Iera. Context-aware information diffusion for alerting messages in 5g mobile social networks. *IEEE Internet of Things Journal*, 4(2):427–436, 2017.
4. L. Atzori, A. Iera, and G. Morabito. SIoT: Giving a social structure to the Internet of Things. *IEEE Communications Letters*, 15(11):1193–1195, 2011. IEEE.
5. G. Baldassarre, P. Lo Giudice, L. Musarella, and D. Ursino. A paradigm for the cooperation of objects belonging to different IoTs. In *Proc. of the International Database Engineering & Applications Symposium (IDEAS 2018)*, pages 157–164, Villa San Giovanni, Italy, 2018. ACM.
6. G. Baldassarre, P. Lo Giudice, L. Musarella, and D. Ursino. The MIoT paradigm: main features and an "ad-hoc" crawler. *Future Generation Computer Systems*, 92:29–42, 2019. Elsevier.
7. F. Buccafurri, V.D. Foti, G. Lax, A. Nocera, and D. Ursino. Bridge Analysis in a Social Internetworking Scenario. *Information Sciences*, 224:1–18, 2013. Elsevier.
8. A. Felfernig, S. Polat-Erdeniz, C. Uran, S. Reiterer, M. Atas, T.N.T. Tran, P. Azzoni, C. Kiraly, and Dolui K. An overview of recommender systems in the internet of things. *Journal of Intelligent Information Systems*, pages 1–25, 2018.

9. A. Forestiero. Multi-agent recommendation system in internet of things. In *Proceedings of the 17th IEEE/ACM International Symposium on Cluster, Cloud and Grid Computing, CCGRID 2017, Madrid, Spain, May 14-17, 2017*, pages 772–775. IEEE Computer Society / ACM, 2017.
10. D. Kempe, J. Kleinberg, and É. Tardos. Maximizing the spread of influence through a social network. In *Proc. of the International ACM SIGKDD Conference on Knowledge Discovery and Data Mining (KDD 2003)*, pages 137–146, Washington, DC, USA, 2003. ACM.
11. R. Lea and M. Blackstock. Smart cities: an iot-centric approach. In *Proceedings of the 2014 International Workshop on Web Intelligence and Smart Sensing, IWWISS '14, Saint Etienne, France, September 1-2, 2014*, pages 12:1–12:2. ACM, 2014.
12. D. Leggio, G. Marra, and D. Ursino. Defining and investigating the scope of users and hashtags in Twitter. In *Proc. of the International Conference on Ontologies, DataBases, and Applications of Semantics (ODBASE 2014)*, pages 674–681, Amantea (CS), Italy, 2014. Lecture Notes in Computer Science. Springer.
13. Z. Ma, A. Sun, and G. Cong. Will this #Hashtag be Popular Tomorrow? In *Proc. of the ACM SIGIR International Conference on Research and Development in Information Retrieval (SIGIR 2012)*, pages 1173 – 1174, Portland, OR, USA, 2012. ACM.
14. Z. Ma, A. Sun, and G. Cong. On Predicting the Popularity of Newly Emerging Hashtags in Twitter. *Journal of the Association for Information Science and Technology*, 64(7):1399–1410, 2013.
15. Z. Miller, B. Dickinson, W. Deitrick, W. Hu, and A. H. Wang. Twitter Spammer Detection Using Data Stream Clustering. *Information Sciences*, 260:64–73, 2014.
16. Z. Ning, X. Wang, X. Kong, and W. Hou. A social-aware group formation framework for information diffusion in narrowband internet of things. *IEEE Internet of Things Journal*, 5(3):1527–1538, 2018.
17. Y. Okada, K. Masui, and Y. Kadobayashi. Proposal of Social Internetworking. In *Proc. of the International Human.Society@Internet Conference (HSI 2005)*, pages 114–124, Asakusa, Tokyo, Japan, 2005. Lecture Notes in Computer Science, Springer.
18. D.M. Romero, W. Galuba, S. Asur, and B.A. Huberman. Influence and passivity in social media. In *Proc. of the International Conference on World Wide Web (WWW'11)*, pages 113–114, Hyderabad, India, 2011. ACM.
19. J. Weng, E. Lim, J. Jiang, and Q. He. TwitterRank: Finding Topic-sensitive Influential Twitterers. In *Proc. of the ACM International Conference on Web Search and Data Mining (WSDM 2010)*, pages 261–270, New York, NY, USA, 2010. ACM.
20. L. Yao, Q. Z. Sheng, A. H. H. Ngu, and X. Li. Things of interest recommendation by leveraging heterogeneous relations in the internet of things. *ACM Transaction on Internet Technology*, 16(2):9:1–9:25, 2016.
21. Z. Zhou, C. Gao, C. Xu, Y. Zhang, S. Mumtaz, and J. Rodriguez. Social big-data-based content dissemination in internet of vehicles. *IEEE Transaction on Industrial Informatics*, 14(2):768–777, 2018.

Querying Influence Graphs over Online Social Networks Effectively and Efficiently (Discussion Paper)

Vincenzo Moscato[1], Antonio Picariello[1], Giancarlo Sperlí[1], and Alfredo Cuzzocrea[2]

[1] DIETI Dept., University of Naples "Federico II", Naples, Italy
{vincenzo.moscato,antonio.picariello,giancarlo.sperli}@unina.it
[2] DIA Dept., University of Trieste, Trieste, Italy
alfredo.cuzzocrea@dia.units.it

Abstract. From the *Social Networks Analysis* (SNA) perspective, *Viral Marketing* has the aim to maximize the number of people that become aware of a given product/service by identifying a few number of individuals, considered more "influential" that can be promoted products or services. In this paper we propose a novel concept of *influence graph* that can be easily derived by querying social network modelled as a graph. Furthermore, spread diffusion model has been defined as a *Combinatorial Multi-Armed Bandit* (CMAB) problem for retrieving the most influential users, without any kind of preliminary knowledge.

Keywords: Social Networks Analytics · Viral Marketing · Influence Diffusion and Maximization · Online Social Networks Models

1 Introduction

The use of *Online Social Networks* or OSNs have rapidly become an essential part of every day life, and today about 2 billions of users are connected on simple smart platforms, where single people or communities of people share personal information, feelings, opinions about their life or on public facts [1, 5], and, of course, such environments represent a novel channel for assessing, choosing and buying goods and services .

Sociologists find out that individuals are frequently, explicitly or implicitly, influenced by their social contacts while deciding whether to adopt an innovation (such as a political idea, or to buy a new product): the way in which new practices spread through a population should so mainly depend on the fact that people influence each others' behavior.

It appears really important for big companies to target "opinion leaders", because if they are able to influence users of a community, it will start a large cascade of further recommendations. One of the main problems here is to maximize the number of people that become aware of a given product, finding the best set of users to start the diffusion and, consequently, to maximize the spread: this is, for example, the basic idea behind each social advertisement campaigns, and it corresponds to solve an *Influence Maximization* (IM) problem, which has the goal to find a small subset of nodes that could maximize the spread of influence over a social network graph.

An application of this strategy in social advertising is surely the so-called *Viral Marketing*. Viral Marketing allows to improve the spread awareness about a given product/service through a sort of "word-of-mouth" advertising. In a nutshell, a company selects a fixed (small) number of individuals, considered more influential, and offers or discounts them the product/services, hoping that they will be recursively recommended: as in epidemic diffusion, the viral effect starts and new products can reach a large number of people. In this way, users will influence their neighbors/friends triggering a "cascade effect". Viral marketing thus capitalizes on the advantages of social networks, and in particular their high capacity of fast and effective information diffusion. In this paper, we propose a novel approach for viral marketing based on modeling OSNs as a *graph database*. Using *regular path queries*, we can then query the database and extract relevant "social paths", by which users influence the other ones, considering a number of different social interactions. Relevant social paths are thus opportunely merged into an *influence graph* that describes the influence spread over a social network, following the *Independent Cascade* (IC) model. Finally, we exploit a particular online learning problem, namely the *Combinatorial Multi-Armed Bandit* (CMAB) framework, to determine the most influential users. The chosen approach allows us to automatically estimate the influence probabilities during the influence maximization stage, without any preliminary knowledge.

2 OSN modeling

Our idea consists in modeling a generic OSN as a *graph database* that is an undirected edge-labeled graph $G = (V, L, E)$ where:

- V is the set of graph vertices, representing the main entities of a social network;
- L is a set of labels, usually belonging to a given vocabulary and describing the different kinds of relationships that can occur among the social network entities;
- $E \subseteq V \times L \times V$ is the set of edges;
- V and E are abstract data types with a set of properties (expressed using several attributes that can be different depending on the type of nodes/edges).

To better explain the proposed approach, we consider a case study based on YELP social network. YELP is an On-line Social Network in which users can build friendship relationships and submit reviews about business objects, described by a set of attributes (i.e. business hour, accessibility and parking and so on), across all industries. Furthermore, an evaluation metrics based on a 5-point rating is assigned to both entities for estimating their relevance with respect to their reviews and actions on YELP.

Considering our model, we can represent Yelp as a graph in which the vertices set is composed by *Users* and *Business objects* while friendship and reviews represent respectively the relationships between two users or a user and business object. Furthermore, vertices and edges can be described by a set of attributes.

Using this general model we have defined a methodology to analyze users' behavior, proposing the novel concepts of "social path".

A *social path* is a particular edge-labeled path, i.e. a sequence $p = (v_1, l_1, v_2, \ldots, l_k, v_{k+1})$ with $(v_i, l_i, v_{i+1}) \in E$ for each $i \in \{1, , k\}$.

Given the graph in Figure 1, examples of social paths connecting two users belonging to YELP are: $p_1 = (vinni, friendship, giank)$ and $p_2 = (vinni, review, gamberorosso, review, giank)$.

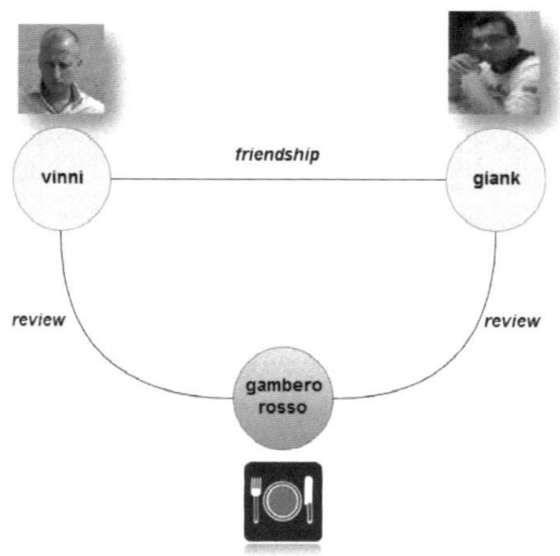

Fig. 1: An example of OSN graph using YELP data.

From a social paths, we can derive *relevant social paths*, i.e. special social paths that may be used in a variety of Social Networks Analytics applications. The elements belonging to a relevant social path must match a set of conditions Θ, defined on the attributes of nodes and edges belonging to the path.

For example, in YELP, the paths p_1 and p_2 can be relevant for an influence analysis problem and represent different ways by which a user can "influence" another one.

We explicitly note that a relevant social path can be expressed by regular path queries on a graph database [4]. A *regular path query* (RPQ) over the set of edge labels L is expressed as a regular expression over L. [3] In other terms, RPQs have the form $Q(x, y) : (x, R, y)$, R being a regular expression over the vocabulary of edge labels.

To extract the set of nodes' pairs connected by relevant social paths, we can first exploit regular path queries and then filtering the obtained results on the base of Θ conditions.

As an example, the query $Q(u_i, u_j) : (u_i, review, review, u_j)$ returns the set of users pairs that have performed a review on the same business object, and in particular, it can be represented using the graph in Figure 2.

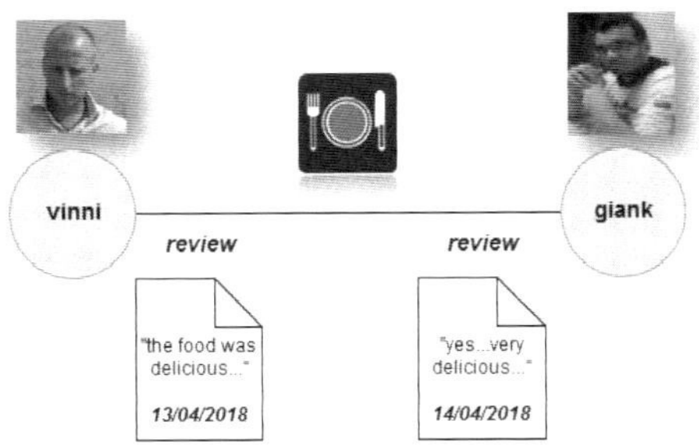

Fig. 2: An example of graph generated using RPQs on YELP.

Exploiting as further condition $\Theta = (e_2.t - e_1.t) \leq \delta t \wedge (e_1.m = e_2.m)$ (m and t respectively being the mood and timestamp of a given review), we can select only the set of users pairs in which the user u_j has performed a review immediately after u_i with the same mood.

3 Influence analysis: building an Influence Graph from an OSN

We can express more complex social paths using *conjunctive* RPQs [4]. As an example, the query $Q(u_i, u_j) : (u_i, review, review, u_j) \wedge (u_i, friendship, u_j)$ returns the set of users pairs that have performed a review on the same business object and are friends.

We define *influential paths* all the social paths that are relevant for an influence analysis problem. The execution of specific RPQS describing influential paths on the database graph (representing a particular social network) allows to determine a new homogeneous graph (vertices are only users), that we call "influence graph", we used to effectively model the influence spread over an OSN.

More precisely, an *Influence Graph* is a labeled graph $IG = (\hat{V}, \widehat{E}, \tau)$ where:

[3]The answer $Q(D)$ to a RPQ Q over a database D is the set of pairs of nodes connected in D by a social path traversing a sequence of edges forming a word in the regular language $L(Q)$ defined by Q.

- $\widehat{V}$ is the set of nodes such that each $v \in \widehat{V}$ corresponds to a user $u \in U$;
- $\hat{E} \subseteq \hat{V} \times \hat{V}$ is the set of edge (with no self-loops);
- $\tau : \hat{V} \times \hat{V} \rightarrow [0, 1]$ is a function that assigns to each edge $e = (v_i, v_j)$ a label, representing the probability τ that user u_i can influence user u_j.

To build an influence graph, we used a *sentiment analysis* technique to associate a predefined mood to each YELP review whilst we initially decided to exploit only the influence graph structure/topology, without considering the influence probabilities. In particular, we adopted a *Combinatorial Multi-Armed Bandit* (CMAB) approach [6] that allows us to automatically estimate the influence probabilities during the influence maximization stage. More in detail, the CMAB approach consists of multiple rounds, in each of them we leverage an IM method. Considering that we start without the knowledge of influence probabilities, the obtained spread will be low compared to the optimal solution and we refer to such situation as a *regret*. At each step, we then attempt to reduce the regret and, at the same time, to improve influence probabilities estimation using an *exploration-exploitation* trade-off.

In particular, the regret ρ after n rounds can be described by the Equation 1: it practically represents the difference between spread σ related to the optimal seed set S^* (knowing the right probabilities) and that returned by the CMAB strategy applied to current seed set S^i at iteration i.

$$\rho = n \cdot \sigma(S^*) - \sum_{i=1}^{n} \bar{\sigma}(S^i) \tag{1}$$

Indeed, CMAB is based on the following *exploration-exploitation* trade-off:

- exploration allows us to improve our knowledge, incrementally learning the influence probabilities over the network;
- exploitation allows us to achieve the largest spread by exploiting the current knowledge.

3.1 Modeling Influence maximization as CMAB problem

In our model, we consider m arms each one with a random variable $X_j^i \in [0, 1]$ having μ_j as mean, which represents the obtained reward when the arm j is triggered at the round i. Furthermore, in the CMAB model it is possible to play a superarm A in each round: in this way all arms in A are triggered. We indicate with p_j^A the probability of arm j to be triggered when superarm A is played.

At each round, we then adopt an approximation oracle that leverages the current means' distribution $\hat{\boldsymbol{\mu}} = (\hat{\mu}_1, \hat{\mu}_2, ..., \hat{\mu}_m)$ to find the best (super)arm to play. After that, the superarm is played and consequently several arms are triggered. In the end, we observe the rewards obtained from each arm to update their mean estimation $\hat{\mu}_j$. To this goal, we use the number of times $n_{j,i}$ that an arm j has been triggered until the round i and the process continues until $i = n$.

In other terms, the CMAB relies on the *Independent Cascade* (IC) diffusion model that mimics the spread of an epidemic disease, evolving along discrete steps.

Given an influence graph $IG = (\hat{V}, \widehat{E}, \tau)$, where at each edge $(u, v) \in \widehat{E}$ is assigned a influence probability $\tau_{u,v} \in [0, 1]$, the process starts with an initial set of active nodes S_0 and each node $u \in S_0$ has a single chance to activate each outgoing inactive node v: it happens with probability $\tau_{u,v}$. The node v can become active in the next step and attempt to influence each one of its inactive out-neighbors. In this way the cascade continues until the process converges; the final spread $\sigma(S_n)$ represents the number of nodes that are activated starting from S_0 after n iterations. Thus, IM tries to maximize the final spread using reduced seed sets.

3.2 The IM algorithm

The procedure receives as input an influence graph IG without the knowledge of influence probabilities τ. In the initial step, it is used the vector $\hat{\boldsymbol{\mu}}_0$ that assigns 0 or a low influence probability to each edge (u, v).

At each round, the algorithm attempts to reduce the regret by implementing a particular exploration-exploitation trade-off technique (*coin flip*):

- the exploitation is performed using as approximation oracle the very simple and efficient greedy strategy proposed by the authors in [2,3] that allows to select a seed set S (with $|S| = k$) representing the played superarm A (it requires to solve an IM problem on the graph IG with influence probability estimating through the current means' vector $\hat{\boldsymbol{\mu}}$);
- the exploration is obtained generating a seed set S in a random way.

When a superarm is played, the diffusion process starts and leads to active several inactive nodes by triggering other arms. At the end of the process, it is evaluated the reward considering the number of nodes that are activated. This information is the used to update the means' estimation $\hat{\boldsymbol{\mu}}$ by the following Equation:

$$\hat{\mu}_j = \frac{\sum_{i=1}^{z} n_{j,i}}{z} \tag{2}$$

$n_{j,i}$ being the number of activated nodes playing the arm j at step i and $z \in [1, n]$. Thus, we improve the knowledge to minimize the regret in the next step.

4 System Overview and Implementation Details

Here, we present an overview of the system for viral marketing purposes, whose main components together with the related workflow are shown in Figure 3.

The system relies on a multilayer architecture typical of Big Data infrastructures based on the Apache Hadoop[4] technological stack and supports four main tasks: i) *data ingestion*, ii) *data storing*, iii) *batch computation*, iv) *data visualization*.

During the data ingestion, and using the functionalities provided by an ETL module, information about users' social interactions are:

[4] http://hadoop.apache.org/

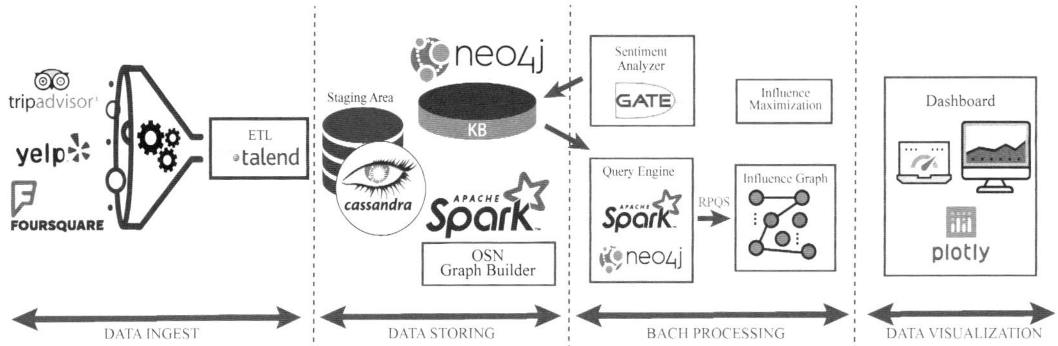

Fig. 3: System Architecture.

- periodically extracted from several OSNs (e.g., YELP, TripAdvisor, etc.) using the related API;
- cleaned and transformed in according to a particular log format containing information on user, timestamp and the performed action with several attributes (as an example ⟨ vinni, 13-05-2018, Gambero Rosso, "the food was delicious", ...⟩);
- loaded into a particular Staging Area.

Concerning implementation details, the ETL module was realized exploiting facilities provided by the Talend[5] tool. In turn, the Staging Area repository was implemented through the Cassandra[6] columnar database.

The data storing task has the goal of generating the OSN graph database by means of OSN Graph Builder module, using data from staging area. For each OSN, the final graph is then stored into system Knowledge Base (KB). The OSN Graph Builder module was realized on the top of Spark[7] engine (choosing Python as programming language), while we exploited Neo4j[8] for the KB.

During the batch computation task several activities are performed:

- textual reviews are processed to infer the related sentiment using Sentiment Analyzer module that is saved as edge property within the KB;
- on the base of a set of RPQs, the KB is queried by a Query Engine module to extract the influence graph;
- an influence maximization procedure (based on the CMAB theory) is applied on the influence graph to determine the most influential users (through Influence Maximization module).

Regarding implementation details, the Sentiment Analyzer module was implemented on the top of Spark engine leveraging several GATE[9] NLP libraries.

[5]https://www.talend.com/l
[6]http://cassandra.apache.org/
[7]https://spark.apache.org/
[8]https://neo4j.com/
[9]https://gate.ac.uk/

GATE detects *sentiment* related to each sentence in the text in terms of *score* (a numeric value for the sentiment), *sarcasm* (a boolean value to indicate whether the sentence is sarcastic or not) and *polarity* (a boolean value that can be **positive** or **negative**). RPQs are expressed in the Cypher Graph Query Language[10] and the Query Engine module was realized using Spark. The IG is stored in a textual raw format directly on HDFS. Eventually, the Influence Maximization module implements the CMAB IM algorithm in Python leveraging Spark graphs' management libraries.

Data visualization task allows to present results of several elaborations (e.g., influence graph, influential users, etc.) thanks to the functionalities provided by Data visualization module implemented using the Jupiter[11] tool.

5 Conclusion

In this paper we presented a novel approach for viral marketing based on modeling OSNs as particular graph databases. In particular, we derive the influence graph by analyzing influence paths and using CMAB technique.

Future works will be devoted to provide more evaluation of the proposed approach and to compare the proposed methodology with different and more recent influence maximization approaches.

References

1. Jordi Albors, Juan C Ramos, and Jose L Hervas. New learning network paradigms: Communities of objectives, crowdsourcing, wikis and open source. *International Journal of Information Management*, 28(3):194–202, 2008.
2. Flora Amato, Antonio Bosco, Vincenzo Moscato, Antonio Picariello, and Giancarlo Sperl. A novel influence diffusion model based on user generated content in online social networks. In *Proceedings of the 6th International Conference on Data Science, Technology and Applications*. SCITEPRESS - Science and Technology Publications, 2017.
3. Flora Amato, Vincenzo Moscato, Antonio Picariello, and Giancarlo Sperlí. Diffusion algorithms in multimedia social networks: a preliminary model. In *Proceedings of the 2017 IEEE/ACM International Conference on Advances in Social Networks Analysis and Mining 2017*, pages 844–851. ACM, 2017.
4. Angela Bonifati, Wim Martens, and Thomas Timm. An analytical study of large sparql query logs. *Proc. VLDB Endow.*, 11(2):149–161, October 2017.
5. Glen Urban. *Don't just relate-advocate!: a blueprint for profit in the era of customer power*. Pearson Education, 2005.
6. Sharan Vaswani, Laks Lakshmanan, Mark Schmidt, et al. Influence maximization with bandits. *arXiv preprint arXiv:1503.00024*, 2015.

[10] https://neo4j.com/cypher-graph-query-language/

[11] http://jupyter.org/

Privacy-Preserving OLAP-based Monitoring of Data Streams: The PP-OMDS Approach (Discussion Paper)

Alfredo Cuzzocrea[1], Assaf Schuster[2], Gianni Vercelli[3], and Massimiliano Nolich[1]

[1] University of Trieste, Trieste, Italy
alfredo.cuzzocrea@dia.units.it, mnolich@units.it
[2] Technion, Haifa, Israel
assaf@cs.technion.ac.il
[3] University of Genoa, Genoa, Italy
gianni.vercelli@unige.it

Abstract. In this paper, we propose PP-OMDS (*Privacy-Preserving OLAP-based Monitoring of Data Streams*), an innovative framework for supporting the *OLAP-based monitoring of data streams*, which is relevant for a plethora of application scenarios (e.g., security, emergency management, and so forth), in a *privacy-preserving manner*. The paper describes motivations, principles and achievements of the PP-OMDS framework, along with technological advancements and innovations. We also incorporate a detailed comparative analysis with competitive frameworks, along with a trade-off analysis.

Keywords: Privacy-Preserving OLAP over Data Streams, OLAP-based Monitoring of Data Streams, Privacy-Preserving OLAP-based Monitoring of Data Streams.

1 Introduction

The PP-OMDS (*Privacy-Preserving OLAP-based Monitoring of Data Streams*) framework focuses the attention on the research challenge represented by *models, techniques and algorithms for supporting privacy-preserving OLAP-based monitoring of data streams*. The investigated research context includes and integrates three distinct components, namely *privacy-preserving OLAP* (e.g., [1,14]), *data stream monitoring* (e.g., [2,15]), and *privacy-preserving data stream monitoring* (e.g., [3]). Even if some sporadic works on supporting *aggregate monitoring queries* in a privacy-preserving manner exist (e.g., [4,5]), the three related issues have not been investigated together under the umbrella of a common framework specially focused to OLAP analysis (rather than the underlying aggregate querying layer), which indeed defines a powerful reference application scenario for a wide spectrum of emerging applications over data streams, such as security (e.g., [6]) and emergency management (e.g., [2]).

Starting from this main motivation, the PP-OMDS framework aims at introducing models, techniques and algorithms for supporting privacy-preserving OLAP-based monitoring of data streams, which is relevant for modern distributed environments such as Clouds. This will fulfil actual limitations of state-of-the-art solutions that do not address the relevant application scenario represented by using OLAP tools and methodologies to support data stream monitoring in a privacy-preserving manner. Application scenarios of the PP-OMDS are many-fold (e.g., security and emergency management). Tangible results of the PP-OMDS framework in real-life applicative settings are represented by relevant research and innovation advancements in the context of models, techniques and algorithms for supporting privacy-preserving OLAP-based monitoring of data streams, which represent the main "result" of the framework. It should be noted that, nowadays, these topics play a critical role as they are "naturally" compliant with the EU H2020 research framework under the topic *Big Data*.

The methodology implemented within the PP-OMDS framework foresees a *multi-step approach* that comprises: (*i*) conceptual analysis and design of case studies and related use cases showing in details how and according to which tasks users/applications interact with the PP-OMDS framework; (*ii*) conceptual analysis and design of models, techniques and algorithms for supporting privacy-preserving OLAP-based monitoring of data streams, which provides a top-down overview of the different PP-OMDS framework's components to be defined and (prototypically) implemented; (*iii*) design of the OLAP-based models and related algorithms for supporting the monitoring of data streams, which represents a more-detailed view of the activity (*ii*) specifically focused on OLAP-analysis aspects of the PP-OMDS framework; (*iv*) design of the privacy-preserving version of the OLAP-based models and related algorithms for supporting the monitoring of data streams, which represents a further refinement of models and algorithms defined by the activity (*iii*) but targeted to embedding privacy-preserving aspects of the PP-OMDS framework in such models and algorithms; (*v*) integration of the OLAP component and the privacy-preserving OLAP component, both oriented to data stream monitoring, into the PP-OMDS framework, according to several alternative computing models.

The scientific contribution of the research carried-out by the PP-OMDS framework is very high because state-of-the-art research, even though focused on the relevant problem of privacy-preserving OLAP over static data, lacks of proposals that are specifically focused on privacy-preserving OLAP over data streams, and, in addition to this, there is not a specific integration with monitoring aspects, which, contrary to this, are indeed very relevant for a wide spectrum of next generation data stream applications and systems.

Summarizing, the main research topics investigated by the PP-OMDS framework are the following:

- models, techniques and algorithms for supporting OLAP-based monitoring of data streams;
- models, techniques and algorithms for supporting the *privacy-preserving version* of OLAP-based monitoring of data streams;

- integration of models, techniques and algorithms devised in the context of the two previous topics/activities, according to several alternative computing models.

The paper describes motivations, principles and achievements of the PP-OMDS framework, along with technological advancements and innovations. We also incorporate a detailed comparative analysis with competitive frameworks, along with a trade-off analysis.

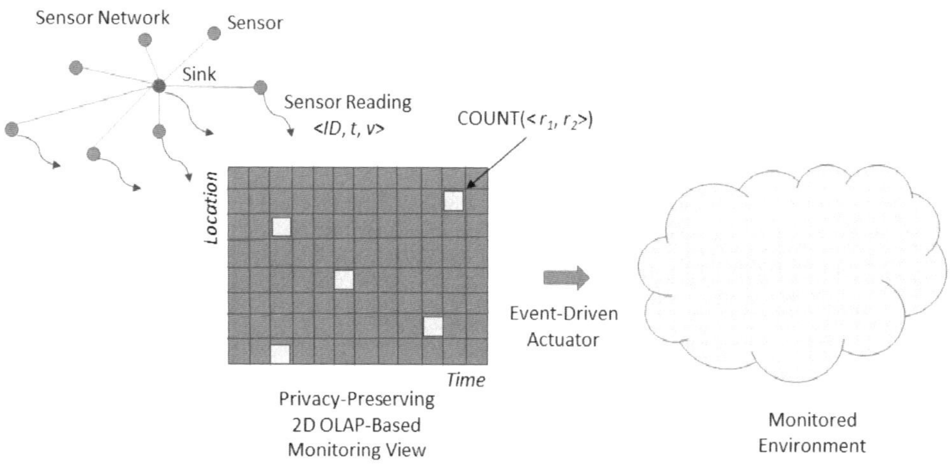

Fig. 1. A Typical Application Scenario for the PP-OMDS Project.

2 Reference Application Scenario

In the PP-OMDS framework, the main research focus is on the issue of supporting privacy-preserving OLAP-based monitoring of data streams, which, has highlighted above, is innovative in actual state-of-the-art research, and it is of relevant interest for a wide spectrum of data stream applications (e.g., security [6], emergency management [2], and so forth). Figure 1 shows a typical application scenario for the PP-OMDS framework. Here, a sensor network, composed by both *sink nodes* and *sensor nodes* (e.g., [7]), produces sensor readings of kind $\langle ID, t, v \rangle$ such that: (*i*) ID is the absolute identifier of the sensor node, (*ii*) t is the timestamp at which the sensor reading is produced, (*iii*) v is the proper reading (i.e., the value). A privacy-preserving 2D OLAP-based monitoring view V is interfaced to the sensor network directly, and it is used to monitor the reading value variable v, based on a complex multidimensional data model [8,9]. In the reference application scenario of Figure 1, the model introduces $Location$ as the first dimension and $Time$ as the second dimension, respectively, and the measure value is defined on top of a COUNT aggregate operator over a two-dimensional range $\langle r_1, r_2 \rangle$, being r_1 and r_2 two one-dimensional ranges along $Location$ and $Time$, respectively, which define the data cube cell. The variable is monitored via suitable aggregate monitoring queries (e.g., [10]) over data cube cells that populate the OLAP view V.

With reference to the so-delineated application scenario, a critical challenge relies on effectively and efficiently computing the OLAP view V over sensor readings (i.e., streaming data), with the additional requirement that V must be computed in a privacy-preserving manner (e.g., [11] – for the static case, [13] – for the dynamic case), i.e. it must preserve the privacy of data sources that originate the sensor readings. The OLAP view V is meant for monitoring goals: when the COUNT-aggregated value of a data cube cell C_i exceeds a fixed threshold τ, then an *event* occurs and a suitable *action* (*trigger*, respectively) is activated in order to modify the target monitored environment. Obviously, the described application scenario is just an instance that represents even more sophisticated multidimensional settings, where the privacy-preserving OLAP-based monitoring view is characterized by multiple dimensions. It is worth to recognize that the described application scenario well-describes a plethora of modern data stream applications, ranging from event detection to complex monitoring queries support, from near-duplicate detection over multimedia streams to anomaly detection, and so forth, all with the innovative and challenging requirement of preserving the privacy of data streams, under OLAP analysis requirements (e.g., [12]), with monitoring purposes, being the latter the three main pillar of the PP-OMDS project.

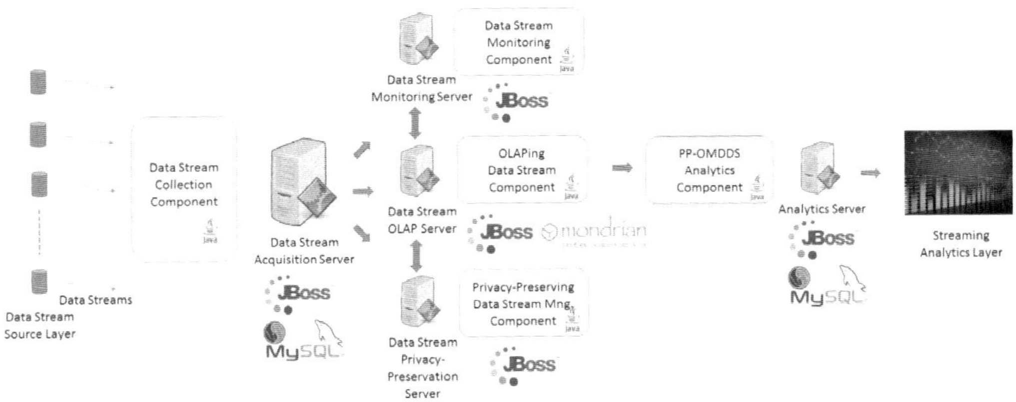

Fig. 2. PP-OMDS Framework Detailed Architecture.

3 PP-OMDS Architecture and Main Functionalities

Figure 2 shows the detailed architecture of the PP-OMDS framework, along with its components and reference technologies. These are:

- *Data Stream Source Layer* – The layer where data streams are produced by a target process (e.g., sensor networks, logistic networks, etc.). Technology used: arbitrary (at the input layer).
- *Data Stream Acquisition Server* – The server devoted to acquire data streams (by also providing the initial pre-processing – e.g., cleaning) and to make the necessary data model transformations. Technology used: *Java programming language*; *JBoss application server*, *MySQL database server*. In particular: (*i*) JBoss provides the necessary Java execution runtime environment for the *Data Stream Collection Component*, which is the component that implements classes and functions supporting the data

stream acquisition phase; (*ii*) My SQL database server provides the necessary data storage (even buffer-oriented) and management functionalities.

- *Data Stream Monitoring Server* – The server devoted to the monitoring of data streams, by implementing the algorithms proposed in the PP-OMDDS framework. It fully interacts with the *Data Stream OLAP Server* and the *Data Stream Privacy-Preservation Server*, respectively, in order to achieve the overall privacy-preserving OLAP-based monitoring of data streams pursued by the PP-OMDDS project. Technology used: Java programming language; JBoss application server. In particular, JBoss provides the necessary Java execution runtime environment for the *Data Stream Monitoring Component*, which is the component that implements classes and functions supporting the data stream monitoring phase.
- *Data Stream OLAP Server* – The server devoted to support OLAP over of data streams, by implementing the algorithms proposed in the PP-OMDDS framework. It fully interacts with the *Data Stream Monitoring Server* and the *Data Stream Privacy-Preservation Server*, respectively, in order to achieve the overall privacy-preserving OLAP-based monitoring of data streams pursued by the PP-OMDDS project. Technology used: Java programming language; JBoss application server, *Mondrian OLAP server*. In particular: (*i*) JBoss provides the necessary Java execution runtime environment for the OLAPing Data Stream Component, which is the component that implements classes and functions supporting OLAP analysis over data streams; (*ii*) Mondrian OLAP server provides the necessary multidimensional data storage and management functionalities.
- *Data Stream Privacy-Preservation Server* – The server devoted to support privacy-preserving management of data streams, by implementing the algorithms proposed in the PP-OMDDS project. It fully interacts with the *Data Stream Monitoring Server* and the *Data Stream OLAP Server*, respectively, in order to achieve the overall privacy-preserving OLAP-based monitoring of data streams pursued by the PP-OMDDS project. Technology used: Java programming language; JBoss application server. In particular, JBoss provides the necessary Java execution runtime environment for the *Privacy-Preserving Data Stream Management Component*, which is the component that implements classes and functions supporting the privacy-preserving data stream management phase.
- *Analytics Server* – The server devoted to support data stream analytics, according to the privacy-preserving OLAP-based vision pursued by the PP-OMDS framework. Technology used: Java programming language; JBoss application server; MySQL database server. In particular: (*i*) JBoss provides the necessary Java execution runtime environment for the *PP-OMDS Analytics Component*, which is the component that implements classes and functions supporting the PP-OMDS analytics phase; (*ii*) My SQL database server provides the necessary data storage (even buffer-oriented) and management functionalities.

- *Streaming Analytics Layer* – The layer where streaming analytics functionalities are finally implemented and delivered to the client applications/users, based on specific analytics goals (e.g., emergency detection and management, security, etc.). Technology used: arbitrary (at the output layer).

The PP-OMDS framework exploits software and hardware solutions that are currently available and completely technologically-feasible (even considering open-source solutions, in the case of software). Indeed, looking at the hardware architecture of the PP-OMDS framework, we identify an (hardware) architecture that makes use of standard solutions for (*i*) collecting data streams, (*ii*) monitoring data streams, (*iii*) aggregating data streams, (*iv*) providing privacy-preserving methods over data streams, and (*v*) supporting OLAP-like query answering over data streams. All these components are commonly delivered on top of well-known architectures composed by (*i*) data servers, (*ii*) OLAP servers, (*iii*) application servers, (*iv*) client components (e.g., desktop computers, laptops, mobile devices, etc.). As regards the software architecture of the PP-OMDS framework, we identify a (software) architecture populated by software components that can be developed by means of standard high-level programming languages (e.g., Java, C++, etc.) and standard data access and manipulation methods (e.g., JDBC, ODBC, etc.). It should be noted that, for both the hardware architecture and the software architecture of the PP-OMDS framework, the components to be developed adhere to well-assessed and mature technologies (both hardware and software) that clearly make the PP-OMDS framework completely-feasible. In addition to this, all the components of the PP-OMDS framework are already Cloud-enabled, hence the framework can be easily extended towards a Cloud-based application (hence, improving performance, reliability and availability).

4 Comparative Analysis with Competitive Frameworks

The software product context of the PP-OMDS framework is represented by the wide area of streaming analytics tools and systems, and, in particular, those devoted to support stream monitoring. Nevertheless, it does not exist a solution that specifically focuses on the relevant problem of supporting privacy-preserving, OLAP-based monitoring of distributed data streams, as delineated by the PP-OMDS framework's motivations. This confirms to us the innovativeness of our proposal.

In the following, we focus the attention on the specific block-founding problems that characterizes the PP-OMDS framework. For what regards the basic distributed data stream monitoring problem, some relevant tools and systems that are currently available are the following ones:

- *APAMA Streaming Analytics*, from Software AG;
- *Stream Computing*, from IBM;
- *Event Stream Processor*, from SAP;
- *Apache Spark*, from Cloudera.

For what regards both the basic OLAP analysis over data streams problem and the basic privacy-preserving data stream management problem, there do not exist direct tools and systems currently available, although vertical solutions on top of existing streaming analytics platforms can be devised.

The most critical limitation of competitor frameworks is represented by the fact that they all adhere to a common deployment model, i.e. providing a general platform for supporting data stream analytics. While on top of such (common) platform personalized solutions can still be developed (via ad-hoc IDE and functional programming environments), they do not focus on the specialized problem of supporting privacy-preserving OLAP-based monitoring of distributed data streams, despite the relevance of this problem and its target application scenarios (e.g., emergency management, security, and so forth).

On the other hand, developing personalized solutions on general-purpose streaming analytics platforms poses critical challenges for what regards a wide spectrum of issues, ranging from complexity overheads to (software) maintenance problems, from heterogeneous data format integration issues to analytical front-end tools that are not focused to the peculiarities of the target application (thus making the whole knowledge discovery from big streaming data harder), and so forth. All these considerations clearly suggest the adoption of an all-inside, self-contained analytical framework that, still being focused on the specific goal of supporting privacy-preserving OLAP-based distributed data stream monitoring, can be further specialized on particular, vertical application settings (still falling in the reference technological area).

Table 1. Comparative Analysis of Competitor Frameworks and the PP-OMDS Framework.

	Distributed Data Stream Monitoring	OLAP Analysis over Data Streams	Privacy-Preserving Data Stream Management	Support for General-Purpose Applications	Support for Vertical Applications
APAMA Streaming Analytics	✓	×	×	✓	×
Stream Computing	✓	×	×	✓	×
Event Stream Processor	✓	×	×	✓	×
Apache Spark	✓	×	×	✓	×
PP-OMDS	✓	✓	✓	✓	✓

In addition to this, the competitor frameworks do not provide an explicit support neither to OLAP analysis tools over data streams neither to privacy-preserving data stream management, making for them hard to follow the paradigms dictated by the PP-OMDS framework's paradigms. Table 1 proposes a summary on the comparative analysis of the competitor frameworks against the PP-OMDS framework, along the above-discussed parameters/functionalities.

5 Conclusions

In this paper, we propose have proposed PP-OMDS, an innovative framework for supporting the OLAP-based monitoring of data streams, which is relevant for a plethora of application scenarios (e.g., security, emergency management, and so forth), in a privacy-preserving manner.

References

1. R. Agrawal, R. Srikant, D. Thomas: Privacy-Preserving OLAP, *SIGMOD*, pp. 251-262, 2005
2. M. Gan, H. Dai: Detecting and monitoring abrupt emergences and submergences of episodes over data streams. *Information Systems 39*:277-289, 2014
3. C. Dwork, T. Pitassi, M. Naor, G.N. Rothblum: Differential privacy under continual observation, *STOC*, 2010
4. E. Shi, T.-H. H. Chan, E.G. Rieffel, R. Chow, D. Song: Privacy-preserving aggregation of time-series data, *NDSS*, 2011
5. L. Fan, L. Xiong. Real-time aggregate monitoring with differential privacy, *CIKM*, 2012
6. J. Zhou, O.C. Au, G. Zhai, Y.Y. Tang, X. Liu: Scalable Compression of Stream Cipher Encrypted Images Through Context-Adaptive Sampling. *IEEE Transactions on Information Forensics and Security 9(11)*:1857-1868, 2014
7. A. Cuzzocrea: Optimization issues of querying and evolving sensor and stream databases. *Information Systems 39*:196-198, 2014
8. Gray J., et al. Data Cube: A Relational Aggregation Operator Generalizing Group-By, Cross-Tab, and Sub-Totals. *Data Mining and Knowledge Discovery, 1(1)*: 29-54, 1997
9. A. Cuzzocrea: CAMS: OLAPing Multidimensional Data Streams Efficiently. *DaWaK*, pp. 48-62, 2009
10. A. Bulut, N. Koudas, A. Meka, A.K. Singh, D. Srivastava: Optimization Techniques for Reactive Network Monitoring. *IEEE Trans. Knowl. Data Eng. 21(9)*: 1343-1357, 2009
11. A. Cuzzocrea, V. Russo, D. Saccà: A Robust Sampling-Based Framework for Privacy Preserving OLAP. *DaWaK*, pp. 97-114, 2008
12. A. Cuzzocrea: Retrieving Accurate Estimates to OLAP Queries over Uncertain and Imprecise Multidimensional Data Streams. *SSDBM*, 2011, pp. 575-576
13. A. Cuzzocrea, E. Bertino: Privacy Preserving OLAP over Distributed XML Data: A Theoretically-Sound Secure-Multiparty-Computation Approach. *Journal of Computer and System Sciences 77(6)*: 965-987, 2011
14. A. Cuzzocrea, V. Russo: Privacy Preserving OLAP and OLAP Security. *Encyclopedia of Data Warehousing and Mining 2009*, pp. 1575-1581, 2009
15. A. Beimel, K. Nissim, E. Omri. Distributed private data analysis: Simultaneously solving how and what, *CRYPTO*, pp. 451-468, 2008

Exotic Compilers as a Malware Evasion Technique (Discussion Paper)

Michele Ianni[1], Elio Masciari[2], and Domenico Saccà[1]

[1] DIMES, University of Calabria, Rende, Italy {mianni, sacca}@dimes.unical.it
[2] ICAR, CNR, Rende, Italy
elio.masciari@icar.cnr.it

Abstract. The increasing complexity of new malware and the constant refinement of detection mechanisms are driving malware writers to rethink the malware development process. In this respect, compilers play a key role and can be used to implement evasion techniques able to defeat even the new generation of detection algorithms. In this paper we provide an overview of the endless battle between malware writers and detectors and we discuss some considerations on the benefits of using high level languages and even exotic compilers (e.g. single instruction compilers) in the process of writing malicious code.

Keywords: Metamorphic malware · Obfuscation · Malware detection · Single instruction compilers.

1 Introduction

History of malware, short for malicious software, is characterized by the endless battle between malware writers and detectors. Since detection strategies are becoming more and more complex, malware writers have to invent new techniques in order to evade detection. Today we can find many viruses that can be considered as pieces of art because they employ several clever ideas in order to keep themselves as stealth as possible. The increasing complexity of new malware is posing new intriguing challenges both from the malware writer perspective and detection mechanisms. In order to implement complex malware, able to spread itself on various operating systems and architectures, it could be useful to move from pure assembly implementations, to malware written using high level languages. In this respect the use of compilers is a key concept to take into account. Compilers, in fact, can be used to implement metamorphic techniques and obfuscation and can build executables able to defeat new detection mechanisms based on the extraction of semantic patterns from the binaries. The paper is organized as follows: in section 2 we describe several techniques used by malware writers in order to avoid detection. In section 3 we show some of the strategies used by antivirus software to detect malicious code and we focus our attention on CFG based detection. In section 4 we discuss the benefits related to the use of compilers in the process of writing malicious code and we show the advantages of using single instruction compilers as an evasion technique. Finally in section 5 we draw our conclusions.

2 Evasion techniques

The most widespread technique used by commercial anti-malware systems in order to detect viruses is based on malware signatures [21]. They are invariant patterns, usually taken from the program's code or raw file content, used to uniquely identify the given malware. To evade signature based scanners many today viruses (called metamorphic) are able to transform themselves during the propagation phase, without losing their capabilities [47]. To achieve this goal several metamorphic transformation are used, including code permutation, garbage code insertion, code shrinking and expansion, register renaming, encryption [2,3,15]. The result of these transformations is a brand new virus that, while keeping the functionality of its predecessor, present a different structure and then a different signature, thus evading detection [47]. As explained in [4], we define $M \subset P$ to be the set of malicious programs, where P is the set of all programs and $\mathbb{S}$ to be the set of signatures. A detector is then a function $D : P \times M \to \{0, 1\}$. A program p is detected if there is a signature $m \in \mathbb{S}$ such that $D(p, m) = 1$. In the case of malwares $D(p, m) = 1 \iff m$ is a pattern derived from p.

Using signature for malware detection is efficient only if it is applied to known malware. This technique, compared to dynamic analysis techniques, has less scanning time, lower false-positive ratio and doesn't suffer of the risks of system infection due to the execution of the malware. The use of code obfuscation techniques allows to easily generate variants of known malware resulting in new malware that cannot be detected by signature based scanners and are harder to comprehend for an human analyst. As stated in [31] more than 80% of malware is packed, in accordance to [41] almost 50% of new malware in 2006 were existing malware obfuscated with packing techniques. The same trend is linked to the use of other obfuscation approaches. There exist many examples of code obfuscation designed to avoid AV scanners detection [17,23,32,34] and all of them are able to easily evade signature based malware detectors.

As described in [47] except for packing, the first obfuscation technique historically used is encryption [36,37,45]. The executable body is crypted and the malware adds to it a decryptor that provides decryption of the body at program runtime. Since at every infection the cryptographic keys used are different the crypted virus body will be always different. One of the first viruses that developed this strategy is Cascade, followed by Win95/Mad and Win95 Zombie [42]. Some of this kind of viruses use also multiple layers of encryption (Win32/Coke). The major limitation of this approach is that in most cases the decryption is in clear text and, since it is always the same, it can be used in order to generate a signature. To overcome this limitation malware writers created new malware able to change also decryptor code. This led to the birth of polymorphic malware [34], that, using many different techniques [11,26,45] are able to generate always different decryptors, without invariant patterns that could be used as signatures. The first viruses that used a real 32-bit polymorphic engine were Win95/Marburg and Win95/HPS. They have been developed and spreaded online many polymorphic engines, among these we can cite *"The Mutation Engine"*

(*MtE*) [36] that is able to easily convert non obfuscated code into polymorphic malware. Altough polymorphic malware are effective against signature based detection, they can be detected using more refined techniques. After the decryption phase, in fact, the body of the virus will be always the same. Using sandboxing techniques [36, 37] the detectors are able to emulate malware in a controlled environment, allowing the decryptor to decrypt malware body in memory. At this point it is still possible to use signature based techniques on the decrypted body. To prevent malware emulation several armoring techniques have been proposed [36] but the improvements in sandboxing mechanisms brought many of them to be ineffective. To overcome all these limitations malware writers brought obfuscation to a new level: metamorphic malware [17, 23] [11, 26, 37, 45]. They are malware able to transform their own body during infection phase. At each iteration metamorphic malware is rewritten so that each succeeding version of the code is different from the preceding one.

There are numerous techniques used by this kind of malware (and often by polymorphic malware too):

- *Register swapping*: is a technique used, for example, by Vecna's Win95/Regswap virus [45]. It consists in changing registers used in various instructions during the evolution from generation to generation. Wildcard searching makes this technique ineffective.
- *Instruction substitution*: it is based on substituting single, or groups, of instructions with other instructions (or groups of them). The new instructions will be equivalent to the previous ones in functionalities but syntactically different [26].
- *Garbage instructions insertion*: is a technique based on the insertion of garbage instructions, that are useless for the execution of the program. Their only goal is to vary malware body [1, 26, 45]. They can be single instructions or sequences that perform useless operations leaving unaltered the state of the program or even instructions located in areas of the program that will never be executed. In this case we are talking about *dead-code*.
- *Transposition*: this name is used to define many instruction reordering techniques that leave unaltered the flow of the program [11]. One of these technique consist in randomly reordering some instructions then using unconditional jumps to reconstruct the original flow. In a more elegant way it is possible to isolate independent groups of instructions then modify their order. In this case, since the sequences are independent, there is no need to make use of unconditional jumps. Finding independent groups of instructions is not an easy task to perform, so, often developers use easier techniques, which can be considered a variant of the first one. It is based on the reordering of the various subroutines that are present inside the malware [11]. One of the malware that used this approach is Win32/Ghost. If we have n subroutines we are able to generate up to $n!$ different variants.
- *Code integration*: is the most sophisticated technique used to obfuscate code. It has been introduced by the virus writer Zombie in Win95/Zmist (Zombie Mistfall). It consists in decompiling the program to infect in distinct parts and then inserting malware code between them. At the end the original program and the malware are reassembled in a single executable.

3 Malware detection

Although several theoretical studies [10, 14] have proved that an algorithm able to detect all types of malware can not exist, a lot of effort has been put to improve detection mechanisms. Several methods have been proposed, varying from support vector machine (SVM) [7], to decision trees [25,33], to Naive Bayes Method [38]. There are two different approaches in malware detection: *static* and *dynamic analysis*. The first analyzes a binary without executing it. Since this technique is safer, faster and easier to implement than dynamic analysis, it is the most widespread approach, even if it is more limited than the latter. Some examples of operations that are performed by static analysis are finding patterns on executables and code flow analysis. In addition to be fast and safe, static analysis has the advantage of reaching complete application code coverage, thus reducing the number of false positives in malware detection. The main problem in using static analysis is that it is very difficult to detect unknown malware. Dynamic analysis, instead, runs malware in a sandbox simulating the behaviour of a real environment, monitoring all system calls. It is clear that the speed of performing this kind of analysis is much slower than static analysis techniques. In addition to that, several techniques have been proposed from malware writers in order to check if the infected executable is running inside a virtual machine, and, in that case, changing its own behaviour in a non offensive one. To overcome the limitation of static analysis they have been introduced many techniques based on the concept of *code normalization*. These techniques try to reduce obfuscated code to a base form that is the same for all obfuscated variants of the same executable. Many different approaches to code normalization have been proposed. Among them we can cite Christodorescu et al. [12], Walenstein et al. [44] and Lakhotia et al. [28]. In the latter the base form is called "zero form" and the process to reduce an executable to that form is called "zeroing". As herm1t states in [20] if this kind of approach was perfect a tool that could perform zeroing reducing all possible variants of a virus into a single "normalized" form (not necessarily optimal), could then use this strategy with every algorithm thus proving or refuting their identity. That's known to be indecidable. The effort of the creators of detectors is then focused on capturing semantic pattern inside an executable rather than invariant synctactic features. These techniques vary from API call analysis [35] to Control Flow Graph analysis.

As explained in [40] a *Control Flow Graph* (*CFG*) is a graph in which the nodes are basic blocks of execution and the edges are possible control flow transfers between them. They are used both for malware detection and vulnerability discovery. CFG recovery is a widely discussed topic in literature, we can cite [13, 24, 27, 39, 43, 46].

Many CFG recovery algorithms deal with the problem of indirect jumps. An indirect jump occurs when the control flow is transferred to a target represented by a value in a register or to a memory location. This makes flow analysis much harder because the destination of the jump is not easily resolvable. This is because it could depend from computations specified in code, from the application context or even from function pointers used in object oriented languages to implement object polymorphism [40].

Control Flow Graph based malware detection As previously stated, due to the difficulty on isolating invariant synctactic features of a self-mutating malware, the effort of the creators of detectors is focused on capturing semantic patterns. CFG are widely used to find similiarities among executables [18] and, more in detail, among malwares [4–6,8,9,19,22,30]. The techniques proposed in literature are based on generating the CFG of a program P to analyze. The generated CFG is the compared to a set of CFGs of known viruses in order to find isomorphic components. Usually ([6]) before extracting the CFG from a program P a set of normalization operations [28] are performed on the binary. This step aims to reduce the effects of mutation techniques. The normalized binary is then used to extract the CFG which is then compared to CFG extracted by normalized known malware. If the CFG of the normalized program contain a subgraph isomorphic to the CFG of a malware, then the executable is marked as malicious.

4 Using compilers to evade detection

The advances in malware detection and the plethora of different devices and operating systems in use nowadays, pose new intriguing challenges to malware writers. The use of assembly language is becoming more and more painful, because of the difficulties involved to write portable and easy-to-support code. In the forward-looking article "Recompiling the metamorphism" [20], the author, herm1t, suggests to make use of high level languages in order to overcome the difficulties involved in developing malware in pure assembly. He outlines how using a high level language gives to the developer the opportunity to easily extract additional information from the code, rather than builtin support for features like hashes, iterators or objects. The idea of "recompiling the metamorphism" is without any doubt interesting and introduces many advantages to the virus writer, however, not all the benefits of using compilers have been considered in detail. In order to evade new anti-malware techniques based on the extraction of semantic patterns from executables, compilers could play an important role. They, in fact, are able to generate executables characterized by very different structures and could be used in order to defeat detection mechanisms. In this respect we take into accounts the benefits introduced by using exotic compilers, like the `M/o/Vfuscator2` [3] in order to obtain different CFGs, thus fooling the CFG based detection.

Single instruction compilers as an evasion technique In [16], Dolan demonstrates the Turing-completeness of the `x86` instruction `mov`. After the publication of the article many people started to implement, most of the time for fun, single instruction compilers, capable to compile arbitrary programs into lists of only `mov` instructions. Several different instruction turned out to be Turing-complete, so many different single instruction compilers arose [4]. Even if at first sight it may seem just like a funny fact, the use of single instruction compilers has very interesting consequences. Since in single instruction compiled programs comparisons, jumps, function calls are all implemented with a single instruction, the resulting CFG is a single (usually long) basic block. This result is very interesting, because having a CFG composed by a single basic block make ineffective all detection mechanisms based on CFG isomorphism detection. Using a single instruction

[3] https://github.com/xoreaxeaxeax/movfuscator

[4] https://github.com/xoreaxeaxeax/movfuscator/tree/master/post

compiler, however, has its drawbacks. First of all a program compiled with a single instruction compiler could be considered suspicious, thus marked as malicious. In addition to that, the size of a program compiled with a single instruction compiler, is, most of the time, much bigger than the size of the same program compiled using the entire set of instructions. This introduces some problems to virus writers that in many cases have a limited space in the binary they are going to infect, so they should keep the malicious code as small as possible. Sometimes even the performances of the malicious code is important and programs compiled with a single instruction compiler usually are slower than traditional ones in terms of execution speed. These problems lead to rethink the way single instruction compilers are used for evasion purposes. A simple but effective solution could be splitting the source code at compilation time. In our implementation we mark with source code annotation the functions that we want to compile with a single instruction compiler, then at compilation time, making use of the tools provided by LLVM [29] we are able to build an executable that uses the full set of instructions for the code that cannot be used to determine its malicious behaviour and a single instruction for the malware routines. In this way we are able to build a much smaller executable that is still able to fool CFG based malware detection. It is important to underline that the single block of single instruction compiled code can be furtherly modified using the metamorphic techniques described in section 2. This single block can be also manipulated in order to obtain different CFGs, this can be easily done by inserting jumps or comparisons, thus creating branches in the graph. To further variate the result of the obfuscation, several different single instruction compilers can be adopted, resulting in a great variety of CFGs, making very hard for the detectors to extract signatures, both syntactically, due to metamorphic transformation, and semantically, thanks to the always changing CFG.

5 Conclusions

In this paper we presented and overview of the techniques used by malware in order to avoid detection as well as some detection mechanisms. We showed the benefits related to the use of compilers on the process of malware creation and we proposed the use of single instruction compilers as an evasion mechanisms for CFG based malware detection. In order to overcome the limitations of this kind of compilers we proposed several solutions that can greatly increase the ability of malware to hide itself from detectors.

References

1. Balakrishnan, A., Schulze, C.: Code obfuscation literature survey. CS701 Construction of compilers **19** (2005)
2. Barak, B., Goldreich, O., Impagliazzo, R., Rudich, S., Sahai, A., Vadhan, S., Yang, K.: On the (im) possibility of obfuscating programs. In: Annual International Cryptology Conference. pp. 1–18. Springer (2001)
3. Beaucamps, P., Filiol, É.: On the possibility of practically obfuscating programs towards a unified perspective of code protection. Journal in Computer Virology **3**(1), 3–21 (2007)

4. Bonfante, G., Kaczmarek, M., Marion, J.Y.: Control flow graphs as malware signatures. In: International workshop on the Theory of Computer Viruses (2007)
5. Briones, I., Gomez, A.: Graphs, entropy and grid computing: Automatic comparison of malware. Virus Bulletin pp. 1–12 (2008)
6. Bruschi, D., Martignoni, L., Monga, M.: Detecting self-mutating malware using control-flow graph matching. In: International Conference on Detection of Intrusions and Malware, and Vulnerability Assessment. pp. 129–143. Springer (2006)
7. Burges, C.J.: A tutorial on support vector machines for pattern recognition. Data mining and knowledge discovery **2**(2), 121–167 (1998)
8. Cesare, S., Xiang, Y.: Classification of malware using structured control flow. In: Proceedings of the Eighth Australasian Symposium on Parallel and Distributed Computing-Volume 107. pp. 61–70. Australian Computer Society, Inc. (2010)
9. Cesare, S., Xiang, Y.: A fast flowgraph based classification system for packed and polymorphic malware on the endhost. In: 2010 24th IEEE International Conference on Advanced Information Networking and Applications. pp. 721–728. IEEE (2010)
10. Chess, D.M., White, S.R.: An undetectable computer virus. In: Proceedings of Virus Bulletin Conference. vol. 5, pp. 1–4 (2000)
11. Christodorescu, M., Jha, S.: Static analysis of executables to detect malicious patterns. Tech. rep., WISCONSIN UNIV-MADISON DEPT OF COMPUTER SCIENCES (2006)
12. Christodorescu, M., Kinder, J., Jha, S., Katzenbeisser, S., Veith, H.: Malware normalization. Tech. rep., University of Wisconsin (2005)
13. Cifuentes, C., Van Emmerik, M.: Recovery of jump table case statements from binary code. Science of Computer Programming **40**(2-3), 171–188 (2001)
14. Cohen, F.: Computer viruses. Computers & security **6**(1), 22–35 (1987)
15. Collberg, C., Thomborson, C., Low, D.: A taxonomy of obfuscating transformations. Tech. rep., Department of Computer Science, The University of Auckland, New Zealand (1997)
16. Dolan, S.: mov is turing-complete. Tech. rep., Tech. rep. 2013 (cit. on p. 153) (2013)
17. Driller, M.: Metamorphism in practice. 29A Magazine **1**(6) (2002)
18. Dullien, T., Rolles, R.: Graph-based comparison of executable objects (english version). SSTIC **5**, 1–3 (2005)
19. Eskandari, M., Hashemi, S.: Metamorphic malware detection using control flow graph mining. Int. J. Comput. Sci. Network Secur **11**(12), 1–6 (2011)
20. herm1t: Recompiling the metamorphism. https://83.133.184.251/virensimulation.org/lib/vhe11.html (2002), accessed: 2018-11-13
21. Idika, N., Mathur, A.P.: A survey of malware detection techniques. Purdue University **48** (2007)
22. Jeong, K., Lee, H.: Code graph for malware detection. In: 2008 International Conference on Information Networking. pp. 1–5. IEEE (2008)
23. Julus, L.: Metamorphism. 29A Magazine **1**(5) (2000)
24. Kinder, J., Veith, H.: Jakstab: A static analysis platform for binaries. In: International Conference on Computer Aided Verification. pp. 423–427. Springer (2008)
25. Kolter, J.Z., Maloof, M.A.: Learning to detect malicious executables in the wild. In: Proceedings of the tenth ACM SIGKDD international conference on Knowledge discovery and data mining. pp. 470–478. ACM (2004)
26. Konstantinou, E., Wolthusen, S.: Metamorphic virus: Analysis and detection. Royal Holloway University of London **15**, 15 (2008)
27. Kruegel, C., Robertson, W., Valeur, F., Vigna, G.: Static disassembly of obfuscated binaries. In: USENIX security Symposium. vol. 13, pp. 18–18 (2004)
28. Lakhotia, A., Mohammed, M.: Imposing order on program statements to assist anti-virus scanners. In: Reverse Engineering, 2004. Proceedings. 11th Working Conference on. pp. 161–170. IEEE (2004)

29. Lattner, C., Adve, V.: Llvm: A compilation framework for lifelong program analysis & transformation. In: Proceedings of the international symposium on Code generation and optimization: feedback-directed and runtime optimization. p. 75. IEEE Computer Society (2004)
30. Lee, J., Jeong, K., Lee, H.: Detecting metamorphic malwares using code graphs. In: Proceedings of the 2010 ACM symposium on applied computing. pp. 1970–1977. ACM (2010)
31. Lyda, R., Hamrock, J.: Using entropy analysis to find encrypted and packed malware. IEEE Security & Privacy **5**(2), 40–45 (2007)
32. Mohanty, D.: Anti-virus evasion techniques and countermeasures. Published online at http://www. hackingspirits. com/eth-hac/papers/whitepapers. asp. **18** (2005)
33. Moser, A., Kruegel, C., Kirda, E.: Exploring multiple execution paths for malware analysis. In: Security and Privacy, 2007. SP'07. IEEE Symposium on. pp. 231–245. IEEE (2007)
34. Rajaat: Polimorphism. 29A Magazine **1**(3) (1999)
35. Sathyanarayan, V.S., Kohli, P., Bruhadeshwar, B.: Signature generation and detection of malware families. In: Australasian Conference on Information Security and Privacy. pp. 336–349. Springer (2008)
36. Schiffman, M.: A brief history of malware obfuscation: Part 1 of 2. Published online at https://blogs.cisco.com/security/a_brief_history_of_malware_obfuscation_part_1_of_2, accessed: 2018-11-13
37. Schiffman, M.: A brief history of malware obfuscation: Part 2 of 2. Published online at https://blogs.cisco.com/security/a_brief_history_of_malware_obfuscation_part_2_of_2, accessed: 2018-11-13
38. Schultz, M.G., Eskin, E., Zadok, F., Stolfo, S.J.: Data mining methods for detection of new malicious executables. In: Security and Privacy, 2001. S&P 2001. Proceedings. 2001 IEEE Symposium on. pp. 38–49. IEEE (2001)
39. Schwarz, B., Debray, S., Andrews, G.: Disassembly of executable code revisited. In: Reverse engineering, 2002. Proceedings. Ninth working conference on. pp. 45–54. IEEE (2002)
40. Shoshitaishvili, Y., Wang, R., Salls, C., Stephens, N., Polino, M., Dutcher, A., Grosen, J., Feng, S., Hauser, C., Kruegel, C., et al.: Sok:(state of) the art of war: Offensive techniques in binary analysis. In: 2016 IEEE Symposium on Security and Privacy (SP). pp. 138–157. IEEE (2016)
41. Stepan, A.: Improving proactive detection of packed malware. Virus Bulletin **1** (2006)
42. Szor, P., Ferrie, P.: Hunting for metamorphic. In: Virus bulletin conference. Prague (2001)
43. Troger, J., Cifuentes, C.: Analysis of virtual method invocation for binary translation. In: Reverse Engineering, 2002. Proceedings. Ninth Working Conference on. pp. 65–74. IEEE (2002)
44. Walenstein, A., Mathur, R., Chouchane, M.R., Lakhotia, A.: Normalizing metamorphic malware using term rewriting. In: Source Code Analysis and Manipulation, 2006. SCAM'06. Sixth IEEE International Workshop on. pp. 75–84. IEEE (2006)
45. Wong, W., Stamp, M.: Hunting for metamorphic engines. Journal in Computer Virology **2**(3), 211–229 (2006)
46. Xu, L., Sun, F., Su, Z.: Constructing precise control flow graphs from binaries. University of California, Davis, Tech. Rep (2009)
47. You, I., Yim, K.: Malware obfuscation techniques: A brief survey. In: Broadband, Wireless Computing, Communication and Applications (BWCCA), 2010 International Conference on. pp. 297–300. IEEE (2010)

An Information System to Track data and processes for food quality and bacterial pathologies prevention

Giuseppe Tradigo[1], Patrizia Vizza[1], Pierangelo Veltri[1], and Pietro Hiram Guzzi[1]

Surgical and Medical Science Department
Magna Graecia University of Catanzaro
{gtradigo, vizzap, veltri, hguzzi}@unicz.it

Abstract. Agricultural related products need to be tracked and treated to guarantee food quality as well as to minimize bacterial diffusion from production to human use. The main problem is related to the lack of tracking about provenance and detailed information about different aspects as, for example, environmental conditions and production sites, groundwater contamination, animal life quality and nutrition. For instance, tracking food process may help in identifying the contamination of lettuce production with escherichia coli bacteria. A controlled tracking mechanism in food supply chain ensures the wellness of citizens. Blockchain has been recently interested as technology to track production in each transaction of food process (e.g. in food origins and nutrition quality certification).

In this paper we present an information system able to model, monitor and track the entire food supply chain for farmland production which includes also milk production. The proposed framework is able to monitor agricultural areas where high quality land products (such as fruit and vegetables) and animal based foods (such as milk, cheese or meat) are produced, packed and then distributed. Moreover, the system provides different services, from land quality monitor to fruits check and milk control, by inserting and accessing useful information that allow the traceability of products. As future works, blockchain technology applied in the food supply chain could also be introduced to support the traceability process.

Keywords: Traceability · Information system · Food quality.

1 Introduction

The agricultural production has been integrated and improved to answer the always increasing requests from the market [1]. Globalization imposes that all simple rules related to natural time intervals have to be considered for agricultural production. Moreover, natural life cycle products in animal farms (e.g. excrements, dirty waters) need to be monitored due to the high pressure in land exploitation, and thus the arise of possible assimilation issues for the ground, which can lead to bacteria transmitted to agriculture products and thus to human. Geographical distribution, farm positions and logistics, i.e. distribution among animals (e.g., cows and pigs), with respect to plants land positioning have to be considered. The correlation among food productions and human potential diseases risk can be mapped by means of geographical information systems relating infections and disease cases obtained by clinical studies [2]. Moreover, rapid reconstruction of vegetables and fruits production, fresh milk nutrition characteristics as well as food provenance have been more and more required by consumers as well as by nutritionists.

Food traceability is the process of tracking any type of food through all phases of production, processing and distribution [3, 4]. Each step in the food chain needs to be tracked from raw materials (e.g., feed, livestock food, ingredients) to the final product up to the consumer. This is made by marking the documentation concerning the different processes in order to monitor the food safety of the citizen.

Modern foods need to be manipulated, processed and stored properly in order to guarantee low pathogens and security for a population-wide consumption. Nonetheless, the number of processing steps and their operational parameters have to be constantly checked and maintained to low threshold levels. In this way, the whole food process is a guarantee of safety and quality of produced food. In case of any issue, such as the recent USA case of Lettuce related Salmonella [5], it is mandatory to reconstruct the food generation process and distribution to gather the fail production issues. Recent salmonella events in USA were related to the production tainted lettuce that sickened more than 200 people in 36 states. In this case, one of the main relevant problem is the lack of limitation of zoonotic pressure (i.e., the impact of livestock on the environment pollution) on landfill. This can be avoided sampling lands, water sources and production by means of geographic database systems [6]. Data population during the farm production phases as well as the biological controls on farm production are related to managers as well as healthy related specialists that are in charge of monitoring production to control safe productions. Latter are generally demanded to government structures.

Different traceability tools are available [7, 9] to track products, but they do not support both food nutrition and control as well as do not guarantee or certificate safe and secure transactions. More recently, some initiatives and projects on the use of blockchain technology in food traceability have been proposed (see [8]). Nevertheless, they do not integrate functionalities for food traceability, nutrition, genetic analysis and production analytics. For instance, fresh milk requires safety procedures for quality maintaining (e.g., temperature and containment controls) as well as information enrichment by means of proteomics and genomics information.

To overcome these limitations and to support the farm production process, in this paper we propose a framework able to track information about: (i) agricultural production process tracking providing for biological controls on farmland related products, and (ii) data source tracking aiming to track milk, fruits and vegetables from their production processes in the supply chain, supporting storage and manipulation of their organoleptic and nutritional properties. The framework manages the recall of non-compliant products from the market, protecting consumers from flaws in the production process. The proposed framework represents a relevant mechanism able to support: (i) single farm (e.g. to reconstruct production phases in case of quality problems), (ii) food operators team (e.g., to prevent bacterial contamination), (iii) consumers (e.g. to track food provenience and gather nutritional as well as energy related characteristics).

The proposed framework has been used in a research project that involves the University of Catanzaro, with a heterogeneous research team composed by engineers, veterinarians, clinicians and nutritionists as well as an IT company and a farm operating in fresh milk and vegetables production, latter European-wide distributed. Preliminary results of this system have been presented in [10]. The paper presents the framework structure and samples of use case applications; finally, blockchain related solutions have been studying to be included in the framework to guarantee safe and reliable transactions in food productions.

2 The framework for farm production tracking

We report the design and implementation of the framework with particular reference to the farmland side.

2.1 Land control monitoring

We designed the proposed system, called SMAT (Sistema di Monitoraggio Ambientale e Territoriale, that means Environmental and Territorial Monitoring System), as a web-based one developed using the Grails framework and implemented to track the analysis and production phases. First results of this system have been previously published in [11].

In Figure 1 we report the data scheme supporting the analysis phases. Each farm, represented by the Company entity, is associated with a number of Assets (which can be of various types, e.g., vegetables, crops, waters, milk). Each Asset is in relationship with Samples, acquired during an analysis procedure. Figure 2 reports some screenshots about the SMAT subsystem which integrates functionalities for the asset analyses. Figure 2(a) reports the web client view of SMAT home page and Figure 2(b) shows an example of Asset creation. Moreover, Figure 2(c) and Figure 2(d) illustrate two types of analysis and biological tests for single sample viewing the bioanalytes dataset.

The analysis is useful to map and control, for instance, the use of water sources in production. Contaminated water sources affect crop production when

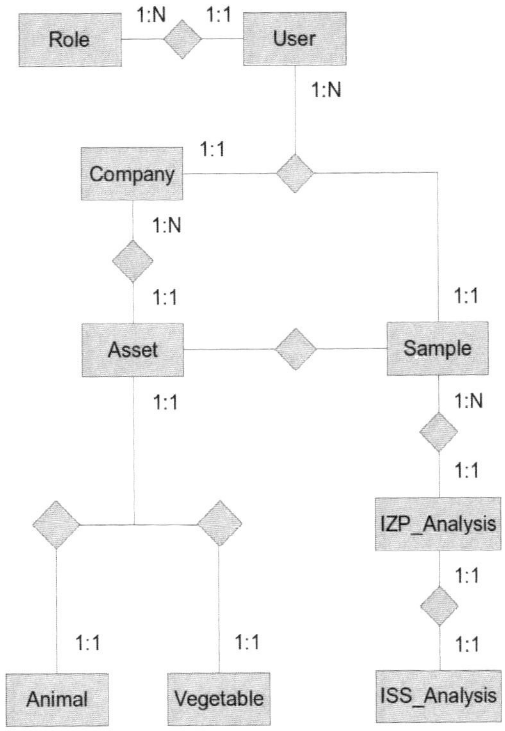

Fig. 1. Conceptual data scheme for the analysis phases.

contaminated water is used with pesticides or herbicides, crop irrigation or washing in post-harvest operations. Similarly, animals may close the cycle need to drink water free from contamination because pathogenic agents can rapidly reach the animal nutritions and then food related productions.

The system is also able to provide geographical modules able to relate productions as well as environmental data associated with indexes reported for instance from different data sources. E.g., in Figure 3 we report analysis of mapping geographically related farm with water source potential pollutions. The land related with water source pollution event (e.g. river) are related to farm that use potentially water pumped from soil. The map shows a part of Calabria (an Italian region) and the green circles indicates the risk area with highest contamination risk related to rivers.

2.2 Production process tracking

We here report the infrastructure related to the production processes and its traceability. The general overview of the traceability processes management system for milk, fruit and vegetables is showed in Figure 4.

We report about two cases. One refers to fruits and vegetables and the other is related to fresh milk. Elements of the traceability process are related to identification of the logistic units (i.e. aggregation of products for delivery) and batches (i.e. aggregation of a certain amount of product) involved in the production pro-

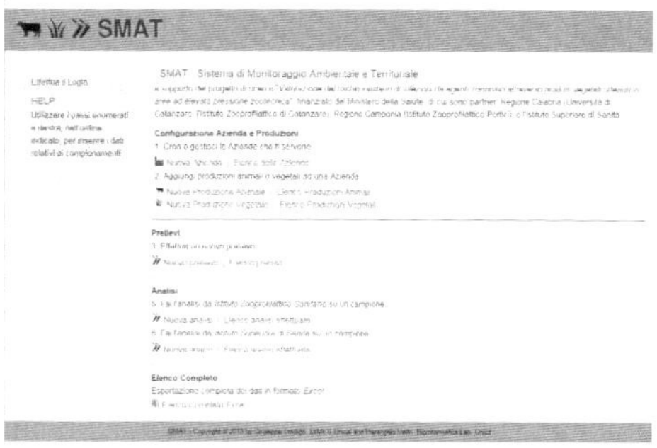

(a) SMAT home page.

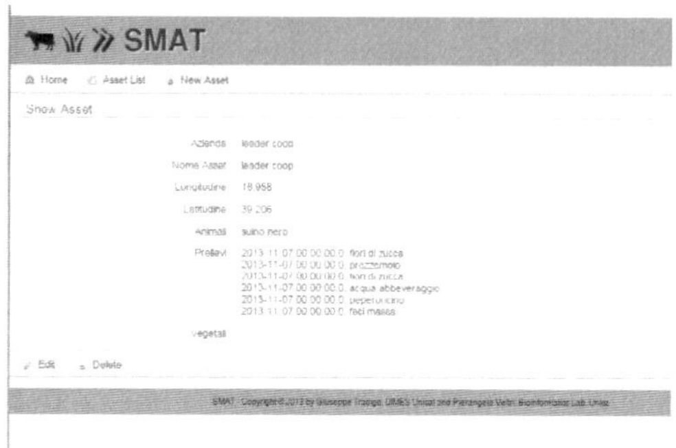

(b) SMAT asset creation.

(c) SMAT ISS analysis.

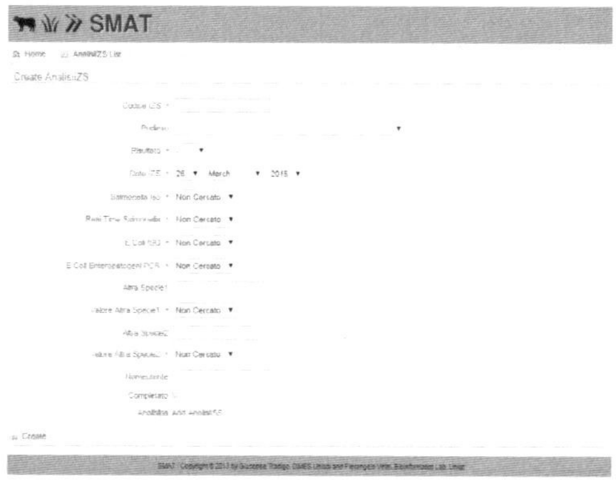

(d) SMAT IZS analsysis.

Fig. 2. SMAT web interfaces.

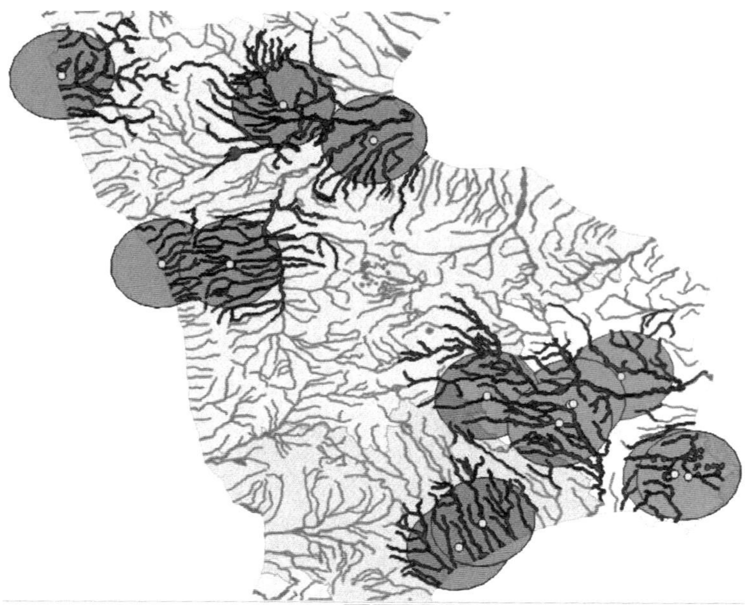

Fig. 3. Risky areas in green with the highest risk of contamination related to rivers.

cess in order to identify at any time the companies that have contributed to the

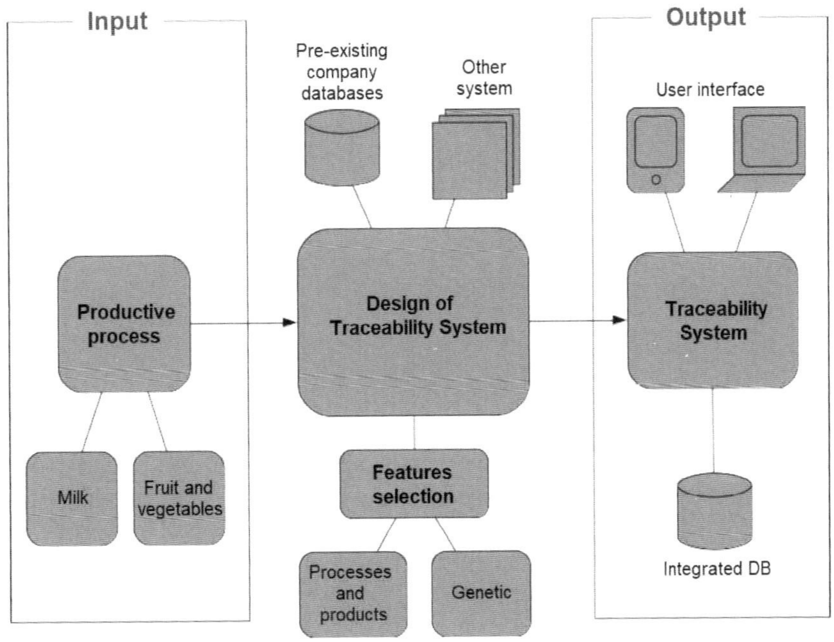

Fig. 4. Overview of the traceability process for milk, fruit and vegetable products with the interaction with external systems.

production of the raw materials. The tracking of the process consists essentially in the selection and registration of relevant information describing overall involved phases of the production process. A good production phase may contain data regarding administration, production, laboratory, packaging, logistics, cows feeding and phytosanitary treatments, functional foods and genetic.

The system aims to support the traceability process removing paper documentation and allowing only digital information. It is also able to track description and flows related to the production process, including check results and indications about the management and the verification of supply chain. The proposed traceability system allows the company to track all information about a specific batch (e.g., in the case of fruit and vegetables: the used fertilizers, harvest date and time, and phytosanitary treatments adopted). Moreover, QR-Code printed on the product label will be used to view all relevant information as the type of product and its variety, information of plants and land source. Indeed, the system is able to store, manage and retrieve these production steps, together with their specific properties. Thus, the possibility of knowing where, when and how a product has been manufactured, sent or stored, guarantees the wellness of consumers in that the process itself is rigorous, well known and also verifiable. Moreover, in case of an issue with any part of production, from a lot to a single product item, each party (e.g. user, company employee) is able to access the traceability system in order to verify all of the information about the product of interest, how and when it has been produced with specific process-related values.

This way, both the company's process awareness and the consumer confidence increase.

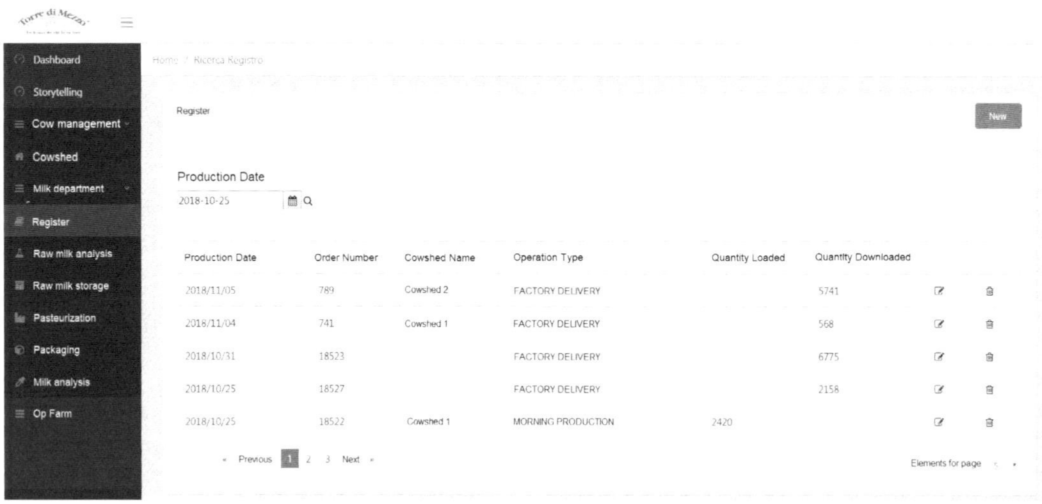

Fig. 5. Register about load/unload activity

An example of traceability system view is shown in Figure 5 reporting the register containing information about loading and unloading of products. It is also possible to shows the dashboard containing information about production trends and organoleptic tests as well as feedbacks that can be recovered from customers or users.

2.3 Customer applications

We now report some example and application of the customer view related to traceability for vegetables. We have information regarding nutraceutic (i.e., science of nutrition) as well as geographic data about production and provenience. Data are recovered from the databases that are loaded during the control and production phases reported above.

An App developed for customer about the track of nutraceutic characteristics and production of vegetables is shown in Figure 6. Figure 6(a) and 6(b) reports land production and nutraceutic information respectively that can be associated to fruits and vegetables. Finally, the customer is also able to track the information by starting reading by means of QR-Code an recovering information about the whole chain related to the fruits or lettuce. For example, Figure 7 reports about the possibility for customer to track information loaded from a QR-Code reported on the milk bottle. It is possible to track and recover information about cold process and cycle, as well as product conservation.

(a) Land production Information. (b) Nutraceutic Information.

Fig. 6. App Tracking Nutraceutic and Production of Vegetables.

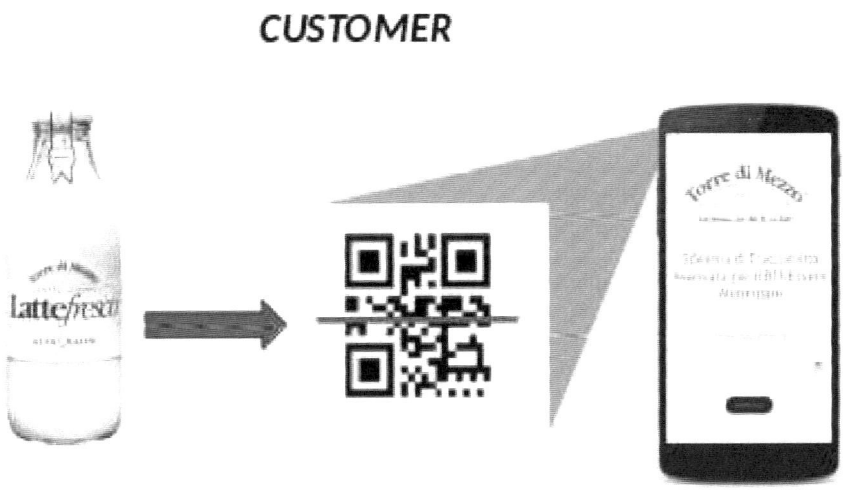

Fig. 7. Tracking nutraceutic information and production for fresh milk.

3 Security and Reliability of Tracking Phases: blockchain investigation

In this contribution, we investigated how blockchain technology can be used to provide greater asset traceability in food supply chains [12].

The food supply chain includes a lot of players (e.g. farmers, processors, distributors, packagers and grocers) often from different regions or countries and with own private record-keeping systems. Blockchain's capability of tracking ownership records and counteracting information tampering can be used to solve many issues in food supply chain as, for example, food fraud, safety recalls, supply chain inefficiency and food traceability [13, 14]. In this context, blockchain could make a positive impact on the food ecosystem.

Traceability is critical for the food supply chain and it can be ensured by the blockchain: each player along the supply chain generates and securely shares data points to create an accountable and traceable system. As a result, the record of a food process, from farm to table, is available to be monitored in real-time, ensuring moreover food safety.

For example, in fresh food supply chain, blockchain technology can provide the following potential use: (i) provenance, for a stronger warranty of origin and chain-of-custody; (ii) recalls, for a faster and more precise recalls; (iii) freshness, for fresher products reducing waste and spoilage; (iv) safety, for minor contamination problems.

We are currently investigating on the impact of this new technology and performing experiments for its integration in our traceability system architecture. This is particularly complex because of the involvement of both private (e.g., farmers, distributors) and public (e.g, Italian Health Agencies) actors in the process.

4 Conclusion

The presented traceability framework represents a valid solution to track and control the whole food process from raw materials up to distribution and marketing. The system is able to manage critical points for production, logistics and work organization, developing a safeness growth for consumer wellness. Moreover, the framework is also able to perform a land monitoring and it furnishes a simply app to be used by customer to obtain production details of the purchased product. Finally, blockchain technology has been introduced as an innovative solution in traceability process.

Acknowledgment

This paper presents results which have been partially funded by POR CALABRIA FESR-FSE 2014-2020 SISTABENE project. We thank Ithea S.r.l. for its contribution to the implementation of the system.

References

1. Lehmann, R. J., Reiche, R., Schiefer, G.: Future internet and the agri-food sector: State-of-the-art in literature and research, Computers and Electronics in Agriculture, 89:158-174, 2012.
2. Tradigo, G., Cannataro, M., Guzzi, P. H., Veltri, P.: Geomedica: a web portal for managing and querying clinical and biological data (Demo Paper). Proceedings of SEBD, 350–353, 2010.
3. Jongen, W. M. F., Meulenberg, M.: Innovation in Agri-food Systems, Wageningen Academic Pub, 2005.
4. Lamine, C., Renting, H., Rossi, A., Wiskerke, J. H., Brunori, G.: Agri-food systems and territorial development: innovations, new dynamics and changing governance mechanisms, In Farming Systems Research into the 21st century: The new dynamic, Springer, Dordrecht, 229-256, 2012.
5. Pretz, K.: How Blockchain Technology Could Track and Trace Food From Farm to Fork. The Institute, The IEEE news source, 2018.
6. Caroprese, L., Zumpano, E.: Integration of Unsound Data in P2P Systems, In Advances in Databases and Information Systems (ADBIS), 278-290, Budapest, Hungary, September 2-5, 2018.
7. Opara, L. U.: Traceability in agriculture and food supply chain: a review of basic concepts, technological implications, and future prospects. Journal of Food Agriculture and Environment, 1, 101–106, 2003.
8. Trusted food provenance on blockchain. Retrieved May 20, 2019, from https://www.trustprovenance.com/
9. Badia-Melis, R., Mishra, P., Ruiz-Garca, L.: Food traceability: New trends and recent advances. A review, Food Control, 57,393–401, 2015.
10. Vizza, P., Tradigo, G., Veltri, P., Lambardi, P., Garofalo, C., Caligiuri, F. M., Caligiuri, G., Guzzi, P. H.: Tracking agricultural products for wellness care. In 2018 IEEE International Conference on Bioinformatics and Biomedicine (BIBM), 2064–2067, 2018.
11. Tradigo, G., Cannataro, M., Guzzi, P. H., Casalinuovo, F., Veltri, P., Graziani, C.: Health risk assessment of zoonotic infections agents through plant products in areas with high livestock pressure. In Proceedings of the First ACM SIGSPATIAL International Workshop on Use of GIS in Public Health, 72–74, 2012.
12. Ge, L., Brewster, C., Spek, J., Smeenk, A., Top, J., van Diepen, F., Klaase, B., Graumans, C., de Wildt, M. D. R.: Blockchain for agriculture and food: Findings from the pilot study (No. 2017-112). Wageningen Economic Research, 2017.
13. Galvez, J. F., Mejuto, J. C., Simal-Gandara, J.: Future challenges on the use of blockchain for food traceability analysis. TrAC Trends in Analytical Chemistry, 107, 222–232, 2018.
14. Chen, S., Shi, R., Ren, Z., Yan, J., Shi, Y., Zhang, J.: A blockchain-based supply chain quality management framework. In 2017 IEEE 14th International Conference on e-Business Engineering (ICEBE), 172–176, 2017.

CNN-based System for Low Resolution Face Recognition (Discussion Paper)

Fabio Valerio Massoli[0000-0001-6447-1301], Giuseppe Amato[0000-0003-0171-4315], Fabrizio Falchi[0000-0001-6258-5313], Claudio Gennaro[0000-0002-0967-5050], and Claudio Vairo[0000-0003-2740-4331]

ISTI-CNR, via G. Moruzzi 1, 56124 Pisa, Italy
{fabio.massoli, giuseppe.amato, fabrizio.falchi, claudio.gennaro, claudio.vairo}@isti.cnr.it

Abstract Since the publication of the AlexNet in 2012, Deep Convolutional Neural Network models became the most promising and powerful technique for image representation. Specifically, the ability of their inner layers to extract high level abstractions of the input images, called deep features vectors, has been employed. Such vectors live in a high dimensional space in which an inner product and thus a metric is defined. The latter allows to carry out similarity measurements among them. This property is particularly useful in order to accomplish tasks such as Face Recognition. Indeed, in order to identify a person it is possible to compare deep features, used as face descriptors, from different identities by means of their similarities. Surveillance systems, among others, utilize this technique. To be precise, deep features extracted from probe images are matched against a database of descriptors from known identities.
A critical point is that the database typically contains features extracted from high resolution images while the probes, taken by surveillance cameras, can be at a very low resolution. Therefore, it is mandatory to have a neural network which is able to extract deep features that are robust with respect to resolution variations.
In this paper we discuss a CNN-based pipeline that we built for the task of Face Recognition among images with different resolution. The entire system relies on the ability of a CNN to extract deep features that can be used to perform a similarity search in order to fulfill the face recognition task.

Keywords: Convolutional Neural Networks · Face Recognition · Ensemble Methods.

1 Introduction

Content based image retrieval (CBIR) is one of the most active research field in the computer vision community. In this context, commonly faced tasks are instance-level retrieval and class retrieval [16]. In the former, given a query image, the goal is to retrieve images that contain the same object regardless of image distortions such as different illumination, rotation or occlusion. Instead, in the latter the purpose is to retrieve all the available images that belong to the same class.

Before the advent of the Convolutional Neural Networks (CNN), the scale-invariant feature transform [12] (SIFT) based methods were among the most frequently used in order to extract global descriptors from the given images. A breakthrough occurred in 2012 when the AlexNet [9] was created and won the ImageNet Large Scale Visual Recognition Competition (ILSRVC) improving upon the state-of-the-art by a noticeable margin. Since then, CNN-based methods for image retrieval received considerably more attention from the scientific community [1], [15].

Under the hood, these methods rely on the ability of deep models to extract the so called deep features from given input images. From a theoretical perspective, the inner layers of a CNN realize an abstraction of the input that describes specific concepts contained inside the data. Moreover, due to the typical structure of deep models architecture, inner layers combine the information available from previous layers thus achieving a higher level of abstraction that summarizes the overall content of the input data. Based on this observation, deep features are usually adopted as global descriptors for input images. Thus, the deeper the layer from which we extract deep features is, the more descriptive of the input they are. It is common practice to extract them from the penultimate layer of a CNN.

As previously said, deep features are high dimensional vectors defined in a space on which it is defined an inner product and thus a metric. This property is fundamental since it allows to evaluate similarities among descriptors, extracted from different images, that can be used as indicators of the similarities of the content of the original data. An example of this principle is sketched in Figure 1.

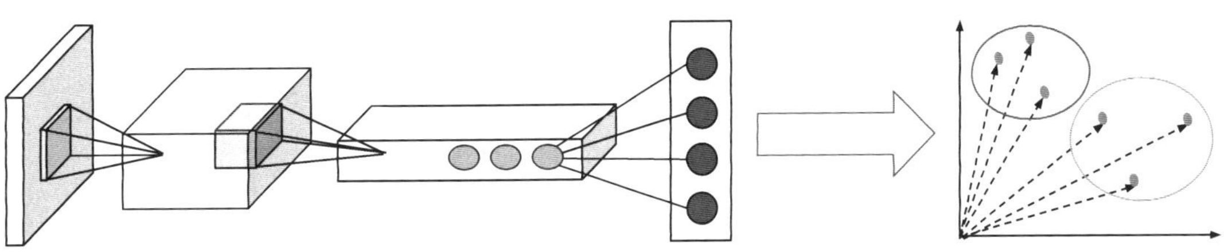

Figure 1. Schematic example of a CNN-based features extraction method for images that belong to two different classes. Vectors from same images tends to cluster in the arrival space.

This concept is typically applied in the context of surveillance systems. Indeed, in a scenario where an input face image is acquired by a camera, its global descriptor is extracted and used in order to perform a similarity search on a database (db) containing a gallery of features vectors that belong to known identities. For example, the research in the db can be accomplished by evaluating the cosine similarity, or the Euclidean distance, among the probe and gallery vectors.

The similarity search becomes even more challenging when gallery and probe come from different resolution domains.

This is the background from which we started the study we present in this paper. Our final goal is to conceive a pipeline for face recognition based on neural networks. In order to extract deep features we used a pre-trained ResNet-50 [7] architecture, with Squeeze-and-Excitation blocks [8]. The extracted descriptors are then used to perform a similarity measurements.

The performance of the deep model used for features extraction has been evaluated on the 1:1 verification protocol on the IARPA Janus Benchmark-B (IJB-B) dataset [17].

1.1 Paper Organization

The remaining part of the paper is organized as follows. In Section 2 we briefly review some related works. In Section 3 we describe in detail the pipeline that we implemented. In Section 4 we present the experimental results. In Section 5 we conclude the paper with a summary of the main results and future perspectives.

2 Related Works

Deep learning techniques are currently experiencing a huge expansion in their field of application mainly as a result of the extremely high computational power reached by the modern GPUs. Moreover, the existence of big datasets [11], [18], [3], [2] and [6] has made it possible to train neural networks and to let them nearly reach human levels of performance when tested against tasks such as image classification [9], object detection [4] and face recognition [14].

Due to its wide range of applications, the task of Face Recognition (FR) is among the hottest topics in the computer vision community. In particular, FR plays a key role in the context of smart surveillance systems [10], [13]. In such systems, the case is usually that a low resolution face image, taken by a surveillance camera, has to be matched against a database containing deep features extracted from high resolution images.

To this end, several techniques have been developed in order to train deep models to deal with low resolution images. Some examples are Super Resolution and Common Space Projection techniques.

Super Resolution is a technique based on the ability of a neural network to synthesize a high resolution image starting from a low resolution one. The recognition task is later fulfilled in the high resolution domain [5].

One of the weaknesses of the super resolution technique is that the identity information can be lost. In [20] they developed a neural network that, together with the super resolution task, tries to recover the initial low resolution image identity in the high resolution one.
Instead, Common Space Projection techniques concern the ability of a neural networks to minimize the distance among deep features, in a common space, extracted from a low resolution image and its high resolution counterpart.
For example, in [19] they train a two-branch CNN to learn a mapping from high/low resolution domain to a common space. Specifically, given a low and high resolution image, the model extracts features vectors of size 2048 and their distance is evaluated and used as loss in order to lead the training towards the desired direction.

3 Pipeline

In this section we briefly describe the main modules of the pipeline we developed. A schematic view is shown in Figure 2.

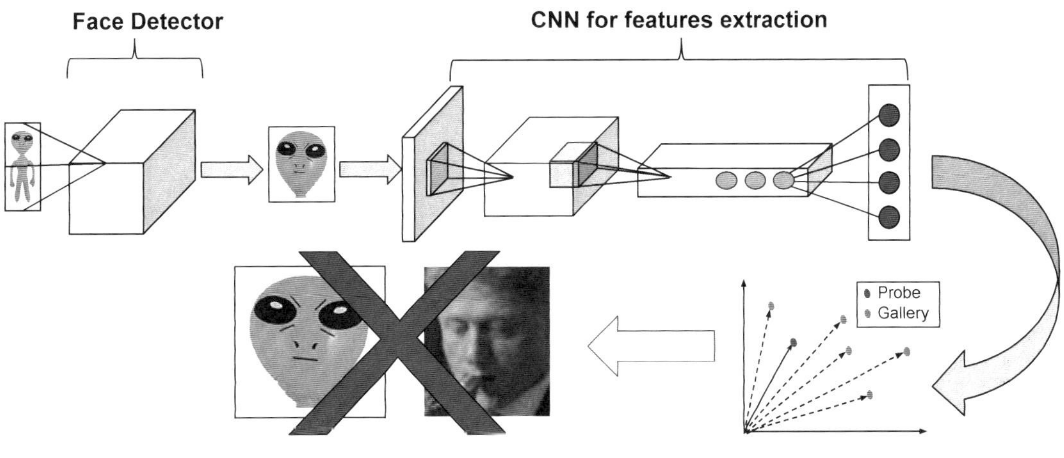

Figure 2. Sketch of the implemented pipeline.

There are three main components at the heart of the system: a face detector, a features extractor and a classifier. We will be focusing on the first two.
The face detection task is accomplished by means of a multi-stage architecture that, given an input image, delivers the coordinates of the bounding boxes that are centred around each face visible in the image. Specifically, we used the Multi-task Cascaded Convolutional Neural Networks (MTCNN) [21]. This step is performed once for each input frame. After all the faces have been identified from the picture, they are cropped, preprocessed and then used as input for the features extractor. The preprocess step includes the rescaling of the image with the shortest side resized at 256 pixels, the cropping of the squared central

region with side of 224 pixels and the normalization of the image
The features extractor module is made of a ResNet-50 [7] architecture, equipped with Squeeze-and-Excitation [8] blocks, that has been pretrained on the VGGFace2 dataset [3].
Features vectors are extracted before the classification layer, they have dimensionality equals to 2048 and they have been L_2-normalized before to evaluate any metric on them.

4 Experimental Tests

In order to test the performance of the features extractor we used the IJB-B dataset [17]. In particular, we tested the model against the 1:1 verification protocol aiming to estimate its ability to extract discriminative features. Due to the low resolution requirements for a surveillance system, we conducted the performance evaluation using the dataset with different resolutions. In Figure 3, we show an example of the various resolution versions of the test images. The first column contains the full resolution test images while from the second to the last column down sampled images in the [8, 256] pixels range are shown.

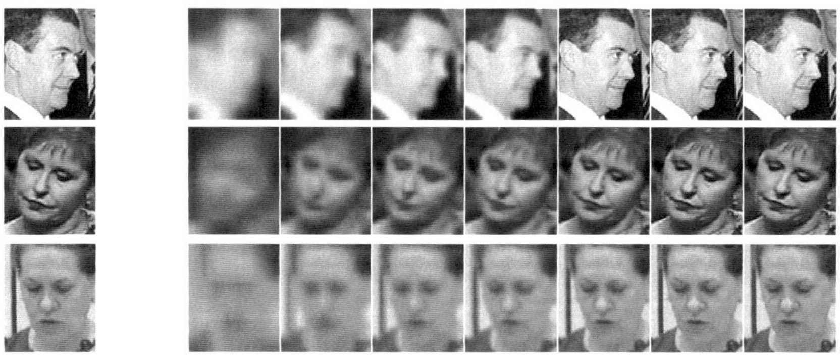

Figure 3. Example of images down sampled at various resolutions. First column: images at full resolutions. Second - Last columns: down sampled images in [8x, 256x] pixels.

The resulting Receiver Operating Characteristic (ROC) for the 1:1 verification task is shown in Figure 4.

In order to evaluate the similarity among the different features vectors we measured the cosine similarity among them. As it is clear from Figure 4 the performance of the features extractor are degraded for lower resolution, especially below 32 pixels. Moreover in Table 1 we reported the True Acceptance Rate (TAR) at a reference value for the False Acceptance Rate (FAR) of $1.e^{-3}$.

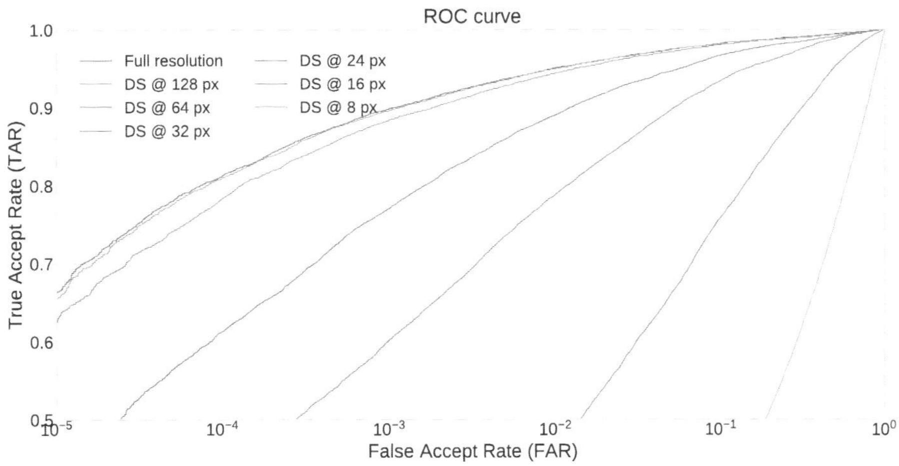

Figure 4. Feature extractor Receiver Operating Characteristic (ROC) for different values of the image resolution (DS stands for "Down Sampled").

Table 1. True Acceptance Rate (TAR @ FAR = $1.e^{-3}$) for different values of the images resolution.

Architecture	**TAR (@ FAR = 1.e−3)**						
	8	**16**	**24**	**32**	**64**	**128**	**256**
Se-ResNet-50	4.8	24.4	60.2	77.0	88.3	89.5	89.8

Up until now, we have considered the case in which the images had the same resolution. In a real scenario it usually happens that probe and gallery have different resolutions. For example, in the case of surveillance systems it is common that the gallery database is populated with high resolution images descriptors while the probe has a lower resolution.
In Table 2 we reported the value for the TAR @ FAR equals to $1.e^{-3}$ for the cross resolution 1:1 verification task.
It is clear from Table 2 that the cross resolution face recognition task is very challenging for a deep neural network model, especially when the images have very low resolutions.

5 Conclusion and Future Experiments

Surveillance systems require high performance from CNN-based systems on the face recognition task. Precisely, the deep models have to be robust with respect to variations of the input image resolution since it is usually the case that low resolution images, from surveillance cameras, have to be matched against a database containing deep features extracted from high resolution images. In fact, the descriptor extracted for each human face have to be robust with respect to resolution variations otherwise any kind of similarity search across the identities

Table 2. True Acceptance Rate (TAR @ FAR = $1.e^{-3}$) for 1:1 verification protocol considering images with mixed resolutions.

		Image Resolution (pixel)						
		8	16	24	32	64	128	256
Image Resolution (pixel)	8	**4.8**						
	16	0.2	**24.4**					
	24	0.2	18.6	**60.2**				
	32	0.2	9.0	65.3	**77.0**			
	64	0.2	2.9	60.4	80.5	**88.3**		
	128	0.2	2.4	57.9	80.1	88.9	**89.5**	
	256	0.2	2.3	57.5	80.1	90.0	89.7	**89.8**

database will fail. We have seen that, even though there are models that perform well on the FR task, their performances suddenly drop when we used low resolution images.

Although we have shown the feasibility of a pipeline for FR based on deep models, we need to improve upon its performance especially in the case of mixed resolutions. Thus, we are planning a new training campaign focused on the low resolution domain below 32 pixels. Finally, we will pay particular attention to the case of FR in which probe and gallery have different resolutions. What we expect from such a campaign is that, even if we might obtain a small drop in the performance at high resolution, the improvement at low and mixed resolutions should outweigh that drop.

References

1. Babenko, A., Slesarev, A., Chigorin, A., Lempitsky, V.: Neural codes for image retrieval. In: European conference on computer vision. pp. 584–599. Springer (2014)
2. Bansal, A., Nanduri, A., Castillo, C.D., Ranjan, R., Chellappa, R.: Umdfaces: An annotated face dataset for training deep networks. In: 2017 IEEE International Joint Conference on Biometrics (IJCB). pp. 464–473. IEEE (2017)
3. Cao, Q., Shen, L., Xie, W., Parkhi, O.M., Zisserman, A.: Vggface2: A dataset for recognising faces across pose and age. In: 2018 13th IEEE International Conference on Automatic Face & Gesture Recognition (FG 2018). pp. 67–74. IEEE (2018)
4. Girshick, R., Donahue, J., Darrell, T., Malik, J.: Region-based convolutional networks for accurate object detection and segmentation. IEEE transactions on pattern analysis and machine intelligence **38**(1), 142–158 (2016)
5. Grm, K., Pernuš, M., Cluzel, L., Scheirer, W., Dobrišek, S., Štruc, V.: Face hallucination revisited: An exploratory study on dataset bias. arXiv preprint arXiv:1812.09010 (2018)
6. Guo, Y., Zhang, L., Hu, Y., He, X., Gao, J.: Ms-celeb-1m: A dataset and benchmark for large-scale face recognition. In: European Conference on Computer Vision. pp. 87–102. Springer (2016)
7. He, K., Zhang, X., Ren, S., Sun, J.: Deep residual learning for image recognition. In: Proceedings of the IEEE conference on computer vision and pattern recognition. pp. 770–778 (2016)

8. Hu, J., Shen, L., Sun, G.: Squeeze-and-excitation networks. arxiv (2017)
9. Krizhevsky, A., Sutskever, I., Hinton, G.E.: Imagenet classification with deep convolutional neural networks. In: Advances in neural information processing systems. pp. 1097–1105 (2012)
10. Lavi, B., Serj, M.F., Ullah, I.: Survey on deep learning techniques for person reidentification task. arXiv preprint arXiv:1807.05284 (2018)
11. Learned-Miller, E., Huang, G.B., RoyChowdhury, A., Li, H., Hua, G.: Labeled faces in the wild: A survey. In: Advances in face detection and facial image analysis, pp. 189–248. Springer (2016)
12. Lowe, D.G.: Distinctive image features from scale-invariant keypoints. International journal of computer vision **60**(2), 91–110 (2004)
13. Nikouei, S.Y., Chen, Y., Song, S., Xu, R., Choi, B.Y., Faughnan, T.: Smart surveillance as an edge network service: From harr-cascade, svm to a lightweight cnn. In: 2018 IEEE 4th International Conference on Collaboration and Internet Computing (CIC). pp. 256–265. IEEE (2018)
14. Parkhi, O.M., Vedaldi, A., Zisserman, A., et al.: Deep face recognition. In: bmvc. vol. 1, p. 6 (2015)
15. Tolias, G., Sicre, R., Jégou, H.: Particular object retrieval with integral max-pooling of cnn activations. arXiv preprint arXiv:1511.05879 (2015)
16. Torresani, L., Szummer, M., Fitzgibbon, A.: Efficient object category recognition using classemes. In: European conference on computer vision. pp. 776–789. Springer (2010)
17. Whitelam, C., Taborsky, E., Blanton, A., Maze, B., Adams, J., Miller, T., Kalka, N., Jain, A.K., Duncan, J.A., Allen, K., et al.: Iarpa janus benchmark-b face dataset. In: Proceedings of the IEEE Conference on Computer Vision and Pattern Recognition Workshops. pp. 90–98 (2017)
18. Wolf, L., Hassner, T., Maoz, I.: Face recognition in unconstrained videos with matched background similarity. IEEE (2011)
19. Zangeneh, E., Rahmati, M., Mohsenzadeh, Y.: Low resolution face recognition using a two-branch deep convolutional neural network architecture. arXiv preprint arXiv:1706.06247 (2017)
20. Zhang, K., Zhang, Z., Cheng, C.W., Hsu, W.H., Qiao, Y., Liu, W., Zhang, T.: Super-identity convolutional neural network for face hallucination. In: Proceedings of the European Conference on Computer Vision (ECCV). pp. 183–198 (2018)
21. Zhang, K., Zhang, Z., Li, Z., Qiao, Y.: Joint face detection and alignment using multitask cascaded convolutional networks. IEEE Signal Processing Letters **23**(10), 1499–1503 (2016)

A Visual Analytics Platform to Measure Performance on University Entrance Tests (Discussion Paper)

Daniele Boncoraglio[3], Francesca Deri[3], Francesco Distefano[3], Daniele Fadda[1,2], Giorgio Filippi[3], Giuseppe Forte[3], Federica Licari[3], Michela Natilli[1,2], Dino Pedreschi[1], and Salvatore Rinzivillo[2]

[1] Computer Science Department - University of Pisa, Italy pedre@di.unipi.it
[2] KDDLab, ISTI-CNR Pisa, Italy {daniele.fadda,michela.natilli, rinzivillo}@isti.cnr.it
[3] CISIA - Consorzio Interuniversitario Sistemi Integrati per l'Accesso, Pisa, Italy name.surname@cisiaonline.it

Abstract. Data visualization dashboards provide an efficient approach that helps to improve the ability to understand the information behind complex databases. It is possible with such tools to create new insights, to represent keys indicators of the activity, to communicate (in real-time) snapshots of the state of the work. In this paper, we present a visual analytics platform created for the exploration and analysis of performance data on entrance tests taken by Italian students when entering the university career. The data is provided by CISIA (Consorzio Interuniversitario Sistemi Integrati per l'Accesso), a non-profit consortium formed exclusively by public universities. With this platform, it is possible to explore the performance of the students along different dimensions, such as gender, high school of provenience, type of test and so on.

Keywords: Data visualization · Performance indicators · University test.

1 Introduction

The effective graphical presentation of information is an essential skill in most scientific disciplines. Visualization is intended to clearly convey and communicate information through graphical means, enabling everyone to comprehend data in a much more explicit way[1]. Through visualization, the results of data processing are made more accessible, straightforward, and user-friendly[2]. Communicating information through visual analytic techniques facilitates understanding of information to those who have no specific technical or domain knowledge[3].

A proper way to describe graphically a complex phenomenon is through the use of dashboards. As stated in [4], "compared to visualization modalities for presentation and exploration, dashboards bring together challenges of at-a-glance reading, coordinated views, tracking data and both private and shared awareness". The access to complex phenomena is made possible through the realization of multiple linked displays [5], where sub-dimensions of the whole data are showed in details and the interaction on one display propagate selection and filtering to the other's views. Thus, the complexity of the data to explore is mitigated through the use of interaction with the observer.

In this paper we present a visual analytic platform created for the exploration and analysis of performance data on entry tests taken by Italian students before entering the university career. The data is provided by CISIA[4] (Consorzio Interuniversitario Sistemi Integrati per l'Accesso), a non-profit consortium formed by public universities. Currently, CISIA consortium counts 45 Universities and the Conferences of Engineering, Architecture and Sciences among the consortium members: the CUIA - Italian University Architecture Conference, the CopI - Conference for Engineering and Con.Scienze - National Conference of Presidents and Structure Directors University of Science and Technology.

The Consortium is open to the participation of all Italian universities; among the different statutory purposes, the main is to organize and coordinate the orientation activities for the access to the universities. Entrance test organized by CISIA serve two different purposes:

- for students enrolling the test, it provides a self-assessment of their preparation and aptitude to undertake the chosen field of studies;
- for the faculties and departments, the tests gives a view of the actual knowledge of the students, and let the management to compare it with the minimum skills and capabilities requirements in order to prepare specific orientation and training activities.

For those course with a restricted number of students, the tests are used as screening and ranking tools. CISIA tests are currently available for six areas: Engineering, Economics, Pharmacy, Sciences, Humanities, and Agriculture.

2 The visual analytics platform

2.1 Problem statement

CISIA Online Test (acronym TOLC) is a tool for orientation and assessment of the knowledge required for access to the Study Programs of Italian Universities, which can be used to select students for access, provided on a computerized platform. TOLC is an individual test, different from student to student, automatically composed for each student by a software. The software follows a set of recipes to guarantee that all the tests generated are equivalent in terms of the level of difficulty. The objective of the platform proposed in this paper is

[4] http://www.cisiaonline.it

to provide an analytic framework where all the performances on each test may be analyzed. Historical data are maintained since 2012, and they register many dimensions from each test: the number of correct answers, high school education of the student attending the test, the geographical origin, the category of each question in the test. Thus the platform should allow an efficient exploration of the many dimensions and should produce an accessible interface where the observer may interact with the data. During the design phase, we identified two kind of users: public visitor of the website of the consortium, and the site managers of the department that organize the tests. The two profiles are managed through a similar web interface, whereas the users with an authorized account may access more detailed data, for example analyzing the performance of the tests organized in her own site.

2.2 Platform design

Accordingly to Sarikaya et al. [4], we may classify our platform as a Communication Dashboard, whose purpose is to inform the public about Consortium activities. Since it is a public dashboard whose primary purpose is to describe social relevant data, great attention was given to the privacy of the users who performed the tests. All data delivered by the platform are anonymized through aggregation and filtering. The subset of data with few representatives (i.e. few users attending the test) is removed from the analysis. This filtering phase allows us to enforce the statistic robustness of the presented data and also to make not identifiable any student in the dataset. One of the main objectives of the platform was the accessibility even for non-expert users. We select only charts that are widely recognizable, mainly bar chart and line chart. To show in details some distributions we also adopted a box plot chart. To guarantee high readability of the result of the chart, we inserted a very detailed explanation of how to read the graph. The user can explore the data through three dimensions: year, area of interest, geographic origin. It is possible to apply a filter to restrict the analysis only on the top 10% ranking tests (best scores). A subset of charts also allows a specialized dimension on gender. The selection of the dimensions to be analyzed can be managed by the user through an integrated toolbox, where the current selection is always visible. When the user modifies one of the dimensions, the visualization is updated.

A schematic representation of the architecture of the CISIAViz platform is presented in Fig.1. The database layer is organized with two levels. The production database used to manage the tests is kept separated from the CISIAViz platform. An ETL (Extract, Transform, and Load) procedure is scheduled to update a staging database for the visualization. During this phase, sensitive information is removed.

The database is running over an instance of MySQL, the same DBMS adopted for the rest of the TOLC system. The data warehouse schema in Fig.2 shows the relations implemented within the DB. The entity *Test* is the main table containing all the results of each test. Since the sections for all the possible tests are limited, we decided to store them into the field within this table. The test

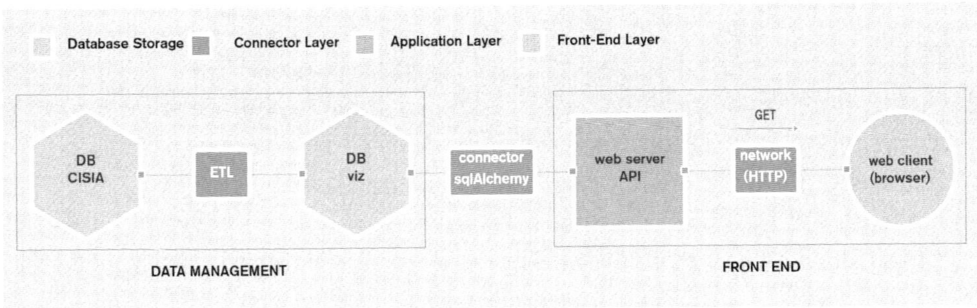

Fig. 1. Web-App schema: Starting from CISIA database, through a process of Extract, Transform, Load (ETL), we build the data warehouse (DB viz). The data warehouse contains only the data that is of interest to the CISIAViz platform. During the ETL phase, new dimensions are calculated (such as the ranking of students by type of test) and some queries are optimized by materializing data (including redundant ones) retrieved from different tables to speed up the subsequent reading phase via web API.

provided in a different area of interests may have different compositions. When a test does not contain a specific section, the corresponding value in the table will be NULL. On one side, this implementation makes the schema of the DB not flexible to accommodate new sections. On the other hand, this allows much faster access during the visualization, as it does not need to create too many joins between the tables.

The relevant dimensions of the star schema are *Geo*, the geographic dimension, and *Time*, the time dimension: the first one is used to explore the origin of the students applying for the test, and the second one allows us to select the time interval to aggregate the tests. Although it is possible to aggregate for an arbitrary temporal interval, to guarantee a sufficient aggregation for sensitive information, the time selection is restricted at the year level.

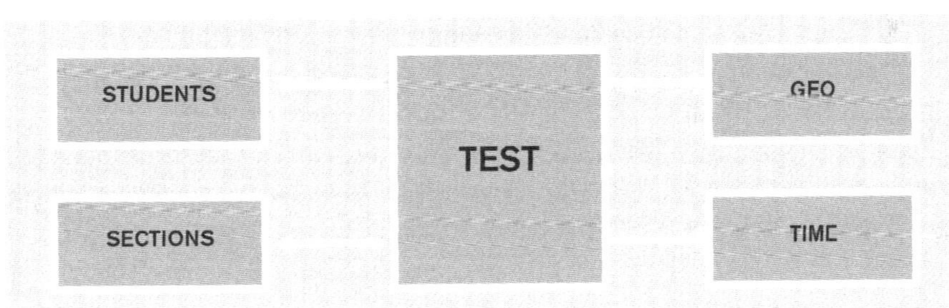

Fig. 2. The schema of the data warehouse. The fact table contains the details of each test performed by each student. This table is linked with the geographical dimension to determine the origin of each student and the temporal dimension to select the time window to analyze.

The access to the database is managed by an application server running a web API implementing the endpoints to access the data. All the interaction of the user with the visualization dashboard will be translated into the corresponding call from the web application. The access to the web API is managed through HTTP GET calls. The authentication, implemented with an SSO system (Single Sign-On) using an IDP (Identification Provider) of the consortium, is performed with HTTP-POST methods. When the user changes the preferences on the dimensions, the web application generates a set of call to the Web API to retrieve the updated data. The application server is implemented in Python, leveraging the Flask library to handle the implementation of the endpoints. The web application running in the front end is a single page application running in Javascript. The dashboard is implemented using the state of the art libraries for managing of user interfaces: *D3.js* to create custom visualization; *Vue.js* to manage the events and selection of the user and to make the internal data representation reactive to new updates; *Plot.ly* to construct high-level charts using configuration descriptors automatically generated by data.

2.3 Backend

The majority of the endpoints of the Web API share a common parameter structure. This design choice allows us to make the front end flexible by composing the set of parameters automatically to be provided to the server. All the selection a user can make on the web interface are projected into a sequence of parameter values that are sent to the web server. All calls that depend on this filter have the following scheme:

```
@ app.route('/api/function_rest/<year>/<area_interest>/<region>/<quantile>')
```

where <year> and <area_interest> are the only mandatory parameters. The parameters reflect the possible combination of the dimensions the user may explore:

<years> Selection of the year in a range between 2012 and the current year

<interest> Select the type of test. Currently, TOLC-I (engineering), TOLC-E (economics), TOLC-F (pharmacy) can be selected.

<region> Selection of the region of origin of the candidates to the tests. In case of missed selection (default status) the value all is used.

<quantile> during the ETL phase, each candidate is associated with a percentile ranking positioning with respect to the score of all the candidates who carried out the test. This filter allows selecting candidates with values higher than a certain percentile. To simplify the exploration for non-expert users, the CISIAViz platform allows selecting only the "best scores", i.e. the score of the top 10th percentile of tests in the DB for the current combination of year and area of interest.

2.4 Front end

The CISIAViz platform is implemented as a single-page web application. The platform is deployed within the website of the consortium[5].

[5] http://www.cisiaonline.it/area-tematica-cisia/report/

The *main* script is the entry point to the application and is responsible for aligning the selection on the interface with the data to the DB, by querying the Web API with new data when needed. Here the event handling of the application is orchestrated and it updates all graphs when new data arrives. Every chart is handled by a general class module *chart*, whose input is transformed accordingly to the type of figure to show using a dedicated *data_transformer*. The configuration and the mapping of transformers to charts are described into the *chart_config*. module. The modules *filter*, *toolbar*, *event_handler* take care of sending the requests to the server.

The web application is composed of a central column showing all the statistics, and a sidebar where the user can manage to insert the constraint for the dimensions to explore: year, area of interest, region of origin, best scores.

The central column is organized into sections, each of them focusing on a specific aspect of the data:

- *Volumes*: the first section shows the number of tests executed with reference to the actual selection, presenting the partial sums for sub-periods of the year.
- *Scores*: this section shows the average score per section in the selected tests and the distribution of each section.
- *Repetition of tests*: here we show how the score varies for those students that repeated the test multiple times.
- *Region of origin*: here we cross filter both the geographical origin and the high school diploma of the students attending the test.
- *Historycal data*: here we show the trends of the test along the years. This section is not affected by the year selection in the sidebar since shows always the statistics of the last five years.

3 Use cases

To demonstrate the efficacy of the web application to deliver high-level knowledge extracted from the data, we show the capabilities of the dashboard through a use case of a person interested in the performance of students. For example, let us consider a journalist interested in documenting the skills of students when entering university: a study of how many individuals take the entry test, how they behave in terms of performance and the presence of differences between types of students, could be an engaging topic for an article on young people. Leveraging the dashboard for the different areas of interest, it is possible to get information on the distribution, among gender, of students taking the tests, as shown in figure 3.

From the figure, it can be seen how, also in the testing phase, the women are underrepresented especially among STEM degree (in this case Engineering). The higher representation of female students is found for Economics and Pharmacy.

It is also possible to compare the performance between male and female students in a different section of the test: for this graph (but also for others) there

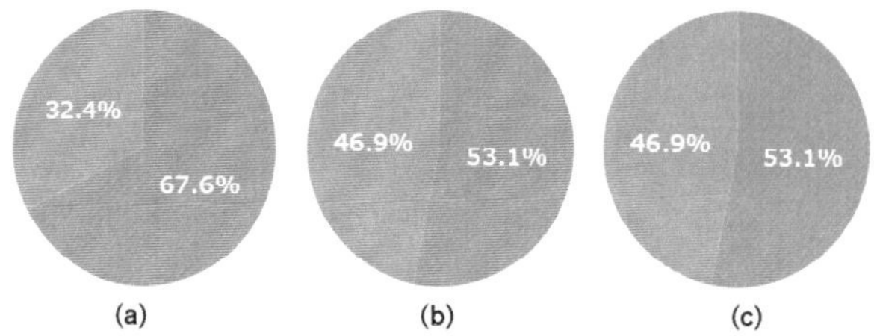

Fig. 3. Distribution of students by gender: percentage of students who took the test in Engineering (a), Economics (b) and Pharmacy (c)

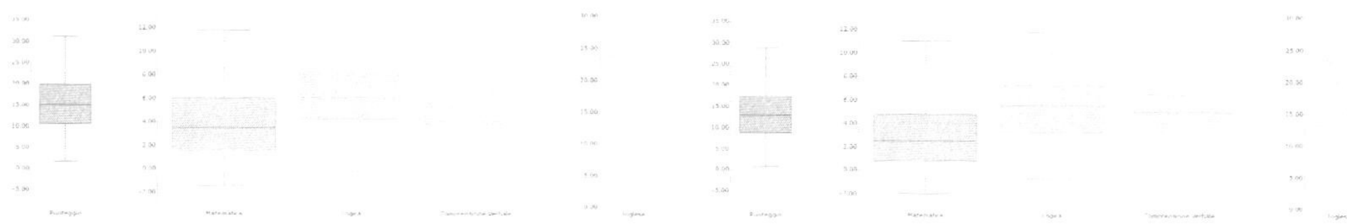

Fig. 4. Distribution of scores on topics: in the graph on left the male distribution of scores, while the graph on the right shows the distribution for female students

are local selectors with which selecting the female, the male or the total population who took a specific test (TOLC). In figure 4 it is shown the distribution of scores among male (top image) and female (bottom image) students. No significant differences can be found between the two genders, except for the results obtained in mathematics, where male students perform better than females. In the figure 4 is reported the distribution of scores for the test for Economics in 2018, but obviously, the same information can be obtained for the other areas (TOLC) and also the trend among years can be seen changing the selector for the years. Another possible comparison can be made among different Italian regions. In figure 5 the average scores obtained to the tests is reported for each region. The results reported in the figure are related to the TOLC in Economics, but the same results can be obtained for Pharmacy or Engineering. In this case average score for each section of the TOLC-Economics of 2018 divided by region and school of origin (all in this specific case). Only regions with a significant number of tests performed are shown. Furthermore, a comparison among different high schools can be made. The detailed average score has been calculated for scientific high school, classical high school, technical institute, technical institute for surveyors, commercial technical institute, professional institute and magistral and pedagogical institute.

The dashboard, therefore, allows you to get a picture of the situation of the students who decide to follow the course of study: a journalist interested in this topic and the differences between students with diverging characteristics (both gender or region of origin), can create his article guided by the data and statistics shown on the portal.

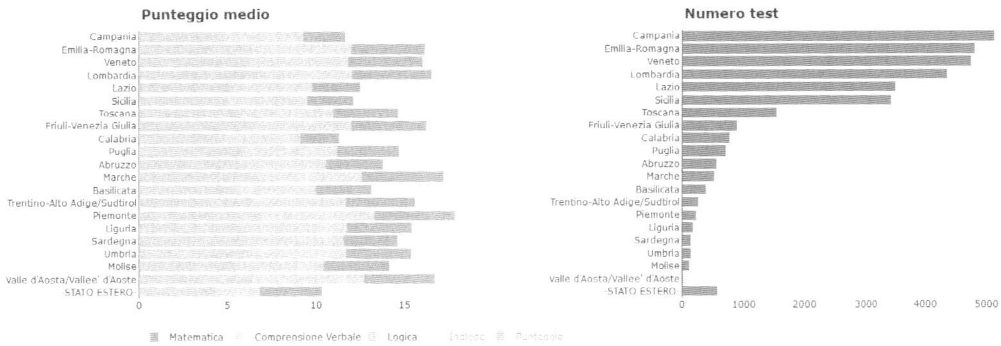

Fig. 5. Average scores among regions: on the left graph the average score made by students in each region, on the right graph the number of administered tests by regions.

4 Conclusions

In this paper we present a visual analytic platform to explore the performances of students when applying for entry tests to the universities. The platform was developed using the state-of-the-art of the technologies for web developing. The visual design of the dashboard was developed to support the user through a set of steps to select sub-dimension of the data. The toolbox which guides the composition of the visual platform is organized in steps and the user may select the relevant parameters to start the exploration. More specific selections, like gender selection or the selection of the high school diploma of origin, are located close to the specific corresponding chart. The system has been deployed and it is used efficiently both by non-expert users and domain experts (with login-based access).

References

1. Lee, M. D., Butavicius, M. A., Reilly, R. E.: Visualizations of binary data: A comparative evaluation. International Journal of Human-Computer Studies, **59**(5), 569-602 (2003).
2. Tao, F., Qi, Q., Liu, A., Kusiak, A.: Data-driven smart manufacturing. Journal of Manufacturing Systems **48**, 157–169 (2018)
3. Gabrielli, L., Rossi, M., Giannotti, F., Fadda, D., Rinzivillo, S.: Mobility Atlas Booklet: an urban dashboard design and implementation. ISPRS Annals of Photogrammetry, Remote Sensing and Spatial Information Sciences, 4 (2018).
4. Sarikaya, A., Correll, M., Bartram, L., Tory, M., Fisher, D.: What Do We Talk About When We Talk About Dashboards?. IEEE transactions on visualization and computer graphics, 25(1), 682-692 (2019).
5. Andrienko, Gennady and Andrienko, N.: Exploring spatial data with dominant attribute map and parallel coordinates. Computers, Environment and Urban Systems, 25(1), (2019).

Querying Cultural Heritage Knowledge Bases in Natural Language: Discussion Paper

Bernardo Cuteri, Kristian Reale, and Francesco Ricca

Department of Mathematics and Computer Science
University of Calabria, Italy
{cuteri,reale,ricca}@mat.unical.it

Abstract. Knowledge Based Question Answering (KBQA) is concerned with the possibility of querying data by posing questions in Natural Language (NL), that is by far, the most (human) common form of expressing an information need. This work reviews an approach to Question Answering that has the goal to transform Natural Language questions into SPARQL queries over cultural heritage knowledge bases. The key idea is to apply a rule-based classification process that we call template matching and that we have implemented in a prototype using logic programming. In the paper we discuss about the application of the prototype in real use-case, and indicate ongoing and future directions of work.

Keywords: Knowledge-based Question Answering · Cultural Heritage.

1 Introduction

Querying data from a database generally requires, at the very least, some programming expertise in the query language of the target database and a good understanding of the database model. Knowledge Based Question Answering (KBQA) is concerned with the possibility of querying data by posing questions in Natural Language (NL), that can be seen as the most (human) common form of expressing an information need.

In this work, we present an ongoing effort in the development of a KBQA system tailored to the cultural heritage domain, whose preliminary version has been developed within the PIUCULTURA project. The PIUCULTURA project, funded by the Italian Ministry for Economic Development, has the goal of devising a multi-paradigm platform that facilitates the fruition of cultural heritage sites in Italy. The prototype QA system described in this work is one of the core components of the platform, that answers to the need of providing a more natural way of obtaining information from the system.

It is worth noting that a system working on the domain of Cultural Heritage can benefit from many existing structured data sources that adhere to international standards. One of the most successful standards is the CIDOC Conceptual

Reference Model [9]. CIDOC-crm provides a common semantic framework for the mapping of cultural heritage information and has been already adopted as a base interchange format by museums, libraries, online data collections and archives all over the world [9,10]. For this reason, CIDOC-crm has been identified as the knowledge reference model for PIUCULTURA. Thus, our Question Answering prototype is applicable to query both general (e.g., online data collections) and specific (e.g., museums databases) CIDOC-compliant knowledge sources.

Our QA approach can be described as a waterfall-like process in which a user question is first processed from a syntactic point of view and then from a semantic point of view. Syntactic processing is based on the concept of *template*, where a template represents a category of syntactically homogeneous sentence patterns and is expressed in terms of Answer Set Programming (ASP) [12,7,6] rules. ASP is a well-established formalism for logic programming, and combines a comparatively high knowledge-modeling power with a robust solving technology [11,17]. ASP has roots in Datalog, that is a language for deductive databases.

On the other hand, the semantic processing is based on the concept of *intent*. By intent we mean the purpose (i.e., the intent) of the question: two questions can belong to two disjoint syntactic categories but have the same intent and vice versa. To give an example: *who created Guernica?* and *who is the author of Guernica?* have a quite different syntactic structure, but have the same intent, i.e., *know who made the work Guernica*. On the other hand, if we consider *who created Guernica?* and *who restored Guernica?* we can say that they are syntactically similar (or homogeneous), but semantically different: the purpose of the two questions is different. Semantic disambiguation, in which intents are mapped to a set of predefined queries on the knowledge base, is done by resorting to the multilingual BabelNet [20] dictionary.

2 Question Answering for Cultural Heritage

2.1 The problem

The goal of our approach is to answer questions on cultural heritage facts stored in a repository modeled according to a standard model of this domain. In particular, the target knowledge base model of the project is the CIDOC conceptual reference model [9]. The CIDOC-crm is a standardized maintained model that has been designed as a common language for the exchange and sharing of data on cultural heritage without loss of meaning, supporting the implementation of local data transformation algorithms towards this model. This standard has been adopted worldwide by a growing number of institutions and provides a more trustable, structured and complete source w.r.t. freely available (often unstructured and non-certified) web resources. Indeed, museums and institutions typically have structured sources in which they store information about their artifacts that can be mapped to CIDOC-crm rather easily (actually, this was one of the main goals of the promoters of CIDOC-crm). On the other hand, the availability of documentary sources is limited. If we take into consideration freely available documentary sources such as Wikipedia, we realize that the percentage coverage of works and authors is low. For example, a museum like the British Museum has about 8 million artifacts (made available in CIDOC-compliant format) while on Wikipedia there are in total about 500 thousand articles about works of art from all over the world. The CIDOC-crm is periodically released in RDFs format [8], thus our Question Answering system has to answer questions by finding the information required on an RDF knowledge base that follows the CIDOC-crm model. The reference query language of RDF is SPARQL [13]. So, in basic terms, the QA system has to map natural language questions into SPARQL queries and produce answers in natural language from query results.

2.2 Overview of the Approach

In this section we present step-by-step our question answering system for cultural heritage. In particular, the question answering process is split into the following phases: **(1) Question NL Processing**: the input question is transformed into a three-level syntactic representation; **(2) Template Matching**: the representation is categorized by a template system that is implemented by means of logical rules; **(3) Intent Determination**: the identified template is mapped to an intent, where the intent identifies precisely the intent (or purpose) of the question; **(4) Query Generation**: an intent becomes a query on the knowledge base; **(5) Query Execution**: the Query is executed on the knowledge base; **(6) Answer Generation**: the result produced by the query is transformed into a natural language answer. Splitting the QA process into distinct phases allowed us to implement a system by connecting loosely-coupled modules dedicated to each phase. In this way we also achieved better maintainability, and extensibility. In the following sections, we analyze in detail the 6 phases just listed.

Question NL Processing The NL processing phase builds a formal and therefore tractable representation of the input question. The question is decomposed and analyzed by highlighting both the atomic components that compose it, and the morphological properties of the components and the relationships that bind them. In this phase we perform the following NLP steps: Named entities recognition, Tokenization, Part-of-speech tagging, and Dependency Parsing.

Named entities recognition (NER) is an NLP task that deals with the identification and categorization of the entities that appear in a text. The named entities are portions of text that identify the names of people, organizations, places or other elements that are referenced by a proper name. For example, in the phrase *Michelangelo has painted the Last Judgment*, we can recognize two entities: *Michelangelo*, that could belong to a *Person* category, and *the Last Judgment* that could belong to an *Artwork* category. When the entities of the text have been recognized, they can be replaced with placeholders that are easier to manage in the subsequent stages of processing of natural language. In our implementation we use CRF++ [14] that implements a supervised model based on conditional random fields that are probabilistic models for segmenting and labeling sequence data [15].

Tokenization consists of splitting text into words (called tokens). A token is an indivisible unit of text. Tokens are separated by spaces or punctuation marks. In western languages, the tokenization phase turns out to be rather simple, as these languages place quite clear word demarcations. In fact, the approaches used for natural language tokenization are based on simple regular expressions. Tokenization is the first phase of lexical analysis and creates the input for the next Part-of-Speech Tagging phase.

The Part-of-Speech tagging phase assigns to each word the corresponding part of the speech. Common examples of parts of speech are adjectives, nouns, pronouns, verbs, or articles. The Part-of-Speech assignment is typically implemented with supervised statistical methods. There are, for several languages, large manually annotated corpora that can be used as training sets to train a statistical system. Among the best performing approaches are those based on Maximum Entropy. For tokenization and POS-tagging we used the Apache OpenNLP library[1] with pretrained models.

Finally, Dependency Parsing is the identification of lexical dependencies of the words of a text according to a grammar of dependencies. The dependency grammar (DG) is a class of syntactic theories that are all based on the dependency relationship (as opposed to the circumscription relation). Dependency is the notion that linguistic units, e.g., words, are connected to one another by directed connections (or dependencies). A dependency is determined by the relationship between a word (a head) and its dependencies. The methods for extracting grammar dependencies are typically supervised and use a reference tag-set and a standard input representation format known as the CoNLL standard developed and updated within the CoNLL scientific conference (Conference on Computational Natural Language Learning). In our implementation we used MaltParser[2] that is a system for data-driven dependency parsing [21].

Template Matching Template matching is in charge of classifying question from the syntactic point of view and extract the question terms that are needed to instantiate the query for retrieving the answer. Basically, a template represents a category of syntactically homogeneous questions. In our system, templates are encoded in terms of ASP rules. By using ASP we can work in a declarative fashion and avoid implementing the template matching procedure from scratch.

To this end, the output of the NLP phase is modeled by using ASP facts that constitute the input of the template matching module. In particular, words are indexed by their position in the sentence and they are associated with their morphological feature by using facts of the following forms:

```
word(pst,wrd).      pos(pst,pos_tag).      gr(pst1,pst2,rel_tag).
```

the first kind of fact associates position of words (`pst`) in a sentence to the word itself (`wrd`); the second associates words (`pst`) with their POS tags (`pos_tag`),

[1] `https://opennlp.apache.org`
[2] `http://www.maltparser.org/`

and the latter models grammatical relations (a.k.a. typed dependencies) specifying the type of grammatical relation (`rel_tag`) holding among pair of words (`pst1,pst2`). The possible tags and relations terms are constants representing the labels produced by the NLP tools mentioned in the previous subsection.

Consider, for example, the question *who painted Guernica?*, the output of the NLP phase would result in the following facts:

```
word(1, "who"). word(2, "painted"). word(3, "Guernica").
word(4, "?"). pos(1, pr). pos(2, vb). pos(3, np). pos(4, f).
gr(2, 1, nsubj). gr(2, 3, dobj). gr(2, 4, punct).
```

In the template matching phase, questions are matched against question templates. Templates identify categories of questions that are uniform from the syntactic point of view and we express them in the form of ASP rules.

Basically, each template rule models a condition under which we identified a possible syntactic question pattern for a template. An example of template rule that matches questions of the form *who action object?* is the following:

```
template(who_action_object, terms_2(V, O), 8) :-
word (1, "who"), word(2, V), word(3, O), word(4, "?"),
pos(1, pr), pos(2, vb), pos(3, np), pos(4, f),
gr(2, 1, nsubj), gr(2, 3, dobj), gr(2, 4, punct).
```

In the example, *who_action_object* is a constant that identifies the template, while $terms(V, W)$ is a function symbol that allows extracting the terms of the input question, respectively the verb V and the object O. The intuitive meaning of a template rule is that whenever all atoms in the body (the part of the rule affter `:-`) are true, then the template matches. The number 8, is the weight of the template rule. The weight is a number expressing the importance of a pattern. By using weights one can freely express preferences; for instance in our implementation we set this number to the size of elements in the body of the ASP template rule to favor more specific templates over more generic ones.

Question templates are intended to be defined by the application designer, which is a reasonable choice in applications like the one we considered, where the number of templates to produce is limited. Nonetheless, to assist the definition of templates we developed a graphical user interface. Such interface helps the user at building template rules by working and generalizing examples, and does not require any previous knowledge of ASP or specific knowledge of NLP tools. The template editing interface is not described in this paper for space reasons.

In our prototype, we used DLV [16] as engine that computes the answer sets (thus the best matches) of the template matching phase, and the DLV Wrapper library to [22] to manage DLV invocations from Java code. DLV has a Datalog subsystem supporting efficient ontological reasoning [4,2,5,3,1].

Intent Determination The identification of a question by templates might be not sufficient to identify its intent or purpose. For example, *who painted Guernica?* and *who killed Caesar?* have similar syntactic structures and may fall into the same template, but they have two different purposes. The intent determination process is based on the lexical expansion of question terms extracted in the template matching phase and has the role of identifying what the question asks (i.e., its intent), starting from the result of the template matching phase. In other words, it disambiguates the intent of questions that fall into the same syntactic category. In the previous example, painting is *hyponym* (i.e., a specific instance) of creating and thus we can understand that the intent is to determine the creator of a work, while killing does not have such relationships and we should, therefore, instantiate a different intent. In the same way, *who painted Guernica?*, *who made Guernica?* are questions that can be correctly mapped with a single template and can be correctly recognized by the same intent thanks to the fact that all three verbs are hyponyms or synonyms of the verb *create*. Words semantic relations can be obtained by using dedicated dictionaries, like wordnet [19] or BabelNet [20]. In our system we implemented the intent determination module in Java and used the BabelNet API library for accessing word relations. In particular, intent determination is implemented as a series of Java conditional checks (possibly nested) on word relations. Such conditional checks are expressed as a question term Q, a word relation R and a target word T. The BabelNet service receives such triple and returns true/false depending on whether Q is in relation R w.r.t. T, R is either synonymy, hyponymy or hyperonymy.

The implementation of intent determination is done by the designer as template definition. Our system implements a set of intents that were identified during the analysis by a partner of the project.

Query Execution The intents identified in the previous phase are mapped one to one with template queries, called prepared statements in programming jargon. In the Query Execution phase, the query template corresponding to the identified event is filled with the slots with terms extracted from the template matching phase and executed over the knowledge base. The CIDOC-crm specification is, by definition, an RDF knowledge base [8], thus we implemented the queries corresponding to intents in the SPARQL language [13]. In our prototype, we store our data and run our queries using Apache Jena, as programmatic query API, and Virtuoso Open-Source Edition as knowledge base service.

Answer Generation Finally, the latest phase of a typical user interaction with the QA system is the so-called Answer Generation. In this phase, the results produced by the execution of the query on the knowledge base are transformed into a natural language answer that is finally presented to the user. To implement this phase, we have designed answer templates that are natural language patterns with parameterized slots that are filled according to the question intent and the terms extracted from the database.

2.3 Preliminary experiments

We conducted an experimental analysis to assess the performance of the system on a set of 60 template rules, which are able to handle basic question forms and types for the cultural heritage domain distributed in 20 different intents.We report, on a sample of 167 questions, an average template matching time of 34 milliseconds (ms) on an Intel i7-7700HQ CPU architecture. For what concerns the other phases of the QA system, the NL phase average execution time is of 30 ms and is at most 50 ms, the intent determination phase average execution time is of 50 ms and is at most 580 ms and the average query execution time is of 8 ms and is at most 32 ms. Overall the system presents good execution times, which are acceptable for a real-time QA system.

3 Discussion and future works

In this work, we presented an approach to the problem of Knowledge-based Question Answering in the Cultural Heritage domain. The presented solution transforms input questions into SPARQL queries that are executed on a knowledge base. The concrete application of the approach to the Cultural Heritage use-case shows that one of the main advantages of the approach is that it is suited for fast prototyping, as it allows the fast integration of new question forms and new question intents. This feature suits the need of closed domains that are characterized by a limited number of intents and question forms. On the other hand a drawback of the approach is that it relies on the manual work of a designer that provides question templates and the strategy for intent matching. This problem is partly solved by some other QA approaches, as the ones based on machine learning that requires less engineering efforts in the implementation of question understanding at the cost of providing a corpora of examples.

The prototype can be seen as a good starting point for many future works. One of the most natural observation that comes in mind is that the intent determination phase can be also encoded using logic programs, thus making also the specification of this step flexible and independent from a static decision made at compile time. Indeed, having the whole question understanding process in ASP makes it more homogeneous and easier to develop and maintain. A prerequisite of implementing intent determination in ASP is to make ASP code interact with the dictionary that provides words semantic relations. We think that this can be achieved either by porting dictionary data in ASP or by using ASP extensions with external computation. Another interesting thing to investigate is how the ASP-based implementation compares with other techniques for question answering, as the ones only based on machine learning (e.g., [23,18]); and develop an architecture where the two can be combined in a single implementation.

References

1. Adrian, W.T., Manna, M., Leone, N., Amendola, G., Adrian, M.: Entity set expansion from the web via ASP. In: ICLP (Technical Communications). OASICS, vol. 58, pp. 1:1–1:5. Schloss Dagstuhl - Leibniz-Zentrum fuer Informatik (2017)
2. Amendola, G., Leone, N., Manna, M.: Finite model reasoning over existential rules. TPLP **17**(5-6), 726–743 (2017)

3. Amendola, G., Leone, N., Manna, M.: Querying finite or arbitrary models? no matter! existential rules may rely on both once again (discussion paper). In: SEBD. CEUR Workshop Proceedings, vol. 2037, p. 218. CEUR-WS.org (2017)
4. Amendola, G., Leone, N., Manna, M.: Finite controllability of conjunctive query answering with existential rules: Two steps forward. In: IJCAI. pp. 5189–5193. ijcai.org (2018)
5. Amendola, G., Leone, N., Manna, M., Veltri, P.: Enhancing existential rules by closed-world variables. In: IJCAI. pp. 1676–1682. ijcai.org (2018)
6. Bonatti, P.A., Calimeri, F., Leone, N., Ricca, F.: Answer set programming. In: 25 Years GULP. Lecture Notes in Computer Science, vol. 6125, pp. 159–182. Springer (2010)
7. Brewka, G., Eiter, T., Truszczyński, M.: Answer set programming at a glance. Communications of the ACM **54**(12), 92–103 (2011)
8. Consortium, W.W.W., et al.: Rdf 1.1 concepts and abstract syntax (2014)
9. Doerr, M.: The cidoc conceptual reference module: an ontological approach to semantic interoperability of metadata. AI magazine **24**(3), 75 (2003)
10. Doerr, M., Gradmann, S., Hennicke, S., Isaac, A., Meghini, C., Van de Sompel, H.: The europeana data model (edm). In: World Library and Information Congress: 76th IFLA general conference and assembly. pp. 10–15 (2010)
11. Gebser, M., Leone, N., Maratea, M., Perri, S., Ricca, F., Schaub, T.: Evaluation techniques and systems for answer set programming: a survey. In: IJCAI. pp. 5450–5456. ijcai.org (2018)
12. Gelfond, M., Lifschitz, V.: Classical negation in logic programs and disjunctive databases. New generation computing **9**(3-4), 365–385 (1991)
13. Harris, S., Seaborne, A., Prud'hommeaux, E.: Sparql 1.1 query language. W3C recommendation **21**(10) (2013)
14. Kudo, T.: Crf++. http://crfpp. sourceforge. net/ (2013)
15. Lafferty, J., McCallum, A., Pereira, F.C.: Conditional random fields: Probabilistic models for segmenting and labeling sequence data (2001)
16. Leone, N., Pfeifer, G., Faber, W., Eiter, T., Gottlob, G., Perri, S., Scarcello, F.: The dlv system for knowledge representation and reasoning. ACM Transactions on Computational Logic (TOCL) **7**(3), 499–562 (2006)
17. Lierler, Y., Maratea, M., Ricca, F.: Systems, engineering environments, and competitions. AI Magazine **37**(3), 45–52 (2016)
18. Lukovnikov, D., Fischer, A., Lehmann, J., Auer, S.: Neural network-based question answering over knowledge graphs on word and character level. In: Proceedings of the 26th international conference on World Wide Web. pp. 1211–1220. International World Wide Web Conferences Steering Committee (2017)
19. Miller, G.: WordNet: An electronic lexical database. MIT press (1998)
20. Navigli, R., Ponzetto, S.P.: Babelnet: The automatic construction, evaluation and application of a wide-coverage multilingual semantic network. Artificial Intelligence **193**, 217–250 (2012)
21. Nivre, J., Hall, J., Nilsson, J., Chanev, A., Eryigit, G., Kübler, S., Marinov, S., Marsi, E.: Maltparser: A language-independent system for data-driven dependency parsing. Natural Language Engineering **13**(2), 95–135 (2007)
22. Ricca, F.: A java wrapper for DLV. In: Answer Set Programming. CEUR Workshop Proceedings, vol. 78. CEUR-WS.org (2003)
23. Zhong, V., Xiong, C., Socher, R.: Seq2sql: Generating structured queries from natural language using reinforcement learning. arXiv preprint arXiv:1709.00103 (2017)

Summarizing social media content for multimedia stories creation
(DISCUSSION PAPER)

Flora Amato[1], Francesco Moscato[3], Vincenzo Moscato[1], Antonio Picariello[1], and Giancarlo Sperli'[3]

[1] University of Naples, Federico II (DIETI)
via Claudio 21, 80125, Naples, Italy {flora.amato,vmoscato,picus}@unina.it
[2] Universita' degli Studi della della Campania
Viale Ellittico, 31, 81100, Caserta, Italy francesco.moscato@unicampania.it
[3] CINI (Consorzio Interuniversitario Nazionale per l'Informatica)
Via Cinthia, 80126, Naples, Italy giancarlo.sperli@consorzio-cini.it

Abstract. This article represents an extended abstract of our previous work on multimedia summarization. In particular, we propose a novel summarization technique of social media content for *multimedia stories* creation, using a graph- based modeling approach and influence analysis methodologies to detect the most important multimedia objects related to one or more topics of interest. Consecutively, from the list of candidates, we obtain a multimedia summary exploiting a summarization model that satisfies several properties such as *Priority* (w.r.t. user keywords), *Continuity*, *Variety* and *not Repetitiveness*. The summary objects are finally arranged in a multimedia story.

Keywords: Social Network Analysis · Summarization · Graph DB.

1 Introduction

Online Social Networks (OSNs) represent interactive platforms where users comment events and facts, express personal opinions on specific topics, report moments of everyday life and so on, by creating on-line profiles and continuously sharing large amount of information (especially multimedia data). Thus, *social media* content coming from OSNs can be considered , without any doubt, the essence of *Big Data*, providing at the same time new opportunities to investigate and analyze social dynamics within these environments. In the last decade, *Social Network Analysis* (SNA) has been introduced to understand OSNs' structure and properties aiming at supporting a wide range of applications : information retrieval, recommendation, viral marketing, event recognition, expert finding, community detection, user profiling, security, social data privacy, etc., and, in particular, summarization [1].

The *summarization* process from OSNs can be considered a "distilling" process of the most important information from a variety of logically related sources, in order to obtain a brief and significant version of the social media content. The heterogeneity of the user generated content leads to the creation of a *multimedia story*, i.e. a sort of summary integrating different kinds of multimedia data (e.g. images, videos, audios, texts, etc.).

Let us consider, for instance, the typical behavior of a user that desires to retrieve particular social media content (e.g., photos posted on Flickr or video on Youtube) related to a specific event (e.g., New year's day in London) described by a set of keywords (e.g. 'London', 'new year's day') and concerning a given topic (e.g., holidays). Once determined the most important objects composing the summary, they have to be properly organized in a multimedia story according to some preferences and needs and delivered to final users[5,7].

Concerning the Related Work on social media content summarization, the majority of approaches focuses on how different features of user generated multimedia content crawled by OSNs can support in several ways visual summaries building related to particular events [4,8,6].

Here, we propose a novel summarization technique of social media content for multimedia stories' creation. In particular, for each *Multimedia Social Network* (MuSN) - i.e. a particular OSN focusing on the management and sharing of multimedia information - we use a graph- based modeling approach and exploit influence analysis methodologies to detect the most important multimedia objects related to one or more topics of interest. Consecutively, from the list of candidate objects we obtain a multimedia summary leveraging a summarization model that considers several properties such as *Priority* (w.r.t. user keywords), *Continuity*, *Variety* and *not Repetitiveness* of generated summaries. The summary objects are finally arranged in a multimedia story and presented/delivered to final users.

2 Multimedia Social Network modeling

The proposed model (see [2,3] for more details) permits to represent in an effective way any kind of entities (i.e., *users* and multimedia *objects*) and relationships (e.g., publishing, sharing, commenting, similarity, etc.) in any type of MuSNs (e.g, YouTube, Flickr, Instagram, Last.fm, etc.). In particular, our idea consists of modeling any MuSN as a particular *database graph.*

Definition 1 (MuSN). *A* MuSN *(Multimedia Social Network) is an undirected edge-labeled graph* $G = (V, L, E)$*,* V *being the set of graph vertices, representing main entities of a social network,* L *being a set of labels (belonging to a given vocabulary), describing the different kinds of relationships that can occur among the social network entities; and* $E \subseteq V \times L \times V$ *being the set of edges;* V *and* E *being abstract data types with a set of properties (expressed using several attributes that can be different depending on the type of nodes and edges).*

Example 1 (Example of MuSN). In the case of *Flickr*, entities of the social network are *Users*, *Groups* and *Photos* ($V = U \cup Gr \cup P$). Users, Groups and Image properties can be described leveraging proper attributes (e.g., username, name, surname, number of followers, etc. for Users; title, description, number of photos, number of users, etc for Groups; and title, description, number of favorites, tags, etc. for Images). Labels correspond to the several activities (L = {'publishing', 'following', 'mark_as_favorite', 'comment', 'visualization', 'add_to_group', 'discussion'}) on the social network (i.e., a user can publish a photo, a user can follow another one, a user can mark as favorite a photo shared by other users, a user can perform a comment on a given photo, a user can visualize a photo, a user or photo can be added to a group and a user can add a discussion to a group). Edges properties are described by proper attributes (e.g., publishing relationships by timestamp and topic, discussion relationships by the timestamp and text of a discussion together with the related answers, etc.).

In addition, particular edge-labeled paths, named *social paths* can be instantiated between two nodes leveraging the different kinds of relationships in MuSN: a given path can "directly" connect two users because they are "friends" , or "indirectly", as they have commented the same photo, or even, two distinct but similar pictures. Among the different types of social paths, the *relevant social paths* ($p = (v_i, e_i, \ldots, e_k, v_j)$) – i.e.particular paths that present certain properties Θ – assume a particular importance for the social network analysis purposes.Eventually, we can easily observe that relevant social paths can be obtained as results of a *Regular Path Query* (RPQ) on the graph database representing the given MuSN. To extract relevant social paths, we can first exploit regular path queries and after filtering the obtained results on the base of Θ.

Example 2 (Influential Paths). A particular kind of relevant social path is constituted by *influential paths* connecting two users; in particular, a user can "influence" in some way other users. As an example, in Flickr a given user u_i influences another user u_j, if u_j adds to her/his favorites any photo of u_i, or if u_j positively comments a photo (or one similar to) that u_i has just published. In Twitter, the influence is mainly related to the re-tweet actions, thus the user u_i influences the user u_j, if u_j has re-tweeted any tweet of u_i. Similarly in Yelp, the user u_i influences u_j, if the user u_j posts a review of the same sentiment of the review previously posted by u_i on the same business object. Indeed, the type of influential paths that can be considered depends on the Social Network and on the analytical goals. Concerning the first case of Flickr, all the influential paths can be extracted using the following RPQ:

$$(u_1, e_1 e_2, u_2) \tag{1}$$

where:

$$e_1.\mathsf{type} = \text{“}publishing'' \wedge e_2.\mathsf{type} = \text{“}mark\_as\_favorite'' \wedge \\ (e_2.\mathsf{time} - e_1.\mathsf{time}) \leq \Delta t$$

constitutes the set of conditions Θ, being Δt a given time.

Example 3 (Recommending Paths). Another kind of relevant path is the *recommending path* that represents a specific path between two objects by which a given object can "recommend" other objects. As an example, in Flickr it is proper to assume that a given object o_i recommends another o_j, if a user visualized/published o_i and o_j in consecutive temporal instants of the same browsing session, and the objects are similar or if a user provided two positive reactions or comments to o_i and o_j in successive times or if a user marked o_i and o_j as favorite in consecutive temporal instants. In the last case, all the recommending paths have the form:

$$o_1, e_1 e_2, o_2 \tag{2}$$

where:

$$e_1.\mathsf{type} = \text{“}mark\_as\_favorite'' \wedge e_2.\mathsf{type} = \text{“}mark\_as\_favorite'' \wedge \\ similar(o_1, o_2) \wedge (e_2.\mathsf{time} - e_1.\mathsf{time}) \leq \Delta t$$

constitutes the set of conditions Θ, being Δt a given time and $similar(o_i, o_j)$ a predicate that is true in the case the two objects are similar in terms of multimedia content. Recommending paths are surely useful for different applications such as recommendation and summarization, being the goal to determine the subset of most relevant objects that could be of interest for a large community of users on the base of their multimedia content. Thus, we can consider recommending paths as a sort of influential paths between objects. The most influential objects are surely good candidates to compose a multimedia summary.

3 Story creation

Our goal is to determine the most *important* objects of a MuSN for summarization purposes exploiting an *Influence Maximization* (IM) strategy that allows to obtain a set of suitable candidates ("influentials"), together with the related overall social *importance* w.r.t. a given topic. We successively apply a summarization algorithm on the influentials in order to generate a summary following a set of optimization criteria.

For the summarization goals, we deal with a particular homogeneous graph – *Summarization Graph* – that is derived from a MuSN topic-based view using relevant paths.

Definition 2 (Summarization Graph). *A* Summarization Graph *is the triple $SG = (V; Es; \omega)$, V being a set of vertices related to specific objects of a MuSN, Es a set of edges and ω a weight function. In particular, there exists a unique edge e between two vertices v_i and v_j for all recommending paths connecting v_i and v_j. For each edge the related weight will be determined as in the following:*

$$\omega(e_{i,j}) = \frac{\sum_{k=1}^{M} \gamma(p_k(v_i, v_j))}{N_j} \tag{3}$$

M being the number of distinct relevant paths between v_i and v_j and N_j the number of relevant paths of having as destination vertex v_j.

It is then possible to apply on the SG all the most diffused models and techniques for influence maximization and diffusion to determine the most important objects (*influentials*) of a MuSN. In particular, we have chosen to model how the influence spreads over a network using an *Independent Cascade* (IC) model, where the "activation" of each node is based on the behavior of its active neighbors, and can occur by a single chance. Among all possible approaches defined in the literature, we have used a biologically inspired technique for influence maximization, in particular the *ABC* algorithm based on the bees' behaviors within a hive (see [2,3] for more details).

In our vision, a *multimedia summary* is a sequence of *summarizable objects* (i.e., influentials represented by multimedia data with topic labels derived from user annotations) that can be semantically correlated (also w.r.t user keywords). On the top of summary definition, we have then introduced four different properties for evaluating the generated summaries (see [2,3] for more details): *Priority*, *Consistence*, *Variety* and *Repetitiveness*.

In more details, the *Priority* criterion measures the relevance of objects in the summary with respect to some user keywords; *Continuity* and *Variety* criteria give more importance to multimedia objects published in the same temporal intervals and by different users, respectively; *Repetitiveness* criterion, eventually, measures how semantically similar are the selected objects. Clearly, it is desirable to have a summary with priority and not repetitive contents that presents a temporal continuity and a certain variety in terms of multimedia sources (i.e. users and social networks).

In the previous work, authors have demonstrated that the optimal summary evaluation is a NP-hard problem. To this aim, we provide a greedy strategy that find a sub-optimal solution for the summary evaluation problem in a more efficient way. Our summarization algorithm is based on genetic programming with the following characteristics (see [2,3] for more details):

- it starts using as input the most important k objects (influentials) computed by the *ABC* influence maximization algorithm applied on the summarization graphs related to all the considered OSNs;
- it works on an initial solution that considers only the priority criterion;
- it uses a *mutation* operator to generate more suitable solutions with respect to all the optimization criteria.

4 System Architecture and Implementation

Figure 1 reports an overview of the proposed summarizer system in terms of main components: the *Data Crawler* – that collects information about users, the related generated content and interactions among users and between users and content) and then store such information into a *Staging Area*: the *MuSN Builder* – that builds the social network using a graph database for each considered MuSN; the *Knowledge Base Manager* – that allows to manage the knowledge related to the different MuSNs; and the *Multimedia Summary Manager*, formed by *Influence Analyzer*, *Summary generator* and the *Summary Presenter*.

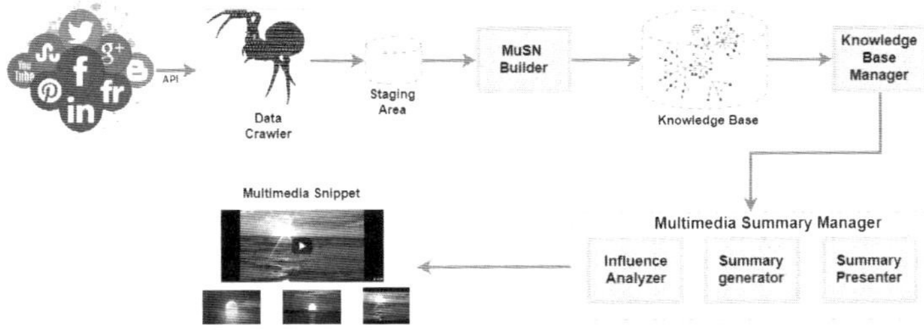

Fig. 1. Overview of the proposed summarizer system

We retrieve data from Flickr and YouTube. The Staging area has been realized using a document oriented database MongoDB that ensures a high horizontal scalability. For the Knowledge Base, we decided to adopt a graph-based approach and to exploit Neo4J functionalities. All the remaining components have been implemented in Scala on the top of Apache Spark, the related data processing libraries and HDFS. Multimedia stories have been realized as HTML pages using javascripts combining AJAX and Jquery technologies.

5 Experiments and Results

We used as dataset the YFCC100M [4] multimedia collection. We have thus instantiated the related MuSN using Flickr images and basic relationships (i.e., publishing, following, visualizations, comments, favorites, etc.). We considered images about *building* and *sport*, obtaining as topic-based view a graph with the characteristics depicted in Table 1.

Dataset	**Vertices**			**Edges**
	Users	**Topic labels**	**Images**	
YFCC100M	1K	40	1.3K	3.8K

Table 1. Topic-based view characterization

We performed a human-based evaluation for generated summaries using the *Recall-Oriented Understudy for Gisting Evaluation* (ROUGE [5]) package.

We asked a group of 25 people[6] to generate, for two distinct triples of keywords ("commercial/residential/government", "soccer/football/rugby"'), two different sets of summaries, each one respectively containing 15, 25 and 50 images from the list of candidates computed by ABC algorithm on the Flickr MuSN.

[4] https://webscope.sandbox.yahoo.com.

[5] http://haydn.isi.edu/ROUGE/

[6] The people involved in the experiments were mainly students from the University of Naples related to the database and multimedia system courses having an account on Flickr.

The first group contains images that according to human judgment maximizing the not repetitiveness criterion and the second one endorses the variety criterion.

After this preliminary step and starting from the 300 obtained summaries, we have built, for each topic, 6 "optimal" summaries (composed by 15, 25 and 50 sentences and respectively giving more importance to variety and not repetitiveness) by considering those objects that have been more frequently chosen by humans. Then, such optimal summaries have been compared with those generated by our summarizer using the same variety and not repetitiveness criteria.

Such combinations have been then considered to obtain all the 12 possible system configurations. We computed system performances in terms of *average recall*, *average precision* and *F-measure* with respect to the human ground truth according to the ROUGE-2 and ROUGE-SU4 methods (see Table 2).

Table 2. Comparison of ROUGE values between system generated summaries and human ground truth.

ROUGE-2			
Configuration	AverageR	AverageP	AverageF
high not repetitiveness, n=25, building	0.40014	0.42331	0.41032
high not repetitiveness, n=25, sport	0.38159	0.41372	0.39409
high variety, n=25, sport	0.38443	0.40959	0.39408
high variety, n=25, building	0.37694	0.40598	0.39104
high not repetitiveness, n=50, sport	0.35801	0.39220	0.37296
high not repetitiveness, n=50, building	0.34689	0.38160	0.36218
high variety, n=50, sport	0.33693	0.35843	0.34691
high variety, n=50, building	0.34627	0.34657	0.34513
high not repetitiveness, n=15, building	0.27698	0.30680	0.28899
high not repetitiveness, n=15, sport	0.29604	0.30803	0.30004
high variety, n=15, building	0.24785	0.26503	0.25412
high variety, n=15, sport	0.23099	0.25431	0.24035

ROUGE-SU4			
Configuration	AverageR	AverageP	AverageF
high not repetitiveness, n=25, building	0.43015	0.45132	0.43802
high not repetitiveness, n=25, sport	0.41684	0.43903	0.42302
high variety, n=25, sport	0.40913	0.44888	0.42691
high variety, n=25, building	0.40713	0.43912	0.42069
high not repetitiveness, n=50, sport	0.37835	0.41433	0.39801
high not repetitiveness, n=50, building	0.38752	0.42374	0.40270
high variety, n=50, sport	0.37023	0.39286	0.37943
high variety, n=50, building	0.37796	0.37801	0.37564
high not repetitiveness, n=15, building	0.32701	0.34106	0.33011
high not repetitiveness, n=15, sport	0.30891	0.34301	0.32201
high variety, n=15, building	0.28032	0.30203	0.28998
high variety, n=15, sport	0.26531	0.29301	0.27632

6 Acknowledgments

This work was co-funded by the European Union's Justice Programme (2014-2020),CREA Project, under grant agreement No. 766463.

References

1. Aggarwal, C., Subbian, K.: Evolutionary network analysis: A survey. ACM Computing Surveys (CSUR) **47**(1), 10 (2014)
2. Amato, F., Castiglione, A., Mercorio, F., Mezzanzanica, M., Moscato, V., Picariello, A., Sperlì, G.: Multimedia story creation on social networks. Future Generation Computer Systems **86**, 412–420 (2018)
3. Amato, F., Castiglione, A., Moscato, V., Picariello, A., Sperlì, G.: Multimedia summarization using social media content. Multimedia Tools and Applications **77**(14), 17803–17827 (2018)
4. Bian, J., Yang, Y., Zhang, H., Chua, T.S.: Multimedia summarization for social events in microblog stream. IEEE Transactions on Multimedia **17**(2), 216–228 (Feb 2015). https://doi.org/10.1109/TMM.2014.2384912
5. d'Acierno, A., Gargiulo, F., Moscato, V., Penta, A., Persia, F., Picariello, A., Sansone, C., Sperlí, G.: A multimedia summarizer integrating text and images. In: Intelligent Interactive Multimedia Systems and Services, pp. 21–33. Springer (2015)
6. Lu, Z., Lin, Y.R., Huang, X., Xiong, N., Fang, Z.: Visual topic discovering, tracking and summarization from social media streams. Multimedia Tools and Applications **76**(8), 10855–10879 (2017)
7. Modani, N., Maneriker, P., Hiranandani, G., Sinha, A.R., Subramanian, V., Gupta, S., et al.: Summarizing multimedia content. In: International Conference on Web Information Systems Engineering. pp. 340–348. Springer (2016)
8. Qian, S., Zhang, T., Xu, C., Shao, J.: Multi-modal event topic model for social event analysis. IEEE Transactions on Multimedia **18**(2), 233–246 (2016)

Counting Database Repairs under Primary Keys Revisited* (DISCUSSION PAPER)

Marco Calautti, Marco Console, and Andreas Pieris

School of Informatics, University of Edinburgh
{mcalautt,mconsole,apieris}@inf.ed.ac.uk

1 Introduction

Consistent query answering (CQA) [2] aims to deliver meaningful answers when queries are evaluated over inconsistent databases. Such answers, called *consistent answers*, must be true in all repairs, which are consistent databases whose difference from the inconsistent one is somehow minimal. Consistent answers only allow us to conclude that a tuple is either entailed by all repairs, or is not entailed by some repair. But, as discussed in [4], the former is too strict, while the latter is not very useful in practice. Instead, we would like to know how often a tuple is consistent, i.e., its relative frequency defined as the ratio between the number of repairs entailing the tuple, and the total number of repairs.

The data complexity, i.e., when the query and the set of constraints are fixed, of the problem of computing the relative frequency of a tuple has been already studied in [6, 7] for conjunctive queries (CQs) and primary keys (i.e., when each relation has at most one key). We know that computing the total number of repairs is feasible in polynomial time. On the other hand, computing the number of repairs that entail the given tuple is #P-complete. Recall that #P is a hard counting complexity class, which, roughly speaking, collects the function problems that ask for the number of solutions to an NP problem. The above #P-hardness relies on polynomial-time Turing, a.k.a. Cook, reductions. However, as observed in the literature [5, 8], there are problems that are "hard-to-count-easy-to-decide" that cannot be complete (under reasonable assumptions) for #P under standard many-one logspace (or even polynomial-time) reductions. Note that the decision version of a counting problem asks whether the count is greater than zero. In our case, it asks whether a repair entailing a given tuple exists. As stated in [8], Cook reductions blur structural differences between counting problems and complexity classes. The reason is that #P is not closed under Cook reductions (under reasonable assumptions). Therefore, for such "hard-to-count-easy-to-decide" problems, a crucial question is whether

* This is a short version of the paper [3].

we can determine their exact complexity w.r.t. subclasses of #P to which they belong. Ideally, we would like to show that such a problem is complete, under logspace reductions, for a class $\mathcal{C} \subseteq$ #P that is closed under such reductions.

Our goal is to perform such a refined analysis for the data complexity of the problem of counting the number of repairs that entail a given tuple in the case of primary keys. We show that for arbitrary first-order queries this problem remains #P-complete. For existential positive queries (and CQs as well), we show that our problem *cannot* be complete (under reasonable assumptions) for #P, or even known classes inside #P. This brings us to our main question whether we can isolate a complexity class $\mathcal{C}$ inside #P that is closed under logspace reductions for which our problem (in the case of positive existential queries) is complete under such reductions. Let us stress that there is no guarantee that such a class $\mathcal{C}$ exists. This is because we focus on the data complexity of our problem. This means, by convention, that we deal with a family of problems and not a single problem; as usual, each query and set of primary keys gives rise to a new problem. Furthermore, establishing a completeness result for a certain complexity class $\mathcal{C}$ boils down to showing that (i) every problem in this family belongs to $\mathcal{C}$, and (ii) there exists one problem that is $\mathcal{C}$-complete. But, there is no guarantee that there exists a problem in this family such that all the other problems of the family are logspace reducible to it. This essentially tells us that the complexity class $\mathcal{C}$ inside #P that we are looking might not exist.

Although we do not give a definite answer to our main question, we make a significant step towards such an answer. We isolate a hierarchy of new complexity classes inside #P, called the Λ-hierarchy, which is of independent interest, and show that if the class $\mathcal{C}$ that we are looking for exists, then it is one of the levels of the Λ-hierarchy. Moreover, whether $\mathcal{C}$ exists boils down to the question whether the Λ-hierarchy collapses. We conjecture that this is not the case.

2 Preliminaries

Relational Databases. A *(relational) schema* $\mathbf{S}$ is a finite set of relation symbols (or predicates) with associated arity. A *database* D over a schema $\mathbf{S}$ is a set of facts of the form $R(\bar{t})$, where $R \in \mathbf{S}$, and $\bar{t} = t_1, \ldots, t_n$ is a tuple of terms that are drawn from a countably infinite set $\mathbf{C}$ of constants. We write $\mathsf{dom}(D)$ for the *active domain* of D, that is, the set of constants occurring in D.

Primary Key Constraints. A *key constraint* (or simply *key*) κ over a schema $\mathbf{S}$ is an expression of the form $\mathsf{key}(R) = \{1, \ldots, m\}$, where $R \in \mathbf{S}$ has arity n, and $m \leq n$. Such an expression is called an R-key. A database D satisfies κ if, for every two facts $R(\bar{t}), R(\bar{s}) \in D$, $\bar{t}[i] = \bar{s}[i]$ for each $i \in \{1, \ldots, m\}$ implies $\bar{t} = \bar{s}$. We say that D is *consistent* w.r.t. a set Σ of keys, written $D \models \Sigma$, if D satisfies each key in Σ; otherwise, it is *inconsistent*. A set of *primary keys* Σ is a set of keys such that, for each predicate R, Σ has at most one R-key. For $\alpha = R(c_1, \ldots, c_n)$, the *key value* of α w.r.t. Σ, denoted $\mathsf{key}_\Sigma(\alpha)$, is defined as $\langle R, \langle c_1, \ldots, c_m \rangle \rangle$, if $\mathsf{key}(R) = \{1, \ldots, m\} \in \Sigma$, and $\langle R, \langle c_1, \ldots, c_n \rangle \rangle$ otherwise. Let $\mathsf{block}_\Sigma(\alpha, D) = \{\beta \in D \mid \mathsf{key}_\Sigma(\beta) = \mathsf{key}_\Sigma(\alpha)\}$, and $\mathsf{block}_\Sigma(D) = \{\mathsf{block}_\Sigma(\alpha, D) \mid \alpha \in D\}$.

A *repair* of D w.r.t. Σ is a database obtained by choosing one fact from each $B \in \mathsf{block}_\Sigma(D)$. We denote the set of repairs of D w.r.t Σ as $\mathsf{rep}(D, \Sigma)$.

Queries. A *first-order query* $Q(\bar{x})$ over a schema $\mathbf{S}$ is an expression $\{\bar{x} \mid \varphi\}$, where φ is a first-order formula with free variables $\bar{x}$ that mentions only atoms over $\mathbf{S}$. We write $\mathbb{FO}$, $\exists\mathbb{FO}^+$ and $\mathbb{CQ}$, for the class of first-order, existential positive, and conjunctive queries, respectively. The answer to $Q(\bar{x})$ over a database D, denoted $Q(D)$, is the set of tuples $\{\bar{c} \in \mathsf{dom}(D)^{|\bar{x}|} \mid D \models \varphi(\bar{c})\}$.

Complexity Toolbox. We recall well-known counting complexity classes, i.e., classes of counting functions of the form $\{0,1\}^* \to \mathbb{N}$. FP contains the functions that are computable in polynomial-time. #P contains the functions that compute the number of accepting computations of an NP machine. SpanL contains the functions that compute the number of *distinct valid* outputs of an NL transducer. The output of a computation is called valid if the machine halts in an accepting state. We know that SpanL $\subseteq$ #P, and the inclusion is strict (under reasonable assumptions) [1]. Consider two counting functions $f, g : \{0,1\}^* \to \mathbb{N}$. We say that f is *Cook reducible* to g, denoted $f \leq^{\mathrm{P}}_{\mathrm{T}} g$, if there exists a polynomial-time deterministic machine M, with access to an oracle for g, such that, for every $x \in \{0,1\}^*$, $f(x) = M(x)$. Moreover, we say that f is *many-one logspace reducible* to g, denoted $f \leq^{\log}_{\mathrm{m}} g$, if there exists a function $h : \{0,1\}^* \to \{0,1\}^*$ that is computable in logarithmic-space such that, for every $x \in \{0,1\}^*$, $f(x) = g(h(x))$. As usual, a complexity class $\mathcal{C}$ is *closed* under $\leq^{\mathrm{P}}_{\mathrm{T}}$ (resp., $\leq^{\log}_{\mathrm{m}}$) if, for every two functions f, g, $f \leq^{\mathrm{P}}_{\mathrm{T}} g$ (resp., $f \leq^{\log}_{\mathrm{m}} g$) and $g \in \mathcal{C}$ implies $f \in \mathcal{C}$.

3 Problem Statement

The main concern of this work is the problem of counting the number of repairs that entail a given tuple defined as follows; $\mathbb{Q}$ denotes a class of queries:

PROBLEM :	$\#\mathsf{CQA}(\mathbb{Q})$
INPUT :	A database D, a set Σ of primary keys, a query $Q(\bar{x}) \in \mathbb{Q}$, and a tuple $\bar{t} \in \mathsf{dom}(D)^{|\bar{x}|}$.
OUTPUT :	$|\{D' \in \mathsf{rep}(D, \Sigma) \mid \bar{t} \in Q(D')\}|$.

As usual, we are interested in the *data complexity* of $\#\mathsf{CQA}(\mathbb{Q})$, where the set of constraints and the query are fixed, and only the database and the tuple are part of the input. To make this notion more precise, we need to define the following problem, where $Q(\bar{x}) \in \mathbb{Q}$ is a query and Σ is a set of primary keys:

PROBLEM :	$\#\mathsf{CQA}(Q(\bar{x}), \Sigma)$
INPUT :	A database D, and a tuple $\bar{t} \in \mathsf{dom}(D)^{|\bar{x}|}$.
OUTPUT :	$|\{D' \in \mathsf{rep}(D, \Sigma) \mid \bar{t} \in Q(D')\}|$.

We say that $\#\mathsf{CQA}(\mathbb{Q})$ is $\mathcal{R}$-complete for $\mathcal{C}$ in data complexity, where $\mathcal{R}$ is a class of reductions and $\mathcal{C}$ a complexity class, if (i) for each query $Q \in \mathbb{Q}$ and set

Σ of primary keys, $\#\mathsf{CQA}(Q, \Sigma)$ is in $\mathcal{C}$, and (ii) there exists $Q' \in \mathbb{Q}$ and set Σ' of primary keys such that $\#\mathsf{CQA}(Q', \Sigma')$ is $\mathcal{R}$-complete for $\mathcal{C}$.

The decision version of $\#\mathsf{CQA}(\mathbb{Q})$, denoted $\#\mathsf{CQA}_{>0}(\mathbb{Q})$, simply asks whether $|\{D' \in \mathsf{rep}(D, \Sigma) \mid \bar{t} \in Q(D')\}| > 0$. The data complexity of $\#\mathsf{CQA}_{>0}(\mathbb{Q})$ is defined in the same way as for $\#\mathsf{CQA}(\mathbb{Q})$. Henceforth, for clarity, we focus on Boolean queries, but all the results hold even if we consider non-Boolean queries.

4 Complexity of #CQA

The complexity of #CQA has been already studied in [6, 7], and we know that $\#\mathsf{CQA}(\mathbb{CQ})$ is $\leq^{\mathrm{P}}_{\mathrm{T}}$-complete for #P.[1] The above result relies on Cook reductions. However, as discussed in Section 1, there are problems that are "hard-to-count-easy-to-decide", which cannot be complete (under reasonable assumptions) for #P under many-one logspace (or polynomial-time) reductions. Hence, the first step is to understand for which classes of queries $\mathbb{Q}$, $\#\mathsf{CQA}(\mathbb{Q})$ is an "easy-to-decide" problem. After a preliminary analysis, we have concluded that in the case of arbitrary first-order queries our problem is not only "hard-to-count", but also "hard-to-decide". In fact, we can show that $\#\mathsf{CQA}_{>0}(\mathbb{FO})$ is $\leq^{\mathrm{log}}_{\mathrm{m}}$-complete for NP, and $\#\mathsf{CQA}(\mathbb{FO})$ is $\leq^{\mathrm{log}}_{\mathrm{m}}$-complete for #P. This indicates that #P is the right complexity for our problem when we focus on first-order queries.

The situation for positive existential queries is more interesting. We can show that in this case we are dealing with a typical "hard-to-count-easy-to-decide" problem. In particular, we can show that $\#\mathsf{CQA}_{>0}(\exists\mathbb{FO}^+)$ is tractable, which in turn implies that $\#\mathsf{CQA}(\exists\mathbb{FO}^+)$ is not $\leq^{\mathrm{log}}_{\mathrm{m}}$-complete for #P (unless P = NP). This tells us that for pinpointing the complexity of $\#\mathsf{CQA}(\exists\mathbb{FO}^+)$ we should look for a subclass of #P, which is closed under logspace reductions. The obvious candidate is SpanL. Indeed, we can show that $\#\mathsf{CQA}(\exists\mathbb{FO}^+)$ is in SpanL. However, $\#\mathsf{CQA}(\exists\mathbb{FO}^+)$ is not $\leq^{\mathrm{log}}_{\mathrm{m}}$-complete for SpanL (unless L = NL). Not much is known about subclasses of SpanL for which our problem can be complete under logspace reductions. This brings us to our main question:

Research Question: *Is there a class $\mathcal{C} \subseteq$ SpanL, which is closed under logspace reductions, such that $\#\mathsf{CQA}(\exists\mathbb{FO}^+)$ is $\leq^{\mathrm{log}}_{\mathrm{m}}$-complete for $\mathcal{C}$?*

Let us stress that since we focus on the data complexity of $\#\mathsf{CQA}(\exists\mathbb{FO}^+)$, as discussed in Section 1, the above question is not trivial in the sense that the existence of the class $\mathcal{C}$ is not guaranteed. Although we cannot give a definite answer to this question, we make a significant step towards such an answer. We isolate a hierarchy of new complexity classes inside #P, called the Λ-hierarchy, and show the following; we write $\Lambda[k]$ for the k-th level of the hierarchy:

Theorem 1. *The following are equivalent:*

[1] All the results for #CQA and $\#\mathsf{CQA}_{>0}$ in the rest of the paper concern their data complexity. Thus, for brevity, we will sometimes avoid to explicitly mention the term data complexity.

1. *There exists a class $\mathcal{C} \subseteq$ SpanL, closed under logspace reductions, such that* $\#\mathsf{CQA}(\exists\mathbb{FO}^+)$ *is* $\leq_{\mathrm{m}}^{\log}$*-complete for* $\mathcal{C}$.
2. *There exists* $k \geq 0$ *such that* $\#\mathsf{CQA}(\exists\mathbb{FO}^+)$ *is* $\leq_{\mathrm{m}}^{\log}$*-complete for* $\Lambda[k]$.
3. *The* Λ*-hierarchy collapses.*

The above theorem essentially tells that either $\#\mathsf{CQA}(\exists\mathbb{FO}^+)$ is $\leq_{\mathrm{m}}^{\log}$-complete for $\Lambda[k]$, for some $k \geq 0$, or there is no complexity class $\mathcal{C} \subseteq$ SpanL, closed under many-one logspace reductions, such that $\#\mathsf{CQA}(\exists\mathbb{FO}^+)$ is $\leq_{\mathrm{m}}^{\log}$-complete for $\mathcal{C}$. Thus, the right complexity class that characterizes the data complexity of our problem, if it exists, is one of the levels of the Λ-hierarchy.

5 The Λ-hierarchy

We now proceed to introduce our hierarchy of complexity classes. The main technical challenge is to understand how to limit the computational power of NL transducers. This will lead to our new complexity classes inside SpanL that allow us to establish Theorem 1. To this end, we give a semi-formal introduction to this hierarchy, by presenting a couple of structural properties enjoyed by the functions therein. For further details, we refer the reader to [3].

5.1 The Guess-Check-Expand Paradigm

There is a generic paradigm, which we call *guess-check-expand*, that an NL transducer can follow in order to place problems inside SpanL, assuming that the following structural properties are fulfilled:

Small Certificates. A solution (in our case, a repair that entails the query) is witnessed via a *small certificate* – by small we mean of logarithmic size – that is verifiable in logspace.

For the next property, we first need to give some auxiliary terminology. Given a sequence of sets $S_1, \ldots, S_n$, an *ℓ-selector* of it, for $\ell \geq 0$, is a sequence of pairs $\sigma = (i_1, e_1), \ldots, (i_\ell, e_\ell)$, where $1 \leq i_1 < \ldots < i_\ell \leq n$, and $e_j \in S_{i_j}$ for each $j \in \{1, \ldots, \ell\}$. Intuitively, a pair (i, e) in σ tells us to "keep the element e from the set S_i". We can then define the *cartesian product of $S_1, \ldots, S_n$ w.r.t. σ*, denoted $[S_1, \ldots, S_n]^\sigma$, as $S_1^\sigma \times \cdots \times S_n^\sigma$, where $S_i^\sigma = \{e\}$ if σ contains a pair (i, e), otherwise, $S_i^\sigma = S_i$. In simple words, $[S_1, \ldots, S_n]^\sigma$ is the cartesian product of $S_1, \ldots, S_n$ with the difference that ℓ sets are first replaced by a singleton set as dictated by the ℓ-selector σ. We can now discuss the second structural property. For an input instance x, we write $\mathsf{sol}(x)$ for the set of solutions, and $\mathsf{cert}(x)$ for the set of certificates that witness a solution of $\mathsf{sol}(x)$.

Solutions via Certificate Expansion. For every input x, there is a sequence of logspace computable sets $S_1, \ldots, S_n$, called *solution domains*, such that

$$|\mathsf{sol}(x)| \;=\; \left| \bigcup_{c \in \mathsf{cert}(x)} [S_1, \ldots, S_n]^{\sigma_c} \right|,$$

where σ_c is an ℓ-selector for $S_1, \ldots, S_n$ determined by the small certificate c. In fact, there exists a bijection enc from $\mathsf{sol}(x)$ to $\bigcup_{c \in \mathsf{cert}(x)} [S_1, \ldots, S_n]^{\sigma_c}$, and $enc(s)$ should be understood as an encoding of the solution s.

A function that enjoys the above structural properties can be shown to be in SpanL via a simple guess-check-expand algorithm:

1. (**Guess**) Guess a candidate small certificate c.
2. (**Check**) If c is not a valid certificate, then reject.
3. (**Expand**) Expand c into an encoding of a solution witnessed by c using $S_1, \ldots, S_n$ as follows: for $i = 1$ to n, if the ℓ-selector σ_c determined by c mentions (i, e), then output e; otherwise, guess $e \in S_i$ and output e.

It is clear that, on an input x, the above transducer uses logspace in the size of x since the small certificates are logspace verifiable, and the solution domains are logspace computable. Moreover, the number of distinct valid outputs of the transducer coincides with $\left|\bigcup_{c \in \mathsf{cert}(x)} [S_1, \ldots, S_n]^{\sigma_c}\right|$, and thus, with $|\mathsf{sol}(x)|$. A transducer of the form above is called k-guess-check-expand, for some integer $k \geq 0$, if the ℓ-selectors are such that $\ell \leq k$.

$\#\mathsf{CQA}(Q, \Sigma)$ via a Guess-Check-Expand Algorithm. It is interesting to observe that the problem $\#\mathsf{CQA}(Q, \Sigma)$, for some UCQ Q and set Σ of primary keys, enjoys the two structural properties defined above; recall that an existential positive query can be rewritten as a UCQ. More precisely, on input D:

- A small certificate for a repair of $\mathsf{rep}(D, \Sigma)$ that entails Q is a pair (Q', h), where Q' is a disjunct of Q, and $h : \mathsf{var}(Q') \rightarrow \mathsf{dom}(D)$, such that $h(Q') \subseteq D$ and $h(Q') \models \Sigma$.
- The sequence of solution domains corresponds to the sequence $B_1, \ldots, B_n$ of the sets of $\mathsf{block}_{\Sigma}(D)$, according to some arbitrary, but fixed ordering. The ℓ-selector $\sigma_{(Q',h)}$ for $B_1, \ldots, B_n$ determined by a certificate (Q', h) mentions the pair $(i, R(\bar{t}))$, i.e., it keeps the fact $R(\bar{t})$ from B_i, iff $h(Q') \cap B_i = \{R(\bar{t})\}$ and Σ has an R-key. The latter implies that ℓ is bounded by the number of atoms with a predicate that has a key over all disjuncts of Q, which does not depend on the input database D. Clearly, the number of repairs of $\mathsf{rep}(D, \Sigma)$ that entail Q is the number

$$\left| \bigcup_{(Q',h) \in \mathsf{cert}(D)} [B_1, \ldots, B_n]^{\sigma_{(Q',h)}} \right|.$$

Therefore, the fact that $\#\mathsf{CQA}(Q, \Sigma)$ is in SpanL can be shown via a k-guess-check-expand algorithm, as the one presented below, where k is the number of atoms in Q with a predicate with a key in Σ:

1. (**Guess**) Guess a candidate small certificate (Q', h).
2. (**Check**) If $h(Q') \nsubseteq D$ or $h(Q') \not\models \Sigma$, then reject.
3. (**Expand**) Expand (Q', h) into an encoding of a solution witnessed by (Q', h) as follows: for $i = 1$ to n, if $h(Q') \cap B_i = \{R(\bar{t})\}$ and Σ has an R-key, then output $R(\bar{t})$; otherwise, guess a fact $\alpha \in B_i$ and output α.

5.2 Semi-formal Definition and Properties

The guess-check-expand paradigm suggests a natural way to define a hierarchy of classes inside SpanL. Intuitively, the k-th level of such hierarchy is defined by considering k-guess-check-expand transducers. This intuition is at the core of the Λ-hierarchy. In particular, for every integer $k \geq 0$, $\Lambda[k]$ is the class of functions $f : \{0,1\}^* \to \mathbb{N}$ such that, for every $x \in \{0,1\}^*$, $f(x)$ is the number of valid distinct outputs of a k-guess-check-expand transducer M_f, with input x. The Λ-hierarchy is defined as the infinite union $\Lambda = \bigcup_{k \geq 0} \Lambda[k]$.

We proceed to discuss some key properties concerning the Λ-hierarchy. The first one states that each level of the hierarchy is closed under logspace reductions, which is crucial for our complexity analysis.

Proposition 1. *For each $k \geq 0$, $\Lambda[k]$ is closed under logspace reductions.*

The next result confirms that Λ is a hierarchy of classes inside SpanL:

Proposition 2. $\Lambda[0] \subseteq \cdots \subseteq \Lambda \subseteq$ SpanL, *and* $\Lambda =$ SpanL *implies* L = NL.

The next result shows that, apart from $\Lambda[0]$ and $\Lambda[1]$, the rest of the hierarchy consists of "hard" complexity classes:

Proposition 3. $\Lambda[1] \subseteq$ FP, *and* $\Lambda[2] \subseteq$ FP *implies* P = NP.

A direct corollary of Proposition 3 is that $\Lambda[1] \subsetneq \Lambda[2]$ (unless P = NP). We do not know whether the inclusions beyond $\Lambda[2]$ are strict. This essentially asks whether there exists an integer $k \geq 2$ such that the Λ-hierarchy collapses to its k-th level, i.e., whether $\Lambda = \Lambda[k]$. This is a non-trivial open question.

6 Establishing our Main Result

Having the Λ-hierarchy in place, we are now ready to explain how Theorem 1 is shown. To this end, we concentrate on a parameterized version of $\#\mathsf{CQA}(\exists\mathbb{FO}^+)$, where the so-called keywidth of the query w.r.t. the set of primary keys is bounded by an integer $k \geq 0$. Formally, the *keywidth function (kw)* maps pairs of the form (Q, Σ), where $Q \in \exists\mathbb{FO}^+$ and Σ is a set of primary keys, to the naturals such that $kw(Q, \Sigma) = |\{R(\bar{t}) \mid R(\bar{t})$ occurs in Q, and Σ has an R-key$\}|$. Then:

PROBLEM :	$\#\mathsf{CQA}^{kw}_{k}(\exists\mathbb{FO}^+)$
INPUT :	A database D, a set Σ of primary keys, and a query $Q \in \exists\mathbb{FO}^+$ such that $kw(Q, \Sigma) = k$.
OUTPUT :	$\lvert\{D' \in \mathsf{rep}(D, \Sigma) \mid D' \models Q\}\rvert$.

The data complexity of the above problem is defined as expected. Then:

Theorem 2. *For each $k \geq 0$, $\#\mathsf{CQA}^{kw}_{k}(\exists\mathbb{FO}^+)$ is $\leq^{\log}_{\mathrm{m}}$-complete for $\Lambda[k]$.*

By exploiting Theorem 2, we can now establish our main result (Theorem 1):

(1) ⇒ (3). By hypothesis, there is a class $\mathcal{C} \subseteq$ SpanL such that $\#\mathsf{CQA}(\exists\mathbb{FO}^+)$ is $\leq_m^{\log}$-complete for $\mathcal{C}$. Thus, for every $Q \in \exists\mathbb{FO}^+$ and set Σ of primary keys, $\#\mathsf{CQA}(Q, \Sigma) \in \mathcal{C}$. Moreover, there exists $\hat{Q}$ and $\hat{\Sigma}$ such that $\#\mathsf{CQA}(\hat{Q}, \hat{\Sigma})$ is $\leq_m^{\log}$-complete for $\mathcal{C}$, which means that, for every $f \in \mathcal{C}$, $f \leq_m^{\log} \#\mathsf{CQA}(\hat{Q}, \hat{\Sigma})$. By Theorem 2, $\#\mathsf{CQA}(\hat{Q}, \hat{\Sigma}) \in \Lambda[kw(\hat{Q}, \hat{\Sigma})]$. Since, by Proposition 1, $\Lambda[kw(\hat{Q}, \hat{\Sigma})]$ is closed under logspace reductions, we conclude that $f \in \mathcal{C}$ implies $f \in \Lambda[kw(\hat{Q}, \hat{\Sigma})]$, or, in other words, $\mathcal{C} \subseteq \Lambda[kw(\hat{Q}, \hat{\Sigma})]$. Hence, for every $Q \in \exists\mathbb{FO}^+$ and set Σ of primary keys, $\#\mathsf{CQA}(Q, \Sigma) \in \Lambda[kw(\hat{Q}, \hat{\Sigma})]$. Since, for every $k \geq 0$, there exists Q' and Σ' such that $\#\mathsf{CQA}(Q', \Sigma')$ is $\leq_m^{\log}$-complete for $\Lambda[k]$, then $\bigcup_{k \geq 0} \Lambda[k] = \Lambda[kw(\hat{Q}, \hat{\Sigma})]$. Hence, the Λ-hierarchy collapses to its $kw(\hat{Q}, \hat{\Sigma})$-th level.

(3) ⇒ (2). By hypothesis, the Λ-hierarchy collapses to its k-the level, for some $k \geq 0$, i.e., $\Lambda = \Lambda[k]$. We proceed to show that (i) for every $Q \in \exists\mathbb{FO}^+$ and set Σ of primary keys, $\#\mathsf{CQA}(Q, \Sigma) \in \Lambda[k]$, and (ii) there exists $\hat{Q}$ and $\hat{\Sigma}$ such that $\#\mathsf{CQA}(\hat{Q}, \hat{\Sigma})$ is $\leq_m^{\log}$-complete for $\Lambda[k]$. For showing (i), fix some query $Q \in \exists\mathbb{FO}^+$ and set Σ of primary keys. By Theorem 2, $\#\mathsf{CQA}(Q, \Sigma) \in \Lambda[kw(Q, \Sigma)]$. Since $\Lambda[kw(Q, \Sigma)] \subseteq \Lambda = \Lambda[k]$, we immediately get that $\#\mathsf{CQA}(Q, \Sigma) \in \Lambda[k]$. Statement (ii) holds trivially since, by Theorem 2, there exists a $\leq_m^{\log}$-complete function for every level of the Λ-hierarchy.

(2) ⇒ (1). Since, for every $k \geq 0$, $\Lambda[k]$ is closed under logspace reductions (Proposition 1), and $\Lambda[k] \subseteq$ SpanL (Proposition 2), the claim follows.

The Next Step. Providing a firm answer to our main question boils down to understanding whether the Λ-hierarchy collapses. Our conjecture is that it does not collapse. Proving or disproving this conjecture is one of our priorities, which will complete the picture concerning the data complexity of $\#\mathsf{CQA}(\exists\mathbb{FO}^+)$.

Acknowledgements. This work was supported by the EPSRC grants S003800 EQUID, M025268 VADA, and N023056 MAGIC.

References

1. Àlvarez, C., Jenner, B.: A very hard log-space counting class. Theor. Comput. Sci. **107**(1), 3–30 (1993)
2. Arenas, M., Bertossi, L.E., Chomicki, J.: Consistent query answers in inconsistent databases. In: PODS. pp. 68–79 (1999)
3. Calautti, M., Console, M., Pieris, A.: Counting database reparis under primary keys revisited. In: PODS (2019), to appear
4. Calautti, M., Libkin, L., Pieris, A.: An operational approach to consistent query answering. In: PODS. pp. 239–251 (2018)
5. Durand, A., Hermann, M., Kolaitis, P.G.: Subtractive reductions and complete problems for counting complexity classes. Theor. Comput. Sci. **340**(3), 496–513 (2005)
6. Maslowski, D., Wijsen, J.: A dichotomy in the complexity of counting database repairs. J. Comput. Syst. Sci. **79**(6), 958–983 (2013)
7. Maslowski, D., Wijsen, J.: Counting database repairs that satisfy conjunctive queries with self-joins. In: ICDT. pp. 155–164 (2014)
8. Pagourtzis, A., Zachos, S.: The complexity of counting functions with easy decision version. In: MFCS. pp. 741–752 (2006)

Multi-Dimensional Contexts for Querying IoT Networks

Claudia Diamantini[1], Antonino Nocera[2], Domenico Potena[1], Emanuele Storti[1], and Domenico Ursino[1]

[1] DII, Polytechnic University of Marche
[2] DIII, University of Pavia

Abstract. The pervasiveness of smart objects in people daily life is increasing, as the capabilities of objects are becoming more and more sophisticated. Objects participate to the Internet of Thing (IoT) with changing contexts and scopes, thus resulting in the rise of multiple networks linked to each other to form a new paradigm, called Multi-IoTs (MIoT). Of course, cooperation strategies among objects must follow this innovative trend as classical strategies based on the concept of co-existence appear no more adequate. In this scenario, this paper proposes a contribution by introducing a complex model for devices and contexts that follows a knowledge representation approach. It adopts dimension hierarchies in the multidimensional perspective typical of OLAP systems to represent roll-up relationships between admissible members of the considered dimensions, enabling the retrieval of relevant objects through a supervised algorithm.

1 Introduction

Nowadays devices and sensors are smart enough to have connection capabilities forming a network also known as Internet of Things (IoT). Furthermore, the variety of types of objects, contexts, and scopes for which devices participate to the IoT push towards the definition of multiple networks linked to each other to form the notion of Multi-IoTs (MIoT). In these scenarios it is of crucial importance the development of techniques for the retrieval of relevant devices and data conveyed by them. As a matter of fact, some contexts, e.g. outdoor applications like intelligent transportation, have largely casual, non pre-determined goals. Moreover, objects move and meet other ones, so that cooperation strategies must be dynamically defined. Some approaches in the literature define some simple criteria to decide about the creation of the network [2]: (a) proximity (objects connect to each other if they are spatially close for a sufficiently long time interval); (b) homogeneity (objects belonging to the same brand and of the same kind, e.g. Samsung community); (c) ownership (objects belonging to the same user); (d) friendship (objects belonging to users that are connected to each other in some social networks). These criteria do not take into account usage and goal context in order to decide for the actual usefulness of the contact. Approaches for the definition of context in IoT have been developed in the literature. This concept has been often intertwined with that of empowering the IoT of social features. Indeed, the idea of studying object contexts has raised from the need of improving the quality of interactions among them. For instance, [13] is the first work in which the idea of filtering contacts on the basis of proximity contexts has been developed. The authors of this work actually suggest to combine the classical notion of proximity with other metrics, such as movements patterns, thus defining a context proximity notion. Several other studies have, then, refined this notion by bringing the notion of context and context matching under the spotlight as a mean to confer social feature to objects in the IoT [6,11].

In this paper we propose an approach to identify and query relevant devices inside a MIoT, that is based on the notion of device's "context", describing its semantics in terms of its customary usage, the interest and behavior (in terms of activities done with the object itself) of the owner, and so forth. Interactions among objects can be then driven by the degree of similarity among their respective contexts. As usually done in the framework of IoT research, a context is defined as a set of couples (p, v), where p is some property, and v represents an admissible value of the property. Differing from other approaches, we adopt a richer model based on a hierarchy of admissible values for each property, in the spirit of the multi-dimensional model typical of OLAP systems. This allows us to introduce different types of relationships among contexts, namely identity, inclusion (similar to the notion of roll-up among members of each context dimension) and a fuzzier relationship of compatibility. On the basis of this model, this paper presents an algorithm to determine the subset of devices that are more likely able to provide relevant answers to a user's query.

Knowledge representation approaches to context modeling have been extensively investigated in the literature [7,4,15] with the aim to accurately describe complex entities, relationships, and constraints [12] forming a context. Many of them adopt logical languages and ontologies to this end [1,8,18,16]. However, the expressiveness of ontologies has complexity as a shortcoming, which can be critical for many applications, like those of the IoT scenario where computing abilities are limited [4]. Furthermore, none of the cited models considers a hierarchical organization of context properties. The Context Dimension Tree, implemented in the PerLa context language for designing and managing wireless sensor network applications [17], considers a tree structure where a *dimension* node is the parent of a set of *concept* nodes. Nesting of more than one dimension level is possible, allowing the representation of structured concepts (namely admissible members). In contrast, the model proposed in this paper adopts dimension hierarchies in the multidimensional perspective typical of OLAP systems, representing roll-up relationships between admissible members of the dimensions.

The above literature focuses on "how" context information can be represented. Another issue is related to "which" information should be included in context. As already noted, this greatly varies from application to application. Authors in [5] recognize a limit inherent in the adoption of knowledge representation methodologies for context modelling, namely the difficulty for a limited group of people to enumerate all the possible concepts and relationships that may be used in a practical mobile or desktop context-aware application. We believe that the multidimensional perspective proposed in this paper offers a more "general-purpose", "application-independent" perspective: in practice, if a dimension is not relevant for a given application, we model it as if any possible admissible value was acceptable, corresponding to a "roll-up all" operation.

The object's network(s) created in this way can be compared to a person's list of contacts in a social network. This view is strongly supported by the research community and, indeed, a number of works have tried to adopt the paradigm of social network in the IoT realm and to combine these worlds improving their usability and the offered services [9,14,3,10]. In [11], the authors propose a social infrastructure allowing access to both humans and objects. In this system, humans can interact with each other offering services through their own objects, or they can interact directly with objects by using the infrastructure as a communication channel. An important step towards the definition of a unified framework for including things in the virtual human communities is described in [3]. This paper provides contribution in both the definition of policies managing the social interaction among objects, so that the result is an accessible and usable social network, and the formalization of an architecture for the IoT, so that objects include all the features needed for an easy and effective integration in existing social sites. As a result of this study the authors propose a new paradigm called Social Internet of Things (SIoT). Very recently, other studies have focused on the social factors that foster the rise of new and stable communication in the IoT. For instance, the work described in [10] first proposes a study on which social aspect improves the quality of object-to-object communication and, after that, provides insights on how to include those aspects in a new framework for creating an IoT-only social community.

Differing from a social network, where peers are not classified according to their profile, or only very naïve manual classification in a predefined set of categories can be done, the proposed model allows a very rich and flexible definition of contexts, and a graded association of profiles to contexts. Furthermore, interaction mechanisms in social networks are typically limited to information sharing by broadcasting (posting information that reaches all node's contacts) or to one-to-one messaging (directly contacting a node via its name/address). In the present paper we also present an algorithm to determine the best set of nodes that can be queried according to given information needs or preferences and contexts, hence producing a projection, or view, of the original overall network, that can be actually exploited for the goal at hand.

This paper is structured as follows: Section 2 presents the model for device contexts in a Multi-IoT scenario, on the top of which a supervised algorithm for device retrieval is presented in Section 3. Experiments to assess the effectiveness of our approach are reported in Section 4, whereas Section 5 ends this paper.

2 A model for devices in a multi-IoT network

This section is devoted to introduce the model used to represent devices and their relations in the context of a multi-IoT network. We define a device Δ_i as a set of sensors $\Delta_i = \{S_1, \ldots, S_n\}$. We refer to the term *context* as a scenario in which the devices operated in the past, are currently operating or may operate in the future. A set P_i of properties are associated with a device, each of which represented as a pair (p, v) where p is a property (e.g., *owner, brand, model, cost, reference measure*) and v is the corresponding value. We discuss in more detail contexts and properties in the following.

2.1 Context of a device

In order to specify a context, we refer to a set of dimensions $\mathcal{D} = \{D_1, \ldots, D_m\}$, which are to be intended as the dimensions in the multidimensional model (e.g., or instance *time, space, goal*). Therefore, from a data perspective, a context may be compared to a fact in a multidimensional model. In this work, we do not assume that all contexts for all devices are defined by the same set of dimensions. According to the information provided by its sensors, each device will specify a context according to available information.

Analogously to the multidimensional model, given a dimension $D_j \in \mathcal{D}$, it is possible to define a hierarchy of levels $L_j = \{l_{j_1}, \ldots, l_{j_m}\}$ such that $l_{j_1} \rightarrow l_{j_2} \rightarrow \cdots \rightarrow l_{j_m}$. The notation $l_{j_p} \rightarrow l_{j_q}$ implies that a functional dependency exists from l_{j_p} to l_{j_q}. To make an example, given the dimension *space*, the following relation holds: $street \rightarrow district \rightarrow city \rightarrow \cdots \rightarrow country$. Given a level l_{j_i} of a dimension D_j, its members $\{\iota_{j_1}, \ldots, \iota_{j_i}\}$ are named instances, e.g. level *city* can include instances *Rome, Venice, Milan.*

The schema of a context C for a device is a set of dimensions $\mathcal{D}$. A context instance $c \in C$ is a tuple $c = (\iota_1, \iota_2, \cdots, \iota_m)$. To make an example, considering a dimensional schema including $\{$ *space, time, goal* $\}$, a possible instance can take the following values: ι_{space}= *Grosseto*, ι_{time}= *June* 16th *2019, 11:00-12:00*, ι_{goal} = *Running.*

Given a dimension $D_j \in \mathcal{D}$, let $\iota_{j_p}, \iota_{j_q} \in D_j$ be two instances of D_j. The following relations are defined between ι_{j_p} and ι_{j_q}:

- $id(\iota_{j_p}, \iota_{j_q})$: it means that ι_{j_p} and ι_{j_q} are identical instances, e.g. *id(Montecitorio square, Montecitorio Sq.)*.
- $inc(\iota_{j_p}, \iota_{j_q})$: it means that ι_{j_p} is included in ι_{j_q}, e.g. *inc(Montecitorio square, Rome)*. In order for this property to hold, it must be that $square \rightarrow city$ and *Montecitorio square* is in Rome. Moreover, given that $square \rightarrow city$ and, in turn, $city \rightarrow nation$, it also holds that *inc(Montecitorio square, Italy)*. In the following we refer to $dist(\iota_{j_p}, \iota_{j_q})$ as the distance between ι_{j_p} and ι_{j_q}, that is the number of steps in the dimensional hierarchy necessary to move from the former to the latter.
- $cpt(\iota_{j_p}, \iota_{j_q})$: it means that $inc(\iota_{j_p}, \iota_{j_r})$, $inc(\iota_{j_q}, \iota_{j_r})$, where $l_{j_p} \rightarrow l_{j_r}$, $l_{j_q} \rightarrow l_{j_r}$ and l_{j_p} (resp., l_{j_q}, l_{j_r}) represents the level of ι_{j_p} (resp., ι_{j_q}, ι_{j_r}). This means

that ι_{j_p} and ι_{j_p} are siblings, e.g. *cpt*(*Rome*,*Milan*), *cpt*(*Italy*, *France*), whereas it does not hold that *cpt*(*Rome*, *Paris*).

Let $c = (\iota_1, \iota_2, \cdots, \iota_m)$ and $c' = (\iota'_1, \iota'_2, \cdots, \iota'_m)$ be two contexts. The following relations are defined among them:

- $id_C(c, c')$, if $id(\iota_i, \iota'_i)$, $1 \leq i \leq m$; for instance *c*=(*Montecitorio square*, [10:00-11:00], *Running*) *c'*=(*Montecitorio sq.*, [10:00-11:00], *Running*).
- $inc_C(c, c')$, if $id(\iota_i, \iota'_i)$ or if $inc(\iota_i, \iota'_i)$, $1 \leq i \leq m$ and $id_C(c, c')$ does not hold; for instance *c*=(*Montecitorio square*, [10:00-11:00], *Running*), *c'*=(*Montecitorio sq.*, *Morning*, *Running*). We define $dist(c, c')$ as a measure of distance between c and c', measured as $\sum_{i=1}^{m} dist(\iota_i, \iota'_i)$, where $dist(\iota_i, \iota'_i) = 0$ if $id(\iota_i, \iota'_i)$.
- $cpt_C(c, c')$, if either $id(\iota_i, \iota'_i)$ or $inc(\iota_i, \iota'_i)$ or $cpt(\iota_i, \iota'_i)$, $1 \leq i \leq m$ and neither $id_C(c, c')$ nor $inc_C(c, c')$ holds; for instance, *c*=(*Montecitorio square*, [09:00-10:00], *Running*) *c*=(*Montecitorio square*, [10:00-11:00], *Running*)

In the following, we define an operator $match(c)$, which returns the set of devices that are matching with the context c. In order for a device Δ_i to match with c, the context provided by Δ_i must be a superset of c, i.e it must provide at least the same dimensions included in c, with the same members.

Definition 1. *(Match operator)*
Given a net $N = \{\Delta_1, \ldots, \Delta_n\}$ including a set of n devices, each with a corresponding context c_i, and given a context $c = (i_1^{D_1}, \ldots, i_m^{D_m})$, $match(c)$=$\{\Delta_i \in N : c \subseteq c_i\}$.

2.2 Properties of devices

Let (p_i, v_i) and (p_j, v_j) be two property-value pairs. We define the following relations between them:

- $id_P(p_i, p_j)$, if $p_i = p_j$ and $v_i = v_j$;
- $cpt_P(p_i, p_j)$, if $p_i = p_j$ and $cpt_V(v_i, v_j)$;
- $cpt_V(v_i, v_j)$, to state an explicit compatibility relation among them. For instance, a device measuring temperature in Farenheit is compatible with another device referring to Celsius.

Let us define $P(d)$ as the set of properties for a device d, i.e. $P = \{(p_1, v_1), (p_2, v_2), \cdots, (p_n, v_n)\}$. We introduce a Jaccard modified operator $J^*(P, P')$ which works on two sets of properties P and P' and returns a float between 0 ed 1 representing the ratio of P that are identical or compatible with P'. It is computed through the following steps:

- the set $I = \{(p, p') | p \in P, p' \in P', id_P(p, p')\}$ is computed, which includes all properties that are identical;
- the set $C = \{(p, p') | p \in P, p' \in P', cpt_P(p, p')\}$ is computed, including those properties that are compatible each other;
- finally, the result of $J^*(P, P')$ is computed as $J^*(P, P') = \frac{|I| + \alpha \cdot |C|}{|P|}$, where $\alpha \in [0, 1]$ allows the contribution of the second factor to be weighted.

3 Retrieval of devices in a multi-IoT network

Given a user and its network, this section presents a supervised algorithm aimed to retrieve the subset of devices satisfying some requirements, that are expressed through a query.

A query q is represented as $q = \langle c, Z \rangle$, where c is the context of interest and $Z = \{(p_1, v_1), (p_2, v_2), \cdots, (p_n, v_n)\}$ represents the properties that the devices must satisfy, expressed as a set of pairs (p, v) indicating the required value v for each property p. The pseudocode is reported in Algorithm 1.

To provide an answer to a query q, the supervised algorithm first executes a $SEARCH$ function, computing all contexts that are respectively identical, included or compatible with c, checking whether there are devices that belong to such contexts. In case there is no answer, the algorithm *rewrites* the query by finding one or more contexts that include c, i.e. that are more general than c (formally the set $\{c' \in C : inc_C(c, c')\}$), and then the $SEARCH$ is performed again. The whole procedure iterates until to: (1) a solution is found, (2) the number of rewritings is above a defined threshold (using the function *dist* discussed in Section 2.1), (3) there are no more general contexts. The pseudocode for the $SEARCH$ function is reported in Algorithm 1, and operates as follows:

1. The Algorithm searches for devices that have contexts identical to or included in c by calling the corresponding function. If there are such devices (line 4) then their properties $P(s)$ are matched against the vector Z to verify if, and to what extent, they satisfy the user query in terms of property values (line 6). Finally, each retrieved device, ranked according to the Jaccard function J^* (discussed in Section 2.2), is added to the output list S_O (line 7).
2. In case no device is found in the previous step, then the algorithm searches for devices having a context compatible with c, through the corresponding function. Similarly to the previous case, for each retrieved device a rank r is computed and the pair $\langle device, rank \rangle$ is added to the output list S_O (line 14). To take into account that such devices have contexts that are compatible, but neither identical to, nor included in, c, the rank is weighted by a parameter $\alpha_{cpt} < 1$.

Finally, the list S_O is returned as output (line 18).

4 Experiments

The supervised algorithm discussed in the previous section has been evaluated. In particular, hereafter, we compare our approach with two baseline algorithms:

- $Baseline_1$ (no contexts): this approach does not consider contexts. Therefore, the query is expressed only as $q = \langle \emptyset, Z \rangle$.
- $Baseline_2$ (only identical): this approach considers contexts but it does not include a knowledge base. Therefore, the supervised approach can only match identical contexts but no reasoning on inclusion or compatibility can be done.

Algorithm 1 Pseudocode for the SEARCH function

Input:

The set S of devices in the user net.

A query q=$\langle c, Z\rangle$ over S, where $c \in C$ is a context and $Z = \{(p_1, v_1), (p_2, v_2), \cdots, (p_n, v_n)\}$ is a set of pairs (property value)

Output:

a ranked set of devices $S_O = \{\langle s_1, r_1\rangle, \ldots, \langle s_n, r_n\rangle\}$, where $s_i \in S$ and $r_i \in [0, 1]$

```
function SEARCH(q)
    S_O ← []
    S' ← FIND_DEVICES_ID(c,S)
    if S' ≠ ∅ then
        for each s ∈ S' do
            r ← J*(Z, P(s))
            S_O ← ⟨s, r⟩
        end for
    else
        S' ← FIND_DEVICES_CPT(c,S)
        if S' ≠ ∅ then
            for each s ∈ S' do
                r ← α_cpt * J*(Z, P(s))
                S_O ← ⟨s, r⟩
            end for
        end if
    end if
    return S_O
end function

function FIND_DEVICES_ID(c, S)
    C' ← IC(c) ∪ INC⁻(c) = {c' ∈ C | id_C(c, c') ∨ inc_C(c', c)}
    S' ← {s ∈ S | s ∈ match(c'), c' ∈ C'}
    return S'
end function

function FIND_DEVICES_CPT(c, S)
    C' ← CPT(c) = {c' ∈ C | cpt_C(c, c') ∨ inc_C(c', c)}
    S' ← {s ∈ S | s ∈ match(c'), c' ∈ C'}
    return S'
end function
```

Firstly, the dataset, the knowledge base and the experimental settings are introduced. Then, we present results aimed to evaluate three different measures: (1) the probability to obtain a response from a query, (2) how the query rewriting approach discussed in Section 3 affects retrieval and (3) how it affects precision of the supervised algorithm. Hereby, we refer to the precision as the ratio $\frac{relevantcontexts}{retrievedcontexts}$, where *retrieved contexts* stands for the contexts belonging to the retrieved sensors, while *relevant contexts* refer to those contexts that are relevant to the query.

Dataset and model In this set of experiments we refer to a dataset that includes 5000 devices, each with a single sensor. Each device belongs to one or more IoT networks, the largest of which includes 500 devices. These are described in terms of their properties, although, in these tests, we consider a single property, namely the "measure" retrieved by the device (e.g., temperature, humidity or pressure), for the sake of simplicity.

The model taken into consideration for these tests includes 3 dimensions, 3 hierarchical levels for each dimension and a branching factor of the dimensional tree equal to 3. In particular, the dimensional tree will include 1 root element at level 1, 3 elements at level 2 and 9 elements at level 3 (i.e. 13 elements in total). The overall number of possible contexts is, therefore, given by all the possible combinations of elements for each dimension, e.g. $|C| = 13^3 = 2197$ in this case. Specific compatibility relationships among members are defined for each dimension. In our experimental setting, each member is defined to be compatible with 5% of the other members in the same level (e.g., given the level "street" of dimension space, each specific member will have 5% of chances to be defined as compatible with any other street).

Experimental settings The initialization includes the following steps:

- Device initialization: a device is picked from the dataset, and the set S of all the devices belonging to its net are extracted. In our test, the following procedure is repeated with 5 devices belonging to nets with sizes $S_1, \ldots, S_5$ from $|S_1| = 100$ to $|S_5| = 500$.
- For each device s $\in S_i$: a context c is randomly assigned to s. The assignment is done according to a strategy following a power law: we randomly assign a context from a small subset of C (i.e., 20% its size) to the large majority of devices (i.e., 80% in our tests), which hereafter we name C_s. We aim to model in such a way as the probable context similarity of devices belonging to the same network. The procedure assigns a random context from the remaining set $C - C_s$ (i.e., in this case corresponding to the remaining 80% of C) to the rest (i.e., the remaining 20% of devices).
- A query $q = \langle c, Z \rangle$ is defined by assigning a context c from C_s and a property value from the list of possible property values seen in the database.
- The query q is launched on the network.

The procedure has been repeated for a number of queries equal to $|C|$, in order to perform a comprehensive evaluation. Results are, then, averaged.

Results Results are summarized in Figure 1. Figure 1(a) shows the performances of the supervised algorithm with increasing net sizes, in terms of percentage of queries with an answer. On the other hand, Figure 1(b) shows how the number of rewritings affects precision (as defined above) and how it affects recall in terms of the increase in the percentage of queries answered when one or more rewritings occur (see Section 3).

The most relevant insights are summarized as follows: the increase in the number of devices in a net has a positive impact, on average, on results. In particular, the larger the size, the greater the ratio of queries with an answer. By rewriting a query c as a query c' (which includes the former), the likelihood of obtaining an answer increases. Indeed, the number of contexts included or compatible in c' is obviously larger than in the former case. A single rewriting is enough to significantly increase the chance to find at least one solution to the query. However, this is achieved at the price of a relaxation of the original query specification and, as a consequence, of a decrease of the precision of results.

A direct comparison with $Baseline_1$ is straightforward, as the number of retrieved devices is purely based on property information. Therefore, with $Baseline_1$ the result set is always larger, but the whole set of sensors in the network must be analysed and matched against the properties, with no guarantee on the correctness of the results. In other terms, recall is not higher whereas precision is much lower. On the other hand, by comparing these results with the $Baseline_2$ approach, it is possible to conclude that our approach allows the retrieval of a much larger number of relevant results. In this respect, $Baseline_2$ is basically equivalent to the evaluation of only identical contexts. Therefore, precision is high, whereas recall is typically much lower. On the other hand, by exploiting the knowledge base, and specifically inclusion relations among contexts, more contexts can be obtained. Moreover, contexts that are compatible are added to the result with a lower rank, meaning that their relevance is lower than the others but can be still useful, depending on the specific application case. Finally, by exploiting inclusion relationships and the notion of rewriting, our approach can optionally lower precision in order to increase the probability to answer a query.

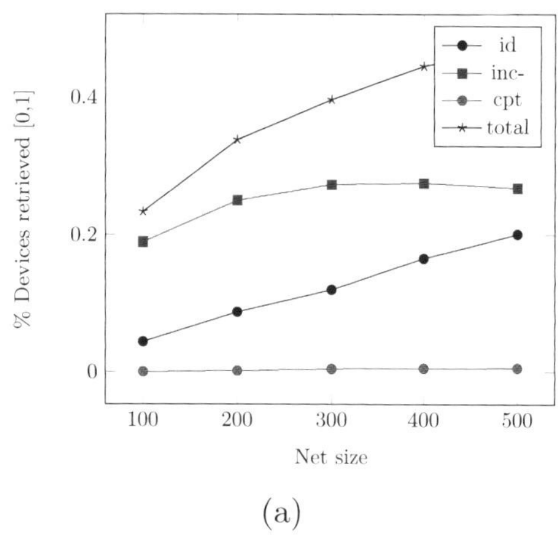

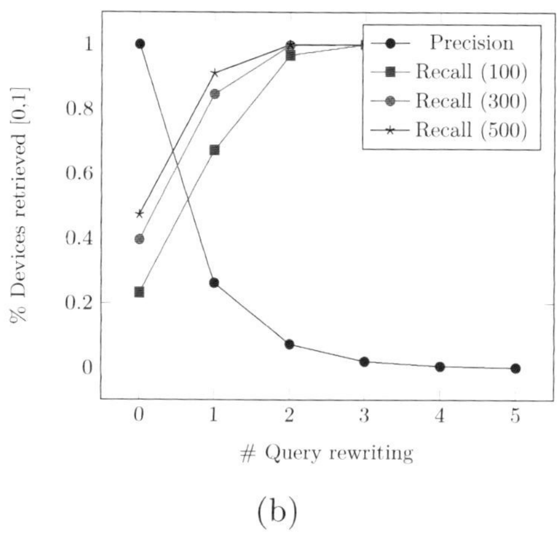

Fig. 1: (a) Percentage of retrieved devices with networks of difference size, (b) precision and recall against the number of query rewritings.

5 Conclusion

This paper has discussed an approach to querying a Multi-IoT network of devices, which relies on a multi-dimensional model for device's contexts that takes also into account its customary usage, user interest and behavior. On top of that, we proposed a supervised algorithm to determine the best set of nodes that can be queried according to given information needs or preferences and contexts, experimentally evaluating its effectiveness. Future works include: (1) the extension of the model with more expressive relations between dimensions members, (2) an unsupervised algorithm that starts with no initial specification of desiderata and automatically generates a query on the basis of its current context and device's properties, and (3) a more comprehensive experimentation.

Acknowledgement

This work was partially funded by the Department of Information Engineering at the Polytechnic University of Marche under the projects "A network-based approach to uniformly extract knowledge and support decision making in heterogeneous application contexts" and "Novel and Optimal Solutions for Metering and Enforcing Security and Privacy in Cloud Systems" (RSA-B 2018).

References

1. Alessandra Agostini, Claudio Bettini, and Daniele Riboni. Hybrid reasoning in the care middleware for context awareness. *International Journal of Web Engineering and Technology*, 5(1):3–23, 2009.
2. Luigi Atzori, Antonio Iera, and Giacomo Morabito. The internet of things: A survey. *Computer networks*, 54(15):2787–2805, 2010.
3. Luigi Atzori, Antonio Iera, Giacomo Morabito, and Michele Nitti. The social internet of things (siot)–when social networks meet the internet of things: Concept, architecture and network characterization. *Computer networks*, 56(16):3594–3608, 2012.
4. Claudio Bettini, Oliver Brdiczka, Karen Henricksen, Jadwiga Indulska, Daniela Nicklas, Anand Ranganathan, and Daniele Riboni. A survey of context modelling and reasoning techniques. *Pervasive and Mobile Computing*, 6(2):161–180, 2010.
5. Preeti Bhargava, Shivsubramani Krishnamoorthy, and Ashok Agrawala. Rocomo: A generic ontology for context modeling, representation and reasoning in a context-aware middleware. In *Proceedings of the 2012 ACM Conference on Ubiquitous Computing*, UbiComp '12, pages 584–585. ACM, 2012.
6. Julian Bleecker. A manifesto for networked objects—cohabiting with pigeons, arphids and aibos in the internet of things. 2006.
7. Oscar Cabrera, Xavier Franch, and Jordi Marco. Ontology-based context modeling in service-oriented computing: A systematic mapping. *Data & Knowledge Engineering*, 110:24–53, 2017.
8. Harry Chen, Tim Finin, and Anupam Joshi. Soupa: standard ontology for ubiquitous and pervasive applications. In *The First Annual International Conference on Mobile and Ubiquitous Systems: Networking and Services, 2004. MOBIQUITOUS 2004*, 2004.
9. Lianhong Ding, Peng Shi, and Bingwu Liu. The clustering of internet, internet of things and social network. In *2010 Third International Symposium on Knowledge Acquisition and Modeling*, pages 417–420. IEEE, 2010.
10. Qinghe Du, Houbing Song, and Xuejie Zhu. Social-feature enabled communications among devices toward the smart iot community. *IEEE Communications Magazine*, 57(1):130–137, 2019.

11. Dominique Guinard, Mathias Fischer, and Vlad Trifa. Sharing using social networks in a composable web of things. In *2010 8th IEEE International Conference on Pervasive Computing and Communications Workshops (PERCOM Workshops)*, pages 702–707. IEEE, 2010.
12. Karen Henricksen and Jadwiga Indulska. Developing context-aware pervasive computing applications: Models and approach. *Pervasive and Mobile Computing*, 2(1):37–64, 2006.
13. Lars Erik Holmquist, Friedemann Mattern, Bernt Schiele, Petteri Alahuhta, Michael Beigl, and Hans-W Gellersen. Smart-its friends: A technique for users to easily establish connections between smart artefacts. In *international conference on Ubiquitous Computing*, pages 116–122. Springer, 2001.
14. Huansheng Ning and Ziou Wang. Future internet of things architecture: like mankind neural system or social organization framework? *IEEE Communications Letters*, 15(4):461–463, 2011.
15. C. Perera, A. Zaslavsky, P. Christen, and D. Georgakopoulos. Context aware computing for the internet of things: A survey. *IEEE Communications Surveys and Tutorials*, 16(1):414–454, 2014.
16. Anand Ranganathan, Robert E McGrath, Roy H. Campbell, and M. Dennis Mickunas. Use of ontologies in a pervasive computing environment. *Knowledge Engineering Review*, 18(3):209–220, 2003.
17. Fabio A. Schreiber, Letizia Tanca, Romolo Camplani, and Diego Viganò. Pushing context-awareness down to the core: more flexibility for the perla language. In *Electronic Proc. PersDB 2012 Workshop (Co-located with VLDB 2012)*, pages 1–6, 2012.
18. Thomas Strang, Claudia Linnhoff-Popien, and Korbinian Frank. Cool: A context ontology language to enable contextual interoperability. In Jean-Bernard Stefani, Isabelle Demeure, and Daniel Hagimont, editors, *Distributed Applications and Interoperable Systems*, pages 236–247. Springer Berlin Heidelberg, 2003.

Simple User Assistance by Data Posting (Discussion Paper)

Elio Masciari, Domenico Saccà, and Irina Trubitsyna
elio.masciari@icar.cnr.it
{sacca,trubitsyna}@dimes.unical.it

ICAR-CNR, DIMES-Università della Calabria, 87036 Rende (CS), Italy

Abstract. Big Data deeply changed both researchers and industries approaches to data management. This impressive amount of data contains a lot of information regarding user suggestions and searches. In this paper, we focus on the effect of users suggestions on their social environment. Suggestions are provided to user by means of simple rules that are defined on the basis of the data being analyzed. We address the reaction of users in a competitive environment when they were invited to judge each other choices. The above mentioned activity is crucial to perform efficient identification of users able to spread their influence across the network, which is a key activity in several scenarios like tourism promotion, personalized marketing, and entertainment suggestion.

1 Introduction

Big Data paradigm is currently driving both research and industrial interests. Many proposals for innovative data analysis for managing impressive amounts of data have been developed. These approaches share the common needs to rethink storage and analysis techniques in order to deal with massive, heterogeneous data, that are fast varying [1]. Indeed, the Big Data revolution has been guided by the continuous advances of the web-based services that have millions of users generating new data everyday. As an example, applications such as Uber, Facebook or Twitter attract millions of people posting information about their habits and activities. Quick analysis of these data is a key activity in several scenarios, such as tourism promotion, personalized marketing and entertainment offers.

To this end in [6] a collaborative network that allows users to cooperate each others for high performance task execution (by partitioning complex tasks in smaller and easier sub-tasks) is described. Each user can operate as client and/or executor. As the tasks assigned to executors may consist in processes defining specific features for a context (e.g., deciding whether a restaurant is better than another), it may happen to deal with inconsistent or incomplete data. Tasks requiring details of all possible solutions obtainable with data exchange process can be solved applying approximate certain query answering algorithms [8–10, 12]. To extract concise data chosen among the possible alternatives on the basis of analyst's indications the data posting framework can be used [2]. The latter formalism allows us to model different situations. However, it requires the ability to manage *count constraints* and *domain relations* (we formally describe these notions in the background section). To simplify the modelling process, we propose to integrate the standard mapping with some parameters, avoiding complex specifications. We call the obtained rules *smart mapping rules* (more details can be found in [13, 14]. As an example, in Section 3 we consider the task of generating user suggestions on the basis of information posted by other peoples and available from the Web. We show how this process can be modelled with smart mapping rules.

Since the sub-tasks are solved by independent executors, payed for their activities, an important problem regards the quality evaluation of the obtained results. In our context the clients can ask for search directions. Once the result is obtained, we can ask the client to evaluate the obtained suggestion, i.e. give a rank for the executor performing this task. Moreover, some credits to executors suggesting useful search directions to clients are assigned. We analyze what happens with users' evaluations when they are aware of the other ones. In particular, we consider a group of users involved in a research project and we let them know mutual preferences on some topics.

We use Exponential Graph Random Models (EGRM) [3] to analyze the network dynamics and to model the revenue flow generated by user interactions. Since the maximum likelihood evaluation is computationally hard, we use two approaches for sampling data: *Metropolis Hastings sampling* and *Clustering based sampling*. Moreover, since the data are continuously updated, we use two type of statistical analysis: *cross-sectional* and *dynamic*.

It has been shown in literature, that in many settings the possibility to observe the other user rankings causes mutual adjustment among raters. In our framework, higher rankings are associated with positive evaluation (thus higher rewards), such that being ranked below others is aversive. To properly measure the above mentioned network dynamics, we compute three values proposed in [11]: (*i*) *Global Nonconformity (GNC)* - indicates how user conforms with others'; (*ii*) *Local Nonconformity (LNC)* - indicates how user conforms with neighbours; (*iii*) *Deference Aversion (DA)* - measures the following phenomenon: if user A ranks B above C ($B > C$), and user C would like rank A above B ($A > B$), since the transitivity of ranking would state that A is above C, user C is influenced negatively to express his ranking as above defined. Based on these measures we performed a deep experimental analysis.

2 Preliminaries

The data posting framework [7] adapts the well-known data exchange techniques to the new Big Data management and analysis challenges we find in real world scenarios. The *data posting setting* $(\mathbf{S}, \boldsymbol{\mathcal{D}}, \mathbf{T}, \Sigma_{st}, \Sigma_t)$ consists of a finite source database schema $\mathbf{S}$, a finite domain database scheme $\boldsymbol{\mathcal{D}}$, a target schema $\mathbf{T}$, a set Σ_{st} of non-deterministic source-to-target TGDs and a set Σ_t of target count constraints. A *non-deterministic source-to-target TGD (NdTGD)* is a dependency over $\langle \mathbf{S}, \boldsymbol{\mathcal{D}}, \mathbf{T} \rangle$ of the form $\forall \mathbf{x} \, [\, \phi_S(\mathbf{x} \cup \tilde{\mathbf{y}}) \rightarrow \phi_T(\mathbf{z}) \,]$, where $\mathbf{x}$ and $\mathbf{z}$ are lists of universally quantified variables; $\tilde{\mathbf{y}}$ is a (possibly empty) list of variables, called *non deterministic*, these variables can occur in ϕ_S only in relations from $\boldsymbol{\mathcal{D}}$; $\mathbf{x} \cap \tilde{\mathbf{y}} = \emptyset$ and $\mathbf{z} \subseteq \mathbf{x} \cup \tilde{\mathbf{y}}$; the formula ϕ_S and ψ_T are conjunctions of atoms with predicate symbols in $\mathbf{S} \cup \boldsymbol{\mathcal{D}}$ and in $\mathbf{T}$, respectively. The structure of NdTGDs ensures that any target database on $\mathbf{T}$ is finite. The NdTGD can be seen as the standard TGD, where existentially quantified variables are replaced with non-deterministic variables, whose values can be chosen from the finite domains defined by domain relations, i.e. relations from $\boldsymbol{\mathcal{D}}$. The mapping process is performed as usual but presumes that for every assignment of $\mathbf{x}$ a subset of all admissible values for $\tilde{\mathbf{y}}$ can be chosen in an arbitrary way. A *count constraint* is a dependency over $\mathbf{T}$ of the form $\forall \mathbf{x} \, [\, \phi_T(\mathbf{x}) \rightarrow \#(\{\mathbf{Y} : \exists \mathbf{z} \, \alpha(\mathbf{x}, \mathbf{Y}, \mathbf{z})\}) \texttt{ <op> } \beta(\mathbf{x}) \,]$, where ϕ_T is a conjunction of atoms with predicate symbol in $\mathbf{T}$, `<op>` is any of the comparison operators ($=$, $>$, $\geq$, $<$ and $\leq$), $H = \{\mathbf{Y} : \exists \mathbf{z} \, \alpha(\mathbf{x}, \mathbf{Y}, \mathbf{z})\}$ is a *set term*, $\#$ is an interpreted function symbol that computes the cardinality of the (possibly empty) set corresponding to H, $\#(H)$ is a *count term*, and $\beta(\mathbf{x})$ is an integer or a variable in $\mathbf{x}$ or another count term with universally quantified variables in $\mathbf{x}$. The lists $\mathbf{x}$, $\mathbf{Y}$ and $\mathbf{z}$ do not share variables, $\alpha(\mathbf{x}, \mathbf{Y}, \mathbf{z})$ is a conjunction of atoms $T_i(\mathbf{x}, \mathbf{Y}, \mathbf{z})$ with $T_i \in \mathbf{T}$. Let I_T be the instance of $\mathbf{T}$. The *active domain* AD_I is the set of all values occurring in I_T. Given a substitution $\mathbf{x}/\mathbf{v}$ assigning values in AD_I to universally quantified variables, $K_{\mathbf{v}} = \{\mathbf{Y} : \exists \mathbf{z} \, \alpha(\mathbf{v}, \mathbf{Y}, \mathbf{z})\}$ defines the set of values in AD_I assigned to the free variables in $\mathbf{Y}$ for which $\exists \mathbf{z} \, \alpha(\mathbf{v}, \mathbf{Y}, \mathbf{z})$ is satisfied by I_T and $\#(K_{\mathbf{v}})$ is the cardinality of this set. We say that I_T satisfies the count constraint if each substitution $\mathbf{x}/\mathbf{v}$ that makes true its body expression, makes also true its head expression. The *data posting problem* is defined as follows: given finite source instance I_S and finite domain instance $I_{\mathcal{D}}$, find a finite target instance I_T such that $\langle I_S, I_{\mathcal{D}}, I_T \rangle$ satisfies both Σ_{st} and Σ_t. This problem is $\mathcal{NP}$-complete under the data complexity. When Σ_{st} does not contain non-deterministic variables, the problem becomes polynomial.

3 Setting up user suggestions

In this section we consider the task requiring generation user suggestions on the basis of information posted in the Web. In the following example we show how this process can be modelled with smart mapping rules.

Example 1. Suppose to have the description of the user ratings (that we call comments) stored in the relation $\mathtt{C(U, N, V)}$ with attributes $\mathtt{U}$ (user identifier), $\mathtt{N}$ (argument of rating) and $\mathtt{V}$ (rating value). Suppose also to have a relation $\mathtt{T(U_1, U_2, L)}$ that represents the trust level $\mathtt{L}$ of user $\mathtt{U_2}$ for the user $\mathtt{U_1}$.

In order to suggest to the user some "relevant" arguments we can set the following criterion: *"An argument n is suggested to the user u if the following conditions hold: 1) it is* sufficiently supported, *i.e. it is "supported" by at least* 20 *users whose trust level towards u is greater than* 70%; *2) if different comments corresponding to the same argument are sufficiently supported, only one can be selected, with the greater level of support"*. In this case, the choice of the comment has to take into account two different needs: 1) deciding if the argument has to be suggested to the user; 2) selecting the rating value for this argument.

This scenario can be modeled as follows:

- `C` and `T` are source relations;
- $\mathtt{Add(U,N,V)}$ is target relation, specifying the comments to be suggested to U;
- the smart mapping rule is reported below:

$$\mathtt{C(u_2,n,v)} \wedge \mathtt{T(u_1,u_2,l)} \wedge \mathtt{l} > \mathtt{0,70} \xrightarrow{\mathtt{u_2,20,\langle v,unique \wedge max\rangle}} \mathtt{Add(u_1,n,v)}$$

Intuitively, the body of the rule allows us to restrict the attention to the users whose trust level towards $\mathtt{u_1}$ is greater than 70%, the selection criterion has been synthesized on the arrow, indicating 1) the support variable $\mathtt{u_2}$, 2) the minimum quantity `20` of support instances to be able to map, and 3) the variable `v` whose value should be chosen from the set of candidate values following the indication $\mathtt{unique} \wedge \mathtt{max}$. □

More formally, a *smart mapping rule* has the form $\forall \mathbf{z}[\, \phi_S(\mathbf{z}) \xrightarrow{\mathbf{y},k,\langle \mathbf{v},f\rangle} r(\mathbf{x},\mathbf{v})\,]$, where $\mathbf{x},\mathbf{y},\mathbf{z},\mathbf{v}$ are vectors of variables, such that $\mathbf{x} \cup \mathbf{y} \cup \mathbf{v} \subseteq \mathbf{z}$ and $\mathbf{x}$, $\mathbf{y}$ and $\mathbf{v}$ do not share the variables; ϕ_S is the conjunction of source relations and expressions involving comparison operators $(>,<,\geq,\leq,=,\neq)$ and variables in $\mathbf{z}$ or constants; r is a target relation; $\mathbf{y}$ is called a *support vector*; k is a natural number (greater than 0) which indicates the support value; the pair $\langle \mathbf{v}, f\rangle$ indicates how the choice for the values of $\mathbf{v}$ should be performed: f can be *max*, *unique*, the conjunction *unique* $\wedge$ *max*, or empty.

We assume that each target relation can be defined by only one smart mapping rule. The smart mapping rule specifies that the tuple $\langle \mathbf{X}, \mathbf{V}\rangle$ is added to r only if it is supported by at least k (different) initializations $\{\mathbf{Y_1}, ...\mathbf{Y_k}\}$ of $\mathbf{y}$, i.e. for each $j \in [1..k]$ there exists an initialization $\mathbf{Z_j}$ of $\mathbf{z}$, that maps $\mathbf{x}$, $\mathbf{y}$ e $\mathbf{v}$ in $\mathbf{X}$, $\mathbf{Y_j}$ and $\mathbf{V}$ respectively, and that makes true $\psi_S(\mathbf{Z_j})$. In the case than no further indications of choice are specified (the third arrow label is $\langle \mathbf{v}, \rangle$) all the tuples supported by at least k (different) initializations of $\mathbf{y}$ are added to r. Otherwise, the set of tuples to be added is further reduced using f content for the selection of values in $\mathbf{v}$.

The $\langle \mathbf{v}, \mathit{unique}\rangle$ constraints specifies that the r relation must obey the functional dependency $\mathbf{x} \rightarrow \mathbf{v}$, i.e. for each assignment of values in $\mathbf{x}$ the assignment of values in $\mathbf{v}$ must be unique. In the case that several tuples are supported by at least k (different) initializations of $\mathbf{y}$ and they have the same values in $\mathbf{x}$, the choice can be made arbitrarily.

The indication $\langle \mathbf{v}, \mathit{max}\rangle$ specifies that, for each $\mathbf{X}$ only tuples supported by a maximum number of initializations of $\mathbf{y}$ must be selected. It is easy to see that this indication does not guarantee the uniqueness of the choice. For example, it is possible that two tuples $\langle \mathbf{X}, \mathbf{V_1} \rangle$ and $\langle \mathbf{X}, \mathbf{V_2} \rangle$ have the same degree of support corresponding to the maximum value.

The indication $\langle \mathbf{v}, \mathit{unique} \land \mathit{max} \rangle$ specifies that, fixed $\mathbf{X}$, only one tuple $\langle \mathbf{X}, \mathbf{V} \rangle$ can be chosen among those supported by a maximum number of (different) initializations of $\mathbf{y}$.

The set of smart mapping rule can be translated into the standard data posting constructs by translating every mapping rule ρ as follows. We introduce the unary domain relation $\mathcal{D}_\rho$. If f is empty $\mathcal{D}_\rho$ contains values -1 and 1, otherwise $\mathcal{D}_\rho$ contains values -1, 0 and 1. We also introduce the target relations $A_\rho(\mathbf{X}, \mathbf{Y}, \mathbf{V})$ and $Add_\rho(\mathbf{X}, \mathbf{V}, Flag)$, where $\mathbf{X}$, $\mathbf{Y}$ and $\mathbf{V}$ represent vectors of attributes corresponding to the vectors of variables $\mathbf{x}$, $\mathbf{y}$, and $\mathbf{v}$, respectively, while the decision weather to select the pair $\langle \mathbf{x}, \mathbf{v} \rangle$ in the target relation r is stored by the attribute $Flag$: -1 or 0 (not added) and 1 (added). The mapping rules are:

$$\phi_S(\mathbf{z}) \rightarrow \mathtt{A}_\rho(\mathbf{x}, \mathbf{y}, \mathbf{v})$$
$$\phi_S(\mathbf{z}) \land \mathcal{D}_\rho(\mathtt{flag}) \rightarrow \mathtt{Add}_\rho(\mathbf{x}, \mathbf{y}, \mathtt{flag})$$

where all the variables are universally quantified. Using the domain relation $\mathcal{D}_\rho$ ensures that only a value among -1, 0 and 1 can be chosen for each initialization of $(\mathbf{x}, \mathbf{y})$ in the relation $\mathtt{Add}_\rho$.

The set of target count constraints is constructed as follows.

1. We start by adding support constraints, that ensure that the value -1 is assigned to the variable $\mathtt{flag}$ iff the degree of support of the combination $\langle \mathbf{x}, \mathbf{v} \rangle$ does not reach k. First, we add constraint for values 1 and -1.

$$\mathtt{Add}_\rho(\mathbf{x}, \mathbf{v}, 1) \rightarrow \#(\{\,\mathbf{Y} : \mathtt{A}_\rho(\mathbf{x}, \mathbf{Y}, \mathbf{v})\}) \geq \mathtt{k}$$
$$\mathtt{Add}_\rho(\mathbf{x}, \mathbf{v}, -1) \rightarrow \#(\{\,\mathbf{Y} : \mathtt{A}_\rho(\mathbf{x}, \mathbf{Y}, \mathbf{v})\}) < \mathtt{k}$$

   If f is not empty, we also add constraint for value 0:

$$\mathtt{Add}_\rho(\mathbf{x}, \mathbf{v}, 0) \rightarrow \#(\{\,\mathbf{Y} : \mathtt{A}_\rho(\mathbf{x}, \mathbf{Y}, \mathbf{v})\}) \geq \mathtt{k}$$

2. When $f = \mathit{unique}$ the *uniqueness choice constraint* is added:

$$\mathtt{Add}_\rho(\mathbf{x}, \_, \mathtt{flag}) \land \mathtt{flag} \geq 0 \rightarrow \#(\{\,\mathbf{V} : \mathtt{Add}_\rho(\mathbf{x}, \mathbf{V}, \mathbf{1})\}) = 1$$

   This constraint ensures that exactly one initialization of $\mathbf{v}$ for each $\mathbf{X}$ is selected.

3. When $f = \mathit{max}$ we add (i) the *optimization constraint*

$$\mathtt{Add}_\rho(\mathbf{x}, \mathbf{v_2}, 1), \mathtt{Add}_\rho(\mathbf{x}, \mathbf{v}, 0) \rightarrow \#(\{\mathbf{Y} : \mathtt{A}_\rho(\mathbf{x}, \mathbf{Y}, \mathbf{v_2})\}) \geq \#(\{\mathbf{Y} : \mathtt{A}_\rho(\mathbf{x}, \mathbf{Y}, \mathbf{v})\})$$

   (ii) the *choice constraint*, ensuring that at least one initialization of $\mathbf{v}$ for each $\mathbf{X}$ is selected

$$\mathtt{Add}_\rho(\mathbf{x}, \_, \mathtt{flag}) \land \mathtt{flag} \geq 0 \rightarrow \#(\{\,\mathbf{V} : \mathtt{Add}_\rho(\mathbf{x}, \mathbf{V}, \mathbf{1})\}) \geq 1$$

4. When $f = \mathit{unique} \land \mathit{max}$ we add the uniqueness choice constraint and the optimization constraint.

The use of the smart mapping rules offers a notable simplification of the data posting framework. The user and/or designer can construct the selection criterion focusing only on the a small set of parameters. The selection criteria modeled by smart mapping rules are the most widespread in practice. The standardization of their representation allows us also to optimize the implementation of the data posting process. Smart mapping rules, initially developed for our application scenario, can be profitable used in different contexts. In particular, we are investigating their application in P2P Deductive Databases [4, 5].

4 Experimental Evaluation

In this section we describe the evaluation of the user ranking behaviours. We report the results obtained on a test set of user searches collected for four months during a research project. We devised for the experimental evaluation an approach similar to the one presented in [2] where the authors leverage ERGM and clustering analysis to partition the user interaction graph in order to tackle the complexity issues due to graph structures.

We provided each user with two different options: 1) they can ask for search suggestion or 2) they can suggest search directions on request. At fixed time intervals, users may evaluate obtained results (both as consumer and provider of information) by assigning a rank ranging from 0 to 10 to their experience. As we implemented a rewarding strategy, i.e. users pay for targeted suggestions and are paid when they suggest a proper search, the effectiveness evaluation is crucial as we do not want user to pay for wrong information.

We model our small network interactions by a random graph that is continuously updated as new links among users appear (i.e. new interactions between a pair of users). In order to better understand the information relevant to our goal we leverage two types of analysis: the first one, referred as cross-sectional (CS), considers only the variation occurring when data are observed while the second one considers each observation as an independent unit, thus it is referred as dynamic (Dyn). In order to be fair and to evaluate the influence excerpted by users each other, every participant is aware of the other's scores.

The latter results in the need to analyze factors that are *endogenous*, i.e., those phenomenon that may arise when users know each the rankings of other thus causing the rankings given by user i to be influenced by other user rankings except i. To this end we measure the values of GNC, LNC and DA.

Evaluation. In order to analyze the evolution of user search effects, we use the following statistics: overall searches number performed by user; keyword total number; mean assigned keyword rank. For the sake of completeness, we use both CS and Dyn analysis combined with clustering (CL) and Metropolis-Hastings (M-H) sampling. The results are shown in Figure 1. For Dyn analysis we compute fifteen graphs (one for each week except the first one) for the CS analysis we have 16 graphs. It is easy to observe that in tables a and b the values obtained for DA are always high since the beginning. It is worth noting that, as we start

Week	GNC	LNC	DA
1	0.000	−0.012	−0.127
2	0.001	−0.014	−0.131
3	0.001	−0.015	−0.127
4	0.001	−0.021	−0.144
5	0.002	−0.024	−0.198
6	0.002	−0.037	−0.223
7	0.003	−0.043	−0.289
8	0.003	−0.039	−0.311
9	0.002	−0.038	−0.327
10	0.0015	−0.041	−0.381
11	0.0015	−0.037	−0.401
12	0.001	−0.035	−0.412
13	0.001	−0.033	−0.423
14	0.001	−0.032	−0.428
15	0.000	−0.030	−0.436
16	0.001	−0.029	−0.441

a) CS, M-H

Week	GNC	LNC	DA
1 → 2	0.000	−0.009	−0.185
2 → 3	0.001	−0.011	−0.190
3 → 4	0.001	−0.015	−0.195
4 → 5	0.001	−0.020	−0.257
5 → 6	0.001	−0.022	−0.289
6 → 7	0.002	−0.023	−0.303
7 → 8	0.002	−0.026	−0.313
8 → 9	0.002	−0.026	−0.357
9 → 10	0.002	−0.029	−0.383
10 → 11	0.001	−0.030	−0.398
11 → 12	0.001	−0.031	−0.401
12 → 13	0.001	−0.031	−0.409
13 → 14	0.001	−0.032	−0.421
14 → 15	0.001	−0.033	−0.435
15 → 16	0.001	−0.033	−0.486

b) Dyn, M-H

Week	GNC	LNC	DA
1	0.000	−0.011	−0.111
2	0.001	−0.012	−0.122
3	0.001	−0.018	−0.1143
4	0.001	−0.020	−0.154
5	0.002	−0.021	−0.161
6	0.003	−0.042	−0.173
7	0.002	−0.048	−0.174
8	0.001	−0.052	−0.176
9	0.001	−0.060	−0.179
10	0.001	−0.061	−0.180
11	0.001	−0.068	−0.182
12	0.001	−0.069	−0.183
13	0.001	−0.071	−0.184
14	0.001	−0.073	−0.184
15	0.001	−0.075	−0.184
16	0.001	−0.079	−0.185

c) CS, CL

Week	GNC	LNC	DA
1 → 2	0.000	−0.008	−0.101
2 → 3	0.000	−0.011	−0.119
3 → 4	0.000	−0.013	−0.127
4 → 5	0.001	−0.019	−0.138
5 → 6	0.000	−0.021	−0.145
6 → 7	0.000	−0.028	−0.167
7 → 8	0.001	−0.031	−0.172
8 → 9	0.000	−0.032	−0.169
9 → 10	0.000	−0.037	−0.166
10 → 11	0.000	−0.041	−0.152
11 → 12	0.001	−0.044	−0.148
12 → 13	0.000	−0.053	−0.145
13 → 14	0.000	−0.057	−0.142
14 → 15	0.000	−0.061	−0.139
15 → 16	0.000	−0.066	−0.132

d) Dyn, CL

Fig. 1. Experiments

rewarding users (at week 4), the DA values further increase. More in detail, both for DYn and CS analysis global nonconformity is not a significant factor. The values reported for the other two factors are, on the whole, significant, but are uniformly smaller in magnitude for dynamic analysis compared to those of the corresponding weeks in the CS analysis and are less precisely estimated (as represented by uniformly greater standard errors). This is because rather than embodying the structure of the whole network, they embody only the structure of changes in the network over the week, thus the only important value to rely on is the weekly changes of values. This means that "instant" social effects (e.g., friendship reciprocation) have been absorbed into the Week 0 observation, which is not modeled in the dynamic analysis.

Moreover, above mentioned phenomena can be considered as a kind of social "envy": users tend to decrease the scores of other users in order to get more requests for themselves and thus getting more rewards. We note that also LNC value is high while GNC is not impressive: in a sense, users tend to agree on the general topics but not on the specific ones. Similar observations can be made for all the analysis reported in Tables c and d. As a final note, we can observe that the results obtained when sampling data by clustering are slightly better. This behaviour can be explained considering that when leveraging cluster approaches, it is more likely to obtain more homogeneous groups (i.e. group of user sharing common interests and features).

5 Conclusion and Future Work

The impressive amount of data shared on the WEB contains a lot of information regarding user suggestions and searches. In this paper we focus on the effect of users suggestions on their social environment. We showed how personalized suggestions can be extracted by using smart mapping rules. This kind of rules, initially developed for our application scenario, can be profitable used in different contexts. For instance, they allow us to define the fragment of data posting framework, where the data posting problem becomes polynomial. We leveraged many interesting mathematical tools to model several psychological and social mechanisms that proved to be effective in our scenario. We are aware that, with respect to population-scale networks, the networks considered in our experiments are fairly small. However, this aspect does not decrease the validity of our approach as ranking data of the form analyzed here is typically of interest only in specific networks, that are by nature fairly small. Thus, highly scalable techniques are less compelling in our setting. Nevertheless, computationally scalable estimation is an interesting challenge for future research in this area and we want to address it in next future.

References

1. D. Agrawal et al. Challenges and opportunities with big data. A community white paper developed by leading researchers across the United States. 2012.
2. E. Bazzi, N. Cassavia, D. Chiggiato, E. Masciari, D. Saccà, A. Spada, and I. Trubitsyna. Evaluating user behaviour in a cooperative environment. *Information*, 9(12):303, 2018.
3. L. D. Brown. Fundamentals of statistical exponential families with applications in statistical decision theory. *Lecture Notes Monograph Series*, 1986.
4. L. Caroprese and E. Zumpano. Aggregates and priorities in P2P data management systems. In *Proc. of (IDEAS 2011), Lisbon, Portugal*, pages 1–7, 2011.
5. L. Caroprese and E. Zumpano. Computing a deterministic semantics for P2P deductive databases. In *Proc. of IDEAS 2017, Bristol, UK*, pages 184–191, 2017.
6. N. Cassavia, S. Flesca, M. Ianni, E. Masciari, and C. Pulice. Distributed computing by leveraging and rewarding idling user resources from P2P networks. *J. Parallel Distrib. Comput.*, 122:81–94, 2018.
7. N. Cassavia, E. Masciari, C. Pulice, and D. Saccà. Discovering user behavioral features to enhance information search on big data. *TiiS*, 7(2):7:1–7:33, 2017.
8. N. Fiorentino, S. Greco, C. Molinaro, and I. Trubitsyna. ACID: A system for computing approximate certain query answers over incomplete databases. In *Proc. of SIGMOD Conference 2018, Houston, TX, USA*, pages 1685–1688, 2018.
9. S. Greco, C. Molinaro, and I. Trubitsyna. Computing approximate query answers over inconsistent knowledge bases. In *Proc. of IJCAI 2018, Stockholm, Sweden.*, pages 1838–1846, 2018.
10. S. Greco, C. Molinaro, and I. Trubitsyna. Approximation algorithms for querying incomplete databases. *Information Systems (2019)*, https://doi.org/10.1016/j.is.2019.03.010, 2019.
11. P. N. Krivitsky and C. T. Butts. Exponential-family random graph models for rank-order relational data. *http://arxiv.org/abs/1210.*
12. T. Lukasiewicz, E. Malizia, and C. Molinaro. Complexity of approximate query answering under inconsistency in datalog+/-. In *Proc. of IJCAI 2018, Stockholm, Sweden.*, pages 1921–1927, 2018.
13. E. Masciari, D. Saccà, and I. Trubitsyna. Simple user assistance by data posting. In *Second IEEE International Conference on Artificial Intelligence and Knowledge Engineering, AIKE 2019, Cagliari, Sardinia, Italy, June 3-5, 2019*, pages 1–8, 2019.
14. E. Masciari, D. Saccà, and I. Trubitsyna. Simplified data posting in practice. In *Proc. of the 23rd International Database Engineering and Applications Symposium (IDEAS 2019), June 10 - 12, 2019, Athens, Greece*, pages 1–6, 2019.

Space Bounds in Ontological Reasoning via Extended Bell Numbers

(DISCUSSION PAPER)

Cinzia Marte[0000−0003−3920−8186]

University of Calabria, Rende, Italy
marte@mat.unical.it

Abstract. In ontology-based query answering a user query is typically evaluated over instances containing both known and anonymous individuals. In this context, the algebraic notion of isomorphism is relevant in many application scenarios, such as the so-called parsimonious chase. Two atoms are isomorphic if there is a bijection among them that, in addition, is the identity on the known individuals. A naive upper bound on the maximum cardinality of any instance containing non-isomorphic atoms is well-known from the literature. However, there are cases in which this bound is far from being optimal. This paper generalizes Bell numbers to provide a tight bound in the above setting. The main result is also relevant in classical databases by characterizing the family of non-equivalent atomic queries.

Keywords: ontology-based query answering · existential rules · parsimonious chase · Bell numbers · atomic queries.

1 Introduction

Ontology-Based Query Answering (OBQA) consists in querying databases by taking ontological knowledge into account. It is a fascinating research topic deeply studied not only in database theory [1,13], but also in artificial intelligence [6,5,11] and in logic [2,3,12]. Moreover, OBQA is strictly related to others important application areas such as data integration [21], data exchange [9], and consistent query answering [23,24]. In particular, OBQA is the problem of answering a query q against a logical theory consisting of an extensional database D paired with an ontology Σ. The goal is to find certain answers to q, i.e. the query must be true in every possible model of the theory [20,7]. Here, we focus on ontologies expressed via existential rules, also known as tuple generating dependencies (TGDs) or $\mathsf{datalog}^{\exists}$ rules. They are at the core of Datalog$^{\pm}$ [14], an emerging family of ontology languages, which collects the basic decidable

 SEBD 2019, June 16-19, 2019, Castiglione della Pescaia, Italy.

classes of TGDs, and generalizes several ontology specification languages such as Description Logics (DLs) [10]. Indeed, $\mathsf{datalog}^{\exists}$ generalizes the well-known language Datalog [16] with existential quantification in the head.

OBQA can be reduced to the problem of answering q over a universal model U that can be homomorphically embedded into every other model of the logical theory. A way to compute a universal model is to employ the so called chase procedure. Starting from D, the chase "repairs" violations of rules by repeatedly adding new atoms –introducing fresh values, called nulls, whenever required by an existential variable– until a fixed point satisfying all rules is reached. Therefore, in the classical setting, the chase is sound and complete. But, unfortunately, the chase does not always terminates [17,18].

Recently, in [22] a new class of $\mathsf{datalog}^{\exists}$ ontologies, called Shy, has been singled out for existential rules. It enjoys a new semantic property called *parsimony* and results in a powerful and decidable class that combines positive aspects of different Datalog$^{\pm}$ classes [4]. The parsimony property is based on the *parsimonious chase* (pchase) procedure that repairs violations of rules only if the (inferred) head atom can not be homomorphically mapped to any atom previously produced. For some classes of Datalog$^{\pm}$, the parsimony property is sound and complete with respect to atomic query answering. Moreover, the termination of the pchase is always guaranteed, and computational complexity has been studied [22]. Understanding the nature of the pchase procedure can lead to obtain practical improvements of existing implementations [22]. Indeed, so far, the research has been focused on establishing the termination of the pchase procedure, thus providing just a very rough upper bound of its maximal size, without any understanding of the relations between the logical theory and the atoms generated by the pchase. We fill this gap deepening this relevant connection. In particular, we need to understand what kind of atoms belong to the pchase. This has as side effect and it is strictly related to count the number of atoms generated by the pchase. An immediate consequence of this better understanding of the chase leads to re-prove computational complexity results, as we improve the upper bounds previously identified in [22]. Indeed, these are very large, as they are aimed at demonstrating computational complexity, and not how many atoms can be produced by the chase.

In this paper, we present contents already set out and published in [8]. In particular, we provide an exact upper bound for the pchase. To this end, we exploit the notion of "equality type" defined in [19], which we show to be strictly related to the form of non-isomorphic atoms of a given predicate. Then, by exploiting the notion of Bell numbers, counting the number of distinct partitions of a finite set, we compute an upper bound for the number of atoms generating by the pchase procedure and we show that there exists a family of ontologies for which the pchase can produce exactly the upper bound previously computed, so that it corresponds to the maximal number of atoms effectively generated by the pchase procedure.

Finally, as a corollary, our estimation of the maximum cardinality of any instance containing non-isomorphic atoms also provides a tight bound on the maximum number of non-equivalent atomic queries over a given relation, where two queries are considered *equivalent* if they give the same answers on every database.

2 Preliminaries

Throughout this paper we use the following notation. Let $\Delta = \Delta_C \cup \Delta_N \cup \Delta_V$ the domain of the *terms*, consisting of the union of the three countably infinite domains of *constants*, *nulls* and *variables*, respectively. We write φ to denote a null; X a variable; $\underline{a}$ an atom, that is an expression of the form $p(\mathbf{t})$, where $p = pred(\underline{a})$ is a predicate, $\mathbf{t} = t_1, \ldots, t_k$ is a *tuple* of terms, $k = arity(\underline{a})$ is the arity of $\underline{a}$ or p, and $\underline{a}[i]$ is the i-th term of $\underline{a}$. Moreover, $const(\underline{a})$ (resp., $vars(\underline{a})$) is the set of constants (resp., variables) occurring in $\underline{a}$. The set of predicates is denoted by $\mathcal{R}$. Let $T \subseteq \Delta$ a nonempty subset, then the set of all atoms that can be formed with predicates of $\mathcal{R}$ and terms from T is denoted by $base(T)$. Moreover, any subset of $base(\Delta_C \cup \Delta_N)$ constitutes an *instance* I, and whenever $I \subseteq base(\Delta_C)$, then it is also called *database*. A *substitution* is a total mapping $s : \Delta \to \Delta$. Let χ_1 and χ_2 be two structures containing atoms. An *homomorphism* $h : \chi_1 \to \chi_2$ is a substitution such that: (1) if $c \in \Delta_C$, then $h(c) = c$; *(ii)* if $\varphi \in \Delta_N$, then $h(\varphi) \in \Delta_C \cup \Delta_N$; *(iii)* $h(\chi_1)$ is a substructure of χ_2. An *existential rule* r is a logical implication of the form $\forall \mathbf{X} \forall \mathbf{Y}(\exists \mathbf{Z}\ \underline{a}(\mathbf{X}, \mathbf{Z}) \leftarrow \phi(\mathbf{X}, \mathbf{Y}))$, where $\mathbf{X}$, $\mathbf{Y}$, and $\mathbf{Z}$ denote sets of variables; $head(r) = \underline{a}(\mathbf{X}, \mathbf{Z})$, while $body(r) = \phi(\mathbf{X}, \mathbf{Y})$ is a conjunction of atoms and can also be empty. We define a $\mathsf{datalog}^{\exists}$ program P as a finite set of existential rules, called ontology and denoted by $dep(P)$ (*dependencies* of P), paired with a database instance, denoted by $data(P)$. Moreover, $pred(P)$ (resp., $const(P)$) represents the set of predicates (resp., constants) occurring in (P) and $arity(P)$ is the maximum arity over $pred(P)$.

Given an instance I, we say that a rule r *is satisfied by* I if whenever there is a homomorphism $h : body(r) \to I$, there is a homomorphism $h' \supset h|_{vars(body(r))}$ s.t. $h' : head(r) \to I$. An instance I is a *model* of a program P if each rule of $dep(P)$ is satisfied by I, and $data(P) \subseteq I$. A *firing homomorphism* for r and I is any homomorphism $h : body(r) \to I$ s.t. $h = h|_{vars(body(r))}$. The *fire* of r via h produces the atom $fire(r, h) = \sigma(h(head(r)))$, where $\sigma = \sigma|_{vars(h(head(r)))}$ (i.e., it replaces each existential variable of r with a different fresh null). Given a firing homomorphism h for a rule r and an instance I, we say that the pair $\langle r, h \rangle$ satisfies the *parsimonious fire condition* w.r.t. an instance $I' \supseteq I$ if there is no homomorphism from $\{h(head(r))\}$ to I'. Finally, given a $\mathsf{datalog}^{\exists}$ program P, the *parsimonious chase* (pchase) of P ($pchase(P)$) is constructed as follows. We start from $I' = data(P)$ and create a copy of it in I. Then, for each r in $dep(P)$, for each unspent firing homomorphism h for the pair $\langle r, I \rangle$ we add the $fire(r, h)$ to I' if $\langle r, h \rangle$ satisfies the parsimonious fire condition w.r.t. I'. If $I \neq I'$, we create a new copy of I' and repeat the previous steps. Otherwise, we return I.

3 Parsimonious Chase Estimation

In this section, we introduce some basic notions that will help us to find a tight upper bound for the pchase. We highlight a main property of the pchase, based on isomorphic atoms, a crucial notion in several Datalog$^{\pm}$ classes [15].

Theorem 1. *Given a program P, $pchase(P)$ does not contain isomorphic atoms.*

Proof. Assume, by contradiction, that there are two isomorphic atoms $\underline{a}$ and $\underline{a}'$ in $pchase(P)$. Thus, there is a homomorphism h from $\{\underline{a}\}$ to $\{\underline{a}'\}$ s.t. h^{-1} is a homomorphism from $\{\underline{a}'\}$ to $\{\underline{a}\}$. W.l.o.g. assume that $\underline{a} \in I$, for some I generated during the pchase procedure. As $\underline{a}' \in pchase(P)$, then there is a rule r, an instance $I' \supseteq I$, and an unspent firing homomorphism h' for $\langle r, I' \rangle$, s.t. $fire(r, h') = \underline{a}'$, against the fact that $h^{-1} \circ \sigma$ is a homomorphism from $\{h'(head(r))\}$ to I'. Indeed, $(h^{-1} \circ \sigma)(h'(head(r)) = h^{-1}(\sigma(h'(head(r)) = h^{-1}(fire(r, h')) = h^{-1}(\underline{a}') = \underline{a} \in I \subseteq I'$. □

To provide a precise upper bound for the number of steps execute by the pchase, we introduce the concept of *type* that is equivalent to the notion of equality type defined in.

Definition 1 (Type). *Let m be a positive integer, S an arbitrary partition of $\{1, \ldots, m\}$, C a set with $|C| \leq |S|$, and $f : C \rightarrow S$ an injective map. We define the* type *of S, C and f as the family of sets $\mathcal{T}(S, C, f) = \{s \cup f^{-1}(s) \mid s \in S\}$.*

Example 1. Let $m = 6$, $C = \{c_1, c_2\}$, and let $S = \{\{1, 2\}, \{3, 6\}, \{4\}, \{5\}\}$ be a partition of $\{1, \ldots, 6\}$. Consider the injective map $f : C \rightarrow S$ such that $f(c_1) = \{3, 6\}$ and $f(c_2) = \{5\}$. Then, $\mathcal{T}(S, C, f) = \{\{1, 2\}, \{3, 6, c_1\}, \{4\}, \{5, c_2\}\}$.

Fixed an integer m, our aim is to count the number of all possible types that can be generated from any partition of the set $\{1, \ldots, m\}$, by varying C on a superset D of a fixed size d. In order to do this, we resort to the Bell number B_n, that is the number of ways to partition a set of n labeled elements.

Theorem 2. *Let $m \in \mathbb{N}$, D a finite set of size $d > 0$, and B_n the n-th Bell number. Hence, the number of all possible types generated from all the partitions of the set $\{1, \ldots, m\}$ and all subsets of D is given by $\gamma_m^d = \sum_{h=0}^{m} \binom{m}{h} d^h B_{m-h}$.*

Proof Sketch. Recall that, given two sets A and B with $|A| = \alpha \leq |B| = \beta$, the number of injective maps from A to B is $\frac{\beta!}{(\beta-\alpha)!}$. Then, fixed a partition S of $\{1, ..., m\}$ with $|S| = s$, the number of injective maps from any subset $C \subseteq D$ to S, with $|C| = c \leq s$, is $\frac{s!}{(s-c)!}$, while the number of subsets of size c is $\binom{d}{c}$. Thus, the number of all possible types for the fixed partition S is $\sum_{c=0}^{min\{s,d\}} \binom{d}{c} \cdot \frac{s!}{(s-c)!}$. Hence, the number of types generated from all the partitions of the set $\{1, \ldots, m\}$ and all subsets of D is given by $\sum_{s=1}^{m} S(m, s) \cdot \sum_{c=0}^{min\{s,d\}} \binom{d}{c} \cdot \frac{s!}{(s-c)!}$, where $S(m, s)$

is the Stirling number counting the number of partitions of size s on m elements. It can be shown that it is equivalent to γ_m^d. □

Taking advantage of the notion of type, we can provide a new representation of an arbitrary atom.

Definition 2 (Atom Type). *Given an atom $\underline{a} = p(\mathbf{t})$ of arity m, we define the type of the atom $\underline{a}$ as $T_{\underline{a}} = \mathcal{T}(S, C, f)$, where $C = const(\underline{a})$; $S = \{\{n \mid \underline{a}[n] = t_i\} \mid i = 1, \dots, m\}$; and $f : C \to S$ such that $f(c) = \{n \mid \underline{a}[n] = c\}$.*

Hence, the type of an atom $\underline{a}$ has the form $T_{\underline{a}} = \{\sigma(t_1), \dots, \sigma(t_m)\}$, where σ is such that $\sigma(t_i) = \{n \mid n \in \{1, \dots, m\} \wedge \underline{a}[n] = t_i\} \cup \{t_i\}$ if t_i is a constant, and $\sigma(t_i) = \{n \mid n \in \{1, \dots, m\} \wedge \underline{a}[n] = t_i\}$ otherwise. Intuitively, the type of an atom is formed by the sets of positions where a term occurs, by highlighting positions where constants occur.

Example 2. Let $\underline{a} = p_1(\varphi_1, \varphi_3, \varphi_2, \varphi_1)$ and $\underline{b} = p_2(c, \varphi_1, d, c, \varphi_2, \varphi_2, \varphi_1)$. Then, $T_{\underline{a}} = \{\{1, 4\}, \{2\}, \{3\}\}$ and $T_{\underline{b}} = \{\{1, 4, c\}, \{2, 7\}, \{3, d\}, \{5, 6\}\}$.

Theorem 3. *Let $\underline{a} = p(t_1, \dots, t_k)$ and $\underline{a}' = p(t'_1, \dots, t'_k)$ be two atoms. Then, $\underline{a}$ and $\underline{a}'$ are isomorphic if, and only if, $pred(\underline{a}) = pred(\underline{a}')$ and $T_{\underline{a}} = T_{\underline{a}'}$.*

Proof. Let us consider two atoms $\underline{a}$ and $\underline{a}'$. If $pred(\underline{a}) \neq pred(\underline{a}')$ or $arity(\underline{a}) \neq arity(\underline{a}')$, then of course can not exists an isomorphism between them. Hence, we can take for granted that the two atoms have same predicate and arity.
[⇒] Assume that there is an isomorphism between $\underline{a}$ and $\underline{a}'$, i.e., there is a homomorphism $h : \{\underline{a}\} \to \{\underline{a}'\}$ s.t. $h(t_i) = t'_i$, $i = 1, \dots, k$ and s.t. $h^{-1} : \{\underline{a}'\} \to \{\underline{a}\}$ is a homomorphism. Let $T_{\underline{a}} = \{\sigma(t_1), \dots, \sigma(t_k)\}$ and $T_{\underline{a}'} = \{\sigma'(t_1), \dots, \sigma'(t_k)\}$. We claim that $\sigma(t_i) = \sigma(t'_i)$, for $i = 1, \dots, k$. Assume that $\sigma(t_i) \subseteq \sigma(t'_i)$, and let $n \in \sigma(t_i) \cap \mathbb{N}$, so that $\underline{a}[n] = t_i$. Therefore, we have that $t'_i = h(t_i) = h(\underline{a}[n]) = h(\underline{a})[n] = \underline{a}'[n]$. Hence, $n \in \sigma(t'_i)$. Moreover, if $n = c$ is a constant, by definition of homomorphism, we have $c \in \sigma(t_i) \Rightarrow t_i = c \Rightarrow t'_i = h(t_i) = t_i = c \Rightarrow c \in \sigma(t'_i)$. The reverse inclusion can be easily proved by replacing h by h^{-1}.
[⇐] Let us assume that $\mathcal{T}_{\underline{a}} = \mathcal{T}_{\underline{a}'}$. Let $h : \{\underline{a}\} \to \{\underline{a}'\}$ be s.t. $h(t_i) = t'_i$. First, we prove that h is a homomorphism. Let $t_i = c$ be a constant. Suppose that $c \in \sigma(t_i)$, then by assumption $c \in \sigma(t'_i)$, hence $t'_i = c$. It remains to be shown that h is also injective. Let $t'_i = t'_j$. Then, $\sigma(t'_i) = \sigma(t'_j) \Rightarrow \sigma(t_i) = \sigma(t_j) \Rightarrow t_i = t_j$. □

Now, we are able to provide an upper bound for the maximum number of atoms generating by the pchase procedure.

Theorem 4. *Let P be a program with $arity(P) = w$, $|const(P)| = d$, and l_m the number of predicates in $pred(P)$ of arity m. Then, $|pchase(P)| \leq \sum_{m=0}^{w} l_m \gamma_m^d$.*

Proof. By Theorem 2 and Theorem 3, the total number of non isomorphic atoms over $pred(P)$ and $const(P) \cup \Delta_N$ is given by $\sum_{m=0}^{w} l_m \gamma_m^d$. Moreover, by Theorem 1, we know that $pchase(P)$ does not contain isomorphic atoms. Hence, $|pchase(P)| \leq \sum_{m=0}^{w} l_m \gamma_m^d$. □

Let Γ_w^d be the upper bound in Theorem 4. To show that it is also tight, we introduce an ordering on types that will allow us to build a program with a sequence of firing homomorphisms generating a pchase of size exactly Γ_w^d.

Definition 3 (Type ordering). *Let $T = \mathcal{T}(S, C, f)$ and $T' = \mathcal{T}(S', C', f')$. Then, T* precedes *T', if (i) $|C| < |C'|$, or (ii) $|C| = |C'|$ and $|S| > |S'|$.*

Intuitively, such a program should have a rule for each possible atom tag, whenever constants are allowed in the rules. Otherwise, we need a predicate to collect all constants of the database. To better understand our idea, we give an example of such a program before we provide the formal result.

Example 3. Let C be a finite set of constant, and P be a program such that $data(P) = \{t(c_1), t(c_2)\}$, and $dep(P)$ is given by

$$\begin{array}{rrr}
\exists X, Y, Z p(X, Y, Z) & \exists X, Y p(Z, X, Y) \leftarrow t(Z) & \exists X p(X, Y, Z) \leftarrow t(Y), t(Z) \\
\exists X, Y p(X, X, Y) & \exists X, Y p(X, Z, Y) \leftarrow t(Z) & \exists X p(Y, X, Z) \leftarrow t(Y), t(Z) \\
\exists X, Y p(X, Y, X) & \exists \mathbf{X}, \mathbf{Y} \mathbf{p}(\mathbf{X}, \mathbf{Y}, \mathbf{Z}) \leftarrow \mathbf{t}(\mathbf{Z}) & \exists X p(Y, Z, X) \leftarrow t(Y), t(Z) \\
\exists X, Y p(X, Y, Y) & \exists X p(X, X, Y) \leftarrow t(Y) & p(X, Y, Z) \leftarrow t(X), t(Y), t(Z) \\
\exists X p(X, X, X) & \exists X p(X, Y, X) \leftarrow t(Y) & \\
 & \exists X p(Y, X, X) \leftarrow t(Y) & \exists X t(X)
\end{array}$$

We build $pchase(P)$ by starting from rules in the first column from top to bottom. For each rule r in this ordering, we consider all firing homomorphism h for r. E.g., the rule in bold produces the atoms $\{p(\varphi_1, \varphi_2, c_1), p(\varphi_3, \varphi_4, c_2)\}$. Thus, the number of atoms with predicate p generated by the pchase will be $37 = \gamma_3^2$, and $|pchase(P)| = 40 = \gamma_3^2 + \gamma_1^2$.

Theorem 5. *Let w be a positive integer, D a set of constants of size d, and Γ_w^d as above. Then, there is a family P_w of programs s.t. $|pchase(P_w)| = \Gamma_w^d$.*

Proof Sketch. We build a program P_w having two predicates p (of arity w) and t (of arity 1). We set $data(P_w) = \{t(c) \mid c \in D\}$, and define $dep(P_w)$ as follows. Given a partition $S_i = \{\Lambda_1, \ldots, \Lambda_n\}$ of w, where $n = |S_i|$, we construct a rule r_i with an empty body, by adding $X_1, \ldots, X_n$ existential variables so that $\Lambda_j = \{k \mid p[k] = X_j,\ k \in [w]\}$. Now, fixed a rule r_i with $n > 1$ existential variables, we produce $n - 1$ blocks of rules as follows. We translate j existential variables into universal ones, by adding j atoms over predicate t in the body. Hence, we construct $\binom{n}{j}$ rules. Then, we add the rules $p(X_1, \ldots, X_w) = t(X_1), \ldots, t(X_w)$, and $\exists X t(X)$. Finally, we remove all rules having in the head more than one repeated universal variable. To prove that $|pchase(P_w)| = \Gamma_w^d$, we provide a sequence of $\Gamma_w^d - d$ firing homomorphisms. To each rule r in $dep(P_w)$ we associate uniquely an atom $g(head(r))$, where g maps existential variables to fresh nulls, and universal variables to a fixed constant. The type ordering on the atoms gives an ordering on the rules, and so to the sequence of firing homomorphisms. □

4 Discussion and Future Work

In this work, we identified the maximal number of distinct atoms generable by the pchase procedure. In particular, γ_m^d improves the bound given in [22], that is $(d+m)^m$. In particular, $d^m \leq \gamma_m^d \leq (d+m)^m$. Since in the OBQA context, normally, d is much bigger than m, it could seem that the effort to find such a precise upper bound can be useless for practical purposes. However, this is not the case, as shown in the paper. Indeed, the search for a precise upper bound led to identify the fundamental notions of type and type ordering that highlighted some qualitative characteristics of the pchase. Moreover, there could be other contexts where m is much bigger than d (think for example to scenarios where tuples encode strings over a certain alphabet, as in complexity proofs based on Turing Machine simulation). In this cases, our bound represents a concrete improvement. As future work, we plan to extend the pchase condition to rules with a complex head, and to compute the maximal number of distinct atoms generable in this case. Then, we will try to analyze the orderings of fire homomorphisms in the generation of the pchase to understand if we can identify a sort of best ordering that minimizes the number of atoms produced. Finally, we will try to apply this metodology to give exact estimations of others chase versions.

References

1. Alviano, M., Pieris, A.: Default negation for non-guarded existential rules. In: Proc of PODS (2015)
2. Amendola, G., Leone, N., Manna, M.: Finite model reasoning over existential rules. TPLP **17**(5-6), 726–743 (2017)
3. Amendola, G., Leone, N., Manna, M.: Querying finite or arbitrary models? no matter! existential rules may rely on both once again (discussion paper). In: SEBD. CEUR Workshop Proceedings, vol. 2037, p. 218. CEUR-WS.org (2017)
4. Amendola, G., Leone, N., Manna, M.: Finite controllability of conjunctive query answering with existential rules: Two steps forward. In: IJCAI. pp. 5189–5193. ijcai.org (2018)
5. Amendola, G., Leone, N., Manna, M., Veltri, P.: Reasoning on anonymity in datalog+/-. In: ICLP (Technical Communications). OASICS, vol. 58, pp. 3:1–3:5. Schloss Dagstuhl - Leibniz-Zentrum fuer Informatik (2017)
6. Amendola, G., Leone, N., Manna, M., Veltri, P.: Enhancing existential rules by closed-world variables. In: IJCAI. pp. 1676–1682. ijcai.org (2018)
7. Amendola, G., Libkin, L.: Explainable certain answers. In: IJCAI. pp. 1683–1690. ijcai.org (2018)
8. Amendola, G., Marte, C.: Extending bell numbers for parsimonious chase estimation. In: JELIA. Lecture Notes in Computer Science, vol. 11468, pp. 490–497. Springer (2019)
9. Arenas, M., Barceló, P., Libkin, L., Murlak, F.: Foundations of Data Exchange. Cambridge University Press (2014)
10. Baader, F., Calvanese, D., McGuinness, D.L., Nardi, D., Patel-Schneider, P.F. (eds.): The Description Logic Handbook. Cambridge University Press (2003)

11. Baget, J., Leclère, M., Mugnier, M., Salvat, E.: On rules with existential variables: Walking the decidability line. Artif. Intell. **175**(9-10), 1620–1654 (2011)
12. Bárány, V., Gottlob, G., Martin Otto: Querying the guarded fragment. LMCS **10**(2) (2014)
13. Bourhis, P., Manna, M., Morak, M., Pieris, A.: Guarded-based disjunctive tuple-generating dependencies. ACM TODS **41**(4) (2016)
14. Calì, A., Gottlob, G., Lukasiewicz, T.: Datalog$^{\pm}$: a unified approach to ontologies and integrity constraints. In: Proc. of ICDT (2009)
15. Calì, A., Gottlob, G., Lukasiewicz, T.: A general datalog-based framework for tractable query answering over ontologies. In: PODS. pp. 77–86. ACM (2009)
16. Ceri, S., Gottlob, G., Tanca, L.: What you always wanted to know about datalog (and never dared to ask). IEEE Trans. Knowl. Data Eng. **1**(1), 146–166 (1989)
17. Deutsch, A., Nash, A., Remmel, J.B.: The chase revisited. In: Proc. of PODS (2008)
18. Fagin, R., Kolaitis, P.G., Miller, R.J., Popa, L.: Data exchange: semantics and query answering. TCS **336**(1), 89–124 (2005)
19. Gottlob, G., Orsi, G., Pieris, A.: Ontological queries: Rewriting and optimization. In: ICDE. pp. 2–13. IEEE Computer Society (2011)
20. Imielinski, T., Lipski, W.: Incomplete information in relational databases. J. ACM **31**(4), 761–791 (1984)
21. Lenzerini, M.: Data integration: A theoretical perspective. In: PODS. pp. 233–246. ACM (2002)
22. Leone, N., Manna, M., Terracina, G., Veltri, P.: Efficiently computable Datalog$^{\exists}$ programs. In: Proc. of KR (2012)
23. Manna, M., Ricca, F., Terracina, G.: Consistent query answering via ASP from different perspectives: Theory and practice. TPLP **13**(2), 227–252 (2013)
24. Manna, M., Ricca, F., Terracina, G.: Taming primary key violations to query large inconsistent data via ASP. TPLP **15**(4-5), 696–710 (2015)

Modelling String Structure in Vector Spaces

Richard Connor[1 [0000-0003-4734-8103]], Alan Dearle[2 [0000-0002-1157-2421]], and Lucia Vadicamo[3 [0000-0001-7182-7038]]

[1] Division of Mathematics and Computing Science, University of Stirling, Scotland
richard.connor@stir.ac.uk
[2] School of Computer Science, University of St Andrews, St Andrews, Scotland
alan.dearle@st-andrews.ac.uk
[3] Institute of Information Science and Technologies (ISTI), CNR, Pisa, Italy
lucia.vadicamo@isti.cnr.it

Abstract. Searching for similar strings is an important and frequent database task both in terms of human interactions and in absolute world-wide CPU utilisation. A wealth of metric functions for string comparison exist. However, with respect to the wide range of classification and other techniques known within vector spaces, such metrics allow only a very restricted range of techniques. To counter this restriction, various strategies have been used for mapping string spaces into vector spaces, approximating the string distances within the mapped space and therefore allowing vector space techniques to be used.
In previous work we have developed a novel technique for mapping metric spaces into vector spaces, which can therefore be applied for this purpose. In this paper we evaluate this technique in the context of string spaces, and compare it to other published techniques for mapping strings to vectors. We use a publicly available English lexicon as our experimental data set, and test two different string metrics over it for each vector mapping. We find that our novel technique considerably outperforms previously used technique in preserving the actual distance.

Keywords: Metric Mapping · n-Simplex projection · Pivoted embedding · String · Jensen-Shannon distance · Levenshtein distance

1 Introduction

Searching over strings has been a central activity of database systems since their inception. In addition to their use in documents composed of character sequences, strings are commonly used to encode the structure of molecules, DNA sequences, product descriptions and many other objects drawn from the real world. The need to search for similar strings arises due to differences in encoding and spelling, textual descriptions being slightly different, and the need to find partial matches. In addition to common tasks such as Web searching, string similarity also plays an important role in many real-world database tasks including deduplication and cleaning. Similarity search is also important in the context of record linkage where similar representations of real word entities require unification. Searching for similar strings is therefore an important and frequent database task both in terms of human interactions and in absolute worldwide CPU utilisation.

A wealth of metric functions for string comparison exist. In previous work, we have identified the *n-Simplex projection* as a way of mapping a class of metric space into lower-dimensionality Euclidean spaces with better indexing properties [1, 5, 6]. Previously we have applied this mapping only to the problem of similarity search: that is, finding those objects which are most similar to a given query object from a very large space. As part of this work we have identified a subclass of proper metrics, called *supermetric*, which are amenable to our techniques. This class includes those spaces which have the so-called four-point property [3], which in turn includes all metric spaces which can be isometrically embedded in Hilbert space. Furthermore, any Hilbert-embeddable space has a deeper property, in that any finite set of n points can be isometrically embedded in an $(n-1)$-dimensional Euclidean space.

So far, we have examined only metrics and data within $\mathbb{R}^n$ spaces. Here, we extend the work beyond metric indexing, and to non-numeric spaces for the first time. Our techniques allow certain string spaces to be represented in vector spaces in such a way that the distances are maintained with various degrees of approximation. Our main contribution is to explain the mapping from the string space to the vector space. Based on a sound mathematical framework, we demonstrate that this mapping into vector spaces is significantly better than those previously known.

2 Background and Related Work

Our domain of interest is string spaces, by which we refer to a (typically large) finite set of character strings $\mathbb{S}$, and a distance function $d : \mathbb{S} \times \mathbb{S} \to \mathbb{R}^+$ which compares them. With only a little loss of generality we restrict our interest further to proper metrics which are common over strings. Such spaces are very important in many domains; not just where strings themselves are the objects of interest (e.g., natural language analysis), but also where another semantic domain is represented in string form (e.g., genome analysis).

Various machine learning techniques have shown great success in the analysis and classification of natural language terms, based on a very large supervised or unsupervised input, which gives a vector space mapping reflecting the semantics of the original text [15, 16]. In such cases, the vector space acts as a semantic proxy space, in that terms with similar meaning will be close when measured in the vector space. In our context, we are interested only the in *structural* similarity of strings, as measured by metrics such as edit distance. The intent is to map into a vector space while preserving the original string distances as far as possible. There are some known techniques for mapping string spaces into vector

Table 1: The nearest few terms from the SISAP lexicon for a selection of four tokens, showing both Levenshtein and Jensen-Shannon Shingle distances

"string"		"metric"		"simplex"		"error"	
lev	jsd	lev	jsd	lev	jsd	lev	jsd
string	string	metric	metric	simples	simple	error	error
strings	stringing	matric	meteoric	dimpled	simples	terror	terror
surfing	strings	eric	metricize	triplex	simpler	mirror	err
tin	striking	dearie	metrical	bingley	simplest	frog	borrower
ringing	stirring	petted	symmetric	names	pimples	racy	emperor
briefing	staring	makeup	mimetic	jugular	simply	petted	horror

spaces, whilst attempting to preserve the integrity of the distance function, but none of these appear to be particularly effective.

This paper presents a mechanism for transforming metric string spaces to vector spaces, which can be applied whenever the distance function d is a proper metric; this includes most edit distances.

2.1 String Metrics

In the literature, many string distance functions have been proposed to measure the dissimilarity between two text strings. In this work we restrict our attention to the *Levenshtein Distance* and *Jensen-Shannon distance* as explained below. These two metrics are representative of the wide range of more or less sophisticated metrics available. For our purposes, we also note a deep mathematical property which is important to our context: the Jensen-Shannon distance is isometrically Hilbert embeddable, whereas the Levenshtein distance is not. The importance of this will be made clear later in the text.

Levenshtein Distance: the best known edit distance between strings defined as the minimum number of single-character edit operations (insertions, deletions or substitutions) needed to transform one string into the other. For example, the distance between "error" and "horror" is 2 (one insertion and one substitution), the distance between "writing" and "writer" is 3 (one deletion, two substitutions). Note that the Levenshtein distance d_{Lev} between two strings of length m and n is at least $|m - n|$, and at most $max(m, n)$.

Jensen-Shannon Distance over Strings: is derived from a distance metric defined over labelled trees [8]. In outline, the technique of digram shingling [13] is used to transform each character string into a very high-dimensional probability space, where each individual character and each character digram is represented as a different event; thus a string represented in a 127-character set will be represented in a space comprising $127^2 + 127$ different events. Each such event is assigned a frequency according to its appearance in the token, including notional start and finish characters denoted ϕ and

ω in the following example. For example, the string "ann" is composed of the characters and diagrams "ϕa","an", "nn" "nω","a", and "n" with corresponding frequencies $\frac{1}{6}, \frac{1}{6}, \frac{1}{6}, \frac{1}{6}, \frac{1}{6}$, and $\frac{1}{3}$.
Jensen-Shannon distance is then applied over these probability ensembles[4].We recall that the Jensen-Shannon distance between two probability vectors x, y is defined as $d_{JS}(x, y) = \sqrt{JSD(x, y)}$, where $JSD(x, y)$ is the Jenson-Shannon divergence.

$$JSD(x, y) = 1 - \frac{1}{2} \sum_i x_i \log_2 x_i + y_i \log_2 y_i - (x_i + y_i) \log_2 (x_i + y_i). \quad (1)$$

To show a characterisation of these two metrics, Table 1 shows the nearest few strings within the SISAP lexicon to an appropriate selection of tokens.

2.2 String space to Vector space mappings

The only information available within our context derives from the distance function over the string domain; this is treated as a "black box" function and therefore any approach to map the string space into a vector space must rely only upon these distances. Usually, the distances between each string and a fixed set of *pivots* (i.e., reference objects) is exploited to map the string space to a vector space. There are however various different ways of using this information, five of are compared in this paper.

In this section we explain three string-to-vector mappings which are variously described in the literature, and indeed are the only methods that we know of other than our own. To introduce a unifying terminology, we refer to these mechanisms by the following terms: *Pivoted Embedding* - ℓ_∞, *Pivoted Embedding* - ℓ_2, *LMDS* - ℓ_2, which we will continue to compare experimentally with two of our own invention, referred to here as *nSimplex* - *lwb* and *nSimplex* - *zen*.

In terms of the construction of a pivot set, it should be noted that in all cases other than LMDS, the selection of n pivot objects leads to the construction of an n-dimensional vector space; in the case of LMDS, the dimension of the constructed space equals the number of positive eigenvalues of the matrix of the squared distance between the pivots, which is at most $n - 1$.

We continue by giving explanations of each of these mechanisms; the first three in this section, the two nSimplex mappings in Section 3.

Pivoted Embedding with ℓ_∞. Pivoted Embedding is a metric space transformation based on the distances between data objects and a set of *pivots*. Given a metric space (U, d), and a set of pivots $\{p_1, \ldots, p_n\}$, the Pivoted Embedding f_P maps an object $o \in U$ to a n-dimensional vector $f_P(o) =$

[4] We appreciate this outline description is insufficient to accurately describe the function used in experiments, however it does succinctly give its essence. The interested reader is referred to the publicly available code base for this paper, which contains full source code for this metric: `bitbucket.org/richardconnor/it_db_conference_2019`.

$[d(o,p_1),\ldots,d(o,p_n)]$. Using the triangle inequality it can be proven that for any $o,q \in U$

$$\max_i |d(o,p_i) - d(q,p_i)| \leq d(o,q) \leq \min_i |d(o,p_i) + d(q,p_i)|. \quad (2)$$

The maximum distance at any dimension is captured by the Chevyshev[5] (ℓ_∞) distance, and therefore the distance $\ell_\infty(f_P(o), f_P(q))$ is guaranteed to be a lower-bound of $d(o,q)$. As the number of pivots increases, this lower-bound distance can reasonably be expected to provide a better approximation to the true distance, and this technique has been used to effect in some metric space contexts, e.g. [7, 19].

Pivoted Embedding with ℓ_2. Other distances over the same pivoted embedding spaces have also been used. For example, in the context of string spaces (i.e. $U = \mathbb{S}$), Spillmann et al [17] used the family of Minkowski metrics, which encompasses the well-known Euclidean distance (ℓ_2). It should be noted that there is no underlying theory for this technique, and in particular the ℓ_2 metric applied over the pivoted embedding space has no formal guarantees that we know of with respect to the string space it is intended to model.

The authors primarily investigate the selection of pivots to best effect within several different contexts, but make no particular justification for their choice of vector representation - except, perhaps, that it is the most straightforward possible mapping.

LMDS. In the general metric space context, perhaps the best known technique is *metric Multidimensional Scaling* (MDS) [12]. MDS aims to preserve *interpoint distances*. Given m objects and the distances $\delta_{i,j}$ between those points, it finds a set of m points $\{x_1,\ldots,x_m\}$ in a Euclidean space $\mathbb{R}^k$ such that $\ell_2(x_i,x_j)$ is close as possible to $\delta_{i,j}$. Those coordinates are computed using spectral analysis of the matrix of the squared interpoint distances.

For any metric which is isometrically Hilbert embeddable, it is possible to find a perfect ℓ_2 embedding for any n objects within $n-1$ Euclidean dimensions [11]. However, when the number m of data points is large the classical MDS is too expensive in practice due to a requirement for $O(m^2)$ distance computations and spectral decomposition of an $m \times m$ matrix.

The *Landmark MDS* (LMDS) [9] is a fast approximation of MDS. LMDS uses a set of k *landmark* points (i.e. pivots) to compute $k \times m$ distances of the data points from the landmark points. It applies classical MSD to the landmark points and uses a distance-based triangulation procedure to project the remaining data points. Specifically if $X_k \in \mathbb{R}^{k\times k}$ is the output of MDS on the pivot set, the embedding of a new point s into $\mathbb{R}^k$ is computed as $x_s = -\frac{1}{2}X_k^+(\delta_s^2 - \delta_\mu^2)$, where $(\delta_s^2)_i = d(s,p_i)$, $(\delta_\mu^2)_j = \frac{1}{n}\sum_{i=1}^n d(p_i,p_j)$ and X_k^+ is the pseudo inverse of X_k.

[5] The Chebyshev distance (ℓ_∞) is a true metric defined on a vector space to be the greatest difference along any coordinate dimension.

3 The n-Simplex Projection

The n-Simplex Projection projection is described in full in [6]; here we give a sketch of the approach. Although it requires a little mathematical background, the outcome is that there exists a relatively simple and efficient mapping from any space with the correct properties into an n-dimensional Euclidean space for an arbitrary choice of n. The mapping is contractive, and the associated error asymptotically approaches zero as n increases.

1. Any metric space (U, d) which is isometrically embeddable in a Hilbert space has the so-called *n-point property*. This means that, for any finite selection of n objects, an isometric embedding of just those objects exists in $(n-1)$-dimensional Euclidean space. That is, for any set $\{u_1, \ldots, u_n\} \subset U$ there exists a mapping $f : \{u_1, \ldots, u_n\} \to \mathbb{R}^{(n-1)}$ such that $d(u_i, u_j) = \ell_2(f(u_i), f(u_j))$ for any two objects u_i, u_j. This background work is attributed to mathematicians such as Blumenthal, Menger, Wilson etc. [3, 14, 18]
2. In practical terms, we have identified that metrics with this property include: Euclidean, Cosine, Jensen-Shannon, Triangular, and Quadratic Form distances [4]. In this context we also note that other proper metrics such as Chebyshev, Levenshtein, and Hamming do *not* possess the property. However, for any metric space (U, d) and any $n \geq 4$ there exist a constant $\alpha_n \leq 1/2$ such that for all the $0 < \alpha \leq \alpha_n$ the space (U, d^α) has the n-point property [10]. Specifically, Blumenthal proved that $\alpha_4 = 1/2$, and thus for any proper metric space (U, d), the space $(U, \sqrt{d})$ has the 4-point property. For $n > 4$, Deza and Maehara [10] proved that $\alpha_n \geq 0.72/n$, thus for any $0 < \alpha \leq 0.72/n$ the space (U, d^α) has the n-point property. Moreover, it is worth noting that for any finite metric space (U, d) of *negative type* [10] (e.g. hypermetric, ℓ_1-embeddedable metric, ultrametric) then $(U, \sqrt{d})$ has the n-point property.
3. In [6], we give the simple corollary of the n-point property that any n objects in the space can be used to form the vertices of a *simplex* in $(n-1)$-dimensional space, such that the edge lengths of the simplex are in one-to-one correspondence with the distances measured in the original space, and furthermore we give an algorithm to construct the Euclidean coordinates of its vertices. This therefore gives a concrete instantiation of the existential function f mentioned above.
4. This function is defined inductively, and at each step constructs a new apex in k dimensions based on a new object and a simplex previously formed in $(k-1)$dimensions, called *base simplex*, according to the distances between the new object and each object represented by the vertices of the base simplex.
5. Finally, we observe that once a base simplex is formed, this may be used to create any number of apexes based on it, using objects from the original space. For a choice of n reference objects, each of these apexes corresponds to a point in n-dimensional Euclidean space.

3.1 Dissimilarity functions over the n-Simplex projected points

For a fixed set of pivots, $\{p_1, \ldots, p_n\}$, let $f_S : U \to \mathbb{R}^n$ be the n-Simplex projection obtained using the pivots to form the vertices of the base simplex. We have shown [6] that for any two objects $o, q \in (U, d)$

$$\sqrt{\sum_{i=1}^{n}(x_i - y_i)^2} \leq d(o,q) \leq \sqrt{\sum_{i=1}^{n-1}(x_i - y_i)^2 + (x_i + y_i)^2}, \quad (3)$$

where $f_S(o) = [x_1, \ldots, x_n]$, $f_S(q) = [y_1, \ldots y_n]$. Thus the Euclidean distance $\ell_2(f_S(o), f_S(q))$ between any two apexes is a lower-bound of the distance between the corresponding objects within the original space, and an upper-bound could be computed as well. Furthermore, as more dimensions are chosen for the base simplex, these distance bounds asymptotically approach the true distance. The lower-bound (d'_{Lwb}) is a proper metric function on $\mathbb{R}^n$, while the upper-bound (d'_{Upb}) is a dissimilarity function but not a proper metric, because it does not satisfy the identity postulate (i.e. $d'_{Upb}(x,x)$ may not be equal to zero).

Other dissimilarity functions over the apex vectors may be considered as well, in particular, any function that is always between the lower-bound and the upper-bound will asymptotically approach the true distance when increasing the number of pivots. An example is the *mean* between the lower- and upper-bound, which as been proved to be particularly effective for similarity search task [1]. Here we introduce the *Zenith* dissimilarity function

$$d'_{Zen}(x,y) = \sqrt{\sum_{i=1}^{n-1}(x_i - y_i)^2 + x_i^2 + y_i^2}, \quad \forall x, y \in \mathbb{R}^n \quad (4)$$

which always satisfies $d'_{Lwb}(x,y) \leq d'_{Zen}(x,y) \leq d'_{Upb}(x,y)$, but has a geometrical interpretation stronger than the arithmetic mean between the upper- and the lower-bound. In fact, the Zenith distance, as well as the lower-bound and the upper-bound, can be interpreted as the Euclidean distance between two points in $\mathbb{R}^{n+1}$. Figure 2 shows the case $n = 2$.

In general, given the pivots $\{p_1, \ldots, p_n\}$ and two objects o, q we know that there exists an *isometric* embedding of those $n+2$ points into $\mathbb{R}^{n+1}$.

Let $v_o, v_q, v_{p_1}, \ldots, v_{p_n}$ be the mapped points, i.e. vectors such that $d(o,q) = \ell_2(v_o, v_q)$, $d(o, p_i) = \ell_2(v_o, v_{p_i})$, $d(q, p_i) = \ell_2(v_q, v_{p_i})$, $d(p_i, p_j) = \ell_2(v_{p_1}, v_{p_j})$, for all $i, j = 1 \ldots, n$. The points $v_{p_1}, \ldots, v_{p_n}$ are the vertices of the so-called base simplex, which lies in a $(n-1)$dimensional subspace. The points $v_{p_1}, \ldots, v_{p_n}$ and v_o lies in a hyperplane of $\mathbb{R}^{n+1}$, which we refer to as H. By rotating v_q around the base simplex (i.e. rotate the point while preserving the distances to the pivots) we have two possible projections onto the hyperplane H (one above and one below the base simplex). Let v_q^+ and v_q^- be those points, which coincide with the intersections of hyperplane H and the n balls of centre p_i and radius $d(p_i, q)$. In general, we don't explicitly know the distance $d(o,q)$, so we don't know the true altitude of the vertex v_q over the hyperplane H. The vertices

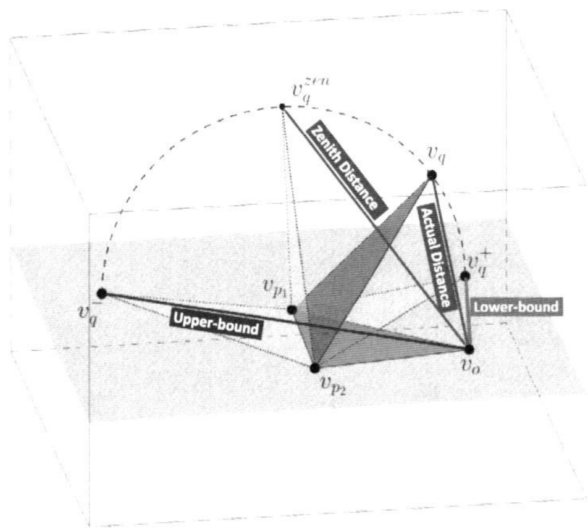

Fig. 1: Example of n-Simplex projection for $n = 2$, where the two pivots p_1, p_2 and two data objects o, q are first isometrically embedded in 3D Euclidean space and then projected in 2D Euclidean plane. The mapped points are indicated with $v_{p_1}, v_{p_2}, v_o, v_q$ in the graph. By rotating v_q around the edge $\overline{v_{p_1} v_{p_2}}$ until it is coplanar with v_{p_1}, v_{p_2}, v_o, we obtain two possible apices (v_q^+ and v_q^-), that are the intersections of the hyperplane containing v_{p_1}, v_{p_2}, v_o, and the the two balls centred in v_{p_1}, v_{p_2} and radii $d(q, p_1)$, $d(q, p_2)$, respectively. The apex v_q^{zen} is that at the highest altitude over the hyperplane that still preserves the distance to the two pivots.

v_q^+ and v_q^- are those obtained by approximating v_q with points at zero altitude such that the distances to the pivots are preserved. Another possible choice is considering the *zenith* point v_q^{zen} which is the point at the highest altitude over H that still preserves the distances to the pivots. In [6] we show that the quantities $\ell_2(v_o, v_q^+)$ and $\ell_2(v_o, v_q^-)$ provide a lower-bound and an upper-bound of $d(o, q)$. By construction, the quantity $\ell_2(v_o, v_q^{zen})$ will always been between those bounds, and it corresponds to the *quadratic mean* of the lower- and upper-bounds, i.e. $d'_{Zen} = \sqrt{\frac{(d'_{Lwb})^2 + (d'_{Upb})^2}{2}}$.

3.2 Application of n-Simplex to Levenshtein

As previously mentioned, with respect to our techniques there is one essential difference between the two metrics we are testing: Jensen-Shannon distance is Hilbert-embeddable, and therefore has the n-point property; Levenshtein does not. This means that, in the form defined above, it cannot be used to build a simplex in n-dimensional space for some arbitrary n.

However, as observed above, for any $n > 4$ there exists some exponent α_n with $0.72/n \leq \alpha_n \leq 0.5$, such that for any $\alpha \in (0, \alpha_n]$ the space $(\mathbb{S}, d_{lev}^{\alpha})$ satisfies the n-point property [10]. Therefore, for a fixed α in the desired range we can use the n-simplex projection to transform the space $(\mathbb{S}, d_{lev}^{\alpha})$ into $(\mathbb{R}^n, d')$, where d' is a dissimilarity function over the projected points (e.g., the n-simplex lower-bound or the zenith measure). If $v_i, v_j \in \mathbb{R}^n$ are the projections of the strings $s_i, s_j \in \mathbb{S}$, then we can approximate the actual distance $d_{lev}(s_i, s_j)$ with $(d'(v_i, v_j))^{1/\alpha}$. It is worth noting that using the value $\tilde{\alpha}_n = 0.72/n$ guarantees that $(U, d^{\tilde{\alpha}_n})$ has the n-point property for *any* metric space (U, d); however for a specified metric space it is possible to find a suitable exponent that is greater than $\tilde{\alpha}_n$. We experimentally observed that, in our context, $\alpha = 0.5$ works well for $(\mathbb{S}, d_{lev})$; in fact we have found no counter-examples where it is impossible to embed any n objects from our domain into an $(n-1)$-dimensional Euclidean space. Thus we applied the n-Simplex projection on $(\mathbb{S}, \sqrt{d_{lev}})$. Note we do not claim this property for $\mathbb{S}$ in general, although we are interested in pursuing this further as we suspect it to be the case.

Given the above, when comparing the n-Simplex techniques in the context of the Levenshtein distance, we first cast the space $(\mathbb{S}, d_{lev})$ into $(\mathbb{S}, \sqrt{d_{lev}})$ to create the vector space, and then square the results before comparison. In terms of intrinsic dimensionality, or discriminability, this is very undesirable; the application of this metric-preserving transformation decreases the variance of measured distances, which makes a proximity query more unstable as the the square-rooted distance has less power in discriminating between nearest and furthest neighbour [2]. Thus, the techniques which do not require to perform this mapping should benefit considerably in terms of relative error. This effect shows in some of our results, as mentioned later.

4 Experimental Analysis

To test the five techniques outlined above, we use a single collection of strings drawn from a public English lexicon of 69,069 words[6] and consider Levenshtein distance (d_{Lev}) and Jensen-Shannon distance (d_{JS}) over this collection. For varying numbers of pivots, we apply the five different methods and measure distortion, relative error, and absolute squared error.

For each measured number n of pivots, we repeatedly select a subset random subset of n strings to act as pivots, and a further random selection of 10,000 strings to act as the finite data set. We consider all $\binom{n}{2}$ pairwise distances within the set, i.e. nearly 50 million distances, and for each pair measure both the original distance and the mapped distance to calculate the properties listed. We repeat this process until the standard error of the mean for each measurement is within an acceptable limit, and then report the mean values obtained.

Notationally, we refer to an original metric space $(\mathbb{S}, d)$ which is mapped into a new space $(\bar{\mathbb{S}}, \bar{d})$, where $s_i, s_j \in \mathbb{S}$ map to $s'_i, s'_j \in \bar{\mathbb{S}}$ and so on. We measure the following properties of the mapped data:

Distortion For each mapping, the distortion is the minimum $R \geq 1$ such that there exists a multiplying factor $r > 0$ such that, for all $s_i, s_j \in \mathbb{S}$,

$$r \cdot \bar{d}(s'_i, s'_j) \leq d(s_i, s_j) \leq rR \cdot \bar{d}(s'_i, s'_j).$$

[6] available from `www.sisap.org`

Note that distortion gives a "worst case" analysis and is driven by outliers within the mapping rather than typical errors; the larger the sample of distances, the larger the distortion is likely to be.

Average Relative Error For each pair of distances $d(s_i, s_j)$ and $\bar{d}(s'_i, s'_j)$ we calculate the ratio, and use the mean of these ratios as a scaling factor γ. Then the average relative error is calculated as

$$\frac{1}{\binom{|\mathbb{S}|}{2}} \sum_{i,j} \frac{|d(s_i, s_j) - \gamma \cdot \bar{d}(s'_i, s'_j)|}{d(s_i, s_j)}$$

Mean Squared Error For each pair of distances $d(s_i, s_j)$ and $\bar{d}(s'_i, s'_j)$ we calculate the ratio, and use the mean of these ratios as a scaling factor γ. Then the mean squared error is calculated as

$$\frac{1}{\binom{|\mathbb{S}|}{2}} \sum_{i,j} (d(s_i, s_j) - \gamma \cdot \bar{d}(s'_i, s'_j))^2$$

4.1 Results

The results of these experiments are plotted in Figure 2.

The clearest observation is that, for almost all measures, the nSimplex-Zenith projection is the best. It is clearly by far the best estimator for all measures over Jensen-Shannon distance, and also for Levenshtein in all aspects other than distortion. Note the scale of the improvement is quite dramatic, the Y axis being given in log scale for all charts. It is also notable how little the performance degrades when less pivots are used compared with the other projections.

The n-Simplex lower-bound estimator also performs well, and our conclusion is that, at least for the Jensen-Shannon space, the n-Simplex projection is clearly preferable to any of the other established methods.

The difference between the two metrics is, we believe, due to the presence of the Hilbert embedding property of the Jensen-Shannon metric, and thus we expect this behaviour to extend to other such metrics. The problem with Levenshtein, which again we would expect to extend to other non-embeddable metrics, is that in order to apply the projection it is necessary to scale the original distance into a much less discriminable form; this we believe in particular is the reason for the relatively poor figures for distortion. This effect deserves further attention to give a better understanding.

5 Conclusions

We have described the use of the n-Simplex projection to create mappings from strings into vector spaces, and compared properties of these mappings with three others. This is the first time n-Simplex has been demonstrated over string functions, and in particular we have introduced for the first time the Zenith estimator function. This has been shown to be significantly better in terms of the accuracy of estimations in the mapped space than any previously published mapping.

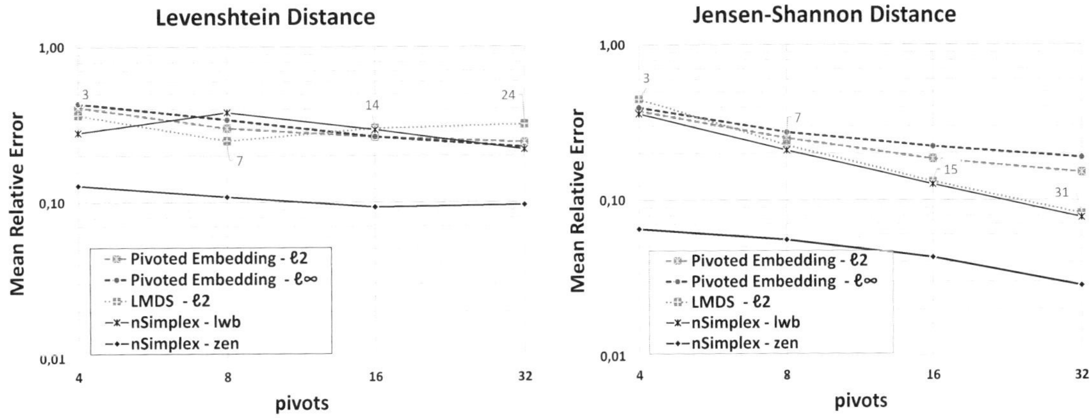

(a) Mean Relative Error

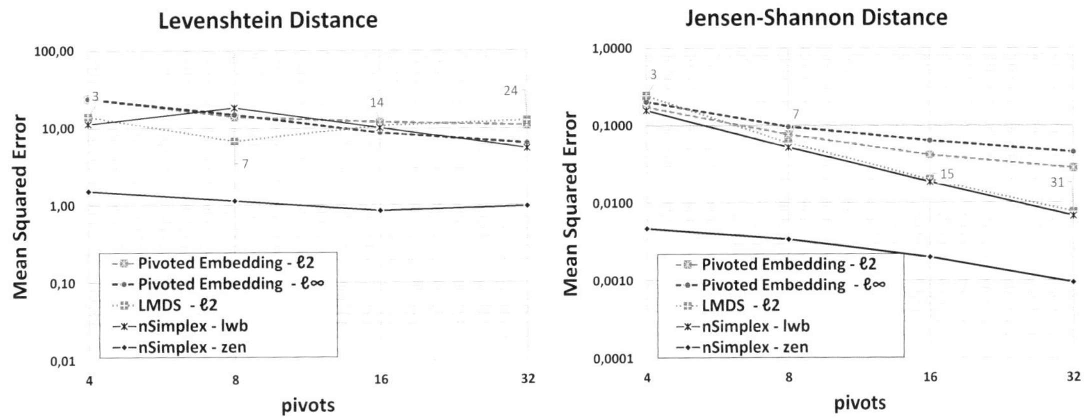

(b) Mean Squared Error

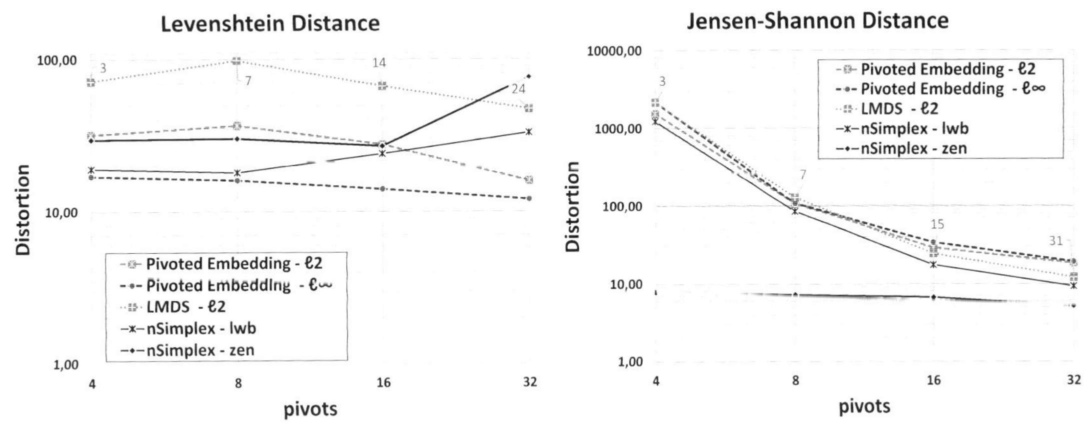

(c) Distortion

Fig. 2: Results from varying the number n of pivots. Left figures give measurements for Levenshtein Distance, the right for Jensen-Shannon Distance. We recall that both Pivoted Embedding and n-Simplex projection provide a mapping into n dimensions. For the LMDS approach, the dimensionality of the projected space equals the number of positive eigenvalues of the matrix of the squared distance between the pivots. These are indicated by the numbers along the LMDS lines in the graphs.

Acknowledgements

Lucia Vadicamo acknowledges financial support from the VISECH ARCO-CNR project, CUP B56J17001330004, and the Italian National Research Council (CNR) for a Short-Term Mobility Grant (STM) at the University of Stirling.

References

1. Amato, G., Chávez, E., Connor, R., Falchi, F., Gennaro, C., Vadicamo, L.: Re-ranking permutation-based candidate sets with the n-Simplex projection. In: Proceedings of SISAP 2018. pp. 3–17. Springer (2018)
2. Beyer, K., Goldstein, J., Ramakrishnan, R., Shaft, U.: When is nearest neighbor meaningful? In: Proceedings of ICDT 1999. pp. 217–235. Springer (1999)
3. Blumenthal, L.M.: Theory and applications of distance geometry. Clarendon Press (1953)
4. Connor, R., Cardillo, F.A., Vadicamo, L., Rabitti, F.: Hilbert exclusion: Improved metric search through finite isometric embeddings. ACM T Inform. Syst. **35**(3), 17:1–17:27 (Dec 2016)
5. Connor, R., Vadicamo, L., Cardillo, F.A., Rabitti, F.: Supermetric search. Inform. Syst. **80**, 108 – 123 (2019)
6. Connor, R., Vadicamo, L., Rabitti, F.: High-dimensional simplexes for supermetric search. In: Proceedings of SISAP 2017. pp. 96–109. Springer (2017)
7. Connor, R.C.H., MacKenzie-Leigh, S., Moss, R.: High dimensional search using polyhedral query. In: Proceedings of SISAP 2014. pp. 176–188. Springer (2014)
8. Connor, R.C.H., Simeoni, F., Iakovos, M., Moss, R.: A bounded distance metric for comparing tree structure. Inform. Syst. **36**(4), 748–764 (2011)
9. deSilva, V., Tenenbaum, J.B.: Global versus local methods in nonlinear dimensionality reduction. In: Proceedings NIPS. vol. 15, p. 721728 (2003)
10. Deza, M., Maehara, H.: Metric transforms and euclidean embeddings. T Am. Math. Soc. **317**(2), 661–671 (1990)
11. Dokmanic, I., Parhizkar, R., Ranieri, J., Vetterli, M.: Euclidean distance matrices: Essential theory, algorithms, and applications. IEEE Signal Proc. Mag. **32**(6), 12–30 (Nov 2015)
12. Kruskal, J.B.: Multidimensional scaling by optimizing goodness of fit to a nonmetric hypothesis. Psychometrika **29**(1), 1–27 (Mar 1964)
13. Manber, U.: Finding similar files in a large file system. In: USENIX Winter 1994 Technical Conference. pp. 1–10 (1994)
14. Menger, K.: New Foundation of Euclidean Geometry. Amer. J. Math. **53**(4), 721–745 (1931)
15. Mikolov, T., Sutskever, I., Chen, K., Corrado, G.S., Dean, J.: Distributed representations of words and phrases and their compositionality. In: Proceedings of NIPS 2013, pp. 3111–3119. Curran Associates, Inc. (2013)
16. Pennington, J., Socher, R., Manning, C.: Glove: Global vectors for word representation. In: Proceedings of EMNLP 2014. pp. 1532–1543 (2014)
17. Spillmann, B., Neuhaus, M., Bunke, H., Pekalska, E., Duin, R.: Transforming strings to vector spaces using prototype selection. In: Structural, Syntactic, and Statistical Pattern Recognition. pp. 287–296. Springer (09 2006)
18. Wilson, W.A.: A Relation Between Metric and Euclidean Spaces. Amer. J. Math. **54**(3), 505–517 (1932)
19. Zezula, P., Amato, G., Dohnal, V., Batko, M.: Similarity search: the metric space approach, vol. 32. Springer Science & Business Media (2006)

Multiple Instance Learning algorithm for medical image classification

(Discussion Paper)

Annabella Astorino[1 [0000-0002-3439-180X]], Antonio Fuduli[2 [0000-0002-1657-0257]], Manlio Gaudioso[3[0000-0002-3022-7041]] and Eugenio Vocaturo[3[0000-0001-7457-7118]]

[1]ICAR-CNR National Research Council, Rende, Italy
annabella.astorino@icar.cnr.it

[2]Department of Mathematics and Computer Science,
University of Calabria, Rende, Italy
antonio.fuduli@unical.it

[3]DIMES - Department of Computer Engineering, Modelling, Electronic and System
University of Calabria, Rende, Italy
{gaudioso, e.vocaturo}@dimes.unical.it

Abstract. After an overview on most relevant methods for image classification, we focus on a recently proposed Multiple Instance Learning (MIL) approach, suitable for image processing applications and based on a mixed integer nonlinear optimization problem. In particular, the algorithm has been preliminarily applied to a set of color images, with the aim to identify images containing some specific color pattern, and successively to a medical dataset, containing photos of melanoma and common nevi. Since the results appear promising, this technique could be at the basis of computer vision systems that act as a filter mechanism to support physicians in detecting melanomas cancer.

Keywords: Image Classification, Multiple Instance Learning, Lagrangian Relaxation.

1 Introduction

Nowadays, continuous development of digital technologies and ICT solutions implies a great availability of digital images in various fields, such as scientific, medical and industrial. Use of this information requires navigation, searching, indexing, classification and retrieval. Image classification is aimed at classifying images according to their visual contents: a particular application is in the medical field, where medical images classification can support the diagnosis of some diseases.
Interesting algorithms to evaluate image similarities have been proposed in [9, 13]: they work by extracting first the features vectors from the image and then by using the vector distances as a measure of similarity. Since these methods, based on object recognition techniques, are sensitive to the noise and do not satisfactorily work when there are no

distinct objects in the images, De Bonet and Viola [8] proposed an algorithm that works well with natural scenes and single object test sets. Ravela et al. [16] proposed a method to evaluate the similarity by means a correlation measure: the application of this system involves a collection of regions of interest, but possible limitations are connected to the difficulties in identifying such regions. A General Image Retrieval (GIR) model that calculates the similarities between query image and the images in the image database was proposed in [11], while R. da Silva Torres et al. [19] released an interesting overview on content based image retrieval and its applications on digital libraries, crime prevention, medicine, fingerprint identification and biodiversity information systems. P.N. Shinde and A.A. Manjrekar [17] proposed different schemes to check similarity between two images: the images are classified, re-ranked and retrieved using an algorithm based on score histogram computation.
In this paper, we face image classification by means of a Multiple Instance Learning approach [1, 6] based on a Lagrangian relaxation technique [3]. Multiple instance learning (MIL) is a recent paradigm of machine learning that performs well in the context of medical images and video analysis [15]. Manual segmentation, typically needed in the training phase, is no more necessary since the supervision is based on global labels, unlike traditional single-instance learning algorithms. The paper is organized as follows. In the next section, we recall the main concepts at the basis of the Multiple Instance Learning paradigm, focusing on the binary case. In Section 3, we shortly describe the algorithm proposed in [3], while in Section 4 we report some preliminary numerical results performed on the classification of some artificial color images and on a data set of dermoscopic images. Finally, some conclusions are drawn in Section 5.

2 Multiple Instance Learning

The objective of the Multiple Instance Learning (MIL) is to discriminate among sets of points: the sets to be classified are called bags, while the points inside the bags are named instances. In the image classification, an image is represented by a bag, whereas the sub-regions forming the images are the instances. In a MIL problem, during the learning phase only the labels of the bags are known, whereas the labels of the instances are unknown. This is different from a classical supervised classification approach, where the label of each point is known. In this work, we focus on the binary MIL classification, whose objective is to discriminate between positive and negative images. Two different approaches are mainly possible: one is in the instance-space and the other one is in the bag-space. In the instance-space, the learning process looks only at the characteristics of each individual instance, without considering the more global characteristics of the entire bag. Vice-versa, in the bag-space case, the learning phase is more global, because each bag is treated as a whole entity: the classification consists in separating directly the positive bags from the negative ones. There exists also a compromise between these two approaches. It consists in representing each bag by means of some of its instances containing maximal similarities and it is referred as the embedding-space approach [6]. An important issue in binary MIL problems is to specify what a positive bag is. The standard assumption is that a bag is negative if all its instances are negative and positive whenever at least one instance is positive: as a consequence, under such an assumption, only the labels of the instances inside the positive bags are to be predicted. An extensive survey on classification of medical images by means of MIL techniques is reported in [15]. The proposed classification method, described in the next section, is a heuristic optimization algorithm [3] based on the SVM (Support Vector Machine) type model introduced in [2].We recall that optimization techniques, aimed at obtaining separation surfaces, play a relevant role in every machine learning problem and in literature various mathematical programming models have been proposed to face a binary MIL classification problem, such as [5, 12].

3 The Classification Algorithm

In this section we describe the heuristics optimization MIL algorithm proposed in [3], which is suitable for image classification. This method is based on the SVM type model introduced by Andrews et al. in [2]. In particular, let J^+ and J^- the index sets corresponding to m positive bags and k negative ones. The two sets are therefore defined respectively as: $J^+ = \{J_1^+, \dots, J_m^+\}$ and $J^- = \{J_1^-, \dots, J_k^-\}$. Let p be the total number of points (the instances) inside the bags.

The j_{th} instance, $j = (1, \dots, p)$ is represented by a vector $x_j \in \mathbb{R}^n$ and its class label $y_j \in \{-1,1\}$ is supposed to be unknown. Differently from the class label of the instances, the class label of each bag is known: it is equal to +1 for each positive bag $J_i^+ = 1, \dots, m$ and it is equal to -1 for each negative bag $J_i^- = 1, \dots, k$.

We hypothesize to work under the MIL standard assumption: we suppose that a bag is positive if it contains at least a positive instance, while it is negative if it contains only negative instances. The objective is to determine a hyperplane:

$$H(w,b) \triangleq \{x \in \mathbb{R}^n \mid w^T x + b = 0\}$$

separating the two classes of bags, where $w \in \mathbb{R}^n$ is the normal to the hyperplane and $b \in \mathbb{R}$ is the bias. Since a negative bag is defined containing only negative instances, only the class label $y_j \in \{-1,1\}$ of the instances inside the positive bags are actually unknown. If in addition we want to minimize a measure of the classification error of all the instances inside the bags, the optimization model [2] is the following:

$$P \begin{cases} z^* = min_{w,b,y} f(w,b,y) \\ \displaystyle\sum_{j \in J_i^+} \frac{y_j + 1}{2} \geq 1, \qquad i = 1, \dots, m \\ y_j \in \{-1,1\}, \qquad j \in J_i^+ \; i = 1, \dots, m \end{cases}$$

where

$$f(w,b,y) \triangleq \frac{1}{2} \parallel w \parallel^2 + C \sum_{i=1}^{k} \sum_{j \in J_i^-} max\{0, 1 + (w^T x_j + b)\} + C \sum_{i=1}^{m} \sum_{j \in J_i^+} max\{0, 1 - y_j(w^T x_j + b)\}.$$

Note that problem P is a constrained, nonlinear, nonconvex and mixed integer program. Moreover, if variables y_j were fixed, we would obtain a classical supervised SVM model [7]. The objective function in problem P is the sum of three terms: the first one is aimed at maximizing the margin, while the other two ones are aimed at minimizing a measure of the classification error of the points belonging to the negative bags and of the points belonging to the positive bags, respectively. Note that the presence of the unknown labels y_j in the third term allows the possibility to allocate some points of positive bags in the negative part with respect to the separating hyperplane. Finally, by means of the constraints:

$$\sum_{j\in J_i^+} \frac{y_j+1}{2} \geq 1, \qquad i = 1, \dots, m \qquad (1)$$

we impose that, for each positive bag, at least one point must be labelled as a positive point. In [2], the authors proposed two different heuristic techniques, based on solving approximately problem P. Our optimization heuristic algorithm (see [3]) is based on the Lagrangian relaxation [10] of problem P, obtained by relaxing the linear constraints (1), i.e.:

$$P_{LR}(\lambda) \begin{cases} z_{LR}(\lambda) \triangleq min_{w,b,y}\, f_\lambda(w,b,y) \\ y_j \in \{-1,1\}, \qquad j \in J_i^+ \;\; i = 1, \dots, m \end{cases}$$

with

$$f_\lambda(w,b,y) \triangleq f(w,b,y) \sum_{i=1}^{m} \lambda_i \left(1 - \sum_{j\in J_i^+} \frac{y_j+1}{2} \right)$$

where $\lambda \geq 0$ is the vector of the Lagrangian multipliers in $\mathbb{R}^m$. Any optimal solution of $P_{LR}(\lambda)$, denoted by $(w(\lambda), b(\lambda), y(\lambda))$, provides a lower bound for problem P, that is $z_{LR} \leq z^*$ for any $\lambda \geq 0$. The Lagrangian dual problem is defined as:

$$P_{LD} \begin{cases} z_{LD} \triangleq max_{\lambda\geq 0}\, z_{LR}(\lambda) = max_{\lambda\geq 0}\, min_{w,b,y}\, f_\lambda(w,b,y) \\ y_j \in \{-1,1\}, \quad j \in J_i^+ \quad i = 1, \dots, m \end{cases}$$

with, of course, $z_{LD} \leq z^*$. In [3] it has been shown that $z_{LD} = z^*$: as a consequence, in solving P_{LD} it is possible to obtain an optimal solution to P by using any dual ascent method. Since problem P_{LD} is nondifferentiable, the use of nonsmooth optimization techniques is in order. We adopt the subgradient method [18], that we stop after a pre-fixed maximum number of iterations. Note that, at each iteration, it is necessary to evaluate the objective function $z_{LR}(\lambda)$. This is a difficult task because it requires in turn to face problem $P_{LR}(\lambda)$, that we solve approximately by means of a Block Coordinate Descent (BCD) algorithm [20]. In fact we alternately fix the value of vector y and of the couple (w, b): for any $\lambda \geq 0$, when variables y_j are kept fixed, problem $P_{LR}(\lambda)$, reduces to solving a classical SVM quadratic program; vice-versa, when the couple (w, b) is fixed, it is possible to solve it, with respect to y, by inspection.

In case BCD provides an infeasible solution to the original problem, such solution may be easily modified to obtain feasibility, giving, in this way, an upper bound (the incumbent) on the optimal solution of P. A simplified scheme of the MIL algorithm is reported in Figure 1; further details can be found in [3].

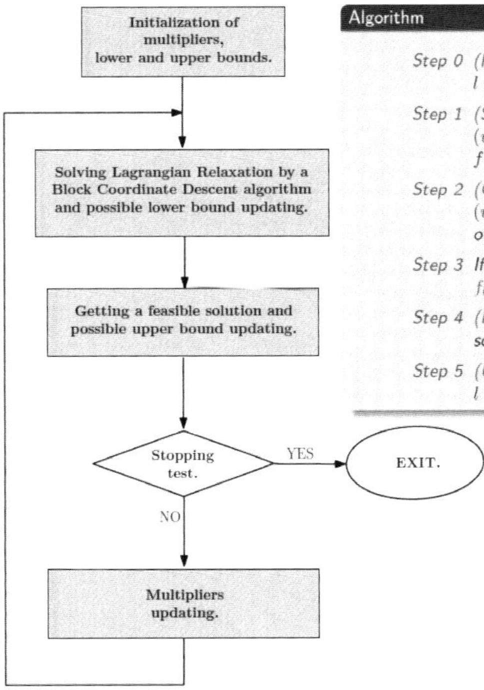

Algorithm

Step 0 (Initialization) Fix $\lambda^{(0)} \geq 0$; set $f_U = +\infty$, $f_L = -\infty$ and $l := 0$.

Step 1 (Solving by BCD the Lagrangian problem) Compute $(w^{(l)}, b^{(l)}, y^{(l)})$ as a solution to problem $P_{LR}(\lambda^{(l)})$. Set $f^{(l)} := f(w^{(l)}, b^{(l)}, y^{(l)})$. If $f^{(l)} > f_L$, set $f_L := f^{(l)}$.

Step 2 (Checking feasibility) If $(w^{(l)}, b^{(l)}, y^{(l)})$ is feasible, set $(\bar{w}, \bar{b}, \bar{y}) := (w^{(l)}, b^{(l)}, y^{(l)})$, $\bar{f} := f(\bar{w}, \bar{b}, \bar{y})$ and go to Step 3; otherwise go to Step 4.

Step 3 If $\bar{f} < f_U$, set $(w_U, b_U, y_U) := (\bar{w}, \bar{b}, \bar{y})$ and $f_U := f(w_U, b_U, y_U)$. Go to Step 5.

Step 4 (Recovering feasibility) From $(w^{(l)}, b^{(l)}, y^{(l)})$ recover a feasible solution $(\bar{w}, \bar{b}, \bar{y})$ and set $\bar{f} := f(\bar{w}, \bar{b}, \bar{y})$. Go to Step 3.

Step 5 (Updating the Lagrangian multipliers) Compute $\lambda^{(l+1)}$, set $l := l + 1$ and go to Step 1.

Fig. 1. The MIL Lagrangian relaxation approach.

4 Numerical Experiments

The algorithm presented in the previous section has been adopted in two types of numerical experimentations: preliminarily for classifying color images and successively for classifying dermoscopic images.

In the first numerical preliminary experiment (see [4]) we have generated one hundred color images of 128x128 pixels dimension, divided into two different classes, positive and negative. We have considered positive each image (bag) containing the yellow color and negative the images without yellow (Figure 2).

We have performed a segmentation process by means of some image processing standard Matlab routines. In particular, given a bitmap image, this image is read by the "*imread*" Matlab routine, which provides a 128x128 matrix, the indexed image, each element corresponding to a pixel and containing a triplet which represents the RGB (red, green, blue) scale. In fact, the first value of each triplet represents the red pixel intensity, the second one represents the green pixel intensity and the last one represents the blue pixel intensity. Once the indexed image has been generated, the successive step consists in converting each indexed image (and the corresponding color map) into an RGB image by means of the "*ind2rgb*" Matlab subroutine. After that, we have proceeded by grouping the pixels in square sub-regions of appropriate dimension: each sub-region forms the so called "*blob*". For each blob, we have computed the average of the RGB intensities and the differences between this value and the same quantity calculated for the adjacent blobs (up, down, left, right).

We recall that a crucial issue in a Support Vector Machine type approach is the choice of parameter C, which generally is performed among a grid of possible values.

We report the results obtained fixing C = 10, since in correspondence to this value the classification algorithm has exhibited the best performance. In discriminating between positive and negative color images, we have considered the following two cases. In the first one we have generated, for ten times, a testing set by choosing ten different images (five positive and five negative), so that each time the remaining ninety ones (forty-five positive and forty-five negative) have constituted the training set.
In the table reported in Figure 2, for each trial, we report the training and the testing correctness percentage, respectively, with the average for both of them in the last row.

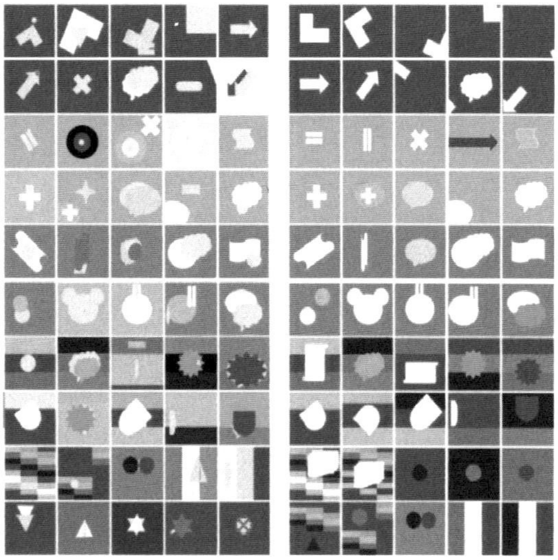

#	Training correctness	Testing correctness
1	81.11	100
2	81.11	80
3	84.44	90
4	83.33	80
5	82.22	80
6	81.11	90
7	83.33	80
8	85.56	70
9	84.44	70
10	84,44	70
Average	83.11	81

Fig. 2. MIL-RL Results for Color Image classification

In the second case, we have performed a leave-one-out cross validation, obtaining 84.07% and 83% as training and testing correctness, respectively. We have noted that, among the seventeen failures in the testing set, fifteen are positive images and two are negative images. Considering the fifteen misclassified positive images it is worth noting that, apart two images, all of them contain a very small yellow colored region.
In the second type of numerical experiment, the MIL classification algorithm proposed in [3] has been applied to classification of some medical dermoscopic images drawn from the database PH_2 [14]. The image are in 8-bit RGB color with a resolution of 768x560 pixels. These images have been classified as common nevus or melanoma by expert dermatologists considering the manual segmentation of the skin lesion, the clinical and histological diagnosis and dermoscopic criteria (asymmetry, colors, pigment network, particular structures).
In our experiments, none of the features resulting from the manual analysis was used in the automatic classification process. We have only considered negative the images of common nevi and positive the images of melanomas. The dataset considered consists of 40 images of melanoma and 40 images of common nevi. To contain the number of instances, we first reduced the image resolution to 128x128 pixels and subsequently we have considered square blobs of 32x32 pixel size. We have adopted a be-level 10-fold cross-validation, listing the corresponding results in Figure 3, where we report, for each fold, the testing correctness, the testing sensitivity, the testing specificity and the CPU time. The results are very promising, even because they have been obtained from photos

with a small resolution (128x128 pixels): we note in fact that in three cases (folds n. 2, 4 e 7) the algorithm has been able to correctly classify all the images in the testing set. We conclude this section by noting that the healthy image with the green box (see Figure 3), characterized by a lot of hair, is the unique misclassified image belonging to the testing set of fold n. 10. This suggests that better results could be obtained by using preprocessing techniques aimed at eliminating the presence of possible noises.

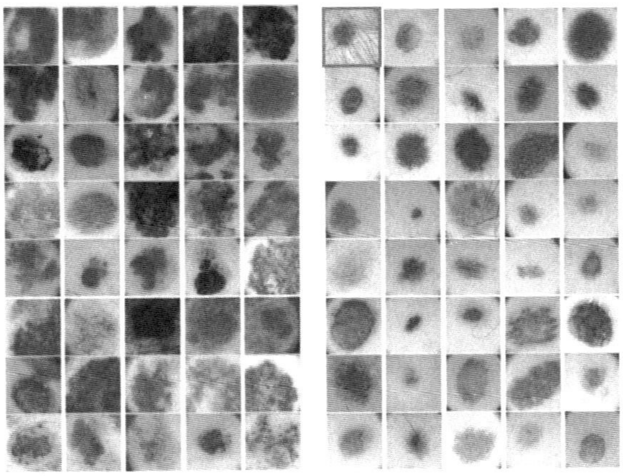

Melanomas **Common Nevi**

Fold number	Testing correctness	Testing sensitivity	Testing specificity	CPU Time
1	87.50	83.33	100.00	0.27
2	100.00	100.00	100.00	0.37
3	75.00	50.00	83.33	0.47
4	100.00	100.00	100.00	0.38
5	87.50	80.00	100.00	0.32
6	62.50	50.00	75.00	0.43
7	100.00	100.00	100.00	0.45
8	75.00	100.00	66.67	0.44
9	62.50	50.00	100.00	0.22
10	87.50	100.00	83.33	0.39
Average	83.75	81.33	90.83	0.37

Fig. 3. MIL-RL Results for Melanoma Image classification

5 Conclusion

In this paper, we have presented an application of a Multiple Instance Learning approach on color and melanoma images, obtaining promising results, both in terms of classification accuracy and CPU times. MIL paradigm fits very well on image classifications because it is able to detect global information (bags) by working at the local level (instance-level). Future research could consist in designing more sophisticated segmentation techniques, aiming to improve the classification performance. Moreover, it would be useful also to test the performance of the proposed algorithm considering preprocessing steps for the optimization of medical images [22]. The inclusion of geometry and textures features may also enrich the classification performance of the proposed model [21]. As for a future extension, we plan to integrate the proposed method into a more general purpose medical information system in order to test and validate its effectiveness on larger datasets also related to different diseases [23, 24].

References

1. Amores, J.: *Multiple instance classification: Review, taxonomy and comparative study*. Artificial intelligence 201, 81-105 (2013)
2. Andrews, S., Tsochantaridis, I., Hofmann, T.: *Support vector machines for multiple-instance learning*. In: Advances in neural information processing systems. pp. 577-584 (2003)
3. Astorino, A., Fuduli, A., Gaudioso, M.: *A Lagrangian relaxation approach for binary multiple instance classification*. IEEE Transactions on Neural Networks and Learning Systems, DOI:10.1109/TNNLS.2018.2885852 (2019)

4. Astorino, A., Fuduli, A., Gaudioso, M., Vocaturo, E.: *A multiple instance learning algorithm for color images classification*. In: Proceedings of the 22nd International Database Engineering & Applications Symposium, IDEAS 2018, Villa San Giovanni, Italy, June 18-20, 2018. pp. 262-266 (2018)
5. Bergeron, C., Moore, G., Zaretzki, J., Breneman, C., Bennett, K.: *Fast bundle algorithm for multiple instance learning*. IEEE Transactions on Pattern Analysis and Machine Intelligence 34(6), 1068-1079 (2012)
6. Carbonneau, M.A., Cheplygina, V., Granger, E., Gagnon, G.: *Multiple instance learning: A survey of problem characteristics and applications*. Pattern Recognition 77, 329-353 (2018)
7. Cristianini, N., Shawe-Taylor, J., et al.: *An introduction to support vector machines and other kernel-based learning methods*. Cambridge university press (2000)
8. De Bonet, J.S., Viola, P.A.: *Structure driven image database retrieval*. In: Advances in Neural Information Processing Systems. pp. 866-872 (1998)
9. Grosky, W.I., Mehrotra, R.: *Index-based object recognition in pictorial data management*. Computer vision, Graphics, and Image processing 52(3), 416-436 (1990)
10. Guignard, M.: Lagrangean relaxation. Top 11(2), 151-200 (2003)
11. Li, X., Shou, L., Chen, G., Hu, T., Dong, J.: *Modeling image data for effective indexing and retrieval in large general image databases*. IEEE Transactions on Knowledge and Data Engineering 20(11), 1566-1580 (2008)
12. Mangasarian, O.L., Wild, E.W.: *Multiple instance classification via successive linear programming*. Journal of Optimization Theory and Applications 137(3), 555-568 (2008)
13. Mehrotra, R., Gary, J.E.: *Similar-shape retrieval in shape data management*. Computer (9), 57-62 (1995)
14. Mendonca, T., Celebi, M., Mendonca, T., Marques, J.: *Ph_2: A public database for the analysis of dermoscopic images*. In: Dermoscopy image analysis. CRC Press (2015)
15. Quellec, G., Cazuguel, G., Cochener, B., Lamard, M.: *Multiple-instance learning for medical image and video analysis*. IEEE reviews in biomedical engineering 10, 213-234 (2017)
16. Ravela, S., Manmatha, R., Riseman, E.M.: *Image retrieval using scale-space matching*. In: European Conference on Computer Vision. pp. 273-282. Springer (1996)
17. Shinde, P.N., Manjrekar, A.: *Retrieval of efficiently classified, re-ranked images using histogram based score computation algorithm extended with the elimination of duplicate images*. International Conference for Convergence for Technology 2014. pp. 1-7. IEEE (2014)
18. Shor, N.Z.: *Minimization methods for non-differentiable functions*, vol. 3. Springer Science & Business Media (2012)
19. da Silva Torres, R., Falcao, A.X.: *Content-based image retrieval: theory and applications*. RITA 13(2), 161-185 (2006)
20. Tseng, P.: *Convergence of a block coordinate descent method for non-differentiable minimization*. Journal of Optimization Theory and Applications (2001)
21. Vocaturo, E., Zumpano, E., Veltri, P.: *Features for melanoma lesions characterization in computer vision systems*. In: 9th International Conference on Information, Intelligence, Systems and Applications, IISA 2018, Zakynthos, Greece, July 23-25, 2018. pp. 1-8 (2018)
22. Vocaturo, E., Zumpano, E., Veltri, P.: *Image pre-processing in computer vision systems for melanoma detection*. In: IEEE International Conference on Bioinformatics and Biomedicine, BIBM 2018, Madrid, Spain, December 3-6, 2018. pp. 2117-2124 (2018)
23. Zumpano E. et al., *SIMPATICO 3D: A Medical Information System for Diagnostic Procedures*, BIBM 2018, pp. 2125-2128.
24. Iaquinta P. et al., *eIMES 3D: An innovative medical images analysis tool to support diagnostic and surgical intervention*. FNC/MobiSPC 2017: 459-464.

Well Founded Semantics for P2P Deductive Databases

(Discussion Paper)

Luciano Caroprese and Ester Zumpano

DIMES, University of Calabria, 87036 Rende, Italy
{l.caroprese, e.zumpano}@dimes.unical.it

Abstract. This paper stems from previous works of the same authors in which a declarative semantics for *Peer-to-Peer* (P2P) systems, defined in terms of *Preferred Weak Models*, is proposed. Under this semantics only facts not making the local databases inconsistent can be imported. As in the general case a P2P system may admit many preferred weak models whose computational complexity is prohibitive, the paper looks for a more pragmatic solution. It assigns to a P2P system its *Well Founded Model*, a partial deterministic model that captures the intuition that if an atom is true in a preferred weak model, but it is false in another one, then it is undefined in the well founded model.

1 Introduction

Different works investigate topic related to the integration of information and the computation of queries in P2P systems [5, 6, 18, 23, 25, 8, 2, 16]. This paper follows the proposal in [7, 8] in which the *Preferred Weak Semantics* has been proposed. Under this semantics only facts not making the local databases inconsistent can be imported, and the preferred weak models are the consistent scenarios in which peers import maximal sets of facts not violating constraints.

Example 1. Consider a P2P in which the peer: (i) $\mathcal{P}_3$ contains two atoms: $r(a)$ and $r(b)$; (ii) $\mathcal{P}_2$ imports data from $\mathcal{P}_3$ using the (mapping) rule $q(X) \hookleftarrow r(X)$ (Please, note the special syntax we use for mapping rules.). Moreover imported atoms must satisfy the constraint $\leftarrow q(X), q(Y), X \neq Y$ stating that the relation q may contain at most one tuple; (iii) $\mathcal{P}_1$ imports data from $\mathcal{P}_2$, using the (mapping) rule $p(X) \hookleftarrow q(X)$. $\mathcal{P}_1$ also contains the rules $s \leftarrow p(X)$ stating that s is *true* if the relation p contains at least one tuple, and $t \leftarrow p(X), p(Y), X \neq Y$, stating that t is *true* if the relation p contains at least two distinct tuples. The intuition is that, with $r(a)$ and $r(b)$ *true* in $\mathcal{P}_3$, either $q(a)$ or $q(b)$ could be imported in $\mathcal{P}_2$ and, consequently, only one tuple is imported in the relation p of the peer $\mathcal{P}_1$. Note that whatever is the derivation in $\mathcal{P}_2$, s is derived in $\mathcal{P}_1$ while t is not derived. Therefore, s and t are, respectively, *true* and *false* in $\mathcal{P}_1$. □

A P2P system may admits many preferred weak models and the computational complexity is prohibitive. Therefore, a more pragmatic solution is needed. This paper presents the *Well Founded Model Semantics*: a deterministic model a deterministic model whose computation is polynomial time. As for future extension we plan to extend the semantics of P2P system by considering logic programs with function symbols [3, 4].

2 P2P Systems: Syntax and Semantics

Familiarity is assumed with deductive database [1], logic programming, stable models, head cycle free (HCF) program, well founded model and computational complexity [17, 21, 22, 24]. A *(peer) predicate symbol* is a pair $i : p$, where i is a *peer identifier* and p is a predicate symbol. A *(peer) atom* is of the form $i : A$, where i is a *peer identifier* and A is a standard atom. A *(peer) literal* is a peer atom $i : A$ or its negation $not\ i : A$. A conjunction $i : A_1, \ldots, i : A_m, not\ i : A_{m+1}, \ldots, not\ i : A_n, \phi$, where ϕ is a conjunction of built-in atoms, will be also denoted as $i : \mathcal{B}$, with $\mathcal{B}$ equals to $A_1, \ldots, A_m, not\ A_{m+1}, \ldots, not\ A_n, \phi$.

A *(peer) rule* can be of one of the following three types:

- STANDARD RULE. It is of the form $i : H \leftarrow i : \mathcal{B}$, where $i : H$ is an atom and $i : \mathcal{B}$ is a conjunction of atoms and built-in atoms.
- INTEGRITY CONSTRAINT. It is of the form $\leftarrow i : \mathcal{B}$, where $i : \mathcal{B}$ is a conjunction of literals and built-in atoms.
- MAPPING RULE. It is of the form $i : H \hookleftarrow j : \mathcal{B}$, where $i : H$ is an atom, $j : \mathcal{B}$ is a conjunction of atoms and built-in atoms and $i \neq j$.

$i : H$ is called *head* while $i : \mathcal{B}$ (resp. $j : \mathcal{B}$) is called *body*. Negation is allowed just in the body of integrity constraints. The definition of a predicate $i{:}p$ consists of the set of rules in whose head the predicate symbol $i{:}p$ occurs. A predicate can be of three different kinds: *base predicate*, *derived predicate* and *mapping predicate*. A base predicate is defined by a set of ground facts; a derived predicate is defined by a set of standard rules and a mapping predicate is defined by a set of mapping rules. An atom $i : p(X)$ is a *base atom* (resp. *derived atom*, *mapping atom*) if $i : p$ is a base predicate (resp. standard predicate, mapping predicate). Given an interpretation M, $M[\mathcal{D}]$ (resp. $M[\mathcal{LP}]$, $M[\mathcal{MP}]$) denotes the subset of base atoms (resp. derived atoms, mapping atoms) in M.

Definition 1. P2P SYSTEM. A *peer* $\mathcal{P}_i$ is a tuple $\langle \mathcal{D}_i, \mathcal{LP}_i, \mathcal{MP}_i, \mathcal{IC}_i \rangle$, where (i) $\mathcal{D}_i$ is a set of facts (*local database*); (ii) $\mathcal{LP}_i$ is a set of standard rules; (iii) $\mathcal{MP}_i$ is a set of mapping rules and (iv) $\mathcal{IC}_i$ is a set of constraints over predicates defined by $\mathcal{D}_i$, $\mathcal{LP}_i$ and $\mathcal{MP}_i$. A *P2P system* $\mathcal{PS}$ is a set of peers $\{\mathcal{P}_1, \ldots, \mathcal{P}_n\}$. □

Given a P2P system $\mathcal{PS} = \{\mathcal{P}_1, \ldots, \mathcal{P}_n\}$, where $\mathcal{P}_i = \langle \mathcal{D}_i, \mathcal{LP}_i, \mathcal{MP}_i, \mathcal{IC}_i \rangle$, $\mathcal{D}, \mathcal{LP}, \mathcal{MP}$ and $\mathcal{IC}$ denote, respectively, the global sets of ground facts, standard rules, mapping rules and integrity constraints, i.e. $\mathcal{D} = \bigcup_{i \in [1..n]} \mathcal{D}_i$, $\mathcal{LP} = \bigcup_{i \in [1..n]} \mathcal{LP}_i$, $\mathcal{MP} = \bigcup_{i \in [1..n]} \mathcal{MP}_i$ and $\mathcal{IC} = \bigcup_{i \in [1..n]} \mathcal{IC}_i$. In the rest of this paper, with a little abuse of notation, $\mathcal{PS}$ will be also denoted both with the tuple $\langle \mathcal{D}, \mathcal{LP}, \mathcal{MP}, \mathcal{IC} \rangle$ and the set $\mathcal{D} \cup \mathcal{LP} \cup \mathcal{MP} \cup \mathcal{IC}$.

We now review the *Preferred Weak Model* semantics in [8]. For each peer $\mathcal{P}_i = \langle \mathcal{D}_i, \mathcal{LP}_i, \mathcal{MP}_i, \mathcal{IC}_i \rangle$, the set $\mathcal{D}_i \cup \mathcal{LP}_i$ is a *positive normal program*, thus it admits just *one minimal model* that represents the *local knowledge* of $\mathcal{P}_i$. It is assumed that each peer is *locally consistent*, i.e. its local knowledge satisfies $\mathcal{IC}_i$ (i.e. $\mathcal{D}_i \cup \mathcal{LP}_i \models \mathcal{IC}_i$). Therefore, inconsistencies may be introduced just when the peer imports data. The intuitive meaning of a mapping rule $i : H \hookleftarrow j : \mathcal{B} \in \mathcal{MP}_i$ is that if the body conjunction $j : \mathcal{B}$ is *true* in the source peer $\mathcal{P}_j$ the atom $i : H$ can be imported in $\mathcal{P}_i$ only if it does not imply (directly or indirectly) the violation of some constraint in $\mathcal{IC}_i$.

Given a mapping rule $r = H \hookleftarrow \mathcal{B}$, the corresponding standard logic rule $H \leftarrow \mathcal{B}$ will be denoted as $St(r)$. Analogously, given a set of mapping rules $\mathcal{MP}$, $St(\mathcal{MP}) = \{St(r) \mid r \in \mathcal{MP}\}$ and given a P2P system $\mathcal{PS} = \mathcal{D} \cup \mathcal{LP} \cup \mathcal{MP} \cup \mathcal{IC}$, $St(\mathcal{PS}) = \mathcal{D} \cup \mathcal{LP} \cup St(\mathcal{MP}) \cup \mathcal{IC}$.

Given an interpretation M, an atom H and a conjunction of atoms $\mathcal{B}$:
- $val_M(H \leftarrow \mathcal{B}) = val_M(H) \geq val_M(\mathcal{B})$,
- $val_M(H \hookleftarrow \mathcal{B}) = val_M(H) \leq val_M(\mathcal{B})$.
Therefore, if the body is *true*, the head of a standard rule *must* be *true*, whereas the head of a mapping rule *could* be *true*. Intuitively, a *weak model* M is an interpretation that satisfies all standard rules, mapping rules and constraints of $\mathcal{PS}$ and such that each atom $H \in M[\mathcal{MP}]$ (i.e. each mapping atom) is *supported* from a mapping rule $H \hookleftarrow \mathcal{B}$ whose body $\mathcal{B}$ is satisfied by M. A *preferred weak model*is a weak model containing a maximal subset of mapping atoms.

Definition 2. (PREFERRED) WEAK MODEL. Given a P2P system $\mathcal{PS} = \mathcal{D} \cup \mathcal{LP} \cup \mathcal{MP} \cup \mathcal{IC}$, an interpretation M is a *weak model* for $\mathcal{PS}$ if $\{M\} = \mathcal{MM}(St(\mathcal{PS}^M))$, where $\mathcal{PS}^M$ is the program obtained from *ground*$(\mathcal{PS})$ by removing all mapping rules whose head is *false* w.r.t. M. Given two weak models M and N, M is said to *preferable* to N, and is denoted as $M \sqsupseteq N$, if $M[\mathcal{MP}] \supseteq N[\mathcal{MP}]$. Moreover, if $M \sqsupseteq N$ and $N \not\sqsupseteq M$, then $M \sqsupset N$. A weak model M is said to be *preferred* if there is no weak model N such that $N \sqsupset M$. The set of weak models for a P2P system $\mathcal{PS}$ will be denoted by $\mathcal{WM}(\mathcal{PS})$, whereas the set of preferred weak models will be denoted by $\mathcal{PWM}(\mathcal{PS})$. □

Theorem 1. *For every consistent P2P system $\mathcal{PS}$, $\mathcal{PWM}(\mathcal{PS}) \neq \emptyset$.*

Example 2. Consider a P2P system $\mathcal{PS}$ in which the peer: $\mathcal{P}_2$ contains the facts $q(a)$ and $q(b)$, whereas $\mathcal{P}_1$ contains the mapping rule $p(X) \hookleftarrow q(X)$ and the constraint $\leftarrow p(X), p(Y), X \neq Y$. $\mathcal{WM}(\mathcal{PS})$ are: $M_0 = \{q(a), q(b)\}$, $M_1 = \{q(a), q(b), p(a)\}$ and $M_2 = \{q(a), q(b), p(b)\}$, whereas $\mathcal{PWM}(\mathcal{PS})$ are M_1 and M_2 as they import maximal sets of atoms from $\mathcal{P}_2$. □

3 Computing the Preferred Weak Model Semantics

This section presents an alternative characterization of the preferred weak model semantics, that allows to model a P2P system $\mathcal{PS}$ with a single logic program $Rew_t(\mathcal{PS})$. Let's firstly introduce some preliminaries. Given an atom $A = i : p(x)$, A^t denotes the atom $i : p^t(x)$ and A^v denotes the atom $i : p^v(x)$. A^t will be called the *testing atom*, whereas A^v will be called the *violating atom*.

Definition 3. Given a conjunction
$\mathcal{B} = A_1, \ldots, A_h, not\ A_{h+1}, \ldots, not\ A_n, B_1, \ldots, B_k, not\ B_{k+1}, \ldots, not\ B_m, \phi$ (1)
where A_i $(i \in [1..\ n])$ is a mapping atom or a derived atom, B_i $(i \in [1..\ m])$ is a base atom and ϕ is a conjunction of built in atoms, we define
$\mathcal{B}^t = A_1^t, \ldots, A_h^t, not\ A_{h+1}^t, \ldots, not\ A_n^t, B_1, \ldots, B_k, not\ B_{k+1}, \ldots, not\ B_m, \phi$ (2)

Therefore, given a negation free conjunction $\mathcal{B} = A_1, \ldots, A_h, B_1, \ldots, B_k, \ldots, \phi$, then $\mathcal{B}^t = A_1^t, \ldots, A_h^t, B_1, \ldots, B_k, \phi$. In the following, the rewriting of a P2P system is reported.

Definition 4. Rewriting of an integrity constraint. Given an integrity constraint $i = \ \leftarrow \mathcal{B}$ (that is of the form (1)) its rewriting is defined as $Rew_t(i) = \{A_1^v \vee \ldots \vee A_h^v \leftarrow \mathcal{B}^t\}$. □

If $\mathcal{B}^t$ (of the form (2)), is *true*, at least one of the violating atoms $A_1^v, \ldots, A_h^v$ is *true*. Therefore, at least one of the atoms $A_1, \ldots, A_h$ cannot be inferred.

Definition 5. Rewriting of a standard rule. Given a standard rule $s = H \leftarrow \mathcal{B}$, its rewriting is defined as $Rew_t(s) = \{H \leftarrow \mathcal{B};\ H^t \leftarrow \mathcal{B}^t;\ A_1^v \vee \ldots \vee A_h^v \leftarrow \mathcal{B}^t, H^v\ \}$. □

In order to find the mapping atoms that, if imported, generate some inconsistencies (i.e. in order to find their corresponding violating atoms), all possible mapping testing atoms are imported and the derived testing atoms are inferred. In the previous definition, if $\mathcal{B}^t$ is *true* and the violating atom H^v is *true*, then the body of the disjunctive rule is *true* and therefore it can be deduced that at least one of the violating atoms $A_1^v, \ldots, A_h^v$ is *true* (i.e. to avoid such inconsistencies at least one of atoms $A_1, \ldots, A_h$ cannot be inferred).

Definition 6. Rewriting of a mapping rule. Given a mapping rule $m = H \hookleftarrow \mathcal{B}$, its rewriting is defined as $Rew_t(m) = \{H^t \leftarrow \mathcal{B};\ H \leftarrow H^t, not\ H^v\ \}$. □

Intuitively, to check whether a mapping atom H generates some inconsistencies, if imported in its target peer, a testing atom H^t is imported in the same peer. Rather than violating some integrity constraint, it (eventually) generates, by rules obtained from the rewriting of standard rules and integrity constraints, the atom H^v. In this case H, cannot be inferred and inconsistencies are prevented.

Definition 7. Rewriting of a P2P system. Given a P2P system $\mathcal{PS} = \mathcal{D} \cup \mathcal{LP} \cup \mathcal{MP} \cup \mathcal{IC}$, then: $Rew_t(\mathcal{MP}) = \bigcup_{m \in \mathcal{MP}} Rew_t(m)$, $Rew_t(\mathcal{LP}) = \bigcup_{s \in \mathcal{LP}} Rew_t(s)$, $Rew_t(\mathcal{IC}) = \bigcup_{i \in \mathcal{IC}} Rew_t(i)$ and $Rew_t(\mathcal{PS}) = \mathcal{D} \cup Rew_t(\mathcal{LP}) \cup Rew_t(\mathcal{MP}) \cup Rew_t(\mathcal{IC})$ □

Definition 8. TOTAL STABLE MODEL. Given a P2P system $\mathcal{PS}$ and a stable model M for $Rew_t(\mathcal{PS})$, the interpretation obtained by deleting from M its violating and testing atoms, denoted as $\mathcal{T}(M)$, is a *total stable model* of $\mathcal{PS}$. The set of total stable models of $\mathcal{PS}$ is denoted as $\mathcal{TSM}(\mathcal{PS})$. □

Example 3. Consider the P2P system $\mathcal{PS}$ in Ex. 2. From Def. (7) we obtain:
$Rew_t(\mathcal{PS}) = \{q(a);\ q(b);\ p^t(X) \leftarrow q(X);\ p(X) \leftarrow p^t(X), not\ p^v(X);$
$p^v(X) \vee p^v(Y) \leftarrow p^t(X), p^t(Y), X \neq Y\}$
The stable models of $Rew_t(\mathcal{PS})$ are: $M_1 = \{q(a), q(b), p^t(a), p^t(b), p^v(a), p(b)\}$, $M_2 = \{q(a), q(b), p^t(a), p^t(b), p(a), p^v(b)\}$. Then, the total stable models of $\mathcal{PS}$ are $\mathcal{TSM}(\mathcal{PS}) = \{\{q(a), q(b), p(b)\}, \{q(a), q(b), p(a)\}\}$. □

Theorem 2. *For every P2P system $\mathcal{PS}$, $\mathcal{TSM}(\mathcal{PS}) = \mathcal{PWM}(\mathcal{PS})$.* □

4 Well Founded Semantics and Distributed Computation

A P2P system may admit many preferred weak models whose computational complexity has been shown to be prohibitive [7]. Therefore, a deterministic model whose computation is guaranteed to be polynomial time is needed. In more details, the rewriting presented in Section 3 allows modeling a P2P system by a single disjunctive logic program. By assuming that this program is HCF, it can be rewritten into an equivalent normal program for which a *Well Founded Model Semantics* can be adopted. Such a semantics allows to compute in polynomial time a deterministic model describing the P2P system, by capturing the intuition that if an atom is *true* in a total stable (or preferred weak) *model* of $\mathcal{PS}$ and is *false* in another one, then it is *undefined* in the well founded model.

Theorem 3. *Let $\mathcal{PS} = \mathcal{D} \cup \mathcal{LP} \cup \mathcal{MP} \cup \mathcal{IC}$ be a P2P system, then $Rew_t(\mathcal{PS})$ is HCF iff there are not two distinct atoms occurring in the body of a rule in $ground(\mathcal{LP} \cup \mathcal{IC})$ mutually dependent by positive recursion.* □

we assume each P2P system $\mathcal{PS}$ is s.t. $Rew_t(\mathcal{PS})$ is HCF. $\mathcal{PS}$ will be called as *HCF P2P system*. From previous hypothesis, it follows that $Rew_t(\mathcal{PS})$ can be normalized as $\mathcal{SM}(Rew_t(\mathcal{PS})) = \mathcal{SM}(Normalized(Rew_t\ (\mathcal{PS})))$.

Definition 9. REWRITING OF AN HCF P2P SYSTEM. Given an HCF P2P system $\mathcal{PS}$, $Rew_w(\mathcal{PS}) = Normalized(Rew_t(\mathcal{PS}))$. □

Therefore, the preferred weak models of an HCF P2P system $\mathcal{PS}$ corresponds to the stable models of the normal program $Rew_w(\mathcal{PS})$. Next step is to adopt for $Rew_w(\mathcal{PS})$ a three-valued semantics that allows computing *deterministic models* and in particular the *well founded model*.

Definition 10. WELL FOUNDED SEMANTICS. Given an HCF P2P system $\mathcal{PS}$ and the well founded model of $Rew_w(\mathcal{PS})$, say $\langle T, F \rangle$, the *well founded model semantics* of $\mathcal{PS}$ is given by $\langle \mathcal{T}(T), \mathcal{T}(F) \rangle$. □

Example 4. The rewriting of the HCF P2P system $\mathcal{PS}$ in Example 3 is:

$$Rew_w(\mathcal{PS}) = \{q(a);\ q(b);\ p^t(X) \leftarrow q(X);\ p(X) \leftarrow p^t(X), not\ p^v(X);$$
$$p^v(X) \leftarrow p^t(X), p^t(Y), X \neq Y, not\ p^v(Y);$$
$$p^v(Y) \leftarrow p^t(X), p^t(Y), X \neq Y, not\ p^v(X)\}$$

The well founded model of $Rew_w(\mathcal{PS})$ is $\langle\{q(a), q(b), p^t(a), p^t(b)\}, \emptyset\rangle$ and the well founded semantics of $\mathcal{PS}$ is given by $\langle\{q(a), q(b)\}, \emptyset\rangle$. The atoms $q(a)$ and $q(b)$ are *true*, while the atoms $p(a)$ and $p(b)$ are *undefined*. □

Theorem 4. *Let $\mathcal{PS}$ be a HCF P2P system, then deciding: (i) whether an interpretation M is a preferred weak model of $\mathcal{PS}$ is P-time; (ii) whether an atom A is* true *in some preferred weak model of $\mathcal{PS}$ is $\mathcal{NP}$-complete; (iii) whether an atom A is* true *in every preferred weak model of $\mathcal{PS}$ is co$\mathcal{NP}$-complete; (iv) whether an atom A is* true *in the well founded model of $\mathcal{PS}$ is P-time.* □

$Rew_w(\mathcal{PS})$ allows to compute the well founded semantics of $\mathcal{PS}$ in polynomial time. In this section we present a technique allowing to compute the well founded model in a distributed way. The basic idea is that each peer computes its own portion of the "unique logic program", sending to the other peers the result.

Definition 11. *Let $\mathcal{PS}$= be an HCF P2P system, where $\mathcal{P}_i = \langle \mathcal{D}_i, \mathcal{LP}_i, \mathcal{MP}_i, \mathcal{IC}_i\rangle$, for $i \in [1..n]$. Then, $Rew_w(\mathcal{P}_i) = Rew_w(\mathcal{D}_i \cup \mathcal{LP}_i \cup \mathcal{MP}_i \cup \mathcal{IC}_i)$.*

Previous definition allows to derive a single normal logic program for each peer. Observe that, $Rew_w(\mathcal{PS}) = \bigcup_{i\in[1..n]} Rew_w(\mathcal{P}_i)$.

Example 5. The rewritings located on peers $\mathcal{P}_1$ and $\mathcal{P}_2$ of Ex. 2 are:

$$Rew_w(\mathcal{P}_1) = \{p^t(X) \leftarrow q(X);\ p(X) \leftarrow p^t(X), not\ p^v(X);$$
$$p^v(X) \leftarrow p^t(X), p^t(Y), not\ p^v(Y), X \neq Y;$$
$$p^v(Y) \leftarrow p^t(X), p^t(Y), not\ p^v(X), X \neq Y\}.$$
$$Rew_w(\mathcal{P}_2) = \{\mathrm{q(a);\ q(b)}\}.$$
□

The idea is the following: if a peer receives a query, then it will recursively query the peer to which it is connected through mapping rules, before being able to calculate its answer. Formally, a local query submitted by a user to a peer does not differ from a remote query submitted by another peer. Once retrieved the necessary data from neighbor peers, the peer computes its well founded model and evaluates the query (either local or remote) on that model; then if the query is a remote query, the answer is sent to the requesting peer. For the sake of presentation, a partial model reports, using the syntax $[T, U]$, the sets of true and undefined atoms, instead of the sets of true and false atoms.

Example 6. Consider the P2P system in Example 2. If $\mathcal{P}_1$ receives the query $p(X)$, it submits the query $p(X)$ to the peer $\mathcal{P}_2$. Once $\mathcal{P}_2$ receives the query $q(X)$, it computes its well founded model $W_2 = [\{q(a), q(b)\}, \emptyset]$. $\mathcal{P}_1$ receives the data, populates its local database and computes its well founded model $W_1 = [\{p^t(a), p^t(b)\}, \{p^v(a), p^v(b), p(a), p(b)\}]$ and finally, evaluates the query $p(X)$ over W_1. The answer will be $[\emptyset, \{p(a), p(b)\}]$. Observe that, the peer replies providing two undefined atoms: $p(a)$ and $p(b)$. □

Algorithm: $ComputeAnswer_i$
input: 1) $i : q(X)$ - a query
2) s - a sender which is a peer $\mathcal{P}_k$ (remote query) or *null* (local query)
output: $[T, U]$ where T (resp. U) is the set of *true* (resp. *undefined*) atoms
begin
while true
wait for an input $i : q(X)$ and s;
$P = Rew_w(\mathcal{P}_i)$;
for each $(i : h(X) \hookleftarrow j : b(X)) \in \mathcal{MP}_i$
$[T, U] = ComputeAnswer_j(j : b(X), \mathcal{P}_i)$;
$P = P \cup T \cup \{a \leftarrow not\ a \mid a \in U\}$;
end for
$[T_w, U_w] = ComputeWellFoundedModel(P)$;
$answer = [\{i : q(x) \mid i : q(x) \in T_w\}, \{i : q(x) \mid i : q(x) \in U_w\}]$;
if $isNull(s)$ **then** $show(answer)$;
else $send(answer, \mathcal{P}_k)$;
end if
end while
end

We associate to a P2P system, $\mathcal{PS}$, a graph $g(\mathcal{PS})$ whose nodes are the peers of $\mathcal{PS}$ and whose edges are the pairs $(\mathcal{P}_i, \mathcal{P}_j)$ s.t. $(i : H \hookleftarrow j : \mathcal{B}) \in \mathcal{PS}$. We say that $\mathcal{PS}$ is acyclic if $g(\mathcal{PC})$ is acyclic. In order to guarantee the termination of the computation, from now on we assume that our P2P systems are acyclic. Without loss of generality, we assume that each mapping rule is of the form $i : p(X) \hookleftarrow j : q(X)$. The behavior of the peer $\mathcal{P}_i = \langle \mathcal{D}_i, \mathcal{LP}_i, \mathcal{MP}_i, \mathcal{IC}_i \rangle$ within the P2P system can be modeled by the algorithm $ComputeAnswer_i$, running on the peer $\mathcal{P}_i$. It receives in input a query $i : q(X)$ submitted by a sender s which can be another peer or a user. For each mapping rule $i : h(X) \hookleftarrow j : b(X)$, the peer $\mathcal{P}_i$ queries the peer $\mathcal{P}_j$ asking for $j : b(X)$. $\mathcal{P}_i$ will receive true and undefined tuples that will enrich the local knowledge. Observe that, true atoms will be simply inserted into P while for each undefined atom a, a rule $a \leftarrow not\ a$ allowing to infer the correct truth value for a (undefined) in the well founded model, is inserted. Once the local knowledge has been updated, the local well founded model is computed by means of the function $ComputeWellFoundedModel$ and the answer for the query is extracted. If the sender is a user then the answer is simply shown, otherwise (if it is a peer) it is sent back to it. A system prototype for query answering in a P2P network based on the proposed semantics has been implemented. The system has been developed using Java.

The communication among peers is performed by using JXTA libraries [20]. XSB [26] is a logic programming and deductive database system used for computing the answer to a given query using the well founded semantics. InterProlog [19] is an open source front-end that provides Java with the ability to interact with XSB engine.

References

1. Abiteboul,S., Hull,R., Vianu,V., *Foundations of Databases*. Addison-Wesley, 1994.
2. Bertossi, L. and Bravo, L. Query Answering in Peer-to-Peer Data Exchange Systems. *EDBT Workshops*, 2004.
3. M. Calautti, S. Greco, I. Trubitsyna: Detecting Decidable Classes of Finitely Ground Logic Programs with Function Symbols. ACM Trans. Comput. Log. 18(4): 28:1-28:42 (2017)
4. M. Calautti, S. Greco, F. Spezzano, I. Trubitsyna: Checking termination of bottom-up evaluation of logic programs with function symbols. TPLP 15(6): 854-889 (2015)
5. Calì, A., Calvanese, D., De Giacomo, G., and M. Lenzerini, On the decidability and complexity of query answering over inconsistent and incomplete databases. *PODS*, 260-271, 2003.
6. Calvanese, D., De Giacomo, G., and M. Lenzerini, and Rosati, R., Logical foundations of peer-to-peer data integration. *PODS*, 241-251, 2004.
7. Caroprese, L., Zumpano, E., A Logic Framework for P2P Deductive Databases, TPLP 2019.
8. Caroprese, L., Zumpano, E., Modeling Cooperation in P2P Data Management Systems. ISMIS 2008: 225-235.
9. Caroprese, L., Zumpano, E., P2P Deductive Databases: Well Founded Semantics and Distributed Computation. ADBIS 2017: 91-99
10. Caroprese, L., Zumpano, E., A Declarative Semantics for P2P Systems. CD-MAKE 2017: 315-329
11. Caroprese, L., Zumpano, E., Computing a Deterministic Semantics for P2P Deductive Databases. IDEAS 2017: 184-191
12. Caroprese, L., Zumpano, E., P2P deductive databases: a system prototype. iiWAS 2017: 258-265
13. Caroprese, L., Zumpano, E., Integration of Unsound Data in P2P Systems. ADBIS 2018: 278-290
14. Caroprese, L., Zumpano, E., Generalized Maximal Consistent Answers in P2P Deductive Databases. DEXA (2) 2016: 368-376.
15. Caroprese, L., Zumpano, E., A Deterministic Model for P2P Deductive Databases. IDEAS 2016: 193-198.
16. Franconi, E., Kuper, G. M., Lopatenko, A., Zaihrayeu,I., A Robust Logical and Computational Characterisation of Peer toPeer Database Systems. *DBISP2P*, 64-76, 2003.
17. Gelfond, M., Lifschitz, V., The Stable Model Semantics for Logic Programming, *Proc. Fifth Conf. on Logic Programming*, 1070-1080, 1998.
18. Halevy, A., Ives, Z., Suciu, D., and Tatarinov, I., Schema mediation in peer data management systems. *int. Conf. on Database Theory*, pages 505-516, 2003.
19. InterProlog. `http://www.declarativa.com/interprolog/`.
20. Project JXTA, `http://www.jxta.org/`.
21. Lonc, Z., Truszczynski, M., On the Problem of Computing the Well-Founded Semantics. Computational Logic 2000: 673-687.
22. J. W. Lloyd, Foundations of Logic Programming. Springer-Verlag, 1987.
23. Madhavan, J., and Halevy, A. Y., Composing mappings among data sources. *VLDB*, 572-583, 2003.
24. Papadimitriou, C. H., *Computational Complexity*. Addison-Wesley, 1994.
25. Tatarinov, I., Halevy., A., Efficient Query reformulation in Peer Data Management Systems, *SIGMOD*, pages 539-550, 2004.
26. XSB Project. `http://xsb.sourceforge.net`.

Image Analysis in Technical Documentation (Discussion Paper)

Fabio Carrara[1], Franca Debole[1], Claudio Gennaro[1], and Giuseppe Amato[1]

Institute of Information Science and Technologies (ISTI), Italian National Research Council (CNR), Via G. Moruzzi 1, 56124 Pisa, Italy
name.surname@isti.cnr.it

Abstract. In the era of Big Data, manufacturing companies are overwhelmed by a lot of disorganized information: the large amount of digital content that is increasingly available in the manufacturing process makes the retrieval of accurate information a critical issue. In this context, and thanks also to the Industry 4.0 campaign, the Italian manufacturing industries have made a lot of effort to ameliorate their knowledge management system using the most recent technologies, like big data analysis and machine learning methods. This paper presents the on-going work done within the ADA project, with special emphasis on the specific image analysis work carried out to extract information from images contained in the so different document of the manufacturing companies, partners of the project.

Keywords: Image Analysis · Machine Learning · Big Data · Manufacturing companies

1 Introduction

Manufacturing companies, which produce complex products and manage large plants, generate a consistent flow of data and information throughout the company processes, from acquisition to production and maintenance of the products themselves. In this amount of data, a significant part consists of texts, graphics, and images obtained as a transposition of the know-how of human personnel.

Collecting and retrieving all this data and information quickly and easily is vital for speeding up internal business activities. For example, during the design phases of a new product, it is useful to be able to identify, in past projects, specifications, data and information contained in lessons learned, in risk analysis, to carry out more reliable and innovative design activities. In case of plants maintenance, it is invaluable for operators to have immediate access to the information necessary to carry out their work quickly and effectively.

The needs of the manufacturing companies described above, however, clash with the complexity of knowledge management, due both to the large quantity and to the heterogeneity of the data and documents to be processed: the technological tools currently available on the market are not able to rise this challenge and effectively meet these needs. In this context, therefore, the main target of the ADA project is to design and develop a platform based on big data analytics systems that allows for the acquisition, organization, and automatic retrieval of information from technical texts and images in the different phases of acquisition, design & development, testing, installation and maintenance of products.

In this paper, we illustrate the work carried out in the ADA project focusing on the image content retrieval part: the images contained in the corporate documents constitute a relevant source of information that could be relevant in the manufacturing work flow. On this context, we developed specific techniques for the extraction, classification, recognition, and tagging of images within technical documentation. The architecture and the methodologies of our work are presented on Section 3 and Section 4, respectively.

2 Related Work

Image recognition techniques have been extensively studied in the last decade in the field of computer vision and the recovery of multimedia information. Deep learning techniques, such as those based on Convolutional Neural Networks (CNNs), represent today the state of the art for the most varied computer vision activities such as image classification, image recovery and object recognition [4]. Furthermore, the use of intermediate layer activation as a high-level descriptor (feature) of visual image content has become very popular and has proven to be effective as demonstrated by many scientific papers [11]. Convolutional neural networks exploit the computing power provided by the GPU-based architectures, in order to learn from huge collections of multimedia information (e.g. images). One of the limitations of this approach is that many collections of images available were created for academic purposes (e.g. ImageNet [9]) and can not be used effectively for applications such as those discussed in the ADA project.

In the project, the development of tools to search for graphic symbols belonging to technical schemes within the technical documentation is of particular importance. To this end, some works [5, 10] that try to tackle the problem by using CNNs seem to be promising. However, as Elyan et al. claim in [5], the application of CNNs to detect and localize symbols in drawings is still a challenging task. This is probably due to the complexity of the problem and also to the lack of sufficient annotated examples or publicly available data sets.

Elyan et al. [5] presented a semi-automatic and heuristic-based approach to localise symbols within engineering drawings, and then applied a CNN to classify the detected symbols. Similarly, Quan et al. [10] used an AlexNet to classify point symbols in color topographic maps.

3 Image Analysis Component

The technical documents of manufacturing companies often contain a large number of heterogeneous images such as graphics, wiring diagrams, mechanical drawings, etc. While on the one hand the images are almost always accompanied by text such as captions, descriptions, and labels, being able to recognize their content without using text is an increasingly requested feature: images represent a rich source of information.

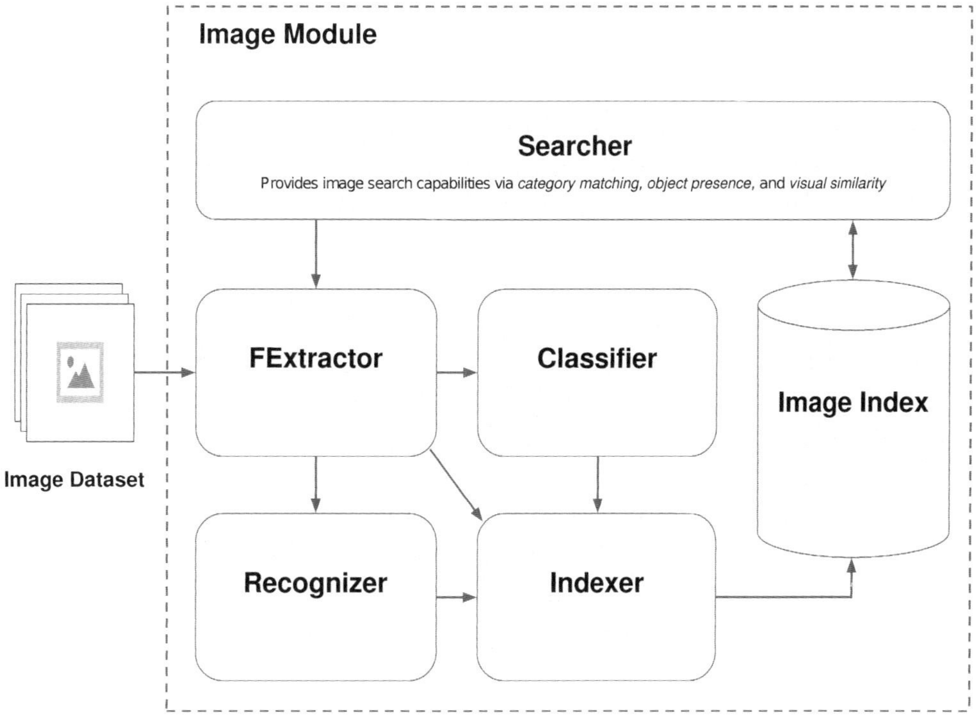

Fig. 1. A general view of the Image Analysis Module architecture.

The Image Analysis Module (Fig. 1) aims to enable companies to extract information from images contained within their technical documentation. This information is necessary to perform a search and classification of images based on visual content. The module in particular deals with the identification and extraction from the images the content, classifying them, recognizing some graphic elements, such as symbols, within them and looking for similar ones.

The Image Analysis Module is composed by the following sub-components:

FExtractor Module. This component is intended to extract from one image one or more visual descriptors (features) that allow one to perform searches based on visual similarity using an image as a query.

Classifier Module. The classifier component deals with the classification of the images in the various possible types in the field of technical and patent documentation (e.g. technical drawing in perspective, sections, electronic circuit, flow chart, etc.). The tool relies on modern Machine Learning techniques based on Deep Learning. The automatic classification is based on training a neural network on a number of examples for each of the types of images to be classified. The accuracy of the tool is strictly correlated to the number of training examples provided.
Recognizer Module. This component allows the automatic recognition of objects within the images classified by the classification tool: once the images are classified through the classification tool, the objects are automatically recognized within the image. For each type of image, the tool will have a number of examples related to the objects to be identified. Another result of this component is to automatically associate one or more tags with an image: the tags can be further enriched or corrected by analyzing the text in the document that refers to the image itself.
Indexer Module. This component deals with the appropriate indexing of both the visual features of the images and the context features related to the image: the image is decomposed into a visual part and into a symbolic part. For each image in fact, we will have both the global visual features necessary to perform visual similarity queries, and local features to perform queries able to detect and localize specific symbols contained in the image.
Searcher Module. This module deals with sorting the various types of search supported (see the details below).

The search component allows the user to perform different types of searches using the index created by the Indexer module:

1. Textual Search on the text correlated or extracted from the images.
2. Similarity Search on images: search by similarity of the basic elements (symbols) in an image archive using an example as a query.
3. Search for the categories to which an image belongs.

Furthermore, the Searcher Module is able to automatically handle external queries, i.e. using images that are not present in the index, as well as internal queries, i.e. using images already present in the database as queries. For the external queries, the Searcher Module uses FExtractor Module to extract features from the query image.

In the next section, we will describe the specific methodologies exploited for the realization of the four main mentioned modules: FExtractor, Classifier, Recognizer, and Indexer.

4 Methods

Due to their astonishing effectiveness on perceptual tasks, we resort to state-of-the-art Deep Learning techniques based on Convolutional Neural Networks

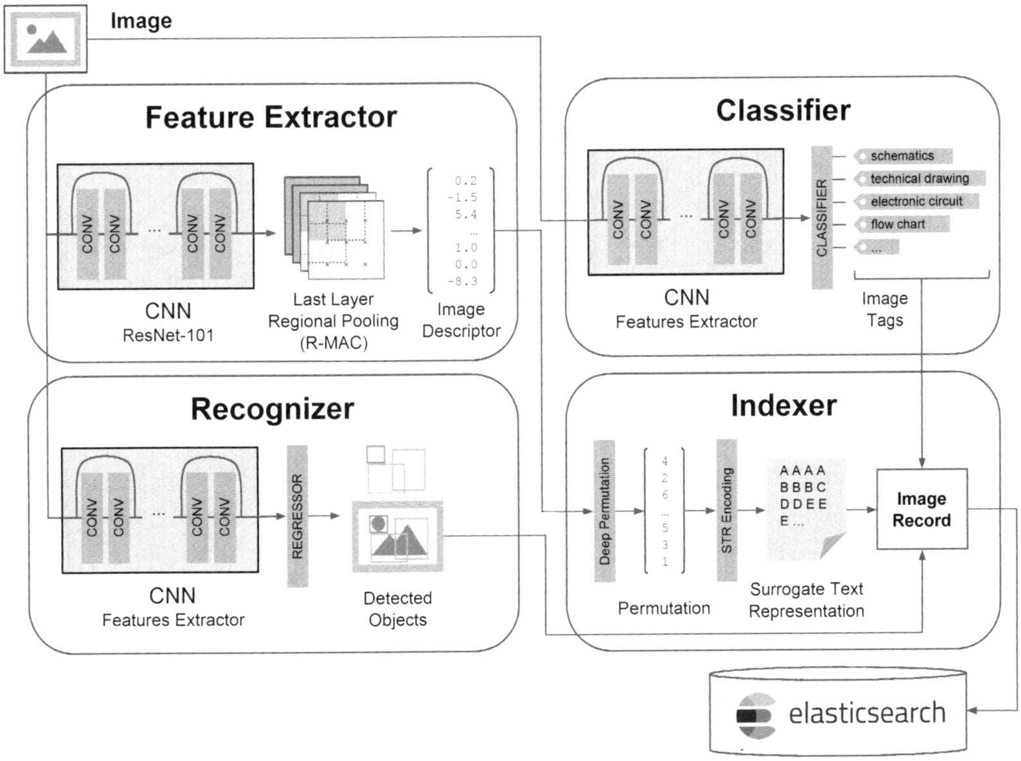

Fig. 2. Image Analysis Module: actual sub-components and their interaction.

(CNN) to implement the visual analyses conducted by the aforementioned modules.

In the following, we will describe in details the methods chosen to implement the main functions of the Image Analysis Module, and how they are distributed among its sub-components. As depicted on Figure 2, for each image on the dataset:

- we extract the features (FExtractor) as descriptors of the image on the index (Indexer); the extracted features are also made available to the Recognizer and Classifier modules;
- for specific categories, we use ad-hoc techniques for the object recognition (Recognizer) and the classification of the image (Classifier); we rely on simpler techniques based on previously extracted features otherwise;
- all the information deriving from FExtractor, Recognizer and Classifier are memorized in the Image Record on a specific index (Indexer).

4.1 Visual Similarity Search

For the implementation of the visual similarity search, we employ state-of-the-art global image descriptors extracted from CNN specifically tailored for image retrieval. Specifically, we select the Region Maximum Activation of Convolution (R-MAC) descriptors [14] as a compact and expressive image descriptors, which enables our system to support instance-level visual object retrieval on both natural photos and schematics/synthetic images.

Given an image, the **FExtractor** module first feeds it to a pre-trained convolutional network to extract the output of the last convolutional layer, which is composed by multiple feature maps having two spatial dimensions. Then, we compute the R-MAC descriptor by pooling and aggregating different parts (or regions) of those feature maps. The feature maps are max-pooled over several regions on their spatial dimensions, and the obtained vectors are aggregated by summation and the result l2-normalized.

The choice of the pre-trained CNN for the extraction of the feature maps is essential: instead of choosing a network trained on generic object recognition tasks (such as ImageNet), we select the model developed by [6], a ResNet-101 convolutional network trained specifically for the task of same-object retrieval. With this configuration, we obtain 2048-dimensional image descriptors that can be compared with the cosine similarity to search for visual matches.

As already mentioned on Section 3, part of the work done for the ADA project is to make use also of the text correlated or extracted from the image. In the following paragraph, we will explain how we realized an appropriate index supporting both the visual and textual features of the images in an efficient way.

4.2 Indexing of Image Descriptors

While textual information, such as labels and tags, can be stored in a relational database, we need a similarity search index structure to store high-dimensional image features and efficiently compute the cosine-similarity to perform retrieval. Despite open-source indexes for efficient similarity search exist [8], they still come with caveats and, in general, are not mature and well-supported as the scalable disk-based textual indexes such as Elastichsearch.

Seeking for simplicity, we propose to adopt Elasticsearch in the **Indexer** and **Searcher** modules as database for all the information extracted by the visual analysis modules, and adapt our similarity search needs to the full-text search engine provided by the software. Specifically, the adoption of two techniques, *Deep Permutations* [3] and *Surrogate Text Representation* [1, 2], permit us to represent our image descriptors as text, index them using a full-text search engine based on inverted indexes, and perform similarity queries without the need of a image-specific similarity index.

The **Deep Permutations** technique is based on the fact that in high-level deep-learned features, each dimension represents an abstract visual concept, and its value specifies the importance of that concept. Similar features tend to have the same relative importance among visual concepts, and thus, we can approximate a float vector of features by sorting its dimensions in descending order and keeping the sorting permutation (an integer vector). By truncating the permutation to the top elements only, Amato et al. [3] demonstrated that this coarse approximation is sufficient to obtain state-of-the-art trade-offs between efficiency and effectiveness, permitting large-scale searches with query time in the order of seconds.

The **Surrogate Text Representation** technique aims at encoding a given integer vector in the term frequency values of a full-text search engine by generating an appropriate textual string. Used in combination with Deep Permutations, it permits us to store sparse truncated permutation in the inverted index for textual data and leverage the vector document model of full-text search engines to perform cosine similarity searches.

4.3 Image Categorization and Object Detection

For certain documentation, the **Classifier** module needs to assign each image to one or more categories defined by the system users. Thus, we have to implement a multi-class multi-label image classifier. For the categories with a considerable number of training examples, a CNN can be trained to implement the image classifier. Instead of defining and training a new model from scratch, we propose to leverage the *transfer learning* practice, exploiting the knowledge of popular CNNs that have been successfully trained in large-scale generic object recognition tasks. Specifically, we plan to use the ResNet-50 [7] model pre-trained on ImageNet1k, replacing the last classification layer to match our number of classes and to perform fine-tuning on the available training samples. When training samples are scarce, we resort to a simpler kNN classifier based on visual similarity: we reuse the same features extracted by the **FExtractor** module and the cosine similarity matching function in the implementation of the kNN classifier.

For specific categories of images, the **Recognizer** module needs to detect the presence of particular objects of interest. If the location of the object is not required, R-MAC features matching can be used to reveal object presence. Being an aggregation of local region descriptors, matching the R-MAC descriptor of a sub-region of an image against the whole image descriptor will yield a high score. Thus, we can perform object detection via instance-level similarity search reusing the same modules. Instead, if more fine-grained information about detected objects is required, such as the specific localization in the image, and enough training samples are available, we resort to more complex object detection techniques based on Deep Learning, such as region based CNNs [13] or single-stage detectors [12], that can be fine-tuned on the specific object category to detect.

Both the information extracted by the **Classifier** and **Recognizer** modules are stored by the **Indexer** module in Elasticsearch as additional fields of the image record, and accordingly searchable through the **Searcher** module.

5 Conclusions

This paper briefly introduces the on-going work on image analysis in the ADA project, whose main aim is to support the innovation of the production process of the manufacturing companies. We focused on the description of the methodologies carried out to extract relevant information from images contained in the different document provided by the project partners.

Acknowledgments

This work was partially funded by "Automatic Data and documents Analysis to enhance human-based processes" (ADA), CUP CIPE D55F17000290009. We gratefully acknowledge the support of NVIDIA Corporation with the donation of a Tesla K40 GPU used and a Jetson TX2 board used for this research.

References

1. Amato, G., Bolettieri, P., Carrara, F., Falchi, F., Gennaro, C.: Large-scale image retrieval with elasticsearch. In: The 41st International ACM SIGIR Conference on Research & Development in Information Retrieval. pp. 925–928. ACM (2018)
2. Amato, G., Carrara, F., Falchi, F., Gennaro, C.: Efficient indexing of regional maximum activations of convolutions using full-text search engines. In: Proceedings of the 2017 ACM on International Conference on Multimedia Retrieval. pp. 420–423. ACM (2017)
3. Amato, G., Falchi, F., Gennaro, C., Vadicamo, L.: Deep permutations: Deep convolutional neural networks and permutation-based indexing. In: International Conference on Similarity Search and Applications. pp. 93–106. Springer (2016)
4. Donahue, J., Jia, Y., Vinyals, O., Hoffman, J., Zhang, N., Tzeng, E., Darrell, T.: Decaf: A deep convolutional activation feature for generic visual recognition. arXiv preprint arXiv:1310.1531 (2013)
5. Elyan, E., Garcia, C.M., Jayne, C.: Symbols classification in engineering drawings. In: 2018 International Joint Conference on Neural Networks (IJCNN). pp. 1–8. IEEE (2018)
6. Gordo, A., Almazán, J., Revaud, J., Larlus, D.: End-to-end learning of deep visual representations for image retrieval. International Journal of Computer Vision **124**(2), 237–254 (2017)
7. He, K., Zhang, X., Ren, S., Sun, J.: Deep residual learning for image recognition. arXiv preprint arXiv:1512.03385 (2015)
8. Johnson, J., Douze, M., Jégou, H.: Billion-scale similarity search with gpus. arXiv preprint arXiv:1702.08734 (2017)
9. Krizhevsky, A., Sutskever, I., Hinton, G.E.: Imagenet classification with deep convolutional neural networks. In: Advances in neural information processing systems. pp. 1097–1105 (2012)
10. Quan, Y., Shi, Y., Miao, Q., Qi, Y.: A combinatorial solution to point symbol recognition. Sensors **18**(10), 3403 (2018)
11. Razavian, A.S., Azizpour, H., Sullivan, J., Carlsson, S.: CNN features off-the-shelf: an astounding baseline for recognition. In: Computer Vision and Pattern Recognition Workshops (CVPRW), 2014 IEEE Conference on. pp. 512–519. IEEE (2014)
12. Redmon, J., Farhadi, A.: Yolo9000: better, faster, stronger. In: Proceedings of the IEEE conference on computer vision and pattern recognition. pp. 7263–7271 (2017)
13. Ren, S., He, K., Girshick, R., Sun, J.: Faster r-cnn: Towards real-time object detection with region proposal networks. In: Advances in neural information processing systems. pp. 91–99 (2015)
14. Tolias, G., Sicre, R., Jégou, H.: Particular object retrieval with integral max-pooling of cnn activations. arXiv preprint arXiv:1511.05879 (2015)

A Novel Approach to Controlled Query Evaluation in *DL-Lite* (DISCUSSION PAPER)

Domenico Lembo[1], Riccardo Rosati[1], Domenico Fabio Savo[2]

[1] Sapienza Università di Roma
`lastname@dis.uniroma1.it`

[2] Università degli Studi di Bergamo
`domenicofabio.savo@unibg.it`

Abstract. In Controlled Query Evaluation (CQE) confidential data are protected through a declarative *policy* and a (optimal) *censor*, which guarantees that answers to queries are maximized without disclosing secrets. In this paper we consider CQE over Description Logic ontologies and study *query answering* over *all* optimal censors. We establish data complexity of the problem for ontologies specified in *DL-Lite*$_R$ and for variants of the censor language, which is the language used by the censor to enforce the policy. In our investigation we also analyze the relationship between CQE and the problem of Consistent Query Answering.

1 Introduction

In Controlled Query Evaluation (CQE), a policy, i.e., a set of logical assertions, regulates the access to a database or knowledge base by specifying the information that must be kept secret, and a *censor* alters answers to queries so that confidential data cannot be inferred by the users on the basis of the queries they ask. The notion of censor traces back to [16], and since then it has been investigated for propositional closed databases [6], incomplete databases [7], and, more recently, Description Logic (DL) ontologies [10,11]. In this latter context, *optimal* censors are defined as those censors that modify query answers in a "minimal" way. Intuitively, such censors hide data to preserve confidentiality according to the policy, without restricting unnecessarily the ability of the system to return answers to users' queries.

Previous work on CQE in DLs has mainly focused on the tasks of establishing the *existence* of an optimal censor and characterizing the complexity of computing it. However, considering only one such censor means making an arbitrary selection among several optimal censors. To avoid such a discretionary choice, in this paper we adopt a different approach and study *query answering over all optimal censors*. Intuitively, given a query q, this amounts to compute the answers to q that are returned by all optimal censors. This form of reasoning can also be considered as the application of a single censor corresponding to an "intersection" of all the optimal censors, which is thus a semantically well-founded (i.e., sound) approximation of any optimal censor. This idea has been also previously discussed in [10].

Our approach has similarities with the work on Consistent Query Answering (CQA), a framework for inconsistency management based on the notion of repair [3,5]. Roughly speaking, in DL, a repair of a possibly inconsistent ontology $\mathcal{O}$ is any ABox for $\mathcal{O}$ (i.e., the extensional component of $\mathcal{Q}$) that is consistent with the TBox (i.e., the intensional component of $\mathcal{O}$), and that differs "minimally" from the original ABox. Then, computing query answers in CQA amounts to reasoning over all repairs and the TBox. The connection between CQE and CQA in DL is based on the intuition that the assertions in the policy in CQE seems to act as the class of assertions in $\mathcal{T}$ that may be violated by the data of the ABox.

Some connections between CQA and a declarative approach for privacy preservation had already been discussed in [4]. The framework in that paper is similar to ours, with so-called secrecy views playing essentially the role of the policy. However, the setting considered there is relational and without intensional knowledge (TBox), and secrecy views are enforced through suitable virtual modifications of database values with SQL NULLs, so that this approach is incomparable with ours. Nonetheless, in this paper we elaborate on the intuition of [4] and investigate in depth the relationship between our CQE framework and CQA in DLs. We provide some general conditions ensuring that the two problems are mutually reducible, and we show cases of practical interest for which such conditions are satisfied and cases for which they are not. This also allows us to highlight the differences between the two frameworks.

The ultimate goal of this paper is to investigate data complexity of answering conjunctive queries (CQs) in CQE. In our analysis we consider ontologies specified in *DL-Lite*$_{\mathcal{R}}$ [9]. We also consider some variants of the *censor language* $\mathcal{L}_{\mathcal{C}}$. Intuitively, $\mathcal{L}_{\mathcal{C}}$ is the language in which the censor expresses the sentences implied by the ontology that can be disclosed to the users without violating the policy. We provide data complexity results for the cases when: (i) $\mathcal{L}_{\mathcal{C}}$ is the ABox of the ontology; (ii) $\mathcal{L}_{\mathcal{C}}$ coincides with the set of ground atoms expressed over the signature of the ontology; and (iii) $\mathcal{L}_{\mathcal{C}}$ is the language of CQs expressed over the signature of the ontology. Some of the complexity results follow from the correspondence between CQA and CQE; we provide novel techniques for the cases in which the CQE problem does not have a CQA counterpart. The complexity results proved in this paper are shown in Figure 1.

This paper is an extended abstract of [15], where also complexity results for ontologies specified in $\mathcal{EL}_{\bot}$ [1] are provided.

2 Preliminaries

We consider a signature Σ of predicates and constants, and a countably infinite alphabet of variables $\mathcal{V}$. To simplify the presentation, we consider only languages containing FO sentences, i.e., formulas without free variables (our results applies to open formulas as well, modulo standard encoding of open formulas into closed ones). We use **FO** to indicate the language of all function-free FO sentences over Σ and $\mathcal{V}$. Every language considered in this paper is a subset of **FO**.

Given a set $\mathcal{K} \subseteq \mathbf{FO}$, $Mod(\mathcal{K})$ indicates the set of models of $\mathcal{K}$, i.e., the FO interpretations $\mathcal{I}$ such that $\phi^{\mathcal{I}}$ (i.e., the interpretation of ϕ in $\mathcal{I}$) evaluates to true, for each sentence $\phi \in \mathcal{K}$. If $\mathcal{I}$ is a model of $\mathcal{K}$, we say that $\mathcal{I}$ satisfies $\mathcal{K}$ and write $\mathcal{I} \models \mathcal{K}$. $\mathcal{K}$ is consistent if it has at least one model, i.e., if $Mod(\mathcal{K}) \neq \emptyset$, inconsistent otherwise. $\mathcal{K}$ entails a FO sentence ϕ, denoted $\mathcal{K} \models \phi$, if $\phi^{\mathcal{I}}$ is true in every $\mathcal{I} \in Mod(\mathcal{K})$.

A Boolean conjunctive query (BCQ) q is a FO sentence of the form $\exists \boldsymbol{x}.conj(\boldsymbol{x})$, where $conj(\boldsymbol{x}) = \alpha_1(\boldsymbol{x}) \wedge \ldots \wedge \alpha_n(\boldsymbol{x})$, $\boldsymbol{x}$ is a sequence of variables, and each $\alpha_i(\boldsymbol{x})$ is an atom (possibly with constants) with predicate α_i and variables in $\boldsymbol{x}$. The *length* of a BCQ q is the number of its atoms, denoted by $length(q)$.

In the following, $\mathbf{CQ}$ denotes the language of BCQs over Σ and $\mathcal{V}$, $\mathbf{CQ}_k$ the language of BCQs from $\mathbf{CQ}$ whose maximum length is k, and $\mathbf{GA}$ the language of ground atoms. Obviously, for every integer k, $\mathbf{GA} \subset \mathbf{CQ}_k \subset \mathbf{CQ}$. Verifying whether $\mathcal{K} \models \alpha$ for $\mathcal{K} \subseteq \mathbf{FO}$ and $\alpha \in \mathbf{GA}$ is also called *instance checking*.

A DL ontology $\mathcal{O}$ is specified as $\mathcal{T} \cup \mathcal{A}$, where $\mathcal{T}$ is the *TBox* and $\mathcal{A}$ is the *ABox* [2]. Throughout the paper an ABox is always a set of ground atoms. We are interested in *DL-Lite*$_R$ DL ontologies [9]. A *DL-Lite*$_R$ TBox is a finite set of assertions of the form: $B_1 \sqsubseteq B_2$, $B_1 \sqsubseteq \neg B_2$, $R_1 \sqsubseteq R_2$, $R_1 \sqsubseteq \neg R_2$, where: each R_i, with $i \in \{1, 2\}$, is an *atomic role* $Q \in \Sigma$, or its inverse Q^-; each B_i, with $i \in \{1, 2\}$, is an *atomic concept* $A \in \Sigma$, or a concept of the form $\exists Q$ (resp. $\exists Q^-$), i.e., unqualified existential restriction, which denotes the set of objects occurring as first (resp. second) argument of Q.

We also consider *denial assertions* (or simply *denials*) over concepts and roles, i.e., sentences of the form: $\forall \boldsymbol{x}.conj(\boldsymbol{x}) \rightarrow \bot$ where $conj(\boldsymbol{x})$ is such that $\exists \boldsymbol{x}.conj(\boldsymbol{x})$ is a BCQ whose atoms use only unary and binary predicates. The *length* of the denial is the length of such query. A denial is satisfied by an ontology $\mathcal{O}$ if $\mathcal{O} \not\models \exists \boldsymbol{x}.conj(\boldsymbol{x})$.

In the following, given an ontology $\mathcal{O}$ and a language $\mathcal{L} \subseteq \mathbf{FO}$, we denote with $\mathcal{L}(\mathcal{O})$ the subset of formulas of $\mathcal{L}$ over the predicates and constants occurring in $\mathcal{O}$.

All the complexity results we provide refer to *data complexity*, that in our framework is the complexity computed only with respect to the size of the ontology ABox.

3 CQE Framework

Our CQE framework is adapted from [11]. An $\mathcal{L}$ *CQE instance* $\mathcal{E}$ is a quadruple $\langle \mathcal{T}, \mathcal{A}, \mathcal{P}, \mathcal{L}_C \rangle$, where $\mathcal{T}$ is a TBox in the DL $\mathcal{L}$, $\mathcal{A}$ is an ABox such that $\mathcal{T} \cup \mathcal{A}$ is consistent, $\mathcal{P}$ is the policy, i.e., a set of denial assertions over the signature of $\mathcal{T} \cup \mathcal{A}$, such that $\mathcal{T} \cup \mathcal{P}$ is consistent, and $\mathcal{L}_C \subseteq \mathbf{FO}(\mathcal{T} \cup \mathcal{A})$ is the *censor language*. Intuitively: $\mathcal{T}$ is the schema a user interacts with to pose her queries; $\mathcal{A}$ is the dataset underlying the schema; $\mathcal{P}$ specifies the knowledge that cannot be disclosed for confidentiality reasons, in the sense that the user will never get, through query answers, sufficient knowledge to violate the denials in $\mathcal{P}$; and $\mathcal{L}_C$ is the language with respect to which the censor is specified, that is, the censor establishes which are the sentences in $\mathcal{L}_C$ implied by $\mathcal{T} \cup \mathcal{A}$ that can be divulged to the user while preserving the policy (cf. Definition 1). To simplify the notation, we will sometimes omit to specify that a certain censor language is limited to the signature of $\mathcal{T} \cup \mathcal{A}$ (e.g., we will use $\mathbf{GA}$ instead of $\mathbf{GA}(\mathcal{T} \cup \mathcal{A})$).

We then define a censor in terms of its underlying theory.

Definition 1. *The* theory $\mathsf{Th}_{\mathsf{cens}}$ of a censor cens *for a CQE instance* $\langle \mathcal{T}, \mathcal{A}, \mathcal{P}, \mathcal{L}_{\mathcal{C}} \rangle$ *is a subset of* $\mathcal{L}_{\mathcal{C}}$ *such that:* (i) $\mathcal{T} \cup \mathcal{A} \models \phi$*, for each* $\phi \in \mathsf{Th}_{\mathsf{cens}}$*, and* (ii) $\mathcal{T} \cup \mathcal{P} \cup \mathsf{Th}_{\mathsf{cens}}$ *is consistent.*

A censor c is *optimal* if there is no censor c' such that $\mathsf{Th}_c \subset \mathsf{Th}_{c'} \subseteq \mathcal{L}_{\mathcal{C}}$. The set of theories of all the optimal censors of a CQE instance $\mathcal{E}$ is denoted by Th_{oc}-$Set(\mathcal{E})$.

Example 1. A CQE instance $\mathcal{E} = (\mathcal{T}, \mathcal{A}, \mathcal{P}, \mathbf{CQ})$ is used by an international humanitarian organization for regulating the access to the information about its volunteer staff. In $\mathcal{E}$, $\mathcal{T}$ is an empty TBox, $\mathcal{A} = \{\mathsf{workedIn}(v_1, c_A), \mathsf{workedIn}(v_1, c_B), \mathsf{workedIn}(v_2, c_A)\}$, and $\mathcal{P} = \{\forall x.\mathsf{workedIn}(x, c_A) \wedge \mathsf{workedIn}(x, c_B) \rightarrow \bot\}$. In words, the policy specifies as confidential the fact that a volunteer worked in both country A and country B, given that these countries are currently at war with each other.

Below we provide the definition of entailment in CQE[1].

Definition 2. ***(CQE-entailment)*** *Given a CQE instance* $\mathcal{E}$ *and a FO sentence* ϕ*, decide whether* $\mathsf{Th} \models \phi$ *for every* $\mathsf{Th} \in Th_{oc}$-$Set(\mathcal{E})$*. If this is the case, we write* $\mathcal{E} \models_{CQE} \phi$*.*

As usual, when the language of ϕ is restricted to ground atoms (i.e., ABox assertions), CQE-entailment is called (CQE-)*instance checking*.

Example 2. For the CQE instance $\mathcal{E}$ of Example 1, we have, for instance, that $\mathcal{E} \models_{CQE} \exists x.\mathsf{workedIn}(v_1, x)$ and $\mathcal{E} \models_{CQE} \exists x.\mathsf{workedIn}(x, c_B)$, but $\mathcal{E} \not\models_{CQE} \mathsf{workedIn}(v_1, c_B)$.

4 Relationship between CQE and CQA

In this section we discuss the relationship between the CQE framework we have just defined and CQA. To this aim, we first provide a general definition for CQA.

A $\mathcal{L}$ *CQA instance* $\mathcal{J}$ is a triple $\langle \mathcal{T}, \mathcal{A}, \mathcal{L}_{\mathcal{R}} \rangle$ where $\mathcal{T}$ is a consistent TBox in the DL $\mathcal{L}$, $\mathcal{A}$ is an ABox, and $\mathcal{L}_{\mathcal{R}} \subseteq \mathbf{FO}(\mathcal{T} \cup \mathcal{A})$ is the *repair language*. The *consistent entailment set in a language* $\mathcal{L}$ of a (possibly inconsistent) theory $\mathcal{T} \cup \mathcal{A}$, denoted by $CES(\mathcal{T}, \mathcal{A}, \mathcal{L})$, is the set $\{\phi \mid \phi \in \mathcal{L}$ and there exists a $\mathcal{A}' \subseteq \mathcal{A}$ such that $\mathcal{T} \cup \mathcal{A}'$ is consistent and $\mathcal{T} \cup \mathcal{A}' \models \phi\}$. A repair for a CQA instance is defined as follows.

Definition 3. *A repair* $\mathcal{R}$ *for a CQA instance* $\mathcal{J} = \langle \mathcal{T}, \mathcal{A}, \mathcal{L}_{\mathcal{R}} \rangle$ *is a subset of* $\mathcal{L}_{\mathcal{R}}$ *such that:* (i) $\mathcal{R} \subseteq CES(\mathcal{T}, \mathcal{A}, \mathcal{L}_{\mathcal{R}})$ *and;* (ii) $\mathcal{T} \cup \mathcal{R}$ *is consistent and;* (iii) *there does not exist any* $\mathcal{R}'$ *such that* $\mathcal{R} \subset \mathcal{R}' \subseteq CES(\mathcal{T}, \mathcal{A}, \mathcal{L}_{\mathcal{R}})$ *and* $\mathcal{T} \cup \mathcal{R}'$ *is consistent. We denote by* $\mathsf{RepSet}(\mathcal{J})$ *the set of repairs of* $\mathcal{J}$.

Definition 3 captures some notions of repair proposed in the literature, such as the repair at the basis of the prototypical *AR*-semantics, or the repair adopted by the *CAR*-semantics [13,14]. Indeed, given an ontology $\mathcal{O} = \mathcal{T} \cup \mathcal{A}$, repairs in the *AR*-semantics aim to preserve as many facts as possible of those in $\mathcal{A}$. This means that, in a CQA instance adopting the *AR*-semantics, the language $\mathcal{L}_{\mathcal{R}}$ has to be set to $\mathcal{A}$. Differently, the *CAR*-semantics aims to preserve as many facts as possible of those implied by $\mathcal{T}$ and

[1] Due to space limits, we give a simplified definition and refer to [15] for other formal details.

each subset of $\mathcal{A}$ consistent with $\mathcal{T}$. Thus, to encode such semantics $\mathcal{L}_{\mathcal{R}}$ has to coincide with the set $\mathbf{GA}(\mathcal{O})$ of ground atoms over the predicates and constants in $\mathcal{O}$.

We now provide some conditions on CQE and CQA instances that allow to establish correspondences between (theories of) censors and repairs.

Definition 4. *A CQE instance $\langle \mathcal{T}, \mathcal{A}, \mathcal{P}, \mathcal{L}_{\mathcal{C}} \rangle$ is* CQA-reducible *if:*
(i) *for every $\phi \in \mathcal{L}_{\mathcal{C}}$ such that $\mathcal{T} \cup \mathcal{A} \models \phi$ and $\{\phi\} \cup \mathcal{T} \cup \mathcal{P}$ is consistent, there exists $\mathcal{A}' \subseteq \mathcal{A}$ such that $\mathcal{T} \cup \mathcal{A}' \cup \mathcal{P}$ is consistent and $\mathcal{T} \cup \mathcal{A}' \models \phi$;*
(ii) *for every $\phi \in \mathcal{L}_{\mathcal{C}}$ and every $\mathcal{A}' \subseteq \mathcal{A}$ such that $\mathcal{T} \cup \mathcal{A}' \cup \mathcal{P}$ is consistent, if $\mathcal{T} \cup \mathcal{A}' \cup \mathcal{P} \models \phi$ then $\mathcal{T} \cup \mathcal{A}' \models \phi$.*

In words, condition (i) imposes that every logical consequence of $\mathcal{T} \cup \mathcal{A}$ that is consistent with the policy and the TBox belongs to $CES(\mathcal{T} \cup \mathcal{P}, \mathcal{A}, \mathcal{L}_{\mathcal{C}})$. Condition (ii) instead says that in a CQA-reducible instance the sentences in the policy act as constraints on top of $\mathcal{T} \cup \mathcal{A}$, since they never contribute to infer new formulas from $\mathcal{L}_{\mathcal{C}}$ if added to $\mathcal{T} \cup \mathcal{A}$.

Example 3. The instance $\mathcal{E} = \langle \mathcal{T}, \mathcal{A}, \mathcal{P}, \mathcal{L}_{\mathcal{C}} \rangle$ with $\mathcal{T} = \{A \sqsubseteq B\}$, $\mathcal{A} = \{A(d)\}$, $\mathcal{P} = \{\forall x.A(x) \rightarrow \bot\}$, and $\mathcal{L}_{\mathcal{C}} = \mathbf{GA}$ is not CQA-reducible, since it does not respect condition (i), even though it satisfies condition (ii) (in a trivial way). Instead, $\mathcal{E} = \langle \mathcal{T}, \mathcal{A}', \mathcal{P}', \mathcal{L}_{\mathcal{C}} \rangle$ with $\mathcal{A}' = \{A(d), B(d)\}$, $\mathcal{P} = \{\forall x.A(x) \wedge B(x) \rightarrow \bot\}$, and $\mathcal{T}$ and $\mathcal{L}_{\mathcal{C}}$ as before is CQA-reducible.

Theorem 1. *Let $\mathcal{E} = \langle \mathcal{T}, \mathcal{A}, \mathcal{P}, \mathcal{L}_{\mathcal{C}} \rangle$ be a CQE instance, such that $\mathcal{E}$ is a CQA-reducible. Then Th_{oc}-Set$(\langle \mathcal{T}, \mathcal{A}, \mathcal{P}, \mathcal{L}_{\mathcal{C}} \rangle) = \mathsf{RepSet}(\langle \mathcal{T} \cup \mathcal{P}, \mathcal{A}, \mathcal{L}_{\mathcal{C}} \rangle)$.*

Below we consider reducibility of CQA instances into CQE ones.

Definition 5. *A CQA instance $\langle \mathcal{T}, \mathcal{A}, \mathcal{L}_{\mathcal{R}} \rangle$ is* CQE-reducible *if there exists a partition $\mathcal{T}_P \cup \mathcal{T}_N$ of $\mathcal{T}$ such that $\mathcal{T}_P \cup \mathcal{A}$ is consistent, $\mathcal{T}_N$ is equivalent to a set of denials, and:*
(i) *for every $\phi \in \mathcal{L}_{\mathcal{R}}$, such that $\mathcal{T}_P \cup \mathcal{A} \models \phi$ and $\{\phi\} \cup \mathcal{T}$ is consistent, there exists $\mathcal{A}' \subseteq \mathcal{A}$ such that $\mathcal{T} \cup \mathcal{A}'$ is consistent and $\mathcal{T} \cup \mathcal{A}' \models \phi$;*
(ii) *for every $\phi \in \mathcal{L}_{\mathcal{R}}$ and every $\mathcal{A}' \subseteq \mathcal{A}$ such that $\mathcal{T} \cup \mathcal{A}'$ is consistent, if $\mathcal{T} \cup \mathcal{A}' \models \phi$ then $\mathcal{T}_P \cup \mathcal{A}' \models \phi$.*

Intuitively, the above definition says that in a CQE-reducible instance we can identify a portion $\mathcal{T}_N$ of $\mathcal{T}$ such that its assertions act as constraints on the ontology $\mathcal{T}_P \cup \mathcal{A}$ (cond. (ii)), thus $\mathcal{T}_N$ behaves as a policy in a CQE instance. At the same time, each logical consequence of $\mathcal{T}_P \cup \mathcal{A}$ consistent with $\mathcal{T}$ must belong to $CES(\mathcal{T}, \mathcal{A}, \mathcal{L}_{\mathcal{R}})$ (cond. (i)). CQE-reducible instances have the following property.

Theorem 2. *Let $\mathcal{J} = \langle \mathcal{T}, \mathcal{A}, \mathcal{L}_{\mathcal{R}} \rangle$ be a CQA instance, such that $\mathcal{J}$ is CQE-reducible with $\mathcal{T} = \mathcal{T}_P \cup \mathcal{T}_N$. Then $\mathsf{RepSet}(\langle \mathcal{T}_P \cup \mathcal{T}_N, \mathcal{A}, \mathcal{L}_{\mathcal{R}} \rangle) = Th_{oc}$-Set$(\langle \mathcal{T}_P, \mathcal{A}, \mathcal{T}_N, \mathcal{L}_{\mathcal{R}} \rangle)$.*

We now rephrase entailment in CQA [14]: given a CQA instance $\mathcal{J} = \langle \mathcal{T}, \mathcal{A}, \mathcal{L}_{\mathcal{R}} \rangle$ and a FO sentence ϕ, decide whether $\mathcal{T} \cup \mathcal{R} \models \phi$ for every $\mathcal{R} \in \mathsf{RepSet}(\mathcal{J})$. This is denoted by $\mathcal{J} \models_{CQA} \phi$. The following results follow from Theorem 1 and Theorem 2.

Corollary 1. *Let $\mathcal{E} = \langle \mathcal{T}, \mathcal{A}, \mathcal{P}, \mathcal{L}_{\mathcal{C}} \rangle$ be a CQA-reducible CQE instance and ϕ a FO sentence. Then, $\mathcal{E} \models_{CQE} \phi$ iff $\mathcal{J} \models_{CQA} \phi$, where $\mathcal{J} = \langle \mathcal{T} \cup \mathcal{P}, \mathcal{A}, \mathcal{L}_{\mathcal{C}} \rangle$. Furthermore, Let $\mathcal{J} = \langle \mathcal{T}, \mathcal{A}, \mathcal{L}_{\mathcal{R}} \rangle$ be a CQE-reducible CQA instance with $\mathcal{T} = \mathcal{T}_P \cup \mathcal{T}_N$, and ϕ a FO sentence. Then, $\mathcal{J} \models_{CQA} \phi$ iff $\mathcal{E} \models_{CQE} \phi$, where $\mathcal{E} = \langle \mathcal{T}_P, \mathcal{A}, \mathcal{T}_N, \mathcal{L}_{\mathcal{R}} \rangle$.*

5 CQE under Restricted Censor Languages

In this section we establish data complexity of instance checking and CQ entailment for *DL-Lite*$_R$ CQE instances, when the censor language $\mathcal{L}_C$ coincides with the ABox $\mathcal{A}$, and with the set of ground atoms $\mathbf{GA}$. For the former case, we establish our complexity results by exploiting a mutual reduction between entailment in CQE and CQA. For the latter case, the two frameworks behave in a slightly different way, and thus we also need to use techniques tailored to the CQE setting.

We start with $\mathcal{L}_C = \mathcal{A}$, and show that CQE instances are CQA-reducible, but also that CQA-instances are CQE-reducible when the repair language coincides with $\mathcal{A}$.

Theorem 3. *Each DL-Lite*$_R$ *CQE instance* $\langle \mathcal{T}, \mathcal{A}, \mathcal{P}, \mathcal{A} \rangle$ *is CQA-reducible, and each DL-Lite*$_R$ *CQA instance* $\langle \mathcal{T}, \mathcal{A}, \mathcal{A} \rangle$ *is CQE-reducible.*

The following result follows from Theorem 3 and the fact that CQ entailment in *DL-Lite*$_{R,den}$ CQA instances under *AR*-semantics is coNP-complete, already for instance checking [14].

Theorem 4. *Both instance checking and CQ entailment are coNP-complete in data complexity for DL-Lite*$_R$ *CQE instances* $\langle \mathcal{T}, \mathcal{A}, \mathcal{P}, \mathcal{A} \rangle$.

We now consider $\mathcal{L}_C = \mathbf{GA}$. In this case, *DL-Lite*$_R$ CQE instances are *not* always CQA-reducible, as shown in Example 3. Reducibility in the other way round is also not always possible. However, we can show some weaker, but useful, properties.

Proposition 1. *Each DL-Lite*$_R$ *CQE instance* $\langle \mathcal{T}, \mathcal{A}, \mathcal{P}, \mathbf{GA} \rangle$*, such that* $\mathcal{T} \cup \mathcal{P} \cup \{\alpha\}$ *is satisfiable for each* $\alpha \in \mathcal{A}$*, is CQA-reducible. Also, each DL-Lite*$_R$ *CQA instance* $\langle \mathcal{T}, \mathcal{A}, \mathbf{GA} \rangle$*, such that* $\mathcal{T} \cup \{\alpha\}$ *is satisfiable for each* $\alpha \in \mathcal{A}$*, is CQE-reducible.*

For *DL-Lite*$_R$ CQE instances satisfying the conditions mentioned in Proposition 1 we can establish computational complexity of query answering by mutual reduction between CQE and CQA under *CAR*-semantics, similarly to what we have done to prove Theorem 4. In fact, we are able to exactly characterize the complexity for general *DL-Lite*$_R$ CQE instances by using tailored proofs, which are inspired to those used in CQA to establish both upper and lower complexity bounds.

Theorem 5. *Instance checking and CQ entailment are respectively in* AC^0 *and coNP-complete in data complexity, for DL-Lite*$_R$ *CQE instances* $\langle \mathcal{T}, \mathcal{A}, \mathcal{P}, \mathbf{GA} \rangle$.

6 CQE under Full Censor Language

In this section we study CQE-entailment when the censor language $\mathcal{L}_C$ is $\mathbf{CQ}$. We start with the following property that is central for our analysis.

Theorem 6. *Let* $\mathcal{T}$ *be a DL-Lite*$_R$ *TBox, let* $\mathcal{A}$ *be an ABox such that* $\mathcal{T} \cup \mathcal{A}$ *is consistent, let* $\mathcal{P}$ *be a policy, let* q *be a BCQ, and let* $k = \max(h, length(q))$*, where* h *is the maximum length of a denial assertion in* $\mathcal{P}$*. Then,* $\langle \mathcal{T}, \mathcal{A}, \mathcal{P}, \mathbf{CQ} \rangle \models_{CQE} q$ *iff* $\langle \mathcal{T}, \mathcal{A}, \mathcal{P}, \mathbf{CQ_k} \rangle \models_{CQE} q$.

	$\mathcal{L}_C = \mathcal{A}$	$\mathcal{L}_C = \mathbf{GA}$	$\mathcal{L}_C = \mathbf{CQ}$
Instance Checking	coNP-complete	in AC^0	in PTIME
CQ Entailment	coNP-complete	coNP-complete	in PTIME

Fig. 1: Data complexity of entailment over *DL-Lite*$_R$ CQE instances $\langle \mathcal{T}, \mathcal{A}, \mathcal{P}, \mathcal{L}_C \rangle$

In the rest of the section, without loss of generality, we assume that, in every CQE instance of the form $\langle \mathcal{T}, \mathcal{A}, \mathcal{P}, \mathbf{CQ_k} \rangle$, all formulas of the language $\mathbf{CQ_k}$ (as well as the query q of the CQE-entailment problem) use the set of $2k$ variables $\{x_1, \ldots, x_{2k}\}$.

We now define the *CQE-Ent-DL-Lite*$_R$ algorithm for deciding CQE-entailment of BCQs for *DL-Lite*$_R$ KBs.

Algorithm *CQE-Ent-DL-Lite*$_R(\mathcal{T}, \mathcal{A}, \mathcal{P}, q)$
Input: *DL-Lite*$_R$ TBox $\mathcal{T}$, ABox $\mathcal{A}$ s. t. $\mathcal{T} \cup \mathcal{A}$ is consistent, policy $\mathcal{P}$, BCQ q
Output: true if $\langle \mathcal{T}, \mathcal{A}, \mathcal{P}, \mathbf{CQ} \rangle \models_{CQE} q$, false otherwise
let h be the maximum length of a denial in $\mathcal{P}$;
let $k = \max(h, \mathit{length}(q))$;
$\Phi = \mathit{CQEntailedSubset}(\mathcal{T}, \mathcal{A}, k)$;
for $i = 1$ to k **do**
remove from Φ every subset Φ' such that $|\Phi'| = i$
and $\mathcal{T} \cup \mathcal{P} \cup \Phi'$ is inconsistent;
if $q \in \Phi$ **then** return true **else** return false

In the algorithm, $\mathit{CQEntailedSubset}(\mathcal{T}, \mathcal{A}, k)$ is the function returning the set of BCQs from $\mathbf{CQ_k}$ that are entailed by $\mathcal{T} \cup \mathcal{A}$.

Informally, the algorithm first computes an integer k, based on the length of q and of the denials in $\mathcal{P}$; then, it computes the set Φ that represents the intersection of the theories of the optimal censors for the CQE instance $\langle \mathcal{T}, \mathcal{A}, \mathcal{P}, \mathbf{CQ_k} \rangle$: this is done by eliminating from Φ all formulas that belong to minimal subsets of Φ that are inconsistent with $\mathcal{T} \cup \mathcal{P}$; finally, it checks the presence of q among the queries in the above set Φ.

Theorem 7. *Let $\mathcal{E} = \langle \mathcal{T}, \mathcal{A}, \mathcal{P}, \mathbf{CQ} \rangle$ be a DL-Lite$_R$ CQE instance, and q a BCQ. Then, $\mathcal{E} \models_{CQE} q$ iff CQE-Ent-DL-Lite$_R(\mathcal{T}, \mathcal{A}, \mathcal{P}, q)$ returns true.*

Algorithm *CQE-Ent-DL-Lite*$_R(\mathcal{T}, \mathcal{A}, \mathcal{P}, q)$ runs in PTIME in the size of the ABox, since $\mathit{CQEntailedSubset}(\mathcal{T}, \mathcal{A}, k)$ can be computed in polynomial time in the size of $\mathcal{A}$ and checking the consistency of $\mathcal{T} \cup \mathcal{P} \cup \Phi'$ can be reduced to checking the consistency of a *DL-Lite*$_{R,den}$ ontology, which is polynomial in data complexity [14].

Theorem 8. *Entailment of CQs is in PTIME in data complexity for DL-Lite$_R$ CQE instances $\langle \mathcal{T}, \mathcal{A}, \mathcal{P}, \mathbf{CQ} \rangle$.*

7 Conclusions

Our results (cf. Figure 1) show a surprising aspect: the complexity of CQ entailment for restricted censor languages is harder than when $\mathcal{L}_C = \mathbf{CQ}$. Indeed, in this latter case,

CQ entailment can be established through the computation of the intersection of (a finite and polynomial representation of) all the theories of optimal censors, which can be done in polynomial time. This does not hold for $\mathcal{L}_C$ equal to $\mathcal{A}$ or $\mathbf{GA}$.

Our research work can be extended in many directions. First, the PTIME upper bound for CQE over *DL-Lite*$_R$ TBoxes and $\mathbf{CQ}$ censor language should be refined. We believe that an AC^0 bound can be shown in this case. Then, the complexity analysis of CQE could be extended to other DLs, as well as to other policy and censor languages. Also, based on the complexity analysis presented in this paper, it would be important to look for practical techniques allowing for the implementation of CQE extensions of current DL reasoners and Ontology-based Data Access systems [8,12].

References

1. F. Baader, S. Brandt, and C. Lutz. Pushing the $\mathcal{EL}$ envelope. In *Proc. of IJCAI*, pages 364–369, 2005.
2. F. Baader, D. Calvanese, D. McGuinness, D. Nardi, and P. F. Patel-Schneider, editors. *The Description Logic Handbook: Theory, Implementation and Applications*. Cambridge University Press, 2nd edition, 2007.
3. L. E. Bertossi. *Database Repairing and Consistent Query Answering*. Synthesis Lectures on Data Management. Morgan & Claypool Publishers, 2011.
4. L. E. Bertossi and L. Li. Achieving data privacy through secrecy views and null-based virtual updates. *IEEE Trans. Knowl. Data Eng.*, 25(5):987–1000, 2013.
5. M. Bienvenu and C. Bourgaux. Inconsistency-tolerant querying of description logic knowledge bases. In *RW Tutorial Lectures*, pages 156–202, 2016.
6. J. Biskup and P. A. Bonatti. Controlled query evaluation for enforcing confidentiality in complete information systems. *Int. J. Inf. Sec.*, 3(1):14–27, 2004.
7. J. Biskup and T. Weibert. Keeping secrets in incomplete databases. *Int. J. Inf. Sec.*, 7(3):199–217, 2008.
8. D. Calvanese, B. Cogrel, S. Komla-Ebri, R. Kontchakov, D. Lanti, M. Rezk, M. Rodriguez-Muro, and G. Xiao. Ontop: Answering SPARQL queries over relational databases. *Semantic Web J.*, 8(3):471–487, 2017.
9. D. Calvanese, G. De Giacomo, D. Lembo, M. Lenzerini, and R. Rosati. Tractable reasoning and efficient query answering in description logics: The *DL-Lite* family. *J. of Automated Reasoning*, 39(3):385–429, 2007.
10. B. Cuenca Grau, E. Kharlamov, E. V. Kostylev, and D. Zheleznyakov. Controlled query evaluation over OWL 2 RL ontologies. In *Proc. of ISWC*, pages 49–65, 2013.
11. B. Cuenca Grau, E. Kharlamov, E. V. Kostylev, and D. Zheleznyakov. Controlled query evaluation for Datalog and OWL 2 profile ontologies. In *Proc. of IJCAI*, pages 2883–2889, 2015.
12. G. De Giacomo, D. Lembo, M. Lenzerini, A. Poggi, R. Rosati, M. Ruzzi, and D. F. Savo. MASTRO: A reasoner for effective Ontology-Based Data Access. In *Proc. of ORE*, 2012.
13. D. Lembo, M. Lenzerini, R. Rosati, M. Ruzzi, and D. F. Savo. Inconsistency-tolerant semantics for description logics. In *Proc. of RR*, pages 103–117, 2010.
14. D. Lembo, M. Lenzerini, R. Rosati, M. Ruzzi, and D. F. Savo. Inconsistency-tolerant query answering in ontology-based data access. *J. of Web Semantics*, 33:3–29, 2015.
15. D. Lembo, R. Rosati, and D. F. Savo. Revisiting controlled query evaluation in Description Logics. In *Proc. of IJCAI*, 2019. To appear.
16. G. L. Sicherman, W. de Jonge, and R. P. van de Riet. Answering queries without revealing secrets. *ACM Trans. Database Syst.*, 8(1):41–59, 1983.

Surrogate Text Representation of Visual Features for Fast Image Retrieval

Fabio Carrara[0000−0001−5014−5089]
Supervised by Dr. Giuseppe Amato, Dr. Claudio Gennaro, and Prof. Francesco Marcelloni.

Institute of Information Science and Technologies (ISTI), Italian National Research Council (CNR), Via G. Moruzzi 1, 56124 Pisa, Italy
fabio.carrara@isti.cnr.it

Abstract. We propose a simple and effective methodology to index and retrieve image features without the need for a time-consuming codebook learning step. We employ a scalar quantization approach combined with Surrogate Text Representation (STR) to perform large-scale image retrieval relying on the latest text search engine technologies. Experiments on large-scale image retrieval benchmarks show that we improve the effectiveness-efficiency trade-off of current STR approaches while performing comparably to state-of-the-art main-memory methods without requiring a codebook learning procedure.

Keywords: image retrieval · deep features · surrogate text representation · inverted index

1 Intruduction

As part of the contributions of our thesis, we explore new approaches for making image retrieval as similar as possible to text to reuse the technologies and platforms exploited today for text retrieval without the need for dedicated access methods. In a nutshell, the idea is to use image representation extracted from a CNN, often referred to as *deep features*, and to transform them into a surrogate text that standard text search engine can index. Our general approach is based on the transformation of deep features, which are (dense) vectors of real numbers, into sparse vectors of integer numbers that can be mapped in term frequencies. Moreover, sparseness is necessary to achieve sufficient levels of efficiency as it does for search engines for text documents. We introduce and evaluate a novel approach for surrogate text representation of deep features based on Scalar Quantization (SQ).

2 Surrogate Text Representation

We define a family of transformations that map a feature vector into a textual representation without the need for tedious training procedures. We require that such transformations preserve as much as possible the proximity relations between the data, i.e., similar feature vectors are mapped to similar textual documents. This basic idea was firstly exploited in [2], where the authors defined the Surrogate Text Representation (STR) to represent a generic metric object, i.e., an object living in a space where a distance function is defined [7]. The STR of an object is a space-separated concatenation of some alphanumeric codeword selected from a pre-defined dictionary. We observe that a surrogate text representation for an object o of a data domain $\mathcal{X}$ can be obtained more generally by defining a transformation

$$\begin{aligned} f : \mathcal{X} &\to \mathbb{N}^n \\ o &\mapsto \boldsymbol{f}_o = [f_o^{(1)}, \ldots, f_o^{(n)}] , \end{aligned} \tag{1}$$

where $\boldsymbol{f}_o$ will act as the vector of the term frequencies of a synthetic text document t_o with respect to a dictionary of n words. Given a dictionary $\{\tau_1, \ldots, \tau_n\}$ and the transformation $f : \mathbb{R}^m \to \mathbb{N}^n$, we define the surrogate text $t_o = \text{STR}_f(o)$ as

$$\text{STR}_f(o) = \bigcup_{i=1}^{n} \bigcup_{j=1}^{f_o^{(i)}} \tau_i \tag{2}$$

where, by abuse of notation, we denote the space-separated concatenation of the codewords with the union operator $\cup$. Thus, by construction, the integer values of the i-th component of the vector $\boldsymbol{f}_o$ is the frequency of the codeword τ_i in the text $\text{STR}_f(o)$. For example, given $\boldsymbol{f}_o = [1, 3, 0, 2]$ and a codebook $\{\tau_1 = \text{“}A''$, $\tau_2 = \text{“}B''$, $\tau_3 = \text{“}C''$, $\tau_4 = \text{“}D''\}$, we have $\text{STR}_f(o) = \text{“}A\,B\,B\,B\,D\,D''$. Using this representation, the search engine indexes the text by using inverted files, i.e., each object o is stored in the posting lists associated to the codewords appearing in $\text{STR}_f(o)$. We demonstrate indexing and searching *D-dimensional vectors* compared with the dot product, i.e. $\mathcal{X} = \mathbb{R}^D$.

3 Scalar Quantization-Based Approach

The first step in our approach is the application of an random orthogonal transformation to the vectors $\mathbf{v} \to R(\mathbf{v} - \boldsymbol{\mu}), \mathbf{q} \to R\mathbf{q}$, where $\mathbf{v}$ and $\mathbf{q}$ are vectors of database and query images, R is a *random* orthogonal matrix ($\|R\|_2 = 1$), and $\boldsymbol{\mu} \in \mathbb{R}^D$ can be arbitrary chosen. The benefit of this transformation is manyfold: a) it re-balances the variance of the components of the feature vectors [4], thus preventing unbalanced posting lists in the inverted file; b) it is ordering-preserving with respect to the dot-product: given a rotation matrix $R \in \mathbb{R}^{D \times D}$ and a vector $\boldsymbol{\mu} \in \mathbb{R}^D$, then

$$\forall\, \mathbf{q}, \mathbf{v}_1, \mathbf{v}_2 \in \mathbb{R}^D \quad \mathbf{q} \cdot \mathbf{v}_1 \leq \mathbf{q} \cdot \mathbf{v}_2 \Rightarrow R\mathbf{q} \cdot R(\mathbf{v}_1 - \boldsymbol{\mu}) \leq R\mathbf{q} \cdot R(\mathbf{v}_2 - \boldsymbol{\mu}) . \tag{3}$$

Then, we transform the rotated vectors into integer term-frequency vectors by scaling and quantization: $\mathbf{v} \to \lfloor s\mathbf{v} \rfloor$ where $\lfloor \cdot \rfloor$ denotes the floor function, and $s > 1$ is the *quantization factor*. This process introduces a quantization error due to the representation of float components in integers that does not affect the retrieval effectiveness. In summary, the SQ-based STR is obtained using the transformation $f_{\text{SQ}} : \mathbf{v} \mapsto \lfloor sR(\mathbf{v} - \boldsymbol{\mu}) \rfloor$. For instance, suppose after the random rotation we have the feature vector $\mathbf{v} = [0.1, 0.3, 0.4, 0, 0.2]$, by adopting a multiplication factor $s = 10$, we obtain the term frequencies vector will be $f_{\text{SQ}}(\mathbf{v}) = [1, 3, 4, 0, 2]$, and thus $\text{STR}_{f_{\text{SQ}}}(\mathbf{v}) = $ "$A\,B\,B\,B\,C\,C\,C\,C\,E\,E$".

In order to sparsify the term frequency vectors, that is, to cancel the less significant components of the vectors, we adopt thresholding

$$\mathbf{v}_\gamma(i) = \begin{cases} \mathbf{v}(i) & \text{if} \quad \mathbf{v}(i) \geq \frac{1}{\gamma} \\ 0 & \text{otherwise} \end{cases}, \tag{4}$$

where $\mathbf{v}(i)$ indicates the i-th dimension of $\mathbf{v}$. To optimize this step, we set $\boldsymbol{\mu}$ of Eq. (3) to the mean vector to obtain zero-centered components. Thresholding alone ignores the negative components of the original real-valued feature vectors, discarding useful information. In order to prevent this, before our proposed transformation, we also apply the Concatenated ReLU (CReLU) transformation to feature vectors, defined as $\mathbf{v}^+ = \max([\mathbf{v}, -\mathbf{v}], \mathbf{0})$, where $\max(\cdot, 0)$ is applied element-wise. Notice that in general, the CReLU operation is lossy since the dot product between vectors is not preserved, i.e., $\mathbf{v}_1 \cdot \mathbf{v}_2 \leq \mathbf{v}_1^+ \cdot \mathbf{v}_2^+$. However, this transformation allows us not to completely neglect the negative components.

4 Experimental Evaluation and Discussion

To validate our approach, we extract R-MAC features [6] — a 2048-dimensional real-valued feature vector — from the images of INRIA Holidays + MIR-Flickr1M [3] — a standard benchmark for image retrieval. We evaluate our approach for different values of the thersholding parameter γ. We compare with Deep Permutations (DP) [1], a permutation-based STR approach. We generate different sets of permutations from the original and CReLU-ed features by considering the top-k truncated sorting permutations at different values of k. We also compared with state-of-the-art main-memory approximate nearest neighbor algorithms based on Product Quantization FAISS [5]. For a fair comparison, we use a configuration for FAISS which gives the best trade-off between effectiveness and efficiency; we choose a relatively big code size ($C = 1,024$) and optimal number of Voronoi cells ($N = 16$k), resulting in 1GB in main memory against about 0.7GB of our solution in secondary memory in the larger configuration. Since FAISS methods need to learn a codebook from data, we report results with two different training datasets: the indexed dataset itself, on which the mAP evaluation is performed, and T4SA, an uncorrelated dataset of Twitter images. Results in Figure 1 show a satisfactory trade-off trend between effectiveness and query selectivity and the general benefit introduced by the CReLU preprocessing. We notice that the impact of codebook learning on PQ-based methods is

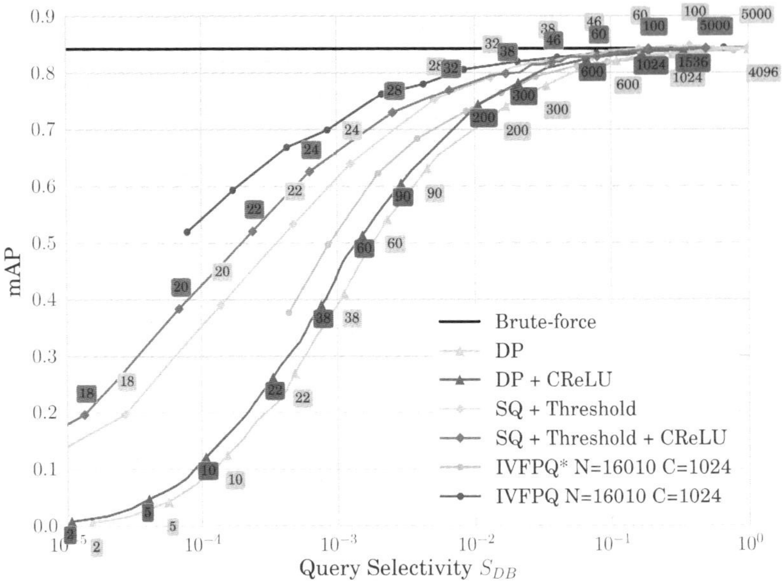

Fig. 1. Performance on Holidays + MIRFlickr1M dataset. The curves are obtained varying k (for deep permutations), γ (for thresholded SQ), and the number of Voronoi cell accessed P (for IVFPQ). Values of k and γ are reported near each point. The horizontal line represents the mAP obtained using the original R-MAC vectors and performing a sequential scan of all the dataset (brute-force approach).

really strong, and it could, in real applications, influence the scalability of the system or require continuous codebook adjustments, forcing to re-indexing the data periodically. Our solution has an intermediate performance but does not require any training procedure and therefore any re-adjustments.

References

1. Amato, G., Bolettieri, P., Carrara, F., Falchi, F., Gennaro, C.: Large-scale image retrieval with elasticsearch. In: The 41st International ACM SIGIR Conference on Research & Development in Information Retrieval. pp. 925–928. ACM (2018)
2. Gennaro, C., Amato, G., Bolettieri, P., Savino, P.: An approach to content-based image retrieval based on the lucene search engine library. In: International Conference on Theory and Practice of Digital Libraries. pp. 55–66. Springer (2010)
3. Jegou, H., Douze, M., Schmid, C.: Hamming embedding and weak geometric consistency for large scale image search. In: European conference on computer vision. pp. 304–317. Springer (2008)
4. Jégou, H., Douze, M., Schmid, C., Pérez, P.: Aggregating local descriptors into a compact image representation. In: Computer Vision and Pattern Recognition (CVPR), 2010 IEEE Conference on. pp. 3304–3311. IEEE (2010)
5. Johnson, J., Douze, M., Jégou, H.: Billion-scale similarity search with gpus. arXiv preprint arXiv:1702.08734 (2017)
6. Tolias, G., Sicre, R., Jégou, H.: Particular object retrieval with integral max-pooling of cnn activations (2016)
7. Zezula, P., Amato, G., Dohnal, V., Batko, M.: Similarity search: the metric space approach, vol. 32. Springer Science & Business Media (2006)

Social mining from Wi-Fi campus data

Roberto Puccetti [1]
supervised by Dino Pedreschi[1] - Mirco Nanni [2]

[1] Pisa University, Pisa - Italy
[2] CNR Pisa – Italy
roberto.puccetti@unipi.it

Abstract. This research deals with methods and algorithms for analyzing Wi-Fi data of individuals at the scale of a large campus area, studying personality traits, class attendance, mobility and social network structure of students. In particular, the main driving application will be the study of whether and how such elements influence academic performances.

1 Introduction

Data mining has been used in telecommunication industry for several applications including marketing, security and network reliability. The exploration data in educational field using Data Mining techniques concerns with extracting a pattern to discover hidden information from educational data. In the case of academic performance studies, a number of behavioral patterns have been linked such as time allocation, active social ties, sleep duration and sleep quality, or participation in sport activity. While most of the existing studies suffer from biases and limitations often associated with surveys and self-reports, our research is directed towards a Wi-Fi network in an urban campus area and therefore it analyses a large set of data that are not biases influenced. We want first to address the problem to analyze such data to discover their quality and then to develop a tool to enable the extraction of latent knowledge in dynamic and multidimensional networks. As an application area of the studies, we use the movements within a university campus and then the study of the influence of daily behavior on students' performance.

2 Related Works

We can define our research as multidisciplinary, in the sense that it approaches and uses many fields of information science: Wi-Fi Data Analysis, Social Networks (Construction [1], Topological properties [2] and Study of community [3]) and Privacy issues [4]. However the most of survey work done is about Prediction of Students' Academic Performance [5] [6], [7] [8], [9], [10]. In these works there are many aspect similar to our research but the most innovative aspects we have introduced are: no survey from questionnaires but directly from their behavior using a large dataset collected from students (about 50k) by their tab-

SEBD 2019, June 16-19, 2019, Castiglione della Pescaia, Italy.

let/smartphones, plurality in course of study, and Social network observations from campus Wi-Fi data (their visited places and physical proximity at the same time).

3 Research plan

To gain the goal of the research, activity includes the following main tasks: to adopt or develop methods and algorithms to analyze wi-fi data on the scale of a large campus, to develop a software prototype, on top of such methods and algorithms, that can be used for solving a selected set of problems as, for example, to predict students' academic performance. Finally, we want to collect a "so-big dataset" from a campus area as a case study to test the prototype. From the viewpoint of the case study, we are planning: i) to extract and evaluate the importance of different sets of features for supervised learning models in particular for students' performance prediction; ii) to identify individual and network factors that best correlate with students' performances; iii) to predict students' performance; iv) to investigate significant differences among performance groups, in terms of the most important individual and network features. Data used to build the case study come from a consistent dataset: Wi-Fi access logs and exam results from the University of Pisa, described in better detail later.

4 Preliminary results

The Wi-fi data usually suffer from various issues, such as sparse data, noise, uncertainty and so on, which need to be dealt with before any analysis-based task. We start our work by studying and trying to remove (or to mitigate) them.

4.1 Semantic labelling of Access Points

Another preliminary work is to understand the role of each Access Point connection in the people activity. This means to understand two main important features of the access points: collocation in area and purpose of their use. So, we aggregated APs to calculate and display interactively the daily use (see Fig.1) and we identified 11 classes of use (Didactics, Central Administration, Study area, Recreational activities, Dormitory, etc.). This second task has two approaches: *Top-Down*, supervised (based on collocation, and *Data-Driven*, using visual tools and Data Time Warping algorithm to validate what prefixed in arbitrary way.

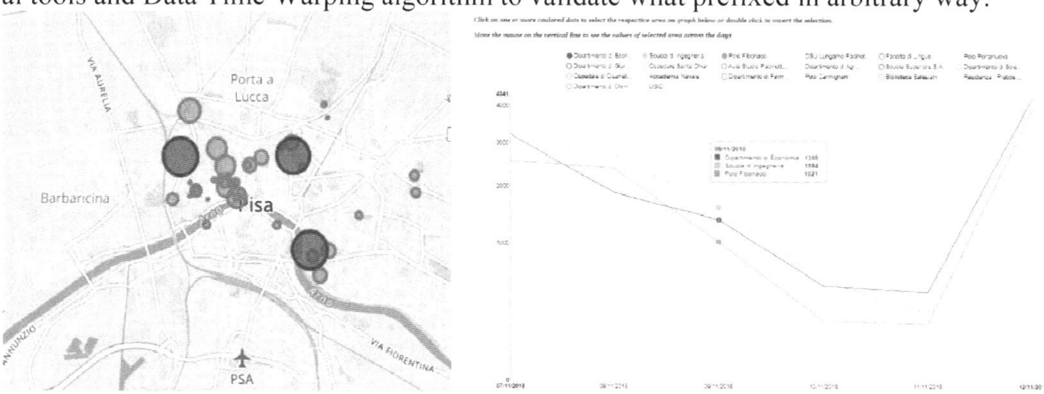

Fig. 1. The 3 main used areas (from http://sintetik.altervista.org/visual/)

4.2 Students clustering

We use two different clustering methods to study users' ties: **behavior similarity**, that wants to analyze how much students use APs in percentage and for which purpose, and **physical collocation**, that presupposes the friendship between two individuals who habitually attend the same places. The first, for each AP classification gathers a score from 1 to 2 to "weight" the importance of the location frequency, for instance assigning higher weights to spaces devoted to study and (secondarily) social activities. Then, for each category, each student is represented by an array describing the percentage of his time spent in it. This representation of a student allows the direct comparison of two individuals through a simple weighted sum (basically a L1-norm where each feature has an associated importance). Distance from student *i* to student *j* is

$$d(i,j) = \sum_{n=1}^{K} abs(V_{i_n} - V_{j_n}) * W_n$$

$k = number\ of\ item \quad V_{i_n} = Value\ of\ item\ n\ in\ array\ i \quad W_n = weight\ of\ item\ n$

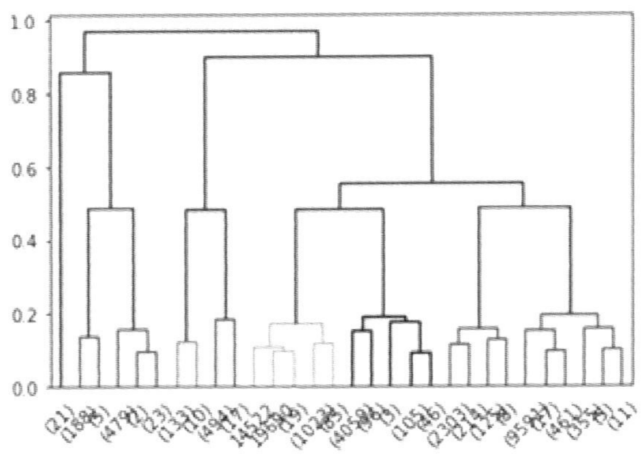

Fig. 2. Hierarchical clusters dendrogram of students' similarity

In such a way, we create a student's *weighted disctance matrix* to measure distance for clustering operations, aimed to group students that spend their time in a similar way (Fig.2).

Instead, the physical location approach considers the simultaneous use of the access point as similarity factor. Staring from the time logs, we study the overlapping time in function of the APs use to determine the reasonable cut factor. We decided to consider 20 minutes as reasonable overlapping time. With this parameter and adopting Jaccard distance index, we construct the relationship matrix for social network methods to determine the student's community. Using two different methods (DEMON and LOUVAIN), in both we collect the same number of communities. This means that in students' environment we have a strong clustering in function of place frequency.

5 Conclusions and next steps

After community's discovery, in function of students' behaviors analysis, we want to correlate them with their performance. The first and simplest method we will use to calculate the performance is to combine exam results with their importance and their timeliness (e.g. it penalizes exams that are late on schedule):

$$p(x) = \sum_{n=1}^{K} \left(R_n * Cr_n * \frac{Cy_n}{Sy(x)} \right)$$

k = number of exam successes in session;
R_i = exam result
Cr_i = exam credits
Cy_i = Year of exam course;
$Sy(x)$ = Year of student course

Finally, based on this score and on cluster membership descripted above, we will profile the students. This process will be done studying how to optimize the accuracy of profiling. Defining such accuracy in a well-founded way is part of the challenge.

References

[1] L.Kovanen, J.Saram and K.Kaski, "Reciprocity of mobile phone calls.," *JDySES,* vol. 2, no. 2, pp. 138-151, 2011.

[2] D.J.Watts and S.H.Strogatz, "Collective dynamics of small-world networks," *Nature,* vol. 393, no. 6684, pp. 440-442, 1998.

[3] K.Kianmehr and R.Alhajj, "Calling communities analysis and identification using machine learning techniques," *Expert Systems with Applications,* vol. 36, no. 3, pp. 6218-6226, 2009.

[4] L.Sweeney, "k-anonymity: a model for protecting privacy," *International Journal of Uncertainty, Fuzziness and Knowledge-Based Systems,* vol. 10, no. 5, pp. 557-570, 2012.

[5] D.Gaševi´c, R.Janzen and A.Zouaq, "Choose your classmates, your GPA is at stake!" The association of cross-class social ties and academic performance," *Am Behav Sci,* vol. 57, no. 10, p. 1460–1479, 2013.

[6] M.P.Vitale, G.C.Porzio and P.Doreian, "Examining the effect of social influence on student performance through network autocorrelation models," *J Appl Stat,* vol. 43, no. 1, p. 115–127, 2016.

[7] PV.Marsden and KE.Campbell, "Measuring tie strength," *Soc Forces,* vol. 63, no. 2, p. 482–501, 1984.

[8] F.Ahmad, N.Hafieza and I.A.A.Aziz, "The Prediction of Students' Academic Performance Using Classification Data Mining Technique," *Applied Mathematical Sciences,* vol. Vol. 9, no. 2015, pp. 6415 - 6426, 2015.

[9] I.Smirnov and S.Thurner, "Formation of homophily in academic performance: students prefer to change their friends rather than performance," *https://arxiv.org/abs/1606.09082,* 2016.

[10] V.Kassarnig, E.Mones, A.Bjerre-Nielsen, P.Sapiezynski, L.D.Dreyer and S.L.Jørgensene, "Academic performance and behavioral patterns," *Epj Data Science,* vol. 7, no. 10, 2018.

Behavioral Analysis For a Continuous User Authentication

Giacomo Giorgi
Supervised by Fabio Martinelli and Andrea Saracino

Istituto di Informatica e Telematica-Consiglio Nazionale Delle Ricerche
{firstname.lastname}@iit.cnr.it

Abstract. New generation devices are pervasive in nature and provide a number of security sensitive functionalities, which might expose the user private information to serious security and privacy threats. The main countermeasure used to prevent unauthorized access is the user authentication. Most of these devices are still protected by traditional authentication mechanisms (PIN, password), which are exposed to well known security limitations. These issues are mitigated by the introduction of new physical biometric authentication mechanisms. Biometric authentication, basing on user physical traits and requiring the user presence at the authentication time, makes the system more secure. Despite the new mechanisms overcome some data security issues, they still suffer from other usability problems. In this paper we explore a new unobtrusive authentication mechanism based on human behavior.

Keywords: Machine learning · Authentication · Human behavior.

1 Introduction

The most common user authentication mechanisms used are based on the concepts of: (i) what the user knows, (ii) what the user has, (iii) what the user is, (iv) what the user does. The traditional authentication mechanisms (i, ii) as explained in literature [4] are not considered much safe to provide security to the users because of many flaws in the conventional systems. These security issues are mitigated by the introduction of the physical biometric authentication mechanisms. However the systems based on physical biometrics require more users cooperation since such traits cannot be analyzed unobtrusively, thereby reducing the usability of the system. The main open challenges of an authentication system are: (i) Identification of a discriminative biometric trait, (ii) Limited resource available, (iii) Robustness over biometric trait variation, (iv) unobtrusiveness. In this paper is described the structure of a new authentication mechanism based on the physical human behavior analysis exploiting the user interaction with its smart devices.

2 Related work

Use sensor data to identify and authenticate smartphone users based on a person's movements is a topic already treated in literature. In the paper [2], they collect individuals data related to walk, jog, and climb stairs having a mobile phone equipped with the sensor and they demonstrated to function as biometric signatures. In a similar way [3], demonstrated that the way a phone is held or kept at different positions through motions can be used to authenticate users.

3 Approach

The approach proposed in order to solve the aforementioned issues, is based on the aggregation of different behavioral analysis classified in: (i) behavioral user actions, (ii) user interactions with the smart devices and reported in Table 1. In

Action	behavioral user action	Device interaction
Free texting sitting/walking	x	v
Unlock from table/pocket/bag	x	v
Web page browsing	x	v
Walking up and down inclination ground	v	x
Running up and down inclination ground	v	x

Table 1. User's actions

order to avoid the direct user interaction with the system and make it less intrusive, data are collected transparently from the devices' sensors (accelerometer and gyroscope). Basing on the fact that each user can has a unique distinctive behavior in doing these actions, it is possible build a system ables to recognize a user starting from the analysis of its behavior. The system is composed by two main components: (i) Human Action Recognition (HAR), (ii) User verification. The HAR component performs the task of identifying the specific movement or action of a person based on sensor data, while the user verification component is used to verify the identity of who has performed the action. Figure 1 shows the complete pipeline.

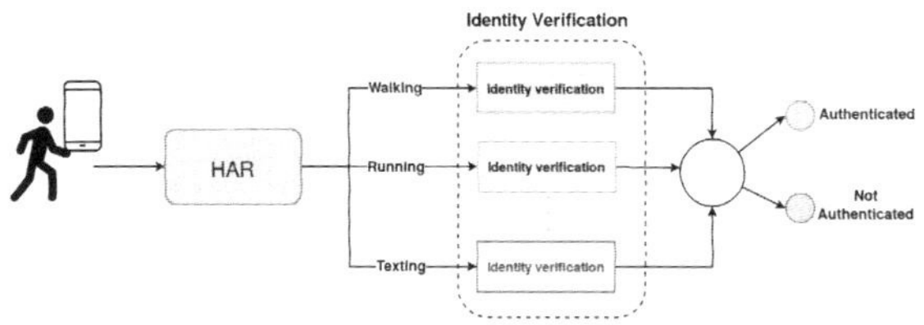

Fig. 1. Behavioral Authentication System

3.1 Implementation

As first step has been implemented an Android application ables to fetch data from the main smartphone sensors. The application requires to the user to perform the specific actions listed in Table 1 in order to catch sensors' values associated to the action required. The data collected will be used to train a Human Action Recognition in recognizing the new type of actions defined. The *Identity verification* component, as showed in Figure 1 is composed by a set of sub components, each of one dedicated to the verification of the identity through the analysis of a different action. One of the sub component analyzed is the *Gait recognition component.* As explained in the paper [1] a deep neural network

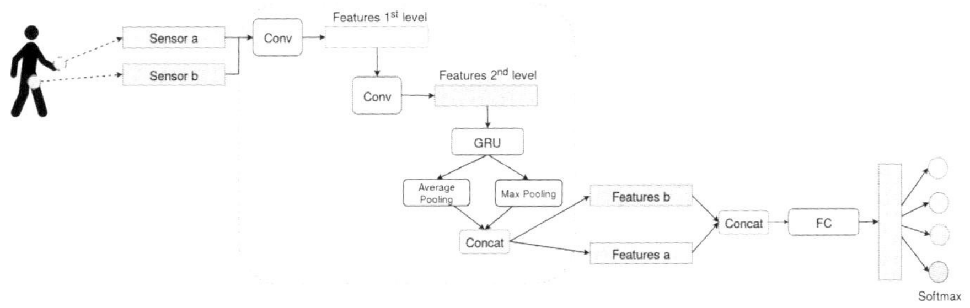

Fig. 2. Gait recognition architecture

architecture is applied to the problem on identifying 153 person exploiting 2 inertial sensors located on the right wrist and on right side of pelvis. Given a gait cycle (walking cycle that starts with initial contact of the right heel and it continues until the right heel contacts the ground again), the task is to determine to which person the cycle belongs. The network extracts, from a single input gait cycle, features of two different abstraction level (through two 1D convolutional layers) and applies a temporal aggregation on the features extracted in the second level (bidirectional recurrent layers). The result is a temporal aggregation feature vectors that are concatenated and passed to a fully connected layer composed by 153 softmax units which compute the probability of the input gait cycle to belong to a specific identity. Figure 2 shows the architecture.

4 Experiments

The experiments are done on the ZJU-gaitAcc dataset that is described in [5]. The dataset contains the gait acceleration series of records collected from 153 subjects gathered in two walking sessions. The aim of our experiments is to learn user identity starting from its walking path. To this end we considered two scenarios in which we experimented the recognition ability in the same session (walking gaits recorded in the same day) and in different sessions (walking gaits recorded over time). Figures 3 and 4, show the CMC curve reporting the recognition accuracy for both scenarios. The real case, right side of the pelvis-right wrist (S3-S1), reaches 94% and 96% of accuracy at rank-1 respectively in cross sessions and single session scenario.

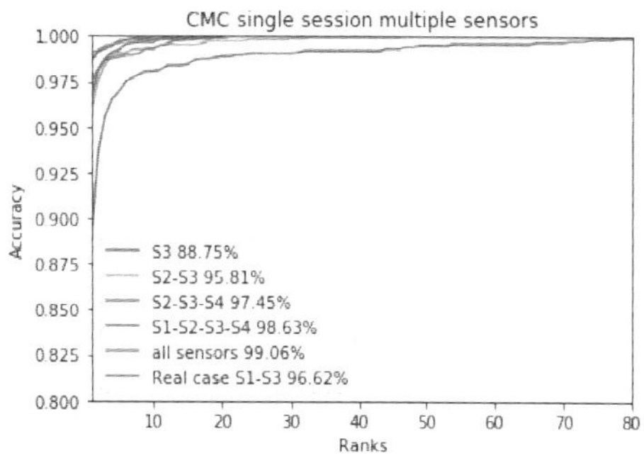

Fig. 3. CMC curve single session

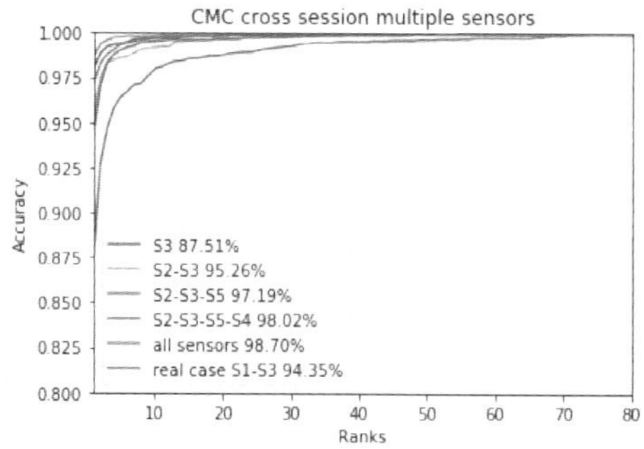

Fig. 4. CMC curve cross session

5 Conclusion and Future work

As showed in Section 3.1, the gait identification network reaches an high accuracy in recognizing a person among 153 different identities, that result is very promising in perspective of the implementation of a verification network. As future work, starting from the gait identification network, we plan to implement a siamese architecture to better adapt to verification problem. In addition we plan to reproduce the experiments on the data collected through smartphone and finally extend the verification to other user actions in combination with a HAR based on the actions showed in Table 1.

References

1. Giorgi, G., Martinelli, F., Saracino, A., Sheikhalishahi, M.: Walking through the deep: Gait analysis for user authentication through deep learning. In: IFIP International Conference on ICT Systems Security and Privacy Protection. pp. 62–76. Springer (2018)
2. Kwapisz, J.R., Weiss, G.M., Moore, S.A.: Cell phone-based biometric identification. In: 2010 Fourth IEEE International Conference on Biometrics: Theory, Applications and Systems (BTAS). pp. 1–7. IEEE (2010)
3. Primo, A., Phoha, V.V., Kumar, R., Serwadda, A.: Context-aware active authentication using smartphone accelerometer measurements. In: Proceedings of the IEEE conference on computer vision and pattern recognition workshops. pp. 98–105 (2014)
4. Raza, M., Iqbal, M., Sharif, M., Haider, W.: A survey of password attacks and comparative analysis on methods for secure authentication. World Applied Sciences Journal **19**(4), 439–444 (2012)
5. Zhang, Y., Pan, G., Jia, K., Lu, M., Wang, Y., Wu, Z.: Accelerometer-based gait recognition by sparse representation of signature points with clusters. IEEE transactions on cybernetics **45**(9), 1864–1875 (2014)

Synthesis of Strategies for Robotic Process Automation

Simone Agostinelli
supervised by prof. Andrea Marrella

DIAG, Sapienza University of Rome, Italy
agostinelli@diag.uniroma1.it

Abstract. Robotic Process Automation (RPA) is an umbrella term for tools that run on an end user's computer, emulating tasks previously executed through a user interface by means of a *software robot*. Nowadays, only simple, predictable tasks can be automated in situations where there is no room for interpretation, while more sophisticated work is still left to human experts. The here proposed research aims at tackling this issue through a paradigm shift in conceiving software robots that are able to behave intelligently and flexibly in many dynamic and knowledge-intensive situations that are common in today's application scenarios.

Keywords: Robotic Process Automation · Human Computer Interaction · Process Mining · Automated Planning

1 Summary of proposal

A today's recurrent question is "*What should be automated and what should be done by humans?*" [2]. The recent developments in Artificial Intelligence (AI) force us to revisit this question continuously. RPA [10] is one of these developments based on the notion of *software robot*. The robot is developed to capture the execution of the tasks previously performed by a human user on the UI of a computer system, and then to emulate the automation of such tasks in place of the user. To date, software robots are manually developed by a human designer through a *trial-and-error* approach, which consists of designing a *flowchart diagram* that determines the *behaviour* of the robot and of verifying its ability to properly mimic the flow of user's actions required to execute a task on the UI [9]. Instead of manually pre-defining the behaviour of a robot, the target of this research is on leveraging a combined use of techniques from the fields of Human-Computer Interaction [5], Process Mining [1], and Automated Planning in AI [7] for: *(i) identifying* and *interpreting* the robot's behaviour by looking at the *interaction logs* that record the concrete user actions taking place during a run of the system; *(ii)* automatically *discovering* the flowchart diagram that describes all possible behaviours of a robot; and *(iii) orchestrating* the behaviours of single robots in order to synthesize complex *execution strategies* able to emulate the enactment not just of single tasks, but of interconnected and large workflows.

2 State of the art

Most of the actual deployments of RPA are industry-specific, e.g., financial and business services [2], and the market for RPA solutions is developing rapidly. Nowadays, robots are mainly used for automating repetitive office tasks in operations like accounting, billing and customer service. Robots are capable of log into applications, connect to system APIs, copy and paste data, extract semi-structured data from documents, read and write to databases, open e-mail and attachments, fill in forms, make calculations, etc. Despite the capabilities of software robots, the RPA technology is still in its infancy, even if similar solutions have been around for a long time. For instance, closely related to software robots, *chatbots* have been using for years to accept voice-based or keyboard inputs and guide customers to find relevant information in web-based applications [8]. Differently from chatbots, RPA can be seen as an evolution of traditional *screen scraping* solutions [4], which sought to visualize screen display data from legacy applications (having no means for automated interfacing) in order to display such data using modern UIs. The strength of RPA is that it does not replace existing applications or manipulate their code, but rather works with them in a way similar to a human user. However, it is worth to notice that the current generation of software robots is guided by procedural rules rather than AI. To be more specific, a software robot can be developed by a human designer through a *trial-and-error* approach consisting of 2 steps that are repeated until success [9]:

- First, the designer produces a *flowchart diagram* that includes the single actions to be performed by the robot on the UI to emulate a task of the system.
- Second, the designer checks if the robot's behaviour during the execution of the task on the UI is capable to properly reproduce the behaviour of a human user that executes the same task. If any misalignment exists, the designer adjusts the flowchart diagram to fix the identified gap.

While this approach is particularly effective for executing simple rules-based logic in situations where there is no room for interpretation, it becomes time-consuming and error-prone in presence of tasks that are less predictable or require some level of human judgment. As a consequence, RPA is not yet able to fully replace human work. Only simple, predictable tasks can be automated. In cases where the rule set does not contain a suitable response for a specific situation, robots allow for escalation to a human supervisor . This is particularly true in today's application scenarios, where also predictable tasks become less-predictable, due to the huge amount of data and events produced in these contexts that may influence their enactment.

3 Research objectives and methodology

This research falls within the scope of RPA, and its overall objective is to devise an approach to automatically synthesize intelligent execution strategies for enacting software robots in dynamic and knowledge-intensive situations, without the need of manually pre-defining the behaviours of such robots. Fig.1 shows an overview of the *three-steps approach* described in Section 1, for achieving the aforementioned objective.

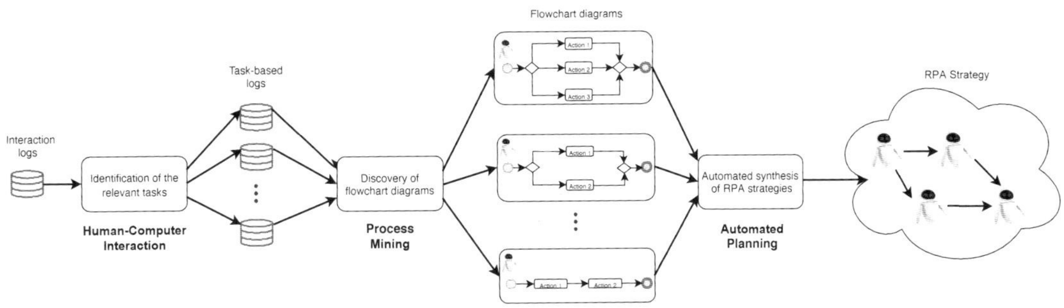

Fig. 1. Approach overview

Objective 1: Identify the relevant tasks to be emulated through software robots by looking at the interaction logs that keep track of the user actions taking place during a run of the system.
Methodology: Development of a novel method in HCI [6] to analyse interaction logs for: *(i)* understanding which user actions have to be captured; *(ii)* interpreting their semantics (also) on the basis of their granularity and *(iii)* identifying the boundaries of relevant tasks. As a result, the list of user actions associated to a complete execution of a relevant task during a run of the system will be recorded into specific execution *traces*. Then, all the traces associated to a relevant task will be clustered in a *task-based log*.

Objective 2: Once identified the relevant tasks to be emulated and the user actions that constitute them (i.e., the task-based logs), the target will be to automatically generate the flowchart diagrams describing the behaviours of software robots required to successfully executing a systems relevant task.
Methodology: Identify which state-of-the-art algorithms suit better to extract the base structure of flowchart diagrams from a task-based log by resorting on discovery algorithms from the Process Mining [1] field, and also on trace alignment [3] techniques.

Objective 3: Automated synthesis of RPA strategies starting from the flowchart diagrams discovered from the task-based logs.
Methodology: The idea is to leverage automated planning techniques in AI [7] for the synthesis of complex execution strategies, in order to emulate the enactment not just of single tasks but of interconnected and large workflows as the composition of many relevant tasks of interest.

4 Results, impacts and benefits

The major results that will be obtained by achieving the objectives of this research are: the *(i) automated identification of relevant tasks*, the *(ii) automated generation of robots' behaviour* and the *(iii) automated synthesis of RPA strategies*. Apart from the ability of automatically generating robots' behaviour and complex strategies of execution for robots starting just from an interaction log, this research proposal aim at also improving the *auditability* (interaction logs are auditable), *upgradability* (flowchart diagrams describing robots' behaviour will be always updated to the current state of system's execution, by employing trace alignment techniques) and the *resiliency* (the ability of having software robots that are always upgraded to deal with new behaviours make them very robust and resilient to any contextual change that may arise during a task execution) of software robots. Furthermore, *scalability* will be improved as well. Human capacity is difficult to scale in situations where demand fluctuates, instead software robots operate at whatever speed is demanded by the work volume. Finally, we also envision that the proposed research will provide long-term benefits on the companies workforce, e.g., improving the customer service in the front office while at the same time reducing the back office tasks. Last but not least, the synthesis of RPA strategies will allow multiple robots to be deployed when demand exceeds the capacity of a single robot increasing the overall productivity.

References

1. van der Aalst, W.M.P.: Process Mining: Data Science in Action. Springer, Heidelberg, 2 edn. (2016). https://doi.org/10.1007/978-3-662-49851-4
2. van der Aalst, W.M., Bichler, M., Heinzl, A.: Robotic process automation (2018)
3. Adriansyah, A., Sidorova, N., van Dongen, B.F.: Cost-based fitness in conformance checking. 2011 Eleventh International Conference on Application of Concurrency to System Design pp. 57–66 (2011)
4. Bisbal, J., Lawless, D., Wu, B., Grimson, J.: Legacy information systems: Issues and directions. IEEE software **16**(5), 103–111 (1999)
5. Dix, A.: Human-computer Interaction. In: Encyclopedia of Database Systems, pp. 1327–1331. Springer (2009)
6. Dumais, S., Jeffries, R., Russell, D.M., Tang, D., Teevan, J.: Understanding user behavior through log data and analysis. In: Ways of Knowing in HCI, pp. 349–372. Springer (2014)
7. Ghallab, M., Nau, D., Traverso, P.: Automated Planning: theory and practice. Elsevier (2004)
8. Hill, J., Ford, W.R., Farreras, I.G.: Real conversations with artificial intelligence: A comparison between human–human online conversations and human–chatbot conversations. Computers in Human Behavior **49**, 245–250 (2015)
9. Volodymyr, L., Dumas, M., Maggi, F.M., La Rosa, M.: Multi-perspective process model discovery for robotic process automation. CAiSE Doctoral Consortium **2114**(9), 37–45 (Jun 2018), `http://ceur-ws.org/Vol-2114/paper5.pdf`
10. Willcocks, L.: Service automation : robots and the future of work. Steve Brookes Publishing, Warwickshire, United Kingdom (2016)